Generalized Sylvester Equations

Unified Parametric Solutions

Generalized Sylvester Equations

Unified Parametric Solutions

Guang-Ren Duan

CRC Press
Taylor & Francis Group
Boca Raton London New York

CRC Press is an imprint of the
Taylor & Francis Group, an **informa** business

MATLAB® and Simulink® are trademarks of The MathWorks, Inc. and are used with permission. The MathWorks does not warrant the accuracy of the text or exercises in this book. This book's use or discussion of MATLAB® and Simulink® software or related products does not constitute endorsement or sponsorship by The MathWorks of a particular pedagogical approach or particular use of the MATLAB® and Simulink® software.

CRC Press
Taylor & Francis Group
6000 Broken Sound Parkway NW, Suite 300
Boca Raton, FL 33487-2742

First issued in paperback 2020

ISBN 13: 978-0-367-57570-0 (pbk)
ISBN 13: 978-1-4822-4396-3 (hbk)

Library of Congress Cataloging-in-Publication Data

Duan, Guangren.
  Generalized Sylvester equations : unified parametric solutions / Guang-Ren Duan.
    pages cm
  Summary: "Generalized Sylvester equations (GSEs) have found applications in many fields, including applied mathematics, systems and control, and signal processing. This book presents a unified parametric approach for solving the various types of GSEs, with proofs theorems and some technical results used. It provides a unified parametric solution formula, in an extremely neat and elegant matrix form, for all the various types of GSEs"-- Provided by publisher.
  Includes bibliographical references and index.
  ISBN 978-1-4822-4396-3 (hardback)
  1. Sylvester equations. 2. Control theory--Mathematics. I. Title.

  QA196.7.D83 2015

  515'.642--dc23

                                                                    2014040866

Visit the Taylor & Francis Web site at
http://www.taylorandfrancis.com

and the CRC Press Web site at
http://www.crcpress.com

Contents

Preface

Goal

The following Sylvester equation,

$$AX + XB = C,$$

with A, B, and C being the coefficient matrices of appropriate dimensions and X the unknown, is very well known in the fields of applied mathematics and systems and control theory. Yet it has many generalized forms that we may not be quite aware of. These generalized forms are as well useful in many control systems analysis and design applications, such as eigenstructure assignment (ESA), observer design, signal tracking, and disturbance decoupling and attenuation.

Since 1992, I have been working on parametric solutions to the various types of generalized Sylvester equations (GSEs) and have also applied these solutions to various control system designs. Later, from 2005, some of my PhD students gradually took part in this research under my guidance and have done some work in this aspect along several directions. While the work in one stream is systematic and relatively complete, the goal of this book is to summarize systematically our research work in this stream on parametric solutions to the several types of GSEs.

GSEs, no matter how complicated in forms, are linear in nature. Hence, they can be easily solved using the stretching operation, or the Kronecker product, when all the coefficient matrices are known. However, in practical applications it is desirable to solve a GSE with certain coefficient matrices not prescribed *a priori*. Taking, for example, the following one:

$$EVF - AV = BW + R,$$

which might have gained the most attention in the literature, the coefficient matrices E, A, and B are usually given, V and W are the unknowns to be solved, and F and R may not be given *a priori*, but to be used as design parameters to be optimized in the application designs. Therefore, in this book, the purpose of solving this GSE is really to answer the following question:

■ *Can we find, when the matrices F and R are unknown or only partially known, a parametric solution (V, W) to the GSE that is*
  – In a simple and neat explicit analytical closed form?
  – Complete in the sense that it provides all the degrees of freedom?

The goal of this book is to provide a complete answer to this question related to all the considered different types of GSEs.

Coverage

The book has nine chapters and an appendix.

Chapter 1 introduces the various types of GSEs discussed in the book and also gives a brief overview on solutions to GSEs, Chapter 2 demonstrates the importance of GSEs with four typical control design applications, and Chapter 3 introduces and discusses the F-coprimeness of a pair of polynomial matrices, which plays a fundamental role in the book.

Chapters 4 through 7 deal with solutions to GSEs. Specifically, solutions to general homogeneous and nonhomogeneous GSEs are presented in Chapters 4 and 5, respectively. In Chapter 6, by simplifying the results in Chapters 4 and 5, general solutions to a special type of GSEs, namely, fully actuated GSEs, which are often encountered in applications, are proposed, and the results are further generalized in Chapter 7 to GSEs with varying coefficients.

In Chapter 8, general higher-order rectangular normal Sylvester equations (NSEs) are proposed, and it is shown that these rectangular NSEs are just different representations of GSEs. Therefore, parametric solutions to these equations are naturally obtained based on those for homogeneous and nonhomogeneous GSEs proposed in Chapters 4 and 5.

In Chapter 9, by simplifying the results in Chapter 6 for homogeneous fully actuated GSEs, analytical solutions to square NSEs, including the well-known continuous- and discrete-time Lyapunov equations, are derived.

The appendix provides the proofs of some of the theorems in Chapters 3 through 5.

I have to mention that many researchers in the world have made great contribution to the solution of GSEs. However, the purpose of this book is really to summarize one aspect of my work on GSEs, and therefore reported results of other researchers are not included, and some of them may not even been cited. I extend my apologies to these researchers.

As highlighted in Chapter 2, the importance of GSEs really lies in their applications. Yet this book only concentrates on the parametric solutions of GSEs, which have already proven to be a sound base for parametric control systems design, while the results on applications of these solutions in parametric control systems design are only briefly mentioned in order to demonstrate the main point of parametric control designs but are really not included in this book. They will indeed be systematically summarized in forthcoming books.

Features and Audience

This book possesses many important features; here, we mention the several main ones:

- *General suitability*: It covers several types of very general GSEs, including GSEs with arbitrary orders, arbitrary dimensions, and almost arbitrary parameters in the sense that they are subject to very weak conditions, or even GSEs with unknown parameter matrices F and R.
- *Completeness in freedom*: It presents complete parametric solutions to the proposed GSEs in simple and neat analytical closed-forms with all degrees of freedom, and the parameter matrices F and R may even be set undetermined and used as a part of the degrees of freedom as well.
- *High unification*: It proposes a whole set of highly unified solutions to the GSEs under very weak conditions. As a matter of fact, all we propose in the book is one single formula that gives the solutions to all the various types of equations (see Figure 1.8).

Due to the wide application range of GSEs, this book suits a very large scope of readership. More specifically, it targets two types of readers.

First, this book can be used as a primary or a secondary textbook for some courses for senior undergraduate and postgraduate students specializing in the fields of applied mathematics and control system theory and applications, and possibly for those specializing in mechanical engineering, electrical engineering, and aerospace engineering.

Second, this book can also be used as a reference book by postgraduates, researchers, scientists, engineers, and university lecturers in the fields of control systems and applications, applied mathematics, mechanical engineering, electrical engineering, and aerospace engineering.

Acknowledgments

All those students who took the graduate course "Parametric Control Systems Design" at Harbin Institute of Technology during 2013–2014 have offered tremendous help in finding the errors and typos in the manuscript. Many of my own students have also helped a lot. Specifically, my master's students, including Feng Zhang, Zhao Lu, Wen-Bin Tang, and Xiu-Wei Huang, have helped with the establishment of the reference database of the book, while quite a few of my PhD students helped with the examples, references, and indices, as well as with proofreading certain parts of the book. Among the latter, three of them deserve my special thanks for their tremendous help during the final stages of this book. They are Yan-Mei Hu, Zhi-Kai Zhang, and Gang Xu.

Several people have proofread the manuscript, including Professor June Feng from Shandong University, Professor Yuan Gao from Heilongjiang University, and also several of my former PhD students—Professor Haihua Yu from Heilongjiang University, Professor Guosheng Wang from the Academy of Armored Force Engineering, and Professor Biao Zhang from Harbin Institute of Technology. Their review has greatly improved the quality of the manuscript and is indeed very much appreciated.

Inspired by my earlier works on this topic, several of my former PhD students have made considerable contribution to the solution of the various types of Sylvester matrix equations under my guidance. These include Professors Aiguo Wu and Ying Zhang from Shenzhen Graduate School of Harbin Institute of Technology, Professors Bin Zhou and Biao Zhang from Harbin Institute of Technology, Professor Haihua Yu from Heilongjiang University, and Professor Guosheng Wang from the Academy of Armored Force Engineering. They have all made considerable contributions in this field. Particularly, Professor Aiguo Wu and Ying Zhang have greatly contributed to the solution of complex conjugate Sylvester-type matrix equations (Wu and Zhang 2015). Their contribution, although most of it may not have been included in this book, is very much appreciated.

Taking this opportunity, I gratefully acknowledge the financial support kindly provided by the many sponsors, including NSFC (the National Natural Science Foundation of China), the Chinese Ministry of Science and Technology, the Aerospace Industry Companies of China, and the Ministry of Education of China, for relevant projects, particularly for those funded by the Program of the National Science Fund for Distinguished Young Scholars, the Innovative Scientific Research Team Program, the National Key Basic Research and Development Program (973 Program), and the Program of ChangJiang Scholars.

Finally, I thank in advance all the readers for choosing to read and use this book. I would be grateful if you could possibly provide via e-mail, to g.r.duan@hit.edu.cn, your feedback and suggestions. Your help will certainly make any future editions of the book much better.

Guang-Ren Duan
Harbin Institute of Technology
Harbin, Heilongjiang, China

Notations

$\mathbb{R}$	Set of all real numbers
$\mathbb{R}^+$	Set of all positive real numbers
$\mathbb{R}^-$	Set of all negative real numbers
$\mathbb{C}$	Set of all complex numbers
$\mathbb{C}^+$	Right-half complex plane
$\mathbb{C}^-$	Left-half complex plane
$\mathbb{R}^n$	Set of all real vectors of dimension n
$\mathbb{C}^n$	Set of all complex vectors of dimension n
$\mathbb{R}^{m \times n}$	Set of all real matrices of dimension $m \times n$
$\mathbb{R}^{m \times n}[s]$	Set of all polynomial matrices of dimension $m \times n$ with real coefficients
$\mathbb{C}^{m \times n}$	Set of all complex matrices of dimension $m \times n$
$\varnothing$	The null set

Notations Related to Vectors and Matrices

0_n	Zero vector in $\mathbb{R}^n$
$0_{m \times n}$	Zero matrix in $\mathbb{R}^{m \times n}$
I_n	Identity matrix of order n
A^{-1}	Inverse matrix of matrix A
A^{T}	Transpose of matrix A
$\det(A)$	Determinant of matrix A
$\mathrm{adj}(A)$	Adjoint matrix of matrix A
$\mathrm{rank}(A)$	Rank of matrix A
$\mathrm{eig}(A)$	Set of all eigenvalues of matrix A
$\mathrm{svd}(A)$	Set of all singular values of matrix A
$\lambda_i(A)$	ith eigenvalue of matrix A
$\sigma_i(A)$	ith singular value of matrix A
$\|A\|_2$	Spectral norm of matrix A
$\|A\|_{fro}$	Frobenius norm of matrix A
$\|A\|_1$	Row-sum norm of matrix A
$\|A\|_\infty$	Column-sum norm of matrix A

$\dot{x}(t)$ First-order derivative of vector x with respective to t

$\ddot{x}(t)$ Second-order derivative of vector x with respective to t

$\dddot{x}(t)$ Third-order derivative of vector x with respective to t

$x^{(i)}(t)$ ith-order derivative of vector x with respective to t

Notations of Relations and Manipulations

$\Longrightarrow$ Imply

$\Longleftrightarrow$ If and only if

$\in$ Belong to

$\subset$ Subset

$\cap$ Intersection

$\cup$ Union

$\forall$ Arbitrarily chosen

$\exists$ Exist

s.t.   Subject to

$A \otimes B$ Kronecker product of matrices A and B

Other Notations

deg   Degree n of a polynomial matrix $P_0 + P_1 s + \cdots + P_n s^n$

diag $\mathrm{diag}(d_1, d_2, \ldots, d_n)$ or $\mathrm{diag}(d_i, \; i = 1, 2, \ldots, n)$, the diagonal matrix with diagonal elements $d_i, \; i = 1, 2, \ldots, n$

blockdiag $\mathrm{blockdiag}(D_1, D_2, \ldots, D_n)$ or $\mathrm{blockdiag}(D_i, \; i = 1, 2, \ldots, n)$, the block diagonal matrix with matrix diagonal elements $D_i, \; i = 1, 2, \ldots, n$

Abbreviations

DPE   Diophantine equation
ESA   Eigenstructure assignment
GSE   Generalized Sylvester equation
NSE   Normal Sylvester equation
RCF   Right coprime factorization
SFR   Smith form reduction
SVD   Singular value decomposition

Chapter 1

Introduction

In order to introduce the whole family of Sylvester matrix equations, three types of dynamical models for linear systems need to be first mentioned.

1.1 Three Types of Linear Models

1.1.1 First-Order Systems

In certain applications, we often encounter a type of first-order linear systems, which are represented by the following model:

$$\begin{cases} E\dot{x} - Ax = B_1\dot{u} + B_0u \\ y = Cx + Du, \end{cases} \tag{1.1}$$

where

- $x \in \mathbb{R}^q$, $y \in \mathbb{R}^m$, and $u \in \mathbb{R}^r$ are the state vector, output vector, and the control vector, respectively
- $E, A \in \mathbb{R}^{n \times q}$, $B_1, B_0 \in \mathbb{R}^{n \times r}$, $C \in \mathbb{R}^{m \times q}$, and $D \in \mathbb{R}^{m \times r}$ are the system coefficient matrices

This is a general first-order rectangular system (Duan 2010, Fletcher 1997, Habets et al. 2006, Hou 2004, Ishihara and Terra 2001, Zhang 2006). Although rectangular systems are often encountered, in most applications, we deal with square systems, that is, systems in the above form, but with $q = n$.

In the case of $B_1 = 0$, the above model (1.1) reduces to the following well-known descriptor linear system model (see, e.g., Duan 2010, Duan et al. 2012):

$$\begin{cases} E\dot{x} = Ax + Bu \\ y = Cx + Du. \end{cases} \tag{1.2}$$

The coefficient matrix E in the above system may be singular, while when this matrix is nonsingular, the above system becomes a normal linear system, which can be represented by the following first-order state space model:

$$\begin{cases} \dot{x} = Ax + Bu \\ y = Cx + Du. \end{cases} \tag{1.3}$$

Theories about the analysis and control of the normal first-order linear system (1.3) have been quite mature, and can be found in many text books (e.g., Chen 1984, Duan 2004a). The first-order descriptor linear system (1.1), which is although a slight extension of system (1.3) in form, has a complete parallel context of theories (see, e.g., Dai 1989, Duan 2010, Lewis 1986, Zhang and Yang 2003).

The following definition clarifies two basic concepts related to system (1.1).

Definition 1.1 *For the first-order linear system (1.1),*

- *$sE - A$ is called the characteristic polynomial matrix of the system.*
- *Furthermore, when $q = n$, $\det(sE - A)$ is called the characteristic polynomial of the system, and the roots of $\det(sE - A)$ are called the poles of the system.*

1.1.2 Second-Order Systems

Many practical systems can be represented by the following second-order dynamical linear model

$$M\ddot{x} + D\dot{x} + Kx = B_2\ddot{u} + B_1\dot{u} + B_0u, \tag{1.4}$$

where

- $x \in \mathbb{R}^q$ and $u \in \mathbb{R}^r$ are the state vector and the control vector, respectively
- $M, D, K \in \mathbb{R}^{n \times q}$, and $B_0, B_1, B_2 \in \mathbb{R}^{n \times r}$, are the system coefficient matrices

Again in applications, often the case of $q = n$ is encountered.

The above system (1.4), with the matrix M being nonzero but possibly singular, is called a second-order descriptor linear system. The following definition further clarifies some basic concepts about the system.

Definition 1.2 *Consider the second-order linear system (1.4).*

- *It is called a second-order descriptor linear system if $M \neq 0$. Particularly, it is called a second-order normal linear system if $\det M \neq 0$.*

- $Ms^2 + Ds + K$ is called the characteristic polynomial matrix of the system.
- When $q = n$, $\det\left(Ms^2 + Ds + K\right)$ is called the characteristic polynomial of the system, and the roots of $\det\left(Ms^2 + Ds + K\right) = 0$ are called the poles of the system.

In many applications, the matrices M and K are symmetric positive (semipositive) definite, and the matrix D is symmetric or skew-symmetric. In these cases, these matrices M, D, and K are called the mass matrix, the structural damping matrix, and the stiffness matrix, respectively.

When $B_1 = B_2 = 0$, and $B \triangleq B_0$, the above system becomes

$$M\ddot{x} + D\dot{x} + Kx = Bu. \tag{1.5}$$

This form must be more familiar, since it is encountered in many applications, such as vibration and structural analysis (Ashour and Nayfeh 2002, Tamaki et al. 1996, Zhang 2002), aerospace control (Balas 1982, Bhaya and Desoer 1985, Duan and Yu 2013, Zou et al. 2012), flexible structures (Juang et al. 1989, Meirovitch et al. 1983), robotic systems (Asada and Slotine 1986, Papadopoulos and Dubowsky 1991, Ulrich and Sasiadek 2010), etc., and has attracted much attention (see, e.g., Chu and Datta 1996, Duan 2004c, Duan and Liu 2002, Duan and Zhou 2006, Rincon 1992, Zhang 2002).

There are two facts which make second-order systems very commonly meet in applications:

1. Many systems are second order in nature; when Newton's Law, the Euler–Lagrangian equation, the theorem of inertia momentum, etc. are applied to establish the dynamical model of a system, the system model appears eventually in a second-order form.
2. Very often a dynamical system is composed of two or more first-order dynamical subsystems, while the overall system possesses a second-order dynamical model.

The above first point can be well accepted, since most readers have experience with modeling using Newton's Law. To demonstrate the above second point, let us consider the cascade system shown in Figure 1.1. Suppose that the model for the plant is given by

$$\dot{x} = A_p x + B_p u + \tau, \tag{1.6}$$

where

- $x \in \mathbb{R}^n$ is the plant state vector
- $\tau \in \mathbb{R}^n$ is the system input, which may be a force or a torque vector

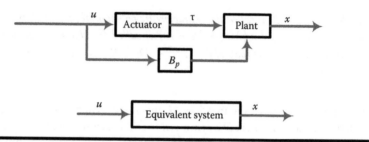

Figure 1.1   Cascaded system.

The actuator is modeled by

$$\dot{\tau} = A_a\tau + B_au, \tag{1.7}$$

where $u \in \mathbb{R}^r$ is the driving control vector. The coefficient matrices A_p, B_p and A_a, B_a are of appropriate dimensions. The following proposition states that second-order systems are often the cascading results of first-order systems.

Proposition 1.1   *For the cascade system shown in Figure 1.1 with the plant and the actuator modeled by (1.6) and (1.7), respectively, the equivalent system with input u and output x is given by the following second-order linear model:*

$$A_2\ddot{x} + A_1\dot{x} + A_0x = B_1\dot{u} + B_0u, \tag{1.8}$$

where

$$\begin{cases} A_2 = I \\ A_1 = -(A_p + A_a) \\ A_0 = A_aA_p, \end{cases} \tag{1.9}$$

and

$$\begin{cases} B_1 = B_p \\ B_0 = B_a - A_aB_p. \end{cases} \tag{1.10}$$

Proof.   Rewrite the actuator model (1.6) as follows:

$$\tau = \dot{x} - A_px - B_pu. \tag{1.11}$$

Taking differentiation over both sides of (1.6), and using (1.7) and (1.11), gives

$$\ddot{x} = A_p \dot{x} + B_p \dot{u} + \dot{\tau}$$
$$= A_p \dot{x} + B_p \dot{u} + (A_a \tau + B_a u)$$
$$= A_p \dot{x} + B_p \dot{u} + A_a \left(\dot{x} - A_p x - B_p u \right) + B_a u$$
$$= \left(A_p + A_a \right) \dot{x} - A_a A_p x + B_p \dot{u} + \left(B_a - A_a B_p \right) u,$$

that is,

$$\ddot{x} - \left(A_p + A_a \right) \dot{x} + A_a A_p x = B_p \dot{u} + \left(B_a - A_a B_p \right) u.$$

This is the second-order model (1.8) with coefficients given in (1.9) and (1.10). ■

1.1.3 Higher-Order Systems

When dealing with some more complicated applications, higher-order dynamical linear systems described by the following model are often encountered (Duan and Yu 2008, Yu and Duan 2009a):

$$A_m x^{(m)} + \cdots + A_1 \dot{x} + A_0 x = B_m u^{(m)} + \cdots + B_1 \dot{u} + B_0 u, \tag{1.12}$$

where

- $x \in \mathbb{R}^q$ and $u \in \mathbb{R}^r$ are the state vector and the control vector, respectively
- $A_i \in \mathbb{R}^{n \times q}$, $B_i \in \mathbb{R}^{n \times r}$, $i = 0, 1, \ldots, m$, are the system coefficient matrices

Because of system physical realizability, it is required that $A_m \neq 0$, and in this case, m is called the order of the system.

Equation (1.12) represents a general higher-order rectangular system. It becomes a square one when $q = n$. In practical applications, often square systems are encountered.

For this type of systems, let us mention that the following scalar one

$$a_m x^{(m)} + \cdots + a_1 \dot{x} + a_0 x = b_m u^{(m)} + \cdots + b_1 \dot{u} + b_0 u, \tag{1.13}$$

with $a_i, b_i \in \mathbb{R}$, $i = 0, 1, \ldots, m$, being scalar coefficients, may be familiar to all readers, since it has appeared in many control context books, for example, Golnaraghi and Kuo (2009), Ogata (2009), Dorf and Bishop (2010), and Duan (2004a).

Let s denote the differential operator, then the system (1.12) can be represented in the following operator form:

$$A(s)x(s) = B(s)u(s),$$

where $x(s)$ and $u(s)$ are the Laplace transforms of $x(t)$ and $u(t)$, respectively, and

$$A(s) = A_m s^m + \cdots + A_2 s^2 + A_1 s + A_0, \qquad (1.14)$$

$$B(s) = B_m s^m + \cdots + B_2 s^2 + B_1 s + B_0. \qquad (1.15)$$

When $B_i = 0$, $i = 1, 2, \ldots, m$, and B_0 is substituted by B, the system becomes

$$A_m x^{(m)} + \cdots + A_1 \dot{x} + A_0 x = Bu, \qquad (1.16)$$

which is encountered more often than (1.12) in practical applications.

Parallel to Definition 1.2, we here give the following one.

Definition 1.3 *Consider the mth order linear system (1.12).*

- *It is called a mth order descriptor linear system if $A_m \neq 0$, and particularly a mth order normal linear system if $\det A_m \neq 0$.*
- *$A(s)$ is called the characteristic polynomial matrix of the system.*
- *When $q = n$, $\det A(s)$ is called the characteristic polynomial of the system, and the roots of $\det A(s) = 0$ are called the poles of the system.*

According to the above definition, the set of poles of the system (1.12) is

$$\aleph = \{s \mid \det A(s) = 0\}.$$

Consider the cascade system shown in Figure 1.1 again. Suppose that the model for the plant is given by

$$M_p \ddot{x} + D_p \dot{x} + K_p x = B_p u + \tau, \qquad (1.17)$$

where

- $x \in \mathbb{R}^n$ is the plant state vector
- $\tau \in \mathbb{R}^n$ is the system input, which may be a force or a torque vector

The actuator is modeled by

$$\ddot{\tau} + D_a \dot{\tau} + K_a \tau = B_a u, \qquad (1.18)$$

where $u \in \mathbb{R}^r$ is the driving control vector. The coefficient matrices M_p, D_p, K_p, B_p and D_a, K_a, B_a are of appropriate dimensions. The following proposition states that higher-order systems are often the cascading results of lower order ones.

Proposition 1.2   *For the cascade system shown in Figure 1.1 with the plant and the actuator modeled by (1.17) and (1.18), respectively, the equivalent system with input u and output x is given by the following fourth-order linear model:*

$$A_4 x^{(4)} + A_3 \dddot{x} + A_2 \ddot{x} + A_1 \dot{x} + A_0 x = B_2 \ddot{u} + B_1 \dot{u} + B_0 u, \qquad (1.19)$$

where

$$\begin{cases} A_4 = M_p \\ A_3 = D_p + D_a M_p \\ A_2 = K_p + D_a D_p + K_a M_p \\ A_1 = D_a K_p + K_a D_p \\ A_0 = K_a K_p, \end{cases} \qquad (1.20)$$

and

$$\begin{cases} B_2 = B_p \\ B_1 = D_a B_p \\ B_0 = K_a B_p + B_a. \end{cases} \qquad (1.21)$$

Proof.   Taking differentiation of both sides of (1.17) gives

$$M_p \dddot{x} + D_p \ddot{x} + K_p \dot{x} = B_p \dot{u} + \dot{\tau}. \qquad (1.22)$$

Thus, from (1.17) and (1.22), we have the following:

$$\tau = M_p \ddot{x} + D_p \dot{x} + K_p x - B_p u,$$
$$\dot{\tau} = M_p \dddot{x} + D_p \ddot{x} + K_p \dot{x} - B_p \dot{u}.$$

Substituting the above two relations into (1.18) produces

$$\ddot{\tau} = -D_a \left(M_p \dddot{x} + D_p \ddot{x} + K_p \dot{x} - B_p \dot{u} \right)$$
$$- K_a \left(M_p \ddot{x} + D_p \dot{x} + K_p x - B_p u \right) + B_a u. \qquad (1.23)$$

Again, differentiating both sides of the equation (1.22) yields

$$M_p x^{(4)} + D_p \dddot{x} + K_p \ddot{x} = B_p \ddot{u} + \ddot{\tau}. \qquad (1.24)$$

Substituting the relation (1.23) into the above equation, and making some simplification, yields the fourth-order equations (1.19) with coefficients given by (1.20) and (1.21). ■

Remark 1.1 It is obvious that the mth order system (1.12) reduces to a second-order descriptor linear system when m takes the value of 2, and a first-order descriptor linear system when m takes the value of 1. On the other side, through state extension, the mth order system (1.12) can also be converted into an extended first-order linear system in the form of (1.3) or (1.1). We point out that although such a conversion allows usage of control theories and techniques for first-order control systems, it is not preferable in most practical analysis and design problems because of the following several reasons:

1. It gives additional computation load and makes the treatment more complicated.
2. It brings numerical error in the first very step of conversion, and this error will be carried to the final analysis or design results and thus will make the final results inaccurate.
3. It destroys the physical meanings of the original system parameters, and more importantly.
4. It enables a first-order system design, which is often worse than a direct design in the higher-order system format in terms of both simplicity and closed-loop system performance.

1.2 Examples of Practical Systems

For two purposes, in this section we give some examples of practical systems, one is to support the system models introduced in Section 1.1, the other is to use them as examples in the later chapters to demonstrate proposed theories and methods.

1.2.1 Circuit System

Example 1.1

Consider the circuit shown in Figure 1.2, where R_0, R_1, and R_2 are the values of the resistors, i_1 and i_2 are the mesh currents passing directly through the voltage sources U_{s1} and U_{s2}, while i_3 and i_4 are the currents passing through the capacitors C_1 and C_2, respectively.

For the mesh i_1, according to Kirchhoff's Law of voltage, we have

$$U_{s1}(t) = R_1 i_3(t) + \frac{1}{C_1} \int i_3(t) dt. \tag{1.25}$$

The differential form of the equation (1.25) can be written as

$$C_1 \frac{d}{dt} U_{s1}(t) = R_1 C_1 \frac{d}{dt} i_3(t) + i_3(t). \tag{1.26}$$

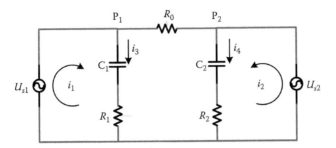

Figure 1.2 A network containing voltage sources.

Similarly, for the mesh i_2, we have

$$U_{s2}(t) = R_2 i_4(t) + \frac{1}{C_2} \int i_4(t) dt. \tag{1.27}$$

The differential form of this equation can be written as

$$C_2 \frac{d}{dt} U_{s2}(t) = R_2 C_2 \frac{d}{dt} i_4(t) + i_4(t). \tag{1.28}$$

Again, according to Kirchhoff's Law of current, at node P_1, we have

$$i_3(t) = i_1(t) + \frac{1}{R_0} (U_{s2}(t) - U_{s1}(t)), \tag{1.29}$$

while at node P_2, we have

$$i_4(t) = i_2(t) + \frac{1}{R_0} (U_{s1}(t) - U_{s2}(t)). \tag{1.30}$$

Substituting (1.29) into (1.26) gives

$$C_1 \frac{d}{dt} U_{s1}(t) = R_1 C_1 \frac{d}{dt} i_1(t) + \frac{R_1}{R_0} C_1 \frac{d}{dt} (U_{s2}(t) - U_{s1}(t))$$
$$+ i_1(t) + \frac{1}{R_0} (U_{s2}(t) - U_{s1}(t)),$$

which can be rearranged into the following form:

$$R_1 C_1 \frac{d}{dt} i_1(t) + i_1(t) = C_1 \left(1 + \frac{R_1}{R_0}\right) \frac{d}{dt} U_{s1}(t)$$
$$- \frac{R_1}{R_0} C_1 \frac{d}{dt} U_{s2}(t) - \frac{1}{R_0} (U_{s2}(t) - U_{s1}(t)). \tag{1.31}$$

Similarly, substituting (1.30) into (1.28) gives

$$C_1 \frac{d}{dt} U_{s2}(t) = R_2 C_2 \frac{d}{dt} \left(i_2(t) + \frac{1}{R_0} (U_{s1}(t) - U_{s2}(t)) \right)$$

$$+ i_2(t) + \frac{1}{R_0} (U_{s1}(t) - U_{s2}(t)),$$

which can be written as

$$R_2 C_2 \frac{d}{dt} i_2(t) + i_2(t) = C_2 \left(1 + \frac{R_2}{R_0} \right) \frac{d}{dt} U_{s2}(t)$$

$$- \frac{R_2}{R_0} C_2 \frac{d}{dt} U_{s1}(t) - \frac{1}{R_0} (U_{s1}(t) - U_{s2}(t)). \qquad (1.32)$$

Defining the state and input vectors as

$$x = \begin{bmatrix} i_1(t) \\ i_2(t) \end{bmatrix} \text{ and } u = \begin{bmatrix} U_{s1}(t) \\ U_{s2}(t) \end{bmatrix},$$

respectively, from equations (1.31) and (1.32), we can obtain the state-space model of the system as

$$E\dot{x} - Ax = B_1 \dot{u} + B_0 u, \qquad (1.33)$$

with

$$E = \begin{bmatrix} R_1 C_1 & 0 \\ 0 & R_2 C_2 \end{bmatrix}, A = \begin{bmatrix} -1 & 0 \\ 0 & -1 \end{bmatrix},$$

$$B_1 = \frac{1}{R_0} \begin{bmatrix} C_1 (R_0 + R_1) & -C_1 R_1 \\ -C_2 R_2 & C_2 (R_0 + R_2) \end{bmatrix}, B_0 = \frac{1}{R_0} \begin{bmatrix} 1 & -1 \\ -1 & 1 \end{bmatrix}.$$

When the system parameter values are taken as

$$C_1 = C_2 = 1,$$

$$R_0 = R_1 = R_2 = 0.5,$$

we have

$$E = \begin{bmatrix} 0.5 & 0 \\ 0 & 0.5 \end{bmatrix}, A = \begin{bmatrix} -1 & 0 \\ 0 & -1 \end{bmatrix},$$

$$B_1 = \begin{bmatrix} 2 & -1 \\ -1 & 2 \end{bmatrix}, B_0 = \begin{bmatrix} 2 & -2 \\ -2 & 2 \end{bmatrix}.$$

1.2.2 Multiagent Kinematic Systems

Consider p objects moving along a track (see Figure 1.3). A case of four objects is treated in Chen (1984).

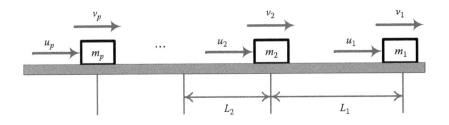

Figure 1.3 Moving objects along a track.

For $i = 1, 2, \ldots, p$, denote by m_i and v_i the mass and the velocity of the ith object, respectively, and let u_i be the force acting on the ith object, and y_i be the position of the ith object. Further, denote by L_i, $i = 1, 2, \ldots, p - 1$, the relative distance between the ith and the $(i + 1)$th object. Then we have the following equations describing the motion of the p objects:

$$\begin{cases} \dot{y}_i = v_i \\ m_i \dot{v}_i + k v_i = u_i, \quad i = 1, 2, \ldots, p, \end{cases} \tag{1.34}$$

where k is the friction factor.

The purpose of control is to let all the objects move with a fixed velocity v_0, and at the same time, to let any neighboring objects keep a fixed distance L_0. Toward this purpose, let us define

$$\begin{cases} L_i^r = L_i - L_0, & i = 1, 2, \ldots, p - 1 \\ v_i^r = v_i - v_0, & i = 1, 2, \ldots, p \\ u_i^r = u_i - k v_0, & i = 1, 2, \ldots, p, \end{cases} \tag{1.35}$$

then, using (1.34) and (1.35), we have

$$\dot{L}_i^r = \dot{L}_i$$
$$= \dot{y}_i - \dot{y}_{i+1}$$
$$= v_i^r - v_{i+1}^r, \quad i = 1, 2, \ldots, p - 1 \tag{1.36}$$

and

$$m_i \dot{v}_i^r + k v_i^r = m_i \dot{v}_i + k (v_i - v_0)$$
$$= u_i - k v_0$$
$$= u_i^r, \quad i = 1, 2, \ldots, p - 1. \tag{1.37}$$

Denote

$$q_i = \begin{bmatrix} v_i^r \\ L_i^r \end{bmatrix}, \quad i = 1, 2, \ldots, p - 1,$$

and choose the state, output, and control vectors as

$$x = \begin{bmatrix} q_1 \\ q_2 \\ \vdots \\ q_{p-1} \\ v_p \end{bmatrix}, \quad y = \begin{bmatrix} L_1^r \\ L_2^r \\ \vdots \\ L_{p-1}^r \end{bmatrix}, \quad u = \begin{bmatrix} u_1^r \\ u_2^r \\ \vdots \\ u_{p-1}^r \\ u_p \end{bmatrix},$$

respectively, we can obtain, by combining the equations in (1.36) and (1.37) and the last equation in (1.34), the dynamical model of the system represented in the standard descriptor form (1.2), with

$$E = \text{diag}\left(m_1, 1, m_2, 1, \ldots, m_{p-1}, 1, m_p\right),$$

$$A = \begin{bmatrix} -k & 0 & 0 & & & & & \\ 1 & 0 & -1 & & & & & \\ & & -k & 0 & 0 & & & \\ & & 1 & 0 & -1 & & & \\ & & & & \ddots & \ddots & & \\ & & & & & -k & 0 & 0 \\ & & & & & 1 & 0 & -1 \\ & & & & & & & -k \end{bmatrix},$$

$$B = \begin{bmatrix} 1 & 0 & & & & \\ 0 & 0 & & & & \\ & & 1 & 0 & & \\ & & 0 & 0 & & \\ & & & & \ddots & \ddots \\ & & & & 1 & 0 \\ & & & & 0 & 0 \\ & & & & & 1 \end{bmatrix},$$

and

$$C = \begin{bmatrix} 0 & 1 & & & \\ & & 0 & 1 & \\ & & & & \ddots & \ddots \\ & & & & & 0 & 1 \end{bmatrix},$$

where in the above matrices A, B, and C the empty entries are all zeros.

Example 1.2

In the case of $p = 3$, the system is described by the equation (1.2), with

$$E = \text{diag}\,(m_1, 1, m_2, 1, m_3),$$

$$A = \begin{bmatrix} -k & 0 & 0 & 0 & 0 & 0 \\ 1 & 0 & -1 & 0 & 0 & 0 \\ 0 & 0 & -k & 0 & 0 & 0 \\ 0 & 0 & 1 & 0 & -1 & 0 \\ 0 & 0 & 0 & 0 & 0 & -k \end{bmatrix}, \tag{1.38}$$

and

$$B = \begin{bmatrix} 1 & 0 & 0 \\ 0 & 0 & 0 \\ 0 & 1 & 0 \\ 0 & 0 & 0 \\ 0 & 0 & 1 \end{bmatrix}, \quad C = \begin{bmatrix} 0 & 1 & 0 & 0 & 0 \\ 0 & 0 & 0 & 1 & 0 \end{bmatrix}. \tag{1.39}$$

Choosing the parameters as

$$k = 0.1, \quad m_i = 2i + 6\,\text{kg}, \quad i = 1, 2, 3,$$

we have

$$E = \text{diag}\,(8, 1, 10, 1, 12), \tag{1.40}$$

and

$$A = \begin{bmatrix} -0.1 & 0 & 0 & 0 & 0 \\ 1 & 0 & -1 & 0 & 0 \\ 0 & 0 & -0.1 & 0 & 0 \\ 0 & 0 & 1 & 0 & -1 \\ 0 & 0 & 0 & 0 & -0.1 \end{bmatrix}, \tag{1.41}$$

while the B and C matrices are still the same as in (1.39).

1.2.3 Constrained Linear Mechanical Systems

Constrained linear mechanical systems can be described as follows (Duan 2010):

$$M\ddot{z} + D\dot{z} + Kz = Lf + J^T\mu, \tag{1.42}$$

$$G\dot{z} + Hz = 0, \tag{1.43}$$

where

- $z \in \mathbb{R}^n$ is the displacement vector
- $f \in \mathbb{R}^n$ is the vector of known input forces
- $\mu \in \mathbb{R}^n$ is the vector of Lagrangian multipliers

- M is the inertial matrix which is usually symmetric and positive definite
- D is the damping gyroscopic matrix
- K is the stiffness and circulator matrix
- L is the force distribution matrix
- J is the Jacobian of the constraint equation
- G and H are the coefficient matrices of the constraint equation

All matrices in (1.42) and (1.43) are known and constant ones of appropriate dimensions.

Equation (1.42) is the dynamical equation, while (1.43) is the constraint equation.

1.2.3.1 Matrix Second-Order Form

By choosing the state vector and the input vector as

$$x = \begin{bmatrix} z \\ \mu \end{bmatrix} \text{ and } u = f,$$

respectively, then the above equations (1.42) and (1.43) can be written in the following second-order descriptor linear system form:

$$A_2\ddot{x} + A_1\dot{x} + A_0x = Bu, \tag{1.44}$$

with

$$A_2 = \begin{bmatrix} M & 0 \\ 0 & 0 \end{bmatrix}, \ A_1 = \begin{bmatrix} D & 0 \\ G & 0 \end{bmatrix},$$

$$A_0 = \begin{bmatrix} K & -J^{\mathrm{T}} \\ H & 0 \end{bmatrix}, \ B = \begin{bmatrix} L \\ 0 \end{bmatrix}.$$

1.2.3.2 Matrix First-Order Form

If we choose the state vector and the input vector as

$$x = \begin{bmatrix} z \\ \dot{z} \\ \mu \end{bmatrix} \text{ and } u = f,$$

respectively, then the above equations (1.42) and (1.43) can be written in the following descriptor linear system form:

$$E\dot{x} = Ax + Bu, \tag{1.45}$$

where

$$E = \begin{bmatrix} I & 0 & 0 \\ 0 & M & 0 \\ 0 & 0 & 0 \end{bmatrix}, \quad B = \begin{bmatrix} 0 \\ L \\ 0 \end{bmatrix}$$

and

$$A = \begin{bmatrix} 0 & I & 0 \\ -K & -D & J^{\mathrm{T}} \\ H & G & 0 \end{bmatrix}.$$

Example 1.3

Consider a mechanical system shown in Figure 1.4. This system consists of two one-mass oscillators connected by a dashpot element (Duan 2010, Schmidt 1994). Let

$$m_1 = m_2 = 1\,\text{kg}, \ d = 1\,\text{N-s/m}, \ k_1 = 2\,\text{N/m}, \ k_2 = 1\,\text{N/m}.$$

Then the equations (1.42) and (1.43) for this system can be obtained as follows:

$$\begin{bmatrix} 1 & 0 \\ 0 & 1 \end{bmatrix}\begin{bmatrix} \ddot{z}_1 \\ \ddot{z}_2 \end{bmatrix} + \begin{bmatrix} 1 & 1 \\ 1 & 1 \end{bmatrix}\begin{bmatrix} \dot{z}_1 \\ \dot{z}_2 \end{bmatrix} + \begin{bmatrix} 2 & 0 \\ 0 & 1 \end{bmatrix}\begin{bmatrix} z_1 \\ z_2 \end{bmatrix} = \begin{bmatrix} 1 \\ -1 \end{bmatrix} f + \begin{bmatrix} 1 \\ 1 \end{bmatrix} \mu,$$

$$\begin{bmatrix} 1 & 1 \end{bmatrix}\begin{bmatrix} z_1 \\ z_2 \end{bmatrix} = 0.$$

Therefore, we have

$$M = \begin{bmatrix} 1 & 0 \\ 0 & 1 \end{bmatrix}, \ D = \begin{bmatrix} 1 & 1 \\ 1 & 1 \end{bmatrix}, \ K = \begin{bmatrix} 2 & 0 \\ 0 & 1 \end{bmatrix},$$

$$L = \begin{bmatrix} 1 \\ -1 \end{bmatrix}, \ J^{\mathrm{T}} = \begin{bmatrix} 1 \\ 1 \end{bmatrix},$$

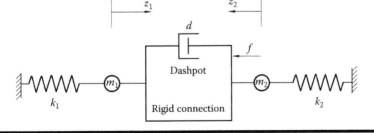

Figure 1.4 **Two connected one-mass oscillators. (With kind permission from Springer Science+Business Media:** *Analysis and Design of Descriptor Linear Systems,* **Advances in Mechanics and Mathematics, 2010, Duan, G.R., Springer, New York.)**

and

$$G = \begin{bmatrix} 0 & 0 \end{bmatrix}, \ H = \begin{bmatrix} 1 & 1 \end{bmatrix}.$$

Based on these matrices, the coefficient matrices in the matrix second-order form (1.44) can be obtained as

$$A_2 = \begin{bmatrix} 1 & 0 & 0 \\ 0 & 1 & 0 \\ 0 & 0 & 0 \end{bmatrix}, \ A_1 = \begin{bmatrix} 1 & 1 & 0 \\ 1 & 1 & 0 \\ 0 & 0 & 0 \end{bmatrix}, \tag{1.46}$$

$$A_0 = \begin{bmatrix} 2 & 0 & -1 \\ 0 & 1 & -1 \\ 1 & 1 & 0 \end{bmatrix}, \ B = \begin{bmatrix} 1 \\ -1 \\ 0 \end{bmatrix}. \tag{1.47}$$

If written in the first-order descriptor linear system form (1.45), then the system coefficients are

$$E = \begin{bmatrix} 1 & 0 & 0 & 0 & 0 \\ 0 & 1 & 0 & 0 & 0 \\ 0 & 0 & 1 & 0 & 0 \\ 0 & 0 & 0 & 1 & 0 \\ 0 & 0 & 0 & 0 & 0 \end{bmatrix} \tag{1.48}$$

and

$$A = \begin{bmatrix} 0 & 0 & 1 & 0 & 0 \\ 0 & 0 & 0 & 1 & 0 \\ -2 & 0 & -1 & -1 & 1 \\ 0 & -1 & -1 & -1 & 1 \\ 1 & 1 & 0 & 0 & 0 \end{bmatrix}, \ B = \begin{bmatrix} 0 \\ 0 \\ 1 \\ -1 \\ 0 \end{bmatrix}. \tag{1.49}$$

1.2.4 Flexible-Joint Robots

This flexible-joint robot example has been studied by Spong et al. (2008), Slotine and Li (1991), and Marino and Spong (1986).

Consider a flexible-joint mechanism shown in Figure 1.5, which represents a link driven by a model through a torsional spring (a single-link flexible-joint robot), in the vertical plane. It consists of an actuator (DC-motor) whose rotor inertia I is connected through a spring to a rigid link with inertia J about the axis of rotation. For simplicity, a linear spring with stiffness k is considered. In the following discussion, the generalized coordinates are taken to be the link angle q_1 and the motor shaft angle q_2.

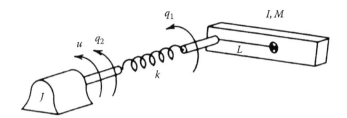

Figure 1.5 A flexible-joint mechanism. (From Spong, M.W. et al., *Robot Dynamics and Control*, 2nd edn., John Wiley & Sons, New York.)

Example 1.4

When the dynamics of the motor is approximated by a zero-order system, the equations of motion of this mechanism can be easily derived as

$$\begin{cases} I\ddot{q}_1 + D_1\dot{q}_1 + k\left(q_1 - q_2\right) = 0 \\ J\ddot{q}_2 + D_2\dot{q}_2 - k\left(q_1 - q_2\right) = u, \end{cases} \tag{1.50}$$

where u is the motor torque, which is proportional to the DC-motor voltage input.

Denote

$$x = \begin{bmatrix} q_1 \\ q_2 \end{bmatrix},$$

then this system can be easily arranged into the standard matrix second-order form of (1.5), with

$$M = \begin{bmatrix} I & 0 \\ 0 & J \end{bmatrix}, \quad D = \begin{bmatrix} D_1 & 0 \\ 0 & D_2 \end{bmatrix}, \quad K = \begin{bmatrix} k & -k \\ -k & k \end{bmatrix}$$

and

$$B = \begin{bmatrix} 0 \\ 1 \end{bmatrix}.$$

When the system parameters are taken as

$$\begin{cases} I = J = 0.0004 \text{ N-ms}^2/\text{rad} \\ D_2 = 0.015 \text{ N-ms/rad} \\ D_1 = 0.0 \text{ N-ms/rad} \\ k = 0.8 \text{ N-m/rad}, \end{cases} \tag{1.51}$$

we have

$$M = 0.0004 \begin{bmatrix} 1 & 0 \\ 0 & 1 \end{bmatrix}, \quad D = \begin{bmatrix} 0 & 0 \\ 0 & 0.015 \end{bmatrix}, \quad K = 0.8 \begin{bmatrix} 1 & -1 \\ -1 & 1 \end{bmatrix}.$$

Example 1.5

In Example 1.4, the dynamics of the motor producing the torque u is considered to be a zero-order system, while in many cases, for example, when the rotating rate is high enough, the dynamics of the motor needs to be modeled by a first- or a second-order dynamical system. Suppose now the dynamics of the motor is given by

$$\dot{u} = a_0 u + v, \tag{1.52}$$

where

■ v is the voltage input
■ a_0 is a proper negative real number

Let us now establish the overall model for this case.

Taking differentiation over both sides of the second equation in (1.50) gives

$$J\dddot{q}_2 + D_2\ddot{q}_2 - k\left(\dot{q}_1 - \dot{q}_2\right) = \dot{u}.$$

Substituting (1.52) into the above equation further produces

$$
\begin{aligned}
J\dddot{q}_2 + D_2\ddot{q}_2 - k\left(\dot{q}_1 - \dot{q}_2\right) \\
= a_0 u + v \\
= a_0 \left(J\ddot{q}_2 + D_2\dot{q}_2 - k\left(q_1 - q_2\right)\right) + v \\
= a_0 J\ddot{q}_2 + a_0 D_2\dot{q}_2 - a_0 k q_1 + a_0 k q_2 + v,
\end{aligned}
$$

that is,

$$J\dddot{q}_2 + \left(D_2 - a_0 J\right)\ddot{q}_2 - k\dot{q}_1 + \left(k - a_0 D_2\right)\dot{q}_2 + a_0 k q_1 - a_0 k q_2 = v.$$

Therefore, in this case, the dynamical equation for this flexible-joint mechanism is given by

$$
\begin{cases}
I\ddot{q}_1 + D_1\dot{q}_1 + k\left(q_1 - q_2\right) = 0 \\
J\dddot{q}_2 + \left(D_2 - a_0 J\right)\ddot{q}_2 - k\dot{q}_1 + \left(k - a_0 D_2\right)\dot{q}_2 + a_0 k q_1 - a_0 k q_2 = v,
\end{cases} \tag{1.53}
$$

which can be arranged into the matrix third-order standard form of

$$A_3 \dddot{q} + A_2 \ddot{q} + A_1 \dot{q} + A_0 = Bv, \tag{1.54}$$

with

$$A_3 = \begin{bmatrix} 0 & 0 \\ 0 & J \end{bmatrix}, \quad A_2 = \begin{bmatrix} I & 0 \\ 0 & D_2 - a_0 J \end{bmatrix}$$

and

$$A_1 = \begin{bmatrix} D_1 & 0 \\ -k & k - a_0 D_2 \end{bmatrix}, \ A_0 = \begin{bmatrix} k & -k \\ a_0 k & -a_0 k \end{bmatrix}, \ B = \begin{bmatrix} 0 \\ 1 \end{bmatrix}.$$

When the system parameters are given as in (1.51) and $a_0 = -0.95$, we have

$$A_3 = \begin{bmatrix} 0 & 0 \\ 0 & 0.0004 \end{bmatrix}, \ A_2 = 10^{-3} \times \begin{bmatrix} 0.4 & 0 \\ 0 & 15.38 \end{bmatrix}$$

and

$$A_1 = \begin{bmatrix} 0 & 0 \\ -0.8 & 0.814\,25 \end{bmatrix}, \ A_0 = \begin{bmatrix} 0.8 & -0.8 \\ -0.76 & 0.76 \end{bmatrix}, \ B = \begin{bmatrix} 0 \\ 1 \end{bmatrix}.$$

1.3 Sylvester Family

In this book, the family of Sylvester matrix equations are classified into four categories, namely, first-order generalized Sylvester equations (GSEs), second-order GSEs, higher-order GSEs, and normal Sylvester equations (NSEs).

1.3.1 First-Order GSEs

1.3.1.1 Homogeneous GSEs

When dealing with analysis and design problems associated with the first-order descriptor linear system (1.1), we often encounter a type of GSEs in the form of

$$EVF - AV = B_1 WF + B_0 W, \tag{1.55}$$

where

- the matrices $E, A \in \mathbb{R}^{n \times q}$, $B_1, B_0 \in \mathbb{R}^{n \times r}$, and $F \in \mathbb{C}^{p \times p}$ are the parameter matrices
- the matrices $V \in \mathbb{C}^{q \times p}$ and $W \in \mathbb{C}^{r \times p}$ are the ones to be determined

In the case of $B_1 = 0$ and denote $B_0 \triangleq B$, the above GSE (1.55) reduces to the following more familiar form:

$$EVF - AV = BW. \tag{1.56}$$

Further, when $E = I_q$, this equation becomes the following one:

$$VF - AV = BW, \tag{1.57}$$

which is often encountered when dealing with the analysis and design problems associated with the first-order normal linear system (1.3).

Obviously, setting $W = -I_p$, $E = -I_q$, and $r = p$, in (1.56), gives the following well-known NSE

$$VF + AV = B, \tag{1.58}$$

and setting $W = I_p$, $A = I_q$, and $r = p$ yields the following generalized discrete-time Lyapunov algebraic matrix equation, or Kalman–Yakubovich equation

$$EVF - V = B, \tag{1.59}$$

which turns, when $E = F^T$, further into the well-known discrete-time Lyapunov algebraic matrix equation, or the Stein equation

$$F^T VF - V = B. \tag{1.60}$$

While setting $W = -I_p$, $E = -I_q$, $A = F^T$ in (1.56) produces the following well-known continuous-time Lyapunov algebraic matrix equation

$$F^T V + VF = B. \tag{1.61}$$

1.3.1.2 Nonhomogeneous GSEs

With many system analysis and design applications, for example, disturbance attenuation design, the following type of nonhomogeneous GSEs in the following form are also often encountered:

$$EVF - AV = B_1 WF + B_0 W + R, \tag{1.62}$$

where $R \in \mathbb{C}^{n \times p}$, and again the matrices $V \in \mathbb{C}^{q \times p}$ and $W \in \mathbb{C}^{r \times p}$ are the ones to be determined. In the case of $B_1 = 0$ and $B \triangleq B_0$, this equation reduces to

$$EVF - AV = BW + R. \tag{1.63}$$

Further, when $E = I$, it becomes

$$VF - AV = BW + R. \tag{1.64}$$

These two GSEs (1.63) and (1.64) correspond to the descriptor linear system (1.2) and the normal linear system (1.3), respectively.

1.3.2 Second-Order GSEs

Many control problems, such as pole assignment and eigenstructure assignment (ESA), disturbance decoupling and observer designs, associated with the second-order linear system (1.4), are closely related to a type of GSEs in the following form:

$$MVF^2 + DVF + KV = B_2 WF^2 + B_1 WF + B_0 W + R, \tag{1.65}$$

where

- M, D, $K \in \mathbb{R}^{n \times q}$, B_2, B_1, $B_0 \in \mathbb{R}^{n \times r}$, $F \in \mathbb{C}^{p \times p}$, and $R \in \mathbb{C}^{n \times p}$ are the parameter matrices
- $V \in \mathbb{C}^{q \times p}$ and $W \in \mathbb{C}^{r \times p}$ are the matrices to be determined

These types of equations are called second-order nonhomogeneous GSEs. When $R = 0$, the nonhomogeneous equation (1.65) becomes the following homogeneous one:

$$MVF^2 + DVF + KV = B_2 WF^2 + B_1 WF + B_0 W. \qquad (1.66)$$

We point out that in many applications, we often have $q = n$, and also $B_1 = B_2 = 0$, and in latter case, the above two GSEs clearly reduce to

$$MVF^2 + DVF + KV = BW + R \qquad (1.67)$$

and

$$MVF^2 + DVF + KV = BW, \qquad (1.68)$$

where B_0 has been replaced with B for simplicity.

The above two second-order GSEs (1.67) and (1.68) correspond to the second-order linear system (1.5).

1.3.3 Higher-Order GSEs

It can be shown that certain control problems, such as pole/ESA and observer design, associated with the higher-order linear system (1.12), are closely related to a type of equations in the following form (Duan 2005b, 2013b,c,d,f, 2014k,l, Yu and Duan 2009a, 2010):

$$A_m VF^m + \cdots + A_1 VF + A_0 V = B_m WF^m + \cdots + B_1 WF + B_0 W + R, \quad (1.69)$$

where

- $A_i \in \mathbb{R}^{n \times q}$, $B_i \in \mathbb{R}^{n \times r}$, $i = 0, 1, \ldots, m$, $F \in \mathbb{C}^{p \times p}$ and $R \in \mathbb{C}^{n \times p}$ are the parameter matrices
- $V \in \mathbb{C}^{q \times p}$ and $W \in \mathbb{C}^{r \times p}$ are the matrices to be determined

Such an equation is called the mth order rectangular nonhomogeneous GSEs, it becomes a square one when $q = n$.

When the matrix R is restricted to possess the following special form

$$R = C_m R^* F^m + \cdots + C_1 R^* F + C_0 R^*,$$

where $C_i \in \mathbb{R}^{n \times d}$, $i = 0, 1, \ldots, m$, and $R^* \in \mathbb{C}^{d \times p}$ are given matrices, the above nonhomogeneous GSE can be written, compactly, as

$$\sum_{i=0}^{m} A_i V F^i = \sum_{i=0}^{m} B_i W F^i + \sum_{i=0}^{m} C_i R^* F^i. \tag{1.70}$$

When $R = 0$, this equation reduces to the following homogeneous form:

$$A_m V F^m + \cdots + A_1 V F + A_0 V = B_m W F^m + \cdots + B_1 W F + B_0 W. \tag{1.71}$$

In many applications, we have $B_i = 0$, $i = 1, 2, \ldots, m$, and in this case, the above two GSEs obviously become (Duan 2005b), when B_0 is replaced with B,

$$A_m V F^m + \cdots + A_1 V F + A_0 V = B W + R, \tag{1.72}$$

and

$$A_m V F^m + \cdots + A_1 V F + A_0 V = B W. \tag{1.73}$$

Obviously, the above higher-order GSE includes both the first- and second-order GSEs as special cases. For convenience, we introduce for the above higher-order GSE the following definition.

Definition 1.4 *Given the mth-order GSE (1.69) or (1.71), the following polynomial matrix pair $(A(s), B(s))$ defined by*

$$\begin{cases} A(s) = A_m s^m + \cdots + A_1 s + A_0 \\ B(s) = B_m s^m + \cdots + B_1 s + B_0 \end{cases}$$

is called the polynomial matrix pair associated with the GSE (1.69) or (1.71); particularly, the polynomial matrix $A(s)$ is called the characteristic polynomial matrix of the GSE (1.69) or (1.71).

1.3.4 NSEs

Letting $B = I_n$ in the homogeneous GSE (1.73) gives the following equation:

$$A_m V F^m + \cdots + A_1 V F + A_0 V = W, \tag{1.74}$$

which is called, when the matrix W is known and $\det A_m \neq 0$, a NSE of mth order.

When the matrix W possesses the following special form

$$W = C_m W^* F^m + \cdots + C_1 W^* F + C_0 W^*,$$

where $C_i \in \mathbb{R}^{n \times d}$, $i = 0, 1, \ldots, m$, and $W^* \in \mathbb{C}^{d \times p}$ are given matrices, the above NSE (1.74) can be written as

$$A_m VF^m + \cdots + A_1 VF + A_0 V = C_m W^* F^m + \cdots + C_1 W^* F + C_0 W^*. \quad (1.75)$$

When $m = 2$, and $A_2 = M$, $A_1 = D$, and $A_0 = K$, the above NSE (1.74) reduces to the following second-order NSE:

$$MVF^2 + DVF + KV = W. \quad (1.76)$$

When $m = 1$, and $A_1 = E$, and $A_0 = -A$, equation (1.74) reduces to the following first-order NSE:

$$EVF - AV = W. \quad (1.77)$$

Further letting in (1.77) $E = I_n$ gives the following most well-known NSE:

$$VF - AV = W. \quad (1.78)$$

As a matter of fact, equation (1.78) is really the Sylvester equation, which is well known in the literature. Equation (1.77) is a slightly generalized form of (1.78), which is often encountered when dealing with the design problems of the first-order descriptor linear system (1.1). Due to this reason, we call both (1.78) and (1.77) the first-order NSEs, and call (1.76) the second-order NSE, while (1.74) the mth-order NSE.

Letting $E = I_n$, $A = -F^{\mathrm{T}}$ in the first-order NSE (1.77), or simply $A = -F^{\mathrm{T}}$ in (1.78), gives the following well-known Lyapunov algebraic equation for continuous-time systems:

$$VF + F^{\mathrm{T}} V = W. \quad (1.79)$$

If we let in the NSE (1.77) $A = I_n$, we obtain the following generalized discrete-time Lyapunov algebraic equation, or the Kalman–Yakubovich equation:

$$EVF - V = W, \quad (1.80)$$

which clearly turns, when $E = F^{\mathrm{T}}$, into the following conventional discrete-time Lyapunov algebraic equation:

$$F^{\mathrm{T}} VF - V = W. \quad (1.81)$$

Remark 1.2 This set of equations (1.74) through (1.81) can also be easily obtained from the nonhomogeneous equation (1.69) through letting $B_i = 0$, $i = 0, 1, \ldots, m$,

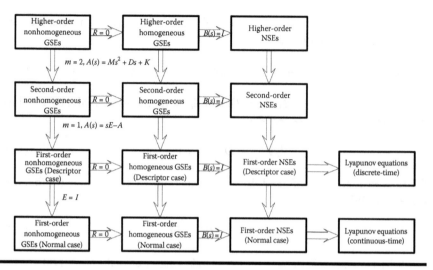

Figure 1.6 **Relations among GSEs (NSEs).**

or letting $r = 0$, that is, the number of columns in the matrix B_i, $i = 0, 1, \ldots, m$, is zero. In this case, the W matrix in the equations (1.74) through (1.81) should be replaced by R.

Remark 1.3 When all the matrices A_i, B_i, $i = 0, 1, \ldots, m$, F, and R are known, perhaps the most direct way to solve the matrix equation (1.69) is via the Kronecker product or the stretching operation (Wu et al. 2008d), which produces equivalent linear vector equations in the forms of (A.24) and (A.25). However, for analysis and design purposes, we often need an explicit complete parametric solution. Furthermore, in certain cases, we still need to have a general solution to this equation even when the matrices F and R are unknown or only partially known. One of the main purposes of this book is to provide such solutions for the GSEs (1.69) and (1.71) as well as their spacial cases.

Within the frame of this book, (1.69) is the most general form treated. Figure 1.6 gives the relations among the several types of GSEs and NSEs introduced in this section.

1.4 An Overview: Work by Other Researchers

In this section, we give a brief overview on results related to GSEs and GSE-based applications. We remark that the author's work is not included in this section, since it will really be presented systematically in this book and/or will be commented in the Notes and References Sections in the later chapters. Three of the Notes and References Sections, which are closely related to this overview section, are Sections 2.4, 4.8, and 5.9.

1.4.1 GSEs Related to Normal Linear Systems

The GSE, which attracts the most attention in the literature, should be the first-order homogeneous GSE (1.57), that is,

$$VF - AV = BW. \tag{1.82}$$

This equation is closely related to applications in various design problems related to the normal linear system (1.3) (see also, Chapter 2). The transposed form of this equation is

$$F^{\mathrm{T}}V^{\mathrm{T}} - V^{\mathrm{T}}A^{\mathrm{T}} = W^{\mathrm{T}}B^{\mathrm{T}},$$

which falls into the form of

$$FT - TA = ZC. \tag{1.83}$$

This equation, with unknowns T and Z, is a dual form of (1.82), and is often called a Sylvester-like observer matrix equation.

1.4.1.1 Numerical Solutions

To most researchers, solving the equation means to find the unknowns V and W (or T and Z in the dual form) when all the other involved matrices are known.

For large Sylvester-like observer matrix equations, a numerical method, namely, the Arnoldi method, has attracted considerable attention. This method is proposed by Datta and Saad (1991), when A is large and sparse, and has also been applied to partial spectrum assignment. One drawback to this method is that, due to potential cancelations during computations, the resulting vectors can be far from orthogonal. However, the method can still provide accurate answers, especially when reorthogonalization is used. Several researchers have further studied the Arnoldi method. Calvetti et al. (2001) further investigate numerical aspects of the Datta–Saad method (Datta and Saad 1991), and Robbe and Sadkane (2008) use the near-breakdowns in the block Arnoldi method for solving large Sylvester equations. The numerical experiments show that the proposed iterative scheme performs much better than the classical methods. Datta et al. (2010) further propose a global Arnoldi method for solving the Sylvester-observer equation, which is a particular generalization of the Arnoldi method proposed earlier by Datta and Saad (1991) in the single-output case. The proposed method is developed by exploiting an interesting relationship between the initially chosen block-row vector and the block-row vector obtained after m steps of the global Arnoldi method. Furthermore, Heyouni (2011) proposes extended Arnoldi methods for large low-rank Sylvester matrix equations. The numerical results show that the methods are robust and give better results than the LRS-BA (low-rank Sylvester block Arnoldi) and LRS-GA (low-rank Sylvester global Arnoldi) methods.

Besides the Arnoldi method, the Krylov-subspace-based methods have also attracted some attention. Carvalho et al. (2003) propose a new block algorithm for solving the Sylvester-observer equation. The algorithm does not require the reduction of the system matrix A and is then ideally suitable for large and sparse computations by using the recently developed Krylov-subspace-based methods. This algorithm is well suited for implementation on high-performance computing using LAPACK (Linear Algebra PACKage), and it seems to be more accurate compared with similar ones. Also, Jbilou (2006) proposes a matrix Krylov subspace method for low-rank approximate solutions to large Sylvester matrix equations. Numerical tests show that the proposed method is effective for sparse Sylvester matrix equations.

Other algorithms have also been proposed by van Dooren (1984), Barlow et al. (1992), and Carvalho and Datta (2011). In van Dooren (1984), an orthogonal transformation-based algorithm was proposed to solve the Sylvester-observer matrix equation. In this algorithm, the matrix pair (A, C) is first transformed via a unitary state-space transformation to a staircase form. With such a transformation, the solution of the Sylvester-observer matrix equation can be obtained by a lower matrix equation with Schur form. The advantage of this approach is that one can use more degrees of freedom in the equation to find a solution matrix with some desired robustness properties such as minimum norm. Barlow et al. (1992) propose an algorithm for computing the solution to constrained matrix Sylvester equations. Existence conditions for the solution are established, and an algorithm for computing the solution is derived. Conditions under which the matrix $[C^{\mathrm{T}} \ T^{\mathrm{T}}]$ is of full rank are also discussed. The problem arises in control theory in the design of reduced-order observers, which achieve loop transfer recovery. Carvalho and Datta (2011) generalize the observer-Hessenberg algorithm for block-wise solution of the generalized Sylvester-observer equation based on the generalized observer-Hessenberg form. Application to state and velocity estimations in vibrating systems is also treated.

Different from the above, Truhar et al. (2010) carry out analysis of the solution of a Sylvester equation using the low-rank alternating-directional-implicit method (LR-ADI) with exact shifts. New bounds and perturbation bounds on the solution matrix V are obtained. A distinguished feature of these bounds is that they reflect the interplay between the eigenvalue decompositions of A and B and the right-hand side factors.

1.4.1.2 Parametric Solutions

For explicit solutions to the GSE, there are also some results. Zhou and Yan (2008) consider solutions to right coprime factorizations (RCFs) and based on which complete solution with explicit freedom to the generalized Sylvester matrix equation is proposed. The primary feature of this solution is that the matrix F does not need to be transformed into any canonical form.

When F is in Jordan form, an attractive analytical and restriction-free solution is proposed by Tsui (1987).

By using Kronecker map and Sylvester sum and the concept of coefficients of characteristic polynomial of the matrix A, Ramadan et al. (2009) consider the explicit solutions of the Sylvester and the Yakubovich matrix equations. The obtained results show that the methods are very neat and efficient.

1.4.1.3 Solutions with Applications

One of the most successful applications of GSEs is ESA in linear systems by feedback controls. Syrmos and Lewis (1993) consider output-feedback ESA using two Sylvester equations and present a simple algorithm for ESA with output feedback for systems with the sum of the dimensions of the input and output vectors greater than the dimension of the state vector. A computationally efficient algorithm is presented for the solution of these two coupled equations, which leads to the computation of a desired output feedback. Choi (1998) considers left ESA via Sylvester equation. The proposed scheme could be utilized in designing a disturbance attenuation controller because the directions of the assigned left eigenvectors affect the degrees of the control effectiveness and disturbance suppressibility of the system. Furthermore, Choi et al. (1999) consider ESA by the Sylvester equation for both the linear time-invariant system and the linear time-varying system, and propose an ESA scheme for linear systems via the algebraic and differential Sylvester equations based upon newly developed notions.

Other types of natural applications of GSEs are observer and compensator designs. Syrmos and Lewis (1994) consider coupled and constrained Sylvester equations in system design. Several design problems, including reduced observer and compensator design, output feedback, and finite transmission zero assignment, are examined using the vehicle of the coupled Sylvester equations. The Sylvester approach allows the unification of algebraic and geometric approaches, and provides numerical design algorithms through the tool of the Hessenberg form. Emirsajlow (2012) also proposes basic theory and application to observer design using the implemented semigroup concept and develops a mathematical framework for the infinite-dimensional Sylvester equation both in the differential and the algebraic form. The problem of designing an asymptotic state observer for a linear infinite-dimensional control system with a bounded input operator and an unbounded output operator is also studied. Furthermore, Wang and his co-authors have proposed a parameterized design of reduced-order state observer in linear control systems based on the parametric solution for a class of Sylvester matrix equations (Wang et al. 2011), and have also considered the design of robust finite time functional observers in uncertain linear systems based on the parametric solution for a class of Sylvester matrix equations (see, e.g., Wang et al. 2013, 2014, Zhao and Wang 2012).

Different from the above, Syrmos (1994) considers disturbance decoupling using constrained Sylvester equations. First, the author designs a state feedback that rejects the disturbance from the controlled outputs, and second, he constructs an observer that estimates the state under the presence of disturbances. It aims to exhibit the significance of the constrained Sylvester equations to system design problems by showing their close relationship to an elegant geometric theory and to develop a numerically efficient algorithm for the disturbance decoupling problem.

1.4.2 GSEs Related to Descriptor Linear Systems

Corresponding to equation (1.82), the first-order homogeneous GSEs related to descriptor linear system (1.2) take the form of (1.56), that is,

$$EVF - AV = BW. \tag{1.84}$$

The observer form of this equation is

$$FTE - TA = ZC,$$

where again the matrices T and Z are the unknowns.

1.4.2.1 Solutions to the Equations

Castelan and Silva (2005) investigate the solution of a Sylvester equation appearing in descriptor systems control theory under the hypothesis of strong detectability of the descriptor system, a sequence of coordinate transformations is proposed such that the considered problem can be solved through a Sylvester equation associated to a detectable reduced-order normal system. The results can easily be adapted for discrete-time descriptor systems. A numerical example has shown that the linear matrix inequality (LMI)-type technique can provide an interesting framework to implicitly find optimized solutions for the considered constrained Sylvester equation. This problem studied in Castelan and Silva (2005) is also investigated by Darouach (2006), who gives a new and simple algorithm to solve the GSE associated with linear descriptor systems, a simple and direct method is developed.

There are also two approaches providing the explicit solutions to this equation. By using Kronecker map and Sylvester sum and the concept of coefficients of characteristic polynomial of the matrix A, Ramadan et al. (2009) consider the explicit solutions of the Sylvester and the Yakubovich matrix equations. The proposed methods are illustrated by numerical examples, and the obtained results show that the methods are very neat and efficient. Wu et al. (2012d) also consider closed-form solutions to the generalized Sylvester-conjugate matrix equation. They adopt two approaches to solve this matrix equation. The first approach is based on the real representation technique. The basic idea is to transform it into the generalized Sylvester matrix equation. In the second approach, the solution to this matrix equation can be explicitly provided. In order to obtain the explicit solution, two matrices are first constructed, and a relation between these two matrices needs to be derived. The approaches do not require the coefficient matrices to be in any canonical forms.

Very recently, Song et al. (2014b,c) consider solution to Yakubovich equations. Specifically, Song et al. (2014b) consider solution of the so-called Yakubovich-transpose matrix equation, which is actually a special case of (1.84) with $A = I_n$, and provide explicit solutions using the Leverrier algorithm and the associated characteristic polynomial, while Song et al. (2014c) give a real representation method for solving the Yakubovich-j-conjugate quaternion matrix equation $X - A\bar{X}B = CY$ based on the real representation of a quaternion matrix.

Different from the above, Yu and Bi (2014) have investigated GSEs in the form of

$$EVJ - AV = B_1 WJ + B_0 W, \qquad (1.85)$$

and have proposed two analytical general solutions to the matrix equation. Here the matrix J possesses a Jordan matrix form.

1.4.2.2 Solutions with Applications

Carvalho and Datta (2011) propose an algorithm for block-wise solution of the generalized Sylvester-observer equation and apply it to state and velocity estimation. Based on the generalized observer-Hessenberg form, they generalize the observer-Hessenberg algorithm for the Sylvester-observer equation. Yang et al. (2012) provide an iterative method to solutions of the generalized Sylvester matrix equation, and then apply it to ESA in linear systems. Some numerical results show the effectiveness of their proposed approach. Zhang uses the parametric solutions to the GSE to solve the problem of parametric ESA by state feedback in descriptor systems (Zhang 2008), and the problem of eigenvalue assignment in linear descriptor systems via output feedback (Zhang 2013). Based on the parametric solution for a class of Sylvester matrix equations, Liang et al. (2011) give approaches for the design of robust H_∞ fault-tolerant controller against sensor and actuator failures for uncertain descriptor systems.

1.4.3 Other Types of Equations

1.4.3.1 Nonhomogeneous First-Order GSEs

A general, complete parametric solution to the nonhomogeneous generalized Sylvester matrix equation in the form of (1.63), that is,

$$EVF - AV = BW + R, \tag{1.86}$$

is proposed by Wu et al. (2010e). This solution is neatly expressed by index-t and index-φ R-controllability matrices associated with the matrix triple (E, A, B), the generalized symmetric operators, and an index-t observability matrices. One advantage of the proposed solution is that the matrices F and R are in an arbitrary form and can be set undetermined.

Different from Wu et al. (2010e), Ramadan et al. (2013) propose two iterative algorithms for the Sylvester-conjugate matrix equation $AV + BW = E\bar{V}F + C$ and $AV + B\bar{W} = E\bar{V}F + C$. When these two matrix equations are consistent, for any initial matrices, the solutions can be obtained within finite iterative steps in the absence of round-off errors. Some lemmas and theorems are stated and proved where the iterative solutions are obtained.

While general nonhomogeneous GSEs have seldom been studied, many researchers have really drawn their attention on the following special one:

$$VF - BW = R. \tag{1.87}$$

These include Beitia and Gracia (1996), Dehghan and Hajarian (2008a), Hodel and Misra (1996), Huang et al. (2012), Jonsson and Kagstrom (2002), Kagstrom (1994), Kagstrom and Poromaa (1996), Kagstrom and Westin (1989), Lin and Wei (2007), Poromaa (1998), Shahzad et al. (2011), Wang et al. (2002), Wimmer (1994), and Yin et al. (2012).

1.4.3.2 Second- and Higher-Order GSEs

Dehghan and Hajarian (2009) construct an efficient iterative method for solving the second-order Sylvester matrix equation (1.68), that is,

$$MVF^2 + DVF + KV = BW. \tag{1.88}$$

By the iterative method, the solvability of the second-order Sylvester matrix equation can be determined automatically. The algorithm is simple and neat, and does not require the matrix F to be in any canonical form. For the same type of equations, Wang et al. (2010) propose a parametric solution, based on which the vibration control problem in second-order linear systems is investigated.

Different from the above, based on the parametric solution for a class of second-order Sylvester matrix equations, Sun et al. (2010) investigate the robust solution on a class of uncertain second-order matrix equations.

Up till now, for the second-order GSEs in the form of (1.66) and also for the higher-order GSEs in the forms of (1.73) and (1.71), except for the author's work, there have not been any reported results.

Again, for the nonhomogeneous second-order GSEs in the forms of (1.67) and (1.65), and also for the nonhomogeneous higher-order GSEs in the forms of (1.69) and (1.72), except the author's work, there has not been any reported results by now.

Nevertheless, having cooperated with the author on solution to higher-order GSEs and ESA in higher-order systems, Haihua Yu has further done some new applications of parametric solutions to higher-order GSEs. These include robust pole assignment of uncertain higher-order discrete systems with input time-delay (Wang and Yu 2014), ESA in a type of higher-order discrete time-delay linear system via state feedback (Yu and Wang 2013) and ESA in higher-order linear systems via output feedback (Yu and Bi 2012a), and also, parametric approaches for observer design in higher-order descriptor linear systems (Yu and Bi 2012b).

Remark 1.4 Regarding existing solutions on NSEs as well as the continuous- and discrete-time Lyapunov matrix equations and the Kalman–Yakubovich equation, please refer to Section 9.6. Here we make the following two points:

- Rectangular NSEs have been seldom addressed in the literature.
- For square NSEs, most results are concentrated on the first-order case, while higher-order NSEs are not at all widely tackled.

1.5 About the Book

1.5.1 Purposes

1.5.1.1 Showing Applications of GSEs

GSEs have found applications in many fields, such as computer science, signal processing, biocomputation, and control systems designs. One of the purposes of this book is to highlight the applications of the family of Sylvester matrix equations in control systems designs. Our intention is to convince the readers that many control system design problems in linear control system theory are closely related to these GSEs.

It has been seen in the former subsection that both the continuous-time and the discrete-time Lyapunov equations (1.79) and (1.81) are special cases of GSEs. Regarding the applications of these Lyapunov equations (1.79) and (1.81) and the first-order NSEs (1.77) and (1.78) in control systems analysis and designs, it is well known that there have been many results given in the last few decades.

In Chapter 2, we show the applications of the GSEs in control system theory. For the sake of familiarity to the readers, we have only stressed on the case of the first-order GSEs and demonstrated their basic functions in control system theory with several typical control system design problems, namely, the problems of generalized pole/ESA, observer design, model reference tracking, and disturbance decoupling.

1.5.1.2 Highlighting the Sylvester Parametric Approaches

This book focuses on the general parametric solutions to the type of GSEs. It is shown in Chapter 2 that many control system design problems can be formulated in such a way that the solutions to these problems are closely related to certain types of GSEs. Based on this fact and the general complete parametric solutions to these types of GSEs, general Sylvester parametric approaches for control system designs have been proposed by the author and his co-authors, which are effective, simple and convenient, and also very powerful in dealing with multiobjective design requirements.

More specifically, to solve such a control system design problem, one can establish the parametrization of the type of controller to be designed and the specifications to be satisfied based on the general parametric solutions to the type of related GSEs, and then solve the design parameters by forming an optimization problem. Once a set of design parameters are sought, a desired controller can then be immediately obtained via the controller parametrization.

Although this book does not go into the details of the Sylvester parametric design approaches, it gives in Chapter 2 the general idea and explains the power of the Sylvester parametric design approaches (see also, Figure 2.1).

1.5.1.3 Presenting Solutions to GSEs

The main purpose of the book is of course to present solutions to GSEs.

It is clear that solving one of the NSEs (1.77) and (1.78), or the Lyapunov matrix equations (1.79) and (1.81), means to find a matrix V satisfying the corresponding equation. In this case, we have only one unknown to solve, the matrix V, while the other coefficient matrices are all assumed to be known. The matrix W, which may not be known *a priori*, is not a variable to be sought. However, regarding the solution to any of the GSEs (1.57) through (1.69), the aim is to find two unknowns, both the matrices V and W, satisfying the equation.

This book deals with a type of higher-order GSEs in the form of (1.69), which include the first- and second-order GSEs, the NSEs of arbitrary orders, and the well-known continuous- and discrete-time Lyapunov matrix equations all as special cases.

Solvability of the GSEs is first investigated. It is shown that the homogeneous GSEs have more than one solution under very mild conditions. Therefore, it is very important to give a general solution, which provides all the degrees of freedom, since the degrees of freedom can be further utilized in applications to cope with additional design requirements. It is shown that the solvability of a homogeneous GSE and the degrees of freedom in the general solution to this equation are determined by a so-called F-left coprime condition, which is actually equivalent to the eigenvalues of the matrix F are different from the uncontrollable modes of the systems associated with the equations.

General complete parametric solutions to these GSEs are established for three important cases:

- F is an arbitrary square matrix
- F is a general Jordan matrix
- F is a diagonal matrix

As we will see, the first case has applications in problems like observer design, model reference tracking, and disturbance decoupling, while the second and third cases are often required by the pole assignment and ESA problems. By specifying the general parametric solutions to the GSEs, explicit and analytical solutions to the series of NSEs, including the continuous- and discrete-time Lyapunov matrix equations, are also obtained, which allow the matrix W to be set undetermined and used as an extra part of the degrees of freedom in the solutions.

1.5.2 Structure

Besides this introductory chapter, the book has nine chapters and one appendix. The structure and relations within the chapters are shown in Figure 1.7.

The purpose of the book is really to provide solutions to GSEs, and yet it is vital for the readers to know how important and useful the GSEs are. To achieve this, we have especially given in the next chapter some typical control design problems whose solutions are heavily dependent on the related GSEs.

In order to solve the proposed GSEs, as a preliminary, we introduce in Chapter 3 the concept of F-left (right) coprimeness, together with some of its criteria. We remark that this concept as well as the several related necessary and sufficient conditions have performed a very fundamental role in deriving the general solution to both the homogeneous and nonhomogeneous GSEs. Particularly, solvability of the homogeneous GSEs in the form of (1.69) and the degrees of freedom in its general solution are all determined by this so-called F-left coprime condition of the GSEs.

Chapters 4 and 5 give the most basic results in the book.

Chapter 4 treats the parametric solutions of the first-, second-, and higher-order homogeneous GSEs. A general complete parametric solution to the equations for the case of F being an arbitrary square matrix is first given, and then by specifying this F matrix to be a Jordan matrix, we derive a simple complete parametric solution to this equation for the case that the F matrix is in Jordan form. When the Jordan

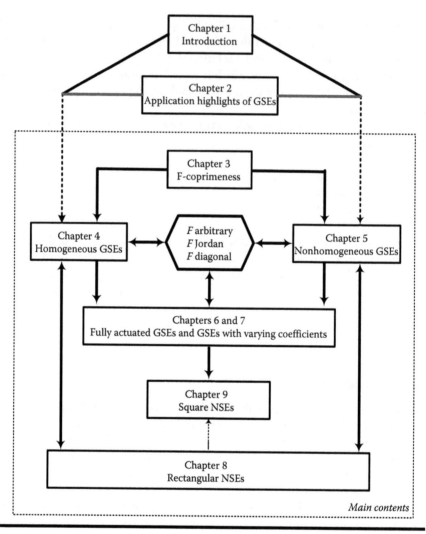

Figure 1.7 Book structure and chapter relations.

matrix is chosen to be a diagonal one, by simplifying the general solution, complete parametric solution to this equation for the case that the F matrix is a diagonal matrix is also obtained, it turns out that this solution appears to be extremely simple and neat.

Chapter 5 deals with the parametric solutions to the higher-order nonhomogeneous GSEs. A particular solution to the equation is firsy sought, and then based on the addition principle for solution of linear equations, general parametric solutions to the nonhomogeneous equations are obtained. Again all the three cases of F being arbitrary, Jordan, and diagonal are treated.

In practical applications such as robot control and satellite attitude control, we often encounter a special type of GSEs, namely, the fully actuated GSEs. By simplifying the results in Chapters 4 and 5, we obtain in Chapter 6 general solutions to both homogeneous and nonhomogeneous fully actuated GSEs. Also, the results are generalized to GSEs with varying coefficient matrices in Chapter 7.

In Chapter 8, it is first discovered that a rectangular NSE is only a different presentation of a GSE, and then by simplifying the results in Chapters 4 and 5, we obtain the general solutions to both homogeneous and nonhomogeneous rectangular NSEs.

Finally, by simplifying the results for fully actuated homogeneous GSEs presented in Chapter 6, analytical solutions to the series of square NSEs (1.74) through (1.81) are obtained in Chapter 9.

1.5.3 Basic Formulas

The approach proposed in this book for solving the various types of GSEs is highly unified. As a matter of fact, all we propose in the whole book is one formula, which appears as follows:

$$
\begin{cases}
V = \left[P^v(s)X \right]\big|_F = P_0^v X + P_1^v XF + \cdots + P_\rho^v XF^\rho \\
W = \left[P^w(s)X \right]\big|_F = P_0^w X + P_1^w XF + \cdots + P_\rho^w XF^\rho,
\end{cases}
\tag{1.89}
$$

where X is a matrix of appropriate dimension, $P^v(s)$ and $P^w(s)$ are two polynomial matrices of the following forms:

$$
\begin{cases}
P^v(s) = P_0^v + P_1^v s + \cdots + P_\rho^v s^\rho \\
P^w(s) = P_0^w + P_1^w s + \cdots + P_\rho^w s^\rho,
\end{cases}
\tag{1.90}
$$

while all the other three sets of formulas can be deduced from this one.

1.5.3.1 Formula Set I for the Case of Arbitrary F

This set of formulas can be directly obtained from (1.89) by further specifying the matrix X and the pair of polynomial matrices $P^v(s)$ and $P^w(s)$. They give a unified general solution to first-order, second-order, and higher-order GSEs with the matrix F being an arbitrary matrix. Specifically,

■ Substituting the matrix X with Z, and replacing the pair of polynomial matrices $P^v(s)$ and $P^w(s)$ with a pair of right coprime polynomial matrices $N(s)$ and $D(s)$ satisfying certain RCF yields our Formula I_H (4.31) which gives a unified general solution to first-order, second-order, and higher-order homogeneous GSEs with the matrix F being an arbitrary matrix; in this case, the matrix Z is a free parameter, which represents the degrees of freedom in the general solution.

▪ Substituting the matrix X with R, and replacing the pair of polynomial matrices $P^v(s)$ and $P^w(s)$ with a pair of polynomial matrices $U(s)$ and $T(s)$ satisfying certain Diophantine equation (DPE) yields our Formula I_N (5.63), which gives a unified specific solution to first-order, second-order, and higher-order nonhomogeneous GSEs with the matrix F being an arbitrary matrix; in this case, the matrix R is the right-hand term in the relevant nonhomogeneous GSE.

▪ By the additional principle for solutions to linear systems of equations, summing up the two Formulas I_H (4.31) and I_N (5.63) side by side gives Formula I_G (5.67), which is the unified general parametric solution to first-order, second-order, and higher-order nonhomogeneous GSEs.

This set of formulas is fundamental, since the other two sets of formulas can be deduced from them.

1.5.3.2 Formula Set II for the Case of Jordan Matrix F

This set of formulas can be deduced from Formula Set I by setting the matrix F to be a Jordan matrix, which gives general parametric solutions to first-order, second-order, and higher-order GSEs with the matrix F being a Jordan matrix. Specifically,

▪ Setting the matrix F to be a Jordan matrix in Formula I_H (4.31) yields Formula II_H (4.65), which gives a unified general solution to first-order, second-order, and higher-order homogeneous GSEs with the matrix F being a Jordan matrix.

▪ Setting the matrix F to be a Jordan matrix in Formula I_N (5.63) yields Formula II_N (5.85), which gives a unified specific solution to first-order, second-order, and higher-order nonhomogeneous GSEs with the matrix F being a Jordan matrix.

▪ By the additional principle for solutions to linear systems of equations, summing up the two Formulas II_H (4.65) and II_N (5.85) side by side gives Formula II_G (5.86), which is the unified general parametric solution to first-order, second-order, and higher-order nonhomogeneous GSEs.

1.5.3.3 Formula Set III for the Case of Diagonal F

This set of formulas are the special case of Formula Set II, which gives the general parametric solutions to first-order, second-order, and higher-order GSEs with the matrix F being a diagonal matrix. Specifically,

Table 1.1   Basic Formulas

Cases	F *Arbitrary*	F *Jordan*	F *Diagonal*
Homogeneous GSEs	Formula I_H	Formula II_H	Formula III_H
Nonhomogeneous GSEs	Formula I_N	Formula II_N	Formula III_N
Nonhomogeneous GSEs	Formula I_G	Formula II_G	Formula III_G

- Setting the matrix F to be a diagonal matrix in Formula II_H (4.65) yields Formula III_H (4.83), which gives a unified general solution to first-order, second-order, and higher-order homogeneous GSEs with the matrix F being a diagonal matrix.
- Setting the matrix F to be a diagonal matrix in Formula II_N (5.85) yields Formula III_N (5.102), which gives a unified specific solution to first-order, second-order, and higher-order nonhomogeneous GSEs with the matrix F being a diagonal matrix.
- By the additional principle for solutions to linear systems of equations, summing up the two Formulas III_H (4.83) and III_N (5.102) side by side gives Formula III_G (5.103), which is the unified general parametric solution to first-order, second-order, and higher-order nonhomogeneous GSEs.

The above three sets of solution formulas for the various GSEs are summarized in Table 1.1, and the relations among these solution formulas are illustrated in Figure 1.8.

Readers are suggested to have a revisit at this subsection when they finish reading the contents in Chapters 4 and 5, since by then the description here will be certainly better understood.

1.5.4 Features

The main purpose of this book is to provide solutions to GSEs. We point out that the solutions proposed in this book to the various types of homogeneous and nonhomogeneous GSEs possess the following features.

1.5.4.1 General Suitability

In this book, we have provided analytical closed-form parametric solutions to a variety of GSEs, including

- GSEs with arbitrary orders
- GSEs with arbitrary dimensions
- GSEs without controllability or regularizability assumption
- GSEs with unknown or partially known parameter matrices F and/or R

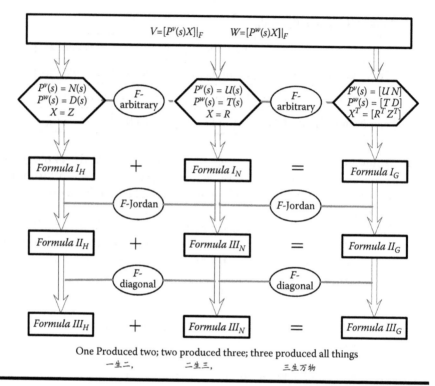

Figure 1.8 Basic solutions and their relations.

1.5.4.2 High Unification

The proposed analytical closed-form parametric solutions for the various GSEs are highly unified in the following senses:

- General solutions to homogeneous GSEs as well as particular and general solutions to nonhomogeneous GSEs are all in the form of (1.89).
- The polynomial matrices $N(s)$ and $D(s)$, which determine the general solution to a homogeneous GSE, are obtained from one unified generalized RCF for all GSEs with arbitrary orders and arbitrary dimensions.
- The polynomial matrices $U(s)$ and $T(s)$, which determine a particular solution to a nonhomogeneous GSE, are obtained from one unified DPE for all GSEs with arbitrary orders and arbitrary dimensions.
- A unified procedure based on Smith form reduction (SFR) exists to obtain the polynomial matrices $N(s)$ and $D(s)$, $U(s)$ and $T(s)$, simultaneously.

1.5.4.3 Completeness in Degrees of Freedom

The general solutions to the homogeneous and nonhomogeneous GSEs are complete in the sense that they provide all the degrees of freedom represented by

- The parameter matrix Z, when the matrix F is an arbitrary matrix
- The parameter vectors $\{z_{ij}\}$, when the matrix F is a Jordan matrix
- The parameter vectors $\{z_i\}$, when the matrix F is a diagonal matrix
- The matrices F and R, which can also be set undetermined and used as a part of the degrees of freedom

In practical applications, these degrees of freedom can be optimized to realize certain optimal properties.

1.5.4.4 Neatness and Simplicity

The analytical closed-form solutions to the various types of GSEs can all be immediately written out as soon as the polynomial matrices $N(s)$ and $D(s)$, or $U(s)$ and $T(s)$, are obtained, and all solutions appear to be very simple and neat, especially,

- The matrix form for the case of arbitrary F is very simple, neat, and also very elegant.
- While the vector form for the case of diagonal F turns out to be extremely simple and neat.

1.5.4.5 Numerical Simplicity and Reliability

The solutions presented in the book are all numerically very simple and reliable, because

- The solution formulas themselves are very simple and do not require complicated manipulations
- The unified procedure for solving the polynomial matrices $N(s)$ and $D(s)$, and/or $U(s)$ and $T(s)$, utilizes only matrix elementary transformations and often gives accurate results as demonstrated by the numerous examples in the book
- In higher-order and large dimension cases, singular value decomposition (SVD) can be called into use to perform the unified procedure, which ensures the numerical reliability of the solutions

Remark 1.5 It is seen from Figure 1.7 that the most general case treated in this book is the nonhomogeneous GSE in Chapter 5. Therefore, the results in Chapter 5 really

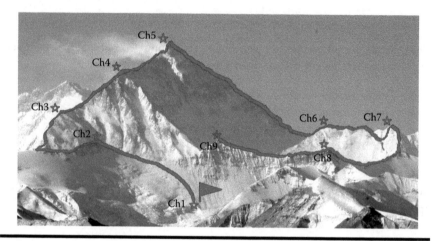

Figure 1.9 We are here, journey started. (Modified from http://go.jutuw.com/ zhumulangmafeng/photo/.)

perform a very fundamental function, since from which all the results in Chapters 6 through 9 can be deduced (Figure 1.9).

Remark 1.6 Some treatments in certain chapters of the book, for example, Chapters 6 and 8, may seem easy and simple, but the results are certainly not trivial. A problem may be solved very complicatedly with one approach while very simply with another. The extensions in the aspects of equation orders, rectangular dimensions, increased degrees of freedom, etc. have been easily tackled within our research framework, while would definitely cause unsolvable difficulties within some other research frameworks.

Chapter 2

Application Highlights of GSEs

Sylvester equations have found applications in many fields and have been investigated by numerous researchers. By searching the website www.amazon.com, we have found that there are over 300 books or book volumes, which use or involve Sylvester equations. Particularly, there are 38 books or book volumes which use GSEs, and these can be classified into the following categories:

- Matrix algebra
  - Matrix computation (Golub and Loan 1996, Higham 1996, Higham 2008)
  - The matrix eigenvalue problem (van Dooren et al. 2001, Watkins 2007)
  - Linear algebra and applications (Hazewinkel 1996, Moonen et al. 2010)
  - Differential-algebraic equations (Ilchmann and Reis 2013)
  - Algebraic geometry (Putinar and Sullivant 2010)
- Numerical methods (Kressner 2005, Wachspress 2013)
- Computer science
  - Parallel computing (Ciegis et al. 2008, Fagerholm et al. 2002, Sorevik et al. 2001, 2006)
  - Parallel processing (Danelutto et al. 2004, Kosch et al. 2003, Luque et al. 2008, Palma et al. 2001)
  - High performance computing (Daydé et al. 2005).
- Circuits and systems (Benner et al. 2005, Datta 1999, Srivastava et al. 2006)
- Signal processing (Havelock et al. 2008, Leondes 1995)
- Control systems

  o Saturated switching systems (Benzaouia 2012)
  o Observer design (Trinh and Fernando 2011)
  o Computer aided design (Anderson et al. 1999, Gray 2001)
  o Descriptor linear systems (Duan 2010)
  o Robust control design (Kucera and Sebek 2005)
  o Periodic control systems (Bittanti and Colaneri 2002)
  o Control designs (Skelton et al. 1997, Voicu 2003)
■ Biocomputing (Altman et al. 2006)
■ Life systems (Fei et al. 2010)
■ Neural networks (Liu et al. 2011)

In this chapter, we describe several typical applications of GSEs in linear control systems design, by only relating certain control design problems to GSEs.

Since the applications of the first-order GSEs are related to the analysis and design problems of the first-order linear systems, which are more familiar to the entire control community, in this chapter, we highlight the applications of the first-order GSEs with a few control problems for first-order linear systems.

It is important to note that all the system models appearing in this chapter are square ones, that is, with $q = n$. This point will not be mentioned again at the specific positions.

2.1 ESA and Observer Designs

In order to show applications of the GSEs in control systems designs, here in this section, we start with the problems of ESA and observer design for first-order linear systems.

2.1.1 Generalized Pole/ESA

Let us start with the state feedback case.

2.1.1.1 State Feedback Case

The problem of generalized pole/ESA in the first-order linear system (1.3) via state feedback can be stated as follows.

Problem 2.1 *Given the first-order linear system (1.3) and a (stable) matrix $F \in \mathbb{C}^{n \times n}$, find a state feedback controller*

$$u = Kx, \quad K \in \mathbb{R}^{r \times n},$$

such that the closed-loop system matrix $A + BK$ is similar to the matrix F.

Due to the requirement of the problem, there must exist a nonsingular matrix $V \in \mathbb{C}^{n \times n}$ such that

$$(A + BK) V = VF. \tag{2.1}$$

Let

$$W = KV, \tag{2.2}$$

then equation (2.1) is converted into the first-order GSE (1.57). Therefore, regarding solution to the above generalized pole/ESA problem, we have the following result (see, e.g., Duan 1992b, 1993b, 1996, 2004a, 2010).

Theorem 2.1 *All the solutions to Problem 2.1 are given by*

$$K = WV^{-1},$$

with

$$(V, W) \in \left\{ (V, W) \mid AV + BW = VF, \ \det V \neq 0, \ WV^{-1} \ real \right\}.$$

Therefore, the key step of solving this generalized pole/ESA problem is to find the general complete parametric solution to the first-order GSE (1.57).

2.1.1.2 Output Feedback Case

The problem of generalized pole/ESA in the first-order linear system (1.3) via output feedback can be stated as follows.

Problem 2.2 *Given the first-order linear system (1.3) and a (stable) matrix $F \in \mathbb{C}^{n \times n}$, find a static output feedback controller*

$$u = Ky, \ \ K \in \mathbb{R}^{r \times m},$$

such that the closed-loop system matrix $A + BKC$ is similar to the matrix F.

Due to the requirement of the above problem, there must exist a pair of nonsingular matrices $T, V \in \mathbb{C}^{n \times n}$ satisfying

$$T^{\mathrm{T}} (A + BKC) = FT^{\mathrm{T}}, \tag{2.3}$$

$$(A + BKC) V = VF, \tag{2.4}$$

and

$$T^T V = I. \tag{2.5}$$

Let

$$Z^T = T^T BK, \quad W = KCV, \tag{2.6}$$

then equation (2.4) is converted into the first-order GSE (1.57), while the equation (2.3) is converted into

$$T^T A + Z^T C = FT^T, \tag{2.7}$$

which is a dual form of the first-order GSE (1.57).

Based on the above deduction, we have the following result about the solution to the above output feedback generalized pole/ESA problem (see Duan 1992a, 1993a, 2004a, 2010, Duan et al. 1991a, 2012).

Theorem 2.2 *All the solutions to Problem 2.2 are determined by the two equations in (2.6) with the matrices $T, V \in \mathbb{C}^{n \times n}$ satisfying the condition (2.5), the first-order GSEs (1.57) and (2.7), and a certain self-complex-conjugate condition to ensure the realness of the matrix K solved from the two equations in (2.6).*

According to the above theorem, to find a general solution to Problem 2.2, one needs to find the general complete parametric expressions for the matrices T, V satisfying (2.5) and the first-order GSEs (1.57) and (2.7), and then solve a parametric expression for the matrix K from the equations in (2.6).

Again, it follows from the above theorem that a key step in solving this output feedback generalized pole/ESA problem is to find the general complete parametric solution to the first-order GSE (1.57).

2.1.1.3 Comments and Remarks

Obviously, the above generalized pole/ESA problems include the usual pole assignment and ESA problems as special cases. For solving the usual pole assignment and ESA problems, many authors have indeed, to certain extent, made use of the GSEs in the form of (1.55) in their developments (see, e.g., Kimura 1977). Furthermore, it is clear that, when the matrix F is chosen to be a real matrix, all the operations, given in the above developments, related to the solution of the proposed problem can be restricted within the real field.

It is seen from the above developments that once a complete parametric solution to the associated GSE is established, a complete parametric approach to the corresponding generalized pole/ESA problem can be proposed. Based on this idea, various

ESA problems have been effectively treated. Different from existing approaches for pole and ESA, the parametric approach provides all the degrees of freedom beyond pole placement, which can be further utilized to achieve additional system design requirements (see, e.g., Duan 1992a, 1993a, Duan et al. 2001b).

Conditions of existence of solutions to these two generalized pole/ESA problems are straightforward. Generally speaking, the problem has a solution if the ESA problem, which assigns the closed-loop Jordan matrix to that of the matrix F, is solvable. Particularly, when the normal linear system (1.3) is controllable, for arbitrary F with distinct eigenvalues, the state feedback generalized pole/ESA problem has a solution.

It is well known that a problem of pole/ESA in a linear system by dynamical output feedback can be converted into a problem of pole/ESA in an extended linear system by constant output feedback. Therefore, once a parametric approach for the generalized pole/ESA by constant output feedback is proposed, a parametric approach for the problem of generalized pole/ESA by dynamical compensators is straightforward.

Finally, we mention that, although the above two generalized pole/ESA problems are proposed for the normal linear system (1.3), they can be easily extended to the descriptor linear system case, as well as the second- and higher-order system cases.

2.1.2 Observer Design

It is well known that the problem of state feedback design based on a full-order state observer for system (1.3) can be converted into a state feedback pole/ESA problem for the dual system of (1.3). Therefore, in view of the solution to Problem 2.1, the solution to the problem of state feedback design based on a full-order state observer is also closely related to first-order GSEs. In the following, we further relate the designs of Luenberger type of observers and the proportional plus integral (PI) state observers with the GSEs.

2.1.2.1 Luenberger Observers

The Luenberger type normal function Kx observers for the descriptor linear system (1.1) possess the following form:

$$\begin{cases} \dot{z} = Fz + Su + Ly \\ w = K\hat{x} = Mz + Ny, \end{cases} \tag{2.8}$$

where

- $z \in \mathbb{R}^p$ is the observer state vector
- F, S, L, M, and N are the observer system coefficient matrices of appropriate dimensions

Problem 2.3 *Given the descriptor linear system (1.1) with $D = 0$, and a matrix $K \in \mathbb{R}^{l \times n}$, find the set of system coefficient matrices F, S, L, M, and N such that the behavior of the combined systems (1.1) and (2.8) satisfies*

$$\lim_{t \to \infty} (Kx(t) - w(t)) = 0, \tag{2.9}$$

for arbitrarily given initial values $x(0)$, $z(0)$, and control input $u(t)$. In this case, we call the system (2.8) a Luenberger type normal function Kx observer for the descriptor linear system (1.1).

The following theorem gives a necessary and sufficient condition for the above observer design problem (Duan 2010, Duan et al. 2012).

Theorem 2.3 *Assume that the descriptor linear system (1.1) is R-controllable and the observer system (2.8) is observable. Then (2.8) is a normal Kx function observer for system (1.1) if and only if the matrix F is stable, and there exists a matrix $T \in \mathbb{R}^{p \times n}$ satisfying*

$$S = TB, \tag{2.10}$$

$$TA - FTE = LC, \tag{2.11}$$

and

$$K = MTE + NC. \tag{2.12}$$

Note that the equation (2.11) in the above theorem is actually a first-order GSE which is in the dual form of (1.56). The problem is therefore converted, partially, into a problem of finding the general parametric solution of first-order GSEs.

2.1.2.2 PI Observers

A PI state observer for the normal linear system (1.3), with $D = 0$, possesses the following form (see, e.g., Duan et al. 2001a and the references therein):

$$\begin{cases} \dot{\hat{x}} = (A - LC)\hat{x} + Bu + Ly + Gw \\ \dot{w} = K(y - C\hat{x}), \end{cases} \tag{2.13}$$

where

- $\hat{x} \in \mathbb{R}^n$ is the estimated state vector
- $w \in \mathbb{R}^p$ is a vector representing the integral of the weighted output estimation error
- $L \in \mathbb{R}^{n \times m}$, $G \in \mathbb{R}^{n \times p}$; and $K \in \mathbb{R}^{p \times m}$ are the observer gains

Specifically, we call the matrices L and G the proportional and integral gain, respectively, and the matrix K the output estimation error weighting gain.

Problem 2.4   *Given the normal linear system (1.3) with $D = 0$, find the observer gains L, G, and K such that the behavior of the combined systems (1.3) and (2.13) satisfies*

$$\lim_{t \to \infty} (\hat{x}(t) - x(t)) = 0, \quad \lim_{t \to \infty} w(t) = 0, \tag{2.14}$$

for arbitrarily given initial values $x(0)$, $\hat{x}(0)$, and control input $u(t)$. In this case, system (2.13) is said to be a PI state observer for the system (1.3).

Summing up the results in Duan et al. (2001a), we have the following theorem about the solution to the above PI observer design problem.

Theorem 2.4   *Let the matrix pair (A, C) be observable, and the matrix C be of full row rank. Then all the gain matrices L and K of the PI observer (2.13) for the system (1.3) are given by*

$$\begin{bmatrix} L \\ K \end{bmatrix} = - \begin{bmatrix} T^{\mathrm{T}} & F^{-1} T^{\mathrm{T}} G \end{bmatrix}^{-1} Z^{\mathrm{T}},$$

where $F \in \mathbb{R}^{(n+p) \times (n+p)}$ is a stable matrix, $T \in \mathbb{R}^{n \times (n+p)}$ and $Z \in \mathbb{R}^{m \times (n+p)}$ are any matrices satisfying the equation

$$T^{\mathrm{T}} A + Z^{\mathrm{T}} C = F T^{\mathrm{T}}. \tag{2.15}$$

Furthermore, the gain matrix $G \in \mathbb{R}^{n \times p}$ can be taken to be an arbitrary matrix which satisfies, together with the matrices T, F, the following condition:

$$\det \begin{bmatrix} T^{\mathrm{T}} & F^{-1} T^{\mathrm{T}} G \end{bmatrix} \neq 0.$$

It is seen from the above theorem that, again, a key step in solving the above PI observer design problem is to derive the general solution to the matrix equation (2.15), which is a dual form of the GSE (1.57).

2.1.2.3 Comments and Remarks

It is shown in the above that the designs of the full-order state observers, the Luenberger function observers, and the PI state observers for linear systems are closely related to a type of GSEs, which are in the dual forms of the ones in the form of (1.55). However, we would like to point out that observers, which can be designed with the help of GSEs, are not limited to these three types. Generally speaking, any kind of linear state observers for a linear system can be related to certain type of GSEs. For such observers, again, once a complete parametric solution to the related GSE is obtained, a parametric approach for the design of this type of observers can be proposed, which provides all the degrees of design freedom.

It is well known that state observers have applications in many theoretical problems, such as observer-based state feedback control and robust fault detection and isolation. In such control applications, if a complete parametric approach is used for the design of the type of observers utilized, a parametric approach for the control application is then proposed. Based on this idea, several parametric approaches for robust fault detection have been proposed (Duan and Patton 1998d, 2001, Duan et al. 2002a).

2.2 Model Reference Tracking and Disturbance Decoupling

This section continues with the introduction of another two types of control systems design applications of GSEs.

2.2.1 Model Reference Tracking

For simplicity, let us only consider model reference tracking in the normal linear system (1.3) using state feedback.

The problem is stated as follows.

Problem 2.5 *Given the first-order linear system (1.3) and the following reference model*

$$\begin{cases} \dot{x}_m = A_m x_m + B_m u_m \\ y_m = C_m x_m + D_m u_m, \end{cases} \tag{2.16}$$

where $x_m \in \mathbb{R}^p$, $u_m \in \mathbb{R}^r$, and $y_m \in \mathbb{R}^m$ are, respectively, the state vector, the input vector, and the output vector of the reference model, and A_m, B_m, C_m, and D_m are known matrices of appropriate dimensions, find a state feedback controller in the form of

$$u = Kx + K_m x_m + Q u_m,$$

such that

1. *The closed-loop system is asymptotically stable, that is, the system matrix $A + BK$ is Hurwitz;*

2. *The following asymptotically tracking requirement*

$$\lim_{t \to \infty} \left(y(t) - y_m(t) \right) = 0 \tag{2.17}$$

is met for arbitrary initial values $x(0)$, $x_m(0)$, and arbitrary reference input $u_m(t) \in \mathbb{R}^r$.

For solution to the above problem, we have the following result (Duan et al. 2001b).

Theorem 2.5 *Problem 2.5 has a solution if and only if there exist matrices $Q \in \mathbb{R}^{r \times r}$, $H \in \mathbb{R}^{r \times p}$, and $G \in \mathbb{R}^{n \times p}$ satisfying the following matrix equations:*

$$AG + BH = GA_m, \tag{2.18}$$

$$CG + DH = C_m, \tag{2.19}$$

$$BQ + GB_m = 0, \tag{2.20}$$

$$DQ + D_m = 0. \tag{2.21}$$

In this case, K_m can be chosen as

$$K_m = H - KG,$$

while K is any real matrix stabilizing the matrix $A + BK$.

It is not hard to tell that the first condition in the above theorem, equation (2.18), is actually a first-order GSE in the form of (1.57), with (G, H) in the position of (V, W), and A_m in the position of F.

By establishing the general complete parametric expressions for the matrices $Q \in \mathbb{R}^{r \times r}$, $H \in \mathbb{R}^{r \times p}$, and $G \in \mathbb{R}^{n \times p}$ satisfying the matrix equations (2.18) through (2.21), a complete parametric approach for the model reference tracking problem can be proposed.

For certain systems, the solution to the above model reference tracking problem is not unique, that is, the matrices $Q \in \mathbb{R}^{r \times r}$, $H \in \mathbb{R}^{r \times p}$, and $G \in \mathbb{R}^{n \times p}$ satisfying the matrix equations (2.18) through (2.21) are not unique. As a consequence, extra degrees of freedom exist in the parametric design. In such a case, the extra degrees of freedom can be used to cope with some robustness requirements. Using this idea, Duan et al. (2001b) have successfully treated the robust model reference control problem for multivariable linear systems subject to parameter uncertainties.

2.2.2 Disturbance Rejection

Disturbance attenuation and rejection is a very important problem in control systems designs. In this subsection, we show that the disturbance attenuation problem is also closely related to GSEs.

In order to describe the problem, let us introduce a normal linear system subject to disturbance:

$$\begin{cases} \dot{x} = Ax + Bu + E_w w \\ y_m = C_m x + D_{mw} w \\ y_r = C_r x + D_{ru} u + D_{rw} w, \end{cases} \tag{2.22}$$

where $x \in \mathbb{R}^n$ and $u \in \mathbb{R}^r$ are, as stated in (1.3), the state vector and the control vector, respectively; $y_m \in \mathbb{R}^{m_1}$ and $y_r \in \mathbb{R}^{m_2}$ are the measured output vector and the to-be-regulated output vector, respectively, while $w \in \mathbb{R}^s$ is the disturbance vector. All the matrices A, B, E_w, C_m, C_r, D_{ru}, D_{mw} and D_{rw} are known system coefficient matrices of appropriate dimensions. Furthermore, the disturbance w is generated by the following exosystem

$$\dot{w} = Fw. \tag{2.23}$$

Problem 2.6 *Given the first-order normal linear system (2.22) and the disturbance generation exosystem (2.23), find an output dynamical compensator in the form of*

$$\begin{cases} \dot{\varsigma} = A_c \varsigma + B_c y_m \\ u = C_c \varsigma + D_c y_m, \end{cases}$$

with $\varsigma \in \mathbb{R}^{n_c}$, such that

1. *The closed-loop system*

$$\begin{cases} \dot{x} = (A + BD_c C_m) x + BC_c \varsigma \\ \dot{\varsigma} = B_c C_m x + A_c \varsigma \end{cases}$$

   is asymptotically stable.
2. *The following asymptotical output regulation requirement*

$$\lim_{t \to \infty} y_r(t) = 0 \tag{2.24}$$

   is met for arbitrary system initial values $x(0) \in \mathbb{R}^n$, $\varsigma(0) \in \mathbb{R}^{n_c}$, and arbitrary disturbance initial value $w(0) \in \mathbb{R}^s$.

In order to make the above problem solvable, we introduce the following three assumptions:

A1. The matrix pair (A, B) is stabilizable.

A2. The matrix F is anti-Hurwitz (since otherwise the disturbance dies itself).

A3. The matrix pair $(\tilde{A}, \tilde{C})$ with

$$\tilde{C} = [C_m \ \ D_{mw}], \quad \tilde{A} = \begin{bmatrix} A & E_w \\ 0 & F \end{bmatrix}$$

is detectable.

For solution to the above problem, we have the following result (Saberi et al. 1999).

Theorem 2.6 *Subject to the above three Assumptions A1 through A3, Problem 2.6 has a solution if and only if there exist matrices $V \in \mathbb{R}^{n \times s}$ and $W \in \mathbb{R}^{r \times s}$ satisfying the following matrix equations*

$$AV + BW = VF - E_w, \tag{2.25}$$

$$C_r V + D_{ru} W = -D_{ru}. \tag{2.26}$$

In this case, a suitable dynamical compensator for the problem is given by

$$\begin{cases} \begin{bmatrix} \dot{\hat{x}} \\ \dot{\hat{w}} \end{bmatrix} = \begin{bmatrix} A & E_w \\ 0 & F \end{bmatrix} \begin{bmatrix} \hat{x} \\ \hat{w} \end{bmatrix} + \begin{bmatrix} K_A \\ K_F \end{bmatrix} \left([C_m \ \ D_{mw}] \begin{bmatrix} \hat{x} \\ \hat{w} \end{bmatrix} - y \right) \\ u = [K \ \ W - KV] \begin{bmatrix} \hat{x} \\ \hat{w} \end{bmatrix}, \end{cases} \tag{2.27}$$

where K is an arbitrary matrix making $A + BK$ Hurwitz, and K_A and K_F are arbitrary matrices making the system (2.27) internally stable, that is, the following matrix

$$A_{ce} = \begin{bmatrix} A & E_w \\ 0 & F \end{bmatrix} + \begin{bmatrix} K_A \\ K_F \end{bmatrix} [C_m \ \ D_{mw}]$$

stable.

Obviously, equation (2.25) is a first-order nonhomogeneous GSE in the form of (1.64). Therefore, the solution to the above disturbance rejection problem is also heavily dependent on the solution to the first-order GSE in the form of (1.64).

By establishing the general complete parametric expressions for the matrices $V \in \mathbb{R}^{n \times s}$ and $W \in \mathbb{R}^{r \times s}$ satisfying the matrix equations (2.25) through (2.26), a complete parametric approach for the disturbance rejection problem can be proposed. As mentioned before, this parametric approach can give all the degrees of design freedom to cope with many additional system design requirements, such as robustness with respect to system coefficient parameter uncertainties, H_2 and H_∞ type of indices as well as control saturation constraints.

2.3 Sylvester Parametric Control Approaches

It has been demonstrated in the above with four types of problems, namely, the generalized pole/ESA problems, the observer design problems, the model reference tracking problems, and the disturbance rejection problems, that many problems in control system designs can be formulated in such a way that the solutions to these problems are closely related to certain types of GSEs. Therefore, by establishing a general complete parametric solution to this type of GSEs, a complete parametric approach for solving the corresponding control problems can then be proposed. Such a parametric approach has the advantage of providing all the degrees of design freedom, which can be further used to meet the various additional design requirements.

The purpose of this section is to give a general picture of the Sylvester parametric control approaches.

2.3.1 General Procedure

Any practical control system should meet not only one single design requirement but a series of design requirements. Therefore, due to the nature of the Sylvester parametric approaches, they can be the most convenient and effective approaches for handling multiobjective control design problems.

It can be observed from the above developments for the four types of control design problems that the general procedure for the Sylvester parametric approaches consists of the following steps:

Step 1. *Relation to GSEs*: Relate a control systems design problem, for example, one of the above proposed problems, to a type of GSEs.

Step 2. *Solving GSEs*: Find a general explicit parametric solution to the related GSEs.

Step 3. *Controller parametrization*: Find, based on the established general complete parametric solution to this type of GSEs, the general parametric expressions for all the coefficient matrices in the controller (or the observer).

Step 4. *Specification parametrization*: Find, based on the general complete parametric solution to this type of GSEs and the general parametric expressions for all the controller (observer) coefficients, the general parametric representations of all the design requirements. This actually gives a series of constraints in terms of the degrees of design freedom.

Step 5. *Parameter optimization*: Find a set of design parameters satisfying the design requirement constraints, usually, by solving a formulated optimization problem that incorporates all the design performance and constraints.

Step 6. *Controller computation*: Substitute the obtained set of parameters into the parametrization of the controller obtained in Step 3 and compute all the coefficient matrices in the controller (or the observer).

The above procedure is illustrated in Figure 2.1.

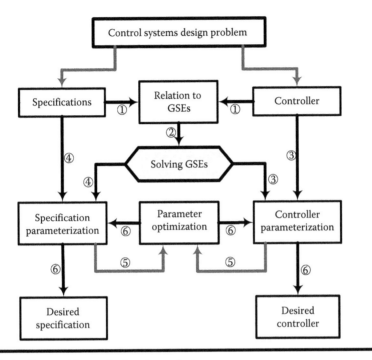

Figure 2.1 Parametric control systems design.

2.3.2 Main Steps

Here we give some further explanation on the main steps in the above procedure.

2.3.2.1 Solving GSEs

This step performs a central role in the Sylvester parametric approaches for control systems design. In fact, the purpose of this book is to present for a wide class of GSEs unified general parametric solutions in closed forms. This book actually proposes two general complete parametric solutions, one for the case of F being an arbitrary square matrix, and the other for the case of F being an arbitrary Jordan matrix. The latter of course includes the case of F being diagonal, in which case the solution turns out to be extremely simple.

As we will find in the later chapters, all the degrees of freedom in the proposed general solutions are given by the matrices R and F as well as a parameter Z, that is,

$$V = V(Z, F, R), \quad W = W(Z, F, R).$$

Please note that for homogeneous GSEs, the parameter matrix R in the above vanishes.

2.3.2.2 Controller Parametrization

The purpose of this step is to derive for the required type of controllers a general parametric expression using the free parameters existing in the solution to the related GSEs. Using the general parametric solutions proposed in this book, the general parametrization of the controller, say a feedback gain K, contains also the matrices Z, F, and R as design parameters, that is,

$$K = K(Z, F, R).$$

2.3.2.3 Specification Parametrization

The purpose of this step is to derive for the system design specifications general parametric representations using the free parameters existing in the solution to the related GSEs. Although there are various kinds of system specification requirements in practical applications, most of them can be generally formulated into the following three types of constraints:

$$\begin{cases} J_k(Z, F, R) \text{ minimized}, & k = 1, 2, \ldots, n_k \\ g_i(Z, F, R) \geq 0, & i = 1, 2, \ldots, n_i \\ p_j(Z, F, R) = 0, & j = 1, 2, \ldots, n_j. \end{cases} \tag{2.28}$$

2.3.2.4 Parameter Optimization

The purpose of this step is to obtain a set of parameters, which meet the system specification requirements. Once the above system specification parametrization (2.28) has been obtained, this can be achieved by solving the following optimization problem:

$$\begin{cases} \min \quad \sum\limits_{k=1}^{n_k} \alpha_k J_k(Z, F, R) \\ \text{s.t.} \quad g_i(Z, F, R) \geq 0, \quad i = 1, 2, \ldots, n_i \\ \qquad p_j(Z, F, R) = 0, \quad j = 1, 2, \ldots, n_j, \end{cases}$$

where $\alpha_k \geq 0$, $k = 1, 2, \ldots, n_k$, are a series of weighting factors.

Control systems designs using Sylvester parametric approaches have been extensively studied by the author and his co-authors (see the brief overview in Section 2.4.2). Particularly, such parametric approaches have also been successfully applied by the author and his co-authors in many applications, such as the robust control of magnetic bearing systems as well as missile and satellite control systems (see, e.g., Cai et al. 2011, Duan and Howe 2003, Duan et al. 2000d, 2001c, 2009b, 2010).

2.4 Notes and References

2.4.1 *Problem of ESA in Higher-Order Systems*

This chapter shows some direct applications of GSEs in control systems designs. All the results are restricted to the first-order GSEs. To highlight the applications of higher-order GSEs, we here consider a generalized ESA problem.

Consider a type of higher-order dynamical linear systems described by the following model:

$$\sum_{i=0}^{m} A_i x^{(i)} = Bu, \qquad (2.29)$$

where

- $x \in \mathbb{R}^n$ and $u \in \mathbb{R}^r$ are the state vector and the control vector, respectively
- $A_i \in \mathbb{R}^{n \times n}$, $i = 0, 1, \ldots, m$, $B \in \mathbb{R}^{n \times r}$, are the system coefficient matrices

Without loss of generality, it is assumed that

$$1 \leq \text{rank} A_m = n_0 \leq n.$$

Applying the following proportional plus derivative feedback controller

$$u = K_0 x + K_1 \dot{x} + \cdots + K_{m-1} x^{(m-1)}$$

to the system (2.29), the closed-loop system is obtained as

$$A_m x^{(m)} + \sum_{i=0}^{m-1} (A_i - BK_i) x^{(i)} = 0, \qquad (2.30)$$

whose extended descriptor state-space system form is

$$E_e \dot{X} = A_e X, \qquad (2.31)$$

with

$$E_e = \text{blockdiag} (I_n, \ldots, I_n, A_m), \qquad (2.32)$$

$$A_e = \begin{bmatrix} 0 & I & \cdots & & 0 \\ \vdots & \ddots & \ddots & & \vdots \\ 0 & \cdots & 0 & & I \\ -A_0^c & \cdots & -A_{m-2}^c & -A_{m-1}^c \end{bmatrix}, \qquad (2.33)$$

where

$$A_i^c = A_i - BK_i, \quad i = 0, 1, \ldots, m - 1. \tag{2.34}$$

The generalized ESA problem in system (2.29) can be stated as follows.

Problem 2.7 *Let $A_i \in \mathbb{R}^{n \times n}$, $i = 0, 1, \ldots, m$, $B \in \mathbb{R}^{n \times r}$, and $F \in \mathbb{R}^{p \times p}$, with $p = (m - 1)n + n_0$. Find some general parametric expressions for series of matrices $K_i \in \mathbb{R}^{r \times n}$, $i = 0, 1, \ldots, m - 1$, and a matrix $V_e \in \mathbb{R}^{mn \times p}$, $rank V_e = p$, satisfying*

$$A_e V_e = E_e V_e F. \tag{2.35}$$

As a consequence of the requirements in the above generalized ESA problem, the eigenvalues of the matrix F are the relative finite eigenvalues of the closed-loop system, or the matrix pair (A_e, B_e), and the matrix V_e is the eigenvector matrix associated with those finite relative eigenvalues given by the eigenvalues of the matrix F (Duan 2010). Particularly, when $n_0 = rank A_m = n$, the closed-loop system has n finite eigenvalues, and now V_e turns out to be the entire eigenvector matrix of the closed-loop system.

Denoting

$$V_e = \begin{bmatrix} V \\ V_1 \\ \vdots \\ V_{m-1} \end{bmatrix},$$

and using (2.32) through (2.35), we obtain

$$V_i = VF^i, \quad i = 1, 2, \ldots, m - 1, \tag{2.36}$$

and

$$\sum_{i=0}^{m} (A_i - BK_i) V_i = 0. \tag{2.37}$$

The relations in (2.36) give

$$V_e = \begin{bmatrix} V \\ VF \\ \vdots \\ VF^{m-1} \end{bmatrix}.$$

Meanwhile, substituting (2.36) into (2.37) produces

$$\sum_{i=0}^{m} (A_i - BK_i) VF^i = 0. \tag{2.38}$$

Letting

$$W = \begin{bmatrix} K_0 & K_1 & \cdots & K_{m-1} \end{bmatrix} V_e \tag{2.39}$$

in (2.38) gives

$$\sum_{i=0}^{m} A_i VF^i = BW. \tag{2.40}$$

This is an mth-order GSE associated with the generalized ESA problem.

It is clearly seen from the above that, in order to solve the generalized ESA problem stated above, it is essential to solve the following problem.

Problem 2.8 *Given the higher-order dynamical system (2.29), and a matrix $F \in \mathbb{R}^{p \times p}$ which may be unknown a priori, find general parametric expressions in explicit closed forms for the matrices V and W, with V nonsingular, satisfying the mth-order GSE (2.40).*

Once a solution to the above problem is sought, under the condition that $n_0 = \mathrm{rank} A_m = n$, we can obtain from (2.39) the gain matrices as

$$\begin{bmatrix} K_0 & K_1 & \cdots & K_{m-1} \end{bmatrix} = WV_e^{-1}. \tag{2.41}$$

For ESA in higher-order systems, interested readers may further refer to Duan (2005b), Duan and Yu (2006b), Duan et al. (2009b), Yu and Duan (2009a), and Yu and Duan (2010). In Section 6.7, we will continue to present a parametric solution to this ESA problem after gaining sufficient knowledge about solution to GSEs.

We point out that, besides ESA, it can also be shown that this type of equations are also closely related to many other control design problems for systems in the form of (2.29).

2.4.2 Author's Work on Sylvester Parametric Approaches

Along the lines of parametric approaches for control systems design, the author and his co-authors have done a great deal of work. Based on our proposed parametric forms for certain types of GSEs, parametric approaches for many types of control system designs are proposed. In this subsection, let us briefly overview some of the main streams of work on parametric control systems designs.

2.4.2.1 ESA

As shown in Section 2.1, the problems of ESA in linear systems via feedback are closely related to GSEs. With the help of the parametric solutions to the concerned GSEs, the author and his co-authors have proposed parametric approaches for ESA in linear control systems via different feedbacks, for example,

■ State feedback (Duan 1991a, 1993b, 1998a, 2002a, Duan and Patton 1997, 1998a, Duan and Xue 2005, Duan and Yu 2006a, Duan et al. 1999d, Wang and Duan 2004b, Xue and Duan 2005a,b, 2006a,b,c, Xue et al. 2006, Zhang and Duan 2002)

■ Output feedback (Duan 1994, 1995, 1999, 2003, Duan et al. 1999c, 2000c, Liu et al. 2000b)

■ Dynamical compensators (Duan 1991b, 1993a, Duan and Howe 2003, Duan et al. 2000a, 2001a, 2003)

Furthermore, the work of the author related to ESA has also covered the cases of

■ First- and second-order descriptor linear systems (Duan 1992b, Duan and Wang 2003, Duan and Wang 2005, Wang et al. 2006d)

■ A class of composite systems (Wang et al. 2005b)

■ Second-order systems (Duan 2004c, Duan and Liu 2002, Duan and Wang 2004, Duan et al. 1999a, 2002c, Wang and Duan 2007, 2008, Wang et al. 2006b, 2007a, 2008b, 2009a, Wu et al. 2005)

■ Higher-order linear systems (Duan 2005b, Duan and Yu 2006b, Duan et al. 2009b, Yu and Duan 2009a, 2010)

Particularly, Duan et al. (2009b), Yu and Duan (2009a), and Yu and Duan (2010) first present general parametric solutions to higher-order GSEs, and then consider parametric control of higher-order normal or descriptor linear systems via proportional plus derivative state feedback and output feedback. By employing the proposed general parametric solutions, complete parametric control approaches for higher-order linear systems are presented. The proposed approaches give simple complete parametric expressions for the feedback gains and the closed-loop eigenvector matrices, and produce all the design degrees of freedom.

Besides the above, other work of the author and his co-authors on ESA covers linear parameter-varying system (Cai et al. 2011), linear time-varying systems (Duan et al. 1991a), mixed performance specifications (Liu and Duan 1998), multiobjective control (He et al. 2004, Liu and Duan 2000), and disturbance decoupling and minimum eigenvalue sensitivities (Wang and Duan 2003), and a complete parametric approach for partial ESA (Duan et al. 1999b).

2.4.2.2 Observer Design

It is well known that state observer designs and feedback control designs are a pair of dual problems, that is, feedback control designs, such as ESAs, make use of the standard GSEs, while the corresponding observer designs make use of the dual forms of GSEs. Such a fact certainly has resulted in many results on parametric approaches for designs of many types of observers, for instance,

- Full order observers (Duan et al. 1999f, Wang et al. 2008a)
- Reduced-order observers (Wu and Duan 2004)
- Function observers (Guan and Duan 1999)
- Luenberger observers (Duan and Ma 1995, Duan and Patton 2001, Duan and Wu 2004b, Duan et al. 2000c, 2004, 2007, Guan et al. 2000c, Zhou and Duan 2006b)
- Unknown input observers (Duan and Wu 2004c, Duan et al. 2002a, Fu et al. 2004, 2006)
- Robust guaranteed cost observers (Fu et al. 2005, 2008, Zhang and Duan 2005)
- Observers for matrix second-order linear systems (Duan and Wu 2004a, Wu and Duan 2005, Wu et al. 2006b)
- Observers for linear discrete periodic systems (Lv and Duan 2010)
- Proportional-integral-derivative (PID) observers (Duan et al. 2001a, 2003, Wang et al. 2006a, 2007b, 2008a, Wu and Duan 2006a,b, 2007a,b, 2008b, Wu et al. 2007a, 2009a, 2012a,b,c)

Other works of the author and his co-authors related to observer design include robust tracking observers (Wang et al. 2006e,f), observers-based fault-tolerant control (Li et al. 2006, Liang and Duan 2004a,b,c), observers-based control (Duan et al. 1991b, Guan et al. 2000a,b, Liu et al. 2000a,c), observers-based output stabilization of integrators system (Zhou et al. 2006), observers for disturbance attenuation (Yan et al. 2005), and observer-based control of self-sensing magnetic bearings (Duan et al. 1999g).

2.4.2.3 Fault Detection

Our controller parametrization based on parametric solutions to GSEs has also been applied to fault detection in linear systems. We have focused our attention on a type of robust fault detection problems, and have proposed parametric approaches for robust fault detection in linear systems with unknown disturbances (Duan and Patton 2001, Duan et al. 1997). Particularly, Duan and Patton (2001) treat robust fault detection using Luenberger-type unknown input observers.

Duan et al. (2002a) and Liang and Duan (2004a) treat fault detection in descriptor linear systems. Duan et al. (2002a) solve the problem of robust fault detection via generalized unknown input observers, Duan et al. (2002a) deal with robust fault detection in descriptor linear systems via generalized unknown input observers, while Liang and Duan (2004a) tackle the problem of observer-based fault-tolerant control.

Our work in fault detection has also covered matrix second-order linear systems. Duan and Wu (2004c) and Duan et al. (2004) give parametric approaches for robust fault detection in matrix second-order linear systems via unknown input observers.

2.4.2.4 Disturbance Decoupling

Based on the parametric forms for certain types of ESA controllers, we have further given the parametric expressions for the disturbance attenuation and disturbance decoupling requirements in the designed control systems; hence, we have given parametric approaches for disturbance decoupling and attenuation.

Duan et al. (1999c), Wu and Duan (2006c), Duan et al. (2000c), and Wang and Duan (2003) have all considered disturbance decoupling. Particularly, Duan et al. (1999c) consider disturbance decoupling with ESA in linear systems via output dynamical feedback control, Wu and Duan (2006c) treat design of Luenberger function observer with disturbance decoupling for matrix second-order linear systems, while Duan et al. (2000c) deal with decoupling in descriptor systems via output feedback, and Wang and Duan (2003) solve the problem of ESA with disturbance decoupling and minimum eigenvalue sensitivities.

As for disturbance attenuation, our work has covered disturbance attenuation in many types of systems, for instance, linear systems via dynamical compensators (Duan et al. 2000a), model following designs of a class of second-order systems (Duan and Huang 2006), and model following designs (Huang et al. 2006). Furthermore, Duan et al. (2000b) consider Luenberger function observer designs, and Yan et al. (2005) consider observer-based controller design for disturbance attenuation in linear systems.

2.4.2.5 Robust Pole Assignment

The importance of parametric control systems designs lies in the fact that they can handle multiple object designs very naturally. As a matter of fact, as long as certain system design requirements can be converted into parametric forms along with the controllers, these design requirements can be handled. Robust pole assignment falls into the scope of such system design requirements, which aims to make the assigned closed-loop poles as insensitive as possible to system parameter perturbations.

Using our general framework, we have proposed algorithms for robust pole assignment in linear systems via different feedback controls, including,

Figure 2.2   We are here. (Modified from http://go.jutuw.com/zhumulangmafeng/ photo/.)

- State feedback (Duan and Yu 2008, Duan and Zhang 2007a, Duan et al. 2002b, Liu et al. 2000c, Wang and Duan 2004a, Wang et al. 2006c, Yu and Duan 2009b, Yu et al. 2005, Zhou et al. 2009d, 2010a)
- Output feedback (Duan 1992a,b, Duan and Zhang 2007c, Duan et al. 2009a)
- Dynamical compensators (Duan 1991b, Liu et al. 2000a,b, 2001)

For other work related to robust pole assignment, please refer to Duan and Patton (1999), Lv et al. (2010), Duan and Huang (2007), Duan and Wu (2005), Duan et al. (1999f), Liu et al. (2000c), Wu et al. (2007c), Zhang and Duan (2012).

For applications for robust pole assignment, please refer to He and Duan (2006) and He et al. (2006).

Besides the above, a comparison research on numerical reliability of pole assignment algorithms via case study has been carried out by Duan (2008), which shows the advantages of our GSE-based parametric approach.

This chapter points out some important applications of GSEs in control system designs. In Chapter 3, we will introduce some fundamental concepts and criterions which are to be used for solutions to GSEs (Figure 2.2).

Remark 2.1   Besides the topics mentioned above, the author and his co-authors have also investigated some other parametric control problems, for example, robust model following control (Duan and Huang 2008), robust model reference control (Duan and Zhang 2006, 2007b, Duan et al. 2001b), and systems reconfiguration (Wang et al. 2005a,b).

Chapter 3

F-Coprimeness

In order to present the solutions to the various types of GSEs, in this chapter, we introduce the concept of *F*-coprimeness of polynomial matrices, which performs a fundamental role in the book. Several criteria for *F*-coprimeness of two polynomial matrices are presented.

3.1 Controllability and Regularizability

Let us begin with a pair of familiar, and yet closely related, concepts, namely, controllability and regularizability.

3.1.1 First-Order Systems

3.1.1.1 Controllability and Stabilizability

Consider a matrix pair (A, B), with $A \in \mathbb{R}^{n \times n}$, $B \in \mathbb{R}^{n \times r}$. According to the well-known Popov–Belevith–Hautus (PBH) criterion for controllability, the matrix pair, or the following linear system

$$\dot{x} = Ax + Bu, \tag{3.1}$$

is controllable if and only if

$$\text{rank} \begin{bmatrix} sI - A & B \end{bmatrix} = n, \quad \forall s \in \mathbb{C}. \tag{3.2}$$

Furthermore, any λ satisfying

$$\text{rank} \begin{bmatrix} \lambda I - A & B \end{bmatrix} < n \tag{3.3}$$

is called an uncontrollable mode of the matrix pair (A, B) or the system (3.1). If we use $\mathcal{U}_c\,(A, B)$ to denote the set of uncontrollable modes of (A, B), then

$$\mathcal{U}_c\,(A, B) = \left\{ \lambda \mid \text{rank}\left[\lambda I - A \quad B\right] < n \right\}.$$

It is obvious that $\mathcal{U}_c\,(A, B)$ is null if and only if (A, B) is controllable.

For the descriptor linear system

$$E\dot{x} = Ax + Bu, \tag{3.4}$$

a similar result holds (Duan 2010).

Theorem 3.1 *A descriptor linear system in the form of (3.4) is R-controllable if and only if*

$$\text{rank}\left[sE - A \quad B\right] = n, \quad \forall s \in \mathbb{C}, \ s \ \text{finite}. \tag{3.5}$$

Similarly, uncontrollable modes for the descriptor linear system can be defined. However, different from the normal system case, the uncontrollable modes of the descriptor linear system (3.4) may be composed of both finite and infinite ones (Duan 2010).

Definition 3.1 *A regular descriptor system in the form of (3.4) is called stabilizable if all of its uncontrollable modes are stable ones.*

Obviously, the descriptor linear system (3.4) is stabilizable if and only if

$$\text{rank}\left[sE - A \quad B\right] = n, \quad \forall s \in \mathbb{C}^+, \tag{3.6}$$

where $\mathbb{C}^+$ denotes the right half complex plane.

3.1.1.2 Regularity and Regularizability

Different from the normal linear system (3.1), for the descriptor linear system (3.4), we may have

$$\det\,(sE - A) = 0, \quad \forall s \in \mathbb{C}.$$

Such a phenomenon gives the following concepts associated with the descriptor linear system (3.4).

Definition 3.2   *The descriptor linear system (3.4) is called regular if*

$$\det(sE - A) \neq 0, \quad \exists s \in \mathbb{C}.$$

It is well known that the importance of regularity of a descriptor linear system lies in the fact that a regular descriptor linear system has a unique solution (Duan 2010).

For an irregular descriptor linear system, we are often interested in the problem of finding a feedback controller for the system such that the closed-loop system is regular. This gives rise to the following definition (Duan 2010).

Definition 3.3   *The descriptor linear system (3.4) is called regularizable if there exists a matrix $K \in \mathbb{R}^{r \times n}$ satisfying*

$$\det[sE - (A + BK)] \neq 0, \quad \exists s \in \mathbb{C}.$$

For regularizability, we have the following sufficient and necessary condition (Duan 2010).

Theorem 3.2   *The descriptor linear system (3.4) is regularizable if and only if*

$$\text{rank}\begin{bmatrix} sE - A & B \end{bmatrix} = n, \quad \exists s \in \mathbb{C}.$$

3.1.2 Higher-Order Systems

3.1.2.1 Controllability and Stabilizability

Now let us consider a type of higher-order systems in the form of (1.16), that is,

$$\sum_{i=0}^{m} A_i x^{(i)} = Bu, \tag{3.7}$$

whose associated polynomial matrix is

$$A(s) = A_m s^m + \cdots + A_1 s + A_0. \tag{3.8}$$

It is easy to show that it can be converted into the following extended first-order state-space model:

$$E_e \dot{z} = A_e z + B_e u, \tag{3.9}$$

with

$$E_e = \text{blockdiag} (I_n, \ldots, I_n, A_m), \tag{3.10}$$

$$A_e = \begin{bmatrix} 0 & I_n & & & \\ & 0 & I_n & & \\ & & \ddots & \ddots & \\ & & & 0 & I_n \\ -A_0 & -A_1 & \cdots & -A_{m-2} & -A_{m-1} \end{bmatrix}, \tag{3.11}$$

and

$$B_e = \begin{bmatrix} 0 & \cdots & 0 & B^T \end{bmatrix}^T. \tag{3.12}$$

The following lemma shows that R-controllability of this extended system can also be checked directly by the original system coefficient matrices.

Lemma 3.1 *Let $A(s) \in \mathbb{R}^{n \times n}[s]$ be given in (3.8), $B \in \mathbb{R}^{n \times r}$. Then the extended first-order system (3.9) through (3.12) is R-controllable if and only if*

$$\text{rank} \begin{bmatrix} A(s) & B \end{bmatrix} = n, \ \forall s \in \mathbb{C}. \tag{3.13}$$

Proof. According to the well-known PBH criterion, we need only to show that the following condition

$$\text{rank} \begin{bmatrix} sE_e - A_e & B_e \end{bmatrix} = mn, \ \forall s \in \mathbb{C} \tag{3.14}$$

is equivalent to (3.13), with E_e, A_e, and B_e given by (3.10) through (3.12).
    Note that

$$\begin{aligned} &\text{rank} \begin{bmatrix} A_e - sE_e & B_e \end{bmatrix} \\ &= \text{rank} \begin{bmatrix} -sI_n & I_n & & & & 0 \\ & \ddots & \ddots & & & \vdots \\ & & -sI_n & I_n & & 0 \\ -A_0 & -A_1 & \cdots & -A_{m-1} - sA_m & B \end{bmatrix}. \end{aligned}$$

Now, starting from the last second column of the right-hand side of the above equation, each column is first multiplied by s and then added to the column by its left side, resulting in the following

$$\text{rank}\left[A_e - sE_e \quad B_e\right]$$

$$= \text{rank}\left[\begin{array}{ccc} 0 & I_{n(m-1)} & 0 \\ -\sum_{i=0}^{m} A_i s^i & * & B \end{array}\right]$$

$$= \text{rank}\left[\begin{array}{ccc} I_{n(m-1)} & 0 & 0 \\ * & \sum_{i=0}^{m} A_i s^i & B \end{array}\right]$$

$$= n(m-1) + \text{rank}\left[A(s) \quad B\right],$$

the conclusion clearly follows. ■

In view of the above result, we may say that $(A(s), B)$ is controllable when (3.13) holds. A further generalization of this suggests the following definition.

Definition 3.4 *Let $A(s) \in \mathbb{R}^{n \times q}[s]$, $B(s) \in \mathbb{R}^{n \times r}[s]$, $q + r > n$. Then*

■ *The polynomial matrix pair $(A(s), B(s))$, or the higher-order system (1.12), is called controllable if*

$$\text{rank}\left[A(s) \quad B(s)\right] = n, \quad \forall s \in \mathbb{C}. \tag{3.15}$$

■ *Any $\lambda \in \mathbb{C}$ satisfying*

$$\text{rank}\left[A(\lambda) \quad B(\lambda)\right] < n \tag{3.16}$$

is called an uncontrollable mode of $(A(s), B(s))$, or, of the higher-order system (1.12).

According to the above definition, the set of uncontrollable modes of $(A(s), B(s))$, denoted by $\mathcal{U}_c(A(s), B(s))$, is

$$\mathcal{U}_c(A(s), B(s)) = \left\{\lambda \mid \text{rank}\left[A(\lambda) \quad B(\lambda)\right] < n\right\}.$$

It is obvious that $\mathcal{U}_c(A(s), B(s))$ is null if and only if $(A(s), B(s))$ is controllable. For convenience, let us introduce the following definition.

Definition 3.5 *Let $M_1(s), M_2(s) \in \mathbb{R}^{m \times n}[s]$. If there exist two unimodular matrices $P(s) \in \mathbb{R}^{m \times m}[s]$, $Q(s) \in \mathbb{R}^{n \times n}[s]$ satisfying*

$$P(s)M_1(s)Q(s) = M_2(s),$$

then we say that the two polynomial matrices $M_1(s)$ and $M_2(s)$ are equivalent.

Using the above definition, we can give the following lemma, which further characterizes $\mathcal{U}_c\,(A(s), B(s))$ in the general case.

Lemma 3.2 *Let $A(s) \in \mathbb{R}^{n \times q}[s]$, $B(s) \in \mathbb{R}^{n \times r}[s]$, $q + r > n$. If $\begin{bmatrix} A(s) & B(s) \end{bmatrix}$ is equivalent to $\begin{bmatrix} \Sigma(s) & 0 \end{bmatrix}$, with $\Sigma(s) \in \mathbb{R}^{n \times n}[s]$, then*

$$\mathcal{U}_c\,(A(s), B(s)) = \{s \mid \det \Sigma(s) = 0\}.$$

Proof. Under the condition of the lemma, a pair of unimodular matrices $P(s)$ and $Q(s)$ exist satisfying

$$P(s) \begin{bmatrix} A(s) & B(s) \end{bmatrix} Q(s) = \begin{bmatrix} \Sigma(s) & 0 \end{bmatrix}, \ \forall s \in \mathbb{C}, \tag{3.17}$$

where $\Sigma(s) \in \mathbb{R}^{n \times n}[s]$. Therefore, it is clear to see that a $\lambda \in \mathbb{C}$ satisfies (3.16) if and only if $\det \Sigma(\lambda) = 0$. The conclusion clearly holds. ∎

The following is a straightforward generalization of the well-known concept of stabilizability.

Definition 3.6 *Let $A(s) \in \mathbb{R}^{n \times q}[s]$, $B(s) \in \mathbb{R}^{n \times r}[s]$, $q + r > n$. Then the pair of polynomial matrices $(A(s), B(s))$ is called stabilizable if all of its uncontrollable modes are stable ones.*

Obviously, $(A(s), B(s))$ is stabilizable if and only if

$$\operatorname{rank} \begin{bmatrix} A(s) & B(s) \end{bmatrix} = n, \ \forall s \in \mathbb{C}^+. \tag{3.18}$$

3.1.2.2 Regularity and Regularizability

Parallely, we can define the concepts of regularity and regularizability.

Definition 3.7 *The polynomial matrix $A(s) \in \mathbb{R}^{n \times q}[s]$ is called regular if*

$$\operatorname{rank} A(s) = \min\{n, q\}, \ \exists s \in \mathbb{C}. \tag{3.19}$$

It clearly follows from the above definition that the polynomial matrix $A(s) \in \mathbb{R}^{n \times q}[s]$ is irregular if and only of

$$\operatorname{rank} A(s) < \min\{n, q\}, \ \forall s \in \mathbb{C}. \tag{3.20}$$

In this case, we can introduce the following so-called essential zeros.

Definition 3.8 *Let $A(s) \in \mathbb{R}^{n \times q}[s]$. Then*

1. *Any λ satisfying*

$$\text{rank} A(\lambda) < \min\{n, q\} \tag{3.21}$$

   is called a zero of $A(s)$;
2. *Any λ satisfying*

$$\text{rank} A(\lambda) < \max_{s \in \mathbb{C}}\{\text{rank} A(s)\} \tag{3.22}$$

   is called an essential zero of $A(s)$.

The following proposition obviously follows from the above definition.

Proposition 3.1 *The polynomial matrix $A(s) \in \mathbb{R}^{n \times q}[s]$ is regular if and only if its sets of zeros and essential zeros coincide with each other.*

The following result reveals the nature of essential zeros of a polynomial matrix in terms of SFR.

Theorem 3.3 *Let the Smith form of $A(s) \in \mathbb{R}^{n \times q}[s]$ be*

$$\begin{bmatrix} \Sigma(s) & 0 \\ 0 & 0 \end{bmatrix},$$

where $\Sigma(s) \in \mathbb{R}^{p \times p}[s]$ is a diagonal polynomial matrix satisfying

$$\det \Sigma(s) \neq 0, \ \exists s \in \mathbb{C}. \tag{3.23}$$

Then the set of essential zeros of $A(s)$ is given by

$$\mathbb{E} = \{s \mid \det \Sigma(s) = 0\}.$$

Proof. Following from (3.23), we have

$$\max_{s \in \mathbb{C}}\{\text{rank} A(s)\} = p.$$

Further, note (3.23) and

$$\text{rank}A(s) = \text{rank} \begin{bmatrix} \Sigma(s) & 0 \\ 0 & 0 \end{bmatrix}$$

$$= \text{rank}\Sigma(s),$$

we can easily get the conclusion following from Definition 3.8. ■

The above result immediately implies the following corollary.

Corollary 3.1 *Equivalent polynomial matrices have the same essential zeros.*

Again, parallely, we can define the concept of regularizability for the polynomial matrix pair $(A(s), B(s))$.

Definition 3.9 *Let $A(s) \in \mathbb{R}^{n \times q}[s]$, $B(s) \in \mathbb{R}^{n \times r}[s]$, $q + r > n$. Then the polynomial matrix pair $(A(s), B(s))$ is called regularizable if*

$$\text{rank} \begin{bmatrix} A(s) & B(s) \end{bmatrix} = n, \quad \exists s \in \mathbb{C}. \tag{3.24}$$

For regularizability of the polynomial matrix pair $(A(s), B(s))$, we obviously have the following result.

Lemma 3.3 *Let $A(s) \in \mathbb{R}^{n \times q}[s]$, $B(s) \in \mathbb{R}^{n \times r}[s]$, $q + r > n$. Then the polynomial matrix pair $(A(s), B(s))$ is regularizable if and only if one of the following conditions is met:*

1. *The set of uncontrollable modes of $(A(s), B(s))$ does not form the whole complex plane, that is,*

$$\mathcal{U}_c (A(s), B(s)) \neq \mathbb{C}.$$

2. *The following relation*

$$\det \Sigma(s) \neq 0, \quad \exists s \in \mathbb{C}, \tag{3.25}$$

holds with $\begin{bmatrix} \Sigma(s) & 0 \end{bmatrix}$ being equivalent to $[A(s) \quad B(s)]$.

It follows from the above definition and result that the polynomial matrix pair $(A(s), B(s))$ is irregularizable if and only if

$$\text{rank}\begin{bmatrix} A(s) & B(s) \end{bmatrix} < n, \quad \forall s \in \mathbb{C}. \tag{3.26}$$

In this case, it is clear that

$$\alpha = \max_{s \in \mathbb{C}} \left\{ \text{rank}\begin{bmatrix} A(s) & B(s) \end{bmatrix} \right\} < n. \tag{3.27}$$

The following proposition summarizes a few obvious conclusions associated with the polynomial matrix pair $(A(s), B(s))$ in terms of zeros of polynomial matrices.

Proposition 3.2 *Let $A(s) \in \mathbb{R}^{n \times q}[s]$, $B(s) \in \mathbb{R}^{n \times r}[s]$, $q + r > n$. Then $(A(s), B(s))$ is*

1. *Controllable if and only if the extended polynomial matrix $[A(s) \ B(s)]$ does not have zeros;*
2. *Stabilizable if and only if all the zeros of the extended polynomial matrix $[A(s) \ B(s)]$ are on the left half complex plane;*
3. *Regularizable if and only if all the zeros of the extended polynomial matrix $[A(s) \ B(s)]$ are essential zeros of the extended polynomial matrix;*
4. *Irregularizable if and only if there exist some zeros of the extended polynomial matrix $[A(s) \ B(s)]$, which are not essential zeros of the extended polynomial matrix.*

To end up this section, let us point out the relations among the three important concepts involved, that is, the controllability of $(A(s), B(s))$ implies the stabilizability of $(A(s), B(s))$, and the stabilizability of $(A(s), B(s))$ implies the regularizability of $(A(s), B(s))$ (see Figure 3.1).

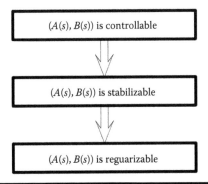

Figure 3.1 Relations among the three concepts.

3.2 Coprimeness

3.2.1 Existing Concepts

It is well known that a pair of polynomial matrices $N(s) \in \mathbb{R}^{n \times r}[s]$ and $D(s) \in \mathbb{R}^{r \times r}[s]$ are right coprime if

$$\text{rank} \begin{bmatrix} N(s) \\ D(s) \end{bmatrix} = r, \ \forall s \in \mathbb{C}, \tag{3.28}$$

and a pair of polynomial matrices $H(s) \in \mathbb{R}^{m \times n}[s]$ and $L(s) \in \mathbb{R}^{m \times m}[s]$ are left coprime if

$$\text{rank} \begin{bmatrix} H(s) & L(s) \end{bmatrix} = m, \ \forall s \in \mathbb{C}. \tag{3.29}$$

By Definitions 3.4 and 3.6, we can easily derive the following result. The first conclusion can be viewed as an extension of the well-known PBH criterion for controllability of first-order systems.

Proposition 3.3 *Let $A(s) \in \mathbb{R}^{n \times n}[s]$, $B(s) \in \mathbb{R}^{n \times r}[s]$. Then the polynomial matrix pair $(A(s), B(s))$ is*

1. *Controllable if and only if $A(s)$ and $B(s)$ are left coprime;*
2. *Stabilizable if all of its uncontrollable modes are stable ones.*

Let $F \in \mathbb{C}^{p \times p}$ be an arbitrary matrix. Duan and Zhou (2006) and Zhou and Duan (2006a) have extended the above concept of coprimeness to the so-called *F*-coprimeness. Specifically, for an arbitrary matrix $F \in \mathbb{C}^{p \times p}$, a pair of polynomial matrices $N(s) \in \mathbb{R}^{n \times r}[s]$ and $D(s) \in \mathbb{R}^{r \times r}[s]$ are said to be *F*-right coprime if

$$\text{rank} \begin{bmatrix} N(s) \\ D(s) \end{bmatrix} = r, \ \forall s \in \text{eig}\,(F), \tag{3.30}$$

and a pair of polynomial matrices $H(s) \in \mathbb{R}^{m \times n}[s]$ and $L(s) \in \mathbb{R}^{m \times m}[s]$ are said to be *F*-left coprime if

$$\text{rank} \begin{bmatrix} H(s) & L(s) \end{bmatrix} = m, \ \forall s \in \text{eig}\,(F). \tag{3.31}$$

Obviously, a pair of polynomial matrices $N(s) \in \mathbb{R}^{n \times r}[s]$ and $D(s) \in \mathbb{R}^{r \times r}[s]$ are right coprime if and only if they are *F*-right coprime for arbitrary $F \in \mathbb{C}^{p \times p}$, $p > 0$, and a pair of polynomial matrices $H(s) \in \mathbb{R}^{m \times n}[s]$ and $L(s) \in \mathbb{R}^{m \times m}[s]$ are left coprime if and only if they are *F*-left coprime for all $F \in \mathbb{C}^{p \times p}$, $p > 0$.

For most practical control systems, controllability is met. However, there do exist circumstances in which controllability is not met. As we are aware of that, satisfactory control can often be achieved under the condition of stabilizability of the considered system. This is to say that the full row rank requirement on $[A(s)\ B(s)]$ can be further relaxed.

3.2.2 Generalized Concepts

With the above background, we can propose the following definition, which will perform important function in the following chapters of this book.

Definition 3.10 *Let $F \in \mathbb{C}^{p \times p}$ be an arbitrary matrix. Then a pair of polynomial matrices $N(s) \in \mathbb{R}^{q \times n}[s]$ and $D(s) \in \mathbb{R}^{r \times n}[s]$, with $q + r > n$, are said to be*

1. *F-right coprime with rank α if*

$$\mathrm{rank} \begin{bmatrix} N(s) \\ D(s) \end{bmatrix} \leq \alpha, \ \forall s \in \mathbb{C}, \tag{3.32}$$

   and

$$\mathrm{rank} \begin{bmatrix} N(s) \\ D(s) \end{bmatrix} = \alpha, \ \forall s \in \mathrm{eig}\,(F)\,; \tag{3.33}$$

2. *F-right coprime if they are F-right coprime with rank n;*
3. *Right coprime with rank α if they are F-right coprime with rank α for arbitrary $F \in \mathbb{C}^{p \times p}$, $p > 0$*

Correspondingly, we also have the following definition for F-left coprimeness.

Definition 3.11 *Let $F \in \mathbb{C}^{p \times p}$ be an arbitrary matrix. Then a pair of polynomial matrices $H(s) \in \mathbb{R}^{n \times q}[s]$ and $L(s) \in \mathbb{R}^{n \times r}[s]$, with $q + r > n$, are said to be*

1. *F-left coprime with rank α if*

$$\mathrm{rank} \begin{bmatrix} H(s) & L(s) \end{bmatrix} \leq \alpha, \ \forall s \in \mathbb{C}, \tag{3.34}$$

   and

$$\mathrm{rank} \begin{bmatrix} H(s) & L(s) \end{bmatrix} = \alpha, \ \forall s \in \mathrm{eig}\,(F)\,; \tag{3.35}$$

2. *F-left coprime if they are F-left coprime with rank n; and*
3. *Left coprime with rank α if they are F-left coprime with rank α for arbitrary $F \in \mathbb{C}^{p \times p}, p > 0$.*

Obviously, the above definitions are generalizations of the F-coprimeness introduced in Duan and Zhou (2006) and Zhou and Duan (2006a).

It clearly follows from the above definition that F-right coprimeness and F-left coprimeness are a pair of dual concepts, that is, $N(s)$ and $D(s)$ are F-right coprime if and only if $N^{\mathrm{T}}(s)$ and $D^{\mathrm{T}}(s)$ are F-left coprime.

3.2.3 Coprimeness of A(s) and B(s)

3.2.3.1 Irregularizable Case

Applying the above definitions to the pair of matrices $A(s)$ and $B(s)$ gives the following definition for F-left coprimeness of $A(s)$ and $B(s)$ with rank α:

$$\begin{cases} \mathrm{rank}\big[A(s) \ \ B(s)\big] \leq \alpha, \ \forall s \in \mathbb{C} \\ \mathrm{rank}\big[A(s) \ \ B(s)\big] = \alpha, \ \forall s \in \mathrm{eig}(F). \end{cases} \tag{3.36}$$

Particularly, the pair of matrices $A(s)$ and $B(s)$ are left coprime with rank α if and only if $A(s)$ and $B(s)$ are F-left coprime with rank α for arbitrary matrix $F \in \mathbb{C}^{p \times p}$, $p > 0$.

In view of the above conditions, and also the definition of essential zeros, we have the following result for the F-left coprimeness of $A(s)$ and $B(s)$ with rank α.

Theorem 3.4 *Let $A(s) \in \mathbb{R}^{n \times q}[s]$, $B(s) \in \mathbb{R}^{n \times r}[s]$, $q + r > n$, $F \in \mathbb{C}^{p \times p}$. Then $A(s)$ and $B(s)$ are F-left coprime with rank α if and only if the eigenvalues of the matrix F are different from the essential zeros of $[A(s) \ \ B(s)]$.*

Proof. Sufficiency. Suppose that the eigenvalues of the matrix F are different from the essential zeros of $[A(s) \ \ B(s)]$, then by the definition of essential zeros we have

$$\mathrm{rank}\big[A(s) \ \ B(s)\big] \geq \alpha, \ \forall s \in \mathrm{eig}(F),$$

where

$$\alpha = \max_{s \in \mathbb{C}} \big\{ \mathrm{rank}\big[A(s) \ \ B(s)\big] \big\}. \tag{3.37}$$

These two relations are clearly equivalent to (3.36).

Necessity. Suppose (3.36) holds, then it is clear that (3.37) is true. Thus, any essential zero s of $[A(s) \ \ B(s)]$ is determined by

$$\text{rank}\begin{bmatrix} A(s) & B(s) \end{bmatrix} < \alpha.$$

Therefore, the second condition in (3.36) indicates that the eigenvalues of the matrix F are different from the essential zeros of $[A(s)\ B(s)]$. ■

3.2.3.2 Regularizable Case

When the pair of matrices $A(s)$ and $B(s)$ are regularizable, we obviously have

$$\alpha = \max_{s \in \mathbb{C}} \left\{ \text{rank}\begin{bmatrix} A(s) & B(s) \end{bmatrix} \right\} = n. \tag{3.38}$$

In view of this fact and Definition 3.11, we immediately have the following results for the F-left coprimeness of $A(s)$ and $B(s)$.

Theorem 3.5 *Let* $A(s) \in \mathbb{R}^{n \times q}[s]$, $B(s) \in \mathbb{R}^{n \times r}[s]$, $q + r > n$, $F \in \mathbb{C}^{p \times p}$. *Then*

1. $(A(s), B(s))$ *is controllable if and only if* $A(s)$ *and* $B(s)$ *are left coprime, that is,* $A(s)$ *and* $B(s)$ *are F-left coprime for arbitrary* $F \in \mathbb{C}^{p \times p}$, $p > 0$;
2. $(A(s), B(s))$ *is stabilizable if and only if* $A(s)$ *and* $B(s)$ *are F-left coprime for arbitrarily unstable matrix* $F \in \mathbb{C}^{p \times p}$, $p > 0$;
3. $A(s)$ *and* $B(s)$ *are F-left coprime (i.e., F-left coprime with rank n) if and only if the eigenvalues of the matrix F are different from the uncontrollable modes of* $(A(s), B(s))$.

To end up this section, we give in Table 3.1 the definitions of the various types of left coprimeness of $A(s)$ and $B(s)$, and also in Figure 3.2 the relations among the various concepts introduced in this section.

Table 3.1 Coprimeness of $A(s)$ and $B(s)$

Terms	Conditions
F-left coprime with rank α	$\begin{cases} \text{rank}\,[A(s)\ \ B(s)] \le \alpha,\ \forall s \in \mathbb{C} \\ \text{rank}\,[A(s)\ \ B(s)] = \alpha,\ \forall s \in \text{eig}(F) \end{cases}$
Left coprime with rank α	$\text{rank}\,[A(s)\ \ B(s)] = \alpha,\ \forall s \in \mathbb{C}$
F-left coprime	$\text{rank}\,[A(s)\ \ B(s)] = n,\ \forall s \in \text{eig}(F)$
Left coprime	$\text{rank}\,[A(s)\ \ B(s)] = n,\ \forall s \in \mathbb{C}$

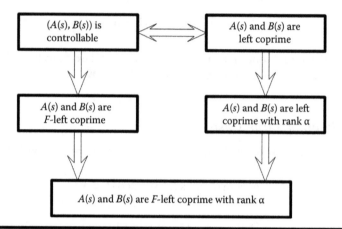

Figure 3.2   Relations among the five concepts.

3.3 Equivalent Conditions

To verify the F-right coprimeness of two polynomial matrices $N(s)$ and $D(s)$ according to the definition, we need to get the eigenvalues of the matrix F. This may involve bad conditioning. While the following is a direct criterion, which uses only the coefficient matrices $N_i, D_i, \ i = 0, 1, \ldots, \omega$, and the matrix F.

Theorem 3.6 *Let $F \in \mathbb{C}^{p \times p}$ be an arbitrary matrix and*

$$
\begin{cases}
N(s) = \sum_{i=0}^{\omega} N_i s^i, \ N_i \in \mathbb{R}^{n \times r} \\
D(s) = \sum_{i=0}^{\omega} D_i s^i, \ D_i \in \mathbb{R}^{m \times r},
\end{cases}
\tag{3.39}
$$

with $m + n > r$. Then $N(s)$ and $D(s)$ are F-right coprime with rank α if and only if

$$
\mathrm{rank} \left[\sum_{i=0}^{\omega} \left(F^i \otimes \begin{bmatrix} N_i \\ D_i \end{bmatrix} \right) \right] = \alpha p.
\tag{3.40}
$$

For a proof of the above theorem, please refer to the appendix.

In the rest of this chapter, we will further look into some equivalent conditions, which will be used in the later chapters, and our emphasis is laid on the left coprimeness of the matrix pair $(A(s), B(s))$.

3.3.1 SFR

By carrying out the SFR of $[A(s) \ -B(s)]$, we can find two unimodular matrices $P(s)$ and $Q(s)$ with appropriate dimensions satisfying

$$P(s) \begin{bmatrix} A(s) & -B(s) \end{bmatrix} Q(s) = \begin{bmatrix} \Sigma(s) & 0 \\ 0 & 0 \end{bmatrix}, \tag{3.41}$$

with $\Sigma(s) \in \mathbb{R}^{\alpha \times \alpha}[s]$ a diagonal polynomial matrix satisfying

$$\det \Sigma(s) \neq 0, \quad \exists s \in \mathbb{C}.$$

It follows from Theorem 3.3 that the set of all essential zeros of $[A(s) \ B(s)]$ is given by

$$\mathbb{E} = \{s | \det \Sigma(s) = 0\}.$$

The following result actually reveals the essence of F-coprimeness in terms of SFR.

Theorem 3.7 *Let $A(s) \in \mathbb{R}^{n \times q}[s]$, $B(s) \in \mathbb{R}^{n \times r}[s]$, $q + r > n$, and (3.41) be their related SFR. Then $A(s)$ and $B(s)$ are*

1. *F-left coprime with rank α if and only if*

$$\Delta(s) = \det \Sigma(s) \neq 0, \quad \forall s \in \text{eig}(F); \tag{3.42}$$

2. *Left coprime with rank α if and only if $\Sigma(s) = I_\alpha$.*

The above theorem can be easily shown with the help of Theorems 3.3 and 3.4. However, a direct proof is given below.

Proof. It is obvious that when

$$\text{rank} \begin{bmatrix} A(s) & B(s) \end{bmatrix} \leq \alpha, \quad \forall s \in \mathbb{C},$$

$[A(s) \ -B(s)]$ admits a SFR in the form of (3.41). With this reduction, it is clear that

$$\text{rank} \begin{bmatrix} A(s) & B(s) \end{bmatrix} = \alpha, \quad \forall s \in \text{eig}(F)$$

$$\Longleftrightarrow \text{rank} \begin{bmatrix} \Sigma(s) & 0 \\ 0 & 0 \end{bmatrix} = \alpha, \quad \forall s \in \text{eig}(F)$$

$$\Longleftrightarrow (3.42).$$

Thus, the first conclusion is true by the definition of F-right coprimeness with rank α.

When the pair of polynomial matrices $A(s)$ and $B(s)$ are left coprime with rank α, using (3.41), we have

$$\text{rank} \begin{bmatrix} A(s) & B(s) \end{bmatrix} = \alpha, \quad \forall s \in \mathbb{C}$$

$$\Leftrightarrow \text{rank} \begin{bmatrix} \Sigma(s) & 0 \\ 0 & 0 \end{bmatrix} = \alpha, \quad \forall s \in \mathbb{C}$$

$$\Leftrightarrow \Sigma(s) = I_\alpha.$$

This indicates that $\begin{bmatrix} A(s) & B(s) \end{bmatrix}$ admits a SFR with $\Sigma(s) = I_\alpha$. ■

3.3.2 Generalized RCF

Given $A \in \mathbb{R}^{n \times n}$, $B \in \mathbb{R}^{n \times r}$, it is well known that, when (A, B) is controllable, there exist a pair of right coprime polynomial matrices $N(s) \in \mathbb{R}^{n \times r}[s]$ and $D(s) \in \mathbb{R}^{r \times r}[s]$ satisfying

$$(sI - A)^{-1} B = N(s)D^{-1}(s). \tag{3.43}$$

This is the well-known so-called RCF of the matrix pair (A, B).

The above RCF can be written in the form of

$$(sI - A) N(s) - BD(s) = 0. \tag{3.44}$$

With this representation, it is not necessary to restrict the columns of $N(s) \in \mathbb{R}^{n \times r}[s]$ and $D(s) \in \mathbb{R}^{r \times r}[s]$ to be equal to that of the B matrix. The need for this relaxation is underlying in the following fact:

When (A, B) is not controllable, there do not exist a pair of right coprime polynomial matrices $N(s) \in \mathbb{R}^{n \times r}[s]$ and $D(s) \in \mathbb{R}^{r \times r}[s]$ satisfying (3.43). However, there may exist a maximum $\beta \leq r$, and a pair of right coprime polynomial matrices $N(s) \in \mathbb{R}^{n \times \beta}[s]$ and $D(s) \in \mathbb{R}^{r \times \beta}[s]$, satisfying (3.44). While applications based on $N(s) \in \mathbb{R}^{n \times r}[s]$ and $D(s) \in \mathbb{R}^{r \times r}[s]$ satisfying (3.43) under the controllability of (A, B) can still be carried out based on the $N(s) \in \mathbb{R}^{n \times \beta}[s]$ and $D(s) \in \mathbb{R}^{r \times \beta}[s]$ satisfying (3.44) when controllability of (A, B) is not met.

Due to the above fact, it is necessary to generalize (3.43) into (3.44), and we call (3.44) a generalized RCF.

Further, we can also replace $(sI - A)$ and B with two general polynomial matrices $A(s) \in \mathbb{R}^{n \times q}[s]$ and $B(s) \in \mathbb{R}^{n \times r}[s]$, $q + r > n$, and obtain the following generalized form of RCF.

$$A(s)N(s) - B(s)D(s) = 0. \tag{3.45}$$

When $q = n$, and the polynomial $\det A(s)$ is not identically zero, $A(s)$ is invertible. Under the assumption that $D(s)$ is also invertible, the above relation (3.45) can be rewritten in the form of the following so-called right factorization

$$A^{-1}(s)B(s) = N(s)D^{-1}(s). \qquad (3.46)$$

This form certainly looks familiar, but the generalized form (3.45) allows rectangular $A(s)$ and $D(s)$.

Recall that $A_m \neq 0$, then the transfer function $A^{-1}(s)B(s)$ is physically realizable, and so is $N(s)D^{-1}(s)$. Thus, the maximum degree of polynomial matrices $N(s)$ and $D(s)$ is determined by that of $D(s)$. If we denote $D(s) = \left[d_{ij}(s)\right]_{r\times\beta}$ and

$$\omega = \max\left\{\deg\left(d_{ij}(s)\right), \quad i = 1, 2, \ldots, r, \quad j = 1, 2, \ldots, \beta\right\},$$

then a pair of $N(s)$ and $D(s)$ satisfying (3.45) can be written in the form of

$$\begin{cases} N(s) = \sum\limits_{i=0}^{\omega} N_i s^i, \ N_i \in \mathbb{R}^{q\times\beta} \\ D(s) = \sum\limits_{i=0}^{\omega} D_i s^i, \ D_i \in \mathbb{R}^{r\times\beta}. \end{cases} \qquad (3.47)$$

The following result gives a condition for two polynomial matrices to be F-left coprime with rank α in terms of the generalized form of RCF (3.45).

Theorem 3.8 *The polynomial matrices $A(s) \in \mathbb{R}^{n\times q}[s]$ and $B(s) \in \mathbb{R}^{n\times r}[s]$, with $q + r > n$, are F-left coprime with rank α for some $F \in \mathbb{C}^{p\times p}$ if and only if*

1. *There exists a pair of right coprime polynomial matrices $N(s) \in \mathbb{R}^{q\times\beta}[s]$ and $D(s) \in \mathbb{R}^{r\times\beta}[s]$, with $\beta = q + r - \alpha$, satisfying the generalized RCF (3.45) for all $s \in \mathbb{C}$;*
2. *There does not exist a pair of right coprime polynomial matrices $N(s)$ and $D(s)$, with columns greater than $\beta = q + r - \alpha$, satisfying the generalized RCF (3.45) for any $s \in \mathrm{eig}\,(F)$.*

Proof. It follows from Theorem 3.7 that $A(s)$ and $B(s)$ are F-left coprime with rank α if and only if there exist two unimodular matrices $P(s)$ and $Q(s)$ with appropriate dimensions satisfying (3.41) and (3.42). Thus, we need only to show that there exist two unimodular matrices $P(s)$ and $Q(s)$ with appropriate dimensions satisfying (3.41) and (3.42) if and only if there exist a pair of right coprime polynomial matrices $N(s) \in \mathbb{R}^{q\times\beta}[s]$ and $D(s) \in \mathbb{R}^{r\times\beta}[s]$, with $\beta = q + r - \alpha$, satisfying the generalized RCF (3.45).

Necessity. Suppose $A(s)$ and $B(s)$ are F-left coprime with rank α for some $F \in \mathbb{C}^{p \times p}$, then there exist two unimodular matrices $P(s)$ and $Q(s)$ with appropriate dimensions satisfying (3.41) and (3.42). Partition the unimodular matrix $Q(s)$ as follows:

$$Q(s) = \begin{bmatrix} * & N(s) \\ * & D(s) \end{bmatrix}, \quad N(s) \in \mathbb{R}^{q \times \beta}[s], \quad D(s) \in \mathbb{R}^{r \times \beta}[s], \tag{3.48}$$

then we immediately have, from (3.41),

$$\begin{bmatrix} A(s) & -B(s) \end{bmatrix} \begin{bmatrix} N(s) \\ D(s) \end{bmatrix} = 0. \tag{3.49}$$

This clearly gives the generalized RCF (3.45). Furthermore, this pair of $N(s)$ and $D(s)$ is also coprime, since $Q(s)$ is unimodular. Thus, the first condition holds. The second one also holds because of (3.42).

Sufficiency. When there exist a pair of right coprime polynomial matrices $N(s) \in \mathbb{R}^{q \times \beta}[s]$ and $D(s) \in \mathbb{R}^{r \times \beta}[s]$ satisfying the generalized RCF (3.45), or equivalently, (3.49), and also, when the second condition holds, we can find a unimodular matrix $Q(s)$ in the form of (3.48) by expansion, which gives

$$\begin{bmatrix} A(s) & -B(s) \end{bmatrix} Q(s) = \begin{bmatrix} C(s) & 0 \end{bmatrix}, \tag{3.50}$$

with $C(s) \in \mathbb{R}^{n \times \alpha}[s]$ satisfying

$$\mathrm{rank}\, C(s) = \alpha, \quad \forall s \in \mathrm{eig}\,(F). \tag{3.51}$$

Therefore,

$$\mathrm{rank} \begin{bmatrix} A(s) & -B(s) \end{bmatrix} \le \alpha, \quad \forall s \in \mathbb{C}. \tag{3.52}$$

Further, note that $Q(s)$ is unimodular and (3.51) holds, we also have

$$\mathrm{rank} \begin{bmatrix} A(s) & -B(s) \end{bmatrix} = \alpha, \quad \forall s \in \mathrm{eig}\,(F). \tag{3.53}$$

This, together with (3.52), implies that the polynomial matrices $A(s) \in \mathbb{R}^{n \times q}[s]$ and $B(s) \in \mathbb{R}^{n \times r}[s]$ are F-left coprime with rank α. ▪

Remark 3.1 It is important to note that, for the case of $A(s)$ and $B(s)$ being left coprime with rank α, the second condition in the above theorem vanishes.

3.3.3 DPE

Let $A(s) \in \mathbb{R}^{n \times q}[s]$, $B(s) \in \mathbb{R}^{n \times r}[s]$, and $C(s) \in \mathbb{R}^{n \times \alpha}[s]$. Then an equation of the following form

$$A(s)U(s) - B(s)T(s) = C(s) \qquad (3.54)$$

is called a DPE, where $U(s) \in \mathbb{R}^{q \times \alpha}[s]$ and $T(s) \in \mathbb{R}^{r \times \alpha}[s]$ are two polynomial matrices to be sought. Zhou et al. (2010b) have given a solution to this type of equations.

Theorem 3.9 *The polynomial matrices $A(s) \in \mathbb{R}^{n \times q}[s]$ and $B(s) \in \mathbb{R}^{n \times r}[s]$ are F-left coprime with rank α if and only if there exist a pair of polynomial matrices $U(s) \in \mathbb{R}^{q \times \alpha}[s]$ and $T(s) \in \mathbb{R}^{r \times \alpha}[s]$ satisfying the DPE (3.54) with*

$$\mathrm{rank}\, C(s) = \alpha, \quad \forall s \in \mathrm{eig}\,(F). \qquad (3.55)$$

Proof. Necessity. It follows from Theorem 3.7 that $A(s) \in \mathbb{R}^{n \times q}[s]$ and $B(s) \in \mathbb{R}^{n \times r}[s]$ are F-left coprime with rank α if and only if there exist two unimodular matrices $P(s)$ and $Q(s)$ with appropriate dimensions satisfying (3.41) and (3.42). Partition the unimodular matrix $Q(s)$ as follows:

$$Q(s) = \begin{bmatrix} U(s) & * \\ T(s) & * \end{bmatrix}, \quad U(s) \in \mathbb{R}^{q \times \alpha}[s], \; T(s) \in \mathbb{R}^{r \times \alpha}[s], \qquad (3.56)$$

then we immediately have, from (3.41),

$$\begin{bmatrix} A(s) & -B(s) \end{bmatrix} \begin{bmatrix} U(s) \\ T(s) \end{bmatrix} = P^{-1}(s) \begin{bmatrix} \Sigma(s) \\ 0 \end{bmatrix}.$$

This clearly gives the DPE (3.54) with

$$C(s) = P^{-1}(s) \begin{bmatrix} \Sigma(s) \\ 0 \end{bmatrix},$$

which satisfies (3.55) in view of (3.42).

Sufficiency. Suppose there exist a pair of right coprime polynomial matrices $U(s) \in \mathbb{R}^{q \times \alpha}[s]$ and $T(s) \in \mathbb{R}^{r \times \alpha}[s]$ satisfying the DPE (3.54) with $C(s)$ satisfying (3.55), we can find a unimodular matrix $Q(s)$ in the form of (3.48) by expansion, which gives

$$\begin{bmatrix} A(s) & -B(s) \end{bmatrix} Q(s) = \begin{bmatrix} C(s) & 0 \end{bmatrix}. \qquad (3.57)$$

Therefore, there clearly holds

$$\text{rank}\begin{bmatrix} A(s) & -B(s) \end{bmatrix} \leq \alpha, \ \forall s \in \mathbb{C}. \tag{3.58}$$

Further, it follows from (3.55) that

$$\text{rank}\begin{bmatrix} A(s) & -B(s) \end{bmatrix} = \alpha, \ \forall s \in \text{eig}\,(F). \tag{3.59}$$

With the above two equations, we can conclude that the polynomial matrices $A(s) \in \mathbb{R}^{n \times q}[s]$ and $B(s) \in \mathbb{R}^{n \times r}[s]$ are F-left coprime with rank α. ■

3.3.4 Unified Procedure

It must have been clearly seen from the proofs of the above three theorems that the right coprime polynomial matrices $N(s)$ and $D(s)$ satisfying the generalized RCF (3.45), and the pair of polynomial matrices $U(s)$ and $T(s)$ satisfying the DPE (3.54), can be obtained simultaneously.

Lemma 3.4 *Let $A(s) \in \mathbb{R}^{n \times q}[s]$, $B(s) \in \mathbb{R}^{n \times r}[s]$ be F-left coprime with rank α and admit the SFR (3.41) and (3.42). Partition the unimodular matrix $Q(s)$ as follows:*

$$Q(s) = \begin{bmatrix} U(s) & N(s) \\ T(s) & D(s) \end{bmatrix},$$

where $N(s) \in \mathbb{R}^{q \times \beta}[s]$, $D(s) \in \mathbb{R}^{r \times \beta}[s]$, and $U(s) \in \mathbb{R}^{q \times \alpha}[s]$, $T(s) \in \mathbb{R}^{r \times \alpha}[s]$. Then,

1. *The polynomial matrices $N(s)$ and $D(s)$ are right coprime and satisfy the generalized RCF (3.45); and*
2. *The polynomial matrices $U(s)$ and $T(s)$ satisfy the DPE (3.54) with*

$$C(s) = P^{-1}(s) \begin{bmatrix} \Sigma(s) \\ 0 \end{bmatrix}, \ \det \Sigma(s) \neq 0, \ \forall s \in \text{eig}\,(F), \tag{3.60}$$

which reduces to

$$C(s) = P^{-1}(s) \begin{bmatrix} I_\alpha \\ 0 \end{bmatrix}, \tag{3.61}$$

when $A(s)$ and $B(s)$ are left coprime with rank α.

It can be clearly observed from the above lemma that a key step to find the right coprime polynomial matrices $N(s)$ and $D(s)$ satisfying the generalized RCF (3.45) and the polynomial matrices $U(s)$ and $T(s)$ satisfying the DPE (3.54) is to solve the SFR (3.41) – (3.42). The following proposition gives a simple way of solving the SFR (3.41) – (3.42).

Proposition 3.4   *Let $A(s) \in \mathbb{R}^{n \times q}[s]$, $B(s) \in \mathbb{R}^{n \times r}[s]$ be two given polynomial matrices, which are F-left coprime with rank α for some given F. When the following block matrix*

$$\left[\begin{array}{c|cc} I_n & A(s) & -B(s) \\ \hline 0 & & I_{q+r} \end{array} \right]$$

is reduced into the form of

$$\left[\begin{array}{c|cc} P(s) & \Sigma(s) & 0 \\ & 0 & 0 \\ \hline 0 & & Q(s) \end{array} \right], \quad \Sigma(s) \in \mathbb{R}^{\alpha \times \alpha}[s],$$

with a series of elementary row transformations, within only the first n rows, and a series of column elementary transformations, within only the last $q+r$ columns, then $P(s)$ and $Q(s)$ satisfy the SFR relation (3.41) and (3.42).

To end this section, we point out that the results in this section will perform fundamental functions in the forthcoming chapters.

3.4 Regularizable Case

We have given some criteria in the proceeding section for a pair of polynomial matrices $A(s)$ and $B(s)$ to be F-left coprime with rank α. In this section, we further look into the case that $(A(s), B(s))$ is regularizable. Remember that in this case, there exists s such that $[A(s)\ B(s)]$ is of full row rank, that is, we have $\alpha = n$. The purpose of this section is to find criteria for the pair of polynomial matrices $A(s)$ and $B(s)$ to be F-left coprime with rank n for some $F \in \mathbb{C}^{p \times p}$, or, for short, F-left coprime for some $F \in \mathbb{C}^{p \times p}$.

Different from the general case treated in the last section above, in this section, we are tackling the special case of $(A(s), B(s))$ being regularizable, that is,

$$\mathrm{rank}\left[A(s)\ \ -B(s) \right] = n, \ \exists s \in \mathbb{C}. \tag{3.62}$$

3.4.1 F-Left Coprime with Rank n

Recall that a pair of polynomial matrices $A(s)$ and $B(s)$ is said to be F-left coprime (with rank n) for some $F \in \mathbb{C}^{p \times p}$ if

$$\text{rank} \begin{bmatrix} A(s) & -B(s) \end{bmatrix} = n, \ \forall s \in \text{eig}(F). \tag{3.63}$$

In this subsection, we give some criteria for this condition.

3.4.1.1 Equivalent Conditions

The following theorem is a direct corollary of Theorems 3.7 through 3.9.

Theorem 3.10 *Let $A(s) \in \mathbb{R}^{n \times q}[s]$, $B(s) \in \mathbb{R}^{n \times r}[s]$, $q + r > n$, and $F \in \mathbb{C}^{p \times p}$. Then $A(s)$ and $B(s)$ are F-left coprime if and only if one of the following conditions holds:*

1. *There exist two unimodular matrices $P(s)$ and $Q(s)$ of appropriate dimensions satisfying*

$$P(s) \begin{bmatrix} A(s) & -B(s) \end{bmatrix} Q(s) = \begin{bmatrix} \Sigma(s) & 0 \end{bmatrix}, \tag{3.64}$$

where $\Sigma(s) \in \mathbb{R}^{n \times n}[s]$ satisfies

$$\Delta(s) = \det \Sigma(s) \neq 0, \ \forall s \in \text{eig}(F). \tag{3.65}$$

2. *There exist a pair of right coprime polynomial matrices $N(s) \in \mathbb{R}^{q \times \beta_0}[s]$ and $D(s) \in \mathbb{R}^{r \times \beta_0}[s]$, with $\beta_0 = q + r - n$, satisfying the generalized RCF*

$$A(s)N(s) - B(s)D(s) = 0, \ \forall s \in \mathbb{C}, \tag{3.66}$$

and meanwhile, there does not exist a pair of right coprime polynomial matrices $N(s)$ and $D(s)$, with columns greater than β_0, satisfying the generalized RCF (3.66) for any $s \in \text{eig}(F)$.

3. *There exist a pair of right coprime polynomial matrices $U(s) \in \mathbb{R}^{q \times n}[s]$ and $T(s) \in \mathbb{R}^{r \times n}[s]$ satisfying the DPE*

$$A(s)U(s) - B(s)T(s) = \Delta(s)I_n, \tag{3.67}$$

with $\Delta(s)$ being some scalar polynomial satisfying

$$\Delta(s) \neq 0, \ \forall s \in \text{eig}(F). \tag{3.68}$$

Proof. The first two conclusions are straightforward corollaries of Theorems 3.7 and 3.8. In the following, we only prove the third one.

It follows from Theorem 3.9 that the polynomial matrices $A(s)$ and $B(s)$ are F-left coprime if and only if there exists a pair of polynomial matrices $\tilde{U}(s) \in \mathbb{R}^{q \times n}[s]$ and $\tilde{T}(s) \in \mathbb{R}^{r \times n}[s]$ satisfying the DPE:

$$A(s)\tilde{U}(s) - B(s)\tilde{T}(s) = C(s), \tag{3.69}$$

where $C(s) \in \mathbb{R}^{n \times n}[s]$ satisfies

$$\Delta(s) \triangleq \det C(s) \neq 0, \quad \forall s \in \text{eig}(F). \tag{3.70}$$

Due to condition (3.70), $C^{-1}(s)$ exists. Postmultiplying $C^{-1}(s)$ both sides of (3.69) gives

$$A(s)\tilde{U}(s)C^{-1}(s) - B(s)\tilde{T}(s)C^{-1}(s) = I. \tag{3.71}$$

Next, multiplying both sides of the above equation by $\Delta(s)$, and using

$$C^{-1}(s) = \frac{\text{adj}\,C(s)}{\Delta(s)},$$

yields

$$A(s)\tilde{U}(s)\text{adj}\,C(s) - B(s)\tilde{T}(s)\text{adj}\,C(s) = \Delta(s)I. \tag{3.72}$$

Finally, defining

$$U(s) = \tilde{U}(s)\text{adj}\,C(s), \quad T(s) = \tilde{T}(s)\text{adj}\,C(s),$$

in the above equation (3.72), gives the DPE (3.67), while (3.68) clearly follows from (3.70). ■

It should be noted that in the case of $q = n$, we have $\beta_0 = r$. In this case, the generalized RCF (3.66) can be written in the form of

$$A^{-1}(s)B(s) = N(s)D^{-1}(s),$$

when both $A(s)$ and $D(s)$ are nonsingular.

3.4.1.2 Unified Procedure

Parallel to the result in Section 3.3.4, we here give a unified Procedure, which finds simultaneously the right coprime polynomial matrices $N(s)$ and $D(s)$ satisfying the generalized RCF (3.66), and the pair of polynomial matrices $U(s)$ and $T(s)$ satisfying the DPE (3.67).

Lemma 3.5 *Let $A(s) \in \mathbb{R}^{n \times q}[s]$, $B(s) \in \mathbb{R}^{n \times r}[s]$, with $q + r > n$, be F-left coprime and admit the SFR (3.64) and (3.65). Partition the unimodular matrix $Q(s)$ as follows:*

$$Q(s) = \begin{bmatrix} \tilde{U}(s) & N(s) \\ \tilde{T}(s) & D(s) \end{bmatrix},$$

where $N(s) \in \mathbb{R}^{q \times \beta_0}[s]$, $D(s) \in \mathbb{R}^{r \times \beta_0}[s]$, and $\tilde{U}(s) \in \mathbb{R}^{q \times n}[s]$, $\tilde{T}(s) \in \mathbb{R}^{r \times n}[s]$. Then

1. *The polynomial matrices $N(s)$ and $D(s)$ are right coprime and satisfy the generalized RCF (3.66)*
2. *A pair of polynomial matrices $U(s)$ and $T(s)$ satisfying the DPE (3.67) is given by*

$$\begin{cases} U(s) = \tilde{U}(s)\mathrm{adj}\Sigma(s)P(s) \\ T(s) = \tilde{T}(s)\mathrm{adj}\Sigma(s)P(s). \end{cases} \tag{3.73}$$

Parallel to Proposition 3.4, we have the following result, which gives a simple way of finding the unimodular matrices $P(s)$ and $Q(s)$ satisfy the SFR (3.64) and (3.65).

Proposition 3.5 *Let $A(s) \in \mathbb{R}^{n \times q}[s]$, $B(s) \in \mathbb{R}^{n \times r}[s]$ be two given polynomial matrices, which are F-left coprime for some given F. When the following block matrix*

$$\left[\begin{array}{c|c} I_n & A(s) \quad -B(s) \\ \hline 0 & I_{q+r} \end{array} \right]$$

is reduced into the form of

$$\left[\begin{array}{c|c} P(s) & \Sigma(s) \quad 0 \\ \hline 0 & Q(s) \end{array} \right],$$

with a series of elementary row transformations, within only the first n rows, and a series of column elementary transformations, within only the last $q + r$ columns, then $P(s)$ and $Q(s)$ satisfy the SFR relation (3.64) – (3.65).

Example 3.1

Consider the well-known space rendezvous problem described by the following C-W equation

$$\begin{bmatrix} \ddot{x}_r - 2\omega\dot{y}_r - 3\omega^2 x_r \\ \ddot{y}_r + 2\omega\dot{x}_r \\ \ddot{z}_r + \omega^2 z_r \end{bmatrix} = \begin{bmatrix} u_1 \\ u_2 \\ u_3 \end{bmatrix}, \qquad (3.74)$$

where x_r, y_r, and z_r are the relative position variables, and u_i, $i = 1, 2, 3$, are the thrusts acting on the three channels. Let us assume that the thrust u_2 fails. In this case, the system can be easily arranged into the standard matrix second-order form of

$$\ddot{x} + D\dot{x} + Kx = Bu,$$

with

$$D = \begin{bmatrix} 0 & -2\omega & 0 \\ 2\omega & 0 & 0 \\ 0 & 0 & 0 \end{bmatrix}, \quad K = \begin{bmatrix} -3\omega^2 & 0 & 0 \\ 0 & 0 & 0 \\ 0 & 0 & \omega^2 \end{bmatrix}$$

and

$$B = \begin{bmatrix} 1 & 0 \\ 0 & 0 \\ 0 & 1 \end{bmatrix}, \quad x = \begin{bmatrix} x_r \\ y_r \\ z_r \end{bmatrix}.$$

Thus the two polynomial matrices associated with this system are

$$\begin{cases} A(s) = \begin{bmatrix} s^2 - 3\omega^2 & -2\omega s & 0 \\ 2\omega s & s^2 & 0 \\ 0 & 0 & s^2 + \omega^2 \end{bmatrix} \\ B(s) = \begin{bmatrix} 1 & 0 \\ 0 & 0 \\ 0 & 1 \end{bmatrix} \end{cases}$$

hence,

$$\begin{bmatrix} A(s) & -B(s) \end{bmatrix} = \begin{bmatrix} s^2 - 3\omega^2 & -2\omega s & 0 & -1 & 0 \\ 2\omega s & s^2 & 0 & 0 & 0 \\ 0 & 0 & s^2 + \omega^2 & 0 & -1 \end{bmatrix}.$$

Applying a series of column elementary transformations to

$$
\begin{bmatrix}
s^2 - 3\omega^2 & -2\omega s & 0 & -1 & 0 \\
2\omega s & s^2 & 0 & 0 & 0 \\
0 & 0 & s^2 + \omega^2 & 0 & -1 \\
1 & 0 & 0 & 0 & 0 \\
0 & 1 & 0 & 0 & 0 \\
0 & 0 & 1 & 0 & 0 \\
0 & 0 & 0 & 1 & 0 \\
0 & 0 & 0 & 0 & 1
\end{bmatrix}
$$

reduces it into

$$
\begin{bmatrix}
1 & 0 & 0 & 0 & 0 \\
0 & s & 0 & 0 & 0 \\
0 & 0 & 1 & 0 & 0 \\
0 & \frac{1}{2\omega} & 0 & -s & 0 \\
0 & 0 & 0 & 2\omega & 0 \\
0 & 0 & 0 & 0 & 1 \\
-1 & \frac{1}{2\omega}\left(s^2 - 3\omega^2\right) & 0 & -4\omega^2 s - \left(s^2 - 3\omega^2\right)s & 0 \\
0 & 0 & -1 & 0 & s^2 + \omega^2
\end{bmatrix}.
$$

Thus, $P(s) = I_3$,

$$
Q(s) =
\begin{bmatrix}
0 & \frac{1}{2\omega} & 0 & -s & 0 \\
0 & 0 & 0 & 2\omega & 0 \\
0 & 0 & 0 & 0 & 1 \\
-1 & \frac{1}{2\omega}\left(s^2 - 3\omega^2\right) & 0 & -4\omega^2 s - \left(s^2 - 3\omega^2\right)s & 0 \\
0 & 0 & -1 & 0 & s^2 + \omega^2
\end{bmatrix},
$$

and

$$
\Sigma(s) =
\begin{bmatrix}
1 & 0 & 0 \\
0 & s & 0 \\
0 & 0 & 1
\end{bmatrix}.
$$

Therefore,

$$
\begin{cases}
N(s) =
\begin{bmatrix}
-s & 0 \\
2\omega & 0 \\
0 & 1
\end{bmatrix} \\
D(s) =
\begin{bmatrix}
-4\omega^2 s - \left(s^2 - 3\omega^2\right)s & 0 \\
0 & s^2 + \omega^2
\end{bmatrix},
\end{cases}
$$

$$\begin{cases} \tilde{U}(s) = \frac{1}{2\omega} \begin{bmatrix} 0 & 1 & 0 \\ 0 & 0 & 0 \\ 0 & 0 & 0 \end{bmatrix} \\ \tilde{T}(s) = \frac{1}{2\omega} \begin{bmatrix} -2\omega & s^2 - 3\omega^2 & 0 \\ 0 & 0 & -2\omega \end{bmatrix}. \end{cases}$$

Noting that

$$\mathrm{adj}\,\Sigma\,(s) = \begin{bmatrix} s & 0 & 0 \\ 0 & 1 & 0 \\ 0 & 0 & s \end{bmatrix}, \quad \det\Sigma\,(s) = s,$$

we can obtain

$$\begin{cases} U(s) = \tilde{U}(s)\mathrm{adj}\,\Sigma\,(s) = \frac{1}{2\omega} \begin{bmatrix} 0 & 1 & 0 \\ 0 & 0 & 0 \\ 0 & 0 & 0 \end{bmatrix} \\ T(s) = \tilde{T}(s)\mathrm{adj}\,\Sigma\,(s) = \frac{1}{2\omega} \begin{bmatrix} -2\omega s & s^2 - 3\omega^2 & 0 \\ 0 & 0 & -2\omega s \end{bmatrix}, \end{cases}$$

and the system is F-left coprime for arbitrary F, which does not possess zero eigenvalues.

3.4.2 Controllability

In this subsection, let us consider further a very important special case, where the pair of polynomial matrix pair $(A(s), B(s))$ is controllable, or equivalently, left coprime. It should be noted that the pair of polynomial matrices $A(s)$ and $B(s)$ is left coprime means $A(s)$ and $B(s)$ are F-left coprime (with rank n) for arbitrary $F \in \mathbb{C}^{p \times p}$. In such a case we have

$$\mathrm{rank}\begin{bmatrix} A(s) & -B(s) \end{bmatrix} = n, \quad \forall s \in \mathbb{C}. \tag{3.75}$$

In this subsection, we give criteria for this condition.

3.4.2.1 Equivalent Conditions

The following theorem is a direct corollary of Theorem 3.10.

Theorem 3.11 *Let $A(s) \in \mathbb{R}^{n \times q}[s]$, $B(s) \in \mathbb{R}^{n \times r}[s]$, $q + r > n$. Then $(A(s), B(s))$ is controllable if and only if one of the following three conditions holds:*

1. *There exists a unimodular matrix $Q(s)$ with an appropriate dimension satisfying*

$$\begin{bmatrix} A(s) & -B(s) \end{bmatrix} Q(s) = \begin{bmatrix} I_n & 0 \end{bmatrix};$$
(3.76)

2. *There exist a pair of right coprime polynomial matrices $N(s) \in \mathbb{R}^{q \times \beta_0}[s]$ and $D(s) \in \mathbb{R}^{r \times \beta_0}[s]$, with $\beta_0 = q + r - n$, satisfying the generalized RCF*

$$A(s)N(s) - B(s)D(s) = 0;$$
(3.77)

3. *There exist a pair of polynomial matrices $U(s) \in \mathbb{R}^{q \times n}[s]$ and $T(s) \in \mathbb{R}^{r \times n}[s]$ satisfying the DPE*

$$A(s)U(s) - B(s)T(s) = I_n.$$
(3.78)

Proof. *Proof of conclusion 1.* It follows from the first conclusion of Theorem 3.10 that $(A(s), B(s))$ is controllable if and only if there exist a pair of unimodular matrices $P_1(s)$ and $Q_1(s)$ with appropriate dimensions satisfying

$$P_1(s) \begin{bmatrix} A(s) & -B(s) \end{bmatrix} Q_1(s) = \begin{bmatrix} I_n & 0 \end{bmatrix}.$$
(3.79)

Pre-multiplying both sides of the above equation by $P_1^{-1}(s)$ gives

$$\begin{bmatrix} A(s) & -B(s) \end{bmatrix} Q_1(s) = \begin{bmatrix} P_1^{-1}(s) & 0 \end{bmatrix}.$$
(3.80)

Post-multiplying both sides of the above equation by

$$Q_2(s) = \text{blockdiag}\left(P_1(s), I_{q+r-n} \right)$$

yields

$$\begin{bmatrix} A(s) & -B(s) \end{bmatrix} Q_1(s)Q_2(s) = \begin{bmatrix} I_n & 0 \end{bmatrix}.$$
(3.81)

Taking

$$Q(s) = Q_1(s)Q_2(s)$$

in the above equation leads to (3.76).

Proof of conclusion 2. Due to the second conclusion of Theorem 3.10 and (3.76), this conclusion obviously holds.

Proof of conclusion 3. It follows from the first conclusion that $(A(s), B(s))$ is controllable if and only if there exists a unimodular matrix $Q(s)$ with an appropriate dimension satisfying (3.76). Partitioning $Q(s)$ as

$$Q(s) = \begin{bmatrix} U(s) & * \\ T(s) & * \end{bmatrix}, \quad U(s) \in \mathbb{R}^{q \times n}[s], \quad T(s) \in \mathbb{R}^{r \times n}[s], \qquad (3.82)$$

we have from (3.76)

$$\begin{bmatrix} A(s) & -B(s) \end{bmatrix} \begin{bmatrix} U(s) \\ T(s) \end{bmatrix} = I_n. \qquad (3.83)$$

This is clearly equivalent to (3.78). ■

The special DPE (3.78) is also called the generalized Bezout identity, while is called the Bezout identity when

$$A(s) = sI - A, \quad B(s) = B.$$

In Kong et al. (2009), we have given a Stein equation approach for solutions to the Bezout identity and the generalized Bezout identity.

3.4.2.2 Unified Procedure

Parallel to the result in Section 3.3.4, we here give a unified procedure, which finds simultaneously the right coprime polynomial matrices $N(s)$ and $D(s)$ satisfying the generalized RCF (3.77), and the right coprime polynomial matrices $U(s)$ and $T(s)$ satisfying the DPE (3.78).

Lemma 3.6 *Let $A(s) \in \mathbb{R}^{n \times q}[s]$, $B(s) \in \mathbb{R}^{n \times r}[s]$, with $q + r > n$, be left coprime and admit the SFR (3.76). Partition the unimodular matrix $Q(s)$ as follows:*

$$Q(s) = \begin{bmatrix} U(s) & N(s) \\ T(s) & D(s) \end{bmatrix},$$

where $N(s) \in \mathbb{R}^{q \times \beta_0}[s]$, $D(s) \in \mathbb{R}^{r \times \beta_0}[s]$, and $U(s) \in \mathbb{R}^{q \times n}[s]$, $T(s) \in \mathbb{R}^{r \times n}[s]$. Then,

1. *The polynomial matrices $N(s)$ and $D(s)$ are right coprime and satisfy the generalized RCF (3.77); and*
2. *The polynomial matrices $U(s)$ and $T(s)$ satisfy the DPE (3.78).*

Parallel to Propositions 3.4 and 3.5, we have the following result about solution to the unimodular matrix $Q(s)$ satisfying (3.76).

Proposition 3.6 *Let $A(s) \in \mathbb{R}^{n \times q}[s]$, $B(s) \in \mathbb{R}^{n \times r}[s]$ be two given polynomial matrices which are left coprime. When the following block matrix*

$$\left[\begin{array}{c|cc} I_n & A(s) & -B(s) \\ \hline 0 & & I_{q+r} \end{array} \right]$$

is reduced into the form of

$$\left[\begin{array}{c|cc} P_1(s) & I_n & 0 \\ \hline 0 & & Q_1(s) \end{array} \right],$$

with a series of elementary row transformations, within only the first n rows, and a series of column elementary transformations, within only the last $q + r$ columns, then

$$Q(s) = Q_1(s) \text{blockdiag} \left(P_1^{-1}(s), I \right)$$

satisfies the SFR (3.76).

Example 3.2

Consider the circuit system treated in Example 1.1, which has a state-space model of the form

$$E\dot{x} - Ax = B_1\dot{u} + B_0 u, \tag{3.84}$$

with

$$E = \begin{bmatrix} 0.5 & 0 \\ 0 & 0.5 \end{bmatrix}, \quad A = \begin{bmatrix} -1 & 0 \\ 0 & -1 \end{bmatrix},$$

$$B_1 = \begin{bmatrix} 2 & -1 \\ -1 & 2 \end{bmatrix}, \quad B_0 = \begin{bmatrix} 2 & -2 \\ -2 & 2 \end{bmatrix}.$$

Thus,

$$A(s) = \begin{bmatrix} 0.5s + 1 & 0 \\ 0 & 0.5s + 1 \end{bmatrix},$$

and

$$B(s) = \begin{bmatrix} 2s+2 & -s-2 \\ -s-2 & 2s+2 \end{bmatrix}.$$

Thus,

$$[A(s) \quad -B(s)] = \begin{bmatrix} 0.5s+1 & 0 & -2s-2 & s+2 \\ 0 & 0.5s+1 & s+2 & -2s-2 \end{bmatrix}.$$

Applying a series of elementary row transformations, within only the first two rows, and a series of column elementary transformations, within only the last four columns, to

$$\left[\begin{array}{c|c} I_2 & A(s) \quad -B(s) \\ \hline 0 & I_4 \end{array} \right]$$

reduces it into the form of

$$\left[\begin{array}{c|cc} P(s) & I_2 & 0 \\ \hline 0 & Q(s) & \end{array} \right],$$

with $P(s) = I$ and

$$Q(s) = \begin{bmatrix} -4s-4 & 2s+4 & 2 & -1 \\ 2s+4 & -4s-4 & -1 & 2 \\ -s-2 & 0 & \frac{1}{2} & 0 \\ 0 & -s-2 & 0 & \frac{1}{2} \end{bmatrix}.$$

Therefore,

$$N(s) = \begin{bmatrix} 2 & -1 \\ -1 & 2 \end{bmatrix}, \quad D(s) = \frac{1}{2}\begin{bmatrix} 1 & 0 \\ 0 & 1 \end{bmatrix}$$

and

$$U(s) = 2\begin{bmatrix} -2(s+1) & s+2 \\ s+2 & -2(s+1) \end{bmatrix},$$

$$T(s) = (s+2)\begin{bmatrix} -1 & 0 \\ 0 & -1 \end{bmatrix}.$$

3.5 Examples

In order to illustrate the procedures introduced in this chapter for finding the solutions to the generalized RCF (3.45) and the DPE (3.54), here we work out some of the practical examples given in Section 1.2.

3.5.1 First-Order Systems

Example 3.3 (Multiagent Kinematics System)

Consider the multi-agent kinematics system introduced in Example 1.2, which is a first-order system with the following coefficient matrices:

$$E = \begin{bmatrix} 8 & 0 & 0 & 0 & 0 \\ 0 & 1 & 0 & 0 & 0 \\ 0 & 0 & 10 & 0 & 0 \\ 0 & 0 & 0 & 1 & 0 \\ 0 & 0 & 0 & 0 & 12 \end{bmatrix},$$

$$A = \begin{bmatrix} -0.1 & 0 & 0 & 0 & 0 \\ 1 & 0 & -1 & 0 & 0 \\ 0 & 0 & -0.1 & 0 & 0 \\ 0 & 0 & 1 & 0 & -1 \\ 0 & 0 & 0 & 0 & -0.1 \end{bmatrix}, \quad B = \begin{bmatrix} 1 & 0 & 0 \\ 0 & 0 & 0 \\ 0 & 1 & 0 \\ 0 & 0 & 0 \\ 0 & 0 & 1 \end{bmatrix}.$$

So we have

$$\begin{bmatrix} sE - A & -B \end{bmatrix} = \begin{bmatrix} 8s+0.1 & 0 & 0 & 0 & 0 & -1 & 0 & 0 \\ -1 & s & 1 & 0 & 0 & 0 & 0 & 0 \\ 0 & 0 & 10s+0.1 & 0 & 0 & 0 & -1 & 0 \\ 0 & 0 & -1 & s & 1 & 0 & 0 & 0 \\ 0 & 0 & 0 & 0 & 12s+0.1 & 0 & 0 & -1 \end{bmatrix}.$$

By applying elementary row transformations, within the first five rows only, and elementary column transformations, within the last eight columns only, to

$$\begin{bmatrix} I_5 & sE - A & -B \\ \hline 0 & I_8 \end{bmatrix},$$

this matrix can be reduced into the form of

$$\begin{bmatrix} P(s) & I_5 & 0 \\ \hline 0 & Q(s) \end{bmatrix},$$

with

$$P(s) = \begin{bmatrix} 0 & 1 & 0 & 0 & 0 \\ 0 & 0 & 0 & 1 & 0 \\ -1 & 0 & 0 & 0 & 0 \\ 0 & 0 & -1 & 0 & 0 \\ 0 & 0 & 0 & 0 & -1 \end{bmatrix}$$

and

$$Q(s) = [Q_1(s) \quad Q_2(s)],$$

where

$$Q_1(s) = \begin{bmatrix} 0 & 0 & 0 & 0 & 0 \\ 0 & 0 & 0 & 0 & 0 \\ 1 & 0 & 0 & 0 & 0 \\ 0 & 0 & 0 & 0 & 0 \\ 1 & 1 & 0 & 0 & 0 \\ 0 & 0 & 1 & 0 & 0 \\ 10s + 0.1 & 0 & 0 & 1 & 0 \\ 12s + 0.1 & 12s + 0.1 & 0 & 0 & 1 \end{bmatrix},$$

$$Q_2(s) = \begin{bmatrix} 1 & 0 & 0 \\ 0 & 1 & 0 \\ 1 & -s & 0 \\ 0 & 0 & 1 \\ 1 & -s & -s \\ 8s + 0.1 & 0 & 0 \\ 10s + 0.1 & -s(10s + 0.1) & 0 \\ 12s + 0.1 & -s(12s + 0.1) & -s(12s + 0.1) \end{bmatrix}.$$

Therefore, a pair of right coprime polynomial matrices $N(s)$ and $D(s)$ satisfying the generalized RCF (3.77) can be given as

$$N(s) = \begin{bmatrix} 1 & 0 & 0 \\ 0 & 1 & 0 \\ 1 & -s & 0 \\ 0 & 0 & 1 \\ 1 & -s & -s \end{bmatrix}$$

and

$$D(s) = \begin{bmatrix} 8s + 0.1 & 0 & 0 \\ 10s + 0.1 & -s(10s + 0.1) & 0 \\ 12s + 0.1 & -s(12s + 0.1) & -s(12s + 0.1) \end{bmatrix}$$

and a pair of polynomial matrices $U(s)$ and $T(s)$ satisfying the DPE (3.54), with

$$C(s) = P^{-1}(s) = \begin{bmatrix} 0 & 0 & -1 & 0 & 0 \\ 1 & 0 & 0 & 0 & 0 \\ 0 & 0 & 0 & -1 & 0 \\ 0 & 1 & 0 & 0 & 0 \\ 0 & 0 & 0 & 0 & -1 \end{bmatrix},$$

can be given as

$$
U(s) = \begin{bmatrix} 0 & 0 & 0 & 0 & 0 \\ 0 & 0 & 0 & 0 & 0 \\ 1 & 0 & 0 & 0 & 0 \\ 0 & 0 & 0 & 0 & 0 \\ 1 & 1 & 0 & 0 & 0 \end{bmatrix}
$$

and

$$
T(s) = \begin{bmatrix} 0 & 0 & 1 & 0 & 0 \\ 10s + 0.1 & 0 & 0 & 1 & 0 \\ 12s + 0.1 & 12s + 0.1 & 0 & 0 & 1 \end{bmatrix}.
$$

Meanwhile, a pair of polynomial matrices $U(s)$ and $T(s)$ satisfying the DPE (3.78) can be given as

$$
U(s) = \begin{bmatrix} 0 & 0 & 0 & 0 & 0 \\ 0 & 0 & 0 & 0 & 0 \\ 0 & 1 & 0 & 0 & 0 \\ 0 & 0 & 0 & 0 & 0 \\ 0 & 1 & 0 & 1 & 0 \end{bmatrix}
$$

and

$$
T(s) = \begin{bmatrix} -1 & 0 & 0 & 0 & 0 \\ 0 & 10s + 0.1 & -1 & 0 & 0 \\ 0 & 12s + 0.1 & 0 & 12s + 0.1 & -1 \end{bmatrix}.
$$

Example 3.4 (Constrained Mechanical System in First-Order Form)

Consider the constrained system in first-order form given in Example 1.3, which has the following coefficient matrices:

$$
E = \begin{bmatrix} 1 & 0 & 0 & 0 & 0 \\ 0 & 1 & 0 & 0 & 0 \\ 0 & 0 & 1 & 0 & 0 \\ 0 & 0 & 0 & 1 & 0 \\ 0 & 0 & 0 & 0 & 0 \end{bmatrix},
$$

$$
A = \begin{bmatrix} 0 & 0 & 1 & 0 & 0 \\ 0 & 0 & 0 & 1 & 0 \\ -2 & 0 & -1 & -1 & 1 \\ 0 & -1 & -1 & -1 & 1 \\ 1 & 1 & 0 & 0 & 0 \end{bmatrix}, \quad B = \begin{bmatrix} 0 \\ 0 \\ 1 \\ -1 \\ 0 \end{bmatrix}.
$$

Thus, we have

$$[sE - A \quad -B] = \begin{bmatrix} s & 0 & -1 & 0 & 0 & 0 \\ 0 & s & 0 & -1 & 0 & 0 \\ 2 & 0 & s+1 & 1 & -1 & -1 \\ 0 & 1 & 1 & s+1 & -1 & 1 \\ -1 & -1 & 0 & 0 & 0 & 0 \end{bmatrix}.$$

By applying elementary column transformations, within only the last six columns, and elementary row transformations, within the first five rows only, to

$$\left[\begin{array}{c|c} I_5 & sE - A \quad -B \\ \hline 0 & I_6 \end{array} \right],$$

this matrix can be reduced into the form of

$$\left[\begin{array}{c|cc} P(s) & I_5 & 0 \\ \hline 0 & Q(s) \end{array} \right],$$

with $P(s) = I_5$ and

$$Q(s) = \begin{bmatrix} 0 & 0 & 0 & 0 & 0 & 1 \\ 0 & 0 & 0 & 0 & -1 & -1 \\ -1 & 0 & 0 & 0 & 0 & s \\ 0 & -1 & 0 & 0 & -s & -s \\ -\frac{1}{2}s - 1 & -\frac{1}{2}s - 1 & -\frac{1}{2} & -\frac{1}{2} & -\frac{1}{2}(s+1)^2 & \frac{1}{2} \\ -\frac{1}{2}s & \frac{1}{2}s & -\frac{1}{2} & \frac{1}{2} & \frac{1}{2}s^2 + \frac{1}{2} & s^2 + \frac{3}{2} \end{bmatrix}.$$

Partitioning $Q(s)$ as

$$Q(s) = \begin{bmatrix} N(s) & U(s) \\ D(s) & T(s) \end{bmatrix},$$

we obtain

$$N(s) = \begin{bmatrix} 1 \\ -1 \\ s \\ -s \\ \frac{1}{2} \end{bmatrix}, \quad D(s) = s^2 + \frac{3}{2},$$

and

$$U(s) = \frac{1}{2} \begin{bmatrix} 0 & 0 & 0 & 0 & 0 \\ 0 & 0 & 0 & 0 & -2 \\ -2 & 0 & 0 & 0 & 0 \\ 0 & -2 & 0 & 0 & -2s \\ -s-2 & -s-2 & -1 & -1 & -(s+1)^2 \end{bmatrix},$$

$$T(s) = \frac{1}{2} \begin{bmatrix} -s & s & -1 & 1 & s^2+1 \end{bmatrix}.$$

3.5.2 Second-Order Systems

Example 3.5 (Constrained Mechanical System in Second-Order Form)

Consider the constrained mechanical system treated in Example 1.3, which is in a matrix second-order form with the following coefficient matrices:

$$A_2 = \begin{bmatrix} 1 & 0 & 0 \\ 0 & 1 & 0 \\ 0 & 0 & 0 \end{bmatrix}, A_1 = \begin{bmatrix} 1 & 1 & 0 \\ 1 & 1 & 0 \\ 0 & 0 & 0 \end{bmatrix},$$

$$A_0 = \begin{bmatrix} 2 & 0 & -1 \\ 0 & 1 & -1 \\ 1 & 1 & 0 \end{bmatrix}, B = \begin{bmatrix} 1 \\ -1 \\ 0 \end{bmatrix}.$$

Thus, we have

$$\begin{aligned} & \begin{bmatrix} A_2 s^2 + A_1 s + A_0 & -B \end{bmatrix} \\ & = \begin{bmatrix} s^2+s+2 & s & -1 & -1 \\ s & s^2+s+1 & -1 & 1 \\ 1 & 1 & 0 & 0 \end{bmatrix}. \end{aligned}$$

Applying a series of column elementary transformations, within only the last four columns, and a series of row elementary transformations within the first three rows only, to the augmented matrix

$$\left[\begin{array}{c|cc} I_3 & A_2 s^2 + A_1 s + A_0 & -B \\ \hline 0 & & I_4 \end{array} \right],$$

this matrix can be reduced into the form of

$$\left[\begin{array}{c|cc} P(s) & I_3 & 0 \\ \hline 0 & & Q(s) \end{array} \right],$$

with

$$P(s) = \begin{bmatrix} 1 & 1 & 0 \\ 0 & 1 & 0 \\ 0 & 0 & 1 \end{bmatrix},$$

$$Q(s) = \begin{bmatrix} 0 & 0 & 0 & 1 \\ 0 & 0 & 1 & -1 \\ -\frac{1}{2} & 0 & \frac{1}{2}(s+1)^2 & \frac{1}{2} \\ -\frac{1}{2} & 1 & -\frac{1}{2}s^2 - \frac{1}{2} & s^2 + \frac{3}{2} \end{bmatrix},$$

which gives

$$N(s) = \frac{1}{2}\begin{bmatrix} 2 \\ -2 \\ 1 \end{bmatrix}, \quad D(s) = s^2 + \frac{3}{2},$$

and

$$U(s) = \frac{1}{2}\begin{bmatrix} 0 & 0 & 0 \\ 0 & 0 & 2 \\ -1 & -1 & (s+1)^2 \end{bmatrix},$$

$$T(s) = \frac{1}{2}\begin{bmatrix} -1 & 1 & -s^2 - 1 \end{bmatrix}.$$

Example 3.6 (Flexible-Joint Mechanism—Case of Second-Order Model)

The flexible-joint mechanism treated in Example 1.4 is modeled by a system in a matrix second-order form with the following parameters:

$$M = 0.0004 \times \begin{bmatrix} 1 & 0 \\ 0 & 1 \end{bmatrix}, \quad D = \begin{bmatrix} 0 & 0 \\ 0 & 0.015 \end{bmatrix},$$

$$K = 0.8 \times \begin{bmatrix} 1 & -1 \\ -1 & 1 \end{bmatrix}, \quad B = \begin{bmatrix} 0 \\ 1 \end{bmatrix}.$$

Thus,

$$\begin{bmatrix} Ms^2 + Ds + K & -B \end{bmatrix}$$
$$= \begin{bmatrix} 0.0004s^2 + 0.8 & -0.8 & 0 \\ -0.8 & 0.0004s^2 + 0.015s + 0.8 & -1 \end{bmatrix}.$$

By applying a series of elementary column transformations to this matrix, a unimodular matrix $Q(s)$ is found to satisfy

$$\begin{bmatrix} Ms^2 + Ds + K & -B \end{bmatrix} Q(s) = \begin{bmatrix} I_2 & 0 \end{bmatrix},$$

where

$$Q(s) = \begin{bmatrix} Q_1(s) & Q_2(s) \end{bmatrix},$$

with

$$Q_1(s) = \begin{bmatrix} 0 & 0 \\ -\frac{5}{4} & 0 \\ -0.0005s^2 - 0.01875s - 1.0 & -1 \end{bmatrix}$$

$$Q_2(s) = \begin{bmatrix} 2000 \\ s^2 + 2000 \\ 0.0004s^4 + 0.015s^3 + 1.6s^2 + 30s \end{bmatrix}.$$

Therefore, by adjusting a proper cofactor, we obtain

$$N(s) = \begin{bmatrix} 2000 \\ s^2 + 2000 \end{bmatrix},$$

$$D(s) = s\left(4 \times 10^{-4}s^3 + 0.015s^2 + 1.6s + 30\right),$$

and

$$U(s) = \begin{bmatrix} 0 & 0 \\ -\frac{5}{4} & 0 \end{bmatrix},$$

$$T(s) = \begin{bmatrix} -0.000\,5s^2 - 0.01875s - 1.0 & -1 \end{bmatrix}.$$

3.5.3 Higher-Order Systems

Example 3.7 (Flexible-Joint Mechanism—Case of Third-Order Model)

The flexible-joint mechanism treated in Example 1.5 is modeled by a system in matrix third-order form with the following parameters:

$$A_3 = \begin{bmatrix} 0 & 0 \\ 0 & 0.0004 \end{bmatrix}, \quad A_2 = 10^{-3} \times \begin{bmatrix} 0.4 & 0 \\ 0 & 15.38 \end{bmatrix},$$

and

$$A_1 = \begin{bmatrix} 0 & 0 \\ -0.8 & 0.814\,25 \end{bmatrix}, \quad A_0 = \begin{bmatrix} 0.8 & -0.8 \\ -0.76 & 0.76 \end{bmatrix}, \quad B = \begin{bmatrix} 0 \\ 1 \end{bmatrix}.$$

Thus,

$$A(s) = A_3 s^3 + A_2 s^2 + A_1 s + A_0$$

$$= \begin{bmatrix} 0.0004s^2 + 0.8 & -0.8 \\ -0.8s - 0.76 & 0.000\,4s^3 + 0.01538s^2 + 0.81425s + 0.76 \end{bmatrix}$$

and

$$[A(s) \quad -B]$$

$$= \begin{bmatrix} 0.0004s^2 + 0.8 & -0.8 & 0 \\ -0.8s - 0.76 & 0.000\,4s^3 + 0.01538s^2 + 0.81425s + 0.76 & -1 \end{bmatrix}.$$

By applying a series of elementary row transformations, within only the first two rows, and a series of elementary column transformations, within only the last three columns, to

$$\left[\begin{array}{c|cc} I_2 & A_3s^3 + A_2s^2 + A_1s + A_0 & -B \\ \hline 0 & & I_3 \end{array}\right],$$

this matrix can be reduced into the form of

$$\left[\begin{array}{c|cc} P(s) & I_2 & 0 \\ \hline 0 & & Q(s) \end{array}\right],$$

with

$$P = \begin{bmatrix} -\frac{10}{8} & 0 \\ 0 & -1 \end{bmatrix}$$

and

$$Q(s) = [Q_1(s) \quad Q_2(s)],$$

where

$$Q_1(s) = \begin{bmatrix} 0 & 0 \\ 1 & 0 \\ 0.0004s^3 + 0.01538s^2 + 0.81425s + 0.76 & 1 \end{bmatrix},$$

$$Q_2(s) = \begin{bmatrix} 2000 \\ s^2 + 2000 \\ s\left(0.0004s^4 + 0.01538s^3 + 1.6143s^2 + 31.52s + 28.5\right) \end{bmatrix}.$$

Therefore,

$$N(s) = \begin{bmatrix} 2000 \\ s^2 + 2000 \end{bmatrix},$$

$$D(s) = s\left(0.0004s^4 + 0.01538s^3 + 1.6143s^2 + 31.52s + 28.5\right),$$

and

$$U(s) = \frac{1}{8}\begin{bmatrix} 0 & 0 \\ -10 & 0 \end{bmatrix},$$

$$T(s) = \frac{1}{8}\left[-0.004s^3 - 0.1538s^2 - 8.1425s - 7.6 \quad -8\right].$$

3.6 Numerical Solution Based on SVD

Let

$$\begin{cases} A(s) = A_0 + A_1 s + \cdots + A_m s^m \\ B(s) = B_0 + B_1 s + \cdots + B_m s^m, \end{cases}$$

where $A_i \in \mathbb{R}^{n \times q}$, $B_i \in \mathbb{R}^{n \times r}$, $i = 0, 1, \ldots, m$, are the coefficient matrices. In this section, we once again treat the case that the matrix pair $(A(s), B(s))$ is controllable, that is,

$$\text{rank}\, [A(s)\ B(s)] = n, \quad \forall s \in \mathbb{C}. \tag{3.85}$$

3.6.1 Problem Description

We have known from Section 3.4.2 that a pair of polynomial matrices $(A(s), B(s))$ is controllable if and only if one of the following three conditions is met:

1. There exist a pair of unimodular matrices $P(s)$ and $Q(s)$ of appropriate dimensions satisfying

$$P(s) \left[A(s)\quad -B(s) \right] Q(s) = \left[I_n\ \ 0 \right]; \tag{3.86}$$

2. There exist a pair of right coprime polynomial matrices $N(s) \in \mathbb{R}^{q \times \beta}[s]$ and $D(s) \in \mathbb{R}^{r \times \beta}[s]$, with $\beta = q + r - n$, satisfying the generalized RCF (3.77), that is,

$$A(s)N(s) - B(s)D(s) = 0; \tag{3.87}$$

3. There exist a pair of right coprime polynomial matrices $U(s) \in \mathbb{R}^{q \times n}[s]$ and $T(s) \in \mathbb{R}^{r \times n}[s]$ satisfying the DPE (3.78), that is,

$$A(s)U(s) - B(s)T(s) = I_n. \tag{3.88}$$

Also, we learnt from Section 3.4.2 that once a pair of unimodular matrices $P(s)$ and $Q(s)$ of appropriate dimensions satisfying (3.76) are found, a pair of right coprime polynomial matrices $N(s) \in \mathbb{R}^{q \times \beta}[s]$ and $D(s) \in \mathbb{R}^{r \times \beta}[s]$, with $\beta = q + r - n$, satisfying the generalized RCF (3.77), and a pair of polynomial matrices $U(s) \in \mathbb{R}^{q \times n}[s]$ and $T(s) \in \mathbb{R}^{r \times n}[s]$ satisfying the DPE (3.78), can be immediately given by the columns of $Q(s)$. Therefore, the key problem involved is to find a pair of unimodular matrices $P(s)$ and $Q(s)$ of appropriate dimensions satisfying (3.76).

Although we have given an approach for solving a general SFR in the previous two sections, the approach is applicable to only lower order and lower dimension cases.

While the purpose of this section is to give a numerical algorithm for solving a pair of unimodular matrices $P(s)$ and $Q(s)$ of appropriate dimensions satisfying (3.76).

Problem 3.1   Let $A(s) \in \mathbb{R}^{n \times q}[s]$, $B(s) \in \mathbb{R}^{n \times r}[s]$, and $(A(s), B(s))$ be controllable. Further, choose a group of distinct complex numbers s_i, $i = 0, 1, \ldots, N$, with N being a sufficiently large integer. Find a pair of unimodular matrices $P(s)$ and $Q(s)$ of appropriate dimensions satisfying (3.86) based on the data

$$[A(s_i) \quad B(s_i)], \quad i = 0, 1, \ldots, N. \tag{3.89}$$

3.6.2 Main Steps

3.6.2.1 Data Generation via SVD

As the first step toward the solution to the above Problem 3.1, we need to obtain the data

$$P(s_i), \quad Q(s_i), \quad i = 0, 1, \ldots, N, \tag{3.90}$$

which are determined by

$$P(s_i) [A(s_i) \quad -B(s_i)] Q(s_i) = [I_n \quad 0], \tag{3.91}$$
$$i = 0, 1, \ldots, N.$$

To do this, we apply SVD to the matrices in (3.89) and obtain

$$U_i [A(s_i) \quad -B(s_i)] V_i = [\Sigma_i \quad 0], \tag{3.92}$$
$$i = 0, 1, \ldots, N,$$

where $U_i, V_i, \; i = 0, 1, \ldots, N$, are orthogonal matrices of appropriate dimensions, and

$$\Sigma_i = \mathrm{diag}(\sigma_{i1}, \sigma_{i2}, \ldots, \sigma_{in}),$$

with

$$\sigma_{ij} \in \mathrm{svd}([A(s_i) \quad -B(s_i)]), \quad i = 0, 1, \ldots, N, \quad j = 1, 2, \ldots, n,$$

and satisfying

$$\sigma_{i1} \geq \sigma_{i2} \geq \cdots \geq \sigma_{in} > 0. \tag{3.93}$$

It should be noted that all the singular values are greater than zero because of the controllability condition (3.85).

Rewrite (3.92) as

$$\Sigma_i^{-1} U_i \left[A(s_i) \quad -B(s_i) \right] V_i = \left[I_n \quad 0 \right], \tag{3.94}$$
$$i = 0, 1, \ldots, N,$$

then comparison of (3.91) with (3.92) gives the following conjecture:

$$\begin{cases} Q(s_i) = V_i \\ P(s_i) = \Sigma_i^{-1} U_i, \quad i = 0, 1, \ldots, N. \end{cases} \tag{3.95}$$

3.6.2.2 Polynomial Recovering

Having obtained the values of the polynomial matrices $P(s)$ and $Q(s)$ in (3.90), the next step we need to recover the two polynomial matrices from these data. The problem can be stated as follows:

Problem 3.2 *Let $s_i, i = 0, 1, \ldots, N$, be a group of arbitrarily chosen distinct self-conjugate complex numbers, with N being a sufficiently large integer. Let*

$$X(s) = X_0 + X_1 s + \cdots + X_n s^n \in \mathbb{R}^{q \times r}[s] \tag{3.96}$$

be a real-coefficient polynomial matrix, whose known function values at $s_i, i = 0, 1, \ldots, N$, are given by

$$Y_i = X(s_i), \quad i = 0, 1, \ldots, N. \tag{3.97}$$

Find both the order n and the coefficients $X_i, i = 0, 1, \ldots, n$, of the polynomial $X(s)$ based on the data in (3.97).

In finding a solution to the above problem, the most natural way is to apply the least square method. Write (3.97) as

$$Y_i = X(s_i)$$
$$= X_0 + X_1 s_i + \cdots + X_n s_i^n$$
$$= \begin{bmatrix} X_0 & X_1 & \cdots & X_n \end{bmatrix} \begin{bmatrix} I_r \\ s_i I_r \\ \vdots \\ s_i^n I_r \end{bmatrix},$$
$$i = 0, 1, \ldots, N,$$

or, more compactly, as

$$Y = \begin{bmatrix} X_0 & X_1 & \cdots & X_n \end{bmatrix} V(N),$$

where

$$Y = \begin{bmatrix} Y_0 & Y_1 & \cdots & Y_N \end{bmatrix}, \tag{3.98}$$

$$V(N) = \begin{bmatrix} I_r & I_r & \cdots & I_r \\ s_0 I_r & s_1 I_r & \cdots & s_N I_r \\ \vdots & \vdots & \cdots & \vdots \\ s_0^n I_r & s_1^n I_r & \cdots & s_N^n I_r \end{bmatrix}. \tag{3.99}$$

Then, the least square solution of the polynomial coefficient matrices is given by

$$\begin{bmatrix} X_0 & X_1 & \cdots & X_n \end{bmatrix} = Y V^{\mathrm{T}}(N) \begin{bmatrix} V(N) V^{\mathrm{T}}(N) \end{bmatrix}^{-1}. \tag{3.100}$$

Alternatively, we can also use the following result to find the solution.

Theorem 3.12 *Let $S_i \in \mathbb{C}^{r \times r}$, $i = 0, 1, \ldots, n$, be a group of arbitrarily chosen commutative matrices satisfying*

$$\mathrm{eig}(S_i) \cap \mathrm{eig}(S_j) = \emptyset, \quad i \neq j, \ i, j = 0, 1, 2, \ldots, N.$$

Then

1. *The following generalized Vandermonde matrix*

$$V_{an} = \begin{bmatrix} I & I & \cdots & I \\ S_0 & S_1 & \cdots & S_n \\ \vdots & \vdots & \cdots & \vdots \\ S_0^n & S_1^n & \cdots & S_n^n \end{bmatrix} \tag{3.101}$$

   is nonsingular;
2. *The coefficient matrices of a polynomial matrix $X(s) \in \mathbb{R}^{q \times r}[s]$ in the form of (3.96) are uniquely determined by the data*

$$Y_i = X(S_i), \quad i = 0, 1, \ldots, n, \tag{3.102}$$

   as

$$\begin{bmatrix} X_0 & X_1 & \cdots & X_n \end{bmatrix} = \begin{bmatrix} Y_0 & Y_1 & \cdots & Y_n \end{bmatrix} V_{an}^{-1}. \tag{3.103}$$

This theorem can be easily proven. The first conclusion is guaranteed by a result in Duan and Yuan (1991).

3.6.3 Numerical Solution

Based on the results in the above subsection, we can now present the following algorithm for solving Problem 3.1.

Algorithm 3.1 (Solution to Problem 3.1)

Step 1. Perform the series of SVDs in (3.92). If any Σ_i is singular, terminate the algorithm since the controllability condition is not satisfied.

Step 2. Obtain the data of the polynomial matrices $P(s_i)$ and/or $Q(s_i)$ in (3.90) according to data (3.95).

Step 3. Find the polynomial matrices $P(s)$ and/or $Q(s)$ using least square method (3.100) or the Vandermonde method (3.103) based on the data in (3.95).

Regarding the SVDs in (3.92), for any integer $0 \leq i \leq N$, we have the following observations:

- The relation (3.92) still holds when any two columns within the last r ones in V_i are exchanged.
- The relation (3.92) still holds when any corresponding two columns in U_i and V_i are exchanged, and at the same time, the corresponding positions of the singular values in Σ_i are swapped (it should be noted that the relation in (3.93) no longer holds).

Due to the above observations, without loss of generality, we can always require

$$\det U_i = \det V_i = 1, \quad i = 0, 1, \ldots, N. \tag{3.104}$$

The main result of this section is given as follows.

Theorem 3.13 *Let the conditions of Problem 3.1 be satisfied, and assume that the SVDs in (3.92) hold with both U_i and V_i being orthogonal matrices satisfying (3.104). Then Algorithm 3.1 provides a unique pair of polynomial matrices $P(s)$ and $Q(s)$, which are both unimodular and satisfy the relation (3.86).*

The proof of this theorem is provided in the appendix.

Remark 3.2 As we know that once the polynomial matrix $Q(s)$ is found, the pair of right coprime polynomial matrices $N(s) \in \mathbb{R}^{q \times \beta}[s]$ and $D(s) \in \mathbb{R}^{r \times \beta}[s]$, with $\beta = q + r - n$, satisfying the generalized RCF (3.77), is given directly by the last β columns of $Q(s)$. However, in order that the first n columns of $Q(s)$ give a pair of polynomial matrices $U(s) \in \mathbb{R}^{q \times n}[s]$ and $T(s) \in \mathbb{R}^{r \times n}[s]$ satisfying the DPE (3.78), one should make sure that $P(s) = I_n$. To realize this, we need to reform the values of $Q(s_i)$, $i = 0, 1, \dots, N$, as follows:

$$Q(s_i) = V_i \begin{bmatrix} \Sigma_i^{-1} U_i & 0 \\ 0 & I \end{bmatrix}, \quad i = 0, 1, \dots, N. \tag{3.105}$$

Remark 3.3 In applications often it is the pair of right coprime polynomial matrices $N(s) \in \mathbb{R}^{q \times \beta}[s]$ and $D(s) \in \mathbb{R}^{r \times \beta}[s]$, with $\beta = q + r - n$, satisfying the generalized RCF (3.77), or the pair of polynomial matrices $U(s) \in \mathbb{R}^{q \times n}[s]$ and $T(s) \in \mathbb{R}^{r \times n}[s]$ satisfying the DPE (3.78), that is used. Of course, we can first get the unimodular matrix $Q(s)$, and then obtain these polynomial matrices by partitioning the matrix $Q(s)$ as follows:

$$Q(s) = \begin{bmatrix} U(s) & N(s) \\ T(s) & D(s) \end{bmatrix}. \tag{3.106}$$

Alternatively, we may get the data

$$N(s_i), \ D(s_i), \quad i = 0, 1, \dots, N, \tag{3.107}$$

or

$$U(s_i), \ T(s_i), \quad i = 0, 1, \dots, N, \tag{3.108}$$

from $Q(s)$ by the relation (3.106), and then directly solve $N(s)$ and $D(s)$, or $U(s)$ and $T(s)$, instead of $P(s)$ and $Q(s)$, in the third step of Algorithm 3.1 based on data in (3.107) or (3.108).

Example 3.8

Consider again the flexible-joint system of third-order treated in Examples 1.5 and 3.7, in which we have

$$A_3 = \begin{bmatrix} 0 & 0 \\ 0 & 0.0004 \end{bmatrix}, \ A_2 = 10^{-3} \times \begin{bmatrix} 0.4 & 0 \\ 0 & 15.38 \end{bmatrix},$$

$$A_1 = \begin{bmatrix} 0 & 0 \\ -0.8 & 0.81425 \end{bmatrix}, \ A_0 = \begin{bmatrix} 0.8 & -0.8 \\ -0.76 & 0.76 \end{bmatrix}, \ B = \begin{bmatrix} 0 \\ 1 \end{bmatrix}.$$

In the following, we find the unimodular matrix $Q(s)$ following Algorithm 3.1.

Step 1. Choose $N = 100$, and

$$s_i = -0.8 - 0.15i, \quad i = 1, 2, \ldots, N.$$

Using MATLAB®, we obtain the following matrices satisfying (3.92):

$$U_i, V_i, \Sigma_i, \quad i = 0, 1, \ldots, N.$$

Step 2. In order to find a pair of $P(s)$ and $Q(s)$ with $P(s) = I$, we need to reset the values of $Q(s_i)$ as

$$Q(s_i) = V_i \begin{bmatrix} \Sigma_i^{-1} U_i & 0 \\ 0 & I \end{bmatrix}, \quad i = 0, 1, \ldots, N.$$

Step 3. Choosing the order of $Q(s)$ to be 5, and using the least square solution (3.100), the polynomial matrix $Q(s)$ is obtained as follows (rounded off to seven significant figures):

$$Q(s) = Q_0 + Q_1 s + Q_2 s^2 + Q_3 s^3 + Q_4 s^4 + Q_5 s^5,$$

where

$$Q_0 = \begin{bmatrix} 0.6255370 & -0.0002122 & 0.7071669 \\ -0.6246203 & -0.0002096 & 0.7071619 \\ -0.9538445 & -1.0001623 & -0.0001427 \end{bmatrix},$$

$$Q_1 = \begin{bmatrix} 0.0078865 & 0.0066119 & 0.0001481 \\ 0.0074906 & 0.0066189 & 0.0001362 \\ -1.0188594 & -0.0003963 & 0.0097318 \end{bmatrix},$$

$$Q_2 = 10^{-1} \times \begin{bmatrix} 0.1543176 & 0.0742285 & -0.0007428 \\ 0.1536496 & 0.0743012 & 0.0026900 \\ -0.1921711 & -0.0026437 & 0.1083799 \end{bmatrix},$$

$$Q_3 = 10^{-2} \times \begin{bmatrix} 0.8551964 & 0.0214671 & -0.0015885 \\ 0.8377301 & 0.0221941 & -0.0019809 \\ -0.4651373 & 0.0058661 & 0.0444892 \end{bmatrix},$$

$$Q_4 = 10^{-3} \times \begin{bmatrix} 0.4529907 & -0.0316473 & -0.0324625 \\ 0.4169516 & -0.0267640 & -0.0331099 \\ -0.9839919 & 0.0953915 & -0.0179649 \end{bmatrix},$$

$$Q_5 = 10^{-4} \times \begin{bmatrix} -0.0590530 & -0.0101880 & -0.0247530 \\ -0.0689572 & -0.0072061 & -0.0246009 \\ -0.4502768 & 0.0732408 & -0.0050057 \end{bmatrix}.$$

A pair of right coprime polynomial matrices $N(s)$ and $D(s)$ satisfying the following generalized RCF (3.87), and a pair of polynomial matrices $U(s)$ and $T(s)$ satisfying the DPE (3.88), can be obtained via partitioning the obtained polynomial matrix $Q(s)$ as

$$Q(s) = \begin{bmatrix} U(s) & N(s) \\ T(s) & D(s) \end{bmatrix},$$

which gives

$$\begin{cases} N(s) = N_0 + N_1 s + N_2 s^2 + N_3 s^3 + N_4 s^4 + N_5 s^5 \\ D(s) = D_0 + D_1 s + D_2 s^2 + D_3 s^3 + D_4 s^4 + D_5 s^5 \\ U(s) = U_0 + U_1 s + U_2 s^2 + U_3 s^3 + U_4 s^4 + U_5 s^5 \\ T(s) = T_0 + T_1 s + T_2 s^2 + T_3 s^3 + T_4 s^4 + T_5 s^5, \end{cases}$$

with

$$N_0 = \begin{bmatrix} 0.7071669 \\ 0.7071619 \end{bmatrix}, \qquad U_0 = \begin{bmatrix} 0.6255370 & -0.0002122 \\ -0.6246203 & -0.0002096 \end{bmatrix},$$

$$N_1 = 10^{-3} \times \begin{bmatrix} 0.1481246 \\ 0.1362151 \end{bmatrix}, \qquad U_1 = 10^{-2} \times \begin{bmatrix} 0.7886536 & 0.6611921 \\ 0.7490588 & 0.6618868 \end{bmatrix},$$

$$N_2 = 10^{-3} \times \begin{bmatrix} -0.0742837 \\ 0.2690009 \end{bmatrix}, \qquad U_2 = 10^{-1} \times \begin{bmatrix} 0.1543176 & 0.0742285 \\ 0.1536496 & 0.0743012 \end{bmatrix},$$

$$N_3 = 10^{-4} \times \begin{bmatrix} -0.1588480 \\ -0.1980903 \end{bmatrix}, \qquad U_3 = 10^{-2} \times \begin{bmatrix} 0.8551964 & 0.0214671 \\ 0.8377301 & 0.0221941 \end{bmatrix},$$

$$N_4 = 10^{-4} \times \begin{bmatrix} -0.3246255 \\ -0.3310990 \end{bmatrix}, \qquad U_4 = 10^{-3} \times \begin{bmatrix} 0.4529907 & -0.0316473 \\ 0.4169516 & -0.0267640 \end{bmatrix},$$

$$N_5 = 10^{-5} \times \begin{bmatrix} -0.2475304 \\ -0.2460089 \end{bmatrix}, \qquad U_5 = 10^{-5} \times \begin{bmatrix} -0.5905300 & -0.1018800 \\ -0.6895723 & -0.0720610 \end{bmatrix},$$

and

$$D_0 = -1.4268069 \times 10^{-4}, \quad T_0 = \begin{bmatrix} -0.9538445 & -1.0001623 \end{bmatrix},$$

$$D_1 = 0.0097318, \qquad\qquad T_1 = \begin{bmatrix} -1.0188594 & -0.0003963 \end{bmatrix},$$

$$D_2 = 0.0108380, \qquad\qquad T_2 = 10^{-1} \times \begin{bmatrix} -0.1921711 & -0.0026437 \end{bmatrix},$$

$$D_3 = 4.4489200 \times 10^{-4}, \quad T_3 = 10^{-2} \times \begin{bmatrix} -0.4651373 & 0.0058661 \end{bmatrix},$$

$$D_4 = -1.7964926 \times 10^{-5}, \quad T_4 = 10^{-3} \times \begin{bmatrix} -0.9839919 & 0.0953915 \end{bmatrix},$$

$$D_5 = -5.0057040 \times 10^{-7}, \quad T_5 = 10^{-4} \times \begin{bmatrix} -0.4502768 & 0.0732408 \end{bmatrix}.$$

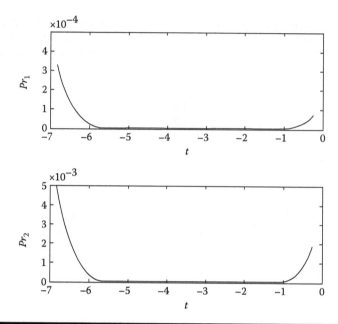

Figure 3.3   Precisions of obtained polynomial matrices.

In order to check the correctness of the above results, we define the following two indices:

$$P_{r1}(t) = \left\| [A(t)N(t) - B(t)D(t)] \right\|_{fro},$$

$$P_{r2}(t) = \left\| A(t)U(t) - B(t)T(t) - I_2 \right\|_{fro},$$

and have computed their values at

$$t_k = -7.0 + 0.15k, \quad k = 0, 1, 2, \ldots, 45.$$

These values are also plotted in Figure 3.3.

It is clearly seen from Figure 3.3 that within the interval $[-5, -1]$, both indices give values less than 1×10^{-4}. Therefore, the polynomial matrix $Q(s)$ obtained by the proposed method gives a good estimate with a very high precision within this working interval.

3.7 Notes and References

In this chapter, the concept of F-left coprimeness with rank α for a pair of polynomial matrices $A(s) \in \mathbb{R}^{n \times q}$ and $B(s) \in \mathbb{R}^{n \times r}$ is introduced. Several special cases, including the case that $(A(s), B(s))$ is controllable, are considered. Conditions in terms of SFR, RCF, and DPE are presented.

Table 3.2 Variables Associated with Coprimeness of $A(s)$ and $B(s)$

Terms	$\Sigma(s)$	β	$C(s)$
F-left coprime with rank α	$\in \mathbb{R}^{\alpha \times \alpha}$	$q + r - \alpha$	$P^{-1}(s)\begin{bmatrix} \Sigma(s) \\ 0 \end{bmatrix}$
Left coprime with rank α	I_α	$q + r - \alpha$	$P^{-1}(s)\begin{bmatrix} I_\alpha \\ 0 \end{bmatrix}$
F-left coprime	$\in \mathbb{R}^{n \times n}$	$q + r - n$	$\Delta(s)I_n$
Left coprime	I_n	$q + r - n$	I_n

For a summarization of the definitions of the various type of coprimeness, please refer to Table 3.1. For a relation among these concepts, please refer to Figure 3.2. Table 3.2 further gives some variables associated with the SFR, RCF, and DPE conditions for certain type of coprimeness of a pair of polynomial matrices $A(s) \in \mathbb{R}^{n \times q}$ and $B(s) \in \mathbb{R}^{n \times r}$. In the following we give some further comments related to SFRs, RCFs, and DPEs.

3.7.1 Coprime Factorizations

Coprime factorization for linear systems is a basic problem in control system theory, and has been investigated by a number of researchers. However, most of the researches are really restricted to the following one associated with first-order linear systems:

$$(sE - A)^{-1} B = N(s)D^{-1}(s),$$

with the matrix E being the identity matrix in most cases.

Coprime factorization has applications in many problems. Green (1992) proposes a coprime factorization approach to the synthesis of H_∞ controllers. While Armstrong (1994) considers robust stabilization using a coprime factorization approach. Ohishi et al. (1996) propose a new speed servo system for a wide speed range based on a doubly coprime factorization and an instantaneous speed observer. Besides the above, Duan (1993b) has shown that a coprime factorization can be used to parameterize all the solutions to a generalized type of Sylvester matrix equations ((Duan 1992b, 1993b, 1996), and has important applications in ESA ((Duan 1992b, 1993b, 1994, 1995, 1998a, Duan and Patton 1997, 1998a), robust pole assignment ((Duan 1992a, 1993a), and robust fault detection ((Duan and Patton 1998d).

For solutions, Beelen and Veltkamp (1987) propose a numerical computational algorithm for solution of a coprime factorization of a transfer function. Bongers and Heuberger (1990) develop a reliable algorithm to perform a normalized coprime factorization of proper discrete-time finite-dimensional linear time-invariant systems. Almuthairi and Bingulac (1994) and Bingulac and Almuthairi (1995) propose new computationally simple algorithms for calculating coprime matrix descriptions, and also consider the minimal state space realization problems based on coprime factorization.

Besides the above, Duan (1998b) considers RCF for single-input systems using Hessenberg forms, and Duan (2001) gives a numerically stable iterative algorithm for RCFs of multiple-input linear systems. The latter is later generalized into the case of descriptor linear systems in Duan (2002b). Also, we have given a Stein matrix equation approach for computing coprime matrix fraction description (Zhou et al. 2009b).

3.7.2 Unified Procedure

Linked by the introduced concept of F-coprimeness with rank α, this chapter has presented a unified procedure based on elementary transformations for solving SFR, RCF, and DPE together, while these topics, as we know, are generally treated separately in the literature. The importance of this unified procedure lies, of course, in giving the solutions to specific SFRs, RCFs, and DPEs, but also in recovering the relations among these three important concepts.

This procedure has a former version that solves the corresponding SFR, RCF, and DPE problems associated with first-order systems only (see, e.g., Duan 1992b, 1993b, 1996, Kong et al. 2009, Zhou et al. 2009b). It was really discovered in the author's research of ESA (see comments in Section 2.4). More specifically, we link the problem of ESA in linear systems with relevant GSEs, while the general analytical parametric solutions to GSEs are presented in terms of the associated RCF, and meanwhile, we gave a way of solving the RCFs through conducting the relevant SFRs.

In order to overcome the drawback of the procedure that it applies to only lower dimension system cases when operated by hand, effective general MATLAB functions `rcfsolve.m`, and `smith.m`, have also been produced for the first-order system case, as basic M-files in a Toolbox named `ParaConD` for parametric control systems design, which is produced by the author.

3.7.3 Numerical Algorithm Using SVD

We must confess that, for the SFR, RCF, and DPE problems associated with generalized higher-order systems of the form

$$A(s)x(s) = B(s)u(s),$$

it is very hard to produce a MATLAB realization of the above unified procedure for the general case based on elementary transformations. As a matter of fact, many of the other existing approaches may simply fail as well in reaching such a purpose, or may even fail to be generalized in theory to fit in such a general higher-order system case at all. It is true that the system can be converted into a first-order one, and then existing numerical algorithms for fist-order systems can be readily applied. Yet one needs also to convert the final result for the extended first-order system back to that for the higher-order system if a direct higher-order system design approach is to be used as we have been always suggesting.

As we have seen in this chapter, under the controllability of $(A(s), B(s))$, an algorithm has been given to solve the SFR, RCF, and DPE problems associated with the generalized higher-order systems, simultaneously if needed. The crucial idea in this scheme is to generate the values of the polynomials to be sought at certain points using SVDs. Such an idea is a great one! It avoids the difficulties of tackling the complicated structures of $A(s)$ and $B(s)$, and also makes the algorithm possess the following very important features:

- It is extremely simple compared with those approaches which involve manipulations directly on the coefficients of $A(s)$ and $B(s)$.
- It possesses very good numerical reliability, since the main computation involved in the algorithm is a set of SVDs, while SVD has been proven to be a numerically stable tool.

This chapter plays a fundamental function in the book. From Chapter 4 onward, we will start examining solutions to GSEs (Figure 3.4).

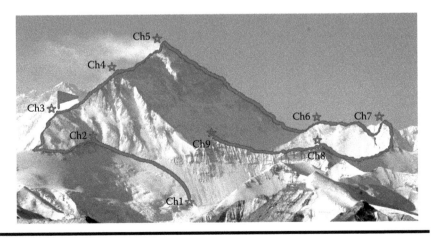

Figure 3.4   We are here. (Modified from http://go.jutuw.com/zhumulangmafeng/ photo/.)

Chapter 4

Homogeneous GSEs

In this chapter, we start to investigate solution to homogeneous GSEs. The first section introduces an operation that is frequently used in this chapter as well as the other sequential chapters. The following three sections treat the general case of F being an arbitrary matrix and provide complete general parametric expressions for the matrices V and W satisfying the GSE. The primary feature of this solution is that the matrix F does not need to be in any canonical form and may be even unknown *a priori*. The rest of the sections consider special cases of the matrix F. In Sections 4.5 and 4.6, cases of F being a Jordan matrix and a diagonal matrix are treated, and some examples follow in Section 4.7.

The results provide great convenience to the computation and analysis of the solutions to this class of equations and can perform important functions in many analysis and design problems in control system theory.

4.1 Sylvester Mappings

Before presenting the general solutions to the homogeneous GSEs, let us first introduce the so-called Sylvester mappings, which will be used frequently in this book.

4.1.1 Definition and Operations

Let $P(s) \in \mathbb{R}^{m \times n}[s]$ be a polynomial defined as

$$P(s) = P_0 + P_1 s + \cdots + P_k s^k. \tag{4.1}$$

Then for an arbitrary matrix $X \in \mathbb{C}^{n \times p}$, we introduce the following notation:

$$P(s)\big|_X \triangleq P_0 + P_1 X + \cdots + P_k X^k.$$

Noting that for an arbitrary matrix $Z \in \mathbb{C}^{n \times p}$, we have

$$P(s) Z = P_0 Z + P_1 Zs + \cdots + P_k Zs^k,$$

for an arbitrary matrix $F \in \mathbb{C}^{p \times p}$ we have

$$[P(s) Z]\big|_F \triangleq P_0 Z + P_1 ZF + \cdots + P_k ZF^k. \tag{4.2}$$

The above notation $[P(s) Z]\big|_F$ in (4.2) defines a mapping from $\mathbb{C}^{n \times p}$ to $\mathbb{C}^{m \times p}$, which is called in this book the Sylvester mapping, and is frequently used in the book.

Please note that, generally,

$$[P(s)Z]\big|_F \neq P(F)Z = P_0 Z + P_1 FZ + \cdots + P_k F^k Z.$$

Let $P_1(s)$ and $P_2(s)$ be polynomial matrices of appropriate dimensions, then by definition (4.2), we clear have

$$\left[\begin{bmatrix} P_1(s) \\ P_2(s) \end{bmatrix} Z \right]\bigg|_F = \begin{bmatrix} [P_1(s)Z]\big|_F \\ [P_2(s)Z]\big|_F \end{bmatrix}. \tag{4.3}$$

Also by definition, it is easily seen that

$$[P_0 Z]\big|_F = P_0 Z$$

holds for a constant matrix P_0.

Now in the following theorem, we give some further operation rules regarding Sylvester mappings.

Theorem 4.1 *Let $P(s) \in \mathbb{R}^{m \times n}[s]$ be given by (4.1). Then*

1. *For any two commutative matrices $F, G \in \mathbb{R}^{p \times p}$, there holds*

$$[P(s) ZG]\big|_F = [P(s) Z]\big|_F G, \ \forall Z \in \mathbb{C}^{n \times p}. \tag{4.4}$$

2. *There exists a $Z \in \mathbb{C}^{n \times p}$ satisfying*

$$\left[P\left(s \right) Z \right] \big|_F = 0, \quad \forall F \in \mathbb{C}^{p \times p}, \tag{4.5}$$

if and only if

$$P\left(s \right) Z = 0, \quad \forall s \in \mathbb{C}, \tag{4.6}$$

or, equivalently

$$P_i Z = 0, \quad i = 0, 1, \ldots, k. \tag{4.7}$$

3. *For $Q(s) \in \mathbb{R}^{n \times r}[s]$, $X \in \mathbb{C}^{r \times p}$, there holds*

$$\left[P\left(s \right) \left[Q\left(s \right) X \right] \big|_F \right] \big|_F = \left[P\left(s \right) Q\left(s \right) X \right] \big|_F, \quad \forall F \in \mathbb{C}^{p \times p}. \tag{4.8}$$

4. *For $\tilde{P}\left(s \right) \in \mathbb{R}^{m \times q}[s]$, $\tilde{Z} \in \mathbb{C}^{q \times p}$, and $Z \in \mathbb{C}^{n \times p}$, there holds*

$$\left[P(s)Z + \tilde{P}(s)\tilde{Z} \right] \big|_F = \left[P(s)Z \right] \big|_F + \left[\tilde{P}(s)\tilde{Z} \right] \big|_F, \quad \forall F \in \mathbb{C}^{p \times p}, \tag{4.9}$$

or

$$\left[P(s)Z + \tilde{P}(s)\tilde{Z} \right] \big|_F = \left[R\left(s \right) Z_e \right] \big|_F, \quad \forall F \in \mathbb{C}^{p \times p}, \tag{4.10}$$

where

$$R\left(s \right) = \left[P(s) \quad \tilde{P}(s) \right], \quad Z_e = \begin{bmatrix} Z \\ \tilde{Z} \end{bmatrix}.$$

For a proof of the above theorem, please refer to the appendix. Let $\Delta\left(s \right)$ be a scalar polynomial. Then it is easy to show

$$F\Delta\left(F \right) = \Delta\left(F \right) F, \tag{4.11}$$

that is, F and $\Delta\left(F \right)$ are commutative. Then it follows from the first conclusion in the above theorem that

$$\left[P\left(s \right) Z\Delta\left(F \right) \right] \big|_F = \left[P\left(s \right) Z \right] \big|_F \Delta\left(F \right). \tag{4.12}$$

4.1.2 Representation of GSEs

Using the above introduced Sylvester mappings, we can give a representation of the general higher-order GSEs.

Let $A_i \in \mathbb{R}^{n \times q}$, $B_i \in \mathbb{R}^{n \times r}$, $i = 0, 1, \ldots, m$, and $F \in \mathbb{C}^{p \times p}$, and define

$$\begin{cases} A(s) = \sum_{i=0}^{m} A_i s^i, \ A_i \in \mathbb{R}^{n \times q} \\ B(s) = \sum_{i=0}^{m} B_i s^i, \ B_i \in \mathbb{R}^{n \times r}, \end{cases} \tag{4.13}$$

then by the definition of Sylvester mappings, we have

$$[A(s)\,V]\big|_F = \sum_{i=0}^{m} A_i V F^i, \tag{4.14}$$

and

$$[B(s)\,W]\big|_F = \sum_{i=0}^{m} B_i W F^i. \tag{4.15}$$

Therefore, the mth order homogeneous GSE

$$\sum_{i=0}^{m} A_i V F^i = \sum_{i=0}^{m} B_i W F^i, \tag{4.16}$$

can be represented, using Sylvester mappings, as

$$[A(s)\,V]\big|_F = [B(s)\,W]\big|_F, \tag{4.17}$$

which can be equivalently written, using the fourth conclusion of the above theorem, as

$$\left[\begin{bmatrix} A(s) & -B(s) \end{bmatrix} \begin{bmatrix} V \\ W \end{bmatrix} \right]\Bigg|_F = 0. \tag{4.18}$$

Particularly, it follows from the second conclusion in the above theorem that

$$[A(s)\,V]\big|_F - [B(s)\,W]\big|_F = 0, \ \forall F \in \mathbb{C}^{p \times p} \tag{4.19}$$

is equivalent to

$$A(s)\,V - B(s)\,W = 0, \ \forall s \in \mathbb{C}. \tag{4.20}$$

Remark 4.1 We would emphasize that the Sylvester mappings introduced in this section will be frequently used in the sequential part of the book. As a matter of fact, all our parametric solutions to both the homogeneous and nonhomogeneous GSEs are represented in terms of Sylvester mappings.

4.2 First-Order GSEs

Let us start with the solution to the first-order homogeneous GSE

$$EVF - AV = B_0 W + B_1 WF, \tag{4.21}$$

where $E, A \in \mathbb{R}^{n \times q}$, $B_1, B_0 \in \mathbb{R}^{n \times r}$, $q + r > n$, $F \in \mathbb{C}^{p \times p}$ are coefficient matrices, and the matrix F may be undetermined, while V and W are the unknowns to be determined. Obviously, two important special forms of this GSE are

$$EVF - AV = BW, \tag{4.22}$$

and

$$VF - AV = BW. \tag{4.23}$$

It is obvious that $V = 0$ and $W = 0$ satisfy the GSE (4.21), therefore, the GSE (4.21) always has a solution. Regarding the degrees of freedom in the general solution (V, W) to the GSE (4.21), we have the following result, which is proven in the appendix.

Theorem 4.2 *Let $A, E \in \mathbb{R}^{n \times q}, B_1, B_0 \in \mathbb{R}^{n \times r}, q + r > n$. Then the maximum degrees of freedom in the general solution (V, W) to the GSE (4.21) is $p\beta$, with $\beta = q + r - \alpha$, if and only if $sE - A$ and $B_1 s + B_0$ are F-left coprime with rank α, that is,*

$$\text{rank} \begin{bmatrix} sE - A & B_1 s + B_0 \end{bmatrix} \leq \alpha, \ \forall s \in \mathbb{C}, \tag{4.24}$$

and

$$\text{rank} \begin{bmatrix} sE - A & B_1 s + B_0 \end{bmatrix} = \alpha, \ \forall s \in \text{eig}(F). \tag{4.25}$$

Due to the above result, in this section we impose

Assumption 4.1 *$sE - A$ and $B_1 s + B_0$ are F-left coprime with rank α.*

4.2.1 General Solution

As a direct consequence of Assumption 4.1, it follows from the results in Section 3.3 that there exist two unimodular matrices $P(s)$ and $Q(s)$ with appropriate dimensions satisfying

$$P(s) \begin{bmatrix} sE - A & -(B_1 s + B_0) \end{bmatrix} Q(s) = \begin{bmatrix} \Sigma(s) & 0 \\ 0 & 0 \end{bmatrix}, \tag{4.26}$$

with $\Sigma(s) \in \mathbb{R}^{\alpha \times \alpha}[s]$ being a diagonal polynomial matrix satisfying

$$\det \Sigma(s) \neq 0, \ \forall s \in \text{eig}(F). \tag{4.27}$$

Partition the unimodular matrix $Q(s)$ as follows:

$$Q(s) = \begin{bmatrix} * & N(s) \\ * & D(s) \end{bmatrix}, \ N(s) \in \mathbb{R}^{q \times \beta}[s], \ D(s) \in \mathbb{R}^{r \times \beta}[s].$$

Then the polynomial matrices $N(s)$ and $D(s)$ are right coprime and satisfy

$$(sE - A)N(s) - (B_1 s + B_0)D(s) = 0. \tag{4.28}$$

Further, when $q = n$ and (E, A) is regular, that is $(sE - A)$ is invertible, we have $\alpha = n$, and the above equation can be rewritten in the form of the following so-called right factorization:

$$(sE - A)^{-1}(B_1 s + B_0) = N(s)D^{-1}(s). \tag{4.29}$$

If we denote $D(s) = \left[d_{ij}(s)\right]_{r \times \beta}$ and

$$\omega = \max\left\{\deg\left(d_{ij}(s)\right), \quad i = 1, 2, \ldots, r, \quad j = 1, 2, \ldots, \beta\right\},$$

then $N(s)$ and $D(s)$ can be rewritten in the form of

$$\begin{cases} N(s) = \sum\limits_{i=0}^{\omega} N_i s^i, \ N_i \in \mathbb{R}^{q \times \beta} \\ D(s) = \sum\limits_{i=0}^{\omega} D_i s^i, \ D_i \in \mathbb{R}^{r \times \beta}. \end{cases} \tag{4.30}$$

With the above polynomial matrices $N(s)$ and $D(s)$ satisfying the generalized RCF (4.28), we have the following result about the general solution to the GSE (4.21).

Theorem 4.3 *Let $E, A \in \mathbb{R}^{n \times q}$, $B_1, B_0 \in \mathbb{R}^{n \times r}$, $q + r > n$, $F \in \mathbb{C}^{p \times p}$ and Assumption 4.1 hold. Further, let $N(s) \in \mathbb{R}^{q \times \beta}[s]$ and $D(s) \in \mathbb{R}^{r \times \beta}[s]$ be a pair of right coprime polynomial matrices in the form of (4.30) and satisfy (4.28). Then all the solutions $V \in \mathbb{C}^{q \times p}$ and $W \in \mathbb{C}^{r \times p}$ to the GSE (4.21) are given by*

Formula I_H

$$\begin{cases} V = [N(s)Z]\big|_F = N_0Z + N_1ZF + \cdots + N_\omega ZF^\omega \\ W = [D(s)Z]\big|_F = D_0Z + D_1ZF + \cdots + D_\omega ZF^\omega, \end{cases} \qquad (4.31)$$

where $Z \in \mathbb{C}^{\beta \times p}$ is an arbitrary parameter matrix.

Proof. Using (4.30), we have

$$(sE - A)N(s)$$

$$= \sum_{i=0}^{\omega} EN_i s^{i+1} - \sum_{i=0}^{\omega} AN_i s^i$$

$$= EN_\omega s^{\omega+1} + \sum_{i=1}^{\omega} EN_{i-1} s^i - \sum_{i=1}^{\omega} AN_i s^i - AN_0$$

$$= EN_\omega s^{\omega+1} + \sum_{i=1}^{\omega} (EN_{i-1} - AN_i) s^i - AN_0,$$

and

$$(B_1 s + B_0)D(s)$$

$$= \sum_{i=0}^{\omega} B_1 D_i s^{i+1} + \sum_{i=0}^{\omega} B_0 D_i s^i$$

$$= B_1 D_\omega s^{\omega+1} + \sum_{i=1}^{\omega} B_1 D_{i-1} s^i + \sum_{i=1}^{\omega} B_0 D_i s^i + B_0 D_0$$

$$= B_1 D_\omega s^{\omega+1} + \sum_{i=1}^{\omega} (B_1 D_{i-1} + B_0 D_i) s^i + B_0 D_0.$$

Substituting the above two relations into (4.28), and equating the coefficients of s^i on both sides, gives the following group of relations:

$$\begin{cases} AN_0 = -B_0 D_0 \\ EN_{i-1} - AN_i = B_1 D_{i-1} + B_0 D_i, \quad i = 1, 2, \ldots, \omega \\ EN_\omega = B_1 D_\omega. \end{cases} \qquad (4.32)$$

With the help of the above set of relations, we can now show that the matrices V and W given by (4.31) satisfy the matrix equation (4.21).

Using the expressions in (4.31), we have

$$EVF - AV$$

$$= \sum_{i=0}^{\omega} EN_i ZF^{i+1} - \sum_{i=0}^{\omega} AN_i ZF^i$$

$$= -(AN_0) Z - \sum_{i=1}^{\omega} AN_i ZF^i + \sum_{i=1}^{\omega} EN_{i-1} ZF^i + EN_\omega ZF^{\omega+1}$$

$$= -(AN_0) Z + \sum_{i=1}^{\omega} (EN_{i-1} - AN_i) ZF^i + EN_\omega ZF^{\omega+1}, \qquad (4.33)$$

and

$$B_0 W + B_1 WF$$

$$= \sum_{i=0}^{\omega} B_0 D_i ZF^i + \sum_{i=0}^{\omega} B_1 D_i ZF^{i+1}$$

$$= B_0 D_0 Z + \sum_{i=1}^{\omega} B_0 D_i ZF^i + \sum_{i=1}^{\omega} B_1 D_{i-1} ZF^i + B_1 D_\omega ZF^{\omega+1}$$

$$= B_0 D_0 Z + \sum_{i=1}^{\omega} (B_1 D_{i-1} + B_0 D_i) ZF^i + B_1 D_\omega ZF^{\omega+1}. \qquad (4.34)$$

Using the equations in (4.32), it can be easily seen that the right-hand sides of the above two equations are equal. Equating the left-hand sides of the above two equations produces the GSE (4.21). This states that the matrices V and W given by (4.31) satisfy the matrix equation (4.21).

Proof of the completeness of the solution (4.31) is given in the appendix. ■

Remark 4.2 The proposed solution (4.31) is very simple and neat, and it is also beautiful and elegant. Yet it is no doubt very useful as well. The simple closed-form can give convenience to many analysis problem, and the linearity in the free parameter matrix Z is certainly an advantage. Furthermore, we remark that numerical stable result is ensured using the formula because the main procedure in obtaining the result according to this formula is to find the pair of polynomial matrices, which can be either obtained accurately by hand with low-dimension problems or obtained via SVD as discussed in Section 3.6.

Remark 4.3 Another advantage of the solution formula (4.31) is that it allows the matrix F to be set undetermined, because it is not needed until the general frame is given and then all one needs to do is to put the matrix F in position. Such a property may give great convenience and advantages to some analysis and design problems in control system theory. In some practical applications, the matrix F, together with the parameter matrix Z, can be utilized as the design degrees of freedom, and optimized to achieve some additional performance.

4.2.2 Example

Example 4.1

Consider a first-order GSE in the form of (4.21) with the following parameters:

$$E = \begin{bmatrix} 1 & 0 & 0 \\ 0 & 1 & 0 \\ 0 & 0 & 0 \end{bmatrix}, \ A = \begin{bmatrix} 0 & 1 & 0 \\ 0 & 0 & 1 \\ 0 & 0 & -1 \end{bmatrix},$$

$$B_1 = \begin{bmatrix} 0 & 0 \\ 0 & 1 \\ 0 & 0 \end{bmatrix}, \ B_0 = \begin{bmatrix} 0 & 0 \\ 1 & 0 \\ 0 & 1 \end{bmatrix}.$$

Following the procedures in Lemma 3.4, we obtain

$$P(s) = \begin{bmatrix} 1 & 0 & 0 \\ 0 & 1 & -s \\ 0 & 0 & 1 \end{bmatrix}, \ Q(s) = \begin{bmatrix} 0 & 0 & 0 & 1 & 0 \\ -1 & 0 & 0 & s & 0 \\ 0 & 0 & 0 & 0 & 1 \\ -s & -1 & 0 & s^2 & -s-1 \\ 0 & 0 & -1 & 0 & 1 \end{bmatrix},$$

which satisfy

$$P(s) \begin{bmatrix} sE - A & -(B_1 s + B_0) \end{bmatrix} Q(s) = \begin{bmatrix} I & 0 \end{bmatrix}.$$

Thus a pair of polynomial matrices $N(s)$ and $D(s)$ satisfying the RCF (4.28) can be obtained as follows:

$$N(s) = \begin{bmatrix} 1 & 0 \\ s & 0 \\ 0 & 1 \end{bmatrix}, \ D(s) = \begin{bmatrix} s^2 & -1-s \\ 0 & 1 \end{bmatrix}.$$

So we have

$$D_0 = \begin{bmatrix} 0 & -1 \\ 0 & 1 \end{bmatrix}, \ D_1 = \begin{bmatrix} 0 & -1 \\ 0 & 0 \end{bmatrix}, \ D_2 = \begin{bmatrix} 1 & 0 \\ 0 & 0 \end{bmatrix}, \tag{4.35}$$

and

$$
N_0 = \begin{bmatrix} 1 & 0 \\ 0 & 0 \\ 0 & 1 \end{bmatrix}, \ N_1 = \begin{bmatrix} 0 & 0 \\ 1 & 0 \\ 0 & 0 \end{bmatrix}, \ N_2 = \begin{bmatrix} 0 & 0 \\ 0 & 0 \\ 0 & 0 \end{bmatrix}. \tag{4.36}
$$

According to Theorem 4.3, for an arbitrary matrix $F \in \mathbb{C}^{p \times p}$, a complete analytical and explicit solution to the GSE in the form of (4.21) can be parameterized as

$$
\begin{cases} V = N_0 Z + N_1 ZF + N_2 ZF^2 \\ W = D_0 Z + D_1 ZF + D_2 ZF^2, \end{cases}
$$

where $Z \in \mathbb{C}^{2 \times p}$ is an arbitrary parameter matrix. Particularly, let

$$
F = \begin{bmatrix} -\lambda & 1 \\ 0 & -\lambda \end{bmatrix}, \ Z = \begin{bmatrix} z_{11} & z_{12} \\ z_{21} & z_{22} \end{bmatrix},
$$

we have

$$
V = \begin{bmatrix} z_{11} & z_{12} \\ -\lambda z_{11} & z_{11} - \lambda z_{12} \\ z_{21} & z_{22} \end{bmatrix},
$$

and

$$
W = \begin{bmatrix} z_{11}\lambda^2 + z_{21}\lambda - z_{21} & \lambda z_{22} - z_{22} - 2\lambda z_{11} - z_{21} + \lambda^2 z_{12} \\ z_{21} & z_{22} \end{bmatrix}.
$$

Further, specially choosing $\lambda = z_{11} = 1$, $z_{12} = z_{21} = z_{22} = 0$, we get the following special solutions:

$$
V = \begin{bmatrix} 1 & 0 \\ -1 & 1 \\ 0 & 0 \end{bmatrix}, \ W = \begin{bmatrix} 1 & -2 \\ 0 & 0 \end{bmatrix}.
$$

4.3 Second-Order GSEs

In this section, we treat the type of second-order homogeneous GSEs in the form of

$$
MVF^2 + DVF + KV = B_2 WF^2 + B_1 WF + B_0 W, \tag{4.37}
$$

where $M, D, K \in \mathbb{R}^{n \times q}$, $B_2, B_1, B_0 \in \mathbb{R}^{n \times r}$, $q + r > n$, and $F \in \mathbb{C}^{p \times p}$ are the coefficient matrices. In many applications, the system coefficient matrices M, D, and K are called the mass matrix, the structural damping matrix, and the stiffness matrix, respectively. The matrix F does not need to be prescribed and may be even set undetermined, and $V \in \mathbb{C}^{q \times p}$ and $W \in \mathbb{C}^{r \times p}$ are the unknown matrices to be determined.

Again, it is obvious that $V = 0$ and $W = 0$ satisfy the second-order GSE (4.37), therefore the second-order GSE (4.37) actually always has a solution. Regarding the degrees of freedom in the solution (V, W), we have the following result, which is proven in the appendix.

Theorem 4.4 *Let $M, D, K \in \mathbb{R}^{n \times q}$, B_2, B_1, $B_0 \in \mathbb{R}^{n \times r}$, $q + r > n$. Then the degrees of freedom in the solution (V, W) to the second-order GSE (4.37) is $p\beta$, with $\beta = q + r - \alpha$, if and only if $Ms^2 + Ds + K$ and $B_2 s^2 + B_1 s + B_0$ are F-left coprime with rank α, that is,*

$$\text{rank} \left[Ms^2 + Ds + K \quad B_2 s^2 + B_1 s + B_0 \right] \leq \alpha, \ \forall s \in \mathbb{C}, \tag{4.38}$$

and

$$\text{rank} \left[Ms^2 + Ds + K \quad B_2 s^2 + B_1 s + B_0 \right] = \alpha, \ \forall s \in \text{eig}(F). \tag{4.39}$$

Due to Theorem 4.4, in this section we impose

Assumption 4.2 *$Ms^2 + Ds + K$ and $B_2 s^2 + B_1 s + B_0$ are F-left coprime with rank α.*

As we will see, the treatment heavily depends on the following two Polynomials:

$$\begin{cases} A(s) = Ms^2 + Ds + K \\ B(s) = B_2 s^2 + B_1 s + B_0. \end{cases} \tag{4.40}$$

They are called the coefficient polynomial matrices associated with GSE (4.37).

4.3.1 General Solution

As a direct consequence of Assumption 4.2, it follows from the results in Section 3.3 that there exist two unimodular matrices $P(s)$ and $Q(s)$ with appropriate dimensions satisfying

$$P(s) \left[(Ms^2 + Ds + K) \quad -(B_2 s^2 + B_1 s + B_0) \right] Q(s) = \begin{bmatrix} \Sigma(s) & 0 \\ 0 & 0 \end{bmatrix}, \tag{4.41}$$

with $\Sigma(s) \in \mathbb{R}^{\alpha \times \alpha}$ being a diagonal polynomial matrix satisfying

$$\det \Sigma(s) \neq 0, \ \forall s \in \text{eig}(F). \tag{4.42}$$

Partition the unimodular matrix $Q(s)$ as follows:

$$Q(s) = \begin{bmatrix} * & N(s) \\ * & D(s) \end{bmatrix}, \quad N(s) \in \mathbb{R}^{q \times \beta}[s], D(s) \in \mathbb{R}^{r \times \beta}[s].$$

Then the polynomial matrices $N(s)$ and $D(s)$ are right coprime and satisfy

$$\left(Ms^2 + Ds + K\right) N(s) - \left(B_2 s^2 + B_1 s + B_0\right) D(s) = 0. \tag{4.43}$$

When $q = n$ and the polynomial $\det A(s)$ is not identically zero, $A(s)$ is invertible. Under the assumption that $D(s)$ is invertible, we have $\beta = r$, and the above equation can be rewritten in the form of the following so-called right factorization

$$\left(Ms^2 + Ds + K\right)^{-1} \left(B_2 s^2 + B_1 s + B_0\right) = N(s) D^{-1}(s). \tag{4.44}$$

If we denote $D(s) = \left[d_{ij}(s)\right]_{r \times \beta}$ and

$$\omega = \max\left\{\deg\left(d_{ij}(s)\right), \quad i = 1, 2, \ldots, r, \quad j = 1, 2, \ldots, \beta\right\},$$

then $N(s)$ and $D(s)$ can be written in the form of

$$\begin{cases} N(s) = \sum_{i=0}^{\omega} N_i s^i, \ N_i \in \mathbb{R}^{q \times \beta} \\ D(s) = \sum_{i=0}^{\omega} D_i s^i, \ D_i \in \mathbb{R}^{r \times \beta}. \end{cases} \tag{4.45}$$

Utilizing the above pair of polynomial matrices $N(s)$ and $D(s)$, we can give the following result about the general solution to the second-order GSE (4.37).

Theorem 4.5 *Let $M, D, K \in \mathbb{R}^{n \times q}$, $B_2, B_1, B_0 \in \mathbb{R}^{n \times r}$, $q + r > n$, and Assumption 4.2 hold. Further, let $N(s) \mathbb{R}^{q \times \beta}[s]$ and $D(s) \in \mathbb{R}^{r \times \beta}[s]$ be a pair of right coprime polynomial matrices given by (4.45) and satisfy (4.44). Then, all the solutions $V \in \mathbb{C}^{q \times p}$ and $W \in \mathbb{C}^{r \times p}$ to the second-order GSE (4.37) are given by*

$$\boxed{\begin{aligned} &\text{Formula } I_H \\ &\begin{cases} V = [N(s) Z]\big|_F = N_0 Z + N_1 ZF + \cdots + N_\omega ZF^\omega \\ W = [D(s) Z]\big|_F = D_0 Z + D_1 ZF + \cdots + D_\omega ZF^\omega, \end{cases} \end{aligned}} \tag{4.46}$$

where $Z \in \mathbb{C}^{\beta \times p}$ is an arbitrary parameter matrix.

Proof. Using (4.45), we can get

$$\left(Ms^2 + Ds + K\right) N\left(s\right)$$

$$= \sum_{i=0}^{\omega} MN_i s^{i+2} + \sum_{i=0}^{\omega} DN_i s^{i+1} + \sum_{i=0}^{\omega} KN_i s^i$$

$$= MN_\omega s^{\omega+2} + MN_{\omega-1} s^{\omega+1} + \sum_{i=2}^{\omega} MN_{i-2} s^i$$

$$+ DN_\omega s^{\omega+1} + \sum_{i=2}^{\omega} DN_{i-1} s^i + DN_0 s$$

$$+ \sum_{i=2}^{\omega} KN_i s^i + KN_1 s^1 + KN_0$$

$$= MN_\omega s^{\omega+2} + (MN_{\omega-1} + DN_\omega) s^{\omega+1}$$

$$+ \sum_{i=2}^{\omega} (MN_{i-2} + DN_{i-1} + KN_i) s^i$$

$$+ (KN_1 + DN_0) s^1 + KN_0,$$

and

$$\left(B_2 s^2 + B_1 s + B_0\right) D\left(s\right)$$

$$= \sum_{i=0}^{\omega} B_2 D_i s^{i+2} + \sum_{i=0}^{\omega} B_1 D_i s^{i+1} + \sum_{i=0}^{\omega} B_0 D_i s^i$$

$$= B_2 D_\omega s^{\omega+2} + B_2 D_{\omega-1} s^{\omega+1} + \sum_{i=2}^{\omega} B_2 D_{i-2} s^i$$

$$+ B_1 D_\omega s^{\omega+1} + \sum_{i=2}^{\omega} B_1 D_{i-1} s^i + B_1 D_0 s$$

$$+ \sum_{i=2}^{\omega} B_0 D_i s^i + B_0 D_1 s^1 + B_0 D_0$$

$$= B_2 D_\omega s^{\omega+2} + (B_2 D_{\omega-1} + B_1 D_\omega) s^{\omega+1}$$

$$+ \sum_{i=2}^{\omega} (B_2 D_{i-2} + B_1 D_{i-1} + B_0 D_i) s^i$$

$$+ (B_0 D_1 + B_1 D_0) s^1 + B_0 D_0.$$

Substituting the above two relations into the generalized RCF (4.43), and comparing the coefficients of s^i on both sides, gives

$$
\begin{cases}
KN_0 = B_0 D_0 \\
KN_1 + DN_0 = B_0 D_1 + B_1 D_0 \\
MN_{i-2} + DN_{i-1} + KN_i \\
\quad = B_2 D_{i-2} + B_1 D_{i-1} + B_0 D_i, \\
\quad i = 2, 3, \ldots, \omega \\
MN_{\omega-1} + DN_\omega = B_2 D_{\omega-1} + B_1 D_\omega \\
MN_\omega = B_2 D_\omega.
\end{cases}
\tag{4.47}
$$

Now with the help of the above set of relations we can show that the matrices V and W given by (4.46) satisfy the matrix equation (4.37).

In fact, using the expressions in (4.46), we have

$$
MVF^2 + DVF + KV
$$

$$
= M\left(\sum_{i=0}^{\omega} N_i ZF^i\right) F^2 + D\left(\sum_{i=0}^{\omega} N_i ZF^i\right) F + K\sum_{i=0}^{\omega} N_i ZF^i
$$

$$
= (KN_0) Z + (DN_0 + KN_1) ZF
$$

$$
+ \sum_{i=0}^{\omega-2} (MN_i + DN_{i+1} + KN_{i+2}) ZF^{i+2}
$$

$$
+ (MN_{\omega-1} + DN_\omega) ZF^{\omega+1} + (MN_\omega) ZF^{\omega+2},
\tag{4.48}
$$

and

$$
B_2 WF^2 + B_1 WF + B_0 W
$$

$$
= B_2\left(\sum_{i=0}^{\omega} D_i ZF^i\right) F^2 + B_1\left(\sum_{i=0}^{\omega} D_i ZF^i\right) F + B_0\sum_{i=0}^{\omega} D_i ZF^i
$$

$$
= (B_0 D_0) Z + (B_1 D_0 + B_0 D_1) ZF
$$

$$
+ \sum_{i=0}^{\omega-2} (B_2 D_i + B_1 D_{i+1} + B_0 D_{i+2}) ZF^{i+2}
$$

$$
+ (B_2 D_{\omega-1} + B_1 D_\omega) ZF^{\omega+1} + (B_2 D_\omega) ZF^{\omega+2}.
\tag{4.49}
$$

Comparing the right-hand sides of the above relations, and using the relations in (4.47), gives the equation (4.37). Therefore, the matrices V and W given by (4.46) are solutions to the GSE (4.37).

Completeness of the solution (4.46) is shown in the appendix. ■

Remark 4.4 It is clearly observed that for the second-order GSEs we have derived the same solution formula as for the first-order GSEs. The only difference is that now for the second-order GSEs the pair of right coprime polynomials $N(s)$ and $D(s)$ are determined by (4.44) instead of (4.28). Yet it is easy to see that (4.44) is also a very natural generalization of (4.28). As in the first-order case, the result allows the matrix F to be set undetermined, hence can be optimized, together with the parameter matrix Z, to achieve some additional properties required in applications.

4.3.2 Example

Example 4.2

Consider a second-order GSE in the form of (4.37) with the following parameters:

$$M = \begin{bmatrix} 1 & 0 & 0 \\ 0 & 1 & 0 \\ 0 & 0 & 0 \end{bmatrix}, \ D = \begin{bmatrix} 1 & 0 & 1 \\ 0 & 2 & -1 \\ 1 & -1 & 3 \end{bmatrix},$$

$$K = \begin{bmatrix} 2 & -1 & 0 \\ -1 & 1 & 2 \\ 0 & 2 & 1 \end{bmatrix},$$

$$B_2 = B_1 = 0, \ B_0 = \begin{bmatrix} 1 & 0 \\ 0 & 0 \\ 0 & 1 \end{bmatrix}.$$

Following Lemma 3.4, a pair of polynomial matrices $N(s)$ and $D(s)$ satisfying the RCF (4.44) can be obtained as

$$N(s) = \begin{bmatrix} s^2 + 2s + 1 & -s + 2 \\ 1 & 0 \\ 0 & 1 \end{bmatrix},$$

$$D(s) = \begin{bmatrix} s^4 + 3s^3 + 5s^2 + 5s + 1 & -s^3 + s^2 + s + 4 \\ s^3 + 2s^2 + 2 & -s^2 + 5s + 1 \end{bmatrix}.$$

So we have

$$D_0 = \begin{bmatrix} 1 & 4 \\ 2 & 1 \end{bmatrix}, \ D_1 = \begin{bmatrix} 5 & 1 \\ 0 & 5 \end{bmatrix}, \ D_2 = \begin{bmatrix} 5 & 1 \\ 2 & -1 \end{bmatrix},$$

$$D_3 = \begin{bmatrix} 3 & -1 \\ 1 & 0 \end{bmatrix}, \ D_4 = \begin{bmatrix} 1 & 0 \\ 0 & 0 \end{bmatrix},$$

and

$$N_0 = \begin{bmatrix} 1 & 2 \\ 1 & 0 \\ 0 & 1 \end{bmatrix}, \ N_1 = \begin{bmatrix} 2 & -1 \\ 0 & 0 \\ 0 & 0 \end{bmatrix}, \ N_2 = \begin{bmatrix} 1 & 0 \\ 0 & 0 \\ 0 & 0 \end{bmatrix}.$$

According to Theorem 4.5, for an arbitrary matrix $F \in \mathbb{C}^{p \times p}$, a complete analytical and explicit solution to the second-order GSE in the form of (4.37) can be parameterized as

$$\begin{cases} V = N_0 Z + N_1 ZF + N_2 ZF^2 \\ W = D_0 Z + D_1 ZF + D_2 ZF^2 + D_3 ZF^3 + D_4 ZF^4, \end{cases}$$

where $Z \in \mathbb{C}^{2 \times p}$ is an arbitrary parameter matrix. Denote

$$F = \begin{bmatrix} -\lambda & 1 \\ 0 & -\lambda \end{bmatrix}, \quad Z = \begin{bmatrix} z_{11} & z_{12} \\ z_{21} & z_{22} \end{bmatrix},$$

we then have

$$V = \begin{bmatrix} v_{11} & v_{12} \\ z_{11} & z_{12} \\ z_{21} & z_{22} \end{bmatrix}, \quad W = \begin{bmatrix} w_{11} & w_{12} \\ w_{21} & w_{22} \end{bmatrix},$$

with

$$v_{11} = z_{11} + 2z_{21} + \lambda(z_{21} - 2z_{11}) + \lambda^2 z_{11},$$

$$v_{12} = 2z_{11} + z_{12} - z_{21} + 2z_{22}$$
$$- 2\lambda z_{11} + \lambda(z_{22} - 2z_{12}) + \lambda^2 z_{12},$$

and

$$w_{11} = z_{11} + 4z_{21} + \lambda^3(z_{21} - 3z_{11}) + \lambda^2(5z_{11} + z_{21})$$
$$- \lambda(5z_{11} + z_{21}) + \lambda^4 z_{11},$$

$$w_{12} = 5z_{11} + z_{12} + z_{21} + 4z_{22} - 3\lambda^2(z_{21} - 3z_{11})$$
$$+ \lambda^3(z_{22} - 3z_{12}) + \lambda^2(5z_{12} + z_{22}) - 2\lambda(5z_{11} + z_{21})$$
$$- \lambda(5z_{12} + z_{22}) - 4\lambda^3 z_{11} + \lambda^4 z_{12},$$

$$w_{21} = 2z_{11} + z_{21} - \lambda^2(z_{21} - 2z_{11}) - 5\lambda z_{21} - \lambda^3 z_{11},$$

$$w_{22} = 2z_{12} + 5z_{21} + z_{22} - \lambda^2(z_{22} - 2z_{12}) - 5\lambda z_{22}$$
$$+ 2\lambda(z_{21} - 2z_{11}) + 3\lambda^2 z_{11} - \lambda^3 z_{12}.$$

Further, specially choosing $\lambda = 1$ and

$$Z = \begin{bmatrix} 1 & 0 \\ 0 & 0 \end{bmatrix},$$

we get a pair of specific solutions

$$V = \begin{bmatrix} 0 & 0 \\ 1 & 0 \\ 0 & 0 \end{bmatrix}, \quad W = \begin{bmatrix} -1 & 0 \\ 3 & -1 \end{bmatrix}.$$

4.4 Higher-Order GSEs

This section considers parametric solution to the following higher-order homogeneous GSE

$$\sum_{i=0}^{m} A_i V F^i = \sum_{i=0}^{m} B_i W F^i, \tag{4.50}$$

where $A_i \in \mathbb{R}^{n \times q}$, $B_i \in \mathbb{R}^{n \times r}$, $i = 0, 1, \ldots, m$, $q + r > n$, and $F \in \mathbb{C}^{p \times p}$ are the coefficient matrices, and the matrix F may not be prescribed. The matrices $V \in \mathbb{C}^{q \times p}$ and $W \in \mathbb{C}^{r \times p}$ are the unknown variables to be determined. The polynomial matrices associated with this GSE are

$$\begin{cases} A(s) = \sum_{i=0}^{m} A_i s^i, \ A_i \in \mathbb{R}^{n \times q} \\ B(s) = \sum_{i=0}^{m} B_i s^i, \ B_i \in \mathbb{R}^{n \times r}. \end{cases} \tag{4.51}$$

Again, it is clear that $V = 0$ and $W = 0$ satisfy the mth order GSE (4.50). Regarding the degrees of freedom existing in the solution, we have the following result, which is proven in the appendix.

Theorem 4.6 *Let $A(s)$ and $B(s)$ be given in (4.51). Then the degrees of freedom in the solution (V, W) to the mth order GSE (4.50) is $p\beta$, with $\beta = q + r - \alpha$, if and only if $A(s)$ and $B(s)$ are F-left coprime with rank α, that is,*

$$\text{rank}\begin{bmatrix} A(s) & B(s) \end{bmatrix} \leq \alpha, \ \forall s \in \mathbb{C}, \tag{4.52}$$

and

$$\text{rank}\begin{bmatrix} A(s) & B(s) \end{bmatrix} = \alpha, \ \forall s \in \text{eig}(F). \tag{4.53}$$

Due to the above result, in this section we impose

Assumption 4.3 *$A(s)$ and $B(s)$ are F-left coprime with rank α.*

From Theorem 3.4, the above assumption is equivalent to that the eigenvalues of the matrix F are different from the essential zeros of $[A(s) \ B(s)]$.

4.4.1 General Solution

As a direct consequence of Assumption 4.3, it follows from the results in Section 3.3 that there exist two unimodular matrices $P(s)$ and $Q(s)$ with appropriate dimensions satisfying

$$P(s)\left[A(s) \ -B(s)\right]Q(s) = \begin{bmatrix} \Sigma(s) & 0 \\ 0 & 0 \end{bmatrix}, \tag{4.54}$$

with $\Sigma(s) \in \mathbb{R}^{\alpha \times \alpha}$ being a diagonal polynomial matrix satisfying

$$\det \Sigma(s) \neq 0, \quad \forall s \in \text{eig}(F). \tag{4.55}$$

Partition the unimodular matrix $Q(s)$ as follows:

$$Q(s) = \begin{bmatrix} * & N(s) \\ * & D(s) \end{bmatrix}, \ N(s) \in \mathbb{R}^{q \times \beta}[s], D(s) \in \mathbb{R}^{r \times \beta}[s].$$

Then the polynomial matrices $N(s)$ and $D(s)$ are right coprime and satisfy

$$A(s)N(s) - B(s)D(s) = 0. \tag{4.56}$$

Particularly, when $q = n$ and the polynomial $\det A(s)$ is not identically zero, $A(s)$ is invertible. Under the assumption that $D(s)$ is invertible, the above equation can be rewritten in the form of the following so-called right factorization

$$A(s)^{-1}B(s) = N(s)D^{-1}(s). \tag{4.57}$$

If we denote $D(s) = \left[d_{ij}(s)\right]_{r \times \beta}$ and

$$\omega = \max\left\{\deg\left(d_{ij}(s)\right), \quad i = 1, 2, \ldots, r, \quad j = 1, 2, \ldots, \beta\right\},$$

then $N(s)$ and $D(s)$ can be written in the form of

$$\begin{cases} N(s) = \sum\limits_{i=0}^{\omega} N_i s^i, \ N_i \in \mathbb{R}^{q \times \beta} \\ D(s) = \sum\limits_{i=0}^{\omega} D_i s^i, \ D_i \in \mathbb{R}^{r \times \beta}. \end{cases} \tag{4.58}$$

Regarding the general solution to the mth order GSE (4.50), we have the following result represented in terms of the above polynomial matrices $N(s)$ and $D(s)$.

Theorem 4.7 *Let $A(s)$ and $B(s)$ be given in (4.51), and Assumption 4.3 hold. Further, let $N(s) \in \mathbb{R}^{q \times \beta}[s]$ and $D(s) \in \mathbb{R}^{r \times \beta}[s]$ be a pair of right coprime polynomial matrices given by (4.58) and satisfy the generalized RCF (4.56). Then all the solutions $V \in \mathbb{C}^{q \times p}$ and $W \in \mathbb{C}^{r \times p}$ to the mth order GSE (4.50) are given by*

$$\textit{Formula } I_H$$
$$\begin{cases} V = [N(s)Z]\big|_F = N_0 Z + N_1 ZF + \cdots + N_\omega ZF^\omega \\ W = [D(s)Z]\big|_F = D_0 Z + D_1 ZF + \cdots + D_\omega ZF^\omega, \end{cases} \tag{4.59}$$

where $Z \in \mathbb{C}^{\beta \times p}$ is an arbitrary parameter matrix.

Proof. Using the expressions of $A(s)$ and $B(s)$ in (4.51) and those of $N(s)$ and $D(s)$ in (4.58), we have

$$A(s)N(s) = \sum_{i=0}^{m} A_i s^i \sum_{j=0}^{\omega} N_j s^j$$
$$= \sum_{i=0}^{m} \sum_{j=0}^{\omega} A_i N_j s^{i+j}$$
$$= \sum_{k=0}^{m+\omega} \left(\sum_{i=0}^{k} A_i N_{k-i} \right) s^k,$$

and

$$B(s)D(s) = \sum_{i=0}^{m} B_i s^i \sum_{j=0}^{\omega} D_j s^j$$
$$= \sum_{i=0}^{m} \sum_{j=0}^{\omega} B_i D_j s^{i+j}$$
$$= \sum_{k=0}^{m+\omega} \left(\sum_{i=0}^{k} B_i D_{k-i} \right) s^k,$$

where $A_i = 0$, $B_i = 0$, when $i > m$, and $N_i = 0$, $D_i = 0$, when $i > \omega$. Thus, by the generalized RCF (4.56) we have

$$A(s)N(s) - B(s)D(s)$$
$$= \sum_{k=0}^{m+\omega} \left(\sum_{i=0}^{k} A_i N_{k-i} \right) s^k - \sum_{k=0}^{m+\omega} \left(\sum_{i=0}^{k} B_i D_{k-i} \right) s^k$$
$$= \sum_{k=0}^{m+\omega} \left(\sum_{i=0}^{k} A_i N_{k-i} - \sum_{i=0}^{k} B_i D_{k-i} \right) s^k$$
$$= 0.$$

Setting the coefficients of s^k in the left-hand side of the above equation to zero gives

$$\sum_{i=0}^{k} A_i N_{k-i} = \sum_{i=0}^{k} B_i D_{k-i}, \quad k = 1, 2, \ldots, \omega + m. \tag{4.60}$$

On the other side, using the solution given in (4.59), we have

$$\sum_{i=0}^{m} A_i V F^i = \sum_{i=0}^{m} A_i \left(\sum_{j=0}^{\omega} N_j Z F^j \right) F^i$$

$$= \sum_{i=0}^{m} \sum_{j=0}^{\omega} A_i N_j Z F^{i+j}$$

$$= \sum_{k=0}^{m+\omega} \left(\sum_{i=0}^{k} A_i N_{k-i} \right) Z F^k,$$

and

$$\sum_{i=0}^{m} B_i W F^i = \sum_{i=0}^{m} B_i \left(\sum_{j=0}^{\omega} D_j Z F^j \right) F^i$$

$$= \sum_{i=0}^{m} \sum_{j=0}^{\omega} B_i D_j Z F^{i+j}$$

$$= \sum_{k=0}^{m+\omega} \left(\sum_{i=0}^{k} B_i D_{k-i} \right) Z F^k.$$

With the relations in (4.60), it is easily seen that the right-hand sides of the above two relations are equal, hence the left-hand sides are also equal to each other, that is,

$$\sum_{i=0}^{m} A_i V F^i = \sum_{i=0}^{m} B_i W F^i.$$

This states that the matrices V and W given by (4.59) satisfy the GSE (4.50).

The proof of the completeness of the solution (4.59) is given in the appendix.
∎

Remark 4.5 It is seen from the above theorem that the general parametric solution (4.59) for a higher-order GSE turns out to be exactly the same as those for a first-order GSE and a second-order one. The only difference lies in solving the pair of right coprime polynomial matrices $N(s)$ and $D(s)$ used in the solution. Yet, as we have seen, the pair of right coprime polynomial matrices $N(s)$ and $D(s)$ are also defined in the same way. These facts state that the solution proposed for the homogeneous GSEs is a highly unified one.

Remark 4.6 We would like to mention again the simplicity, neatness, and elegancy of the general parametric solution (4.59), and again the linearity of the solution with respect to the free parameter matrix Z. Let us also mention that, as in first- and second-order cases, the matrix F can also be set undetermined, and sought together with the parameter matrix Z, to achieve additional requirements in applications.

Remark 4.7 In many other researches of this aspect, controllability of $(A(s), B(s))$ (often a special pair) is assumed. Under this assumption, it is clearly seen from our results that the degrees of freedom in the general solution is $(q + r - n)p$. While our research not only has relaxed the assumption to regularizable case, but also to irregularizable case, and the degrees of freedom provided in the general solution is shown to be $(q + r - \alpha)p$. Note that in the irregularizable case we have $\alpha < n$, thus this general case provides more degrees of freedom in the general solution to the homogeneous GSE.

Remark 4.8 For a larger application scope, we have allowed the matrices V, W and F in the GSE (4.50) to take complex values. However, it can be easily observed that, once the matrix F is restricted to be real (but may possess complex eigenvalues), our proposed solution (4.59) also provides real matrices V and W.

4.4.2 Example

Example 4.3

Consider a third-order GSE in the form of (4.50) with

$$A_3 = \begin{bmatrix} 1 & 0 & 0 \\ 0 & 1 & 0 \\ 0 & 0 & 0 \end{bmatrix}, \ A_2 = \begin{bmatrix} 1 & 0 & 1 \\ 0 & 2 & -1 \\ 1 & -1 & 3 \end{bmatrix},$$

$$A_1 = \begin{bmatrix} 2 & 0 & 0 \\ 0 & 1 & 2 \\ 0 & 2 & 1 \end{bmatrix}, \ A_0 = \begin{bmatrix} 0 & -1 & 0 \\ -1 & 1 & 2 \\ 0 & 1 & 1 \end{bmatrix},$$

and

$$B_3 = B_2 = B_1 = 0, \ B_0 = \begin{bmatrix} 1 & 0 \\ 0 & 0 \\ 0 & 1 \end{bmatrix}.$$

Following Lemma 3.4, a pair of polynomial matrices $N(s)$ and $D(s)$ satisfying the generalized RCF (4.56) are obtained as

$$N(s) = \begin{bmatrix} s^3 + 2s^2 + s + 1 & -s^2 + 2s + 2 \\ 1 & 0 \\ 0 & 1 \end{bmatrix},$$

$$D(s) = \begin{bmatrix} s^6 + 3s^5 + 5s^4 + 6s^3 + 3s^2 + 2s - 1 \\ s^5 + 2s^4 + s^3 + 2s + 1 \end{bmatrix}$$

$$\begin{bmatrix} -s^5 + s^4 + 2s^3 + 7s^2 + 4s \\ -s^4 + 2s^3 + 5s^2 + s + 1 \end{bmatrix}.$$

Thus, we have

$$N_0 = \begin{bmatrix} 1 & 2 \\ 1 & 0 \\ 0 & 1 \end{bmatrix}, \quad N_1 = \begin{bmatrix} 1 & 2 \\ 0 & 0 \\ 0 & 0 \end{bmatrix},$$

$$N_2 = \begin{bmatrix} 2 & -1 \\ 0 & 0 \\ 0 & 0 \end{bmatrix}, \quad N_3 = \begin{bmatrix} 1 & 0 \\ 0 & 0 \\ 0 & 0 \end{bmatrix},$$

and

$$D_0 = \begin{bmatrix} -1 & 0 \\ 1 & 1 \end{bmatrix}, \quad D_1 = \begin{bmatrix} 2 & 4 \\ 2 & 1 \end{bmatrix},$$

$$D_2 = \begin{bmatrix} 3 & 7 \\ 0 & 5 \end{bmatrix}, \quad D_3 = \begin{bmatrix} 6 & 2 \\ 1 & 2 \end{bmatrix},$$

$$D_4 = \begin{bmatrix} 5 & 1 \\ 2 & -1 \end{bmatrix}, \quad D_5 = \begin{bmatrix} 3 & -1 \\ 1 & 0 \end{bmatrix}, \quad D_6 = \begin{bmatrix} 1 & 0 \\ 0 & 0 \end{bmatrix}.$$

According to Theorem 4.7, for an arbitrary matrix $F \in \mathbb{C}^{p \times p}$, a complete analytical and explicit general solution to this third-order GSE in the form of (4.50) can be parameterized as

$$\begin{cases} V = \sum_{i=0}^{3} N_i Z F^i \\ W = \sum_{i=0}^{6} D_i Z F^i, \end{cases}$$

where $Z \in \mathbb{C}^{2 \times p}$ is an arbitrary parameter matrix. Let

$$F = \begin{bmatrix} -\lambda & 1 \\ 0 & -\lambda \end{bmatrix}, \quad Z = \begin{bmatrix} 0 & 1 \\ -1 & 0 \end{bmatrix}, \tag{4.61}$$

we have

$$V = \begin{bmatrix} \lambda^2 + 2\lambda - 2 & -\lambda^3 + 2\lambda^2 - 3\lambda - 1 \\ 0 & 1 \\ -1 & 0 \end{bmatrix},$$

and

$$W = \begin{bmatrix} w_{11} & w_{12} \\ w_{21} & w_{22} \end{bmatrix},$$

with

$$\begin{cases} w_{11} = -\lambda^5 - \lambda^4 + 2\lambda^3 - 7\lambda^2 + 4\lambda \\ w_{12} = \lambda^6 - 3\lambda^5 + 10\lambda^4 - 2\lambda^3 - 3\lambda^2 + 12\lambda - 5 \\ w_{21} = \lambda^4 + 2\lambda^3 - 5\lambda^2 + \lambda - 1 \\ w_{22} = -\lambda^5 + 2\lambda^4 - 5\lambda^3 - 6\lambda^2 + 8\lambda. \end{cases}$$

Specially choosing $\lambda = 1$ gives the following pair of specific solutions

$$V = \begin{bmatrix} 1 & -3 \\ 0 & 1 \\ -1 & 0 \end{bmatrix}, \quad W = \begin{bmatrix} -3 & 10 \\ -2 & -2 \end{bmatrix}. \tag{4.62}$$

4.5 Case of *F* Being in Jordan Form

In pole assignment designs or ESA designs of linear systems, it is often required that the coefficient matrix F is in Jordan form (Duan 1991a, 1993a,b, 1994, 1995, 1998a, 1999, 2003, Duan and Patton 1997, 1998a, 1999). In this section, we will derive, based on the general solution (4.59), a complete parametric solution to the homogeneous GSE (4.50) for the case that the matrix $F \in \mathbb{C}^{p \times p}$ is a Jordan matrix of the following form:

$$
\begin{cases}
F = \text{blockdiag}\,(F_1, F_2, \ldots, F_w) \\
F_i = \begin{bmatrix} s_i & 1 & & & \\ & s_i & \ddots & & \\ & & & \ddots & 1 \\ & & & & s_i \end{bmatrix}_{p_i \times p_i}
\end{cases}
\tag{4.63}
$$

where $s_i \in \mathbb{C}$, $i = 1, 2, \ldots, w$, are obviously the eigenvalues of the matrix F, and p_i, $i = 1, 2, \ldots, w$, are the geometric multiplicities corresponding to the eigenvalues s_i, $i = 1, 2, \ldots, w$, and satisfy

$$
\sum_{i=1}^{w} p_i = p.
$$

Corresponding to the structure of the above F Jordan matrix, we introduce the following convention.

Convention C1. Any matrix X possessing p columns corresponds by the structure of F to a group of vectors x_{ij}, $j = 1, 2, \ldots, p_i$, $i = 1, 2, \ldots, w$, in the following manner:

$$
\begin{cases}
X = \begin{bmatrix} X_1 & X_2 & \cdots & X_w \end{bmatrix} \\
X_i = \begin{bmatrix} x_{i1} & x_{i2} & \cdots & x_{ip_i} \end{bmatrix}.
\end{cases}
\tag{4.64}
$$

By the structure of the above F matrix, the columns of the matrices V and W, namely, v_{ij} and w_{ij}, are well defined according to Convention C1.

Also, when the matrix F is given in the form of (4.63), Assumption 4.3 becomes

Assumption 4.4 $\quad \begin{cases} \text{rank} \begin{bmatrix} A(s) & B(s) \end{bmatrix} \leq \alpha, \ \forall s \in \mathbb{C} \\ \text{rank} \begin{bmatrix} A(s_i) & B(s_i) \end{bmatrix} = \alpha, \quad i = 1, 2, \ldots, w. \end{cases}$

4.5.1 General Solution

Based on Theorem 4.7, we can obtain the general solution to the homogeneous GSE (4.50) with F being given by (4.63).

Theorem 4.8 *Let Assumption 4.4 hold. Further, let $F \in \mathbb{C}^{p \times p}$ be a Jordan matrix given by (4.63), $N(s) \in \mathbb{R}^{q \times \beta}[s]$ and $D(s) \in \mathbb{R}^{r \times \beta}[s]$ be a pair of right coprime*

polynomial matrices satisfying (4.56). Then all the solutions of the homogeneous GSE (4.50) are parameterized by

---

Formula II_H

$$\begin{bmatrix} v_{ij} \\ w_{ij} \end{bmatrix} = \sum_{k=0}^{j-1} \frac{1}{k!} \frac{d^k}{ds^k} \begin{bmatrix} N(s_i) \\ D(s_i) \end{bmatrix} z_{i,j-k},$$

$$j = 1, 2, \ldots, p_i, \quad i = 1, 2, \ldots, w,$$

(4.65)

---

which has the expanded form

$$\begin{bmatrix} v_{ij} \\ w_{ij} \end{bmatrix} = \begin{bmatrix} N(s_i) \\ D(s_i) \end{bmatrix} z_{ij} + \frac{1}{1!} \frac{d}{ds} \begin{bmatrix} N(s_i) \\ D(s_i) \end{bmatrix} z_{i,j-1}$$

$$+ \cdots + \frac{1}{(j-1)!} \frac{d^{j-1}}{ds^{j-1}} \begin{bmatrix} N(s_i) \\ D(s_i) \end{bmatrix} z_{i1},$$

(4.66)

$$j = 1, 2, \ldots, p_i, \quad i = 1, 2, \ldots, w,$$

where $z_{ij} \in \mathbb{C}^\beta$, $j = 1, 2, \ldots, p_i$, $i = 1, 2, \ldots, w$, are an arbitrary group of parameter vectors.

In order to prove the above result, we need the following lemma.

Lemma 4.1 *Let $P(s)$ be a polynomial matrix in the form of*

$$P(s) = P_0 + P_1 s + \cdots + P_l s^l,$$

(4.67)

and define

$$\Theta(l - k) = \sum_{i=0}^{k} \left(s^i C_{i+l-k}^{l-k} P_{i+l-k} \right), \quad k = 0, 1, \ldots, l.$$

(4.68)

Then

$$\Theta(l - k) = \frac{1}{(l-k)!} \frac{d^{l-k}}{ds^{l-k}} P(s), \quad k = 0, 1, 2, \ldots, l.$$

(4.69)

Proof. By (4.68), we have

$$\Theta(l - k) = C_{l-k}^{l-k} P_{l-k} + s^1 C_{1+l-k}^{l-k} P_{1+l-k} + \cdots + s^k C_l^{l-k} P_l.$$

Inserting $k = 0, 1, 2, \ldots, l$, into the above formula yields

$$\begin{cases} \Theta(l) = C_l^l P_l \\ \Theta(l-1) = C_{l-1}^{l-1} P_{l-1} + s^1 C_l^{l-1} P_l \\ \Theta(l-2) = C_{l-2}^{l-2} P_{l-k} + s^1 C_{l-1}^{l-2} P_{l-1} + s^2 C_l^{l-2} P_l \\ \vdots \\ \Theta(0) = C_0^0 P_0 + s^1 C_1^0 P_1 + \cdots + s^l C_l^{l-l} P_l. \end{cases} \tag{4.70}$$

On the other hand, according to (4.69), we have

$$\begin{aligned} \Theta(0) &= \frac{1}{0!} \frac{d^0}{ds^0} P(s) \\ &= P_0 + P_1 s + \cdots + P_l s^l \\ &= C_0^0 P_0 + s^1 C_1^0 P_1 + \cdots + s^l C_l^0 P_l, \end{aligned} \tag{4.71}$$

$$\begin{aligned} \Theta(1) &= \frac{1}{1!} \frac{d}{ds} P(s) \\ &= P_1 + 2P_2 s + \cdots + l P_l s^{l-1} \\ &= C_1^1 P_1 + C_2^1 P_2 s + \cdots + l C_l^1 P_l s^{l-1}, \end{aligned} \tag{4.72}$$

and

$$\begin{aligned} \Theta(2) &= \frac{1}{2!} \frac{d^2}{ds^2} P(s) \\ &= \frac{1}{2!} \left(2P_2 + 3 \times 2P_3 s + \cdots + l \times (l-1) P_l s^{l-2} \right) \\ &= C_2^2 P_2 + C_3^2 P_3 s + \cdots + C_l^2 P_l s^{l-2}. \end{aligned} \tag{4.73}$$

Continuing this process, finally yields

$$\Theta(l) = \frac{1}{l!} \frac{d^l}{ds^l} P(s) = C_l^l P_l. \tag{4.74}$$

Comparing the equations in (4.70) with equations (4.71) through (4.74) clearly gives the conclusion. ■

With the help of Lemma A.1 and the above lemma, we can now derive the following main result of this section from Theorem 4.7.

Proof. (*Proof of Theorem* 4.8) Write the Solution Formula I$_H$, that is, (4.59), in the form of

$$\begin{bmatrix} V \\ W \end{bmatrix} = \begin{bmatrix} N_0 \\ D_0 \end{bmatrix} Z + \begin{bmatrix} N_1 \\ D_1 \end{bmatrix} ZF + \cdots + \begin{bmatrix} N_\omega \\ D_\omega \end{bmatrix} ZF^\omega.$$

Then by Convention C1, we have

$$\begin{bmatrix} V_i \\ W_i \end{bmatrix} = \sum_{k=0}^{\omega} \begin{bmatrix} N_k \\ D_k \end{bmatrix} Z_i F_i^k$$

$$= \begin{bmatrix} N_0 \\ D_0 \end{bmatrix} Z_i + \begin{bmatrix} N_1 \\ D_1 \end{bmatrix} Z_i F_i + \cdots + \begin{bmatrix} N_\omega \\ D_\omega \end{bmatrix} Z_i F_i^\omega, \qquad (4.75)$$

$$i = 1, 2, \ldots, w.$$

Note that

$$F_i = s_i I_{p_i} + E_i, \quad i = 1, 2, \ldots, w,$$

with

$$E_i = \begin{bmatrix} 0 & I_{p_i - 1} \\ 0 & 0 \end{bmatrix}_{p_i \times p_i}, \quad i = 1, 2, \ldots, w. \qquad (4.76)$$

Using the second conclusion in Lemma A.1 gives

$$F_i^k = s^k I_{p_i} + s_i^{k-1} C_k^1 E_i^1 + \cdots + s_i^0 C_k^k E_i^k$$

$$= \sum_{j=0}^{k} s_i^{k-j} C_k^j E_i^j. \qquad (4.77)$$

Substituting equation (4.77) into equation (4.75) and through some simplification yields

$$\begin{bmatrix} V_i \\ W_i \end{bmatrix} = \sum_{k=0}^{\omega} \begin{bmatrix} N_k \\ D_k \end{bmatrix} Z_i F_i^k$$

$$= \sum_{k=0}^{\omega} \begin{bmatrix} N_k \\ D_k \end{bmatrix} Z_i \sum_{j=0}^{k} s_i^{k-j} C_k^j E_i^j$$

$$= \sum_{k=0}^{\omega} \sum_{j=0}^{k} \left(s_i^j C_{j+\omega-k}^{\omega-k} \begin{bmatrix} N_{j+\omega-k} \\ D_{j+\omega-k} \end{bmatrix} \right) Z_i E_i^k$$

$$= \Theta_i(0) Z_i I_{p_i} + \Theta_i(1) Z_i E_i + \cdots$$

$$\quad + \Theta_i(\omega - 1) Z_i E_i^{\omega-1} + \Theta_i(\omega) Z_i E_i^\omega, \qquad (4.78)$$

where

$$\Theta_i\left(\omega - k\right) = \sum_{j=0}^{k}\left(\mathcal{I}_i^j C_{j+\omega-k}^{\omega-k}\begin{bmatrix} N_{j+\omega-k} \\ D_{j+\omega-k} \end{bmatrix}\right), \tag{4.79}$$

$$k = 0, 1, \ldots, \omega.$$

Thus based on (4.78) and Convention C1, we can derive

$$\begin{bmatrix} v_{ij} \\ w_{ij} \end{bmatrix} = \Theta_i\left(0\right) z_{ij} + \Theta_i\left(1\right) Z_i\left(E_i\right)_j + \cdots$$

$$+ \Theta_i\left(\omega - 1\right) Z_i\left(E_i^{\omega-1}\right)_j + \Theta_i\left(\omega\right) Z\left(E_i^{\omega}\right)_j. \tag{4.80}$$

Further, using the first conclusion in Lemma A.1, we have

$$Z_i\left(E_i^k\right)_j = z_{i,j-k}, \quad k = 1, 2, \ldots, \omega.$$

Substituting these relations into (4.80) gives

$$\begin{bmatrix} v_{ij} \\ w_{ij} \end{bmatrix} = \Theta_i\left(0\right) z_{ij} + \Theta_i\left(1\right) z_{i,j-1} + \cdots + \Theta_i\left(\omega\right) z_{i,j-\omega},$$

$$j = 1, 2, \ldots, p_i, \quad i = 1, 2, \ldots, w.$$

Finally, using Lemma 4.1, and noticing that z_{ij}, $j \leq 0$, do not exist, we can write the above expression in the form of (4.66). The proof is then completed. ■

4.5.2 Example

Example 4.4

Consider the third-order GSE in the form of (4.50) treated in Example 4.3 again, where

$$A_3 = \begin{bmatrix} 1 & 0 & 0 \\ 0 & 1 & 0 \\ 0 & 0 & 0 \end{bmatrix}, \; A_2 = \begin{bmatrix} 1 & 0 & 1 \\ 0 & 2 & -1 \\ 1 & -1 & 3 \end{bmatrix},$$

$$A_1 = \begin{bmatrix} 2 & 0 & 0 \\ 0 & 1 & 2 \\ 0 & 2 & 1 \end{bmatrix}, \; A_0 = \begin{bmatrix} 0 & -1 & 0 \\ -1 & 1 & 2 \\ 0 & 1 & 1 \end{bmatrix},$$

$$B_3 = B_2 = B_1 = 0, \; B_0 = \begin{bmatrix} 1 & 0 \\ 0 & 0 \\ 0 & 1 \end{bmatrix}.$$

The F matrix is chosen to be

$$F = \begin{bmatrix} -1 & 1 \\ 0 & -1 \end{bmatrix}.$$

Using Lemma 3.4, a pair of polynomial matrices $N(s)$ and $D(s)$ satisfying the RCF (4.56) are obtained as

$$N(s) = \begin{bmatrix} s^3 + 2s^2 + s + 1 & -s^2 + 2s + 2 \\ 1 & 0 \\ 0 & 1 \end{bmatrix},$$

$$D(s) = \left[\begin{matrix} s^6 + 3s^5 + 5s^4 + 6s^3 + 3s^2 + 2s - 1 \\ s^5 + 2s^4 + s^3 + 2s + 1 \end{matrix} \right.$$

$$\left. \begin{matrix} -s^5 + s^4 + 2s^3 + 7s^2 + 4s \\ -s^4 + 2s^3 + 5s^2 + s + 1 \end{matrix} \right].$$

Note that the given matrix F is actually a Jordan matrix. Using Theorem 4.8, we have for this equation the following general solution

$$V = \begin{bmatrix} v_{11} & v_{12} \end{bmatrix}, \quad W = \begin{bmatrix} w_{11} & w_{12} \end{bmatrix},$$

with

$$\begin{bmatrix} v_{11} \\ w_{11} \end{bmatrix} = \begin{bmatrix} N(-1) \\ D(-1) \end{bmatrix} z_{11},$$

and

$$\begin{bmatrix} v_{12} \\ w_{12} \end{bmatrix} = \begin{bmatrix} N(-1) \\ D(-1) \end{bmatrix} z_{12} + \frac{1}{1!} \frac{d}{ds} \begin{bmatrix} N(-1) \\ D(-1) \end{bmatrix} z_{11}.$$

Since

$$\frac{d}{ds} N(s) = \begin{bmatrix} 3s^2 + 4s + 1 & -2s + 2 \\ 0 & 0 \\ 0 & 0 \end{bmatrix},$$

$$\frac{d}{ds} D(s) = \left[\begin{matrix} 6s^5 + 15s^4 + 20s^3 + 18s^2 + 6s + 2 \\ 5s^4 + 8s^3 + 3s^2 + 2 \end{matrix} \right.$$

$$\left. \begin{matrix} -5s^4 + 4s^3 + 6s^2 + 14s + 4 \\ -4s^3 + 6s^2 + 10s + 1 \end{matrix} \right],$$

with the matrix Z given by

$$Z = \begin{bmatrix} 1 & 0 \\ 0 & 1 \\ 3 & 1 \end{bmatrix},$$

we can obtain

$$\begin{bmatrix} v_{11} \\ w_{11} \end{bmatrix} = \begin{bmatrix} 1 & -1 & 0 \\ 1 & 0 & 0 \\ 0 & 1 & 0 \\ -3 & 3 & -1 \\ -1 & 2 & 0 \end{bmatrix} \begin{bmatrix} 1 \\ 0 \\ 3 \end{bmatrix} = \begin{bmatrix} 1 \\ 1 \\ 0 \\ -6 \\ -1 \end{bmatrix},$$

and

$$\begin{bmatrix} v_{12} \\ w_{12} \end{bmatrix} = \begin{bmatrix} 1 & -1 & 0 \\ 1 & 0 & 0 \\ 0 & 1 & 0 \\ -3 & 3 & -1 \\ -1 & 2 & 0 \end{bmatrix} \begin{bmatrix} 0 \\ 1 \\ 1 \end{bmatrix} + \begin{bmatrix} 0 & 4 & 0 \\ 0 & 0 & 0 \\ 0 & 0 & 0 \\ 3 & -13 & 0 \\ 2 & 1 & 0 \end{bmatrix} \begin{bmatrix} 1 \\ 0 \\ 3 \end{bmatrix}$$

$$= \begin{bmatrix} -1 & 0 & 1 & 5 & 4 \end{bmatrix}^{\mathrm{T}}.$$

Therefore, a solution is obtained as

$$V = \begin{bmatrix} 1 & -1 \\ 1 & 0 \\ 0 & 1 \end{bmatrix}, \quad W = \begin{bmatrix} -6 & 5 \\ -1 & 4 \end{bmatrix}.$$

4.6 Case of *F* Being Diagonal

In many applications, the matrix F in the higher-order GSE (4.50) is a diagonal matrix, that is,

$$F = \mathrm{diag}\left(s_1, s_2, \ldots, s_p\right), \tag{4.81}$$

where $s_i \in \mathbb{C}$, $i = 1, 2, \ldots, p$, may not be distinct. Such a special case is often encountered in practical applications and hence is very important. In this section, we provide a complete parametric general solution to the higher-order GSE (4.50) for this important special case.

When the matrix F is diagonal, by Convention C1 the columns v_{i1}, w_{i1}, and z_{i1} of matrices V, W, and Z, respectively, are well-defined. Without loss of generality, we can further denote v_{i1}, w_{i1}, and z_{i1} simply by v_i, w_i, and z_i. This is the following convention.

Convention C2. Any matrix X possessing p columns corresponds by the structure of the diagonal matrix F in (4.81) to a group of vectors x_i, $i = 1, 2, \ldots, p$, in the following manner:

$$X = \begin{bmatrix} x_1 & x_2 & \cdots & x_w \end{bmatrix}. \tag{4.82}$$

It can also be noted that, when the matrix F is in the form of (4.81), Assumption 4.3 simply becomes

Assumption 4.5 $\begin{cases} \operatorname{rank} \begin{bmatrix} A(s) & B(s) \end{bmatrix} \leq \alpha, \ \forall s \in \mathbb{C} \\ \operatorname{rank} \begin{bmatrix} A(s_i) & B(s_i) \end{bmatrix} = \alpha, \quad i = 1, 2, \ldots, p. \end{cases}$

4.6.1 Case of Undetermined F

A diagonal matrix is also a Jordan matrix. Simply by replacing the Jordan matrix F in Theorem 4.8 with the diagonal matrix F in the form of (4.81), we can obtain a general solution to the GSE (4.50) with F being given by (4.81).

Theorem 4.9 *Let $A(s) \in \mathbb{R}^{n \times q}[s]$, $B(s) \in \mathbb{R}^{n \times r}[s]$, $q + r > n$, be given in (4.51), $F \in \mathbb{C}^{p \times p}$ be a diagonal matrix in the form of (4.81), and Assumption 4.5 hold. Further, let $N(s) \in \mathbb{R}^{q \times \beta}[s]$ and $D(s) \in \mathbb{R}^{r \times \beta}[s]$ be given by (4.58) and satisfy the generalized RCF (4.56). Then all the solutions V and W to the GSE (4.50) are given by*

$$\boxed{\begin{array}{l} \textit{Formula III}_H \\[4pt] \begin{bmatrix} v_i \\ w_i \end{bmatrix} = \begin{bmatrix} N(s_i) \\ D(s_i) \end{bmatrix} z_i, \quad i = 1, 2, \ldots, p, \end{array}} \tag{4.83}$$

where $z_i \in \mathbb{C}^{\beta}$, $i = 1, 2, \ldots, p$, are a group of arbitrary parameter vectors that represent the degrees of freedom in the solution.

Simplicity is the ultimate sophistication, is the best art. The above general complete parametric solution Formula III$_H$ given in (4.83) to the GSE (4.50) for the case of F being a diagonal matrix turns out to be just extremely simple. Yet this case is also the mostly encountered one in applications. What is more, with the help of similarity transformations, this diagonal case can also be applied to the case that F is nondefective since a nondefective matrix is similar to a diagonal matrix.

The degrees of freedom existed in this solution Formula III$_H$ (4.83) are represented by the set of vectors z_i, $i = 1, 2, \ldots, p$. Again, this solution allows the eigenvalues of the matrix F to be set undetermined, but restricted to make the polynomial matrices $A(s)$ and $B(s)$ be F-left coprime with rank α. Particularly, in the case that $(A(s), B(s))$ is controllable, the matrix F can be arbitrarily chosen. These degrees of freedom may give great convenience and advantages to many analysis and design problems in control system theory.

In the case of $\beta = r$, and

$$\det D(s_i) \neq 0, \quad i = 1, 2, \ldots, p,$$

we can make the following variable substitution:

$$z_i' = D(s_i) z_i, \quad i = 1, 2, \ldots, p,$$

and now the above solution becomes

$$\begin{bmatrix} v_i \\ w_i \end{bmatrix} = \begin{bmatrix} N(s_i) D^{-1}(s_i) \\ I_r \end{bmatrix} z_i', \quad i = 1, 2, \ldots, p.$$

By the definition of $N(s)$ and $D(s)$, in this case of $q = n$ and

$$\det A(s_i) \neq 0, \quad i = 1, 2, \ldots, p, \tag{4.84}$$

we also have the following solution:

$$\begin{bmatrix} v_i \\ w_i \end{bmatrix} = \begin{bmatrix} A^{-1}(s_i) B(s_i) \\ I_r \end{bmatrix} z_i', \quad i = 1, 2, \ldots, p.$$

The above solution does have a huge advantage, that is, it uses directly the original equation parameter polynomial matrices. However, there is one thing we must bear in mind—it is applicable to only square GSEs satisfying condition (4.84) and is only effective for the case of diagonal matrix F.

Example 4.5

Consider a type of nonrotating missiles described by the model (Duan and Wang 1992)

$$\dot{x} = Ax + Bu, \tag{4.85}$$

with

$$A = \begin{bmatrix} -0.5 & 1 & 0 & 0 & 0 \\ -62 & -0.16 & 0 & 0 & 30 \\ 10 & 0 & -50 & 40 & 5 \\ 0 & 0 & 0 & -40 & 0 \\ 0 & 0 & 0 & 0 & -20 \end{bmatrix}, \quad B = \begin{bmatrix} 0 & 0 \\ 0 & 0 \\ 0 & 0 \\ 4 & 0 \\ 0 & 20 \end{bmatrix}. \tag{4.86}$$

The associated GSE is in the form of

$$VF - AV = BW. \tag{4.87}$$

By Lemma 3.4, we can obtain

$$
N(s) = \begin{bmatrix}
1 & 0 \\
0.5 + s & 0 \\
0 & 1 \\
-\frac{1}{240}[122 + (0.5 + s)(0.16 + s)] & \frac{1}{40}(50 + s) \\
\frac{1}{30}[62 + (0.5 + s)(0.16 + s)] & 0
\end{bmatrix},
$$

and

$$
D(s) = \begin{bmatrix}
-\frac{1}{960}(s^3 + 40.66s^2 + 148) & \frac{1}{160}(s^2 + 90s + 2000) \\
\frac{1}{600}(s^3 + 20.66s^2 + 75.28s + 1241.6) & 0
\end{bmatrix}.
$$

Thus, it follows from Theorem 4.9 that the general solution to the corresponding GSE (4.87) is given by (4.83). In the following, we consider the case of

$$
F = \mathrm{diag}\,(-6 + 4\,\mathrm{i}, -6 - 4\,\mathrm{i}, -70, -60, -30).
$$

In order to find a pair of real matrices V and W, let us choose

$$
z_{1,2} = \begin{bmatrix} z_{11} \pm z_{21}\,\mathrm{i} \\ z_{12} \pm z_{22}\,\mathrm{i} \end{bmatrix}, \quad z_i = \begin{bmatrix} z_{i1} \\ z_{i2} \end{bmatrix}, \quad i = 3, 4, 5.
$$

As a mode decoupling requirement associated with the control design of the missile system (4.85) and (4.86), here we are interested in a class of solutions satisfying the following conditions:

$$
v_1\,(3) = v_2\,(3) = 0,
$$
$$
v_3\,(1) = v_3\,(2) = 0,
$$
$$
v_4\,(1) = v_4\,(2) = 0.
$$

According to formula (4.83), these constraints can be easily converted into constraints on the parameter vectors z_i, $i = 1 \sim 5$, as

$$
z_{12} = z_{22} = z_{31} = 0.
$$

Thus the parameter vectors z_i, $i = 1, 2, 3$, should possess the following structures:

$$
z_1 = \begin{bmatrix} z_{11} + z_{21}\,\mathrm{i} \\ 0 \end{bmatrix}, \quad z_2 = \begin{bmatrix} z_{11} - z_{21}\,\mathrm{i} \\ 0 \end{bmatrix}, \quad z_3 = \begin{bmatrix} 0 \\ z_{32} \end{bmatrix}.
$$

Particularly, specifying the free parameters as

$$\begin{cases} z_{11} = z_{32} = 1 \\ z_{21} = 0.5455 \\ z_{41} = z_{52} = 0 \\ z_{42} = -4 \\ z_{51} = 0.03184, \end{cases}$$

we then obtain the following specific solution:

$$V = \begin{bmatrix} 1+0.5455\,i & 1-0.5455\,i & 0 & 0 & 0.03184 \\ -7.6820+i & -7.6820-i & 0 & 0 & -0.9392 \\ 0 & 0 & 1 & -4 & 0 \\ -0.6786-0.1249\,i & -0.6876+0.1249\,i & -0.5 & 1 & -0.13296 \\ 3.4290-0.0916\,i & 3.4290+0.0916\,i & 0 & 0 & 1 \end{bmatrix},$$

and

$$W = \begin{bmatrix} -5.6432-1.7405\,i & -5.6432+1.7405\,i & 3.75 & -5 & -0.3324 \\ 2.4185+0.6217\,i & 2.4185-0.6217\,i & 0 & 0 & -0.5 \end{bmatrix}.$$

4.6.2 Case of Determined F

In Section 4.6.1, solution to the homogeneous GSE (4.50) with matrix F being diagonal is considered, where the eigenvalues of the matrix F are not needed until the very last step to express the solution, and hence can be set undetermined.

In this subsection, we still treat the case that the matrix F is in the diagonal form of (4.81), but with the eigenvalues s_i, $i = 1, 2, \ldots, p$, being known. The technique applied here is first presented in Section 3.6, with strict proof for the controllable case. The results in this subsection are presented without strict proofs.

It is clearly observed from Section 4.6.1 that, when the matrix F is diagonal, a general solution to the homogeneous GSE (4.50) can be immediately written out when a pair of right coprime polynomial matrices $N(s) \in \mathbb{R}^{q \times \beta}[s]$ and $D(s) \in \mathbb{R}^{r \times \beta}[s]$ given by (4.58) and satisfy (4.56) are obtained. More importantly, it can be observed that it is the values of these polynomials at s_i, $i = 1, 2, \ldots, p$, namely, $N(s_i)$, $D(s_i)$, $i = 1, 2, \ldots, p$, that are really used in the solutions. Therefore, in the case that the eigenvalues s_i, $i = 1, 2, \ldots, p$, are prescribed, we may try to *compute these values $N(s_i)$, $D(s_i)$, $i = 1, 2, \ldots, p$, directly instead of solving the two polynomial matrices.*

In Section 3.6, we have given a numerical method for solving RCF and DPE based on the well-known SVD. In the following, we also adopt SVDs to fulfil this task. The basic idea is the same.

Under Assumption 4.3, or equivalently Assumption 4.5 when F is diagonal, we have, by Theorem 3.7, the following SFR:

$$P(s)\begin{bmatrix}A(s) & -B(s)\end{bmatrix}Q(s) = \begin{bmatrix}\Sigma(s) & 0\\ 0 & 0\end{bmatrix}, \tag{4.88}$$

with $\Sigma(s) \in \mathbb{R}^{\alpha\times\alpha}[s]$ diagonal and satisfying

$$\det \Sigma(s_i) \neq 0, \quad i = 1, 2, \ldots, p. \tag{4.89}$$

Further, it follows from Lemma 3.4 that, when $Q(s)$ is partitioned as

$$Q(s) = \begin{bmatrix}* & N(s)\\ * & D(s)\end{bmatrix}, \quad N(s) \in \mathbb{R}^{q\times\beta}[s], \quad D(s) \in \mathbb{R}^{r\times\beta}[s],$$

the following generalized RCF holds:

$$A(s)N(s) - B(s)D(s) = 0.$$

On the other side, if we apply SVD to $\begin{bmatrix}A(s_i) & -B(s_i)\end{bmatrix}$, we can obtain two orthogonal matrices P_i, Q_i and a nonsingular diagonal matrix Σ_i satisfying the following:

$$P_i\begin{bmatrix}A(s_i) & -B(s_i)\end{bmatrix}Q_i = \begin{bmatrix}\Sigma_i & 0\\ 0 & 0\end{bmatrix}, \quad i = 1, 2, \ldots, p. \tag{4.90}$$

Further, partition the matrix Q_i as

$$Q_i = \begin{bmatrix}* & N_i\\ * & D_i\end{bmatrix}, \quad N_i \in \mathbb{R}^{q\times\beta}, \quad D_i \in \mathbb{R}^{r\times\beta}. \tag{4.91}$$

Then we have from (4.90),

$$A(s_i)N_i - B(s_i)D_i = 0, \quad i = 1, 2, \ldots, p. \tag{4.92}$$

Comparison of the above two aspects clearly suggests that

$$\begin{cases}N_i = N(s_i)\\ D_i = D(s_i), \quad i = 1, 2, \ldots, p.\end{cases} \tag{4.93}$$

With the above preparation, and using Theorem 4.9, we immediately have the following result about a particular solution to the homogeneous GSE (4.50).

Theorem 4.10   *Let $A(s) \in \mathbb{R}^{n\times q}[s]$, $B(s) \in \mathbb{R}^{n\times r}[s]$, $q + r > n$, be given in (4.51), $F \in \mathbb{C}^{p\times p}$ be in the diagonal form of (4.81), and Assumption 4.5 hold. Further, let*

$N_i \in \mathbb{R}^{q \times \beta}$ and $D_i \in \mathbb{R}^{r \times \beta}$, $i = 1, 2, \ldots, p$, be given by (4.90) and (4.91). Then all the solutions V and W to the GSE (4.50) are given by

$$
\boxed{
\begin{array}{l}
\textit{Formula } III^*_H \\[2mm]
\begin{bmatrix} v_i \\ w_i \end{bmatrix} = \begin{bmatrix} N_i \\ D_i \end{bmatrix} z_i, \quad i = 1, 2, \ldots, p,
\end{array}
}
\tag{4.94}
$$

where $z_i \in \mathbb{C}^\beta$, $i = 1, 2, \ldots, p$, are a group of arbitrary parameter vectors that represents the degrees of freedom in the solution.

Obviously, the above general complete parametric solution (4.94) to the GSE (4.50) for the case of F being a known diagonal matrix turns out to be even simpler. This is of course a huge advantage. Besides simplicity, another huge advantage of this solution is its numerical reliability ensured by the well-known numerical stability property of SVDs. Since s_i, $i = 1, 2, \ldots, p$, are used to derive $N_i, D_i, i = 1, 2, \ldots, p$, they are now no longer degrees of freedom. Nevertheless, this solution still provides all the degrees of freedom beyond the eigenvalues of F represented by the group of arbitrary parameter vectors $z_i \in \mathbb{C}^\beta$, $i = 1, 2, \ldots, p$.

Example 4.6

Again, consider the well-known space rendezvous system described by the C-W equation, with a failed thruster, treated in Example 3.1. The system has a standard matrix second-order form of

$$
\ddot{x} + D\dot{x} + Kx = Bu,
$$

with

$$
D = \begin{bmatrix} 0 & -2\omega & 0 \\ 2\omega & 0 & 0 \\ 0 & 0 & 0 \end{bmatrix}, \quad K = \begin{bmatrix} -3\omega^2 & 0 & 0 \\ 0 & 0 & 0 \\ 0 & 0 & \omega^2 \end{bmatrix}, \quad B = \begin{bmatrix} 1 & 0 \\ 0 & 0 \\ 0 & 1 \end{bmatrix}.
$$

As shown in Example 3.1, this system is not controllable, it has an uncontrollable mode at the origin. Also, a pair of right coprime polynomial matrices satisfying the RCF (4.56) are obtained as

$$
\begin{cases}
N(s) = \begin{bmatrix} -s & 0 \\ 2\omega & 0 \\ 0 & 1 \end{bmatrix} \\[4mm]
D(s) = \begin{bmatrix} -4\omega^2 s - (s^2 - 3\omega^2)s & 0 \\ 0 & s^2 + \omega^2 \end{bmatrix}.
\end{cases}
$$

Thus, it follows from Theorem 4.9 that when

$$
z_i = \begin{bmatrix} 1 \\ \alpha_i \end{bmatrix}, \quad i = 1, 2, \ldots, p,
\tag{4.95}
$$

the solutions to the corresponding GSE are given by

$$v_i = \begin{bmatrix} -s_i \\ 2\omega \\ \alpha_i \end{bmatrix}, \quad w_i = \begin{bmatrix} -4\omega^2 s_i - \left(s_i^2 - 3\omega^2\right) s_i \\ \alpha_i \left(s_i^2 + \omega^2\right) \end{bmatrix}, \quad i = 1, 2, \dots, p.$$

In the following let us consider the same GSE using Theorem 4.10. Let us assume that the target is moving on a geosynchronous orbit, with $\omega = 7.292115 \times 10^{-5}$ rad/s. Also, let us choose

$$F = \text{diag}(-1, -2, -3, -4, -5).$$

Then we have

$$N_1 = \begin{bmatrix} 0.707106775546493 & 0 \\ 0.000103126078491 & 0 \\ 0 & 0.707106779306529 \end{bmatrix},$$

$$N_2 = \begin{bmatrix} 0.242535624694947 & 0 \\ 0.000017685976669 & 0 \\ 0 & 0.242535624732878 \end{bmatrix},$$

$$N_3 = \begin{bmatrix} 0.110431526008804 & 0 \\ 0.000005368529249 & 0 \\ 0 & 0.110431526010396 \end{bmatrix},$$

$$N_4 = \begin{bmatrix} 0.062378286134369 & 0 \\ 0.000002274348180 & 0 \\ 0 & 0.062378286134530 \end{bmatrix},$$

$$N_5 = \begin{bmatrix} 0.039968038340357 & 0 \\ 0.000001165806128 & 0 \\ 0 & 0.039968038340384 \end{bmatrix},$$

and

$$D_1 = \begin{bmatrix} 0.707106779306530 & 0 \\ 0 & 0.707106783066566 \end{bmatrix},$$

$$D_2 = \begin{bmatrix} 0.970142500069468 & 0 \\ 0 & 0.970142500221196 \end{bmatrix},$$

$$D_3 = \begin{bmatrix} 0.993883734666458 & 0 \\ 0 & 0.993883734680780 \end{bmatrix},$$

$$D_4 = \begin{bmatrix} 0.998052578481598 & 0 \\ 0 & 0.998052578484179 \end{bmatrix},$$

$$D_5 = \begin{bmatrix} 0.999200958721450 & 0 \\ 0 & 0.999200958722129 \end{bmatrix}.$$

With these matrices determined, the general solution is given by

$$\begin{cases} v_i = N_i z_i \\ w_i = D_i z_i, \quad i = 1, 2, \dots, 5. \end{cases}$$

Particularly, choosing

$$z_i = \begin{bmatrix} 1 \\ 1 \end{bmatrix}, \quad i = 1, 2, \ldots, 5,$$

gives the following solutions,

$$V = \begin{bmatrix} 0.70710678 & 0.24253562 & 0.11043153 & 0.06237827 & 0.03996804 \\ 0.00010313 & 0.00001769 & 0.00000537 & 0.00000227 & 0.00000117 \\ 0.70710678 & 0.24253562 & 0.11043153 & 0.06237829 & 0.03996804 \end{bmatrix},$$

and

$$W = \begin{bmatrix} 0.70710678 & 0.97014250 & 0.99388373 & 0.99805258 & 0.99920096 \\ 0.70710678 & 0.97014250 & 0.99388373 & 0.99805258 & 0.99920096 \end{bmatrix}.$$

It can be verified that with the above obtained matrices V and W, we have

$$\left\| VF^2 + DVF + KV - BW \right\|_{fro} = 3.0758 \times 10^{-7},$$

where $\|.\|_{fro}$ stands for the Frobenius norm.

4.7 Examples

In order to further demonstrate out result for the case of diagonal matrix F, in this section let us consider again the practical examples given in Section 1.2 and treated in Section 3.5.

4.7.1 First-Order Systems

Example 4.7 (Multiagent Kinematics System)

Consider the multiagent kinematics system introduced in Example 1.2, which is a first-order system with the following coefficient matrices:

$$E = \begin{bmatrix} 8 & 0 & 0 & 0 & 0 \\ 0 & 1 & 0 & 0 & 0 \\ 0 & 0 & 10 & 0 & 0 \\ 0 & 0 & 0 & 1 & 0 \\ 0 & 0 & 0 & 0 & 12 \end{bmatrix},$$

$$A = \begin{bmatrix} -0.1 & 0 & 0 & 0 & 0 \\ 1 & 0 & -1 & 0 & 0 \\ 0 & 0 & -0.1 & 0 & 0 \\ 0 & 0 & 1 & 0 & -1 \\ 0 & 0 & 0 & 0 & -0.1 \end{bmatrix}, \quad B = \begin{bmatrix} 1 & 0 & 0 \\ 0 & 0 & 0 \\ 0 & 1 & 0 \\ 0 & 0 & 0 \\ 0 & 0 & 1 \end{bmatrix}.$$

It has been proposed in Example 3.3 that this system is controllable, a pair of right coprime polynomial matrices $N(s)$ and $D(s)$ satisfying the generalized RCF (3.77) are given as

$$N(s) = \begin{bmatrix} 1 & 0 & 0 \\ 0 & 1 & 0 \\ 1 & -s & 0 \\ 0 & 0 & 1 \\ 1 & -s & -s \end{bmatrix},$$

and

$$D(s) = \begin{bmatrix} 8s + 0.1 & 0 & 0 \\ 10s + 0.1 & -s(10s + 0.1) & 0 \\ 12s + 0.1 & -s(12s + 0.1) & -s(12s + 0.1) \end{bmatrix}.$$

Thus according to formula (4.83), the general solution to the corresponding GSE with a diagonal matrix F in the form of (4.81) is given by

$$v_i = \begin{bmatrix} 1 & 0 & 0 \\ 0 & 1 & 0 \\ 1 & -s_i & 0 \\ 0 & 0 & 1 \\ 1 & -s_i & -s_i \end{bmatrix} z_i, \quad i = 1, 2, \ldots, p,$$

and

$$w_i = \begin{bmatrix} 8s_i + 0.1 & 0 & 0 \\ 10s_i + 0.1 & -s_i(10s_i + 0.1) & 0 \\ 12s_i + 0.1 & -s_i(12s_i + 0.1) & -s_i(12s_i + 0.1) \end{bmatrix} z_i, \quad i = 1, 2, \ldots, p.$$

Particularly, choosing

$$F = \text{diag}(-1 \pm 2\,\mathrm{i}, -3, -3, -4),$$

and

$$z_{1,2} = \begin{bmatrix} 1 \pm \mathrm{i} \\ 1 \\ \pm \mathrm{i} \end{bmatrix}, \quad z_3 = \begin{bmatrix} 1 \\ 0 \\ 0 \end{bmatrix},$$

$$z_4 = \begin{bmatrix} 1 \\ 1 \\ 1 \end{bmatrix}, \quad z_5 = \begin{bmatrix} 0 \\ 0 \\ 1 \end{bmatrix},$$

gives the following particular solution to the corresponding GSE:

$$
V = \begin{bmatrix} 1+i & 1-i & 1 & 1 & 0 \\ 1 & 1 & 0 & 1 & 0 \\ 2-i & 2+i & 1 & 4 & 0 \\ i & -i & 0 & 1 & 1 \\ 4 & 4 & 1 & 7 & 4 \end{bmatrix},
$$

and

$$
W = \begin{bmatrix} -23.9+8.1\,i & -23.9-8.1\,i & -23.9 & -23.9 & 0 \\ 0.2+49.9\,i & 0.2-49.9\,i & -29.9 & -119.6 & 0 \\ -47.6+96.0\,i & -47.6-96.0\,i & -35.9 & -251.3 & -191.6 \end{bmatrix}.
$$

Example 4.8 (Constrained Mechanical System in First-Order Form)

Consider the constrained system in first-order form given in Example 1.3, which has the following coefficient matrices:

$$
E = \begin{bmatrix} 1 & 0 & 0 & 0 & 0 \\ 0 & 1 & 0 & 0 & 0 \\ 0 & 0 & 1 & 0 & 0 \\ 0 & 0 & 0 & 1 & 0 \\ 0 & 0 & 0 & 0 & 0 \end{bmatrix},
$$

$$
A = \begin{bmatrix} 0 & 0 & 1 & 0 & 0 \\ 0 & 0 & 0 & 1 & 0 \\ -2 & 0 & -1 & -1 & 1 \\ 0 & -1 & -1 & -1 & 1 \\ 1 & 1 & 0 & 0 & 0 \end{bmatrix}, \; B = \begin{bmatrix} 0 \\ 0 \\ 1 \\ -1 \\ 0 \end{bmatrix}.
$$

It has been shown in Example 3.4 that the system is controllable and a pair of right coprime polynomial matrices $N(s)$ and $D(s)$ satisfying the generalized RCF (3.77) are given as

$$
N(s) = \begin{bmatrix} 1 \\ -1 \\ s \\ -s \\ \frac{1}{2} \end{bmatrix}, \; D(s) = s^2 + \frac{3}{2}.
$$

Thus according to formula (4.83), the general solution to the corresponding GSE with a diagonal matrix F in the form of (4.81) is given by

$$v_i = \begin{bmatrix} 1 \\ -1 \\ s_i \\ -s_i \\ \frac{1}{2} \end{bmatrix} z_i, \quad w_i = \left(s_i^2 + \frac{3}{2} \right) z_i, \quad i = 1, 2, \ldots, p.$$

Particularly, choosing

$$F = \text{diag}(-1, -2, -3),$$

and

$$z_1 = \begin{bmatrix} 1 \\ 0 \\ 0 \end{bmatrix}, \quad z_2 = \begin{bmatrix} 0 \\ 1 \\ 0 \end{bmatrix}, \quad z_3 = \begin{bmatrix} 0 \\ 0 \\ 1 \end{bmatrix},$$

gives the following particular solution to the corresponding GSE:

$$V = \frac{1}{2} \begin{bmatrix} 2 & 2 & 2 \\ -2 & -2 & -2 \\ -2 & -4 & -6 \\ 2 & 4 & 6 \\ 1 & 1 & 1 \end{bmatrix}, \quad W = \frac{1}{2} \begin{bmatrix} 5 & 11 & 21 \end{bmatrix}.$$

4.7.2 Second-Order Systems

Example 4.9 (Constrained Mechanical System in Second-Order Form)

Consider the constrained mechanical system treated in Example 1.3, which is in a matrix second-order form with the following coefficient matrices:

$$A_2 = \begin{bmatrix} 1 & 0 & 0 \\ 0 & 1 & 0 \\ 0 & 0 & 0 \end{bmatrix}, \quad A_1 = \begin{bmatrix} 1 & 1 & 0 \\ 1 & 1 & 0 \\ 0 & 0 & 0 \end{bmatrix},$$

$$A_0 = \begin{bmatrix} 2 & 0 & -1 \\ 0 & 1 & -1 \\ 1 & 1 & 0 \end{bmatrix}, \quad B = \begin{bmatrix} 1 \\ -1 \\ 0 \end{bmatrix}.$$

It has been shown in Example 3.5 that the system is controllable and a pair of right coprime polynomial matrices $N(s)$ and $D(s)$ satisfying the generalized RCF (3.77) are given as

$$N(s) = \frac{1}{2} \begin{bmatrix} 2 \\ -2 \\ 1 \end{bmatrix}, \quad D(s) = s^2 + \frac{3}{2}.$$

Thus according to formula (4.83), the general solution to the corresponding GSE with a diagonal matrix F in the form of (4.81) is given by

$$\begin{cases} v_i = \frac{1}{2} \begin{bmatrix} 2 \\ -2 \\ 1 \end{bmatrix} z_i \\ w_i = \left(s_i^2 + \frac{3}{2} \right) z_i, \quad i = 1, 2, \ldots, p. \end{cases}$$

Particularly, choosing

$$F = \text{diag}\,(-1, -2, -3, -4, -5, -6),$$

and

$$z_i = 1, 2, \ldots, 6,$$

gives the following particular solution to the corresponding GSE:

$$V = \frac{1}{2} \begin{bmatrix} 2 & 4 & 6 & 8 & 10 & 12 \\ -2 & -4 & -6 & -8 & -10 & -12 \\ 1 & 2 & 3 & 4 & 5 & 6 \end{bmatrix},$$

and

$$W = \frac{1}{2} \begin{bmatrix} 5 & 22 & 63 & 140 & 265 & 450 \end{bmatrix}.$$

Example 4.10 (Flexible-Joint Mechanism—Case of Second-Order Model)

The flexible-Joint mechanism treated in Example 1.4 is modeled by a system in a matrix second-order form with the following parameters:

$$M = 0.0004 \times \begin{bmatrix} 1 & 0 \\ 0 & 1 \end{bmatrix}, \quad D = \begin{bmatrix} 0 & 0 \\ 0 & 0.015 \end{bmatrix},$$

$$K = 0.8 \times \begin{bmatrix} 1 & -1 \\ -1 & 1 \end{bmatrix}, \quad B = \begin{bmatrix} 0 \\ 1 \end{bmatrix}.$$

It has been shown in Example 3.6 that the system is controllable and a pair of right coprime polynomial matrices $N\,(s)$ and $D\,(s)$ satisfying the generalized RCF (3.77) are given as

$$N\,(s) = \begin{bmatrix} 2000 \\ s^2 + 2000 \end{bmatrix},$$

$$D\,(s) = s\left(4 \times 10^{-4} s^3 + 0.015 s^2 + 1.6 s + 30 \right).$$

Thus according to formula (4.83), the general solution to the corresponding GSE with a diagonal matrix F in the form of (4.81) is given by

$$v_i = \begin{bmatrix} 2000 \\ s_i^2 + 2000 \end{bmatrix} z_i, \quad i = 1, 2, \ldots, p,$$

and

$$w_i = s_i \left(4 \times 10^{-4} s_i^3 + 0.015 s_i^2 + 1.6 s_i + 30 \right) z_i, \quad i = 1, 2, \ldots, p.$$

Particularly, choosing

$$F = \text{diag}(-1 \pm i, -1, -2),$$

and

$$z_i = 1, \quad i = 1, 2, 3, 4,$$

gives the following particular solution to the corresponding GSE:

$$V = \begin{bmatrix} 2000 & 2000 & 2000 & 2000 \\ 2000 - 2i & 2000 + 2i & 2001 & 2004 \end{bmatrix},$$

and

$$W = \begin{bmatrix} -29.972 + 26.83i & -29.972 - 26.83i & -28.415 & -53.714 \end{bmatrix}.$$

4.7.3 Higher-Order Systems

Example 4.11 (Flexible-Joint Mechanism—Case of Third-Order Model)

The flexible-joint mechanism treated in Example 1.5 is modeled by a system in matrix third-order form with the following parameters:

$$A_3 = \begin{bmatrix} 0 & 0 \\ 0 & 0.0004 \end{bmatrix}, \quad A_2 = 10^{-3} \times \begin{bmatrix} 0.4 & 0 \\ 0 & 15.38 \end{bmatrix},$$

and

$$A_1 = \begin{bmatrix} 0 & 0 \\ -0.8 & 0.814\,25 \end{bmatrix}, \quad A_0 = \begin{bmatrix} 0.8 & -0.8 \\ -0.76 & 0.76 \end{bmatrix}, \quad B = \begin{bmatrix} 0 \\ 1 \end{bmatrix}.$$

It has been shown in Example 3.7 that the system is controllable and a pair of right coprime polynomial matrices $N(s)$ and $D(s)$ satisfying the generalized RCF (3.77) are given as

$$N(s) = \begin{bmatrix} 2000 \\ s^2 + 2000 \end{bmatrix},$$

$$D(s) = s\left(0.0004s^4 + 0.01538s^3 + 1.614\,3s^2 + 31.52s + 28.5\right).$$

Thus according to formula (4.83), the general solution to the corresponding GSE with a diagonal matrix F in the form of (4.81) is given by

$$v_i = \begin{bmatrix} 2000 \\ s_i^2 + 2000 \end{bmatrix} z_i, \quad i = 1, 2, \ldots, p,$$

and

$$w_i = s_i\left(0.0004s_i^4 + 0.01538s_i^3 + 1.6143s_i^2 + 31.52s_i + 28.5\right) z_i,$$

$$i = 1, 2, \ldots, p.$$

Particularly, choosing

$$F = \operatorname{diag}(-1, -2, -3),$$

and

$$z_i = 1, \quad i = 1, 2, 3,$$

gives the following particular solution to the corresponding GSE:

$$V = \begin{bmatrix} 2000 & 2000 & 2000 \\ 2001 & 2004 & 2009 \end{bmatrix},$$

and

$$W = \begin{bmatrix} 1.4207 & 56.399 & 155.74 \end{bmatrix}.$$

4.8 Notes and References

In this chapter, general solutions to the several types of homogeneous GSEs are investigated (Figure 4.1). The main feature of these solutions is that they have a highly unified complete analytical parametric form, and the approach also unifies all the various types of GSEs. Because of this feature, we have not gone to cover all the cases in the text. Those cases that are really tackled in this chapter are shown in Table 4.1. Readers are suggested to give the presentations of the results for the rest cases by themselves.

Figure 4.1   We are here. (Modified from http://go.jutuw.com/zhumulangmafeng/photo/.)

Table 4.1   Homogeneous GSEs Treated in the Chapter

Cases	F *Arbitrary*	F *Jordan*	F *Diagonal*
Higher-order	Yes	Yes	Yes
Second-order	Yes	—	—
First-order (descriptor)	Yes	—	—
First-order (normal)	—	—	—

In the following, we mention some of the author's work related to the contents of this chapter.

The author has drawn attention to parametric solutions of GSEs since 1991. From 2005, a few of his PhD students joined this research under his guidance, and have produced cooperatively quite a few pieces of work, for example, Duan and Zhou (2005), Duan and Zhou (2006), Zhou and Duan (2005), Zhou and Duan (2006a), Zhou and Duan (2007b), Wu et al. (2008a), Wu et al. (2009c), Yu and Duan (2009a), Duan et al. (2009b), Yu and Duan (2010), Wang et al. (2007c), etc.

4.8.1 GSEs Associated with Normal Linear Systems

The first-order GSEs associated with normal linear systems in the form of (1.57), that is,

$$VF - AV = BW,\qquad (4.96)$$

have been one of our main targets for research. Our earliest result on this equation was reported in Duan (1993b). In this work, the author proposes two simple, complete, analytical, and restriction-free solutions with complete and explicit freedom of the matrix equation based on the assumption that (A, B) is known and is controllable, and F is in the Jordan form with arbitrary given eigenvalues. Using the proposed solutions of this matrix equation, a complete parametric approach for ESA in linear systems via state feedback is proposed, and two new algorithms are presented. The proposed solutions of the matrix equation and the ESA result are generalizations of some previous results and are simpler and more effective.

In 2005, a complete, general, and explicit solution to the generalized Sylvester matrix equation $AX - XF = BY$, with the matrix F in a companion form, is proposed by Zhou and Duan (2005). The solution is in an extremely neat form represented by a symmetric operator matrix, a Hankel matrix and the controllability matrix of the matrix pair (A, B). Furthermore, several equivalent forms of this solution are also presented. Based on these presented results, explicit solutions to the NSE and the well-known Lyapunov matrix equation are also established. The results provide great convenience to the analysis of the solution to the equation, and can perform important functions in many analysis and design problems in control system theory. As a demonstration, a simple and effective approach for parametric pole assignment is proposed.

Zhou and Duan (2007a) also propose explicit parametric solutions to the generalized Sylvester matrix equation without any transformation and factorization. The proposed solutions are presented in terms of the Krylov matrix of matrix pair (A, B), a symmetric operator, and the generalized observability matrix of matrix pair (Z, F) where Z is an arbitrary matrix and is used to denote the degrees of freedom in the solution.

Different from the above, Wu et al. (2008c) consider the GSEs of the same form, but with F being an arbitrary matrix. With the help of the Kronecker map, an explicit parametric solution to this matrix equation is established. The proposed solution possesses a very simple and neat form, and allows the matrix F to be set undetermined.

4.8.2 GSEs Associated with Descriptor Linear Systems

The GSEs in the form of (1.56), that is,

$$EVF - AV = BW, \qquad (4.97)$$

have close relation with analysis and design problems of descriptor linear systems and have also attracted great attention.

Our earliest work on parametric solution to this type of equations is Duan (1992b), in which a simple, complete analytical restriction-free parametric solution with complete and explicit freedom of equation is proposed by using the Smith canonical form of the matrix $[sE - A \quad B]$. Based on the presented solution of this equation, an approach for ESA for the continuous descriptor system $E\dot{x} = Ax + Bu$ via descriptor-variable feedback $u = Kx$ is proposed; parametric forms of the gain matrix and the eigenvectors associated with the assigned finite closed loop eigenvalues are given. The approach possesses three advantages:

- It eliminates the requirements on the assigned finite closed loop poles;
- It provides more design parameters;
- It needs less computational work.

Besides the parametric approach proposed in Duan (1992b), the author proposes in Duan (1996) another one for the same equation with the matrix F being in a Jordan form with arbitrary eigenvalues. The approach also uses the Smith canonical form of the matrix $[sE - A \quad B]$, but gives a solution in a simple, direct, complete, and explicit parametric form.

In Zhou and Duan (2006a), a complete parametric solution to the equation is proposed. The primary feature of this solution is that the matrix F does not need to be in any canonical form, and may be even unknown *a priori*. The results provide great convenience to the computation and analysis of the solutions to this class of equations, and can perform important functions in many analysis and design problems in control system theory. Another piece of work on which the author cooperated with B. Zhou is Zhou and Duan (2007b), in which another complete parametric solution to this equation is proposed. The matrix F is firstly transformed into triangular form by Schur decomposition and then unimodular transformation or SVD is employed. The results can be easily extended to second-order case and higher-order case and can provide great convenience to the computation and analysis of the solutions to this class of equations. Also, Zhou and Duan (2009) generalize the results in Zhou and Duan (2005) and propose closed-form solutions to the matrix equation $AX - EXF = BY$ also for the case of F in a companion form.

Another main collaborator of the author on this equation is Aiguo Wu. In Wu and Duan (2007c) and Wu et al. (2008a), explicit solutions to this generalized Sylvester matrix equation are established. Particularly, the one in the latter paper is expressed in terms of the R-controllability matrix of (E, A, B), a generalized symmetric operator matrix and an observability matrix. Based on this solution, solutions to some other matrix equations are also derived. The results may provide great convenience for the analysis and synthesis problems related to these equations. In Wu et al. (2008d), a method for solving the generalized Sylvester matrix equation (4.97) via Kronecker map is proposed. While in Wu et al. (2009c), an explicit solution to the same GSE with the matrix F being a companion matrix is given. This solution is represented in terms of the R-controllability matrix of (E, A, B), generalized symmetric operator and a Hankel matrix. Several equivalent forms of this solution are presented. The obtained results may provide great convenience for many analysis and design problems.

Very recently, the author has investigated first-order homogeneous GSEs in the more general form of (1.55), that is,

$$EVF - AV = B_1 WF + B_0 W, \qquad (4.98)$$

and has proposed a general complete parametric solution in Duan (2013a) based on a generalized version of matrix fraction right factorization. The primary feature of this solution is that the parameter matrix F, which corresponds to the finite closed-loop Jordan matrix in the generalized ESA problem, does not need to be in any canonical form, and may be even unknown *a priori*.

4.8.3 Second-Order GSEs

For the second-order GSEs in the form of (1.68), that is,

$$MVF^2 + DVF + KV = BW, \qquad (4.99)$$

Duan and Zhou (2006) (see also the corresponding conference version Duan and Zhou (2005)) present an explicit parametric general solution for the case that the matrix F is an arbitrary square matrix. The proposed solution can be immediately obtained as soon as a pair of so-called F-right coprime polynomial matrices satisfying the relation

$$(Ms^2 + Ds + K)N(s) - BD(s) = 0$$

are derived. The proposed solution is very simple and neat, and does not require the matrix F to be in any canonical form. Furthermore, it gives all the degrees of freedom represented by the parameter matrix Z, and does not require the matrix F to be prescribed, and hence allow it to be set undetermined and used as a part of the degrees of freedom.

For the case that the matrix F is in a diagonal form, we have proposed in Wang et al. (2007c), under the controllability of the matrix triple (E, A, B), a complete, general, and explicit parametric solution to the second-order GSE in the form of (4.99).

Very recently, the type of second-order GSEs in the form of (1.66), that is,

$$MVF^2 + DVF + KV = B_2 WF^2 + B_1 WF + B_0 W, \qquad (4.100)$$

has been investigated by Duan (2013c). It is first shown that this type of equations are associated with the general ESA of a type of second-order linear systems. Regarding solution to this type of GSEs, degrees of freedom are first investigated using the concept of F-coprimeness, and a complete general parametric solution in a neat explicit closed form is then established using a generalized matrix fraction right factorization. The primary feature of this solution is that the matrix F does not need to be in any canonical form, or may be even unknown *a priori*.

Different from the above, based on a parametric solution for a class of second-order Sylvester matrix equations, we have considered the robust solution to a class of perturbed second-order Sylvester equation (Wang et al. 2009b).

4.8.4 Higher-Order GSEs

For the type of GSEs in the form of (1.73), that is,

$$A_m VF^m + \cdots + A_1 VF + A_0 V = BW, \qquad (4.101)$$

we have also proposed complete parametric solutions (see, Duan 2005a, Duan et al. 2009b, Yu and Duan 2009a, 2010). Particularly, the conference keynote paper Duan (2005a) has given a detailed treatment on this equation and its various special cases.

Duan et al. (2009b) present general parametric solutions to this type of equations for the case that the matrix F is arbitrary. By employing the proposed general parametric solutions, complete parametric control approaches for higher-order linear systems are presented. The proposed approaches give simple complete parametric expressions for the proportional plus derivative state feedback gains and the closed-loop eigenvector matrices, and produce all the design degrees of freedom. Furthermore, important special cases are treated, and an application of the proposed parametric design approaches to two missile control problems is also investigated. The simulation results show that the method is superior to the traditional one in the sense of either global stability or system performance.

Different from the above, both Yu and Duan (2009a) and Yu and Duan (2010) propose parametric solutions to this type of equations for the case that the matrix F is diagonal. The difference between the two approaches is that the one in Yu and Duan (2010) allows the matrix A_m to be singular. Based on the proposed parametric solutions, Yu and Duan (2009a) and Yu and Duan (2010) consider ESA via output feedback, particularly, the former one focuses on normal higher-order linear systems, while the latter focuses on descriptor higher-order linear systems. Parametric expressions for the left and right closed-loop eigenvectors associated with the finite closed-loop eigenvalues and two simple and complete parametric solutions for the feedback gain matrices are obtained on the basis of the parametric solutions of the generalized higher-order Sylvester matrix equations. Both approaches do not impose any restriction on the closed-loop eigenvalues.

The type of higher-order GSEs in the form of (1.71), that is,

$$A_m VF^m + \cdots + A_1 VF + A_0 V = B_m WF^m + \cdots + B_1 WF + B_0 W, \quad (4.102)$$

are investigated by Yu and Duan (2011) and Duan (2013b). Yu and Duan (2011) propose three completely analytical parametric solutions, which are expressed in terms of a set of parameter vectors representing the design degrees of freedom. These solutions do not require the eigenvalues of the matrix F to be distinct or to be different from the roots of $A(s)$, and also numerically very simple. Duan (2013b) first investigated the degrees of freedom using the concept of F-coprimeness and then proposed a complete general parametric solution in a neat explicit closed form using a generalized matrix fraction right factorization. The primary feature of this solution is that the matrix F does not need to be in any canonical form, or may be even unknown *a priori*.

4.8.5 Other Related Results

Besides the above, the author and his coauthors have also worked out quite some results related to solution of GSEs, for example, Zhang et al. (2004), which gives full-column rank solutions of the matrix equation $AV - EVJ = 0$; and Zhou and Duan (2008), which define the concept of the generalized Sylvester mapping and use it to solve some general matrix equations. A large amount of work can be classified into the following two big categories.

4.8.5.1 Numerical Solutions of GSEs

While having proposed general parametric solutions to the various types of GSEs, we have also produced numerical iterative algorithms for solving some of these GSEs. Representative pieces of work include Zhou et al. (2009a), and Zhou et al. (2009f). Specifically, Zhou et al. (2009a) propose a gradient-based iterative algorithm for solving coupled matrix equations; while Zhou et al. (2009f) give a weighted least squares solutions to general coupled Sylvester matrix equations. Among the iterative algorithms for solving GSEs, there exist a type of finite iterative algorithms. Some of our work on this aspect include Wu et al. (2010a), Wu et al. (2011a), and Li et al. (2010).

4.8.5.2 Sylvester-Conjugate Matrix Equations

Besides the GSEs mentioned in the book, we have also considered solution to a big type of GSEs that have simultaneously the unknowns and the conjugates of the unknowns in the equations, namely Sylvester-conjugate matrix equations. For some of these equations, we have also worked out parametric solutions and analytical closed-form solutions (Wu et al. 2010b, 2011b,c). Meanwhile, some iterative algorithms for solving these equations are also proposed (see, Wu et al. 2008b, 2010d,f, 2011a), particularly, we have also given some finite iterative algorithms in Wu et al. (2010a), Wu et al. (2010c), and Wu et al. (2011a).

Chapter 5

Nonhomogeneous GSEs

This chapter considers parametric solution to the following higher-order nonhomogeneous GSE:

$$\sum_{i=0}^{m} A_i V F^i = \sum_{i=0}^{m} B_i W F^i + R, \tag{5.1}$$

where

- $A_i \in \mathbb{R}^{n \times q}$, $B_i \in \mathbb{R}^{n \times r}$, $i = 0, 1, \ldots, m$, $F \in \mathbb{C}^{p \times p}$, and $R \in \mathbb{C}^{n \times p}$ are the parameter matrices
- $V \in \mathbb{C}^{q \times p}$ and $W \in \mathbb{C}^{r \times p}$ are the matrices to be determined

Again, the two polynomial matrices associated with this equation are

$$\begin{cases} A(s) = \sum_{i=0}^{m} A_i s^i, & A_i \in \mathbb{R}^{n \times q} \\ B(s) = \sum_{i=0}^{m} B_i s^i, & B_i \in \mathbb{R}^{n \times r}. \end{cases} \tag{5.2}$$

For linear algebraic equations, generally there holds the so-called additional principle. This certainly applies to the GSE (5.1).

Lemma 5.1 *If $\left(V_p, W_p\right)$ is a particular solution to the GSE (5.1), $\left(V_g, W_g\right)$ is the general solution to the corresponding homogeneous GSE (4.50), then a general solution (V, W) to the nonhomogeneous GSE (5.1) is given by*

$$V = V_g + V_p, \quad W = W_g + W_p. \tag{5.3}$$

Proof. By assumption of the lemma, we have

$$\sum_{i=0}^{m} A_i V_p F^i = \sum_{i=0}^{m} B_i W_p F^i + R, \tag{5.4}$$

and

$$\sum_{i=0}^{m} A_i V_g F^i = \sum_{i=0}^{m} B_i W_g F^i. \tag{5.5}$$

Adding the above two equations side by side gives

$$\sum_{i=0}^{m} A_i \left(V_p + V_g \right) F^i = \sum_{i=0}^{m} B_i \left(W_p + W_g \right) F^i + R, \tag{5.6}$$

which clearly gives the conclusion. ◼

Due to the above additional principle of solutions, in this chapter we will lay a special emphasis on a particular solution to the nonhomogeneous GSE (5.1).

As in Chapter 4, in this section we seek the solution to the nonhomogeneous GSE (5.1) under the following general assumption.

Assumption 5.1 *$A(s)$ and $B(s)$ are F-left coprime with rank α.*

We here remind the reader of the following scalar

$$\beta = q + r - \alpha,$$

introduced in Chapter 3, which is to be used in this chapter.

5.1 Solution Based on RCF and DPE

According to Lemma 5.1, to find the general solution to the nonhomogeneous GSE (5.1), we first need to get a special solution to the nonhomogeneous GSE (5.1).

5.1.1 Particular Solution

According to Theorem 3.9, under the condition that $A(s)$ and $B(s)$ are F-left coprime with rank α, there exist two polynomial matrices $U(s) \in \mathbb{R}^{q \times \alpha}[s]$ and $T(s) \in \mathbb{R}^{r \times \alpha}[s]$ satisfying the following DPE

$$A(s)U(s) - B(s)T(s) = C(s), \tag{5.7}$$

where $C(s) \in \mathbb{R}^{n \times \alpha} [s]$ satisfies the condition

$$\operatorname{rank} C(s) = \alpha, \ \forall s \in \operatorname{eig}(F). \tag{5.8}$$

Denote

$$U(s) = \left[U_{ij}(s)\right]_{q \times \alpha}, \ \ T(s) = \left[T_{ij}(s)\right]_{r \times \alpha},$$

and define

$$\varphi = \max\left\{\deg U_{ij}(s), \deg T_{ij}(s)\right\}, \ 1 \le i, j \le n,$$

then the two polynomial matrices $U(s)$ and $T(s)$ can be written in the following form:

$$\begin{cases} U(s) = \sum_{i=0}^{\varphi} U_i s^i, \ U_i \in \mathbb{R}^{q \times \alpha} \\ T(s) = \sum_{i=0}^{\varphi} T_i s^i, \ T_i \in \mathbb{R}^{r \times \alpha}. \end{cases} \tag{5.9}$$

Further, denote

$$C(s) = C_0 + C_1 s + \cdots + C_\psi s^\psi. \tag{5.10}$$

Then the main result in this subsection can be given as follows.

Theorem 5.1 *Let $A(s) \in \mathbb{R}^{n \times q} [s]$, $B(s) \in \mathbb{R}^{n \times r} [s]$, $q + r > n$, be given by (5.2), and Assumption 5.1 hold. Further, let $U(s) \in \mathbb{R}^{q \times \alpha} [s]$, $T(s) \in \mathbb{R}^{r \times \alpha} [s]$ and $C(s) \in \mathbb{R}^{n \times \alpha}$ be in the forms of (5.9) and (5.10) and given by (5.7) and (5.8). Then*

1. *The nonhomogeneous GSE (5.1) has a solution with respect to (V, W) if and only if there exists a matrix $R' \in \mathbb{C}^{\alpha \times p}$ satisfying*

$$\left[C(s)R'\right]\big|_F = C_0 R' + C_1 R' F + \cdots + C_\psi R' F^\psi = R. \tag{5.11}$$

2. *When such a matrix R' exists, a particular solution to the nonhomogeneous GSE (5.1) is given by*

$$\boxed{\begin{aligned} &\textit{Formula } I_N'' \\ &\begin{cases} V = \left[U(s)R'\right]\big|_F = U_0 R' + U_1 R' F + \cdots + U_\varphi R' F^\varphi \\ W = \left[T(s)R'\right]\big|_F = T_0 R' + T_1 R' F + \cdots + T_\varphi R' F^\varphi. \end{cases} \end{aligned}} \tag{5.12}$$

Proof. Sufficiency. Using the expressions in (5.9), we have

$$A(s)U(s) = \sum_{i=0}^{m} A_i s^i \sum_{i=0}^{\varphi} U_i s^i$$

$$= \sum_{i=0}^{m} \sum_{j=0}^{\varphi} A_i U_j s^{i+j}$$

$$= \sum_{k=0}^{\varphi+m} \left(\sum_{i=0}^{k} A_i U_{k-i} \right) s^k,$$

and

$$B(s)T(s) = \sum_{i=0}^{m} B_i s^i \sum_{i=0}^{\varphi} T_i s^i$$

$$= \sum_{i=0}^{m} \sum_{j=0}^{\varphi} B_i T_j s^{i+j}$$

$$= \sum_{k=0}^{\varphi+m} \left(\sum_{i=0}^{k} B_i T_{k-i} \right) s^k,$$

where $A_i = 0$, $B_i = 0$, when $i > m$, and $U_i = 0$, $T_i = 0$, when $i > \varphi$.
Further, by (5.7), we have

$$A(s)U(s) - B(s)T(s)$$

$$= \sum_{k=0}^{\varphi+m} \left(\sum_{i=0}^{k} (A_i U_{k-i} - B_i T_{k-i}) \right) s^k$$

$$= C_0 + C_1 s + C_2 s^2 + \cdots + C_\psi s^\psi.$$

Note that both sides of the above equation are polynomials in s. By equating the coefficients of the powers of s on both sides, we obtain the following relations:

$$\sum_{i=0}^{k} (A_i U_{k-i} - B_i T_{k-i}) = \begin{cases} C_k, & k = 0, 1, 2, \ldots, \psi \\ 0, & k = \psi + 1, \ldots, \psi + m. \end{cases} \quad (5.13)$$

With the above set of relations, we can now show that the pair of matrices V and W given in (5.12), with R' determined by (5.11), satisfy the GSE (5.1).

Using (5.12), we have

$$
\sum_{i=0}^{m} A_i V F^i = \sum_{i=0}^{m} A_i \left(\sum_{j=0}^{\varphi} U_j R' F^j \right) F^i
$$

$$
= \sum_{i=0}^{m} \sum_{j=0}^{\varphi} A_i U_j R' F^{i+j}
$$

$$
= \sum_{k=0}^{\varphi+m} \left(\sum_{i=0}^{k} A_i U_{k-i} \right) R' F^k,
$$

and

$$
\sum_{i=0}^{m} B_i W F^i = \sum_{i=0}^{m} B_i \left(\sum_{j=0}^{\varphi} T_j R' F^j \right) F^i
$$

$$
= \sum_{i=0}^{m} \sum_{j=0}^{\varphi} B_i T_j R' F^{i+j}
$$

$$
= \sum_{k=0}^{\varphi+m} \left(\sum_{i=0}^{k} B_i T_{k-i} \right) R' F^k.
$$

Further using (5.13) and (5.11), we finally obtain

$$
\sum_{i=0}^{m} A_i V F^i - \sum_{i=0}^{m} B_i W F^i
$$

$$
= \sum_{k=0}^{\varphi+m} \sum_{i=0}^{k} \left(A_i U_{k-i} - B_i T_{k-i} \right) R' F^k
$$

$$
= \sum_{k=0}^{\psi} C_k R' F^k
$$

$$
= R.
$$

This states that V and W given by (5.12), with R' determined by (5.11), satisfy the nonhomogeneous GSE (5.1).

Necessity. Suppose that the nonhomogeneous GSE (5.1) has a solution (V, W), that is, there exist matrices V and W satisfying

$$\sum_{i=0}^{m} A_i V F^i - \sum_{i=0}^{m} B_i W F^i = R. \tag{5.14}$$

Denote

$$\tilde{A}_i = [A_i \ -B_i], \quad i = 0, 1, \ldots, m, \quad \tilde{V} = \begin{bmatrix} V \\ W \end{bmatrix},$$

then the above equation can be written as

$$\sum_{i=0}^{m} \tilde{A}_i \tilde{V} F^i = R. \tag{5.15}$$

Therefore, there exists a matrix $\tilde{V}$ satisfying the above equation (5.15).

On the other hand, we can write the DPE (5.7) as

$$[A(s) \ -B(s)] \begin{bmatrix} U(s) \\ T(s) \end{bmatrix} = C(s), \tag{5.16}$$

or, more compactly, as

$$\tilde{A}(s)\tilde{N}(s) - \tilde{D}(s) = 0, \tag{5.17}$$

where

$$\tilde{A}(s) = [A(s) \ -B(s)],$$

and

$$\tilde{N}(s) = \begin{bmatrix} U(s) \\ T(s) \end{bmatrix}, \quad \tilde{D}(s) = C(s).$$

Now let us view (5.15) as a special homogeneous GSE with variables $\tilde{V}$ and R. Then, since $\tilde{A}_i = [A_i \ -B_i]$, $i = 0, 1, \ldots, m$, are actually the coefficients of the polynomial matrix $\tilde{A}(s)$, (5.17) is a generalized RCF associated with the homogeneous GSE (5.15). Therefore, by Theorem 4.7 we know that there exists an R', such that

$$R = \left[\tilde{D}(s)R' \right]\big|_F = [C(s)R']\big|_F,$$

and

$$\begin{bmatrix} V \\ W \end{bmatrix} = \tilde{V}$$

$$= \left[\tilde{N}(s)R' \right]\big|_F$$

$$= \begin{bmatrix} [U(s)R']\big|_F \\ [T(s)R']\big|_F \end{bmatrix}.$$

These two relations respectively give the condition (5.11) and the solution (5.12). ■

Remark 5.1 It is clearly seen from the above theorem that the solution (5.12) to a nonhomogeneous GSE turns out to be in the same format as that to a homogeneous GSE proposed in Chapter 4. Specifically, the polynomial matrices $U(s)$ and $T(s)$ correspond to $N(s)$ and $D(s)$, while the matrix R' corresponds to Z. Such a coincidence makes our approach highly unified—not only the solutions to the various homogeneous GSEs have a unified single general parametric form, but also the solutions to the homogeneous and nonhomogeneous GSEs can possess the same structure.

5.1.2 General Solution

Using Lemma 5.1, Theorems 4.7 and 5.1, we immediately have the following result about the general solution to the nonhomogeneous GSE (5.1).

Theorem 5.2 *Let* $A(s) \in \mathbb{R}^{n \times q}[s]$, $B(s) \in \mathbb{R}^{n \times r}[s]$ *and* $F \in \mathbb{C}^{p \times p}$ *satisfy Assumption 5.1. Furthermore, let*

1. $U(s) \in \mathbb{R}^{q \times \alpha}[s]$, $T(s) \in \mathbb{R}^{r \times \alpha}[s]$ *and* $C(s) \in \mathbb{R}^{n \times \alpha}$ *be in the forms of (5.9) and (5.10) and satisfy (5.7) and (5.8);*
2. $N(s) \in \mathbb{R}^{q \times \beta}[s]$ *and* $D(s) \in \mathbb{R}^{r \times \beta}[s]$ *be a pair of right coprime polynomial matrices given by (4.58) and satisfy the generalized RCF (4.56).*

Then the general complete solution (V, W) *to the nonhomogeneous GSE (5.1) is given by*

$$\boxed{\begin{array}{l} \textit{Formula } I''_G \\[2mm] \begin{bmatrix} V \\ W \end{bmatrix} = \left[\tilde{Q}(s) \begin{bmatrix} R' \\ Z \end{bmatrix} \right]\Big|_F = \sum_{i=0}^{\tau} \tilde{Q}_i \begin{bmatrix} R' \\ Z \end{bmatrix} F^i, \end{array}} \tag{5.18}$$

where R' is determined by (5.11), $Z \in \mathbb{C}^{\beta \times p}$ is an arbitrary parameter matrix, which represents the degrees of freedom in the solution, and $\tilde{Q}(s)$, as well as $\tilde{Q}_i$ and τ, are determined by

$$\tilde{Q}(s) = \begin{bmatrix} U(s) & N(s) \\ T(s) & D(s) \end{bmatrix} = \sum_{i=0}^{\tau} \tilde{Q}_i s^i. \qquad (5.19)$$

Proof. Using Lemma 5.1, Theorems 4.7 and 5.1, we immediately have the following general solution to the nonhomogeneous GSE (5.1) as

$$\begin{cases} V = [N(s)Z]\big|_F + [U(s)R']\big|_F = \sum_{i=0}^{\omega} N_i Z F^i + \sum_{j=0}^{\varphi} U_j R' F^j \\ W = [D(s)Z]\big|_F + [T(s)R']\big|_F = \sum_{i=0}^{\omega} D_i Z F^i + \sum_{j=0}^{\varphi} T_j R' F^j. \end{cases} \qquad (5.20)$$

This can clearly be re-arranged into the form of (5.18) in view of (5.19). ■

Remark 5.2 It is seen from the aforementioned theorem that the general parametric solution given by Formula I''_G (5.18) to the nonhomogeneous GSE (5.1) is also in the same form as that to the corresponding homogeneous GSE as proposed in Chapter 4. The correspondences are clear as follows:

$$\tilde{Q}(s) \longleftrightarrow \begin{bmatrix} N(s) \\ D(s) \end{bmatrix}, \begin{bmatrix} R' \\ Z \end{bmatrix} \longleftrightarrow Z.$$

This phenomenon is natural since both the general solution to a homogeneous GSE and a particular solution to the nonhomogeneous GSE possess the same structure, while the general solution to a nonhomogeneous GSE is obtained by the additional principle. Perhaps by now it is time for some readers to have a revisit at Section 1.5.3.

5.1.3 Solution to GSE (1.70)

Obviously, when the matrix R in the nonhomogeneous GSE (5.1) is restricted to the following specific form

$$R = \sum_{i=0}^{\psi} H_i R^* F^i, \qquad (5.21)$$

the nonhomogeneous GSE (5.1) becomes the GSE (1.70), that is,

$$\sum_{i=0}^{m} A_i V F^i = \sum_{i=0}^{m} B_i W F^i + \sum_{i=0}^{\psi} H_i R^* F^i. \qquad (5.22)$$

Meanwhile, the condition (5.11) of existence of a solution becomes the following conversion condition:

$$\sum_{i=0}^{\psi} C_i R' F^i = \sum_{i=0}^{\psi} H_i R^* F^i. \tag{5.23}$$

With this observation, and the help of the above Theorem 5.1, we immediately have the following result for solution to the GSE (5.22).

Theorem 5.3 *Let $A(s) \in \mathbb{R}^{n \times q} [s]$, $B(s) \in \mathbb{R}^{n \times r} [s]$, $q + r > n$, be given by (5.2), and Assumption 5.1 hold. Further, let $U(s) \in \mathbb{R}^{q \times \alpha} [s]$, $T(s) \in \mathbb{R}^{r \times \alpha} [s]$ and $C(s) \in \mathbb{R}^{n \times \alpha}$ be in the forms of (5.9) and (5.10) and given by (5.7) and (5.8). Then*

1. *The nonhomogeneous GSE (5.22) has a solution with respect to (V, W) if and only if there exists a matrix $R' \in \mathbb{C}^{\alpha \times p}$ satisfying the conversion condition (5.23);*
2. *When such a matrix R' exists, a particular to the nonhomogeneous GSE (5.1) is given by the Formula I''_N in (5.12).*

Note that the conversion condition automatically holds when

$$R = \sum_{i=0}^{\psi} C_i R' F^i.$$

Such an observation, together with the above Theorem 5.1, obviously gives the following corollary.

Corollary 5.1 *Let $A(s) \in \mathbb{R}^{n \times q} [s]$, $B(s) \in \mathbb{R}^{n \times r} [s]$, $q + r > n$, be given by (5.2), and Assumption 5.1 hold. Further, let $U(s) \in \mathbb{R}^{q \times \alpha} [s]$, $T(s) \in \mathbb{R}^{r \times \alpha} [s]$ and $C(s) \in \mathbb{R}^{n \times \alpha}$ be in the forms of (5.9) and (5.10) and given by (5.7) and (5.8). Then the following GSE*

$$\sum_{i=0}^{m} A_i V F^i = \sum_{i=0}^{m} B_i W F^i + \sum_{i=0}^{\psi} C_i R' F^i, \tag{5.24}$$

always has a solution with respect to (V, W) and a particular can be given by the Formula I''_N in (5.12).

The conversion conditions (5.11) and (5.23) are really NSEs, which are treated in Chapters 8 and 9. Therefore, the results in Chapters 8 and 9 can be of course applied to solve these two equations. In the next section, we will give a way of solving these conditions based on SFR.

5.2 Condition (5.11)

It is clearly seen from Theorem 5.1 that (5.11) is the condition for existence of solutions to the nonhomogeneous GSE (5.1). To solve a nonhomogeneous GSE, a solution to the equation (5.11) needs first to be found. Taking vec(.) both sides of (5.11) gives the following linear equation:

$$\sum_{i=1}^{\varphi} \left(\left(F^i\right)^{\mathrm{T}} \otimes C_i \right) \mathrm{vec}\left(R'\right) = \mathrm{vec}(R).$$

Therefore, when F and R are known, condition (5.11) can be easily checked by solving the above linear equation. However, with applications where the matrices F and R are not fully known *a priori*, this method by stretching operation is not valid. We point out that in this case the theories in Chapters 8 can be used since it can be easily recognized that (5.11) is actually an NSE.

In this section, let us give some equivalent forms of this condition for existence of solutions represented by (5.11) and find its explicit solution. Before proceeding, let us state the following basic result.

Lemma 5.2 *Let*

$$\alpha(s) = \alpha_0 + \alpha_1 s + \alpha_2 s^2 + \cdots + \alpha_q s^q, \tag{5.25}$$

be a scalar polynomial defined on $\mathbb{C}$. *Then*

$$\alpha(s) \neq 0, \ \forall s \in \mathrm{eig}\,(F), \tag{5.26}$$

holds for some square matrix $F \in \mathbb{C}^{p \times p}$ *if and only if*

$$\det \alpha(F) = \det \left(\alpha_0 I + \alpha_1 F + \alpha_2 F^2 + \cdots + \alpha_q F^q \right) \neq 0.$$

Proof. Let J be the Jordan form of F, and X be the corresponding eigenvector matrix, then

$$F = XJX^{-1}.$$

Using this relation and (5.26), we have

$$\det \alpha(F) = \det \left(X\alpha(J)X^{-1} \right)$$
$$= \det \alpha(J)$$
$$= \prod_{i=1}^{p} s_i^{p_i} \neq 0.$$

The proof is then finished. ■

5.2.1 Solution of R'

Let $A(s) \in \mathbb{R}^{n \times q}[s]$, $B(s) \in \mathbb{R}^{n \times r}[s]$, $q + r > n$, be given by (5.2). Then, under Assumption 5.1, there exist two unimodular matrices $P(s) \in \mathbb{R}^{n \times n}[s]$ and $Q(s) \in \mathbb{R}^{(q+r) \times (q+r)}[s]$ and a diagonal polynomial matrix $\Sigma(s) \in \mathbb{R}^{\alpha \times \alpha}[s]$ satisfying the SFR

$$P(s) \left[A(s) \quad -B(s) \right] Q(s) = \begin{bmatrix} \Sigma(s) & 0 \\ 0 & 0 \end{bmatrix}, \tag{5.27}$$

and

$$\Delta(s) = \det \Sigma(s) \neq 0, \ \forall s \in \text{eig}(F). \tag{5.28}$$

Partition the unimodular matrix $Q(s)$ as follows:

$$Q(s) = \begin{bmatrix} U(s) & N(s) \\ T(s) & D(s) \end{bmatrix}, \tag{5.29}$$

where $N(s) \in \mathbb{R}^{q \times \beta}[s]$, $D(s) \in \mathbb{R}^{r \times \beta}[s]$, and $U(s) \in \mathbb{R}^{q \times \alpha}[s]$, $T(s) \in \mathbb{R}^{r \times \alpha}[s]$. Then, according to Lemma 3.4, the polynomial matrices $N(s)$ and $D(s)$ are right coprime and satisfy the generalized RCF (3.45), and the polynomial matrices $U(s)$ and $T(s)$ satisfy the DPE (5.7) with

$$C(s) = P^{-1}(s) \begin{bmatrix} \Sigma(s) \\ 0 \end{bmatrix}. \tag{5.30}$$

Let $\Sigma(s)$ be given by the SFR (5.27), then under the condition that $A(s) \in \mathbb{R}^{n \times q}[s]$, $B(s) \in \mathbb{R}^{n \times r}[s]$ are F-left coprime with rank α, condition (5.28) holds. Therefore, by Lemma 5.2, we have $\det \Delta(F) \neq 0$.

Theorem 5.4 *Let $F \in \mathbb{C}^{p \times p}$, and $A(s) \in \mathbb{R}^{n \times q}[s]$, $B(s) \in \mathbb{R}^{n \times r}[s]$ be F-left coprime with rank α and admit the SFR (5.27), $C(s) \in \mathbb{R}^{n \times \alpha}$ be in the form of (5.30) with $P(s)$ and $\Sigma(s)$ given by the SFR (5.27). Partition $P(s)$ as follows:*

$$P(s) = \begin{bmatrix} P_1(s) \\ P_2(s) \end{bmatrix}, \ P_1(s) \in \mathbb{R}^{\alpha \times n}[s]. \tag{5.31}$$

Then,

1. *There exists a matrix $R' \in \mathbb{C}^{n \times p}$ satisfying condition (5.11) if and only if*

$$P_2(s)R = 0. \tag{5.32}$$

2. *When the above condition is met, there exists a unique matrix*

$$R' = [\text{adj}\,\Sigma(s)P_1(s)R]\big|_F [\Delta(F)]^{-1} \tag{5.33}$$

satisfying condition (5.11).

Proof. Noting that

$$
\begin{aligned}
[C(s)R']\big|_F &- R \\
&= [C(s)R']\big|_F - [R]\big|_F \\
&= [C(s)R' - R]\big|_F,
\end{aligned}
$$

we can write condition (5.11) as

$$[C(s)R' - R]\big|_F = 0.$$

It thus follows from the second conclusion of Theorem 4.1 that condition (5.11) holds for arbitrary $F \in \mathbb{C}^{p \times p}$ if and only if

$$C(s)R' - R = 0, \ \forall s \in \mathbb{C}. \tag{5.34}$$

Recall that the polynomial matrix $C(s)$ possesses the specific form of (5.30), equation (5.34) can be equivalently written as

$$\begin{bmatrix} \Sigma(s) \\ 0 \end{bmatrix} R' - P(s)R = 0, \ \forall s \in \mathbb{C},$$

which can be further decomposed into (5.32) and

$$\Sigma(s)R' - P_1(s)R = 0, \ \forall s \in \mathbb{C}. \tag{5.35}$$

The above equation is clearly equivalent to

$$R' - \Sigma^{-1}(s)P_1(s)R = 0, \ \forall s \in \mathbb{C}. \tag{5.36}$$

At this point, we have proven the first conclusion of the theorem.

Using the following relation

$$\Sigma^{-1}(s) = \frac{\text{adj}\,\Sigma(s)}{\det \Sigma(s)} = \frac{\text{adj}\,\Sigma(s)}{\Delta(s)},$$

equation (5.36) can be written as

$$\det \Sigma(s)R' - \text{adj}\,\Sigma(s)P_1(s)R = 0, \ \forall s \in \mathbb{C}.$$

It follows from the second conclusion of Theorem 4.1 again that the above equation holds if and only if

$$\left[\det \Sigma(s)R'\right]\big|_F = \left[\text{adj}\,\Sigma(s)P_1(s)R\right]\big|_F \qquad (5.37)$$

holds for arbitrary $F \in \mathbb{C}^{p \times p}$. Note that

$$\left[\det \Sigma(s)R'\right]\big|_F = R'\left[\det \Sigma(s)\right]\big|_F$$
$$= R'\left[\Delta(s)\right]\big|_F$$
$$= R'\left[\Delta(F)\right].$$

Submitting this relation into (5.37) gives

$$R'\left[\Delta(F)\right] = \left[\text{adj}\,\Sigma(s)P_1(s)R\right]\big|_F . \qquad (5.38)$$

Further, from Lemma 5.2 we know that $\Delta(F)$ is nonsingular. Hence, (5.33) immediately follows from (5.38). ■

Remark 5.3 Theorem 5.4 actually gives a complete solution to the condition (5.11). We point out that the matrix R may take any special structure, for example, when

$$R = \sum_{i=0}^{\psi} H_i R^* F^i, \qquad (5.39)$$

we can simply insert this expression into (5.32) and (5.33).

5.2.2 Regularizable Case

In Section 5.2.1, we have presented for the case of $C(s)$ possessing the form of (5.30), a complete solution to the equation (5.11), which does not require the matrices F and R to be fully known *a priori*. In this subsection, let us look into the special case of $A(s)$ and $B(s)$ being regularizable, that is,

$$\text{rank}\left[A(s) \quad B(s)\right] = n, \ \exists s \in \mathbb{C}.$$

Under the above regularizability condition, we can find certain matrix F such that $A(s)$ and $B(s)$ are F-left coprime. In this whole subsection, it is taken for granted that each matrix F appeared to belong to this category.

It follows from Theorem 3.10 that, when $A(s) \in \mathbb{R}^{n \times q}[s]$ and $B(s) \in \mathbb{R}^{n \times r}[s]$ are F-left coprime, there exist a pair of right coprime polynomial matrices $U(s) \in \mathbb{R}^{q \times n}[s]$ and $T(s) \in \mathbb{R}^{r \times n}[s]$ satisfying the following DPE

$$A(s)U(s) - B(s)T(s) = \Delta(s)I_n, \qquad (5.40)$$

with $\Delta(s)$ being a scalar polynomial satisfying

$$\Delta(s) \neq 0, \quad \forall s \in \text{eig}(F). \tag{5.41}$$

Thus, in this case, we have $C(s) = \Delta(s)I_n$, and condition (5.11) becomes

$$[\Delta(s)R']\big|_F = R. \tag{5.42}$$

Since

$$[\Delta(s)R']\big|_F = [R'\Delta(s)]\big|_F = R'\Delta(F),$$

the above condition can obviously be written as

$$R'\Delta(F) = R. \tag{5.43}$$

It follows from Lemma 5.2 again that, under the condition that $A(s)$ and $B(s)$ are F-left coprime, or equivalently, under the condition of (5.41), $\Delta(F)$ is nonsingular. Therefore, in this case the above equation has a unique solution

$$R' = R[\Delta(F)]^{-1}. \tag{5.44}$$

When $(A(s), B(s))$ is controllable, we have $C(s) = I_n$, hence $\Delta(s) = 1$ and $\Delta(F) = I$. Therefore, (5.44) becomes

$$R' = R. \tag{5.45}$$

The above fact, together with Theorem 5.1, immediately suggests the following result.

Theorem 5.5 *Let $F \in \mathbb{C}^{p \times p}$, and $A(s) \in \mathbb{R}^{n \times q}[s]$, $B(s) \in \mathbb{R}^{n \times r}[s]$, $q + r > n$, be given by (5.2), and be F-left coprime. Further, let $U(s) \in \mathbb{R}^{q \times \alpha}[s]$, $T(s) \in \mathbb{R}^{r \times \alpha}[s]$ be in the forms of (5.9) and satisfy the DPE (5.40). Then the nonhomogeneous GSE (5.1) always has a solution with respect to (V, W), and a particular solution can be given by Formula I''_N (5.12), with R' given by (5.44).*

Remark 5.4 Parallel to Remark 5.3, again the matrix R may take any special structure. When

$$R = \sum_{i=0}^{\psi} H_i R^* F^i, \tag{5.46}$$

which corresponds to the GSE (5.22), under the F-left coprimeness of $A(s)$ and $B(s)$, we can simply insert this expression of R into (5.44) and obtain the solution of R' as

$$
R' = \left(\sum_{i=0}^{\psi} H_i R^* F^i \right) [\Delta(F)]^{-1}. \tag{5.47}
$$

Furthermore, with this expression, Formula I''_N (5.12) gives a particular solution to GSE (5.22).

5.3 Solution Based on SFR

In Section 5.1, we have given solutions to the nonhomogeneous GSE based on a generalized RCF and a DPE. There are many ways to solve the generalized RCFs and the DPEs. Particularly, they can be solved by conducting the SFR of $[A(s)\ B(s)]$ as shown in Section 3.3, or as reviewed in Section 5.2.

In this section, we will seek the solution to the nonhomogeneous GSE based on SFR (5.27). With the specific form of the polynomial matrix $C(s)$ given by (5.30), it is shown that an alternative form of the condition (5.11) can be obtained based on SFR, hence a different set of solutions to the nonhomogeneous GSE is obtained.

The following technical result is used in the development.

Lemma 5.3 *Let $F \in \mathbb{C}^{p \times p}$, and $\Delta(s)$ be a scalar polynomial satisfying (5.41). Then,*

$$
[\Delta(F)]^{-1} F = F [\Delta(F)]^{-1}, \tag{5.48}
$$

and for an arbitrary matrix Z and a polynomial matrix $P(s)$, of appropriate dimensions, there holds

$$
\left[P(s)Z [\Delta(F)]^{-1} \right] \Big|_F = [P(s)Z] \Big|_F [\Delta(F)]^{-1}. \tag{5.49}
$$

Proof. Since $\Delta(s)$ is a polynomial matrix, it is easy to show that

$$
F [\Delta(F)] = [\Delta(F)] F.
$$

Further, it follows from the given condition and Lemma 5.2 that $[\Delta(F)]^{-1}$ exists. Pre- and postmultiplying both sides of the aforementioned equation by $[\Delta(F)]^{-1}$ gives the relation (5.48). The next conclusion clearly follows from the commutativity of F and $[\Delta(F)]^{-1}$ and the first conclusion of Theorem 4.1. ■

5.3.1 Particular Solution

Using Lemma 3.4, and also Theorems 5.1 and 5.4, we can immediately derive the following result about the solution to the GSE (5.1) based on SFR.

Theorem 5.6 *Let $A(s) \in \mathbb{R}^{n \times q}[s]$, $B(s) \in \mathbb{R}^{n \times r}[s]$, $q + r > n$, be given in (5.2), $F \in \mathbb{C}^{p \times p}$, and Assumption 5.1 hold. Furthermore, let*

- *$P(s) \in \mathbb{R}^{n \times n}[s]$, $Q(s) \in \mathbb{R}^{(q+r) \times (q+r)}[s]$ and $\Sigma(s) \in \mathbb{R}^{\alpha \times \alpha}[s]$ be given by SFR (5.27) and (5.28)*
- *$U(s) \in \mathbb{R}^{q \times \alpha}[s]$, $T(s) \in \mathbb{R}^{r \times \alpha}[s]$ be given by (5.29)*
- *$P_1(s) \in \mathbb{R}^{\alpha \times n}[s]$ and $P_2(s) \in \mathbb{R}^{(n-\alpha) \times n}[s]$ be given by (5.31)*

Then, the GSE (5.1) has a solution if and only if (5.32) holds, and in this case, a particular solution is given by

$$
\boxed{
\begin{aligned}
&\text{Formula } I'_N \\
&\begin{cases}
V\Delta(F) = \left[\hat{U}(s)R \right]\Big|_F = \hat{U}_0 R + \hat{U}_1 RF + \cdots + \hat{U}_\varphi RF^\varphi \\
W\Delta(F) = \left[\hat{T}(s)R \right]\Big|_F = \hat{T}_0 R + \hat{T}_1 RF + \cdots + \hat{T}_\varphi RF^\varphi,
\end{cases}
\end{aligned}
}
\tag{5.50}
$$

where

$$
\begin{bmatrix} \hat{U}(s) \\ \hat{T}(s) \end{bmatrix} = \begin{bmatrix} U(s) \\ T(s) \end{bmatrix} \operatorname{adj}\Sigma(s) P_1(s).
\tag{5.51}
$$

Proof. In view of Lemma 3.4, $U(s) \in \mathbb{R}^{q \times \alpha}[s]$ and $T(s) \in \mathbb{R}^{r \times \alpha}[s]$ are a pair of right coprime polynomial matrices satisfying the DPE (5.7) with $C(s) \in \mathbb{R}^{n \times \alpha}$ given by (5.30). It thus follows from Theorems 5.1 and 5.4 that the GSE (5.1) has a solution if and only if (5.32) holds, and in this case a solution is given by

$$
\begin{cases}
V = [U(s)R']\big|_F \\
W = [T(s)R']\big|_F,
\end{cases}
\tag{5.52}
$$

with

$$
R' = [\operatorname{adj}\Sigma(s) P_1(s) R]\big|_F [\Delta(F)]^{-1}.
\tag{5.53}
$$

Substituting the above expression of R' into (5.52) and applying Lemma 5.3, we further have

$$
\begin{aligned}
V &= \left[U(s)R'\right]\big|_F \\
&= \left[U(s)\left[\mathrm{adj}\,\Sigma(s)P_1(s)R\left[\Delta(F)\right]^{-1}\right]\big|_F\right]\big|_F \\
&= \left[U(s)\left[\mathrm{adj}\,\Sigma(s)P_1(s)R\right]\big|_F\right]\big|_F \left[\Delta(F)\right]^{-1},
\end{aligned}
$$

and

$$
\begin{aligned}
W &= \left[T(s)R'\right]\big|_F \\
&= \left[T(s)\left[\mathrm{adj}\,\Sigma(s)P_1(s)R\left[\Delta(F)\right]^{-1}\right]\big|_F\right]\big|_F \\
&\quad \left[T(s)\left[\mathrm{adj}\,\Sigma(s)P_1(s)R\right]\big|_F\right]\big|_F \left[\Delta(F)\right]^{-1}.
\end{aligned}
$$

Finally, applying the third conclusion of Theorem 4.1 to the above two equations obviously gives the solution (5.50) and (5.51). ■

The following corollary further gives solutions to the nonhomogeneous GSE (5.1) in several special cases.

Corollary 5.2 *Given conditions of Theorem 5.6, then*

1. *When $A(s) \in \mathbb{R}^{n \times q}[s]$, $B(s) \in \mathbb{R}^{n \times r}[s]$ are left coprime with rank α, the GSE (5.1) has a solution if and only if (5.32) holds, and in this case, a particular solution is given by*

$$
\begin{cases}
V = \left[\hat{U}(s)R\right]\big|_F \\
W = \left[\hat{T}(s)R\right]\big|_F,
\end{cases}
\tag{5.54}
$$

where $\hat{U}(s)$ and $\hat{T}(s)$ are defined in (5.51).

2. *When $A(s) \in \mathbb{R}^{n \times q}[s]$, $B(s) \in \mathbb{R}^{n \times r}[s]$ are F-left coprime with rank n, the GSE (5.1) always has a solution, and a particular solution is given by (5.50) with*

$$
\begin{bmatrix} \hat{U}(s) \\ \hat{T}(s) \end{bmatrix} = \begin{bmatrix} U(s) \\ T(s) \end{bmatrix} \mathrm{adj}\,\Sigma(s)\,P(s).
\tag{5.55}
$$

3. *When $A(s) \in \mathbb{R}^{n \times q}[s]$, $B(s) \in \mathbb{R}^{n \times r}[s]$ are left coprime, the GSE (5.1) always has a solution, and a particular solution is given by*

$$\begin{cases} V = [U(s)P(s)R]\big|_F \\ W = [T(s)P(s)R]\big|_F. \end{cases} \tag{5.56}$$

Proof. Let us notice the following:

1. When $A(s) \in \mathbb{R}^{n \times q}[s]$, $B(s) \in \mathbb{R}^{n \times r}[s]$ are left coprime with rank α, we have $\Sigma(s) = I_\alpha$, and in this case,

$$\Delta(F) = [\Delta(F)]^{-1} = I_p.$$

Thus, the solution (5.50) reduces to (5.54).
2. When $A(s) \in \mathbb{R}^{n \times q}[s]$, $B(s) \in \mathbb{R}^{n \times r}[s]$ are F-left coprime with rank n, $P_2(s)$ vanishes, and $P_1(s) = P(s)$. Thus, condition (5.32) vanishes, and the solution (5.50) reduces to (5.55).
3. When $A(s) \in \mathbb{R}^{n \times q}[s]$, $B(s) \in \mathbb{R}^{n \times r}[s]$ are left coprime, we have $\Sigma(s) = I_n$, and also $P_2(s)$ vanishes, and $P_1(s) = P(s)$.

With the above facts, the proofs of the corresponding conclusions are straightforward. ■

Remark 5.5 Theorems 5.1 and 5.6 both give general complete parametric solution to the matrix equation (5.1) under the same condition. Eventually, these two solutions are equivalent to each other. Under the general Assumption 5.1, in order that the nonhomogeneous GSE has a solution the R matrix must possess certain special structure, this is reflected by the condition (5.32) and the matrix R' in Theorem 5.1. While in Theorem 5.6 this factor is coped with by readjusting the polynomial matrices $U(s)$ and $T(s)$.

Remark 5.6 The solution (5.50) is as well very simple and neat. It is in a linear explicit form with respect to R, and therefore allows the matrix R to be set undetermined. Furthermore, note that the only requirement on the matrix F is to maintain the F-left coprimeness of $A(s)$ and $B(s)$, thus the matrix F can be arbitrarily chosen with eigenvalues different from the uncontrollable modes of $(A(s), B(s))$. Such a property may give great convenience and advantages to some analysis and design problems in control system theory. These matrices F and R, together with the parameter matrix Z, can be optimized to achieve some better performance in applications.

5.3.2 General Solution

Again, using Lemma 5.1, Theorems 4.7 and 5.1, we immediately have the following result about the general solution to the nonhomogeneous GSE (5.1).

Theorem 5.7 *Let $A(s) \in \mathbb{R}^{n \times q}[s]$, $B(s) \in \mathbb{R}^{n \times r}[s]$, $q + r > n$, be given in (5.2), $F \in \mathbb{C}^{p \times p}$ and Assumption 5.1 hold. Further, let $P(s) \in \mathbb{R}^{n \times n}[s]$, $Q(s) \in \mathbb{R}^{(q+r) \times (q+r)}[s]$ and $\Sigma(s) \in \mathbb{R}^{\alpha \times \alpha}[s]$ be given by SFR (5.27) and (5.28). Then, the nonhomogeneous GSE (5.1) has a solution if and only if condition (5.32) is met, and in this case a general complete solution (V, W) to the nonhomogeneous GSE (5.1) is given by*

$$
\boxed{
\begin{aligned}
&Formula\ I'_G \\
&\begin{bmatrix} V \\ W \end{bmatrix} = \left. \left[\hat{Q}(s) \begin{bmatrix} R \\ Z \end{bmatrix} \right] \right|_F [\Delta(F)]^{-1},
\end{aligned}
}
\tag{5.57}
$$

where $Z \in \mathbb{C}^{\beta \times p}$ is an arbitrary parameter matrix, which represents the degrees of freedom in the solution, and $\hat{Q}_i$ is determined by

$$
\hat{Q}(s) = Q(s) \begin{bmatrix} \mathrm{adj}\,\Sigma(s) P_1(s) & 0 \\ 0 & I \end{bmatrix}.
\tag{5.58}
$$

If we denote

$$
\hat{Q}(s) = \sum_{i=0}^{\tau} \hat{Q}_i s^i,
$$

then by definition, solution (5.57) can be expressed as

$$
\begin{aligned}
\begin{bmatrix} V \\ W \end{bmatrix} &= \sum_{i=0}^{\tau} \hat{Q}_i \begin{bmatrix} R \\ Z \end{bmatrix} F^i [\Delta(F)]^{-1} \\
&= \sum_{i=0}^{\tau} \hat{Q}_i \begin{bmatrix} R \\ Z \end{bmatrix} [\Delta(F)]^{-1} F^i.
\end{aligned}
\tag{5.59}
$$

Noting that $\Sigma(s)$ is diagonal, both $\mathrm{adj}\,\Sigma^{-1}(s)$ and $\Sigma^{-1}(s)$ are very easy to be solved.

To end this section, let us remark again that, in order to obtain the solution to the GSE (5.22), we suffice only to substitute the matrix R with $\sum_{i=0}^{\psi} H_i R^* F^i$.

5.4 Controllable Case

In this section, let us further consider the solution to the nonhomogeneous GSE (5.1) under the condition that the associated matrices $A(s)$ and $B(s)$ are left coprime, or equivalently, the matrix pair $(A(s), B(s))$ is controllable.

As a matter of fact, the results given in the sections have already covered this case; however, due to the special importance of this controllable case, we here especially give a clear representation of a particular solution to the nonhomogeneous GSE (5.1) under the controllability condition.

5.4.1 Results

By definition, $(A(s), B(s))$ is controllable if and only if

$$\text{rank}\begin{bmatrix} A(s) & B(s) \end{bmatrix} = n, \ \forall s \in \mathbb{C}.$$

In this case, it follows from Theorem 3.11 that there exists a pair of polynomial matrices

$$\begin{cases} U(s) = U_0 + U_1 s + \cdots + U_\varphi s^\varphi \in \mathbb{R}^{q \times n}[s] \\ T(s) = T_0 + T_1 s + \cdots + T_\varphi s^\varphi \in \mathbb{R}^{r \times n}[s] \end{cases} \tag{5.60}$$

satisfying the following DPE

$$A(s)U(s) - B(s)T(s) = I_n. \tag{5.61}$$

Further, it follows from Section 5.2.2 that, under the controllability of $(A(s), B(s))$, the condition (5.11) reduces to

$$R' = R. \tag{5.62}$$

With the above observations, we immediately have the following result for a particular solution to the nonhomogeneous GSE (5.1) under the controllability assumption following Theorem 5.6 or Corollary 5.2.

Theorem 5.8 *Let $A(s) \in \mathbb{R}^{n \times q}[s]$, $B(s) \in \mathbb{R}^{n \times r}[s]$, $q + r > n$, be given in (5.2), and $(A(s), B(s))$ be controllable. Furthermore, let $U(s) \in \mathbb{R}^{q \times n}[s]$ and $T(s) \in \mathbb{R}^{r \times n}[s]$ be a pair of polynomial matrices given by (5.60) and satisfying the DPE (5.61). Then, for an arbitrary $R \in \mathbb{C}^{n \times p}$, the nonhomogeneous GSE (5.1) always has a solution, and, particularly, a solution is given by*

Formula I_N

$$\begin{cases} V = [U(s)R]\big|_F = U_0R + U_1RF + \cdots + U_\varphi RF^\varphi \\ W = [T(s)R]\big|_F = T_0R + T_1RF + \cdots + T_\varphi RF^\varphi. \end{cases} \tag{5.63}$$

Now, let us consider the general solution to the nonhomogeneous GSE (5.1) under the controllability assumption.

It follows from Theorem 3.11 that, under the controllability assumption of $(A(s), B(s))$, there exists a unimodular polynomial matrix $Q(s) \in \mathbb{R}^{(q+r)\times(q+r)}[s]$ satisfying

$$\begin{bmatrix} A(s) & -B(s) \end{bmatrix} Q(s) = \begin{bmatrix} I_n & 0 \end{bmatrix}. \tag{5.64}$$

Partition the matrix $Q(s)$ as follows:

$$Q(s) = \begin{bmatrix} U(s) & N(s) \\ T(s) & D(s) \end{bmatrix},$$

where $U(s) \in \mathbb{R}^{q\times n}[s]$, $T(s) \in \mathbb{R}^{r\times n}[s]$ and $N(s) \in \mathbb{R}^{q\times\beta_0}[s]$, $T(s) \in \mathbb{R}^{r\times\beta_0}[s]$ with $\beta_0 = q + r - n$. Then $U(s)$ and $T(s)$ satisfy the DPE (5.61), while $N(s)$ and $T(s)$ are right coprime and satisfy the generalized RCF

$$A(s)N(s) - B(s)D(s) = 0. \tag{5.65}$$

Recall from Chapter 4 that a complete parametric general solution to the homogeneous GSE corresponding to GSE (5.1) is given by

$$\begin{cases} V = [N(s)Z]\big|_F = N_0Z + N_1ZF + \cdots + N_\omega ZF^\omega \\ W = [D(s)Z]\big|_F = D_0Z + D_1ZF + \cdots + D_\omega ZF^\omega, \end{cases} \tag{5.66}$$

where $Z \in \mathbb{C}^{\beta_0\times p}$ is an arbitrary parameter matrix.

Combining the general solution (5.66) to the homogeneous GSE with the above particular solution (5.63) to the nonhomogeneous GSE yields a general solution to the nonhomogeneous GSE as given in the following theorem.

Theorem 5.9 *Let $A(s) \in \mathbb{R}^{n\times q}[s]$, $B(s) \in \mathbb{R}^{n\times r}[s]$, $q + r > n$, be given in (5.2) and $(A(s), B(s))$ be controllable. Furthermore, let $Q(s) \in \mathbb{R}^{(q+r)\times(q+r)}[s]$ be a* *unimodular polynomial matrix satisfying (5.64). Then, for an arbitrary $R \in \mathbb{C}^{n \times p}$, the nonhomogeneous GSE (5.1) has a solution, and a general solution is given by*

$$\boxed{\begin{array}{l} \text{Formula } I_G \\ \left[\begin{array}{c} V \\ W \end{array}\right] = \left[Q(s) \left[\begin{array}{c} R \\ Z \end{array}\right]\right]\Big|_F \end{array}}, \qquad (5.67)$$

where $Z \in \mathbb{C}^{(q+r-n) \times p}$ is an arbitrary parameter matrix.

Remark 5.7 At least with applications in control systems design the controllability condition is often taken for granted. Thus, this controllable case is very important, and as we have seen from the above two theorems both the particular solution and the general parametric solution to the nonhomogeneous GSE under the controllability condition turn out to be the most simple ones. They own their simplicity, as well as beauty and elegancy. Yet they are the ones to be used most often in control systems designs.

In this controllable case, the nonhomogeneous GSE (5.1) has a solution for arbitrarily given R matrix. Therefore, we can take this matrix to be dependent on the matrix F. Generally, we can assume

$$R = f(F), \qquad (5.68)$$

where $f : \mathbb{R}^{p \times p} \longrightarrow \mathbb{R}^{n \times p}$ is some given mapping. A specific case maybe

$$R = \sum_{i=0}^{\psi} H_i R^* F^{i+\rho}, \qquad (5.69)$$

with ρ being some integers. In the case that the matrix F is nonsingular, the integer ρ can also be chosen negative.

Remark 5.8 Due to the above fact, we suggest the readers not to look upon the GSE (5.1) as a special case of (5.22), but vice versa. The complexity in the expression of (5.22) does not make it more general, but conversely, it makes it more special since this complexity is actually a constraint putting on the matrix R. Due to this point, in the rest of this chapter we are not mentioning solutions of (5.22) again, but only stress on the GSE (5.1).

Remark 5.9 Corresponding to Remark 4.8, we mention that, again, for a larger application scope, we have allowed the matrices F, V, W, and R in the nonhomogeneous GSE (5.1) to take complex values. It can also be easily observed that, once the matrices F and R are restricted to be real (but with the matrix F possessing complex eigenvalues), our proposed solutions for the case of arbitrary matrix F also provide real matrices V and W.

5.4.2 Examples

To demonstrate the above results, let us consider a few examples that have been treated in Chapter 4. Since the homogeneous GSEs associated with these examples have already been proposed in Chapter 4, here we mainly concentrate on a particular solution to the nonhomogeneous GSEs.

Example 5.1

Consider a nonhomogeneous GSE in the form of (4.21) with the following parameters same as in Example 4.1:

$$E = \begin{bmatrix} 1 & 0 & 0 \\ 0 & 1 & 0 \\ 0 & 0 & 0 \end{bmatrix}, \ A = \begin{bmatrix} 0 & 1 & 0 \\ 0 & 0 & 1 \\ 0 & 0 & -1 \end{bmatrix},$$

$$B_1 = \begin{bmatrix} 0 & 0 \\ 0 & 1 \\ 0 & 0 \end{bmatrix}, \ B_0 = \begin{bmatrix} 0 & 0 \\ 1 & 0 \\ 0 & 1 \end{bmatrix}.$$

Following the procedures in Lemma 3.4, in Example 4.1 we have obtained the following polynomial matrices

$$P(s) = \begin{bmatrix} 1 & 0 & 0 \\ 0 & 1 & -s \\ 0 & 0 & 1 \end{bmatrix}, \ Q(s) = \begin{bmatrix} 0 & 0 & 0 & 1 & 0 \\ -1 & 0 & 0 & s & 0 \\ 0 & 0 & 0 & 0 & 1 \\ -s & -1 & 0 & s^2 & -s-1 \\ 0 & 0 & -1 & 0 & 1 \end{bmatrix},$$

which satisfy

$$P(s) \begin{bmatrix} (sE - A) & -(B_1 s + B_0) \end{bmatrix} Q(s) = \begin{bmatrix} I & 0 \end{bmatrix}.$$

Thus, a pair of polynomial matrices $U(s)$ and $T(s)$ satisfying the DPE (5.61) are given by

$$U(s) = \begin{bmatrix} 0 & 0 & 0 \\ -1 & 0 & 0 \\ 0 & 0 & 0 \end{bmatrix} P(s) = \begin{bmatrix} 0 & 0 & 0 \\ -1 & 0 & 0 \\ 0 & 0 & 0 \end{bmatrix},$$

$$T(s) = \begin{bmatrix} -s & -1 & 0 \\ 0 & 0 & -1 \end{bmatrix} P(s) = \begin{bmatrix} -s & -1 & s \\ 0 & 0 & -1 \end{bmatrix},$$

which gives $\varphi = 1$, and

$$U_0 = \begin{bmatrix} 0 & 0 & 0 \\ -1 & 0 & 0 \\ 0 & 0 & 0 \end{bmatrix}, \ U_1 = 0_{3\times3},$$

$$T_0 = \begin{bmatrix} 0 & -1 & 0 \\ 0 & 0 & -1 \end{bmatrix}, \ T_1 = \begin{bmatrix} -1 & 0 & 1 \\ 0 & 0 & 0 \end{bmatrix}.$$

According to Theorem 5.8, for an arbitrary matrix $F \in \mathbb{C}^{p \times p}$, a complete analytical and explicit solution to the corresponding nonhomogeneous GSE can be parameterized as

$$\begin{cases} V_p = U_0 R + U_1 RF \\ W_p = T_0 R + T_1 RF. \end{cases}$$

Letting

$$F = \begin{bmatrix} -\lambda & 1 \\ 0 & -\lambda \end{bmatrix}, \ R = \begin{bmatrix} \gamma_{11} & \gamma_{12} \\ \gamma_{21} & \gamma_{22} \\ \lambda & -\lambda \end{bmatrix},$$

we have

$$V_p = \begin{bmatrix} 0 & 0 \\ -\gamma_{11} & -\gamma_{12} \\ 0 & 0 \end{bmatrix},$$

and

$$W_p = \begin{bmatrix} \lambda(\gamma_{11} - \lambda) - \gamma_{21} & w_{p12} \\ -\lambda & \lambda \end{bmatrix},$$

with

$$w_{p12} = \lambda - \gamma_{22} - \gamma_{11} + \lambda(\gamma_{12} + \lambda).$$

Particularly, choosing

$$\lambda = -1, \quad \begin{bmatrix} \gamma_{11} & \gamma_{12} \\ \gamma_{21} & \gamma_{22} \end{bmatrix} = I_2,$$

we get the following specific solution to the nonhomogeneous GSE as

$$V_p = \begin{bmatrix} 0 & 0 \\ 0 & -1 \\ 0 & 0 \end{bmatrix}, \quad W_p = \begin{bmatrix} 0 & 0 \\ -1 & 1 \end{bmatrix}.$$

Example 5.2

Consider a second-order GSE in the form of (5.1) with the following parameters same as in Example 4.2:

$$M = \begin{bmatrix} 1 & 0 & 0 \\ 0 & 1 & 0 \\ 0 & 0 & 0 \end{bmatrix}, \quad D = \begin{bmatrix} 1 & 0 & 1 \\ 0 & 2 & -1 \\ 1 & -1 & 3 \end{bmatrix}, \quad K = \begin{bmatrix} 2 & -1 & 0 \\ -1 & 1 & 2 \\ 0 & 2 & 1 \end{bmatrix},$$

$$B_2 = B_1 = 0, \quad B_0 = \begin{bmatrix} 1 & 0 \\ 0 & 0 \\ 0 & 1 \end{bmatrix}.$$

For this set of parameters, the general solution to the corresponding homogeneous equation has been given in Example 4.2. Hence, here we only need to solve a particular solution to the nonhomogeneous equation.

Following Theorem 3.7, in Example 4.2 we have conducted the SFR associated with these parameters and obtained $\Sigma(s) = I_3$, $P(s) = -I_3$, and

$$Q(s) = \begin{bmatrix} 0 & 1 & 0 & q_2(s) & -q_3(s) \\ 0 & 0 & 0 & 1 & 0 \\ 0 & 0 & 0 & 0 & 1 \\ 1 & q_1(s) & 0 & q_1(s)q_2(s) - 1 & s - q_3(s)q_1(s) \\ 0 & s & 1 & sq_2(s) - q_3(s) & -s^2 + 5s + 1 \end{bmatrix},$$

where

$$\begin{cases} q_1(s) = s^2 + s + 2 \\ q_2(s) = s^2 + 2s + 1 \\ q_3(s) = s - 2. \end{cases}$$

Thus, it follows from Lemma 3.4 that

$$U(s) = \begin{bmatrix} 0 & 1 & 0 \\ 0 & 0 & 0 \\ 0 & 0 & 0 \end{bmatrix} P(s) = \begin{bmatrix} 0 & -1 & 0 \\ 0 & 0 & 0 \\ 0 & 0 & 0 \end{bmatrix},$$

$$T(s) = \begin{bmatrix} 1 & (s^2+s+2) & 0 \\ 0 & s & 1 \end{bmatrix} P(s) = \begin{bmatrix} -1 & -(s^2+s+2) & 0 \\ 0 & -s & -1 \end{bmatrix}.$$

So we have

$$U_0 = \begin{bmatrix} 0 & -1 & 0 \\ 0 & 0 & 0 \\ 0 & 0 & 0 \end{bmatrix}, \tag{5.70}$$

$$T_0 = \begin{bmatrix} -1 & -2 & 0 \\ 0 & 0 & -1 \end{bmatrix}, \; T_1 = \begin{bmatrix} 0 & -1 & 0 \\ 0 & -1 & 0 \end{bmatrix}, \; T_2 = \begin{bmatrix} 0 & -1 & 0 \\ 0 & 0 & 0 \end{bmatrix}. \tag{5.71}$$

According to Theorem 5.2, for an arbitrary matrix $R \in \mathbb{C}^{3 \times p}$, a solution to the second-order GSE can be parameterized as

$$\begin{cases} V = U_0 R \\ W = T_0 R + T_1 RF + T_2 RF^2. \end{cases}$$

Letting

$$F = \begin{bmatrix} -\lambda & 1 \\ 0 & -\lambda \end{bmatrix}, \; R = \begin{bmatrix} r_{11} & r_{12} \\ r_{21} & r_{22} \\ r_{31} & r_{32} \end{bmatrix},$$

we have

$$V = \begin{bmatrix} -r_{21} & -r_{22} \\ 0 & 0 \\ 0 & 0 \end{bmatrix}, \; W = \begin{bmatrix} w_{11} & w_{12} \\ w_{21} & w_{22} \end{bmatrix},$$

with

$$\begin{cases} w_{11} = -r_{21}\lambda^2 + r_{21}\lambda - r_{11} - 2r_{21} \\ w_{12} = 2\lambda r_{21} - r_{21} - 2r_{22} - r_{12} + \lambda r_{22} - \lambda^2 r_{22} \\ w_{21} = \lambda r_{21} - r_{31} \\ w_{22} = \lambda r_{22} - r_{32} - r_{21}. \end{cases}$$

Further, specially choosing

$$r_{11} = r_{12} = r_{21} = r_{22} = 0,$$

for arbitrary λ, we get a special solution

$$V = 0_{3\times2}, \quad W = -\begin{bmatrix} 0 & 0 \\ r_{31} & r_{32} \end{bmatrix},$$

which happens to be invariant with variable λ.

Example 5.3

Consider a third-order GSE in the form of (5.1) with the following parameters same as in Example 4.3:

$$A_0 = \begin{bmatrix} 0 & -1 & 0 \\ -1 & 1 & 2 \\ 0 & 1 & 1 \end{bmatrix}, \quad A_1 = \begin{bmatrix} 2 & 0 & 0 \\ 0 & 1 & 2 \\ 0 & 2 & 1 \end{bmatrix},$$

$$A_2 = \begin{bmatrix} 1 & 0 & 1 \\ 0 & 2 & -1 \\ 1 & -1 & 3 \end{bmatrix}, \quad A_3 = \begin{bmatrix} 1 & 0 & 0 \\ 0 & 1 & 0 \\ 0 & 0 & 0 \end{bmatrix},$$

$$B_0 = \begin{bmatrix} 1 & 0 \\ 0 & 0 \\ 0 & 1 \end{bmatrix}, \quad B_1 = B_2 = B_3 = 0.$$

It is easy to verify that the corresponding system (1.12) is R-controllable, and using Lemma 3.4 a pair of polynomial matrices $U(s)$ and $T(s)$ satisfying the DPE (5.61) are obtained as

$$U(s) = \begin{bmatrix} 0 & -1 & 0 \\ 0 & 0 & 0 \\ 0 & 0 & 0 \end{bmatrix}, \quad T(s) = -\begin{bmatrix} 1 & s^3 + s^2 + 2s & 0 \\ 0 & s^2 & 1 \end{bmatrix}.$$

From the above expressions for the polynomial matrices $U(s)$ and $T(s)$, we have

$$U_0 = \begin{bmatrix} 0 & -1 & 0 \\ 0 & 0 & 0 \\ 0 & 0 & 0 \end{bmatrix}, \quad U_i = 0_{3\times3}, \quad i = 1, 2, 3,$$

$$T_0 = \begin{bmatrix} -1 & 0 & 0 \\ 0 & 0 & -1 \end{bmatrix}, \quad T_1 = \begin{bmatrix} 0 & -2 & 0 \\ 0 & 0 & 0 \end{bmatrix},$$

$$T_2 = \begin{bmatrix} 0 & -1 & 0 \\ 0 & -1 & 0 \end{bmatrix}, \quad T_3 = \begin{bmatrix} 0 & -1 & 0 \\ 0 & 0 & 0 \end{bmatrix}.$$

According to Theorem 5.9, and using the general solution obtained in Example 4.3 for the corresponding homogeneous GSE, a complete analytical and explicit solution to this third-order GSE with arbitrary matrices $F \in \mathbb{C}^{p \times p}$ and $R \in \mathbb{C}^{3 \times p}$ can be parameterized as

$$
\begin{cases}
V = \sum_{i=0}^{3} N_i Z F^i + U_0 R \\
W = \sum_{i=0}^{6} D_i Z F^i + \sum_{i=0}^{3} T_i R F^i,
\end{cases}
$$

where $Z \in \mathbb{C}^{2 \times p}$ is an arbitrary parameter matrix. Particularly, let

$$
F = \begin{bmatrix} -1 & 1 \\ 0 & -1 \end{bmatrix}, \quad R = \begin{bmatrix} 3 & 1 \\ 0 & 5 \\ 4 & 0 \end{bmatrix}, \tag{5.72}
$$

and specially choose $Z = I_2$, then we get a special solution

$$
V = \begin{bmatrix} 1 & -6 \\ 1 & 0 \\ 0 & 1 \end{bmatrix}, \quad W = \begin{bmatrix} -6 & 15 \\ -5 & -1 \end{bmatrix}. \tag{5.73}
$$

5.5 Case of *F* Being in Jordan Form

In this section, let us consider the case that the matrix F is a Jordan matrix of the following form:

$$
\begin{cases}
F = \text{blockdiag}\,(F_1, F_2, \ldots, F_w) \\
F_i = \begin{bmatrix} s_i & 1 & & \\ & s_i & \ddots & \\ & & \ddots & 1 \\ & & & s_i \end{bmatrix}_{p_i \times p_i},
\end{cases} \tag{5.74}
$$

where $s_i \in \mathbb{C}$, $i = 1, 2, \ldots, w$, are obviously the eigenvalues of the matrix F, and p_i, $i = 1, 2, \ldots, w$, are the geometric multiplicities corresponding to the eigenvalues s_i, $i = 1, 2, \ldots, w$, and satisfy $\sum_{i=1}^{w} p_i = p$.

By the structure of the F matrix, the columns of the matrices V, W, Z, and R, namely, v_{ij}, w_{ij}, z_{ij}, and r_{ij} are well defined according to Convention C1 introduced in Chapter 4. Further, Assumption 5.1 becomes

Assumption 5.2 $\begin{cases} \text{rank}\,[A(s) \ B(s)] \le \alpha, \ \forall s \in \mathbb{C} \\ \text{rank}\,[A(s_i) \ B(s_i)] = \alpha, \quad i = 1, 2, \ldots, w. \end{cases}$

5.5.1 Solution Based on RCF and DPE

Using Lemmas A.1 and 4.1, following the same lines as in the proof of Theorem 4.8, we can easily prove the following lemma.

Lemma 5.4 *With Convention C1, condition (5.11) can be equivalently expressed in the following form:*

$$r_{ij} = \sum_{k=0}^{j-1} \frac{1}{k!} \frac{d^k}{ds^k} C(s_i) r'_{i,j-k}, \tag{5.75}$$

$$j = 1, 2, \ldots, p_i, \quad i = 1, 2, \ldots, w.$$

Obviously, a looser form for condition (5.75) is

$$r_{ij} = C(s_i) r'_{ij} + \frac{1}{1!} \frac{d}{ds} C(s_i) r'_{i,j-1} + \cdots + \frac{1}{(j-1)!} \frac{d^{j-1}}{ds^{j-1}} C(s_i) r'_{i1}.$$

Similar to the proof of Theorem 4.8, using Theorem 5.1 and again Lemmas A.1 and 4.1, we can obtain a special solution to the GSE (5.1) with F being given in the Jordan form (5.74).

Theorem 5.10 *Let $A(s) \in \mathbb{R}^{n \times q}[s]$, $B(s) \in \mathbb{R}^{n \times r}[s]$, $F \in \mathbb{C}^{p \times p}$ be in the Jordan form of (5.74), and Assumption 5.2 hold. Further, let $U(s) \in \mathbb{R}^{q \times n}[s]$ and $T(s) \in \mathbb{R}^{r \times n}[s]$ be given by DPE (5.7) with $C(s)$ satisfying (5.8). Then,*

1. *The nonhomogeneous GSE (5.1) has a solution if and only if there exists an $R' \in \mathbb{C}^{n \times p}$ satisfying (5.75).*
2. *The matrices V and W are given by*

> *Formula II''_N*
>
> $$\begin{bmatrix} v_{ij} \\ w_{ij} \end{bmatrix} = \sum_{k=0}^{j-1} \frac{1}{k!} \frac{d^k}{ds^k} \begin{bmatrix} U(s_i) \\ T(s_i) \end{bmatrix} r'_{i,j-k}, \tag{5.76}$$
>
> $$j = 1, 2, \ldots, p_i, \quad i = 1, 2, \ldots, w,$$

with R' determined from (5.75) (if exists) satisfying the GSE (5.1).

When written in a loose form, solution (5.76) appears to be

$$\begin{bmatrix} v_{ij} \\ w_{ij} \end{bmatrix} = \begin{bmatrix} U(s_i) \\ T(s_i) \end{bmatrix} r'_{ij} + \frac{1}{1!} \frac{d}{ds} \begin{bmatrix} U(s_i) \\ T(s_i) \end{bmatrix} r'_{i,j-1}$$

$$+ \cdots + \frac{1}{(j-1)!} \frac{d^{j-1}}{ds^{j-1}} \begin{bmatrix} U(s_i) \\ T(s_i) \end{bmatrix} r'_{i1}.$$

Using Lemma 5.1, Theorems 4.8 and 5.1, we immediately have the following result about the general solution to the nonhomogeneous GSE (5.1).

Theorem 5.11 *Let $A(s) \in \mathbb{R}^{n \times q}[s]$, $B(s) \in \mathbb{R}^{n \times r}[s]$, $q + r > n$, be given in (5.2), $F \in \mathbb{C}^{p \times p}$ be in the Jordan form of (5.74), and Assumption 5.2 hold. Further, let*

- *$N(s) \in \mathbb{R}^{q \times \beta}[s]$ and $D(s) \in \mathbb{R}^{r \times \beta}[s]$ be a pair of right coprime polynomial matrices given by (4.58) and satisfy the generalized RCF (4.56)*
- *$U(s) \in \mathbb{R}^{q \times \alpha}[s]$ and $T(s) \in \mathbb{R}^{r \times \alpha}[s]$ be given by (5.7) with $C(s)$ satisfying (5.8)*

Then, a general complete parametric solution (V, W) to the nonhomogeneous GSE (5.1) is given by

---

Formula II$''_G$

$$\begin{bmatrix} v_{ij} \\ w_{ij} \end{bmatrix} = \sum_{k=0}^{j-1} \frac{1}{k!} \frac{d^k}{ds^k} \begin{bmatrix} U(s_i) & N(s_i) \\ T(s_i) & D(s_i) \end{bmatrix} \begin{bmatrix} r'_{i,j-k} \\ z_{i,j-k} \end{bmatrix}, \qquad (5.77)$$

$$j = 1, 2, \ldots, p_i, \quad i = 1, 2, \ldots, w,$$

---

where R' is determined by (5.75) (if exists), and $z_{ij} \in \mathbb{C}^{\beta}$, $j = 1, 2, \ldots, p_i$, $i = 1, 2, \ldots, w$, are a group of arbitrary parameter vectors representing the degrees of freedom in the solution.

When written in a loose form, the above solution (5.77) clearly appears as

$$\begin{bmatrix} v_{ij} \\ w_{ij} \end{bmatrix} = \begin{bmatrix} U(s_i) & N(s_i) \\ T(s_i) & D(s_i) \end{bmatrix} \begin{bmatrix} r'_{ij} \\ z_{ij} \end{bmatrix}$$

$$+ \frac{1}{1!} \frac{d}{ds} \begin{bmatrix} U(s_i) & N(s_i) \\ T(s_i) & D(s_i) \end{bmatrix} \begin{bmatrix} r'_{i,j-1} \\ z_{i,j-1} \end{bmatrix}$$

$$+ \cdots + \frac{1}{(j-1)!} \frac{d^{j-1}}{ds^{j-1}} \begin{bmatrix} U(s_i) & N(s_i) \\ T(s_i) & D(s_i) \end{bmatrix} \begin{bmatrix} r'_{i1} \\ z_{i1} \end{bmatrix}.$$

5.5.2 Solution Based on SFR

Similarly, using Theorems 5.7 and 5.4 and also Lemmas A.1 and 4.1, we can obtain a special solution to the nonhomogeneous GSE (5.1) with F being given in the Jordan form (5.74).

Theorem 5.12 *Let $A(s) \in \mathbb{R}^{n \times q}[s]$, $B(s) \in \mathbb{R}^{n \times r}[s]$, $q + r > n$, be given in (5.2), $F \in \mathbb{C}^{p \times p}$ be in the Jordan form of (5.74), and Assumption 5.2 hold. Further, let*

- $P(s) \in \mathbb{R}^{n \times n}[s]$, $Q(s) \in \mathbb{R}^{(q+r) \times (q+r)}[s]$ *and* $\Sigma(s) \in \mathbb{R}^{\alpha \times \alpha}[s]$ *be given by SFR (5.27) and (5.28)*
- $U(s) \in \mathbb{R}^{q \times \alpha}[s]$, $T(s) \in \mathbb{R}^{r \times \alpha}[s]$ *be given by (5.29)*
- $P_1(s) \in \mathbb{R}^{\alpha \times n}[s]$ *and* $P_2(s) \in \mathbb{R}^{(n-\alpha) \times n}[s]$ *be given by (5.31)*

Then, the GSE (5.1) has a solution if and only if (5.32) holds, and in this case, a particular solution is given by

$$
\begin{cases}
V = \hat{V} \left[\Delta(F) \right]^{-1} \\
W = \hat{W} \left[\Delta(F) \right]^{-1},
\end{cases}
\tag{5.78}
$$

with

> **Formula** II'_N
>
> $$
> \begin{bmatrix} \hat{v}_{ij} \\ \hat{w}_{ij} \end{bmatrix} = \sum_{k=0}^{j-1} \frac{1}{k!} \frac{d^k}{ds^k} \begin{bmatrix} \hat{U}(s_i) \\ \hat{T}(s_i) \end{bmatrix} r_{i,j-k},
> \tag{5.79}
> $$
>
> $$
> j = 1, 2, \ldots, p_i, \quad i = 1, 2, \ldots, w,
> $$

where $\hat{U}(s)$ and $\hat{T}(s)$ are given by (5.51).

Now, using Lemma 5.1, Theorems 4.7 and 5.1, we immediately have the following result about the general solution to the nonhomogeneous matrix equation (5.1).

Theorem 5.13 *Let $A(s) \in \mathbb{R}^{n \times q}[s]$, $B(s) \in \mathbb{R}^{n \times r}[s]$, $q + r > n$, be given in (5.2), $F \in \mathbb{C}^{p \times p}$ be in the Jordan form of (5.74), and Assumption 5.2 hold. Further, let $P(s) \in \mathbb{R}^{n \times n}[s]$, $Q(s) \in \mathbb{R}^{(q+r) \times (q+r)}[s]$ and $\Sigma(s) \in \mathbb{R}^{\alpha \times \alpha}[s]$ be given by SFR (5.27) and (5.28). Then the nonhomogeneous GSE (5.1) has a solution if and only* *if condition (5.32) is met, and in this case a general complete solution* (V, W) *to the nonhomogeneous GSE (5.1) is given by*

$$\begin{cases} V = \hat{V} \left[\Delta(F) \right]^{-1} \\ W = \hat{W} \left[\Delta(F) \right]^{-1}, \end{cases} \tag{5.80}$$

with

Formula II'_G

$$\begin{bmatrix} \hat{v}_{ij} \\ \hat{w}_{ij} \end{bmatrix} = \sum_{k=0}^{j-1} \frac{1}{k!} \frac{\mathrm{d}^k}{\mathrm{d}s^k} \hat{Q}(s_i) \begin{bmatrix} r_{i,j-k} \\ z_{i,j-k} \end{bmatrix}, \tag{5.81}$$

$$j = 1, 2, \ldots, p_i, \quad i = 1, 2, \ldots, w,$$

---

where $\hat{Q}(s)$ *is defined as in (5.58),* $z_{ij} \in \mathbb{C}^{(q+r-n)}$, $j = 1, 2, \ldots, p_i$, $i = 1, 2, \ldots, w$, *are a group of arbitrary parameter vectors representing the degrees of freedom in the solution.*

Corresponding to Corollary 5.2, we also have the following results.

Corollary 5.3 *Given conditions of Theorem 5.12, then,*

1. *When* $A(s) \in \mathbb{R}^{n \times q}[s]$, $B(s) \in \mathbb{R}^{n \times r}[s]$ *are left coprime with rank* α, *the GSE (5.1) has a solution if and only if (5.32) holds, and in this case, a particular solution is given by*

$$\begin{bmatrix} v_{ij} \\ w_{ij} \end{bmatrix} = \sum_{k=0}^{j-1} \frac{1}{k!} \frac{\mathrm{d}^k}{\mathrm{d}s^k} \begin{bmatrix} \hat{U}(s_i) \\ \hat{T}(s_i) \end{bmatrix} r_{i,j-k}, \tag{5.82}$$

$$j = 1, 2, \ldots, p_i, \quad i = 1, 2, \ldots, w,$$

where $\hat{U}(s)$ *and* $\hat{T}(s)$ *are defined in (5.51).*

2. *When* $A(s) \in \mathbb{R}^{n \times q}[s]$, $B(s) \in \mathbb{R}^{n \times r}[s]$ *are F-left coprime, the GSE (5.1) always has a solution, and a particular solution is given by (5.78) and (5.79) with*

$$\begin{bmatrix} \hat{U}(s) \\ \hat{T}(s) \end{bmatrix} = \begin{bmatrix} U(s) \\ T(s) \end{bmatrix} \mathrm{adj}\, \Sigma(s) P(s). \tag{5.83}$$

3. When $A(s) \in \mathbb{R}^{n \times q} [s]$, $B(s) \in \mathbb{R}^{n \times r} [s]$ are left coprime, the GSE (5.1) always has a solution, and a particular solution is given by (5.82) with

$$\begin{bmatrix} \hat{U}(s) \\ \hat{T}(s) \end{bmatrix} = \begin{bmatrix} U(s) \\ T(s) \end{bmatrix} P(s). \tag{5.84}$$

Further, for the controllable case, we also have the following result.

Corollary 5.4 *Let $A(s) \in \mathbb{R}^{n \times q} [s]$ and $B(s) \in \mathbb{R}^{n \times r} [s]$, $q + r > n$, be given by (5.2) and be left coprime, $F \in \mathbb{C}^{p \times p}$ be in the Jordan form of (5.74). Furthermore, let $Q(s) \in \mathbb{R}^{(q+r) \times (q+r)}[s]$ be a unimodular polynomial matrix satisfying (5.64). Then,*

1. *For an arbitrary $R \in \mathbb{C}^{n \times p}$, the nonhomogeneous GSE (5.1) has a solution, and a particular solution is given by*

   > Formula II_N
   >
   > $$\begin{bmatrix} v_{ij} \\ w_{ij} \end{bmatrix} = \sum_{k=0}^{j-1} \frac{1}{k!} \frac{d^k}{ds^k} \begin{bmatrix} U(s_i) \\ T(s_i) \end{bmatrix} r_{i,j-k}, \tag{5.85}$$
   >
   > $$j = 1, 2, \ldots, p_i, \quad i = 1, 2, \ldots, w;$$

2. *A general solution is given by*

   > Formula II_G
   >
   > $$\begin{bmatrix} v_{ij} \\ w_{ij} \end{bmatrix} = \sum_{k=0}^{j-1} \frac{1}{k!} \frac{d^k}{ds^k} Q(s_i) \begin{bmatrix} r_{i,j-k} \\ z_{i,j-k} \end{bmatrix}, \tag{5.86}$$
   >
   > $$j = 1, 2, \ldots, p_i, \quad i = 1, 2, \ldots, w,$$

   where $z_{ij} \in \mathbb{C}^{(q+r-n)}$, $j = 1, 2, \ldots, p_i$, $i = 1, 2, \ldots, w$, are a group of arbitrary parameter vectors representing the degrees of freedom in the solution.

Suppose that the ith Jordan block in the Jordan matrix F is a third-order one, that is,

$$J_i = \begin{bmatrix} s_i & 1 & 0 \\ 0 & s_i & 1 \\ 0 & 0 & s_i \end{bmatrix},$$

then it follows from formula (5.85) that the vectors $\left(v_{ij},\ w_{ij}\right)$, $j = 1, 2, 3$, in a particular solution $(V,\ W)$ are explicitly given as follows:

$$\begin{cases} \begin{bmatrix} v_{i1} \\ w_{i1} \end{bmatrix} = \begin{bmatrix} U\,(s_i) \\ T\,(s_i) \end{bmatrix} r_{i1} \\[2mm] \begin{bmatrix} v_{i2} \\ w_{i2} \end{bmatrix} = \begin{bmatrix} U\,(s_i) \\ T\,(s_i) \end{bmatrix} r_{i2} + \frac{\mathrm{d}}{\mathrm{d}s} \begin{bmatrix} U\,(s_i) \\ T\,(s_i) \end{bmatrix} r_{i1} \\[2mm] \begin{bmatrix} v_{i3} \\ w_{i3} \end{bmatrix} = \begin{bmatrix} U\,(s_i) \\ T\,(s_i) \end{bmatrix} r_{i3} + \frac{\mathrm{d}}{\mathrm{d}s} \begin{bmatrix} U\,(s_i) \\ T\,(s_i) \end{bmatrix} r_{i2} + \frac{1}{2}\frac{\mathrm{d}^2}{\mathrm{d}s^2} \begin{bmatrix} U\,(s_i) \\ T\,(s_i) \end{bmatrix} r_{i1}. \end{cases} \tag{5.87}$$

Similarly, it follows from formula (5.86) that the vectors $\left(v_{ij},\ w_{ij}\right)$, $j = 1, 2, 3$, in a general solution $(V,\ W)$ are explicitly given as follows:

$$\begin{cases} \begin{bmatrix} v_{i1} \\ w_{i1} \end{bmatrix} = Q\,(s_i) \begin{bmatrix} r_{i1} \\ z_{i1} \end{bmatrix} \\[2mm] \begin{bmatrix} v_{i2} \\ w_{i2} \end{bmatrix} = Q\,(s_i) \begin{bmatrix} r_{i2} \\ z_{i2} \end{bmatrix} + \frac{\mathrm{d}}{\mathrm{d}s} Q\,(s_i) \begin{bmatrix} r_{i1} \\ z_{i1} \end{bmatrix} \\[2mm] \begin{bmatrix} v_{i3} \\ w_{i3} \end{bmatrix} = Q\,(s_i) \begin{bmatrix} r_{i3} \\ z_{i3} \end{bmatrix} + \frac{\mathrm{d}}{\mathrm{d}s} Q\,(s_i) \begin{bmatrix} r_{i2} \\ z_{i2} \end{bmatrix} + \frac{1}{2}\frac{\mathrm{d}^2}{\mathrm{d}s^2} Q\,(s_i) \begin{bmatrix} r_{i1} \\ z_{i1} \end{bmatrix}. \end{cases} \tag{5.88}$$

Remark 5.10 The above results give closed-form particular and general complete parametric solutions to the nonhomogeneous GSE (5.1) for the case of F being a Jordan matrix. It may have noticed that both the particular and general solutions possess a same structure as the general solution to the corresponding homogeneous GSE. The correspondence relations are

$$\begin{bmatrix} N(s) \\ D(s) \end{bmatrix} \longleftrightarrow \begin{bmatrix} U(s) \\ T(s) \end{bmatrix} \longleftrightarrow Q(s),$$

and

$$Z \longleftrightarrow R \longleftrightarrow \begin{bmatrix} R \\ Z \end{bmatrix}.$$

Remark 5.11 For the general solution (5.85), all the degrees of freedom are represented by the matrix Z, or equivalently, the set of vectors z_{ij}, $j = 1, 2, \ldots, p_i$, $i = 1, 2, \ldots, w$. Both the particular and general solutions allow the matrix R to be set undetermined, and also allow the eigenvalues of the matrix F to be set undetermined, but restricted to be different from the uncontrollable modes of $(A(s), B(s))$.

Particularly, in the case that $(A(s), B(s))$ is controllable, the matrix F can be arbitrarily chosen. These degrees of freedom may give great convenience and advantages to some analysis and design problems in control system theory.

5.5.3 Example

Example 5.4

In order to demonstrate the proposed approach, let us consider a third-order GSE in the form of (5.1) with

$$A_3 = \begin{bmatrix} 1 & 0 & 0 \\ 0 & 1 & 0 \\ 0 & 0 & 0 \end{bmatrix}, \ A_2 = \begin{bmatrix} 1 & 0 & 1 \\ 0 & 2 & -1 \\ 1 & -1 & 3 \end{bmatrix},$$

$$A_1 = \begin{bmatrix} 2 & 0 & 0 \\ 0 & 1 & 2 \\ 0 & 2 & 1 \end{bmatrix}, \ A_0 = \begin{bmatrix} 0 & -1 & 0 \\ -1 & 1 & 2 \\ 0 & 1 & 1 \end{bmatrix},$$

and

$$B_3 = B_2 = B_1 = 0, \ B = \begin{bmatrix} 1 & 0 \\ 0 & 0 \\ 0 & 1 \end{bmatrix}.$$

It may have been noted that these parameters have appeared in Examples 4.3, 4.4, and 5.3.

Using Lemma 3.4, it is easy to verify that this matrix pair $(A(s), B(s))$ is controllable, and a pair of polynomial matrices $N(s)$ and $D(s)$ satisfying the generalized RCF (4.56) are obtained as

$$N(s) = \begin{bmatrix} s^3 + 2s^2 + s + 1 & -s^2 + 2s + 2 \\ 1 & 0 \\ 0 & 1 \end{bmatrix},$$

$$D(s) = \begin{bmatrix} s^6 + 3s^5 + 5s^4 + 6s^3 + 3s^2 + 2s - 1 & -s^5 + s^4 + 2s^3 + 7s^2 + 4s \\ s^5 + 2s^4 + s^3 + 2s + 1 & -s^4 + 2s^3 + 5s^2 + s + 1 \end{bmatrix},$$

and a pair of polynomial matrices $U(s)$ and $T(s)$ given by (5.40) are obtained as

$$U(s) = \begin{bmatrix} 0 & -1 & 0 \\ 0 & 0 & 0 \\ 0 & 0 & 0 \end{bmatrix}, \ T(s) = -\begin{bmatrix} 1 & s^3 + s^2 + 2s & 0 \\ 0 & s^2 & 1 \end{bmatrix}.$$

Taking the matrix F as in (5.72), that is,

$$F = \begin{bmatrix} -1 & 1 \\ 0 & -1 \end{bmatrix},$$

which is a Jordan matrix, we can also solve this GSE using Theorem 5.2, which gives, for an arbitrary matrix R, the following general solution

$$V = \begin{bmatrix} v_{11} & v_{12} \end{bmatrix}, \quad W = \begin{bmatrix} w_{11} & w_{12} \end{bmatrix},$$

with

$$\begin{bmatrix} v_{11} \\ w_{11} \end{bmatrix} = \begin{bmatrix} N(-1) & U(-1) \\ D(-1) & T(-1) \end{bmatrix} \begin{bmatrix} z_{11} \\ r_{11} \end{bmatrix},$$

and

$$\begin{bmatrix} v_{12} \\ w_{12} \end{bmatrix} = \begin{bmatrix} N(-1) & U(-1) \\ D(-1) & T(-1) \end{bmatrix} \begin{bmatrix} z_{12} \\ r_{12} \end{bmatrix}$$
$$+ \frac{1}{1!} \frac{d}{ds} \begin{bmatrix} N(-1) & U(-1) \\ D(-1) & T(-1) \end{bmatrix} \begin{bmatrix} z_{11} \\ r_{11} \end{bmatrix}.$$

Since

$$\frac{d}{ds} N(s) = \begin{bmatrix} 3s^2 + 4s + 1 & -2s + 2 \\ 0 & 0 \\ 0 & 0 \end{bmatrix},$$

$$\frac{d}{ds} D(s) = \begin{bmatrix} 6s^5 + 15s^4 + 20s^3 + 18s^2 + 6s + 2 \\ 5s^4 + 8s^3 + 3s^2 + 2 \end{bmatrix}$$
$$\begin{matrix} -5s^4 + 4s^3 + 6s^2 + 14s + 4 \\ -4s^3 + 6s^2 + 10s + 1 \end{matrix} \Bigg],$$

and

$$\frac{d}{ds} U(s) = \begin{bmatrix} 0 & 0 & 0 \\ 0 & 0 & 0 \\ 0 & 0 & 0 \end{bmatrix},$$

$$\frac{d}{ds} T(s) = \begin{bmatrix} 0 & 3s^2 + 2s + 2 & 0 \\ 0 & 2s & 0 \end{bmatrix}.$$

As in Example 5.3, choosing $Z = I_2$, and

$$R = \begin{bmatrix} 3 & 1 \\ 0 & 5 \\ 4 & 0 \end{bmatrix},$$

we can obtain

$$\begin{bmatrix} v_{11} \\ w_{11} \end{bmatrix} = \begin{bmatrix} 1 & -1 & 0 & -1 & 0 \\ 1 & 0 & 0 & 0 & 0 \\ 0 & 1 & 0 & 0 & 0 \\ -3 & 3 & -1 & 2 & 0 \\ -1 & 2 & 0 & -1 & -1 \end{bmatrix} \begin{bmatrix} 1 \\ 0 \\ 3 \\ 0 \\ 4 \end{bmatrix} = \begin{bmatrix} 1 \\ 1 \\ 0 \\ -6 \\ -5 \end{bmatrix},$$

and

$$\begin{bmatrix} v_{12} \\ w_{12} \end{bmatrix} = \begin{bmatrix} 1 & -1 & 0 & -1 & 0 \\ 1 & 0 & 0 & 0 & 0 \\ 0 & 1 & 0 & 0 & 0 \\ -3 & 3 & -1 & 2 & 0 \\ -1 & 2 & 0 & -1 & -1 \end{bmatrix} \begin{bmatrix} 0 \\ 1 \\ 1 \\ 5 \\ 0 \end{bmatrix}$$

$$+ \begin{bmatrix} 0 & 4 & 0 & 0 & 0 \\ 0 & 0 & 0 & 0 & 0 \\ 0 & 0 & 0 & 0 & 0 \\ 3 & -13 & 0 & -3 & 0 \\ 2 & 1 & 0 & 2 & 0 \end{bmatrix} \begin{bmatrix} 1 \\ 0 \\ 3 \\ 0 \\ 4 \end{bmatrix} = \begin{bmatrix} -6 \\ 0 \\ 1 \\ 15 \\ -1 \end{bmatrix}.$$

Thus, the solution is given by

$$V = \begin{bmatrix} 1 & -6 \\ 1 & 0 \\ 0 & 1 \end{bmatrix}, \quad W = \begin{bmatrix} -6 & 15 \\ -5 & -1 \end{bmatrix}.$$

5.6 Case of *F* Being Diagonal

A diagonal matrix is a special Jordan matrix. Yet due to its special importance, in this section we further specify the case that the matrix F in the higher-order GSE (5.1) is a diagonal matrix, that is,

$$F = \text{diag}\left(s_1, s_2, \cdots, s_p\right), \tag{5.89}$$

where $s_i \in \mathbb{C}$, $i = 1, 2, \ldots, p$, may not be distinct. Such a special case is often encountered in practical applications and hence is very important.

When the F matrix is diagonal, by Convention C1 the columns v_{i1}, w_{i1}, z_{i1}, r_{i1}, and r'_{i1} of matrices V, W, Z, R, and R', respectively, are well-defined. Without loss of generality, we can further denote, similar to Convention C2, the vectors v_{i1}, w_{i1}, z_{i1}, r_{i1}, and r'_{i1} simply by v_i, w_i, z_i, r_i, and r'_i. Also, in this special case Assumption 5.1 simply becomes

Assumption 5.3 $\begin{cases} \text{rank}\begin{bmatrix} A(s) & B(s) \end{bmatrix} \leq \alpha, \ \forall s \in \mathbb{C} \\ \text{rank}\begin{bmatrix} A(s_i) & B(s_i) \end{bmatrix} = \alpha, \quad i = 1, 2, \ldots, p. \end{cases}$

5.6.1 Solution Based on RCF and DPE

When the matrix F is in the form of (5.89), the solution existence condition (5.75) becomes

$$C(s_i) r'_i = r_i, \quad i = 1, 2, \ldots, p. \tag{5.90}$$

Simply by specifying the matrix F in Theorem 5.10, we can obtain a special solution to the GSE (5.1) with F being given in the diagonal form (5.89).

Theorem 5.14 *Let $A(s) \in \mathbb{R}^{n \times q}[s]$, $B(s) \in \mathbb{R}^{n \times r}[s]$, $q + r > n$, be given in (5.2), $F \in \mathbb{C}^{p \times p}$ be in the diagonal form of (5.89), and Assumption 5.3 hold. Further, let $U(s) \in \mathbb{R}^{q \times \alpha}[s]$ and $T(s) \in \mathbb{R}^{r \times \alpha}[s]$ be given by (5.7) with $C(s)$ satisfying (5.8). Then,*

1. *The GSE (5.1) has a solution if and only if there exists a matrix R' satisfying the equations in (5.90).*
2. *When the above condition is met, the matrices V and W given by*

$$
\boxed{
\begin{aligned}
&\text{Formula III}''_N \\
&\begin{bmatrix} v_i \\ w_i \end{bmatrix} = \begin{bmatrix} U(s_i) \\ T(s_i) \end{bmatrix} r'_i, \quad i = 1, 2, \ldots, p,
\end{aligned}
}
\tag{5.91}
$$

with R' determined by (5.90) satisfy the GSE (5.1).

Further, using Lemma 5.1, Theorems 4.8 and 5.14, we immediately have the following result about the general solution to the nonhomogeneous GSE (5.1).

Theorem 5.15 *Let $A(s) \in \mathbb{R}^{n \times q}[s]$, $B(s) \in \mathbb{R}^{n \times r}[s]$, $q + r > n$, be given in (5.2), $F \in \mathbb{C}^{p \times p}$ be in the diagonal form of (5.89), and Assumption 5.3 hold.*

■ $N(s) \in \mathbb{R}^{q \times \beta}[s]$ and $D(s) \in \mathbb{R}^{r \times \beta}[s]$ be a pair of right coprime polynomial matrices given by (4.58) and satisfy the generalized RCF (4.56)
■ $U(s) \in \mathbb{R}^{q \times \alpha}[s]$ and $T(s) \in \mathbb{R}^{r \times \alpha}[s]$ be given by (5.7) with $C(s)$ satisfying (5.8) and the set of equations in (5.90)

Then, a general complete parametric solution (V, W) to the nonhomogeneous GSE (5.1) is given by

> Formula III''_G
> $$\begin{bmatrix} v_i \\ w_i \end{bmatrix} = \begin{bmatrix} U(s_i) & N(s_i) \\ T(s_i) & D(s_i) \end{bmatrix} \begin{bmatrix} r'_i \\ z_i \end{bmatrix}, \quad i = 1, 2, \dots, p,$$

(5.92)

where R' is determined by (5.90), and $z_i \in \mathbb{C}^\beta$, $i = 1, 2, \dots, p$, are a group of arbitrary parameter vectors representing the degrees of freedom in the solution.

Let Assumption 5.3 be strengthened to

Assumption 5.4 $\operatorname{rank}[A(s_i) \ B(s_i)] = n, \ i = 1, 2, \dots, p,$

which is equivalent to that $A(s)$ and $B(s)$ are F-left coprime. Since in this case we have

$$C(s) = P(s)\Sigma(s),$$

with $P(s)$ a unimodular matrix, and $\Sigma(s)$ a diagonal matrix satisfying

$$\det \Sigma(s) \neq 0, \ \forall s \in \operatorname{eig}(F),$$

the condition (5.90) has a unique solution, which is given by

$$r'_i = C^{-1}(s_i) r_i, \quad i = 1, 2, \dots, p.$$

(5.93)

This fact immediately gives the following corollary.

Corollary 5.5 *Let $A(s) \in \mathbb{R}^{n \times q}[s]$, $B(s) \in \mathbb{R}^{n \times r}[s]$, $F \in \mathbb{C}^{p \times p}$ be in the diagonal form of (5.89), and Assumption 5.4 hold. Further, let $U(s) \in \mathbb{R}^{q \times \alpha}[s]$ and $T(s) \in \mathbb{R}^{r \times \alpha}[s]$ be given by (5.7) with $C(s)$ satisfying (5.8). Then, the GSE (5.1) always has a solution, and particularly, a pair of matrices V and W satisfying the GSE (5.1) are given by*

$$\begin{bmatrix} v_i \\ w_i \end{bmatrix} = \begin{bmatrix} U'(s_i) \\ T'(s_i) \end{bmatrix} r_i, \quad i = 1, 2, \dots, p,$$

(5.94)

with

$$\begin{bmatrix} U'(s) \\ T'(s) \end{bmatrix} = C^{-1}(s) \begin{bmatrix} U(s) \\ T(s) \end{bmatrix}.$$

5.6.2 Solution Based on SFR

When F is given in the diagonal form of (5.89), by simplifying Theorem 5.12, we can obtain a special solution to the nonhomogeneous GSE (5.1).

Theorem 5.16 *Let $A(s) \in \mathbb{R}^{n \times q}[s]$, $B(s) \in \mathbb{R}^{n \times r}[s]$, $q + r > n$, be given in (5.2), $F \in \mathbb{C}^{p \times p}$ be in the diagonal form of (5.89), and Assumption 5.3 be satisfied. Further, let*

- $P(s) \in \mathbb{R}^{n \times n}[s]$, $Q(s) \in \mathbb{R}^{(q+r) \times (q+r)}[s]$ *and* $\Sigma(s) \in \mathbb{R}^{\alpha \times \alpha}[s]$ *be given by SFR (5.27) and (5.28)*
- $U(s) \in \mathbb{R}^{q \times \alpha}[s]$, $T(s) \in \mathbb{R}^{r \times \alpha}[s]$ *be given by (5.29)*
- $P_1(s) \in \mathbb{R}^{\alpha \times n}[s]$ *and* $P_2(s) \in \mathbb{R}^{(n-\alpha) \times n}[s]$ *be given by (5.31)*

Then, the GSE (5.1) has a solution if and only if (5.32) holds, and in this case, a particular solution is given by

$$\boxed{\begin{array}{l} \textit{Formula III}'_N \\[2mm] \begin{bmatrix} v_i \\ w_i \end{bmatrix} = \begin{bmatrix} \mathring{U}(s_i) \\ \mathring{T}(s_i) \end{bmatrix} r_i, \quad i = 1, 2, \ldots, p, \end{array}} \tag{5.95}$$

where

$$\begin{bmatrix} \mathring{U}(s_i) \\ \mathring{T}(s_i) \end{bmatrix} = \frac{1}{\Delta(s_i)} \begin{bmatrix} \hat{U}(s_i) \\ \hat{T}(s_i) \end{bmatrix}$$

$$= \begin{bmatrix} U(s_i) \\ T(s_i) \end{bmatrix} \Sigma^{-1}(s_i) P_1(s_i),$$

$$i = 1, 2, \ldots, p.$$

Proof. According to Theorem 5.12, under condition (5.32), a particular solution to the GSE is given by

$$\begin{cases} V = \hat{V} [\Delta(F)]^{-1} \\ W = \hat{W} [\Delta(F)]^{-1}, \end{cases} \tag{5.96}$$

with

$$\begin{bmatrix} \hat{v}_i \\ \hat{w}_i \end{bmatrix} = \begin{bmatrix} \hat{U}(s_i) \\ \hat{T}(s_i) \end{bmatrix} r_i, \quad i = 1, 2, \ldots, p, \tag{5.97}$$

where $\hat{U}(s)$ and $\hat{T}(s)$ are given by (5.51). Noting the diagonal form of F, we have

$$[\Delta(F)]^{-1} = \text{diag}\left(\frac{1}{\Delta(s_1)}, \frac{1}{\Delta(s_2)}, \ldots, \frac{1}{\Delta(s_p)} \right).$$

Therefore, (5.96) is equivalent to

$$\begin{cases} v_i = \frac{1}{\Delta(s_i)} \hat{v}_i \\ w_i = \frac{1}{\Delta(s_i)} \hat{w}_i, \quad i = 1, 2, \ldots, p. \end{cases}$$

Combining the above equations with those in (5.97) yields our solution (5.95). ■

Now, using Lemma 5.1, Theorems 4.7 and 5.16, we immediately have the following result about the general solution to the nonhomogeneous matrix equation (5.1).

Theorem 5.17 *Let $A(s) \in \mathbb{R}^{n \times q}[s]$, $B(s) \in \mathbb{R}^{n \times r}[s]$, $q + r > n$, be given in (5.2), $F \in \mathbb{C}^{p \times p}$ be in the diagonal form of (5.89), and Assumption 5.3 be met. Further, let $P(s) \in \mathbb{R}^{n \times n}[s]$, $Q(s) \in \mathbb{R}^{(q+r) \times (q+r)}[s]$, and $\Sigma(s) \in \mathbb{R}^{\alpha \times \alpha}[s]$ be given by SFR (5.27) and (5.28). Then, the nonhomogeneous GSE (5.1) has a solution if and only if condition (5.32) is met, and in this case, a general complete parametric solution (V, W) to the nonhomogeneous GSE (5.1) is given by*

$$\boxed{\begin{array}{l} \textit{Formula III}'_G \\[1em] \begin{bmatrix} v_i \\ w_i \end{bmatrix} = \frac{1}{\Delta(s_i)} \hat{Q}(s_i) \begin{bmatrix} r_i \\ z_i \end{bmatrix}, \quad i = 1, 2, \ldots, p, \end{array}} \tag{5.98}$$

where $\hat{Q}(s)$ is defined as in (5.58), $z_i \in \mathbb{C}^{\beta}$, $i = 1, 2, \ldots, p$, are a group of arbitrary parameter vectors, which represent the degrees of freedom in the solution.

Corresponding to Corollary 5.3, we also have the following results.

Corollary 5.6 *Given conditions of Theorem 5.16, then,*

1. *When $A(s) \in \mathbb{R}^{n \times q}[s]$, $B(s) \in \mathbb{R}^{n \times r}[s]$ are left coprime with rank α, the GSE (5.1) has a solution if and only if (5.32) holds, and in this case, a particular solution is given by*

$$\begin{bmatrix} v_i \\ w_i \end{bmatrix} = \begin{bmatrix} \hat{U}(s_i) \\ \hat{T}(s_i) \end{bmatrix} r_i, \quad i = 1, 2, \ldots, p, \tag{5.99}$$

where $\hat{U}(s)$ and $\hat{T}(s)$ are defined in (5.51).

2. *When $A(s) \in \mathbb{R}^{n \times q}[s]$, $B(s) \in \mathbb{R}^{n \times r}[s]$ are F-left coprime, the GSE (5.1) always has a solution, and a particular solution is given by (5.95) with*

$$\begin{bmatrix} \mathring{U}(s_i) \\ \mathring{T}(s_i) \end{bmatrix} = \begin{bmatrix} U(s_i) \\ T(s_i) \end{bmatrix} \Sigma^{-1}(s_i) P(s_i), \quad i = 1, 2, \ldots, p. \tag{5.100}$$

3. *When $A(s) \in \mathbb{R}^{n \times q}[s]$, $B(s) \in \mathbb{R}^{n \times r}[s]$ are left coprime, the GSE (5.1) always has a solution, and a particular solution is given by (5.99) with*

$$\begin{bmatrix} \hat{U}(s) \\ \hat{T}(s) \end{bmatrix} = \begin{bmatrix} U(s) \\ T(s) \end{bmatrix} P(s). \tag{5.101}$$

For the controllable case, we also have the following result.

Corollary 5.7 *Let $F \in \mathbb{C}^{p \times p}$ be in the diagonal form of (5.89), $A(s) \in \mathbb{R}^{n \times q}[s]$, $B(s) \in \mathbb{R}^{n \times r}[s]$, $q + r > n$, be given in (5.2) and $(A(s), B(s))$ be controllable. Furthermore, let $Q(s) \in \mathbb{R}^{(q+r) \times (q+r)}[s]$ be a unimodular polynomial matrix satisfying (5.64). Then,*

1. *For an arbitrary $R \in \mathbb{C}^{n \times p}$, the nonhomogeneous GSE (5.1) has a particular solution, which is given by*

$$\boxed{\begin{array}{l} \textit{Formula III}_N \\ \begin{bmatrix} v_i \\ w_i \end{bmatrix} = \begin{bmatrix} U(s_i) \\ T(s_i) \end{bmatrix} r_i, \quad i = 1, 2, \ldots, p. \end{array}} \tag{5.102}$$

2. *A general solution to the GSE (5.1) is given by*

$$\boxed{\begin{array}{l} \textit{Formula III}_G \\ \begin{bmatrix} v_i \\ w_i \end{bmatrix} = Q(s_i) \begin{bmatrix} r_i \\ z_i \end{bmatrix}, \quad i = 1, 2, \ldots, p, \end{array}} \tag{5.103}$$

where $z_i \in \mathbb{C}^{(q+r-n)}$, $i = 1, 2, \ldots, p$, are a group of arbitrary vectors.

Remark 5.12 Again, simplicity is the ultimate sophistication, is the best art. The results in this section give very simple and neat particular and general complete parametric solutions to the nonhomogeneous GSE (5.1) for the case of F being a diagonal matrix. Particularly, the above Formulas III_N (5.102) and III_G (5.103) appear to be extremely simple.

Remark 5.13 For the general solution (5.103), all the degrees of freedom are represented by the set of vectors z_i, $i = 1, 2, \ldots, p$. The matrix R and the eigenvalues of the matrix F can also be set undetermined in both the particular and general solutions, and used as a part of the degrees of freedom. These degrees of freedom may give great convenience and advantages to some analysis and design problems in control system theory.

5.6.3 Example

Example 5.5

Again, consider the well-known space rendezvous system described by the C-W equation, with a failed thruster, treated in Examples 3.1 and 4.6. The system has a standard matrix second-order form of

$$\ddot{x} + D\dot{x} + Kx = Bu,$$

with

$$D = \begin{bmatrix} 0 & -2\omega & 0 \\ 2\omega & 0 & 0 \\ 0 & 0 & 0 \end{bmatrix}, \ K = \begin{bmatrix} -3\omega^2 & 0 & 0 \\ 0 & 0 & 0 \\ 0 & 0 & \omega^2 \end{bmatrix}, \ B = \begin{bmatrix} 1 & 0 \\ 0 & 0 \\ 0 & 1 \end{bmatrix}.$$

As shown in Example 3.1, this system is not controllable, and it has an uncontrollable mode at the origin. Also, the SFR (5.27) and (5.28) has been obtained with $P(s) = I_3$,

$$Q(s) = \begin{bmatrix} -s & 0 & 0 & \frac{1}{2\omega} & 0 \\ 2\omega & 0 & 0 & 0 & 0 \\ 0 & 1 & 0 & 0 & 0 \\ -4\omega^2 s - (s^2 - 3\omega^2)s & 0 & -1 & \frac{1}{2\omega}(s^2 - 3\omega^2) & 0 \\ 0 & s^2 + \omega^2 & 0 & 0 & -1 \end{bmatrix},$$

and

$$\Sigma(s) = \begin{bmatrix} 1 & 0 & 0 \\ 0 & s & 0 \\ 0 & 0 & 1 \end{bmatrix}.$$

Thus,

$$U(s) = \frac{1}{2\omega} \begin{bmatrix} 0 & 1 & 0 \\ 0 & 0 & 0 \\ 0 & 0 & 0 \end{bmatrix},$$

$$T(s) = \frac{1}{2\omega} \begin{bmatrix} -2\omega & s^2 - 3\omega^2 & 0 \\ 0 & 0 & -2\omega \end{bmatrix},$$

we can then obtain by (5.100), for $i = 1, 2, \ldots, p$,

$$\mathring{U}(s_i) = U(s_i) \Sigma^{-1}(s_i) = \frac{1}{2\omega s_i} \begin{bmatrix} 0 & 1 & 0 \\ 0 & 0 & 0 \\ 0 & 0 & 0 \end{bmatrix},$$

$$\mathring{T}(s_i) = T(s_i) \Sigma^{-1}(s_i) = \frac{1}{2\omega s_i} \begin{bmatrix} -2\omega s_i & s_i^2 - 3\omega^2 & 0 \\ 0 & 0 & -2\omega s_i \end{bmatrix}.$$

Therefore, it follows from formula (5.95) that, when

$$r_i = \begin{bmatrix} 1 \\ 0 \\ \beta_i \end{bmatrix}, \quad i = 1, 2, \ldots, p, \tag{5.104}$$

a particular solution, which does not dependent on the matrix F, to the corresponding nonhomogeneous GSE is given by

$$v_i = 0, \quad w_i = -\begin{bmatrix} 1 \\ \beta_i \end{bmatrix}, \quad i = 1, 2, \ldots, p.$$

5.7 Case of F Being Diagonally Known

In Section 5.6, solution to the nonhomogeneous GSE (5.1) with matrix F being diagonal is considered, where the eigenvalues of the matrix F are not needed until the very last step to express the solutions. In this section, we still treat the case that the matrix F is in the diagonal form of (5.89), but with the eigenvalues s_i, $i = 1, 2, \ldots, p$, being known *a priori*.

The technique applied here is first presented in Section 3.6, with strict proof for the controllable case, and then used in Section 4.6.2 for solving homogeneous GSEs with a prescribed diagonal matrix F. In this section, we are applying the technique to solve a nonhomogeneous GSEs with a prescribed diagonal matrix F. The results are presented without strict proofs.

It is clearly observed from Section 5.6 that, when the matrix F is diagonal, a special solution and the general solution to the nonhomogeneous GSE (5.1) can be immediately written out when the following polynomial matrices are obtained:

- $N(s) \in \mathbb{R}^{q \times \beta}[s]$ and $D(s) \in \mathbb{R}^{r \times \beta}[s]$ given by (4.58) and satisfy (4.56)
- $U(s) \in \mathbb{R}^{q \times \alpha}[s]$ and $T(s) \in \mathbb{R}^{r \times \alpha}[s]$ given by (5.7) with $C(s)$ satisfying (5.8), or $U(s) \in \mathbb{R}^{q \times n}[s]$ and $T(s) \in \mathbb{R}^{r \times n}[s]$ given by (5.40) with $\Delta(s)$ defined in (3.70)
- $P(s) \in \mathbb{R}^{n \times n}[s]$, $Q(s) \in \mathbb{R}^{(q+r) \times (q+r)}[s]$ and $\Sigma(s) \in \mathbb{R}^{\alpha \times \alpha}[s]$ given by SFR (4.54) and (4.55) or SFR (3.64) and (3.65)

More importantly, it can be observed that it is the values of these polynomials at s_i, $i = 1, 2, \ldots, p$, namely, $N(s_i)$, $D(s_i)$, $U(s_i)$, $T(s_i)$, $C(s_i)$, $\Delta(s_i)$, $P(s_i)$, $Q(s_i)$, and $\Sigma(s_i)$, $i = 1, 2, \ldots, p$, which are really used in the solutions. Therefore, in the case that the eigenvalues s_i, $i = 1, 2, \ldots, p$, are prescribed, we would naturally ask the following question:

Can we find a way to compute these values directly instead of solving these polynomials?

In this section, we show that the answer to the above question is positive and the well-known SVD provides a perfect technique to fulfil this task.

5.7.1 SFR and SVD

Under Assumption 5.1, or equivalently Assumption 5.3 when F is diagonal, we have, by Theorem 3.7, the following SFR:

$$P(s)\left[A(s) \quad -B(s)\right]Q(s) = \begin{bmatrix} \Sigma(s) & 0 \\ 0 & 0 \end{bmatrix}, \qquad (5.105)$$

with $\Sigma(s) \in \mathbb{R}^{\alpha \times \alpha}[s]$ diagonal and satisfying

$$\det \Sigma(s_i) \neq 0, \qquad i = 1, 2, \ldots, p. \qquad (5.106)$$

Therefore, the values $P(s_i)$, $Q(s_i)$, and $\Sigma(s_i)$ used in Theorem 5.3 actually should satisfy, besides the nonsingularity of $P(s_i)$ and $Q(s_i)$, relations (5.106) and

$$P(s_i)\left[A(s_i) \quad -B(s_i)\right]Q(s_i) = \begin{bmatrix} \Sigma(s_i) & 0 \\ 0 & 0 \end{bmatrix}, \qquad i = 1, 2, \ldots, p. \qquad (5.107)$$

On the other side, if we apply SVD to $\left[A(s_i) \quad -B(s_i)\right]$, we can obtain two orthogonal matrices P_i, Q_i and a nonsingular diagonal matrix Σ_i satisfying the following:

$$P_i\left[A(s_i) \quad -B(s_i)\right]Q_i = \begin{bmatrix} \Sigma_i & 0 \\ 0 & 0 \end{bmatrix}, \qquad i = 1, 2, \ldots, p. \qquad (5.108)$$

Comparison of the above two equations obviously suggests the following:

$$\begin{cases} P_i = P(s_i) \\ Q_i = Q(s_i) \\ \Sigma_i = \Sigma(s_i), \quad i = 1, 2, \ldots, p. \end{cases} \tag{5.109}$$

5.7.1.1 Discretized RCF and DPE

Partition the matrix Q_i as

$$Q_i = \begin{bmatrix} U_i & N_i \\ T_i & D_i \end{bmatrix}, \quad U_i \in \mathbb{R}^{q \times \alpha}, \quad T_i \in \mathbb{R}^{r \times \alpha}, \tag{5.110}$$

then we have from (5.108),

$$A(s_i)N_i - B(s_i)D_i = 0, \quad i = 1, 2, \ldots, p, \tag{5.111}$$

and

$$A(s_i)U_i - B(s_i)T_i = C_i, \quad i = 1, 2, \ldots, p, \tag{5.112}$$

with

$$C_i = P_i^{-1} \begin{bmatrix} \Sigma_i \\ 0 \end{bmatrix}, \quad i = 1, 2, \ldots, p. \tag{5.113}$$

The above two relations (5.111) and (5.112), together with Lemma 3.4, further suggest that

$$\begin{cases} N_i = N(s_i), \quad D_i = D(s_i) \\ U_i = U(s_i), \quad T_i = T(s_i) \\ C_i = C(s_i), \quad i = 1, 2, \ldots, p. \end{cases} \tag{5.114}$$

5.7.1.2 Discretized Form of Condition (5.11)

Due to (5.114), condition (5.11) is replaced to

$$C_i r_i' = r_i, \quad i = 1, 2, \ldots, p. \tag{5.115}$$

Further, substituting the expression of C_i in (5.113) into the above equations yields

$$\begin{bmatrix} \Sigma_i \\ 0 \end{bmatrix} r_i' = P_i r_i, \quad i = 1, 2, \ldots, p, \tag{5.116}$$

which has a solution with respect to R' if and only if

$$\begin{bmatrix} 0 & I_{n-\alpha} \end{bmatrix} P_i r_i = 0, \quad i = 1, 2, \ldots, p, \tag{5.117}$$

and in this case, R' is uniquely given by

$$r_i' = \Sigma_i^{-1} \begin{bmatrix} I_\alpha & 0 \end{bmatrix} P_i r_i, \quad i = 1, 2, \ldots, p. \tag{5.118}$$

5.7.2 Solution Based on SVD

With the above preparation, and using Theorem 5.14, we immediately have the following result about a particular solution to the nonhomogeneous GSE (5.1).

Theorem 5.18 *Let $A(s) \in \mathbb{R}^{n \times q}[s]$, $B(s) \in \mathbb{R}^{n \times r}[s]$, $q + r > n$, be given in (5.2), $F \in \mathbb{C}^{p \times p}$ be in the diagonal form of (5.89), and Assumption 5.3 hold. Further, let $P_i \in \mathbb{R}^{n \times n}$, $U_i \in \mathbb{R}^{q \times \alpha}$, $T_i \in \mathbb{R}^{r \times \alpha}$, and $\Sigma_i \in \mathbb{R}^{\alpha \times \alpha}$ be given by (5.108), (5.110), and (5.113). Then,*

1. *The nonhomogeneous GSE (5.1) has a solution if and only if (5.117) holds.*
2. *When the above condition is met, the matrices V and W given by*

$$\boxed{\begin{array}{l} \textit{Formula } III_N^* \\[4pt] \begin{bmatrix} v_i \\ w_i \end{bmatrix} = \begin{bmatrix} \hat{U}_i \\ \hat{T}_i \end{bmatrix} r_i, \quad i = 1, 2, \ldots, p, \end{array}} \tag{5.119}$$

with

$$\begin{bmatrix} \hat{U}_i \\ \hat{T}_i \end{bmatrix} = \begin{bmatrix} U_i \\ T_i \end{bmatrix} \Sigma_i^{-1} \begin{bmatrix} I_\alpha & 0 \end{bmatrix} P_i, \tag{5.120}$$

satisfy the nonhomogeneous GSE (5.1).

Again, with the above preparation, and using Theorem 5.17, we immediately have the following result about the general solution to the nonhomogeneous GSE (5.1).

Theorem 5.19 *Let $A(s) \in \mathbb{R}^{n \times q}[s]$, $B(s) \in \mathbb{R}^{n \times r}[s]$, $q + r > n$, be given in (5.2), $F \in \mathbb{C}^{p \times p}$ be in the diagonal form of (5.89), and Assumption 5.3 be satisfied. Further, let $P_i \in \mathbb{R}^{n \times n}$, $Q_i \in \mathbb{R}^{(q+r) \times (q+r)}$, and $\Sigma_i \in \mathbb{R}^{\alpha \times \alpha}$, $i = 1, 2, \ldots, p$, be given by (5.108). Then,*

- *The nonhomogeneous GSE (5.1) has a solution if and only if the equations in (5.117) hold.*
- *When the above condition is met, the general complete solution (V, W) to the nonhomogeneous GSE (5.1) is given by*

$$
\boxed{
\begin{array}{l}
\textit{Formula III}^*_G \\[6pt]
\begin{bmatrix} v_i \\ w_i \end{bmatrix} = \hat{Q}_i \begin{bmatrix} r_i \\ z_i \end{bmatrix}, \quad i = 1, 2, \ldots, p,
\end{array}
}
\tag{5.121}
$$

where

$$
\hat{Q}_i = Q_i \begin{bmatrix} \Sigma_i^{-1} \begin{bmatrix} I_\alpha & 0 \end{bmatrix} P_i & 0 \\ 0 & I_\alpha \end{bmatrix}, \quad i = 1, 2, \ldots, p,
$$

and $z_i \in \mathbb{C}^\beta$, $i = 1, 2, \ldots, p$, are a group of arbitrary parameter vectors representing the degrees of freedom in the solution.

In the above solutions, polynomial matrix operations are no longer needed. This obviously gives great convenience to the computation of the solution. Moreover, note that SVD is well known for its numerical reliability, and the solution can be immediately obtained as soon as the set of SVDs in (5.108) are carried out, the solution procedure of this solution is extremely numerically simple and reliable.

Corresponding to Corollary 5.6, we also have the following results.

Corollary 5.8 *Given conditions of Theorem 5.16, then,*

1. *When $A(s) \in \mathbb{R}^{n \times q}[s]$, $B(s) \in \mathbb{R}^{n \times r}[s]$ are left coprime with rank α, the GSE (5.1) has a solution if and only if (5.117) holds, and in this case, a particular solution is given by (5.119) with*

$$
\begin{bmatrix} \hat{U}_i \\ \hat{T}_i \end{bmatrix} = \begin{bmatrix} U_i \\ T_i \end{bmatrix} \begin{bmatrix} I_\alpha & 0 \end{bmatrix} P_i.
\tag{5.122}
$$

2. *When $A(s) \in \mathbb{R}^{n \times q}[s]$, $B(s) \in \mathbb{R}^{n \times r}[s]$ are F-left coprime with rank n, the GSE (5.1) always has a solution, and a particular solution is given by (5.119) with*

$$
\begin{bmatrix} \hat{U}_i \\ \hat{T}_i \end{bmatrix} = \begin{bmatrix} U_i \\ T_i \end{bmatrix} \Sigma_i^{-1} P_i.
\tag{5.123}
$$

3. *When $A(s) \in \mathbb{R}^{n \times q} [s]$, $B(s) \in \mathbb{R}^{n \times r} [s]$ are left coprime, the GSE (5.1) always has a solution, and a particular solution is given by (5.119) with*

$$\begin{bmatrix} \hat{U}_i \\ \hat{T}_i \end{bmatrix} = \begin{bmatrix} U_i \\ T_i \end{bmatrix} P_i. \tag{5.124}$$

Example 5.6

Again, consider the well-known space rendezvous system described by the C-W equation, with a failed thruster, treated in Examples 3.1 and 4.6. The system has a standard matrix second-order form of

$$\ddot{x} + D\dot{x} + Kx = Bu,$$

with

$$D = \begin{bmatrix} 0 & -2\omega & 0 \\ 2\omega & 0 & 0 \\ 0 & 0 & 0 \end{bmatrix}, \ K = \begin{bmatrix} -3\omega^2 & 0 & 0 \\ 0 & 0 & 0 \\ 0 & 0 & \omega^2 \end{bmatrix}, \ B = \begin{bmatrix} 1 & 0 \\ 0 & 0 \\ 0 & 1 \end{bmatrix}.$$

As shown in Example 3.1, this system is not controllable, and it has an uncontrollable mode at the origin.

In the following, let us consider the same nonhomogeneous GSE as in Example 5.5 using Corollary 5.8. Let us assume that the target is moving on a geosynchronous orbit, with $\omega = 7.292115 \times 10^{-5}$ rad/s.

As in Example 4.6, we also take

$$F = \text{diag}\,(-1, -2, -3, -4, -5).$$

By (5.108), (5.110), and (5.113), the matrices $P_i \in \mathbb{R}^{3 \times 3}$, $U_i \in \mathbb{R}^{3 \times 3}$, $T_i \in \mathbb{R}^{2 \times 3}$, and $\Sigma_i \in \mathbb{R}^{3 \times 3}$ are obtained for $i = 1, 2, \ldots, 5$. Further, according to (5.123), we have

$$\hat{U}_1 = \begin{bmatrix} 0.49999999 & -0.00014584 & 0 \\ 0.00007292 & 0.99999998 & 0 \\ 0 & 0 & 0.50000000 \end{bmatrix},$$

$$\hat{U}_2 = \begin{bmatrix} 0.23529412 & -0.00001823 & 0 \\ 0.00001716 & 0.25000000 & 0 \\ 0 & 0 & 0.23529412 \end{bmatrix},$$

$$\hat{U}_3 = \begin{bmatrix} 0.10975610 & -0.00000540 & 0 \\ 0.00000534 & 0.11111111 & 0 \\ 0 & 0 & 0.10975610 \end{bmatrix},$$

$$\hat{U}_4 = \begin{bmatrix} 0.06225681 & -0.00000228 & 0 \\ 0.00000227 & 0.06250000 & 0 \\ 0 & 0 & 0.06225681 \end{bmatrix},$$

$$\hat{U}_5 = \begin{bmatrix} 0.03993610 & -0.00000117 & 0 \\ 0.00000116 & 0.04000000 & 0 \\ 0 & 0 & 0.03993610 \end{bmatrix},$$

and

$$\hat{T}_1 = \begin{bmatrix} -0.50000000 & 0.00000000 & 0 \\ 0 & 0 & -0.50000000 \end{bmatrix},$$

$$\hat{T}_2 = \begin{bmatrix} -0.05882353 & 0.00000000 & 0 \\ 0 & 0 & -0.05882353 \end{bmatrix},$$

$$\hat{T}_3 = \begin{bmatrix} -0.01219512 & 0.00000000 & 0 \\ 0 & 0 & -0.01219512 \end{bmatrix},$$

$$\hat{T}_4 = \begin{bmatrix} -0.00389105 & 0.00000000 & 0 \\ 0 & 0 & -0.00389105 \end{bmatrix},$$

$$\hat{T}_5 = \begin{bmatrix} -0.00159744 & 0.00000000 & 0 \\ 0 & 0 & -0.00159744 \end{bmatrix}.$$

With these matrices determined, a particular solution is given by

$$\begin{cases} v_i = \hat{U}_i r_i \\ w_i = \hat{T}_i r_i, \quad i = 1, 2, \ldots, 5. \end{cases}$$

Particularly, choosing

$$r_i = \begin{bmatrix} i - 2 \\ -i + 3 \\ 1 \end{bmatrix}, \quad i = 1, 2, \ldots, 5,$$

gives the following solutions:

$$V = \begin{bmatrix} -0.5002917 & -0.0000182 & 0.1097561 & 0.1245159 & 0.1198106 \\ 1.9999270 & 0.2500000 & 0.0000053 & -0.0624955 & -0.0799965 \\ 0.5000000 & 0.2352941 & 0.1097561 & 0.0622568 & 0.0399361 \end{bmatrix},$$

and

$$W = \begin{bmatrix} 0.5000000 & 0.0000000 & -0.0121951 & -0.0077821 & -0.0047923 \\ -0.5000000 & -0.0588235 & -0.0121951 & -0.0038911 & -0.0015974 \end{bmatrix}.$$

With the above obtained matrices V and W, it can be verified that

$$\left\| VF^2 + DVF + KV - BW - R \right\|_{fro} = 1.40125764 \times 10^{-7}.$$

5.8 Examples

In Section 1.2, we have given a few practical examples, for which the solutions to the corresponding generalized RCF (3.45) and the DPE (3.54) are provided in Section 3.5. Furthermore, the corresponding homogeneous GSEs have also been solved in Section 4.7 for the case of F being diagonal.

In this section, we further look into the solutions to the corresponding nonhomogeneous GSEs for the case of F being diagonal. For convenience, with each example we choose here the same corresponding diagonal matrix F as in Section 4.7. Since the general solutions to the corresponding homogeneous GSEs have already been given in Section 4.7, here in this section we only concentrated on some particular solutions of the corresponding nonhomogeneous GSEs.

5.8.1 First-Order Systems

Example 5.7 (Multiagent Kinematics System)

Consider the multiagent kinematics system introduced in Example 1.2, which is a first-order system with the following coefficient matrices:

$$E = \begin{bmatrix} 8 & 0 & 0 & 0 & 0 \\ 0 & 1 & 0 & 0 & 0 \\ 0 & 0 & 10 & 0 & 0 \\ 0 & 0 & 0 & 1 & 0 \\ 0 & 0 & 0 & 0 & 12 \end{bmatrix},$$

$$A = \begin{bmatrix} -0.1 & 0 & 0 & 0 & 0 \\ 1 & 0 & -1 & 0 & 0 \\ 0 & 0 & -0.1 & 0 & 0 \\ 0 & 0 & 1 & 0 & -1 \\ 0 & 0 & 0 & 0 & -0.1 \end{bmatrix}, \ B = \begin{bmatrix} 1 & 0 & 0 \\ 0 & 0 & 0 \\ 0 & 1 & 0 \\ 0 & 0 & 0 \\ 0 & 0 & 1 \end{bmatrix}.$$

As in Example 4.7, we take

$$F = \operatorname{diag}(-1 \pm 2\,\mathrm{i}, -3, -3, -4).$$

Further, we assume

$$R = I_5.$$

It has been proposed in Example 3.3 that this system is controllable, and a pair of polynomial matrices $U(s)$ and $T(s)$ satisfying the DPE (3.78) are given as

$$U(s) = \begin{bmatrix} 0 & 0 & 0 & 0 & 0 \\ 0 & 0 & 0 & 0 & 0 \\ 0 & 1 & 0 & 0 & 0 \\ 0 & 0 & 0 & 0 & 0 \\ 0 & 1 & 0 & 1 & 0 \end{bmatrix},$$

and

$$T(s) = \begin{bmatrix} -1 & 0 & 0 & 0 & 0 \\ 0 & 10s + 0.1 & -1 & 0 & 0 \\ 0 & 12s + 0.1 & 0 & 12s + 0.1 & -1 \end{bmatrix}.$$

Thus by formula (5.102), we can obtain a particular solution to this corresponding nonhomogeneous GSE as

$$V = \begin{bmatrix} 0 & 0 & 0 & 0 & 0 \\ 0 & 0 & 0 & 0 & 0 \\ 0 & 1 & 0 & 0 & 0 \\ 0 & 0 & 0 & 0 & 0 \\ 0 & 1 & 0 & 1 & 0 \end{bmatrix},$$

and

$$W = \begin{bmatrix} -1 & 0 & 0 & 0 & 0 \\ 0 & -9.9 - 20\,i & -1 & 0 & 0 \\ 0 & -11.9 - 24\,i & 0 & -35.9 & -1 \end{bmatrix}.$$

Example 5.8 (Constrained Mechanical System in First-Order Form)

Consider the constrained system in first-order form given in Example 1.3, which has the following coefficient matrices:

$$E = \begin{bmatrix} 1 & 0 & 0 & 0 & 0 \\ 0 & 1 & 0 & 0 & 0 \\ 0 & 0 & 1 & 0 & 0 \\ 0 & 0 & 0 & 1 & 0 \\ 0 & 0 & 0 & 0 & 0 \end{bmatrix},$$

$$A = \begin{bmatrix} 0 & 0 & 1 & 0 & 0 \\ 0 & 0 & 0 & 1 & 0 \\ -2 & 0 & -1 & -1 & 1 \\ 0 & -1 & -1 & -1 & 1 \\ 1 & 1 & 0 & 0 & 0 \end{bmatrix}, \ B = \begin{bmatrix} 0 \\ 0 \\ 1 \\ -1 \\ 0 \end{bmatrix}.$$

As in Example 4.8, we take

$$F = \operatorname{diag}(-1, -2, -3).$$

Further, we assume

$$R = \begin{bmatrix} 0 & 0 & 0 \\ 1 & 0 & 0 \\ 0 & 1 & 0 \\ 0 & 0 & 1 \\ 0 & 0 & 0 \end{bmatrix}.$$

It has been proposed in Example 3.4 that this system is controllable, and a pair of polynomial matrices $U(s)$ and $T(s)$ satisfying the DPE (3.78) are given as

$$U(s) = \frac{1}{2} \begin{bmatrix} 0 & 0 & 0 & 0 & 0 \\ 0 & 0 & 0 & 0 & -2 \\ -2 & 0 & 0 & 0 & 0 \\ 0 & -2 & 0 & 0 & -2s \\ -s-2 & -s-2 & -1 & -1 & -(s+1)^2 \end{bmatrix},$$

$$T(s) = \frac{1}{2} \begin{bmatrix} -s & s & -1 & 1 & s^2+1 \end{bmatrix}.$$

Thus by formula (5.102), we obtain a particular solution to this corresponding nonhomogeneous GSE as

$$V = \begin{bmatrix} 0 & 0 & 0 \\ 0 & 0 & 0 \\ 0 & 0 & 0 \\ -1 & 0 & 0 \\ -\frac{1}{2} & -\frac{1}{2} & -\frac{1}{2} \end{bmatrix},$$

and

$$W = \frac{1}{2} \begin{bmatrix} -1 & -1 & 1 \end{bmatrix}.$$

5.8.2 Second-Order Systems

Example 5.9 (Constrained Mechanical System in Second-Order Form)

Consider the constrained mechanical system treated in Example 1.3, which is in a matrix second-order form with the following coefficient matrices:

$$A_2 = \begin{bmatrix} 1 & 0 & 0 \\ 0 & 1 & 0 \\ 0 & 0 & 0 \end{bmatrix}, \ A_1 = \begin{bmatrix} 1 & 1 & 0 \\ 1 & 1 & 0 \\ 0 & 0 & 0 \end{bmatrix},$$

$$A_0 = \begin{bmatrix} 2 & 0 & -1 \\ 0 & 1 & -1 \\ 1 & 1 & 0 \end{bmatrix}, \ B = \begin{bmatrix} 1 \\ -1 \\ 0 \end{bmatrix}.$$

As in Example 4.9, we take

$$F = \text{diag}\,(-1, -2, -3, -4, -5, -6).$$

Further, we assume

$$R = [I_3 \quad 0_{3\times3}].$$

It has been proposed in Example 3.5 that this system is controllable, and a pair of polynomial matrices $U(s)$ and $T(s)$ satisfying the DPE (3.78) are given as

$$U(s) = \frac{1}{2}\begin{bmatrix} 0 & 0 & 0 \\ 0 & 0 & 2 \\ -1 & -1 & (s+1)^2 \end{bmatrix},$$

$$T(s) = \frac{1}{2}\begin{bmatrix} -1 & 1 & -s^2 - 1 \end{bmatrix}.$$

Thus by formula (5.102), we obtain a particular solution to this corresponding nonhomogeneous GSE as

$$V = \frac{1}{2}\begin{bmatrix} 0 & 0 & 0 & 0 & 0 & 0 \\ 0 & 0 & 2 & 0 & 0 & 0 \\ -1 & -1 & 4 & 0 & 0 & 0 \end{bmatrix},$$

and

$$W = \frac{1}{2}\begin{bmatrix} -1 & 1 & -10 & 0 & 0 & 0 \end{bmatrix}.$$

Example 5.10 (Flexible-Joint Mechanism—Case of Second-Order Model)

The flexible-joint mechanism treated in Example 1.4 is modeled by a system in a matrix second-order form with the following parameters:

$$M = 0.0004 \times \begin{bmatrix} 1 & 0 \\ 0 & 1 \end{bmatrix}, \quad D = \begin{bmatrix} 0 & 0 \\ 0 & 0.015 \end{bmatrix},$$

$$K = 0.8 \times \begin{bmatrix} 1 & -1 \\ -1 & 1 \end{bmatrix}, \quad B = \begin{bmatrix} 0 \\ 1 \end{bmatrix}.$$

As in Example 4.10, we take

$$F = \text{diag}\,(-1 \pm i, -1, -2).$$

Further, we assume

$$R = \begin{bmatrix} 0 & 1 & 0 & 0 \\ -1 & 0 & 0 & 1 \end{bmatrix}.$$

It has been proposed in Example 3.6 that this system is controllable, and a pair of polynomial matrices $U(s)$ and $T(s)$ satisfying the DPE (3.78) are given as

$$U(s) = \begin{bmatrix} 0 & 0 \\ -\frac{5}{4} & 0 \end{bmatrix},$$

$$T(s) = \begin{bmatrix} -0.0005s^2 - 0.01875s - 1.0 & -1 \end{bmatrix}.$$

Thus by formula (5.102), we obtain a particular solution to this corresponding nonhomogeneous GSE as

$$V = \frac{5}{4} \begin{bmatrix} 0 & 0 & 0 & 0 \\ 0 & -1 & 0 & 0 \end{bmatrix},$$

and

$$W = \begin{bmatrix} 1 & -0.98125 + 0.01775\,i & 0 & -1 \end{bmatrix}.$$

5.8.3 Higher-Order Systems

Example 5.11 (Flexible-Joint Mechanism—Case of Third-Order Model)

The flexible-joint mechanism treated in Example 1.5 is modeled by a system in a matrix third-order form with the following parameters:

$$A_3 = \begin{bmatrix} 0 & 0 \\ 0 & 0.0004 \end{bmatrix}, \quad A_2 = 10^{-3} \times \begin{bmatrix} 0.4 & 0 \\ 0 & 15.38 \end{bmatrix},$$

and

$$A_1 = \begin{bmatrix} 0 & 0 \\ -0.8 & 0.814\,25 \end{bmatrix}, \quad A_0 = \begin{bmatrix} 0.8 & -0.8 \\ -0.76 & 0.76 \end{bmatrix}, \quad B = \begin{bmatrix} 0 \\ 1 \end{bmatrix}.$$

As in Example 4.11, we take

$$F = \operatorname{diag}(-1, -2, -3).$$

Further, we assume

$$R = \begin{bmatrix} 1 & 1 & 0 \\ 0 & -1 & -1 \end{bmatrix}.$$

It has been proposed in Example 3.7 that this system is controllable, and a pair of polynomial matrices $U(s)$ and $T(s)$ satisfying the DPE (3.78) are given as

$$U(s) = \frac{1}{8}\begin{bmatrix} 0 & 0 \\ -10 & 0 \end{bmatrix},$$

$$T(s) = \frac{1}{8}\begin{bmatrix} -0.004s^3 - 0.1538s^2 - 8.1425s - 7.6 & -8 \end{bmatrix}.$$

Thus by formula (5.102), we can obtain a particular solution to this corresponding nonhomogeneous GSE as

$$V = \frac{5}{4}\begin{bmatrix} 0 & 0 & 0 \\ -1 & -1 & 0 \end{bmatrix},$$

and

$$W = \begin{bmatrix} 4.9088 \times 10^{-2} & 2.0127 & 1 \end{bmatrix}.$$

5.9 Notes and References

By now, we have finished the most important chapter in the book (Figure 5.1). In this chapter, general solutions to the several types of nonhomogeneous GSEs are investigated. As in Chapter 4, the main feature of these solutions is that they have a highly unified complete analytical parametric form which suits all the various types of nonhomogeneous GSEs mentioned in this book. Because of this feature, as in Chapter 4, we have not gone to cover all the cases. Those cases that are really tackled in this chapter are shown in Table 5.1. Readers may give the presentations of the results for the rest cases by themselves.

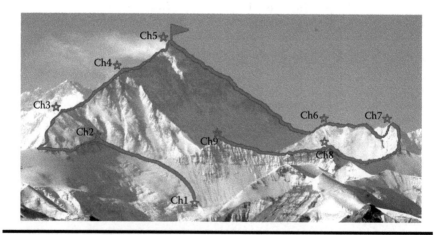

Figure 5.1 We are here, conquered the peak. (Modified from http://go.jutuw.com/zhumulangmafeng/photo/.)

Table 5.1   Nonhomogeneous GSEs Treated in the Chapter

Cases	F Arbitrary	F Jordan	F Diagonal
Higher-order	Yes	Yes	Yes
Second-order	–	–	–
First-order (descriptor)	–	–	–
First-order (normal)	–	–	–

In the following, we mention some of the author's work related to the contents of this chapter.

5.9.1 First-Order GSEs

As we have seen, the first-order nonhomogeneous GSE, which attracts the most attention, takes the form of (1.63), that is,

$$EVF - AV = BW + R. \qquad (5.125)$$

This equation has a close relation with certain control design problems in descriptor linear systems Duan (2010).

When the matrix F is substituted with J, an arbitrary given Jordan matrix, Duan et al. (1999e) propose based on elementary matrix transformations general complete parameterizations of all the matrices V and W satisfying this GSE. Later this result is modified in Duan (2004d), which presents a simple parametric solution to this GSE based on the SFR of the matrix $[A - sE \; B]$. The solution possesses a very simple and neat form, and does not require the eigenvalues of matrix J to be known.

For this GSE, a complete explicit general solution is also established in Wu and Duan (2008a) based on elementary transformations of polynomial matrices. The proposed solution does not involve the derivative of polynomial matrices and not require the eigenvalues of matrix F to be known. When the eigenvalues of matrix F are prescribed, the solution for the pair of matrices V and W can be obtained by carrying out a series of SVDs, thus possesses good numerical stability. An example is employed to illustrate the effect of the proposed approaches.

Besides the above, we have also proposed finite iterative algorithms for generalized Sylvester-conjugate matrix equation in the form of (Wu et al., 2010a)

$$E\bar{V}F - AV = BW + R. \qquad (5.126)$$

When $E = I$, the identity matrix, the GSE (5.125) reduces to

$$VF - AV = BW + R, \qquad (5.127)$$

which has applications in control designs in normal linear systems.

For the first-order GSE (1.64), Zhou and Duan (2007a) propose an explicit parametric solution, which is presented in terms of the Krylov matrix of matrix pair (A, B), a symmetric operator and the generalized observability matrix of matrix pair (Z, F), where Z is an arbitrary matrix representing the degrees of freedom in the solution.

When $A = I_n$, the equation in (5.125) is also called a nonhomogeneous Yakubovich matrix equation. Very recently, Song et al. (2014e) consider solution to nonhomogeneous Yakubovich matrix equations and presented two methods to obtain the closed-form solutions of the nonhomogeneous Yakubovich-transpose matrix equation.

Different from the above, the author has considered GSEs in the more general form of (1.62), that is,

$$EVF - AV = B_1 WF + B_0 W + R, \qquad (5.128)$$

and has proposed in Duan (2013e) a complete general parametric solution in a neat explicit closed form using the F-coprimeness condition. The derived solution has several features:

- It is very simple and neat, and does not require the matrix F to be in any canonical form.
- It gives all the degrees of freedom represented linearly by the parameter matrix Z.
- It does not require the matrices F and R to be prescribed, and hence allows them to be set undetermined and used as a part of the degrees of freedom.
- It is linear in the matrices Z and R, which actually represent the degrees of freedom in practical applications.

5.9.2 Second- and Higher-Order GSEs

The simplest type of nonhomogeneous second-order GSEs is in the form of (1.67), that is,

$$MVF^2 + DVF + KV = BW + R. \qquad (5.129)$$

For this type of GSEs, both the particular and complete parametric general solutions have been proposed in the conference keynote paper Duan (2005a). Very recently, the type of GSEs in the form of (1.65), that is,

$$MVF^2 + DVF + KV = B_2 WF^2 + B_1 WF + B_0 W + R, \qquad (5.130)$$

was investigated by Duan (2013f). A complete general parametric solution in a neat explicit closed form is established using the F-coprimeness condition. The primary feature of this solution is that the matrix F does not need to be in any canonical form, or may be even unknown *a priori*. The matrix R, together with the matrix F, may be both set undetermined and used as degrees of freedom beyond the completely free parameter matrix Z.

For the higher-order GSE

$$A_m VF^m + \cdots + A_1 VF + A_0 V = BW + R, \qquad (5.131)$$

the preliminary paper Duan (2005a) has presented systematic theories and parametric solutions, and has also addressed various of its special cases, including the equation (5.129). Duan (2013d) recently considered the following type of nonhomogeneous higher-order GSEs in the more general form of (1.69), that is,

$$A_m VF^m + \cdots + A_1 VF + A_0 V = B_m WF^m + \cdots + B_1 WF + B_0 W + R. \qquad (5.132)$$

A complete general parametric solution in a neat explicit closed form is established using the feature of F-coprimeness. The primary feature of this solution is that the matrix F does not need to be in any canonical form, or may be even unknown *a priori*. The matrix R, together with the matrix F, may be both set undetermined and used as degrees of freedom beyond the completely free parameter matrix Z.

Finally, let us mention that we have also proposed closed-form solutions to a family of generalized Sylvester matrix equation in form of (1.70) by using Kronecker maps (Wu et al., 2007b), solutions to DPEs (Zhou et al., 2010b), and the so-called Kronecker matrix polynomials (Zhou et al., 2009e).

Chapter 6

Fully Actuated GSEs

In Chapters 4 and 5, we have given general complete parametric solutions to general homogeneous and nonhomogeneous GSEs. In this chapter, we will investigate a special type of homogeneous and nonhomogeneous GSEs, namely, fully actuated GSEs, which are often encountered in practical applications.

6.1 Fully Actuated GSEs

In order to introduce the concept of fully actuated GSEs, we first need to introduce the concept of fully actuated systems.

6.1.1 Fully Actuated Systems

The term "full actuation" really originated from a type of mechanical second-order systems of the following form:

$$M\ddot{x} + D\dot{x} + Kx = Bu, \tag{6.1}$$

where

- M, D, and K are the mass matrix, the damping matrix, and the stiffness matrix, respectively
- B is the control distribution coefficient matrix
- x is the position vector of the system
- u is the force or torque vector acting on the system

We point out that in many cases the matrix B is an identity one, in this case the system certainly has as many input variables as the system state variables, or in other words, the number of effective control channels of the system is equal to the number of the state variables. Such systems are said to be fully actuated systems. More generally, as long as the matrix B is a nonsingular one, that is, $\det B \neq 0$, we say that the system is fully actuated.

This concept can be generalized to higher-order systems of the following form:

$$A_m x^{(m)} + \cdots + A_1 \dot{x} + A_0 x = B_m u^{(m)} + \cdots + B_1 \dot{u} + B_0 u, \qquad (6.2)$$

where

- $x \in \mathbb{R}^q$ and $u \in \mathbb{R}^r$ are the state vector and control vector, respectively
- $A_i \in \mathbb{R}^{n \times q}$, $B_i \in \mathbb{R}^{n \times r}$, $i = 0, 1, \ldots, m$, are the system coefficient matrices

The two polynomial matrices associated with this system are

$$\begin{cases} A(s) = A_m s^m + \cdots + A_2 s^2 + A_1 s + A_0 \\ B(s) = B_m s^m + \cdots + B_2 s^2 + B_1 s + B_0. \end{cases} \qquad (6.3)$$

Definition 6.1 *The above higher-order system is called fully actuated if $B(s) \in \mathbb{R}^{n \times n}[s]$ is unimodular, that is,*

$$\det B(s) \neq 0, \ \forall s \in \mathbb{C}, \qquad (6.4)$$

and is called fully actuated over a matrix $F \in \mathbb{C}^{p \times p}$ if

$$\det B(s) \neq 0, \ \forall s \in \mathrm{eig}(F). \qquad (6.5)$$

Obviously, a system in the form of (6.2) is fully actuated if and only if it is fulled actuated over arbitrary matrix $F \in \mathbb{C}^{p \times p}$. Since there exists a $F \in \mathbb{C}^{p \times p}$ satisfying

$$\mathrm{rank} \begin{bmatrix} A(s) & B(s) \end{bmatrix} = n, \ \forall s \in \mathrm{eig}(F)$$

under condition (6.5); and

$$\mathrm{rank} \begin{bmatrix} A(s) & B(s) \end{bmatrix} = n, \ \forall s \in \mathbb{C},$$

holds under condition (6.4), the following proposition obviously follows from the above definition.

Proposition 6.1 *Consider the system (6.2),*

1. *It is regularizable if it is fully actuated over some matrix $F \in \mathbb{C}^{p \times p}$, $p \geq 1$*
2. *It is controllable if it is fully actuated*

Further, note that condition (6.4) is equivalent to that

$$\mu(s) = \det B(s) = \mu$$

is a nonzero constant. Therefore,

$$B^{-1}(s) = \frac{\text{adj}B(s)}{\det B(s)} = \frac{1}{\mu}\text{adj}B(s)$$

is also a polynomial matrix. Using this property, we can show the following result.

Proposition 6.2 *Every fully actuated system in the form of (6.2) can be converted into the following standard fully actuated form:*

$$A'_\gamma x^{(\gamma)} + \cdots + A'_1 \dot{x} + A'_0 x = u. \tag{6.6}$$

Proof. Note that the frequency domain version of system (6.2) is

$$A(s)x(s) = B(s)u(s),$$

where $x(s)$ and $u(s)$ are the Laplace transforms of $x(t)$ and $u(t)$, respectively. Pre-multiplying both sides of the above equation by $B^{-1}(s)$ gives

$$B^{-1}(s)A(s)x(s) = u(s). \tag{6.7}$$

Recall that $B^{-1}(s)$ is a polynomial matrix, so is

$$\Phi(s) = B^{-1}(s)A(s),$$

and (6.7) turns to be

$$\Phi(s)x(s) = u(s),$$

whose time-domain version is clearly in the form of (6.6). ■

6.1.2 Fully Actuated GSEs

Corresponding to the higher-order system (6.2), we have the following homogeneous and nonhomogeneous GSEs as

$$\sum_{i=0}^{m} A_i V F^i = \sum_{i=0}^{m} B_i W F^i, \tag{6.8}$$

and

$$\sum_{i=0}^{m} A_i VF^i = \sum_{i=0}^{m} B_i WF^i + R, \tag{6.9}$$

respectively. Corresponding to Definition 6.1, we have the following definition for the two GSEs.

Definition 6.2 *The higher-order GSEs (6.8) and (6.9) are said to be fully actuated if their corresponding higher-order system (6.2) is fully actuated, that is, $B(s) \in \mathbb{R}^{n \times n}[s]$ is unimodular.*

Further, corresponding to Proposition 6.2, we also have the following result.

Proposition 6.3 *The higher-order GSEs (6.8) and (6.9) can always be converted into the following standard fully actuated forms of*

$$\sum_{i=0}^{\gamma} A_i' VF^i = W, \tag{6.10}$$

and

$$\sum_{i=0}^{\gamma} A_i' VF^i = W + R', \tag{6.11}$$

respectively.

The above full actuation property requires the system polynomial matrix $B(s) \in \mathbb{R}^{n \times n}[s]$ to be unimodular. We must confess that although there are many fully actuated systems in applications, there do exist systems in which the polynomial matrix $B(s)$ is indeed square but not unimodular. Due to this phenomenon, we introduce the following definition.

Definition 6.3 *The higher-order GSEs (6.8) and (6.9) are said to be F-fully actuated for some $F \in \mathbb{C}^{p \times p}$ if $B(s) \in \mathbb{R}^{n \times n}[s]$ and satisfies*

$$\det B(s) \neq 0, \ \forall s \in \text{eig}(F).$$

The matrix F in the above definition often stands for some matrix containing all or partial of the closed-loop eigenvalues in control applications, the release of the modularity requirement on $B(s)$ in the above definition has really greatly enlarged the application scope.

In the following sections, we will investigate the solutions to fully actuated, or F-fully actuated GSEs, that is, the GSEs (6.8) and (6.9) satisfying one of the following assumptions:

Assumption 6.1 $B(s) \in \mathbb{R}^{n \times n}[s]$, *and it satisfies* $\det B(s) \neq 0$, $\forall s \in \mathrm{eig}(F)$ *for some* F.

Assumption 6.2 $B(s) \in \mathbb{R}^{n \times n}[s]$, *and it satisfies* $\det B(s) \neq 0$, $\forall s \in \mathbb{C}$.

Remark 6.1 The state vector x and the input vector u in the higher-order system (6.2) have clear meanings and are certainly not exchangeable. However, for the higher-order GSE (6.9) the variables V and W are just the unknowns to be determined, and are in parallel positions. Therefore, in the case that $\det A(s) \neq 0$, $\forall s \in \mathbb{C}$, we may turn to consider the following GSE

$$\sum_{i=0}^{m} B_i W F^i = \sum_{i=0}^{m} A_i V F^i - R, \tag{6.12}$$

which is obviously fully actuated. Of course, results for fully actuated GSEs can be applied to the altered GSE.

6.1.3 Examples

The model for space rendezvous provides a typical example for a fully actuated system.

Example 6.1 (Space Rendezvous System)

Consider spacecraft rendezvous as shown in Figure 6.1. The origin of the coordinate system is taken to be the center of mass of the target, x-axis takes the direction from the earth center to the center of the spacecraft, y-axis goes along with the tangent line of the orbit of the target spacecraft, and z-axis is determined by the right-hand coordinate system. Denote by θ the true anomaly, then the coordinate system rotate with the orbital angular rate $\dot{\theta}$, and r_c corresponds in this rotating coordinate system the vector

$$r = [x_r,\ y_r,\ z_r]^{\mathrm{T}},$$

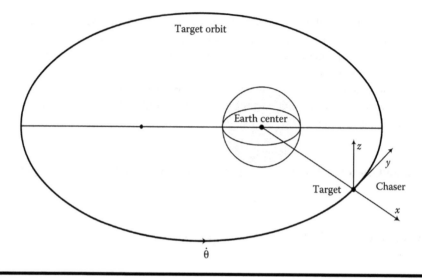

Figure 6.1 Spacecraft rendezvous. (Redrawn from Clohessy, W.H. and Wiltshire, R.S., *J. Aero. Sci.*, 27(9), 653, 1960; Schaub, H. and Junkins, J.L., *Analytical Mechanics of Space Systems*, AIAA Education Series, AIAA, Reston, VA, 2003, pp. 593–601.)

where x_r, y_r, and z_r are the relative position variables. The problem is to adjust the thrusts so as to make these relative position variables x_r, y_r, and z_r tend to zero.

When the chaser and the target are very close to each other, and also, the target orbit is circular, dynamical behavior is governed by the following so-called C-W equation, or Hill equation (Clohessy and Wiltshire 1960, Schaub and Junkins 2003):

$$\begin{bmatrix} \ddot{x}_r - 2\omega\dot{y}_r - 3\omega^2 x_r \\ \ddot{y}_r + 2\omega\dot{x}_r \\ \ddot{z}_r + \omega^2 z_r \end{bmatrix} = u, \qquad (6.13)$$

where $\omega = \dot{\theta}$ is the orbital angular rate of the chaser. Obviously, the above model can be easily arranged into the standard matrix second-order form of (6.1), with $M = B = I_3$, and

$$D = \begin{bmatrix} 0 & -2\omega & 0 \\ 2\omega & 0 & 0 \\ 0 & 0 & 0 \end{bmatrix}, \quad K = \begin{bmatrix} -3\omega^2 & 0 & 0 \\ 0 & 0 & 0 \\ 0 & 0 & \omega^2 \end{bmatrix}. \qquad (6.14)$$

It is clearly a fully actuated system.

Example 6.2 (Satellite Attitude System)

The dynamical model of the attitude system of a satellite is as follows (Duan and Yu 2013):

$$M\ddot{q} + H\dot{q} + Gq = u, \tag{6.15}$$

where

$$q = \begin{bmatrix} \varphi \\ \theta \\ \psi \end{bmatrix}, \quad u = \begin{bmatrix} T_{cx} \\ T_{cy} \\ T_{cz} \end{bmatrix},$$

are the Euler angle vector and the control torque vector, respectively,

$$M = \text{diag}\left(I_x,\ I_y,\ I_z\right),$$

$$H = \omega_0(I_y - I_x - I_z) \begin{bmatrix} 0 & 0 & 1 \\ 0 & 0 & 0 \\ -1 & 0 & 0 \end{bmatrix},$$

and

$$G = \text{diag}\left(4\omega_0^2(I_y - I_z),\ 3\omega_0^2(I_x - I_z),\ \omega_0^2(I_y - I_x)\right),$$

here I_x, I_y and I_z are the inertia matrices of the three channels, $\omega_0 = 7.292115 \times 10^{-5}$ rad/s is, the rotational-angular velocity of the earth.

This system is clearly also a fully actuated system.

Remark 6.2 As we will show in this chapter that, for F-fully actuated GSEs satisfying Assumption 6.1, the general solution can be instantly written out without any computation. However, this huge advantage vanishes if a second- or higher-order GSE is converted into a first-order one. Then, very naturally, one would raise such a question—*How often can this assumption be satisfied?* The answer to this question is two folds:

- For first-order GSEs, this assumption is really seldom satisfied.
- For second-order and higher-order GSEs, this assumption is indeed often satisfied.
- For some systems that do not satisfy such an assumption, when they are converted into a higher-order system this assumption may be granted.

This whole physical world is governed by certain laws, including Newton's law, Kirchhoff's law, etc. Such laws really originally produce system models of second-order. Then why do we not see many of such models in system analysis and control? Because most of such models have been converted into the first-order form at the early stage of modeling for treatment with techniques for first-order systems.

6.2 Homogeneous GSEs: Forward Solutions

In this section, let us consider solution to the homogeneous GSE (6.8), which satisfies Assumption 6.1 or 6.2.

Under Assumption 6.1, we have

$$\mu(s) = \det B(s) \neq 0, \ \forall s \in eig(F),$$

and the following generalized RCF

$$A(s)N(s) - B(s)D(s) = 0 \tag{6.16}$$

obviously holds for

$$\begin{cases} N(s) = \mu(s)I_q \\ D(s) = \mathrm{adj}B(s)A(s). \end{cases} \tag{6.17}$$

When, particularly, Assumption 6.2 holds, $B^{-1}(s)$ is a polynomial matrix, and the pair of polynomial matrices $N(s)$ and $D(s)$ satisfying the generalized RCF (6.16) can be replaced by

$$\begin{cases} N(s) = I_q \\ D(s) = B^{-1}(s)A(s). \end{cases} \tag{6.18}$$

The generalized RCF obviously has indefinite number of solutions with respect to the polynomial matrices $N(s)$ and $D(s)$. The solutions (6.18) and (6.17), which use really the "invertible" property of $B(s)$, are called forward solutions to the RCF (6.16). Correspondingly, the solutions to the homogeneous GSE (6.8) using the solutions (6.18) and (6.17) are also called forward solutions.

It has been seen in Chapter 4 that all we need to do to derive a general solution to the homogeneous GSE (6.8) is to solve a pair of right coprime polynomial matrices $N(s)$ and $D(s)$ satisfying the generalized RCF (6.16). Yet for the type of fully actuated GSEs, even the process of solving $N(s)$ and $D(s)$ is not needed.

6.2.1 General Solutions

6.2.1.1 Case of F Being Arbitrary

Denote

$$\Psi(s) = \mathrm{adj}B(s)A(s)$$

$$= \sum_{k=0}^{\omega} \Psi_k s^k, \ \Psi_k \in \mathbb{R}^{n \times q}. \tag{6.19}$$

Further, when Assumption 6.2 is met, $B^{-1}(s)A(s)$ is also a polynomial matrix, which can be assumed to be in the form of

$$\Phi(s) = B^{-1}(s)A(s)$$

$$= \sum_{k=0}^{\omega} \Phi_k s^k, \quad \Phi_k \in \mathbb{R}^{n \times q}, \tag{6.20}$$

Directly applying Theorem 4.7 to the fully actuated homogeneous GSE (6.8), and using the above mentioned solutions to the generalized RCF (6.16), immediately give the following result.

Theorem 6.1 *Let $A(s) \in \mathbb{R}^{n \times q}[s]$ and $B(s) \in \mathbb{R}^{n \times n}[s]$ be given as in (6.3). Further, let $\Psi(s) \in \mathbb{R}^{n \times q}[s]$ be given by (6.19), and $\Phi(s) \in \mathbb{R}^{n \times q}[s]$ be given by (6.20). Then,*

1. *When Assumption 6.1 is met, all the solutions to the GSE (6.8) are given by*

$$\begin{cases} V = Z\mu(F) \\ W = [\mathrm{adj}B(s)A(s)Z]\big|_F \\ \quad = \Psi_0 Z + \Psi_1 ZF + \cdots + \Psi_\omega ZF^\omega, \end{cases} \tag{6.21}$$

   with $Z \in \mathbb{C}^{q \times p}$ being an arbitrary parameter matrix.
2. *When, particularly, Assumption 6.2 holds, the above solution can also be replaced by*

$$\begin{cases} V = Z \\ W = [B^{-1}(s)A(s)Z]\big|_F \\ \quad = \Phi_0 Z + \Phi_1 ZF + \cdots + \Phi_\omega ZF^\omega. \end{cases} \tag{6.22}$$

Please note that in derivation of (6.21) the following relation has been used:

$$[\mu(s)Z]\big|_F = [Z\mu(s)]\big|_F = Z\mu(F).$$

6.2.1.2 Case of F Being in Jordan Form

In this subsection, let us consider the case that the matrix F is in the Jordan form of (4.63), that is,

$$
\begin{cases}
F = \text{blockdiag}\,(F_1, F_2, \ldots, F_w) \\[6pt]
F_i =
\begin{bmatrix}
s_i & 1 & & & \\
& s_i & \ddots & & \\
& & \ddots & 1 & \\
& & & s_i &
\end{bmatrix}_{p_i \times p_i}
\end{cases}
\tag{6.23}
$$

where s_i, $i = 1, 2, \ldots, w$, are obviously the eigenvalues of the matrix F, and p_i, $i = 1, 2, \ldots, w$, are the geometric multiplicities corresponding to the eigenvalues s_i, $i = 1, 2, \ldots, w$, and satisfy

$$
\sum_{i=1}^{w} p_i = p.
$$

By Convention C1, the columns w_{ij} and z_{ij} are well defined. Applying Theorem 4.8 to the fully actuated homogeneous GSE (6.8) immediately gives the following result.

Theorem 6.2 *Let $A(s) \in \mathbb{R}^{n \times q}[s]$ and $B(s) \in \mathbb{R}^{n \times n}[s]$ be given as in (6.3), F be a Jordan matrix given by (6.23). Then,*

1. *When Assumption 6.1 is met, all the solutions to the GSE (6.8) are given by*

$$
\begin{cases}
v_{ij} = \displaystyle\sum_{k=0}^{j-1} \frac{1}{k!} \frac{d^k}{ds^k} \left[\mu\,(s_i) \right] z_{i,j-k} \\[10pt]
w_{ij} = \displaystyle\sum_{k=0}^{j-1} \frac{1}{k!} \frac{d^k}{ds^k} \left[\text{adj}B\,(s_i)\, A\,(s_i) \right] z_{i,j-k}, \\[10pt]
j = 1, 2, \ldots, p_i, \quad i = 1, 2, \ldots, w,
\end{cases}
\tag{6.24}
$$

   with $z_{ij} \in \mathbb{C}^q$, $j = 1, 2, \ldots, p_i, i = 1, 2, \ldots, w$, being a group of arbitrary parameter vectors.

2. *When, in particular, Assumption 6.2 is met, the above solution can be replaced by*

$$
\begin{cases}
v_{ij} = z_{ij} \\[6pt]
w_{ij} = \displaystyle\sum_{k=0}^{j-1} \frac{1}{k!} \frac{d^k}{ds^k} \left[B^{-1}\,(s_i)\, A\,(s_i) \right] z_{i,j-k}, \\[10pt]
j = 1, 2, \ldots, p_i, \quad i = 1, 2, \ldots, w.
\end{cases}
\tag{6.25}
$$

Comparing the first equations in (6.24) with (6.21) clearly gives the following relation:

$$V = Z\mu(F) \Longleftrightarrow \begin{cases} v_{ij} = \sum_{k=0}^{j-1} \frac{1}{k!} \frac{d^k}{ds^k} \left[\mu(s_i)\right] z_{i,j-k} \\ j = 1, 2, \ldots, p_i, \quad i = 1, 2, \ldots, w. \end{cases} \quad (6.26)$$

6.2.1.3 Case of F Being Diagonal

When the matrix F reduces to the diagonal form of (4.81), that is,

$$F = \text{diag}\left(s_1, s_2, \cdots, s_p\right), \quad (6.27)$$

where s_i, $i = 1, 2, \ldots, p$, may not be distinct, by Convention C1 the columns w_i and z_i are well defined. Furthermore, in this case Assumption 6.1 becomes

$$\mu(s_i) = \det B(s_i) \neq 0, \quad i = 1, 2, \ldots, p.$$

Applying Theorem 4.9 to the fully actuated homogeneous GSE (6.8) immediately gives the solution

$$\begin{cases} v_i = \mu(s_i) z_i' \\ w_i = \text{adj}B(s_i) A(s_i) z_i', \quad i = 1, 2, \ldots, p, \end{cases}$$

where z_i', $i = 1, 2, \ldots, p$, is a group of parameter vectors. If we introduce the new parameter vectors

$$z_i = \mu(s_i) z_i', \quad i = 1, 2, \ldots, p,$$

then we have

$$w_i = \text{adj}B(s_i) A(s_i) z_i'$$

$$= \text{adj}B(s_i) A(s_i) \frac{1}{\mu(s_i)} z_i$$

$$= B^{-1}(s_i) A(s_i) z_i, \quad i = 1, 2, \ldots, p.$$

The above deduction clearly gives the following result.

Theorem 6.3 *Let $A(s) \in \mathbb{R}^{n \times q}[s]$ and $B(s) \in \mathbb{R}^{n \times n}[s]$ be given as in (6.3), $F \in \mathbb{C}^{p \times p}$ be in the diagonal form of (6.27), and Assumption 6.1 hold. Then all the solutions to the GSE (6.8) are given by*

$$\begin{cases} v_i = z_i \\ w_i = B^{-1}(s_i) A(s_i) z_i, \quad i = 1, 2, \ldots, p. \end{cases}$$

with z_i, $i = 1, 2, \ldots, p$, being a group of arbitrary parameter vectors.

6.2.1.4 Standard Fully Actuated GSEs

Using the above three theorems, we have the following result for solution to the standard homogeneous fully actuated GSE (6.10).

Theorem 6.4 *Let $A(s) \in \mathbb{R}^{n \times q}[s]$ be given as in (6.3). Then,*

1. *For arbitrary $F \in \mathbb{C}^{p \times p}$, all the solutions to the standard homogeneous fully actuated GSE (6.10) are given by*

$$\begin{cases} V = Z \\ W = [A(s)Z] \big|_F \\ \quad = A_0 Z + A_1 ZF + \cdots + A_m ZF^m; \end{cases} \tag{6.28}$$

2. *When $F \in \mathbb{C}^{p \times p}$ is in the Jordan form of (6.23), all the solutions to the standard homogeneous fully actuated GSE (6.10) are given by*

$$\begin{cases} v_{ij} = z_{ij} \\ w_{ij} = \sum_{k=0}^{j-1} \frac{1}{k!} \frac{d^k}{ds^k} A(s_i) z_{i,j-k}, \\ \quad j = 1, 2, \ldots, p_i, \quad i = 1, 2, \ldots, w; \end{cases} \tag{6.29}$$

3. *When $F \in \mathbb{C}^{p \times p}$ is in the diagonal form of (6.27), all the solutions to the standard homogeneous fully actuated GSE (6.10) are given by*

$$\begin{cases} v_i = z_i \\ w_i = A(s_i) z_i, \quad i = 1, 2, \ldots, p, \end{cases} \tag{6.30}$$

where in the above solutions the matrix $Z \in \mathbb{C}^{q \times p}$ is an arbitrary parameter matrix.

Remark 6.3 The general solution (6.28) can really be directly derived from the form of the standard homogeneous fully actuated GSE (6.10). This is due to the simplicity of the problem. However, if a higher-order equation had been converted into an extended first-order one, such a simplicity would not have remained or recognized. So, again, in related applications one should use the direct approach whenever possible.

6.2.2 Type of Second-Order GSEs

In many applications, we encounter a type of fully actuated second-order linear systems in the form of

$$M\ddot{x} + D\dot{x} + Kx = Bu,$$

where

- M, D, and K are the mass matrix, the damping matrix, and the stiffness matrix, respectively
- B is a nonsingular coefficient matrix
- x is the position vector of the system
- u is the force or torque vector acting on the system

The corresponding GSE takes the following form:

$$MVF^2 + DVF + KV = BW. \tag{6.31}$$

For the above equation, Assumption 6.2 becomes $\det B \neq 0$.

Using Theorems 6.1 through 6.3, we can immediately have the following corollary.

Corollary 6.1 *Consider the second-order GSE (6.31) satisfying $\det B \neq 0$, and let*

$$\Phi(s) = B^{-1}\left(Ms^2 + Ds + K\right). \tag{6.32}$$

Then,

1. *For an arbitrary matrix $F \in \mathbb{C}^{p \times p}$, all the solutions to the second-order GSE (6.31) are given by*

$$\begin{cases} V = Z \\ W = B^{-1}\left(MZF^2 + DZF + KZ\right), \end{cases} \tag{6.33}$$

with $Z \in \mathbb{C}^{q \times p}$ being an arbitrary parameter matrix.

2. *When F is in the Jordan form of (6.23), all the solutions to the second-order GSE (6.31) are given by*

$$\begin{cases} V = Z \\ w_{i1} = \Phi(s_i) z_{i,1} \\ w_{i2} = \Phi(s_i) z_{i,2} + B^{-1}(2Ms_i + D) z_{i,1} \\ w_{ij} = \Phi(s_i) z_{i,j} + B^{-1}(2Ms_i + D) z_{i,j-1} + B^{-1}Mz_{i,j-2}, \\ \qquad j = 3, 4, \ldots, p_i, \quad i = 1, 2, \ldots, w, \end{cases} \tag{6.34}$$

with $z_{ij} \in \mathbb{C}^q$, $j = 1, 2, \ldots, p_i$, $i = 1, 2, \ldots, w$, being a group of arbitrary parameter vectors.

3. *When F is in the diagonal form of (6.27), all the solutions to the second-order GSE (6.31) are given by*

$$\begin{cases} v_i = z_i \\ w_i = B^{-1}\left(Ms_i^2 + Ds_i + K\right)z_i, & i = 1, 2, \ldots, p, \end{cases} \tag{6.35}$$

with $z_i \in \mathbb{C}^q$, $i = 1, 2, \ldots, p$, being a group of arbitrary parameter vectors.

6.3 Homogeneous GSEs: Backward Solutions

In Section 6.2, general solutions to the fully actuated higher-order GSE (6.8) are obtained via specially choosing a pair of solutions to the generalized RCF

$$A(s)N(s) - B(s)D(s) = 0. \tag{6.36}$$

In this section, we continue the consideration of the fully actuated higher-order GSE (6.8), which satisfies Assumption 6.1 or 6.2. Different general solutions are given by choosing different solutions to the generalized RCF (6.36).

Please note that, constrained by the choices of $N(s)$ and $D(s)$, in this section we require the matrix polynomial matrix $A(s)$ to be square, that is, we assume $q = n$.

Under Assumption 6.1, it is easily observed that the generalized RCF (6.36) holds for

$$\begin{cases} N(s) = \mu(s)\mathrm{adj}A(s) \\ D(s) = \pi(s)\mathrm{adj}B(s), \end{cases} \tag{6.37}$$

where

$$\begin{cases} \mu(s) = \det B(s) \\ \pi(s) = \det A(s). \end{cases} \tag{6.38}$$

If, in particular, Assumption 6.2 holds, the pair of polynomial matrices $N(s)$ and $D(s)$ satisfying the generalized RCF (6.36) can also be replaced by

$$\begin{cases} N(s) = \mathrm{adj}A(s) \\ D(s) = \pi(s)B^{-1}(s). \end{cases} \tag{6.39}$$

Still if, in addition, $A(s)$ is also unimodular, then $A^{-1}(s)$ is also a polynomial matrix, and in this case a pair of polynomial matrices satisfying the generalized RCF (6.36) can also be taken as

$$\begin{cases} N(s) = A^{-1}(s) \\ D(s) = B^{-1}(s). \end{cases} \tag{6.40}$$

The solutions (6.37), (6.39), and (6.40), which use the "inverse property" of $A(s)$, are called backward solutions. While the solutions to the fully actuated GSE (6.8) obtained using the backward solutions (6.37), (6.39), and (6.40) are also called backward solutions. Please bear in mind that these backward solutions are only valid for the square case, that is, the case of $q = n$.

As in Section 6.2, here these two sets of solutions to the generalized RCF can also be immediately obtained using the original equation coefficients, and thus the process of solving $N(s)$ and $D(s)$ is even not needed.

6.3.1 General Solutions

For convenience, in this section we are presenting the solutions using only the Sylvester mapping

$$[P(s)Z]\big|_F$$

but not its expansion.

6.3.1.1 Case of F Being Arbitrary

Applying Theorem 4.7 to the fully actuated GSE (6.8), and using the above mentioned solutions to the generalized RCF (6.36), immediately gives the following result.

Theorem 6.5 *Let $F \in \mathbb{C}^{p \times p}$, and $A(s), B(s) \in \mathbb{R}^{n \times n}[s]$ be given as in (6.3). Then,*

1. *When Assumption 6.1 is met, the general solution to the GSE (6.8) is given by*

$$\begin{cases} V = [\mu(s)\mathrm{adj}A(s)Z]\big|_F \\ W = [\pi(s)\mathrm{adj}B(s)Z]\big|_F, \end{cases} \tag{6.41}$$

with $Z \in \mathbb{C}^{n \times p}$ being an arbitrary parameter matrix.
2. *When, in particular, Assumption 6.2 is met, the above solution can be replaced by*

$$\begin{cases} V = [\mathrm{adj}A(s)Z]\big|_F \\ W = [\pi(s)B^{-1}(s)Z]\big|_F. \end{cases} \tag{6.42}$$

3. *If, in addition, $A(s)$ is also unimodular, the solution can also be given by*

$$\begin{cases} V = [A^{-1}(s)Z]\big|_F \\ W = [B^{-1}(s)Z]\big|_F. \end{cases} \tag{6.43}$$

The above results can also be directly shown using the Sylvester mapping. Taking the solution (6.41), for example, using the properties of Sylvester mapping given in Theorem 4.1, we have

$$[A(s)V]\big|_F = \big[A(s)\left[\mu(s)\mathrm{adj}A(s)Z\right]\big|_F\big]\big|_F$$
$$= [A(s)\mu(s)\mathrm{adj}A(s)Z]\big|_F$$
$$= [\pi(s)\mu(s)Z]\big|_F,$$

and

$$[B(s)W]\big|_F = \big[B(s)\left[\pi(s)\mathrm{adj}B(s)Z\right]\big|_F\big]\big|_F$$
$$= [B(s)\pi(s)\mathrm{adj}B(s)Z]\big|_F$$
$$= [\pi(s)\mu(s)Z]\big|_F.$$

Combining the above two equations yields

$$[A(s)V]\big|_F = [B(s)W]\big|_F. \tag{6.44}$$

This is the Sylvester mapping representation of the GSE (6.8).

6.3.1.2 Case of F Being a Jordan Matrix

When the matrix F is in the Jordan form of (6.23), by Convention C1 the columns v_{ij}, w_{ij} and z_{ij} are well defined. Applying Theorem 4.8 to the fully actuated GSE (6.8), immediately gives the following result.

Theorem 6.6 *Let $A(s)$, $B(s) \in \mathbb{R}^{n\times n}[s]$ be given as in (6.3), $F \in \mathbb{C}^{p\times p}$ be a Jordan matrix given by (6.23). Then,*

1. *When Assumption 6.1 is met, the general solution to the GSE (6.8) is given by*

$$\begin{cases} v_{ij} = \sum_{k=0}^{j-1} \frac{1}{k!} \frac{d^k}{ds^k}\left[\mu\left(s_i\right)\mathrm{adj}A\left(s_i\right)\right]z_{i,j-k} \\[4mm] w_{ij} = \sum_{k=0}^{j-1} \frac{1}{k!} \frac{d^k}{ds^k}\left[\pi\left(s_i\right)\mathrm{adj}B\left(s_i\right)\right]z_{i,j-k}, \\[4mm] \quad j = 1,2,\ldots,p_i, \quad i = 1,2,\ldots,w, \end{cases} \tag{6.45}$$

with $z_{ij} \in \mathbb{C}^n$, $j = 1,2,\ldots,p_i$, $i = 1,2,\ldots,w$, being a group of arbitrary parameter vectors.

2. *When, in particular, Assumption 6.2 is met, the above solution can be replaced by*

$$
\begin{cases}
v_{ij} = \displaystyle\sum_{k=0}^{j-1} \frac{1}{k!} \frac{d^k}{ds^k} \operatorname{adj} A\,(s_i)\, z_{i,j-k} \\[4mm]
w_{ij} = \displaystyle\sum_{k=0}^{j-1} \frac{1}{k!} \frac{d^k}{ds^k} \left[\pi\,(s_i)\, B^{-1}\,(s_i) \right] z_{i,j-k}, \\[4mm]
\qquad j = 1, 2, \ldots, p_i, \quad i = 1, 2, \ldots, w.
\end{cases}
\tag{6.46}
$$

3. *If, in addition, A(s) is also unimodular, the above solutions can also be replaced by*

$$
\begin{cases}
v_{ij} = \displaystyle\sum_{k=0}^{j-1} \frac{1}{k!} \frac{d^k}{ds^k} A^{-1}\,(s_i)\, z_{i,j-k} \\[4mm]
w_{ij} = \displaystyle\sum_{k=0}^{j-1} \frac{1}{k!} \frac{d^k}{ds^k} B^{-1}\,(s_i)\, z_{i,j-k}, \\[4mm]
\qquad j = 1, 2, \ldots, p_i, \quad i = 1, 2, \ldots, w.
\end{cases}
$$

6.3.1.3 Case of F *Being Diagonal*

Further, when the matrix F reduces to the diagonal form of (6.27), by Convention C1 the columns v_i, w_i, and z_i are well defined. Applying Theorem 4.9 to the fully actuated GSE (6.8) immediately gives the following solution

$$
\begin{cases}
v_i = \mu\,(s_i)\, \operatorname{adj} A\,(s_i)\, z_i' \\
w_i = \pi\,(s_i)\, \operatorname{adj} B\,(s_i)\, z_i', \quad i = 1, 2, \ldots, p.
\end{cases}
$$

Substituting $\mu\,(s_i)\, z_i'$ with $\mu\,(s_i)\, z_i$ immediately gives the following result.

Theorem 6.7 *Let $A(s)$, $B(s) \in \mathbb{R}^{n \times n}[s]$ be given as in (6.3), $F \in \mathbb{C}^{p \times p}$ be in the diagonal form of (6.27), and Assumption 6.1 hold. Then the general solution to the GSE (6.8) is given by*

$$
\begin{cases}
v_i = \operatorname{adj} A\,(s_i)\, z_i \\
w_i = \pi\,(s_i)\, B^{-1}\,(s_i)\, z_i, \quad i = 1, 2, \ldots, p,
\end{cases}
$$

with $Z \in \mathbb{C}^{n \times p}$ being an arbitrary parameter matrix. If, in addition,

$$
\pi\,(s_i) = \det A\,(s_i) \neq 0, \quad i = 1, 2, \ldots, p,
$$

the above solutions can also be replaced by

$$\begin{cases} v_i = A^{-1}(s_i) z_i \\ w_i = B^{-1}(s_i) z_i, & i = 1, 2, \ldots, p. \end{cases}$$

6.3.2 Standard Fully Actuated GSEs

In certain cases, the fully actuated higher-order GSEs in the form of (6.8) may be solved by first converting it into standard fully actuated forms. Therefore, giving general parametric solutions to the fully actuated GSE in the standard form of (6.10) is necessary.

Setting $B(s) = I_n$ in the three theorems given in the above subsection, immediately produces the following result.

Theorem 6.8 *Let $F \in \mathbb{C}^{p \times p}$, and $A(s) \in \mathbb{R}^{n \times n}[s]$ be given as in (6.3). Then,*

1. *The general solution to the standard fully actuated GSE (6.10) is given by*

$$\begin{cases} V = [\text{adj}A(s)Z]\big|_F \\ W = Z\pi(F), \end{cases}$$

or, when $A(s)$ is also unimodular, by

$$\begin{cases} V = [A^{-1}(s)Z]\big|_F \\ W = Z, \end{cases}$$

where $Z \in \mathbb{C}^{n \times p}$ is an arbitrary parameter matrix.
2. *When $F \in \mathbb{C}^{p \times p}$ is in the Jordan form of (6.23), the general solution to the standard fully actuated GSE (6.10) is given by*

$$\begin{cases} v_{ij} = \displaystyle\sum_{k=0}^{j-1} \frac{1}{k!} \frac{d^k}{ds^k} \text{adj}A(s_i) z_{i,j-k} \\ \\ w_{ij} = \displaystyle\sum_{k=0}^{j-1} \frac{1}{k!} \frac{d^k}{ds^k} \pi(s_i) z_{i,j-k}, \\ \\ j = 1, 2, \ldots, p_i, \quad i = 1, 2, \ldots, w, \end{cases}$$

or, when A(s) is also unimodular, by

$$
\begin{cases}
w_{ij} = z_{ij} \\
v_{ij} = \displaystyle\sum_{k=0}^{j-1} \frac{1}{k!} \frac{\mathrm{d}^k}{\mathrm{d}s^k} A^{-1}(s_i) z_{i,j-k}, \\
\qquad j = 1, 2, \ldots, p_i, \quad i = 1, 2, \ldots, w,
\end{cases}
$$

with $z_{ij} \in \mathbb{C}^n$, $j = 1, 2, \ldots, p_i$, $i = 1, 2, \ldots, w$, being a group of arbitrary parameter vectors.

3. *When $F \in \mathbb{C}^{p \times p}$ is in the diagonal form of (6.27), the general solution to the standard fully actuated GSE (6.10) reduces to*

$$
\begin{cases}
v_i = \mathrm{adj}A(s_i) z_i \\
w_i = \pi(s_i) z_i, \quad i = 1, 2, \ldots, p,
\end{cases}
$$

or, when $A(s_i)$, $i = 1, 2, \ldots, p$, are all nonsingular, by

$$
\begin{cases}
v_i = A^{-1}(s_i) z_i \\
w_i = z_i, \quad i = 1, 2, \ldots, p,
\end{cases}
$$

with $z_i \in \mathbb{C}^n$, $i = 1, 2, \ldots, p$, being a group of arbitrary parameter vectors.

In Chapter 9, the results in Theorem 6.8 will be adopted to give the solutions to square NSEs.

6.4 Nonhomogeneous GSEs: Forward Solutions

In Sections 6.2 and 6.3, we have shown that the solution to the fully actuated homogeneous GSE (6.8) can be immediately written out. In this section, parallel to Section 6.2, we consider the general type of fully actuated nonhomogeneous GSEs, namely, nonhomogeneous GSEs in the form of (6.9), which satisfy Assumption 6.1 or 6.2.

Recall

$$
\mu(s) = \det B(s). \tag{6.47}
$$

Then, under Assumption 6.1, the following DPE

$$
A(s)U(s) - B(s)T(s) = \mu(s)I_n \tag{6.48}
$$

obviously has a pair of solutions

$$
\begin{cases}
U(s) = \mu(s)I_n \\
T(s) = \mathrm{adj}B(s)\left[A(s) - I_n\right].
\end{cases} \tag{6.49}
$$

If, in particular, Assumption 6.2 is met, then $B^{-1}(s)$ is also a polynomial matrix. In this case, a pair of polynomial matrices $U(s)$ and $T(s)$ satisfying the DPE

$$A(s)U(s) - B(s)T(s) = I_n \tag{6.50}$$

can be given by

$$\begin{cases} U(s) = I_n \\ T(s) = B^{-1}(s)\left[A(s) - I_n\right]. \end{cases} \tag{6.51}$$

As in Section 6.2, the two solutions (6.49) and (6.51) to the DPEs (6.48) and (6.50) are called forward solutions since they use the "inverse" property of $B(s)$, while the solutions to the nonhomogeneous GSEs in the form of (6.9), obtained using (6.49) or (6.51), are called forward solutions to the GSEs.

Two theorems will perform fundamental function in this section and the next section; these are Theorems 5.5 and 5.8. Theorem 5.5 gives solutions of the fully actuated nonhomogeneous GSE (6.9) based on DPE (6.48), while Theorem 5.8 gives solutions of the fully actuated nonhomogeneous GSE (6.9) based on DPE (6.50).

6.4.1 Case of F Being Arbitrary

Denoting

$$\Theta(s) = B^{-1}(s)\left[A(s) - I_n\right]$$

$$= \sum_{k=0}^{\omega} \Theta_k s^k, \ \Theta_k \in \mathbb{R}^{n \times n}, \tag{6.52}$$

and

$$\Gamma(s) = \mathrm{adj}B(s)\left[A(s) - I_n\right]$$

$$= \sum_{k=0}^{\omega} \Gamma_k s^k, \ \Gamma_k \in \mathbb{R}^{n \times n}, \tag{6.53}$$

and observing the following fact:

$$\begin{aligned} \left[\mu(s)R'\right]\big|_F &= \left[\mu(s)R\left[\mu(F)\right]^{-1}\right]\big|_F \\ &= \left[\mu(s)R\right]\big|_F\left[\mu(F)\right]^{-1} \\ &= R\left[\mu(s)\right]\big|_F\left[\mu(F)\right]^{-1} \\ &= R\left[\mu(F)\right]\left[\mu(F)\right]^{-1} \\ &= R, \end{aligned}$$

we can give, based on Theorems 5.5 and 5.8, the following result about a particular solution to the nonhomogeneous GSE (6.9).

Theorem 6.9 Let $A(s)$, $B(s) \in \mathbb{R}^{n \times n}[s]$ be given as in (6.3), $F \in \mathbb{C}^{p \times p}$. Further, let $\Gamma(s) \in \mathbb{R}^{n \times n}[s]$ be given by (6.53), and $\Theta(s) \in \mathbb{R}^{n \times n}[s]$ be given by (6.52). Then,

1. *Under Assumption 6.1, a solution to the nonhomogeneous GSE (6.9) is given by*

$$\begin{cases} V = R \\ W = [\mathrm{adj}B(s)\,[A(s) - I_n]\,R]\,\big|_F\,[\mu(F)]^{-1} \\ \quad = (\Gamma_0 R + \Gamma_1 RF + \cdots + \Gamma_\omega RF^\omega)\,[\mu(F)]^{-1}. \end{cases}$$

2. *Under Assumption 6.2, a solution to the nonhomogeneous GSE (6.9) is given by*

$$\begin{cases} V = R \\ W = \left[B^{-1}(s)\,[A(s) - I_n]\,R\right]\big|_F \\ \quad = \Theta_0 R + \Theta_1 RF + \cdots + \Theta_\omega RF^\omega. \end{cases}$$

Remark 6.4 It can be seen from the previous sections in this chapter that all we need to do to derive a particular solution to the nonhomogeneous GSE (6.9) is to solve a pair of right coprime polynomial matrices $U(s)$ and $T(s)$ satisfying the DPE (6.48) or (6.50). Yet for the type of fully actuated GSEs, even the process of solving $U(s)$ and $T(s)$ is not needed, and a particular solution can be just instantly written out.

Recall Theorem 6.1 in Section 6.2 that all the solutions to the homogeneous GSE (6.8) are given by

$$\begin{cases} V = Z\mu(F) \\ W = [\mathrm{adj}B(s)A(s)Z]\,\big|_F , \end{cases} \tag{6.54}$$

or

$$\begin{cases} V = Z \\ W = \left[B^{-1}(s)A(s)Z\right]\big|_F , \end{cases} \tag{6.55}$$

where $Z \in \mathbb{C}^{n \times p}$ is an arbitrary parameter matrix. Further using Lemma 5.1 and Theorem 6.9, we have the following result about the general solution to the GSE (6.9) satisfying Assumption 6.2.

Theorem 6.10 *Let $F \in \mathbb{C}^{p \times p}$, and $A(s)$, $B(s) \in \mathbb{R}^{n \times n}[s]$ be given as in (6.3). Then,*

1. *When Assumption 6.1 is met, all the solutions to the nonhomogeneous GSE (6.9) are given by*

$$\begin{cases} V = Y \\ W = [\mathrm{adj}\, B(s)\, (A(s)Y - R)]\big|_F\, [\mu(F)]^{-1}, \end{cases} \tag{6.56}$$

with $Y \in \mathbb{C}^{n \times p}$ being an arbitrary parameter matrix.
2. *When, in particular, Assumption 6.2 is met, the above solution can be replaced by*

$$\begin{cases} V = Y \\ W = [B^{-1}(s)\, (A(s)Y - R)]\big|_F. \end{cases} \tag{6.57}$$

Proof. Firstly, let us show the solution (6.57).

It follows from Lemma 5.1 and Theorem 6.9 that the general solution to the GSE (6.9) satisfying Assumption 6.2 is given by

$$\begin{cases} V = Z + R \\ W = [B^{-1}(s)\, [A(s) - I_n]\, R]\big|_F + [B^{-1}(s)\, A(s)\, Z]\big|_F, \end{cases} \tag{6.58}$$

with $Z \in \mathbb{C}^{n \times p}$ being an arbitrary parameter matrix.

Note that

$$\begin{aligned} W &= [B^{-1}(s)\, [A(s) - I_n]\, R]\big|_F + [B^{-1}(s)A(s)Z]\big|_F \\ &= [B^{-1}(s)\, (A(s)R - R + A(s)Z)]\big|_F \\ &= [B^{-1}(s)\, (A(s)\, (Z + R) - R)]\big|_F \\ &= [B^{-1}(s)\, (A(s)Y - R)]\big|_F, \end{aligned} \tag{6.59}$$

with

$$Y = Z + R. \tag{6.60}$$

Substituting (6.59) and (6.60) into (6.58), gives the formula (6.57).

Secondly, let us prove (6.56). Since $\mu(F)$ is nonsingular under Assumption 6.1, we can make a variable substitution as follows:

$$Z' = Z\mu(F),$$

and now the solution (6.54) can be written as

$$\begin{cases} V = Z' \\ W = \left[\mathrm{adj}B(s)A(s)Z' \left[\mu(F) \right]^{-1} \right] \Big|_F \\ \quad = \left[\mathrm{adj}B(s)A(s)Z' \right] \Big|_F \left[\mu(F) \right]^{-1}. \end{cases} \tag{6.61}$$

Again, it follows from Lemma 5.1 and Theorem 6.9 that the general solution to the GSE (6.9) satisfying Assumption 6.1 is given by

$$V = Z' + R, \tag{6.62}$$

and

$$\begin{aligned} W &= \left[\mathrm{adj}B(s) \left[A(s) - I_n \right] R \right] \Big|_F \left[\mu(F) \right]^{-1} \\ &\quad + \left[\mathrm{adj}B(s)A(s)Z' \right] \Big|_F \left[\mu(F) \right]^{-1} \\ &= \left(\left[\mathrm{adj}B(s) \left[A(s) - I_n \right] R \right] \Big|_F + \left[\mathrm{adj}B(s)A(s)Z' \right] \Big|_F \right) \left[\mu(F) \right]^{-1} \\ &= \left[\mathrm{adj}B(s) \left(A(s) \left(Z' + R \right) - R \right) \right] \Big|_F \left[\mu(F) \right]^{-1} \\ &= \left[\mathrm{adj}B(s) \left(A(s)Y - R \right) \right] \Big|_F \left[\mu(F) \right]^{-1}, \end{aligned} \tag{6.63}$$

where

$$Y = Z' + R.$$

Combining (6.62) with (6.63) gives formula (6.56). ■

6.4.2 Case of F *Being in Jordan Form*

When F is in the Jordan form given by (6.23), based on Theorem 5.12, we can give the following result about a particular solution to the nonhomogeneous GSE (6.9).

Theorem 6.11 *Let $A(s)$, $B(s) \in \mathbb{R}^{n \times n}[s]$ be given as in (6.3), $F \in \mathbb{C}^{p \times p}$ be in the Jordan form of (6.23). Then,*

1. *Under Assumption 6.1, a solution to the nonhomogeneous GSE (6.9) is given by*

$$\begin{cases} v_{ij} = r_{ij} = \displaystyle\sum_{k=0}^{j-1} \frac{1}{k!} \frac{\mathrm{d}^k}{\mathrm{d}s^k} \left[\mu \left(s_i \right) \right] r'_{i,j-k} \\ \\ w_{ij} = \displaystyle\sum_{k=0}^{j-1} \frac{1}{k!} \frac{\mathrm{d}^k}{\mathrm{d}s^k} \left[\mathrm{adj}B \left(s_i \right) \left(A \left(s_i \right) - I_n \right) \right] r'_{i,j-k}, \\ \\ j = 1, 2, \dots, p_i, \quad i = 1, 2, \dots, w, \end{cases} \tag{6.64}$$

with

$$R' = R\left[\mu(F)\right]^{-1}.$$

2. *Under Assumption 6.2, a solution to the nonhomogeneous GSE (6.9) is given by*

$$\begin{cases} v_{ij} = r_{ij} \\ w_{ij} = \sum_{k=0}^{j-1} \frac{1}{k!} \frac{d^k}{ds^k} \left[B^{-1}(s_i)(A(s_i) - I_n)\right] r_{i,j-k}, \\ j = 1, 2, \ldots, p_i, \quad i = 1, 2, \ldots, w. \end{cases} \tag{6.65}$$

Recall Theorem 6.2 in Section 6.2 that all the solutions to the homogeneous GSE (6.8) are given by

$$\begin{cases} v_{ij} = \sum_{k=0}^{j-1} \frac{1}{k!} \frac{d^k}{ds^k} \left[\mu(s_i)\right] z_{i,j-k} \\ w_{ij} = \sum_{k=0}^{j-1} \frac{1}{k!} \frac{d^k}{ds^k} \left[\text{adj}B(s_i) A(s_i)\right] z_{i,j-k}, \\ j = 1, 2, \ldots, p_i, \quad i = 1, 2, \ldots, w, \end{cases} \tag{6.66}$$

or

$$\begin{cases} v_{ij} = z_{ij} \\ w_{ij} = \sum_{k=0}^{j-1} \frac{1}{k!} \frac{d^k}{ds^k} \left[B^{-1}(s_i) A(s_i)\right] z_{i,j-k}, \\ j = 1, 2, \ldots, p_i, \quad i = 1, 2, \ldots, w, \end{cases} \tag{6.67}$$

where $Z \in \mathbb{C}^{n \times p}$ is an arbitrary parameter matrix. Further using Lemma 5.1 and Theorem 6.11, we have the following result about the general solution to the GSE (6.9) satisfying Assumption 6.1 or 6.2.

Theorem 6.12 *Let $A(s)$, $B(s) \in \mathbb{R}^{n \times n}[s]$ be given as in (6.3), $F \in \mathbb{C}^{p \times p}$ be a Jordan matrix given by (6.23). Then,*

1. *When Assumption 6.1 is met, all the solutions to the nonhomogeneous GSE (6.9) are given by*

$$
\begin{cases}
v_{ij} = \displaystyle\sum_{k=0}^{j-1} \frac{1}{k!} \frac{d^k}{ds_i^k} \left[\mu\left(s_i\right) \right] y_{i,j-k} \\[2mm]
w_{ij} = \displaystyle\sum_{k=0}^{j-1} \frac{1}{k!} \frac{d^k}{ds_i^k} \left[\mathrm{adj} B\left(s_i\right) \left(A\left(s_i\right) y_{i,j-k} - r'_{i,j-k} \right) \right], \\[2mm]
\qquad j = 1,2,\ldots,p_i, \quad i = 1,2,\ldots,w,
\end{cases}
\tag{6.68}
$$

with $R' = R\left[\mu(F)\right]^{-1}$ and $Y \in \mathbb{C}^{n \times p}$ being an arbitrary parameter matrix.

2. When, in particular, Assumption 6.2 is met, the above solution can be replaced by

$$
\begin{cases}
v_{ij} = y_{ij} \\[2mm]
w_{ij} = \displaystyle\sum_{k=0}^{j-1} \frac{1}{k!} \frac{d^k}{ds_i^k} \left[B^{-1}\left(s_i\right) \left(A\left(s_i\right) y_{i,j-k} - r_{i,j-k} \right) \right], \\[2mm]
\qquad j = 1,2,\ldots,p_i, \quad i = 1,2,\ldots,w.
\end{cases}
\tag{6.69}
$$

Proof. Let us first show (6.69).

It follows from Lemma 5.1 and Theorem 6.11 that the general solution to the GSE (6.9) satisfying Assumption 6.2 is given by

$$
\begin{cases}
v_{ij} = z_{ij} + r_{ij} \\[2mm]
w_{ij} = \displaystyle\sum_{k=0}^{j-1} \frac{1}{k!} \frac{d^k}{ds_i^k} \left[B^{-1}\left(s_i\right) \left(A\left(s_i\right) - I_n \right) r_{i,j-k} + B^{-1}\left(s_i\right) A\left(s_i\right) z_{i,j-k} \right], \\[2mm]
\qquad j = 1,2,\ldots,p_i, \quad i = 1,2,\ldots,w.
\end{cases}
\tag{6.70}
$$

Note that

$$
\begin{aligned}
B^{-1}&\left(s_i\right) \left(A\left(s_i\right) - I_n \right) r_{i,j-k} + B^{-1}\left(s_i\right) A\left(s_i\right) z_{i,j-k} \\
&= B^{-1}\left(s_i\right) \left[A\left(s_i\right) r_{i,j-k} - r_{i,j-k} + A\left(s_i\right) z_{i,j-k} \right] \\
&= B^{-1}\left(s_i\right) \left[A\left(s_i\right) \left(z_{i,j-k} + r_{i,j-k} \right) - r_{i,j-k} \right] \\
&= B^{-1}\left(s_i\right) \left[A\left(s_i\right) y_{i,j-k} - r_{i,j-k} \right],
\end{aligned}
\tag{6.71}
$$

where

$$
y_{i,j-k} = z_{i,j-k} + r_{i,j-k}.
$$

Substituting (6.71) and $y_{ij} = z_{ij} + r_{ij}$ into (6.70), gives the solution (6.69).

Now, let us first show (6.68). Again, it follows from Lemma 5.1 and Theorem 6.11 that the general solution to the GSE (6.9) satisfying Assumption 6.1 is given by

$$
\begin{aligned}
v_{ij} &= \sum_{k=0}^{j-1} \frac{1}{k!} \frac{d^k}{ds^k} \left[\mu\left(s_i\right) \right] z_{i,j-k} + \sum_{k=0}^{j-1} \frac{1}{k!} \frac{d^k}{ds^k} \left[\mu\left(s_i\right) \right] r'_{i,j-k} \\
&= \sum_{k=0}^{j-1} \frac{1}{k!} \frac{d^k}{ds^k} \left[\mu\left(s_i\right) \right] \left(z_{i,j-k} + r'_{i,j-k} \right) \\
&= \sum_{k=0}^{j-1} \frac{1}{k!} \frac{d^k}{ds^k} \left[\mu\left(s_i\right) \right] y_{i,j-k},
\end{aligned}
\tag{6.72}
$$

$$
j = 1, 2, \ldots, p_i, \quad i = 1, 2, \ldots, w,
$$

with

$$
y_{i,j-k} = z_{i,j-k} + r'_{i,j-k},
$$

and

$$
w_{ij} = \sum_{k=0}^{j-1} \frac{1}{k!} \frac{d^k}{ds^k} \left[\operatorname{adj}B\left(s_i\right) \left(A\left(s_i\right) - I_n\right) r'_{i,j-k} + \operatorname{adj}B(s_i)A(s_i)z_{i,j-k} \right],
\tag{6.73}
$$

$$
j = 1, 2, \ldots, p_i, \quad i = 1, 2, \ldots, w.
$$

Note that

$$
\begin{aligned}
&\operatorname{adj}B\left(s_i\right) \left(A\left(s_i\right) - I_n\right) r'_{i,j-k} + \operatorname{adj}B\left(s_i\right) A\left(s_i\right) z_{i,j-k} \\
&= \operatorname{adj}B\left(s_i\right) \left[A\left(s_i\right) \left(z_{i,j-k} + r'_{i,j-k} \right) - r'_{i,j-k} \right] \\
&= \operatorname{adj}B\left(s_i\right) \left[A\left(s_i\right) y_{i,j-k} - r'_{i,j-k} \right].
\end{aligned}
\tag{6.74}
$$

Substituting (6.74) into (6.4.2) gives

$$
w_{ij} = \sum_{k=0}^{j-1} \frac{1}{k!} \frac{d^k}{ds^k} \operatorname{adj}B\left(s_i\right) \left[A\left(s_i\right) y_{i,j-k} - r'_{i,j-k} \right],
\tag{6.75}
$$

$$
j = 1, 2, \ldots, p_i, \quad i = 1, 2, \ldots, w.
$$

Combining (6.72) and (6.4.2) yields (6.68). ■

It should be noted that the solution (6.68) can also be written as

$$
\begin{cases}
V = Y\mu(F) \\
w_{ij} = \sum_{k=0}^{j-1} \frac{1}{k!} \frac{d^k}{ds^k} \left[\mathrm{adj}B\,(s_i) \left(A\,(s_i)\, y_{i,j-k} - r'_{i,j-k} \right) \right], \\
\qquad j = 1, 2, \ldots, p_i, \quad i = 1, 2, \ldots, w.
\end{cases}
\tag{6.76}
$$

6.4.3 Case of F Being Diagonal

When F is in the diagonal form given by (6.27), we can give, based on Theorem 5.16, the following solution to the nonhomogeneous GSE (6.9):

$$
\begin{cases}
v_i = \mu\,(s_i)\, r'_i \\
w_i = \mathrm{adj}B\,(s_i)\,(A\,(s_i) - I_n)\, r'_i, \quad i = 1, 2, \ldots, p,
\end{cases}
\tag{6.77}
$$

where

$$
R' = R\,[\mu(F)]^{-1}.
$$

Further, noting that, when F is given by (6.27),

$$
[\mu(F)]^{-1} = \mathrm{diag}\left(\frac{1}{\mu\,(s_i)}, \quad i = 1, 2, \ldots, p \right),
$$

we thus have

$$
r'_i = \frac{1}{\mu\,(s_i)}\, r_i, \quad i = 1, 2, \ldots, p.
\tag{6.78}
$$

Substituting the above relations in (6.78) into (6.77) immediately gives the following result about a particular solution to the nonhomogeneous GSE (6.9).

Theorem 6.13 *Let $A(s)$, $B(s) \in \mathbb{R}^{n\times n}[s]$ be given as in (6.3), $F \in \mathbb{C}^{p\times p}$ be a diagonal matrix given by (6.27), and Assumption 6.1 hold. Then a solution to the nonhomogeneous GSE (6.9) is given by*

$$
\begin{cases}
v_i = r_i \\
w_i = B^{-1}\,(s_i)\,(A\,(s_i) - I_n)\, r_i, \quad i = 1, 2, \ldots, p.
\end{cases}
\tag{6.79}
$$

Recall Theorem 6.3 in Section 6.2 that all the solutions to the homogeneous GSE (6.8) are given by

$$
\begin{cases}
v_i = z_i \\
w_i = B^{-1}\,(s_i)\, A\,(s_i)\, z_i, \quad i = 1, 2, \ldots, p,
\end{cases}
$$

where $Z \in \mathbb{C}^{n \times p}$ is an arbitrary parameter matrix. Further, using Lemma 5.1 and the above theorem, and observing that

$$B^{-1}(s_i)(A(s_i) - I_n)r_i + B^{-1}(s_i)A(s_i)z_i$$
$$= B^{-1}(s_i)[(A(s_i) - I_n)r_i + A(s_i)z_i]$$
$$= B^{-1}(s_i)[A(s_i)(r_i + z_i) - r_i],$$

we have the following result about the general solution to the GSE (6.9) satisfying Assumption 6.1 or 6.2.

Theorem 6.14 *Let* $A(s)$, $B(s) \in \mathbb{R}^{n \times n}[s]$ *be given as in (6.3),* $F \in \mathbb{C}^{p \times p}$ *be in the diagonal form of (6.27), and Assumption 6.1 hold. Then all the solutions to nonhomogeneous GSE (6.9) are given by*

$$\begin{cases} v_i = y_i \\ w_i = B^{-1}(s_i)[A(s_i)y_i - r_i], & i = 1, 2, \ldots, p, \end{cases} \tag{6.80}$$

with $y_i \in \mathbb{C}^n$, $i = 1, 2, \ldots, p$, *being a group of arbitrary parameter vectors.*

Remark 6.5 For solutions to the standard fully actuated GSE (6.11), we need only to remove the terms $B^{-1}(s)$ and $\mathrm{adj}B(s)$ and $\mu(s)$ in the above three theorems since in this case we have

$$B^{-1}(s) = \mathrm{adj}B(s) = I_n, \quad \mu(s) = 1.$$

6.4.4 Type of Second-Order GSEs

In many applications, we encounter a type of second-order linear systems in the form of

$$M\ddot{x} + D\dot{x} + Kx = Bu,$$

where

- $M, D \in \mathbb{R}^{n \times n}$, and $K \in \mathbb{R}^{n \times n}$ are the inertia matrix, the damping matrix, and the stiffness matrix, respectively
- $B \in \mathbb{R}^{n \times n}$ is a nonsingular coefficient matrix
- x is the position vector of the system
- u is the force or torque vector acting on the system

The corresponding nonhomogeneous GSE takes the following form:

$$MVF^2 + DVF + KV = BW + R. \tag{6.81}$$

Using Theorems 6.10, 6.12, and 6.14, we can immediately have the following corollary.

Corollary 6.2 *Consider the second-order GSE (6.81) satisfying* $\det B \neq 0$, *and denote*

$$\Phi(s) = B^{-1}\left(Ms^2 + Ds + K\right).$$

1. *For arbitrary* $F \in \mathbb{C}^{p \times p}$, *the general solution can be given by*

$$\begin{cases} V = Y \\ W = B^{-1}\left(MYF^2 + DYF + KY - R\right), \end{cases} \tag{6.82}$$

   with $Y \in \mathbb{C}^{n \times p}$ *being an arbitrary parameter matrix.*
2. *When* $F \in \mathbb{C}^{p \times p}$ *is in the Jordan form of (6.23), the general solution is given by*

$$\begin{cases} V = Z \\ w_{i1} = \Phi(s_i)\, y_{i,1} - r_{i,1} \\ w_{i2} = \Phi(s_i)\, y_{i,2} - r_{i,2} + B^{-1}\,(2Ms_i + D)\, y_{i,1} \\ w_{ij} = \Phi(s_i)\, y_{i,j} - r_{i,j} + B^{-1}\,(2Ms_i + D)\, y_{i,j-1} + B^{-1} M y_{i,j-2}, \\ \qquad j = 3, 4, \ldots, p_i, \quad i = 1, 2, \ldots, w, \end{cases} \tag{6.83}$$

   which reduces, when F *is in the diagonal form of (6.27), to*

$$\begin{cases} V = Y \\ w_i = B^{-1}\left[\left(s_i^2 M + s_i D + K\right) y_i - r_i\right], \\ \qquad i = 1, 2, \ldots, p, \end{cases} \tag{6.84}$$

   with $Y \in \mathbb{C}^{n \times p}$ *being an arbitrary parameter matrix.*

Remark 6.6 It is clearly observed from the above that, for a GSE satisfying Assumption 6.1 or 6.2, the solution can be instantly written out without any computation. However, this huge advantage vanishes if the GSE is converted into a first-order one. The advantage that the original second-order or higher-order systems offer us— *when Assumption 6.2 is satisfied, the problem can really be treated extremely simply in the second- or higher-order frame*—should really be taken in applications.

Remark 6.7 Remember that the solution to the DPE (6.48) or (6.50) is not unique. Another natural solution to DPE (6.48) is

$$
\begin{cases}
U(s) = \mu(s)A^{\mathrm{T}}(s) \\
T(s) = \mathrm{adj}B(s)\left[A(s)A^{\mathrm{T}}(s) - I_n\right],
\end{cases}
\tag{6.85}
$$

and correspondingly another to (6.50) can be taken as

$$
\begin{cases}
U(s) = A^{\mathrm{T}}(s) \\
T(s) = B^{-1}(s)\left[A(s)A^{\mathrm{T}}(s) - I_n\right],
\end{cases}
\tag{6.86}
$$

where

$$
\mu(s) = \det B(s),
$$

is a constant when Assumption 6.2 is met.

6.5 Nonhomogeneous GSEs: Backward Solutions

In this section, let us continue to investigate the solution to the fully actuated non-homogeneous GSEs in the form of (6.9) using a different choice of $U(s)$ and $T(s)$. As in Section 6.3, here the polynomial matrix $A(s)$ is also assumed to be square, that is, the case of $q = n$ is considered.

When Assumption 6.1 is satisfied, that is,

$$
\mu(s) = \det B(s) \neq 0, \ \forall s \in \mathrm{eig}(F),
$$

it can be easily verified the following pair of polynomial matrices

$$
\begin{cases}
U(s) = \mu(s)\mathrm{adj}A(s) \\
T(s) = (\pi(s) - 1)\,\mathrm{adj}B(s),
\end{cases}
\tag{6.87}
$$

with

$$
\pi(s) = \det A(s),
$$

satisfy the DPE (6.48).

If, in particular, Assumption 6.2 is satisfied, $\det B(s)$ is constant and $B^{-1}(s)$ is also a polynomial matrix. In this case, the DPE (6.50) has a pair of solutions as follows:

$$
\begin{cases}
U(s) = \mathrm{adj}A(s) \\
T(s) = (\pi(s) - 1)\,B^{-1}(s).
\end{cases}
\tag{6.88}
$$

As in Section 6.3, the solutions to the DPEs (6.48) and (6.50) are called backward solutions since they make use of the "inverse" property of $A(s)$, while the solutions to the nonhomogeneous GSEs in the form of (6.9), obtained using (6.87) or (6.88), are also called a backward solution to the GSE.

6.5.1 Case of F Being Arbitrary

Based on Theorems 5.5 and 5.8, we can obtain the following result about a particular solution to the nonhomogeneous GSE (6.9).

Theorem 6.15 *Let $A(s)$, $B(s) \in \mathbb{R}^{n \times n}[s]$ be given as in (6.3), $F \in \mathbb{C}^{p \times p}$. Then,*

1. *Under Assumption 6.1, a solution to the nonhomogeneous GSE (6.9) is given by*

$$
\begin{cases}
V = \left[\mu(s) \mathrm{adj} A(s) R \right] \big|_F \left[\mu(F) \right]^{-1} \\
W = \left[(\pi(s) - 1) \, \mathrm{adj} B(s) R \right] \big|_F \left[\mu(F) \right]^{-1}.
\end{cases}
\tag{6.89}
$$

2. *Under Assumption 6.2, a solution to the nonhomogeneous GSE (6.9) is given by*

$$
\begin{cases}
V = \left[\mathrm{adj} A(s) R \right] \big|_F \\
W = \left[(\pi(s) - 1) \, B^{-1}(s) R \right] \big|_F.
\end{cases}
\tag{6.90}
$$

Remark 6.8 It has been seen from the previous sections in this chapter that all we need to do in deriving a particular solution to the nonhomogeneous GSE (6.9) is to solve a pair of right coprime polynomial matrices $U(s)$ and $T(s)$ satisfying the DPE (6.48) or (6.50). Yet in this special case of $r = n$ and $\det B(s) \neq 0$, even the process of solving $U(s)$ and $T(s)$ is not needed. Therefore, a particular solution can be instantly written out.

Further, regarding the general solution to the nonhomogeneous GSE (6.9) satisfying Assumption 6.1 or 6.2, we have the following result.

Theorem 6.16 *Let $A(s)$, $B(s) \in \mathbb{R}^{n \times n}[s]$ be given as in (6.3), and $F \in \mathbb{C}^{p \times p}$. Then,*

1. *When Assumption 6.1 is met, a general solution to the nonhomogeneous GSE (6.9) is given by*

$$
\begin{cases}
V = \left[\mu(s) \mathrm{adj} A(s) Y \right] \big|_F \left[\mu(F) \right]^{-1} \\
W = \left[\mathrm{adj} B(s) \, (\pi(s) Y - R) \right] \big|_F \left[\mu(F) \right]^{-1},
\end{cases}
\tag{6.91}
$$

with $Y \in \mathbb{C}^{n \times p}$ being an arbitrary parameter matrix.

2. *When, in particular, Assumption 6.2 is satisfied, the above solution can also be replaced by*

$$\begin{cases} V = \left[\text{adj}A(s)\,Y\right]\big|_F \\ W = \left[B^{-1}(s)\,(\pi(s)\,Y - R)\right]\big|_F. \end{cases} \tag{6.92}$$

Proof. Recall Theorem 6.5 in Section 6.3 that all the solutions to the homogeneous GSE (6.8) under the Assumption 6.2 are given by

$$\begin{cases} V = \left[\text{adj}A(s)Z\right]\big|_F \\ W = \left[\pi(s)B^{-1}(s)Z\right]\big|_F, \end{cases}$$

where $Z \in \mathbb{C}^{n \times p}$ is an arbitrary parameter matrix. Further using Lemma 5.1 and the above theorem, we have the general solution to the GSE (6.9) satisfying Assumption 6.2 as

$$\begin{aligned} V &= \left[\text{adj}A(s)R\right]\big|_F + \left[\text{adj}A(s)Z\right]\big|_F \\ &= \left[\text{adj}A(s)\,(R + Z)\right]\big|_F \\ &= \left[\text{adj}A(s)\,Y\right]\big|_F, \end{aligned}$$

with

$$Y = Z + R,$$

and

$$\begin{aligned} W &= \left[(\pi(s) - 1)\,B^{-1}(s)R\right]\big|_F + \left[\pi(s)B^{-1}(s)Z\right]\big|_F \\ &= \left[B^{-1}(s)\,(\pi(s)R - R + \pi(s)Z)\right]\big|_F \\ &= \left[B^{-1}(s)\,(\pi(s)\,(Z + R) - R)\right]\big|_F \\ &= \left[B^{-1}(s)\,(\pi(s)\,Y - R)\right]\big|_F. \end{aligned}$$

Thus, the formula (6.92) is proven. In the following, let us show the other formula (6.91).

Again, recall Theorem 6.5 in Section 6.3 that all the solutions to the homogeneous GSE (6.8) under the Assumption 6.1 are given by

$$\begin{cases} V = \left[\mu(s)\text{adj}A(s)Z\right]\big|_F \\ W = \left[\pi(s)\text{adj}B(s)Z\right]\big|_F, \end{cases} \tag{6.93}$$

where $Z \in \mathbb{C}^{n \times p}$ is an arbitrary parameter matrix. Again, using Lemma 5.1 and the above theorem, we have the general solution to the GSE (6.9) satisfying Assumption 6.1 as

$$
\begin{aligned}
V &= \left[\mu(s)\mathrm{adj}A(s)R\right]\big|_F \left[\mu(F)\right]^{-1} + \left[\mu(s)\mathrm{adj}A(s)Z\right]\big|_F \\
&= \left[\mu(s)\mathrm{adj}A(s)R'\right]\big|_F + \left[\mu(s)\mathrm{adj}A(s)Z\right]\big|_F \\
&= \left[\mu(s)\mathrm{adj}A(s)\left(R' + Z\right)\right]\big|_F \\
&= \left[\mu(s)\mathrm{adj}A(s)Y\left[\mu(F)\right]^{-1}\right]\big|_F,
\end{aligned}
\tag{6.94}
$$

with

$$
Y = \left(Z + R'\right)\mu(F),
$$

and

$$
\begin{aligned}
W &= \left[(\pi(s) - 1)\,\mathrm{adj}B(s)R\right]\big|_F \left[\mu(F)\right]^{-1} + \left[\pi(s)\mathrm{adj}B(s)Z\right]\big|_F \\
&= \left[(\pi(s) - 1)\,\mathrm{adj}B(s)R'\right]\big|_F + \left[\pi(s)\mathrm{adj}B(s)Z\right]\big|_F \\
&= \left[\mathrm{adj}B(s)\left[(\pi(s) - 1)R' + \pi(s)Z\right]\right]\big|_F \\
&= \left[\mathrm{adj}B(s)\left(\pi(s)\left(R' + Z\right) - R'\right)\right]\big|_F \\
&= \left[\mathrm{adj}B(s)\left(\pi(s)Y\left[\mu(F)\right]^{-1} - R\left[\mu(F)\right]^{-1}\right)\right]\big|_F \\
&= \left[\mathrm{adj}B(s)\left(\pi(s)Y - R\right)\right]\big|_F \left[\mu(F)\right]^{-1}.
\end{aligned}
$$

$$\tag{6.95}$$
$$\tag{6.96}$$

Combining (6.94) and (6.95) gives the formula (6.91). ■

6.5.2 Case of F *Being in Jordan Form*

When F is given by (6.23), we can give, based on Theorem 5.12, the following result about a particular solution to the fully actuated nonhomogeneous GSE (6.9).

Theorem 6.17 *Let $A(s)$, $B(s) \in \mathbb{R}^{n \times n}[s]$ be given as in (6.3), and $F \in \mathbb{C}^{p \times p}$ be a Jordan matrix in the form of (6.23). Then,*

1. *Under Assumption 6.1, a solution to the nonhomogeneous GSE (6.9) is given by*

$$
\begin{cases}
v_{ij} = \sum_{k=0}^{j-1} \frac{1}{k!} \frac{d^k}{ds^k} \left[\mu\left(s_i\right) \mathrm{adj}A\left(s_i\right) \right] r'_{i,j-k} \\[2mm]
w_{ij} = \sum_{k=0}^{j-1} \frac{1}{k!} \frac{d^k}{ds^k} \left[\left(\pi\left(s_i\right) - 1\right) \mathrm{adj}B\left(s_i\right) \right] r'_{i,j-k}, \\[2mm]
j = 1, 2, \ldots, p_i, \quad i = 1, 2, \ldots, w,
\end{cases}
\tag{6.97}
$$

where $R' = R\left[\mu(F)\right]^{-1}$.

2. *Under Assumption 6.2, a solution to the nonhomogeneous GSE (6.9) is given by*

$$
\begin{cases}
v_{ij} = \sum_{k=0}^{j-1} \frac{1}{k!} \frac{d^k}{ds^k} \mathrm{adj}A\left(s_i\right) r_{i,j-k} \\[2mm]
w_{ij} = \sum_{k=0}^{j-1} \frac{1}{k!} \frac{d^k}{ds^k} \left[\left(\pi\left(s_i\right) - 1\right) B^{-1}\left(s_i\right) \right] r_{i,j-k}, \\[2mm]
j = 1, 2, \ldots, p_i, \quad i = 1, 2, \ldots, w.
\end{cases}
\tag{6.98}
$$

Further using Lemma 5.1 and the above theorem, we have the following result about the general solution to the GSE (6.9) satisfying Assumption 6.1 or 6.2.

Theorem 6.18 *Let* $A(s)$, $B(s) \in \mathbb{R}^{n \times n}[s]$ *be given as in (6.3), and* $F \in \mathbb{C}^{p \times p}$ *be in the Jordan form of (6.23). Then,*

1. *When Assumption 6.1 holds, a general solution to the nonhomogeneous GSE (6.9) is given by*

$$
\begin{cases}
v_{ij} = \sum_{k=0}^{j-1} \frac{1}{k!} \frac{d^k}{ds^k} \left[\mu\left(s_i\right) \mathrm{adj}A\left(s_i\right) \right] y_{i,j-k} \\[2mm]
w_{ij} = \sum_{k=0}^{j-1} \frac{1}{k!} \frac{d^k}{ds^k} \left[\mathrm{adj}B\left(s_i\right) \left(\pi\left(s_i\right) y_{i,j-k} - r'_{i,j-k} \right) \right], \\[2mm]
j = 1, 2, \ldots, p_i, \quad i = 1, 2, \ldots, w,
\end{cases}
\tag{6.99}
$$

with $R' = R\left[\mu(F)\right]^{-1}$ *and* $y_{ij} \in \mathbb{C}^n$, $j = 1, 2, \ldots, p_i$, $i = 1, 2, \ldots, w$, *being a group of arbitrary parameter vectors; and*

2. *When, in particular, Assumption 6.2 holds, the above solution can also be replaced by*

$$
\begin{cases}
v_{ij} = \sum\limits_{k=0}^{j-1} \frac{1}{k!} \frac{d^k}{ds_i^k} \mathrm{adj} A\,(s_i)\, y_{i,j-k} \\[2ex]
w_{ij} = \sum\limits_{k=0}^{j-1} \frac{1}{k!} \frac{d^k}{ds_i^k} \left[B^{-1}\,(s_i)\,(\pi\,(s_i)\, y_{i,j-k} - r_{i,j-k}) \right], \\[2ex]
\qquad j = 1, 2, \ldots, p_i, \quad i = 1, 2, \ldots, w.
\end{cases}
\tag{6.100}
$$

Proof. Recall Theorem 6.6 in Section 6.3 that all the solutions to the homogeneous GSE (6.8) are given, under Assumption 6.1, by

$$
\begin{cases}
v_{ij} = \sum\limits_{k=0}^{j-1} \frac{1}{k!} \frac{d^k}{ds_i^k} \mathrm{adj} A\,(s_i)\, z_{i,j-k} \\[2ex]
w_{ij} = \sum\limits_{k=0}^{j-1} \frac{1}{k!} \frac{d^k}{ds_i^k} \left[\pi\,(s_i)\, B^{-1}\,(s_i) \right] z_{i,j-k}, \\[2ex]
\qquad j = 1, 2, \ldots, p_i, \quad i = 1, 2, \ldots, w,
\end{cases}
\tag{6.101}
$$

where $Z \in \mathbb{C}^{n \times p}$ is an arbitrary parameter matrix. Therefore, using Lemma 5.1 and the above Theorem 6.17, we have the general solution to the GSE (6.9) satisfying Assumption 6.2 as

$$
\begin{cases}
v_{ij} = \sum\limits_{k=0}^{j-1} \frac{1}{k!} \frac{d^k}{ds_i^k} \mathrm{adj} A\,(s_i)\, \left(z_{i,j-k} + r_{i,j-k} \right) \\[2ex]
w_{ij} = \sum\limits_{k=0}^{j-1} \frac{1}{k!} \frac{d^k}{ds_i^k} \left[(\pi\,(s_i) - 1)\, B^{-1}\,(s_i)\, r_{i,j-k} + \pi\,(s_i)\, B^{-1}\,(s_i)\, z_{i,j-k} \right], \\[2ex]
\qquad j = 1, 2, \ldots, p_i, \quad i = 1, 2, \ldots, w.
\end{cases}
\tag{6.102}
$$

Note that

$$
\begin{aligned}
(\pi\,(s_i) &- 1)\, B^{-1}\,(s_i)\, r_{i,j-k} + \pi\,(s_i)\, B^{-1}\,(s_i)\, z_{i,j-k} \\
&= B^{-1}\,(s_i) \left[(\pi\,(s_i) - 1)\, r_{i,j-k} + \pi\,(s_i)\, z_{i,j-k} \right] \\
&= B^{-1}\,(s_i) \left[\pi\,(s_i)\, (z_{i,j-k} + r_{i,j-k}) - r_{i,j-k} \right] \\
&= B^{-1}\,(s_i) \left(\pi\,(s_i)\, y_{i,j-k} - r_{i,j-k} \right),
\end{aligned}
\tag{6.103}
$$

where

$$y_{i,j-k} = z_{i,j-k} + r_{i,j-k}. \tag{6.104}$$

Substituting (6.103) and (6.104) into (6.102), gives the formula (6.100). In the following let us prove the other formula (6.99).

Again, recall Theorem 6.6 in Section 6.3 that all the solutions to the homogeneous GSE (6.8) are given, under Assumption 6.1, by

$$
\begin{cases}
v_{ij} = \displaystyle\sum_{k=0}^{j-1} \frac{1}{k!} \frac{d^k}{ds^k} \left[\mu\left(s_i\right) \mathrm{adj} A\left(s_i\right) \right] z_{i,j-k} \\[2mm]
w_{ij} = \displaystyle\sum_{k=0}^{j-1} \frac{1}{k!} \frac{d^k}{ds^k} \left[\pi\left(s_i\right) \mathrm{adj} B\left(s_i\right) \right] z_{i,j-k}, \\[2mm]
\quad j = 1, 2, \ldots, p_i, \quad i = 1, 2, \ldots, w,
\end{cases}
\tag{6.105}
$$

where $z_{ij} \in \mathbb{C}^n$, $j = 1, 2, \ldots, p_i$, $i = 1, 2, \ldots, w$, is a group of arbitrary parameter vectors. Therefore, using Lemma 5.1 and the above Theorem 6.17, we have the general solution to the GSE (6.9) satisfying Assumption 6.1 as

$$
\begin{cases}
v_{ij} = \displaystyle\sum_{k=0}^{j-1} \frac{1}{k!} \frac{d^k}{ds^k} \left[\mu\left(s_i\right) \mathrm{adj} A\left(s_i\right) \right] \left(z_{i,j-k} + r'_{i,j-k} \right) \\[2mm]
w_{ij} = \displaystyle\sum_{k=0}^{j-1} \frac{1}{k!} \frac{d^k}{ds^k} \left[\left[\left(\pi\left(s_i\right) - 1\right) \mathrm{adj} B\left(s_i\right)\right] r'_{i,j-k} + \left[\pi\left(s_i\right) \mathrm{adj} B\left(s_i\right)\right] z_{i,j-k} \right], \\[2mm]
\quad j = 1, 2, \ldots, p_i, \quad i = 1, 2, \ldots, w.
\end{cases}
$$
$$\tag{6.106}$$

Note that

$$
\begin{aligned}
\left[\left(\pi\left(s_i\right) - 1\right) \mathrm{adj} B\left(s_i\right)\right] r'_{i,j-k} &+ \left[\pi\left(s_i\right) \mathrm{adj} B\left(s_i\right)\right] z_{i,j-k} \\
&= \left[\left(\pi\left(s_i\right) - 1\right) \mathrm{adj} B\left(s_i\right)\right] r'_{i,j-k} + \left[\pi\left(s_i\right) \mathrm{adj} B\left(s_i\right)\right] z_{i,j-k} \\
&= \mathrm{adj} B\left(s_i\right) \left[\pi\left(s_i\right) \left(z_{i,j-k} + r'_{i,j-k} \right) - r'_{i,j-k} \right] \\
&= \mathrm{adj} B\left(s_i\right) \left[\pi\left(s_i\right) y_{i,j-k} - r'_{i,j-k} \right],
\end{aligned}
$$

where

$$y_{i,j-k} = z_{i,j-k} + r'_{i,j-k}.$$

Substituting the above two relations into (6.106) gives the formula (6.99). ■

6.5.3 *Case of* F *Being Diagonal*

When F is in the diagonal form of (6.27), we can give, based on Theorem 5.16, the following solution to the nonhomogeneous GSE (6.9) satisfying Assumption 6.1:

$$\begin{cases} v_i = \mu(s_i) \operatorname{adj}A(s_i) r'_i \\ w_i = (\pi(s_i) - 1) \operatorname{adj}B(s_i) r'_i, & i = 1, 2, \dots, p. \end{cases} \qquad (6.107)$$

On the other side, we have

$$r'_i = \frac{1}{\mu(s_i)} r_i, \quad i = 1, 2, \dots, p.$$

Substituting the above relations into solution (6.107), immediately gives the following result.

Theorem 6.19 *Let $A(s)$, $B(s) \in \mathbb{R}^{n \times n}[s]$ be given as in (6.3), $F \in \mathbb{C}^{p \times p}$ be in the diagonal form of (6.27), and Assumption 6.1 hold. Then a solution to the nonhomogeneous GSE (6.9) is given by*

$$\begin{cases} v_i = \operatorname{adj}A(s_i) r_i \\ w_i = (\pi(s_i) - 1) B^{-1}(s_i) r_i, & i = 1, 2, \dots, p. \end{cases} \qquad (6.108)$$

Recall Theorem 6.7 in Section 6.3 that all the solutions to the homogeneous GSE (6.8) are given by

$$\begin{cases} v_i = \operatorname{adj}A(s_i) z_i \\ w_i = \pi(s_i) B^{-1}(s_i) z_i, & i = 1, 2, \dots, p, \end{cases}$$

where $Z \in \mathbb{C}^{n \times p}$ is an arbitrary parameter matrix. Further using Lemma 5.1 and the above theorem, we obtain the general solution to the GSE (6.9) satisfying Assumption 6.2 as

$$\begin{cases} v_i = \operatorname{adj}A(s_i)(z_i + r_i) \\ w_i = B^{-1}(s_i) [\pi(s_i)(z_i + r_i) - r_i], & i = 1, 2, \dots, p, \end{cases}$$

where $z_i \in \mathbb{C}^n$, $i = 1, 2, \dots, p$, is a group of arbitrary parameter vectors. Letting $y_i = z_i + r_i$ in the above solution immediately gives the following result.

Theorem 6.20 *Let $A(s)$, $B(s) \in \mathbb{R}^{n \times n}[s]$ be given as in (6.3), $F \in \mathbb{C}^{p \times p}$ be in the diagonal form of (6.27), and Assumption 6.1 hold. Then a general solution to the* *nonhomogeneous GSE (6.9) is given by*

$$\begin{cases} v_i = \text{adj}A\,(s_i)\,y_i \\ w_i = B^{-1}\,(s_i)\,[\pi\,(s_i)\,y_i - r_i], \quad i = 1, 2, \ldots, p, \end{cases} \tag{6.109}$$

with $y_i \in \mathbb{C}^n$, $i = 1, 2, \ldots, p$, is a group of arbitrary parameter vectors.

6.6 Examples

In this section, let us demonstrate our approaches with two practical examples.

Example 6.3 Space Rendezvous System

Consider again the space rendezvous system described by the well-known C-W equation (see Example 6.1) in the following second-order system form:

$$\ddot{x} + D\dot{x} + Kx = u,$$

where

$$D = \begin{bmatrix} 0 & -2\omega & 0 \\ 2\omega & 0 & 0 \\ 0 & 0 & 0 \end{bmatrix}, \quad K = \begin{bmatrix} -3\omega^2 & 0 & 0 \\ 0 & 0 & 0 \\ 0 & 0 & \omega^2 \end{bmatrix},$$

here ω is the orbital angular rate of the chaser.

The two polynomial matrices associated with this system are $B(s) = I_3$ and

$$A(s) = Is^2 + Ds + K = \begin{bmatrix} s^2 - 3\omega^2 & -2\omega s & 0 \\ 2\omega s & s^2 & 0 \\ 0 & 0 & s^2 + \omega^2 \end{bmatrix}.$$

1. *Homogeneous Equation*

   The homogeneous GSE associated with this system takes the following form:

   $$VF^2 + DVF + KV = W.$$

   For this equation, we have

   $$\begin{cases} N(s) = I_3 \\ D(s) = A(s). \end{cases}$$

Thus, the solution is given by

$$\begin{cases} V = Z \\ W = [A(s)Z]\,|_F \\ \quad = KZ + DZF + ZF^2, \end{cases} \tag{6.110}$$

when $F \in \mathbb{C}^{p \times p}$ is an arbitrary matrix. Particularly, when

$$F = \text{diag}\,(s_i, \quad i = 1, 2, \ldots, p), $$

the above solution can also be replaced by

$$\begin{cases} V = Z \\ w_i = A\,(s_i)\,z_i, \quad i = 1, 2, \ldots, p. \end{cases} \tag{6.111}$$

When

$$F = \begin{bmatrix} -1 & 1 & 0 \\ -1 & -1 & 0 \\ 0 & 0 & F_0 \end{bmatrix}, \quad F_0 = \text{diag}\,(-2, -3, -4, -5), \tag{6.112}$$

and taking

$$Z = [I_3 \;\; I_3], \tag{6.113}$$

we obtain following from (6.110) the solution

$$\begin{cases} V = \begin{bmatrix} 1 & 0 & 0 & 1 & 0 & 0 \\ 0 & 1 & 0 & 0 & 1 & 0 \\ 0 & 0 & 1 & 0 & 0 & 1 \end{bmatrix} \\[6pt] W = \begin{bmatrix} -\omega\,(3\omega - 2) & 2\omega - 2 & 0 & 9 - 3\omega^2 & 8\omega & 0 \\ 2 - 2\omega & 2\omega & 0 & -6\omega & 16 & 0 \\ 0 & 0 & \omega^2 + 4 & 0 & 0 & \omega^2 + 25 \end{bmatrix}. \end{cases}$$

When

$$F = \text{diag}\,(-1 \pm \mathrm{i}, -2, -3, -4, -5), \tag{6.114}$$

and Z is taken to be the same as in (6.113), we obtain following (6.111) the solution

$$\begin{cases} V = \begin{bmatrix} 1 & 0 & 0 & 1 & 0 & 0 \\ 0 & 1 & 0 & 0 & 1 & 0 \\ 0 & 0 & 1 & 0 & 0 & 1 \end{bmatrix} \\[6pt] W = \begin{bmatrix} -3\omega^2 - 2\mathrm{i} & 2\omega\,(\mathrm{i} + 1) & 0 & 9 - 3\omega^2 & 8\omega & 0 \\ 2\omega\,(\mathrm{i} - 1) & 2\,\mathrm{i} & 0 & -6\omega & 16 & 0 \\ 0 & 0 & \omega^2 + 4 & 0 & 0 & \omega^2 + 25 \end{bmatrix}. \end{cases}$$

2. *Nonhomogeneous Equation*

The corresponding nonhomogeneous GSE to this rendezvous system is

$$VF^2 + DVF + KV = W + R.$$

According to formula (6.57), the general solution to this GSE is given by

$$\begin{cases} V = Y \\ W = YF^2 + DYF + KY - R, \end{cases} \qquad (6.115)$$

where F is arbitrary. Particularly, when

$$F = \text{diag}\,(s_i, \quad i = 1, 2, \ldots, 6),$$

the solution can also be given by

$$\begin{cases} V = Y \\ w_i = \left[(s_i^2 I + s_i D + K) y_i - r_i \right], \quad i = 1, 2, \ldots, 6, \end{cases} \qquad (6.116)$$

where in (6.115) and (6.116) $Y \in \mathbb{C}^{3 \times p}$ is an arbitrary parameter matrix.

Again, for the same matrix F as in (6.112) and (6.114), respectively, and the Z matrix is taken as in (6.113) in both cases, the solutions to this nonhomogeneous equation are given, following from (6.115) and (6.116), respectively, by

$$\begin{cases} V = \begin{bmatrix} 1 & 0 & 0 & 1 & 0 & 0 \\ 0 & 1 & 0 & 0 & 1 & 0 \\ 0 & 0 & 1 & 0 & 0 & 1 \end{bmatrix} \\[2em] W = \begin{bmatrix} -3\omega^2 + 2\omega - 1 & 2\omega - 2 & 0 & 8 - 3\omega^2 & 8\omega & 0 \\ 2 - 2\omega & 2\omega - 1 & 0 & -6\omega & 15 & 0 \\ 0 & 0 & \omega^2 + 3 & 0 & 0 & \omega^2 + 24 \end{bmatrix}, \end{cases}$$

and

$$\begin{cases} V = \begin{bmatrix} 1 & 0 & 0 & 1 & 0 & 0 \\ 0 & 1 & 0 & 0 & 1 & 0 \\ 0 & 0 & 1 & 0 & 0 & 1 \end{bmatrix} \\[2em] W = \begin{bmatrix} -3\omega^2 - 1 - 2\mathrm{i} & 2\omega\,(\mathrm{i}+1) & 0 & 8 - 3\omega^2 & 8\omega & 0 \\ 2\omega\,(\mathrm{i}-1) & 2\,\mathrm{i} - 1 & 0 & -6\omega & 15 & 0 \\ 0 & 0 & \omega^2 + 3 & 0 & 0 & \omega^2 + 24 \end{bmatrix}. \end{cases}$$

Example 6.4 Satellite Attitude System

Consider again the dynamical model of the attitude system of a satellite given in Duan and Yu (2013) (see Example 6.2):

$$M\ddot{q} + H\dot{q} + Gq = u, \tag{6.117}$$

where q and u are the Euler angle vector and the control torque vector, respectively, and

$$M = \text{diag}\left(I_x,\ I_y,\ I_z\right),$$

$$H = \omega_0(I_y - I_x - I_z)\begin{bmatrix} 0 & 0 & 1 \\ 0 & 0 & 0 \\ -1 & 0 & 0 \end{bmatrix},$$

and

$$G = \text{diag}\left(4\omega_0^2(I_y - I_z),\ 3\omega_0^2(I_x - I_z),\ \omega_0^2(I_y - I_x)\right),$$

here I_x, I_y, and I_z are the inertia matrix of the three channels, and $\omega_0 = 7.292115 \times 10^{-5}$ rad/s is the rotational-angular velocity of the earth.

For this system, we can obtain

$$
\begin{aligned}
A(s) &= s^2 M + sH + G \\
&= \begin{bmatrix} s^2 I_x + 4\omega_0^2 I_{y,z} & 0 & -s\omega_0 I_0 \\ 0 & s^2 I_y + 3\omega_0^2 I_{x,z} & 0 \\ s\omega_0 I_0 & 0 & s^2 I_z - \omega_0^2 I_{x,y} \end{bmatrix},
\end{aligned}
$$

where

$$
\begin{cases} I_0 = I_x - I_y + I_z \\ I_{a,b} = I_a - I_b, \quad a, b = x, y, z. \end{cases} \tag{6.118}
$$

1. *Homogeneous Equation*

   The corresponding homogeneous GSE to this satellite attitude system is

   $$MVF^2 + HVF + GV = W.$$

   Using Corollary 6.1, we have the following conclusions about the solution to the above homogeneous GSE:

■ For an arbitrary matrix F, the general solution to this GSE is given by

$$\begin{cases} V = Z \\ W = MZF^2 + HZF + GZ. \end{cases} \qquad (6.119)$$

■ When F is taken to be the following Jordan matrix

$$F = \begin{bmatrix} \lambda & 1 & 0 \\ 0 & \lambda & 1 \\ 0 & 0 & \lambda \end{bmatrix}, \qquad (6.120)$$

the general solution can be also given by

$$\begin{cases} V = Z \\ w_{11} = A(\lambda) z_{11} \\ w_{12} = A(\lambda) z_{12} + (2\lambda M + D) z_{11} \\ w_{13} = A(\lambda) z_{13} + (2\lambda M + D) z_{12} + M z_{11}. \end{cases} \qquad (6.121)$$

■ When F is taken to be the following diagonal matrix

$$F = \mathrm{diag}(s_1, s_2, s_3), \qquad (6.122)$$

the general solution to this equation is given by

$$\begin{cases} V = Z \\ w_i = A(s_i) z_i, \quad i = 1, 2, 3; \end{cases} \qquad (6.123)$$

where in the equations in (6.119), (6.121), and (6.123), the matrix $Z \in \mathbb{C}^{3 \times 3}$ represents an arbitrary parameter matrix. Specifically, when

$$F = \mathrm{diag}(-1, -2, -3), \qquad (6.124)$$

and choose $Z = I_3$, both (6.119) and (6.123) give the following solution:

$$\begin{cases} V = I_3 \\ W = \begin{bmatrix} 4I_{y,z}\omega_0^2 + I_x & 0 & 3\omega_0 I_0 \\ 0 & 4I_y + 3\omega_0^2 I_{x,z} & 0 \\ -\omega_0 I_0 & 0 & 9I_z - \omega_0^2 I_{x,y} \end{bmatrix}, \end{cases} \qquad (6.125)$$

where the notions $I_{x,y}$, $I_{x,z}$, $I_{y,z}$, and I_0 are defined in (6.118).

2. *Nonhomogeneous Equation*

The corresponding nonhomogeneous GSE to the satellite attitude system is

$$MVF^2 + HVF + GV = W + R.$$

According to Theorem 6.8, we also have the following:

■ When $F \in \mathbb{C}^{p \times p}$, the general solution to this GSE is given by

$$\begin{cases} V = Y \\ W = MYF^2 + HYF + GY - R, \end{cases} \quad (6.126)$$

with $Y \in \mathbb{C}^{3 \times p}$ being an arbitrary parameter matrix.

■ When F is taken as in (6.120), the general solution can be also given by

$$\begin{cases} V = Y \\ w_{11} = A(\lambda) y_{11} - r_{11} \\ w_{12} = A(\lambda) y_{12} - r_{12} + (2\lambda M + D) y_{11} - r_{11} \\ w_{13} = A(\lambda) y_{13} - r_{13} + (2\lambda M + D) y_{12} - r_{12} + My_{11} - \frac{1}{2} r_{11}. \end{cases}$$
$$(6.127)$$

■ When F is taken as in (6.122), the general solution is given by

$$\begin{cases} V = Y \\ w_i = A(s_i) y_i - r_i, \quad i = 1, 2, 3, \end{cases} \quad (6.128)$$

where in (6.127) and (6.128) $Y \in \mathbb{C}^{3 \times 3}$ is an arbitrary parameter matrix. Particularly, when $R = I_3$, and

$$F = \text{diag}(-1 \pm i, -2),$$

where i represents the imaginary unit, and the parameter matrix Y is taken to be the third-order identity matrix, it can be verified that both the formulas (6.126) and (6.128) give the following same result:

$$\begin{cases} V = I_3 \\ W = \begin{bmatrix} 4w_0^2 I_{y,z} - 1 - 2I_x i & 0 & 2w_0 I_0 \\ 0 & 3w_0^2 I_{x,z} - 1 + 2I_y i & 0 \\ w_0(i-1)I_0 & 0 & 4I_z - w_0^2 I_{x,y} - 1 \end{bmatrix}, \end{cases}$$

where the notions $I_{x,y}$, $I_{x,z}$, $I_{y,z}$, and I_0 are defined in (6.118).

6.7 Notes and References

In this chapter, general solutions to the several types of fully actuated nonhomogeneous GSEs are investigated. The results are deduced from those in Chapters 4 and 5 (Figure 6.2). As in Chapters 4 and 5, the main feature of these solutions is that they possess a highly unified complete analytical parametric form, and the approach also unifies all the cases mentioned. Because of this feature, we have not gone to cover all the cases. Those cases those are really tackled in this chapter are shown in Table 6.1. Again, it is suggested that readers give the presentations of the results for the rest of the cases by themselves.

The main results in this chapter are slight generalizations of the results in two recent conference papers Duan (2014i) and Duan (2014j).

In the following, we try to convince the readers to accept the parametric higher-order system design approaches by both reasoning and demonstrating.

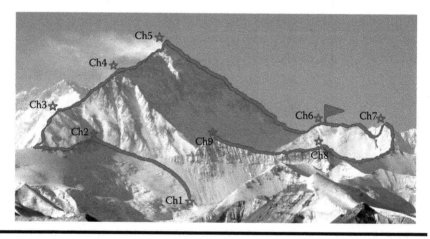

Figure 6.2   We are here. (Modified from http://go.jutuw.com/zhumulangmafeng/photo/.)

Table 6.1   Fully Actuated GSEs Treated in the Chapter

Cases	F Arbitrary	F Jordan	F Diagonal
Higher-order	Yes	Yes	Yes
Second-order	—	—	—
First-order (descriptor)	—	—	—
First-order (normal)	—	—	—

6.7.1 Utilizing the Advantage

As we have seen from the above that, for a second- and a higher-order GSE satisfying Assumption 6.1 or 6.2, the general solution can be instantly written out without any computation. However, this huge advantage vanishes if the equation is converted into a first-order one.

The advantage that the original second-order or higher-order fully actuated systems offer us is indeed vital—*when Assumption 6.1 or 6.2 is satisfied, control problems can be solved extremely simply in the second- or higher-order frame*. Such an advantage should have been taken in applications.

Many researchers would solve a higher-order GSE by first converting it into a first-order one. By doing this, they are refusing this great offer. As seen in this chapter, we have given a unified simple way to solve fully actuated GSEs of arbitrary order. It is strongly suggested that a higher-order GSE be solved in the higher-order frame whenever possible due to the above-mentioned advantage.

6.7.2 ESA in Fully Actuated Systems

In Section 2.4, we have considered generalized ESA in a type of higher-order dynamical linear systems in the form of

$$\sum_{i=0}^{m} A_i x^{(i)} = Bu, \tag{6.129}$$

where $x \in \mathbb{R}^n$ and $u \in \mathbb{R}^r$ are the state vector and the control vector, respectively; $A_i \in \mathbb{R}^{n \times n}$, $i = 0, 1, \ldots, m$, are the system coefficient matrices, and

$$1 \leq \mathrm{rank} A_m = n_0 \leq n.$$

Now let us revisit this problem under the following full actuation assumption:

Assumption 6.3 $r = n$ *and* $\det B \neq 0$.

Recall from Section 2.4, the generalized ESA problem to be solved can be stated as follows.

Problem 6.1   *Let the dynamical system (6.129) satisfy Assumption 6.3. Further, let $F \in \mathbb{R}^{p \times p}$, with $p = (m-1)n + n_0$. Find for the system a proportional plus derivative feedback controller in the form of*

$$u = K_0 x + K_1 \dot{x} + \cdots + K_{m-1} x^{(m-1)},$$

and a matrix $V_e \in \mathbb{R}^{mn \times p}$, with $rankV_e = p$, satisfying

$$A_e V_e = E_e V_e F, \tag{6.130}$$

where

$$E_e = \text{blockdiag}\,(I_n, \ldots, I_n, A_m), \tag{6.131}$$

$$A_e = \begin{bmatrix} 0 & I & \cdots & 0 \\ \vdots & \ddots & \ddots & \vdots \\ 0 & \cdots & 0 & I \\ -A_0^c & \cdots & -A_{m-2}^c & -A_{m-1}^c \end{bmatrix}. \tag{6.132}$$

with

$$A_i^c = A_i - BK, \ i = 0, 1, \ldots, m-1. \tag{6.133}$$

As a consequence of the problem requirement, the closed-loop system possesses the eigenvalues of the matrix F as eigenvalues.

Again, it follows from the result in Section 2.4 that the solution to the problem is given, under the condition that $rankA_m = n_0 = n$ and $p = mn$, by

$$\begin{bmatrix} K_0 & K_1 & \cdots & K_{m-1} \end{bmatrix} = WV_e^{-1}, \tag{6.134}$$

where

$$V_e = \begin{bmatrix} V \\ VF \\ \vdots \\ VF^{m-1} \end{bmatrix}, \tag{6.135}$$

while the matrices V and W are determined by the following mth order GSE:

$$\sum_{i=0}^{m} A_i VF^i = BW. \tag{6.136}$$

Now, let us carry on from here.

When Assumption 6.3 is met, it follows from Theorem 6.1 that all the solutions to GSE (6.136) are characterized by

$$\begin{cases} V = Z \\ W = \left[B^{-1}(s)A(s)Z \right]\big|_F, \end{cases} \tag{6.137}$$

with $Z \in \mathbb{R}^{n \times p}$ being an arbitrary parameter matrix.

With this observation, we immediately have the following result regarding solution to ESA in a higher-order fully actuated linear system.

Theorem 6.21 *Under the condition that $rankA_m = n$ and $p = mn$, all the solutions to Problem 6.1 are given by (6.134) and (6.135), with the matrices V and W given by (6.137), where $Z \in \mathbb{R}^{n \times mn}$ is an arbitrary parameter matrix.*

The above treatment has clearly demonstrated the advantage of fully actuated system, that is, the controller gains can be immediately given without going through any complicated computation procedure. If the higher-order system had been converted into a first-order one, then this huge advantage would simply have been lost.

In the next subsection, let us further demonstrate this design with the space rendezvous control problem.

6.7.3 Space Rendezvous Control

In this subsection, let us apply the generalized ESA design to the space rendezvous system described by the well-known C-W equation (see Examples 6.1 and 6.3). Let us mention that this space rendezvous system is a typical fully actuated system and has attracted great attention in the past decades (Clohessy and Wiltshire 1960, Duan 2012, 2014a, Gao et al. 2012a,b, 2013, Luo et al. 2013, Yamanaka and Ankersen 2002, Zhou et al. 2011, 2012).

As we will soon find out, with our direct parametric approach in the second-order frame, the problem is solved in an extremely simple way.

Recall from Examples 6.1 and 6.3, the space rendezvous system described by the C-W equation can be written in the following second-order system form:

$$\ddot{x} + D\dot{x} + Kx = u,$$

where

$$D = \begin{bmatrix} 0 & -2\omega & 0 \\ 2\omega & 0 & 0 \\ 0 & 0 & 0 \end{bmatrix}, \quad K = \begin{bmatrix} -3\omega^2 & 0 & 0 \\ 0 & 0 & 0 \\ 0 & 0 & \omega^2 \end{bmatrix},$$

where ω is the orbital angular rate of the chaser. The controller to be designed is in the following proportional plus derivative feedback form:

$$u = K_0 x + K_1 \dot{x}. \tag{6.138}$$

Noting that $B(s) = I_3$ and

$$A(s) = s^2 + Ds + K = \begin{bmatrix} s^2 - 3\omega^2 & -2\omega s & 0 \\ 2\omega s & s^2 & 0 \\ 0 & 0 & s^2 + \omega^2 \end{bmatrix}, \quad (6.139)$$

we have the following result regarding this space rendezvous control problem.

Corollary 6.3 *Let $F \in \mathbb{R}^{6\times6}$ have desired eigenvalues. Then, the gains K_0 and K_1 of the controller (6.138) that assigns the eigenvalues of the matrix F to the closed-loop system are given by*

$$[K_0 \quad K_1] = [A(s)Z]\,|_F \begin{bmatrix} Z \\ ZF \end{bmatrix}^{-1}, \quad (6.140)$$

where $Z \in \mathbb{R}^{3\times6}$ is an arbitrary parameter matrix satisfying

$$\det \begin{bmatrix} Z \\ ZF \end{bmatrix} \neq 0. \quad (6.141)$$

As in Example 6.3, choosing

$$F = \begin{bmatrix} -1 & 1 & 0 \\ -1 & -1 & 0 \\ 0 & 0 & F_0 \end{bmatrix}, \quad F_0 = \mathrm{diag}\,(-2, -3, -4, -5), \quad (6.142)$$

and taking

$$Z = [I_3 \quad I_3], \quad (6.143)$$

we obtain

$$[A(s)Z]\,|_F = \begin{bmatrix} -\omega\,(3\omega - 2) & 2\omega - 2 & 0 & 9 - 3\omega^2 & 8\omega & 0 \\ 2 - 2\omega & 2\omega & 0 & -6\omega & 16 & 0 \\ 0 & 0 & \omega^2 + 4 & 0 & 0 & \omega^2 + 25 \end{bmatrix},$$

and

$$\begin{bmatrix} Z \\ ZF \end{bmatrix} = \begin{bmatrix} 1 & 0 & 0 & 1 & 0 & 0 \\ 0 & 1 & 0 & 0 & 1 & 0 \\ 0 & 0 & 1 & 0 & 0 & 1 \\ -1 & 1 & 0 & -3 & 0 & 0 \\ -1 & -1 & 0 & 0 & -4 & 0 \\ 0 & 0 & -2 & 0 & 0 & -5 \end{bmatrix}.$$

Therefore, according to formula (6.140), the gain matrices are given by

$$
[K_0 \quad K_1] = \frac{1}{7}
\begin{bmatrix}
-21\omega^2 - 24 & 20 & 0 & -29 & 5 - 14\omega & 0 \\
-30 & -24 & 0 & 14\omega - 10 & -34 & 0 \\
0 & 0 & 7\omega^2 - 70 & 0 & 0 & -49
\end{bmatrix}.
$$
(6.144)

For the above space rendezvous control problem, many researchers have adopted the first-order system approach in the literature. From the above design, we have seen how simple and convenient the direct second-order system parametric approach is. So, please bear in mind to, with control of fully actuated systems, use the direct higher-order system parametric approach instead of that for extended first-order systems. Furthermore, in certain specific applications, the parameter matrix Z may be properly chosen to meet certain additional system design requirements.

In Section 7.7, this problem is generalized to the nonlinear case, in which a nonlinear feedback controller is designed while the resulting closed-loop system is still a constant linear one.

Chapter 7

GSEs with Varying Coefficients

In this chapter, we further investigate higher-order GSEs with varying coefficients. It is pointed out that the results for GSEs with invariant coefficient matrices, which are treated in Chapters 4 and 5, naturally hold for GSEs with varying coefficients, but the varying property of the coefficients does add a great difficulty and complexity in the computation of the polynomial matrices satisfying the corresponding generalized RCFs or DPEs. However, like the results in Chapter 6, for fully actuated GSEs with varying coefficients, it is shown that these polynomial matrices can be immediately obtained. Hence, general solutions to fully actuated GSEs with varying coefficients can be immediately written out.

Due to the close relation of this chapter with Chapters 4 through 6, it is strongly recommended that readers go over Chapters 4 through 6 before reading this chapter. Furthermore, proofs of most of the results in this chapter are not provided. They can be given similarly as those in the previous chapters for GSEs with constant coefficients.

In order to understand the background of GSEs with varying coefficients, let us start with the introduction of dynamical systems with varying coefficients.

7.1 Systems with Varying Coefficients

As generalizations to the higher-order constant linear systems studied in the former chapters, let us propose a type of higher-order quasilinear time-varying systems described by

$$\sum_{i=0}^{m} A_i \left(X\left(t\right), \theta\left(t\right), t\right) x^{(i)} = \sum_{i=0}^{m} B_i \left(X\left(t\right), \theta\left(t\right), t\right) u^{(i)}, \tag{7.1}$$

where $x \in \mathbb{R}^n$ and $u \in \mathbb{R}^r$ are the state and input vectors, respectively;

$$X\left(t\right) = \begin{bmatrix} x & \dot{x} & \cdots & x^{(m-1)} \end{bmatrix},$$

$\theta\left(t\right) : [0, +\infty) \to \Theta \subset \mathbb{R}^q$, is a time-varying parameter vector, $\Theta \subset \mathbb{R}^q$ is some compact set. Without loss of generality, $\theta\left(t\right)$ is assumed to be piecewise continuous. The polynomial matrices associated with these GSEs are

$$\begin{cases} A\left(X, \theta, t, s\right) = \sum_{i=0}^{m} A_i\left(X, \theta, t\right) s^i \\ B\left(X, \theta, t, s\right) = \sum_{i=0}^{m} B_i\left(X, \theta, t\right) s^i, \end{cases} \tag{7.2}$$

where $A_i\left(X, \theta, t\right) \in \mathbb{R}^{n \times q}$ and $B_i\left(X, \theta, t\right) \in \mathbb{R}^{n \times r}$, $i = 1, 2, \ldots, m$, are matrix functions that are piecewise continuous with respect to both θ and t.

In the rest of this section, we present some of the specific examples of the aforementioned quasilinear time-varying system in the form of (7.1).

7.1.1 Examples of First-Order Systems

7.1.1.1 Nonlinear Systems

As an example of a first-order nonlinear dynamical system, let us consider the longitudinal dynamics of a hypersonic vehicle.

Example 7.1 (Hypersonic Vehicle System—The Nonlinear Case)

Consider the longitudinal dynamics of a hypersonic vehicle system, which is modeled by the following set of equations (Xu et al. 2004, Yang et al. 2013):

$$\begin{cases} \dot{V} = \left(\frac{T \cos \alpha - D}{m} - \frac{\mu_g \sin \gamma}{r_e^2} \right) \\ \dot{\gamma} = \frac{L + T \sin \alpha}{mV} - \frac{\left(\mu_g - V^2 r_e \right) \cos \gamma}{V r_e^2} \\ \dot{h} = V \sin \gamma \\ \dot{\alpha} = q - \dot{\gamma} \\ \dot{q} = M / I_{yy}, \end{cases} \tag{7.3}$$

where the variables include the forward velocity V, the flight-path angle γ, the altitude h, the angle of attack α, and the pitch rate q. Variables m, I_{yy}, and μ_g represent the vehicle mass, the moment of inertia, and the gravity constant, respectively.

L, D, T, M, and r_e represent the lift, drag, thrust forces, pitching moment, and the radial distance from Earth's center, respectively, which are given by

$$\begin{cases} L = \frac{1}{2}\rho V^2 S C_L \\ D = \frac{1}{2}\rho V^2 S C_D \\ T = \frac{1}{2}\rho V^2 S C_T \\ M = \frac{1}{2}\rho V^2 S \bar{c} C_M \\ r_e = h + R_e, \end{cases} \tag{7.4}$$

where C_D, C_L, C_T, and C_M are the coefficients of the drag, lift, thrust, and moment, respectively. The parameters ρ, S, $\bar{c}$ and R_e are the air density, the reference area, the mean aerodynamic chord, and the radius of the Earth, respectively. Their expressions can be given as follows:

$$\begin{cases} C_L = C_{LA}(V) + C_{LB}(V,\alpha)\,\alpha + C_{LC}(V,\alpha)\delta_z \\ C_D = C_{DA}(V) + C_{DB}(V,\alpha)\,\alpha + C_{DC}(V,\alpha)\,\delta_z \\ C_T = C_{TA}(h,V) + C_{TB}(h,V,\alpha)\,\alpha + C_{TC}(h,V,\alpha)\,\phi \\ C_M = C_{MA1}(h,V) + C_{MA2}(q,h,V)\,q \\ \qquad + C_{MB}(\alpha,h,V)\,\alpha + C_{MC}(\alpha,q,h,V)\,\delta_z, \end{cases} \tag{7.5}$$

the functions involved in the equations in (7.5) are often dependent on the specific type of missiles as well as the designers (Keshmiri et al. 2005, Parker et al. 2007).

Obviously, (7.3) through (7.5) is a very complicated nonlinear system.

7.1.1.2 Quasilinear Systems

The nonlinear model (7.3) through (7.5) can be represented in the form of a quasilinear system as shown in the following example.

Example 7.2 (Hypersonic Vehicle System—The Quasilinear Case)

For the hypersonic vehicle system (7.3) through (7.5), denote the state and the input vectors as

$$x = \begin{bmatrix} V \\ \gamma \\ h \\ \alpha \\ q \end{bmatrix}, \quad u = \begin{bmatrix} \delta_z \\ \phi \end{bmatrix},$$

then we have the following result (proof omitted).

Proposition 7.1 *The hypersonic vehicle system (7.3) through (7.5) can be equivalently written in the following matrix form*

$$\dot{x} + A(x)x + f(x) = B(x)u, \tag{7.6}$$

where

$$
A(x) = \begin{bmatrix} a_1 & 0 & 0 & a_2 & 0 \\ a_3 & 0 & 0 & a_4 & 0 \\ -\sin\gamma & 0 & 0 & 0 & 0 \\ -a_3 & 0 & 0 & -a_4 & -1 \\ a_5 & 0 & 0 & a_6 & a_7 \end{bmatrix},
$$

with

$$
\begin{cases}
a_1 = -\frac{1}{mV} QS\left[C_{TA}(h, V)\cos\alpha - C_{DA}(V)\right] \\
a_2 = -\frac{1}{m} QS\left[C_{TB}(h, V, \alpha)\cos\alpha - C_{DB}(V, \alpha)\right] \\
a_3 = -\frac{1}{2m}\rho S\left(C_{LA}(V) + C_{TA}(h, V)\sin\alpha\right) - \frac{\cos\gamma}{r_e} \\
a_4 = -\frac{1}{mV} QS\left(C_{LB}(V, \alpha) + C_{TB}(h, V, \alpha)\sin\alpha\right) \\
a_5 = -\frac{1}{2I_{yy}}\rho V S\bar{c}C_{MA1}(h, V) \\
a_6 = -\frac{1}{I_{yy}} QS\bar{c}C_{MB}(\alpha, h, V) \\
a_7 = -\frac{1}{I_{yy}} QS\bar{c}C_{MA2}(q, h, V),
\end{cases}
\tag{7.7}
$$

$$
B(x) = \begin{bmatrix} b_1 & b_2 V\cos\alpha \\ b_3 & b_2\sin\alpha \\ 0 & 0 \\ -b_3 & -b_2\sin\alpha \\ b_4 & 0 \end{bmatrix},
$$

with

$$
\begin{cases}
b_1 = -\frac{1}{m} QSC_{DC}(V, \alpha) \\
b_2 = \frac{1}{mV} QSC_{TC}(h, V, \alpha) \\
b_3 = \frac{1}{mV} QSC_{LC}(V, \alpha) \\
b_4 = \frac{1}{I_{yy}}\bar{c}QSC_{MC}(\alpha, q, h, V),
\end{cases}
\tag{7.8}
$$

and

$$
f(x) = \frac{\mu_g}{V r_e^2} \begin{bmatrix} V\sin\gamma \\ \cos\gamma \\ 0 \\ -\cos\gamma \\ 0 \end{bmatrix}.
$$

This system, when $f(x)$ is neglected, is clearly in a quasilinear system form.

7.1.2 Examples of Second-Order Systems

Many systems are originally in second-order system forms due to the various nature laws, such as Newton's law, Theorem of Momentum, and Euler–Lagrangian equations. Without some strict assumptions, these systems really do not appear in constant linear forms.

7.1.2.1 Time-Varying Linear Systems

Example 7.3 (Space Rendezvous System—The T-H Equation)

Consider the space rendezvous problem mentioned in Example 6.1 again, when the chaser and the object are relatively close to each other, the relative equation of motion is governed by the following well-known T-H equation or Lawden equation (Yamanaka and Ankersen 2002):

$$
\begin{bmatrix} \ddot{x}_r \\ \ddot{y}_r \\ \ddot{z}_r \end{bmatrix} - \begin{bmatrix} 2k\dot{\theta}^{\frac{3}{2}}x_r + 2\dot{\theta}\dot{y}_r + \dot{\theta}^2 x_r + \ddot{\theta}y_r \\ -k\dot{\theta}^{\frac{3}{2}}y_r - 2\dot{\theta}\dot{x}_r + \dot{\theta}^2 y_r - \ddot{\theta}x_r \\ -k\dot{\theta}^{\frac{3}{2}}z_r \end{bmatrix} = u,
\tag{7.9}
$$

which can be easily arranged into the form of

$$
\ddot{x} + D(\dot{\theta})\dot{x} + K(\dot{\theta}, \ddot{\theta})x = u,
\tag{7.10}
$$

with

$$
x = \begin{bmatrix} x_r & y_r & z_r \end{bmatrix}^{\mathrm{T}},
$$

$$
D(\dot{\theta}) = \begin{bmatrix} 0 & -2\dot{\theta} & 0 \\ 2\dot{\theta} & 0 & 0 \\ 0 & 0 & 0 \end{bmatrix},
\tag{7.11}
$$

$$
K(\dot{\theta}, \ddot{\theta}) = \begin{bmatrix} -2k\dot{\theta}^{\frac{3}{2}} - \dot{\theta}^2 & -\ddot{\theta} & 0 \\ \ddot{\theta} & k\dot{\theta}^{\frac{3}{2}} - \dot{\theta}^2 & 0 \\ 0 & 0 & k\dot{\theta}^{\frac{3}{2}} \end{bmatrix},
\tag{7.12}
$$

where θ is the true anomaly.

This is obviously a time-varying linear system since θ varies with time t. It describes the relative movement of two spacecrafts moving on an orbit, eventually, the system is a periodic one (Zhou and Duan 2012). The two polynomial matrices associated with this system are $B(\theta, t, s) = I_3$ and

$$
A(\theta, t, s) = M(\dot{\theta}, \ddot{\theta})s^2 + D(\dot{\theta}, \ddot{\theta})s + K(\dot{\theta}, \ddot{\theta})
$$

$$
= \begin{bmatrix} s^2 - 2k\dot{\theta}^{\frac{3}{2}} - \dot{\theta}^2 & -2\dot{\theta}s - \ddot{\theta} & 0 \\ 2\dot{\theta}s + \ddot{\theta} & s^2 + k\dot{\theta}^{\frac{3}{2}} - \dot{\theta}^2 & 0 \\ 0 & 0 & s^2 + k\dot{\theta}^{\frac{3}{2}} \end{bmatrix}.
$$

7.1.2.2 Quasilinear Systems

Example 7.4 (Space Rendezvous System—The Nonlinear Case)

When the chaser and the object are not close to each other, neither the C-W equation (6.13) nor the T-H equation (7.9) can describe the relative movement of the two spacecrafts. In such a general, case the equation describing the relative movement of the two spacecrafts is really nonlinear and is given as follows (Duan 2012, 2014a, Yamanaka and Ankersen 2002):

$$
\begin{bmatrix} \ddot{x}_r \\ \ddot{y}_r \\ \ddot{z}_r \end{bmatrix} =
\begin{bmatrix}
\dot{\theta}^2 x_r + 2\dot{\theta}\dot{y}_r + \ddot{\theta}y_r - \frac{\mu(x_r+R)}{\Sigma(x_r,y_r,z_r)} + \frac{\mu}{R^2} \\
-2\dot{\theta}\dot{x}_r - \ddot{\theta}x_r + \dot{\theta}^2 y_r - \frac{\mu y_r}{\Sigma(x_r,y_r,z_r)} \\
-\frac{\mu z_r}{\Sigma(x_r,y_r,z_r)}
\end{bmatrix} + u,
$$

where u is the torque vector, and

$$
\Sigma(x_r, y_r, z_r) = \left[y_r^2 + z_r^2 + (x_r + R)^2 \right]^{\frac{3}{2}}.
$$

This system can also be easily arranged into the following quasilinear system form:

$$
\ddot{x} + D(\dot{\theta})\dot{x} + K(x, \dot{\theta}, \ddot{\theta})x = R(x, \dot{\theta}, \ddot{\theta}) + u, \tag{7.13}
$$

with

$$
x = \begin{bmatrix} x_r & y_r & z_r \end{bmatrix}^{\mathrm{T}},
$$

and

$$
D(\dot{\theta}) = \begin{bmatrix} 0 & -2\dot{\theta} & 0 \\ 2\dot{\theta} & 0 & 0 \\ 0 & 0 & 0 \end{bmatrix}, \tag{7.14}
$$

$$
K(x, \dot{\theta}, \ddot{\theta}) = \begin{bmatrix}
\frac{\mu}{\Sigma(x)} - \dot{\theta}^2 & -\ddot{\theta} & 0 \\
\ddot{\theta} & \frac{\mu}{\Sigma(x)} - \dot{\theta}^2 & 0 \\
0 & 0 & \frac{\mu}{\Sigma(x)}
\end{bmatrix}, \tag{7.15}
$$

$$
R(x, \dot{\theta}, \ddot{\theta}) = \begin{bmatrix} -\frac{\mu R}{\Sigma(x)} + \frac{\mu}{R^2} \\ 0 \\ 0 \end{bmatrix}. \tag{7.16}
$$

The two polynomial matrices associated with this system are $B(\theta, t, s) = I_3$ and

$$
A(x, \theta, t, s) = M(\dot{\theta}, \ddot{\theta})s^2 + D(\dot{\theta}, \ddot{\theta})s + K(\dot{\theta}, \ddot{\theta})
$$

$$
= \begin{bmatrix}
s^2 + \frac{\mu}{\Sigma(x)} - \dot{\theta}^2 & -2\dot{\theta}s - \ddot{\theta} & 0 \\
2\dot{\theta}s + \ddot{\theta} & s^2 + \frac{\mu}{\Sigma(x)} - \dot{\theta}^2 & 0 \\
0 & 0 & s^2 + \frac{\mu}{\Sigma(x)}
\end{bmatrix}.
$$

7.2 GSEs with Varying Coefficients

As generalizations to the homogeneous GSE (6.8) and the nonhomogeneous GSE (6.9), now let us propose, corresponding to the higher-order quasilinear time-varying system (7.1), the following homogeneous GSE with varying coefficients:

$$\sum_{i=0}^{m} A_i\left(\theta\left(t\right), t\right) VF^i = \sum_{i=0}^{m} B_i\left(\theta\left(t\right), t\right) WF^i, \tag{7.17}$$

and the following nonhomogeneous GSE with varying coefficients:

$$\sum_{i=0}^{m} A_i\left(\theta\left(t\right), t\right) VF^i = \sum_{i=0}^{m} B_i\left(\theta\left(t\right), t\right) WF^i + R\left(\theta\left(t\right), t\right), \tag{7.18}$$

where $\theta\left(t\right) : [0, +\infty) \rightarrow \Theta \subset \mathbb{R}^q$, is a time-varying parameter vector, $\Theta \subset \mathbb{R}^q$ is some compact set. Without loss of generality, $\theta\left(t\right)$ is assumed to be piecewisely continuous. The polynomial matrices associated with these GSEs are

$$\begin{cases} A\left(\theta, t, s\right) = \sum_{i=0}^{m} A_i\left(\theta, t\right) s^i \\ B\left(\theta, t, s\right) = \sum_{i=0}^{m} B_i\left(\theta, t\right) s^i, \end{cases} \tag{7.19}$$

where $A_i\left(\theta, t\right) \in \mathbb{R}^{n \times q}$ and $B_i\left(\theta, t\right) \in \mathbb{R}^{n \times r}$, $i = 1, 2, \ldots, \omega$, are matrix functions which are piecewisely continuous with respect to both θ and t.

7.2.1 F-Left Coprimeness

For convenience, let us introduce the following set

$$\Omega = \Theta \times [0, +\infty).$$

It is convented that in the following context it is generally assumed that $(\theta, t) \in \Omega$ even if when this is not mentioned.

As a natural generalization of the concept of F-coprimeness for time-invariant polynomial matrices introduced in Chapter 3, we here give the following definition.

Definition 7.1 *Let $A(\theta, t, s) \in \mathbb{R}^{n \times q}[s]$ and $B(\theta, t, s) \in \mathbb{R}^{n \times r}[s]$, $q + r > n$ be given as in (7.19), and $F \in \mathbb{C}^{p \times p}$ be an arbitrary matrix. Then $A(\theta, t, s)$ and $B(\theta, t, s)$ are said to be*

1. *F-left coprime with rank α over Ω if*

$$\mathrm{rank}\left[A(\theta, t, s) \quad B(\theta, t, s)\right] \leq \alpha, \ \forall (\theta, t) \in \Omega, \ s \in \mathbb{C}, \tag{7.20}$$

$$\mathrm{rank}\left[A(\theta, t, s) \quad B(\theta, t, s)\right] = \alpha, \ \forall (\theta, t) \in \Omega, \ s \in \mathrm{eig}(F). \tag{7.21}$$

2. *F-left coprime over Ω if*

$$\mathrm{rank}\left[A(\theta, t, s) \quad B(\theta, t, s)\right] = n, \ \forall (\theta, t) \in \Omega, \ s \in \mathrm{eig}(F). \tag{7.22}$$

3. *Left coprime with rank α over Ω if they are F-left coprime with rank α for arbitrary $F \in \mathbb{C}^{p \times p}$, $p > 0$.*
4. *Left coprime if they are F-left coprime over Ω for arbitrary $F \in \mathbb{C}^{p \times p}$, $p > 0$.*

For simplicity, here let us only look into the property of the F-left coprimeness of the polynomial matrices $A(\theta, t, s)$ and $B(\theta, t, s)$. Under this condition, there exist two unimodular matrices $P(\theta, t, s)$ and $Q(\theta, t, s)$ satisfying the following relation:

$$P(\theta, t, s)\left[A(\theta, t, s) \ -B(\theta, t, s)\right] Q(\theta, t, s) = \left[\Sigma(\theta, t, s) \ \ 0\right], \tag{7.23}$$

where $\Sigma(\theta, t, s) \in \mathbb{R}^{n \times n}[s]$ is usually a diagonal matrix and satisfies the following condition:

$$\det \Sigma(\theta, t, s) \neq 0, \ \forall (\theta, t) \in \Omega, \ s \in \mathrm{eig}(F).$$

Partition $Q(\theta, t, s)$ as

$$Q(\theta, t, s) = \begin{bmatrix} \tilde{U}(\theta, t, s) & N(\theta, t, s) \\ \tilde{T}(\theta, t, s) & D(\theta, t, s) \end{bmatrix},$$

where $U(\theta, t, s) \in \mathbb{R}^{q \times n}[s]$, $T(\theta, t, s) \in \mathbb{R}^{r \times n}[s]$, $N(\theta, t, s) \in \mathbb{R}^{q \times \beta_0}[s]$, $D(\theta, t, s) \in \mathbb{R}^{r \times \beta_0}[s]$, $\beta_0 = q + r - n$, then it obviously follows from (7.23) that $N(\theta, t, s)$ and $D(\theta, t, s)$ satisfy the following generalized RCF:

$$A(\theta, t, s) N(\theta, t, s) - B(\theta, t, s) D(\theta, t, s) = 0, \tag{7.24}$$

and $U(\theta, t, s)$ and $T(\theta, t, s)$ satisfy the following DPE:

$$A(\theta, t, s) U(\theta, t, s) - B(\theta, t, s) T(\theta, t, s) = \Delta(\theta, t, s) I, \qquad (7.25)$$

where

$$U(\theta, t, s) = \tilde{U}(\theta, t, s) \operatorname{adj}\Sigma(\theta, t, s) P$$
$$T(\theta, t, s) = \tilde{T}(\theta, t, s) \operatorname{adj}\Sigma(\theta, t, s) P$$
$$\Delta(\theta, t, s) = \det \Sigma(\theta, t, s)$$

Let the order of polynomial matrices $N(\theta, t, s)$ and $D(\theta, t, s)$ be ω, we can denote

$$\begin{cases} N(\theta, t, s) = \sum_{i=0}^{\omega} N_i(\theta, t) s^i, \ N_i(\theta, t) \in \mathbb{R}^{q \times \beta_0} \\ D(\theta, t, s) = \sum_{i=0}^{\omega} D_i(\theta, t) s^i, \ D_i(\theta, t) \in \mathbb{R}^{r \times \beta_0}. \end{cases} \qquad (7.26)$$

Similarly, let the order of polynomial matrices $U(\theta, t, s)$ and $T(\theta, t, s)$ be φ, we can denote

$$\begin{cases} U(\theta, t, s) = \sum_{i=0}^{\varphi} U_i(\theta, t) s^i, \ U_i(\theta, t) \in \mathbb{R}^{q \times n} \\ T(\theta, t, s) = \sum_{i=0}^{\varphi} T_i(\theta, t) s^i, \ T_i(\theta, t) \in \mathbb{R}^{r \times n}. \end{cases} \qquad (7.27)$$

In view of this and also recalling similar results in Chapter 3, we give without proof the following result.

Theorem 7.1 *Let $A(\theta, t, s) \in \mathbb{R}^{n \times q}[s]$, $B(\theta, t, s) \in \mathbb{R}^{n \times r}[s]$, $F \in \mathbb{C}^{p \times p}$. Then $A(\theta, t, s)$ and $B(\theta, t, s)$ are F-left coprime over Ω if and only if one of the following two conditions holds:*

- *There exist a pair of polynomial matrices $N(\theta, t, s) \in \mathbb{R}^{q \times \beta_0}[s]$ and $D(\theta, t, s) \in \mathbb{R}^{r \times \beta_0}[s]$ satisfying the generalized RCF (7.24) pointwisely over Ω.*
- *There exist a pair of polynomial matrices $U(\theta, t, s) \in \mathbb{R}^{q \times n}[s]$ and $T(\theta, t, s) \in \mathbb{R}^{r \times n}[s]$ satisfying the DPE (7.25) pointwisely over Ω.*

7.2.2 Solutions

Theoretically, our results in Chapters 4 and 5 can be easily generalized into the case for GSEs with time-varying coefficients. The reason for this is that, as we can easily observe, the proofs of these results involve only algebraic operations.

For simplicity, in this subsection let us consider solutions to GSEs with varying coefficients under the condition that $A(\theta, t, s)$ and $B(\theta, t, s)$ are F-left coprime over Ω.

7.2.2.1 Homogeneous GSEs

For solution to the homogeneous GSE (7.17), we have the following result (proof omitted).

Theorem 7.2 *Let $F \in \mathbb{C}^{p \times p}$, and $A(\theta, t, s)$ and $B(\theta, t, s)$ be F-left coprime over Ω. Further, let $N(\theta, t, s)$ and $D(\theta, t, s)$ be a pair of right coprime polynomial matrices satisfying the generalized RCF (7.24) pointwisely over Ω and be given by (7.26). Then, for $(\theta, t) \in \Omega$, a general solution to the homogeneous GSE (7.17) is given by*

$$
\boxed{
\begin{aligned}
&\text{Formula } I_H \\[4pt]
&\left\{
\begin{aligned}
V(\theta, t) &= \left[N(\theta, t, s)\, Z\right]\Big|_F = \sum_{k=0}^{\omega} N_k(\theta, t)\, Z F^k \\
W(\theta, t) &= \left[D(\theta, t, s)\, Z\right]\Big|_F = \sum_{k=0}^{\omega} D_k(\theta, t)\, Z F^k,
\end{aligned}
\right.
\end{aligned}
}
\tag{7.28}
$$

with $Z \in \mathbb{C}^{\beta_0 \times p}$ being an arbitrary parameter matrix.

7.2.2.2 Nonhomogeneous GSEs

Using (7.28) and the solution structural lemma for GSEs, that is, Lemma 5.1, we have the following result on solution to the nonhomogeneous GSE (7.18).

Theorem 7.3 *Let $F \in \mathbb{C}^{p \times p}$, $A(\theta, t, s)$ and $B(\theta, t, s)$ be F-left coprime, $N(\theta, t, s)$ and $D(\theta, t, s)$ be a pair of polynomial matrices satisfying the generalized RCF (7.24) pointwisely over Ω. Further, let a pair of polynomial matrices $U(\theta, t, s)$ and $T(\theta, t, s)$ satisfying the DPE (7.25) pointwisely over Ω be given by (7.27). Then, for $(\theta, t) \in \Omega$,*

1. *A particular solution to the nonhomogeneous GSE (7.18) is given by*

$$
\boxed{
\begin{aligned}
&\text{Formula } I_N \\[4pt]
&\left\{
\begin{aligned}
V(\theta, t) &= \left[U(\theta, t, s)\, R(\theta, t)\right]\Big|_F = \sum_{k=0}^{\varphi} U_k(\theta, t)\, R(\theta, t)\, F^k \\
W(\theta, t) &= \left[T(\theta, t, s)\, R(\theta, t)\right]\Big|_F = \sum_{k=0}^{\varphi} T_k(\theta, t)\, R(\theta, t)\, F^k.
\end{aligned}
\right.
\end{aligned}
}
\tag{7.29}
$$

2. *A general solution to the nonhomogeneous GSE (7.18) is given by*

$$\begin{cases} V(\theta, t) = [U(\theta, t, s) R(\theta, t)]\big|_F + [N(\theta, t, s) Z]\big|_F \\ W(\theta, t) = [T(\theta, t, s) R(\theta, t)]\big|_F + [D(\theta, t, s) Z]\big|_F, \end{cases} \tag{7.30}$$

which can also be interpreted as

$$\begin{bmatrix} V(\theta, t) \\ W(\theta, t) \end{bmatrix} = \left[\hat{Q}(\theta, t, s) \begin{bmatrix} R \\ Z \end{bmatrix} \right]\Big|_F$$

$$= \sum_{k=0}^{\gamma} \hat{Q}_k(\theta, t) \begin{bmatrix} R \\ Z \end{bmatrix} F^k,$$

where $Z \in \mathbb{C}^{\beta_0 \times p}$ is an arbitrary parameter matrix, $\gamma = \max(\omega, \varphi)$, and

$$\hat{Q}(\theta, t, s) = \begin{bmatrix} U(\theta, t, s) & N(\theta, t, s) \\ T(\theta, t, s) & D(\theta, t, s) \end{bmatrix} = \sum_{k=0}^{\gamma} \hat{Q}_k(\theta, t) s^k.$$

7.2.3 Example

Example 7.5 (Hypersonic Vehicle)

Consider the hypersonic vehicle system introduced in Example 7.2. The related homogeneous GSE is in the form of

$$VF + A(\theta) V = B(\theta) W, \tag{7.31}$$

where

$$A(\theta) = \begin{bmatrix} a_1 & 0 & 0 & a_2 & 0 \\ a_3 & 0 & 0 & a_4 & 0 \\ -\sin\gamma & 0 & 0 & 0 & 0 \\ -a_3 & 0 & 0 & -a_4 & -1 \\ a_5 & 0 & 0 & a_6 & a_7 \end{bmatrix}, \tag{7.32}$$

$$B(\theta) = \begin{bmatrix} b_1 & b_2 V \cos\alpha \\ b_3 & b_2 \sin\alpha \\ 0 & 0 \\ -b_3 & -b_2 \sin\alpha \\ b_4 & 0 \end{bmatrix}, \tag{7.33}$$

the a_is and b_is are defined in (7.7) and (7.8), and naturally, the parameter vector θ comprises the a_is and b_is, that is,

$$\theta = \begin{bmatrix} a_1 & a_2 & \cdots & a_7 & b_1 & b_2 & b_3 & b_4 & V & \gamma \end{bmatrix}^{\mathrm{T}}. \tag{7.34}$$

Due to practical requirement, the following assumption is imposed.

Assumption 7.1 $b_2(t) b_4(t) \cos \alpha(t) \neq 0, \ \forall t \geq 0.$

It follows from Theorem 7.2 that in order to solve the GSE (7.31), the main task is really to solve a pair of right coprime polynomial matrices $N(\theta, t, s) \in \mathbb{R}^{5 \times 2}[s]$ and $D(\theta, t, s) \in \mathbb{R}^{2 \times 2}[s]$ satisfying the generalized RCF (7.24). For this, we have the following proposition (proof omitted).

Proposition 7.2 *Let $A(\theta)$ and $B(\theta)$ be given in (7.32) and (7.33). Then, under Assumption 7.1,*

1. $(A(\theta), B(\theta))$ *is controllable pointwisely if and only if*

$$\theta \in \Theta_{13} = \left\{ \theta \mid \theta \in \mathbb{R}^{13}, \sin \gamma \neq 0 \right\}.$$

2. *A pair of polynomial matrices $N(\theta, t, s) \in \mathbb{R}^{5 \times 2}[s]$ and $D(\theta, t, s) \in \mathbb{R}^{2 \times 2}[s]$ satisfying the generalized RCF (7.24), which are right coprime for $\theta \in \Theta_{13}$, are given by*

$$\begin{cases} N(s) = N_0 + N_1 s + N_2 s^2 + N_3 s^3 + N_4 s^4 \\ D(s) = D_0 + D_1 s + D_2 s^2 + D_3 s^3 + D_4 s^4, \end{cases}$$

where

$$\begin{cases} N_k = \left[N_{ij}^{(k)} \right]_{5 \times 2}, & i = 1, 2, \ldots, 5, \ j = 1, 2, \ k = 0, 1, 2, 3 \\ D_k = \left[D_{ij}^{(k)} \right]_{5 \times 2}, & i = 1, 2, \ j = 1, 2, \ k = 0, 1, \ldots, 4, \end{cases}$$

with

$$N_{11}^{(0)} = N_{41}^{(0)} = N_{51}^{(0)} = 0,$$

$$N_{12}^{(0)} = N_{42}^{(0)} = N_{52}^{(0)} = 0,$$

$$N_{21}^{(0)} = -N_{51}^{(1)} = \Upsilon_2 b_4 \sin \alpha,$$

$$N_{22}^{(0)} = N_{52}^{(1)} = \Upsilon_3 \Upsilon_2,$$

$$N_{31}^{(0)} = -N_{32}^{(0)} = \Upsilon_1 \Upsilon_2 \sin \gamma,$$

$$N_{11}^{(1)} = N_{12}^{(1)} = 0,$$

$$N_{21}^{(1)} = V \Upsilon_3 b_4 \cos \alpha,$$

$$N_{22}^{(1)} = \Upsilon_1 \Upsilon_3 a_7,$$

$$N_{31}^{(1)} = -\Upsilon_1 V b_4 \cos \alpha \sin \gamma,$$

$$N_{32}^{\langle 1 \rangle} = -\Upsilon_1^2 a_7 \sin \gamma,$$

$$N_{41}^{\langle 1 \rangle} = -Vb_4 \left(b_4 \sin \alpha - \Upsilon_3 \right) \cos \alpha,$$

$$N_{42}^{\langle 1 \rangle} = -\Upsilon_1 a_7 \left(\Upsilon_3 + b_4 \sin \alpha \right),$$

$$N_{11}^{\langle 2 \rangle} = N_{12}^{\langle 2 \rangle} = 0,$$

$$N_{21}^{\langle 2 \rangle} = N_{31}^{\langle 2 \rangle} = N_{41}^{\langle 2 \rangle} = 0,$$

$$N_{22}^{\langle 2 \rangle} = -\Upsilon_3 \Upsilon_1,$$

$$N_{32}^{\langle 2 \rangle} = \Upsilon_1^2 \sin \gamma,$$

$$N_{42}^{\langle 2 \rangle} = \Upsilon_1 \left(\Upsilon_3 + b_4 \sin \alpha \right),$$

$$N_{51}^{\langle 2 \rangle} = Vb_4^2 \cos \alpha \sin \alpha,$$

$$N_{52}^{\langle 2 \rangle} = \Upsilon_1 b_4 a_7 \sin \alpha,$$

$$N_{11}^{\langle 3 \rangle} = N_{21}^{\langle 3 \rangle} = N_{31}^{\langle 3 \rangle} = N_{41}^{\langle 3 \rangle} = N_{51}^{\langle 3 \rangle} = 0,$$

$$N_{12}^{\langle 3 \rangle} = N_{22}^{\langle 3 \rangle} = N_{32}^{\langle 3 \rangle} = N_{42}^{\langle 3 \rangle} = 0,$$

$$N_{52}^{\langle 3 \rangle} = -\Upsilon_1 b_4 \sin \alpha,$$

and

$$D_{11}^{\langle 0 \rangle} = -D_{12}^{\langle 0 \rangle} = \frac{1}{b_4} \left(\Upsilon_5 a_6 - \Upsilon_2 \Upsilon_3 a_6 - \Upsilon_2 a_6 b_4 \sin \alpha \right),$$

$$D_{21}^{\langle 0 \rangle} = -D_{22}^{\langle 0 \rangle} = \frac{1}{Vb_2 b_4 \cos \alpha} \left(\Upsilon_5 a_2 b_4 - \Upsilon_6 \Upsilon_2 - \Upsilon_5 b_1 a_6 \right),$$

$$D_{11}^{\langle 1 \rangle} = \frac{1}{b_4} \Upsilon_2 \left(\Upsilon_1 a_5 + a_7 \sin \alpha \right) + Va_6 \left(\Upsilon_3 + b_4 \sin \alpha \right) \cos \alpha,$$

$$D_{12}^{\langle 1 \rangle} = \frac{1}{b_4} \left[\Upsilon_1 a_6 a_7 \left(\Upsilon_3 + b_4 \sin \alpha \right) - \Upsilon_2 \left(\Upsilon_1 a_5 - a_7 \Upsilon_3 \right) \right],$$

$$D_{21}^{\langle 1 \rangle} = \frac{1}{Vb_2 b_4 \cos \alpha} \left(V\Upsilon_6 b_4 \cos \alpha - \Upsilon_4 \Upsilon_2 \right),$$

$$D_{22}^{\langle 1 \rangle} = \frac{1}{Vb_2 b_4 \cos \alpha} \left(\Upsilon_4 \Upsilon_2 - \Upsilon_5 b_1 a_7 + \Upsilon_6 \Upsilon_1 a_7 \right),$$

$$D_{11}^{\langle 2 \rangle} = -V\Upsilon_1 a_5 \cos \alpha - \Upsilon_2 \sin \alpha - Vb_4 a_7 \cos \alpha \sin \alpha,$$

$$D_{12}^{\langle 2 \rangle} = \Upsilon_1 \left(a_7^2 - a_6 \right) \sin \alpha - \frac{1}{b_4} \left(\Upsilon_2 \Upsilon_3 + \Upsilon_1 \Upsilon_3 a_6 + \Upsilon_1^2 a_5 a_7 \right),$$

$$D_{21}^{(2)} = \frac{1}{b_2}\left(\Upsilon_2 b_3 + \Upsilon_4\right),$$

$$D_{22}^{(2)} = \frac{1}{V b_2 b_4 \cos\alpha}\left(\Upsilon_5 b_1 - \Upsilon_1 \Upsilon_6 + \Upsilon_4 \Upsilon_1 a_7\right) - \frac{1}{b_2}\Upsilon_2 b_3,$$

$$D_{11}^{(3)} = V b_4 \cos\alpha \sin\alpha,$$

$$D_{12}^{(3)} = \frac{1}{b_4}a_5 \Upsilon_1^2 + 2\Upsilon_1 a_7 \sin\alpha,$$

$$D_{21}^{(3)} = -\frac{1}{b_2}V b_3 b_4 \cos\alpha,$$

$$D_{22}^{(3)} = -\frac{1}{V b_2 b_4 \cos\alpha}\Upsilon_1 \Upsilon_4 - \frac{1}{b_2}\Upsilon_1 a_7 b_3,$$

$$D_{11}^{(4)} = D_{21}^{(4)} = 0,$$

$$D_{12}^{(4)} = -\Upsilon_1 \sin\alpha,$$

$$D_{22}^{(4)} = \frac{1}{b_2}\Upsilon_1 b_3,$$

and also the variables used in the above expressions are given by

$$\begin{cases} \Upsilon_1 = b_1 \sin\alpha - V b_3 \cos\alpha \\ \Upsilon_2 = b_4\left(a_2 \sin\alpha - V a_4 \cos\alpha\right) - \Upsilon_1 a_6 \\ \Upsilon_3 = \frac{1}{V b_4 \cos\alpha}\Upsilon_1\left[b_4\left(a_7 - a_1\right)\sin\alpha + \Upsilon_1 a_5\right] + \Upsilon_1 a_3 \\ \Upsilon_4 = -\Upsilon_1 a_1 b_4 + \Upsilon_1 b_1 a_5 + b_1 b_4 a_7 \sin\alpha \\ \Upsilon_5 = \Upsilon_2 \Upsilon_3 + \Upsilon_2 b_4 \sin\alpha \\ \Upsilon_6 = a_2 b_4^2 \sin\alpha + \Upsilon_3 a_2 b_4 - \Upsilon_3 b_1 a_6 - b_1 a_6 b_4 \sin\alpha. \end{cases}$$

7.3 Fully Actuated GSEs with Varying Coefficients

In Chapter 6, we have introduced the concept of fully actuated GSEs. In this section, we generalize this concept into the case of GSEs with varying coefficients.

7.3.1 Definitions

Definition 7.2 *The corresponding homogeneous GSE (7.17) and the nonhomogeneous GSE (7.18) are called fully actuated if $B\left(\theta, t, s\right) \in \mathbb{R}^{n\times n}$, and*

$$\det B\left(\theta, t, s\right) \neq 0, \ \forall\left(\theta, t\right) \in \Omega, \ s \in \mathbb{C}. \tag{7.35}$$

In many applications, we really do not need to require the fully actuation condition (7.35), and instead we allow $B\,(\theta, t, s) \in \mathbb{R}^{n \times n}$ to possess certain singular points that are not important or can be avoided. This leads to the following definition of F-fully actuation.

Definition 7.3 *The corresponding homogeneous GSE (7.17) and the nonhomogeneous GSE (7.18) are called F-fully actuated for some matrix $F \in \mathbb{C}^{p \times p}$ if $B\,(\theta, t, s) \in \mathbb{R}^{n \times n}$, and*

$$\det B\,(\theta, t, s) \neq 0, \ \forall\,(\theta, t) \in \Omega, \ s \in \text{eig}\,(F). \tag{7.36}$$

Consider two special types of GSEs in the forms of

$$\sum_{i=0}^{m} A_i\,(\theta\,(t), t)\, VF^i = W, \tag{7.37}$$

and

$$\sum_{i=0}^{m} A_i\,(\theta\,(t), t)\, VF^i = W + R\,(\theta\,(t), t). \tag{7.38}$$

They are obviously special forms of (7.17) and (7.18), respectively. Since

$$B\,(\theta\,(t), t, s) = I_n,$$

they are certainly fully actuated ones.

The two equations (7.37) and (7.38) are clearly generalizations of the standard homogeneous and nonhomogeneous GSEs (6.10) and (6.11) introduced in Chapter 6. In the time-invariant case, any GSE can be equivalently converted into a standard GSE by applying Laplace transforms, while this cannot be realized in the time-varying case.

We have seen in Section 7.2 that, in the general case solving $N\,(\theta, t, s)$ and $D\,(\theta, t, s)$ satisfying the generalized RFC (7.24), and $U\,(\theta, t, s)$ and $T\,(\theta, t, s)$ satisfying the DPE (7.25), is not easy. However, similarly to the case in Chapter 6, for the type of fully actuated GSEs, these polynomial matrices can be easily derived. Therefore, in the rest of this chapter, we will focus on the GSEs (7.17) and (7.18) satisfying the following F-full actuation assumption.

Assumption 7.2 $B\,(\theta, t, s) \in \mathbb{R}^{n \times n}\,[s]$ *and satisfies*

$$\det B\,(\theta, t, s) \neq 0, \ \forall\,(\theta, t) \in \Omega, \ s \in \text{eig}\,(F).$$

In certain circumstances, the above assumption can be further strengthened and appears as follows.

Assumption 7.3 $B(\theta, t, s) \in \mathbb{R}^{n \times n}[s]$ *and satisfies*

$$\det B(\theta, t, s) \neq 0, \ \forall (\theta, t) \in \Omega, \ s \in \mathbb{C}.$$

Let us define the scalar function

$$\mu(\theta, t, s) \triangleq \det B(\theta, t, s). \tag{7.39}$$

Then, Assumption 7.2 is equivalent to

$$\mu(\theta, t, s) \neq 0, \ \forall (\theta, t) \in \Omega, \ s \in \text{eig}(F); \tag{7.40}$$

while Assumption 7.3 is equivalent to

$$\mu(\theta, t, s) \neq 0, \ \forall (\theta, t) \in \Omega, \ s \in \mathbb{C}. \tag{7.41}$$

The latter implies that $\mu(\theta, t, s)$ is a nonzero function, which is invariant of s, that is,

$$\mu(\theta, t, s) = \mu(\theta, t) \neq 0, \ \forall (\theta, t) \in \Omega. \tag{7.42}$$

7.3.2 Examples

Again, the general space rendezvous systems introduced in Examples 7.3 and 7.4 give good examples of fully actuated GSEs.

Example 7.6

Consider the linear time-varying space rendezvous system mentioned in Example 7.3 again, which are given by (7.10) through (7.12). The corresponding homogeneous GSE takes the following form:

$$VF^2 + D(\dot{\theta})VF + K(\dot{\theta}, \ddot{\theta})V = W, \tag{7.43}$$

with

$$D(\dot{\theta}) = \begin{bmatrix} 0 & -2\dot{\theta} & 0 \\ 2\dot{\theta} & 0 & 0 \\ 0 & 0 & 0 \end{bmatrix}, \tag{7.44}$$

$$K(\dot\theta, \ddot\theta) = \begin{bmatrix} -2k\dot\theta^{\frac{3}{2}} - \dot\theta^2 & -\ddot\theta & 0 \\ \ddot\theta & k\dot\theta^{\frac{3}{2}} - \dot\theta^2 & 0 \\ 0 & 0 & k\dot\theta^{\frac{3}{2}} \end{bmatrix},$$ (7.45)

where θ is the true anomaly.

The GSE is obviously a fully actuated one with the associated polynomial matrices $B(\theta, t, s) = I_3$ and

$$A(\theta, t, s) = M(\dot\theta, \ddot\theta)s^2 + D(\dot\theta, \ddot\theta)s + K(\dot\theta, \ddot\theta)$$

$$= \begin{bmatrix} s^2 - 2k\dot\theta^{\frac{3}{2}} - \dot\theta^2 & -2\dot\theta s - \ddot\theta & 0 \\ 2\dot\theta s + \ddot\theta & s^2 + k\dot\theta^{\frac{3}{2}} - \dot\theta^2 & 0 \\ 0 & 0 & s^2 + k\dot\theta^{\frac{3}{2}} \end{bmatrix}.$$

Example 7.7 (Space Rendezvous System—The Nonlinear Case)

Consider the nonlinear space rendezvous system introduced in Example 7.4. The corresponding homogeneous GSE is given by

$$VF^2 + D(\dot\theta)VF + K(x, \dot\theta, \ddot\theta)V = W,$$ (7.46)

with

$$D(\dot\theta) = \begin{bmatrix} 0 & -2\dot\theta & 0 \\ 2\dot\theta & 0 & 0 \\ 0 & 0 & 0 \end{bmatrix},$$ (7.47)

$$K(x, \dot\theta, \ddot\theta) = \begin{bmatrix} \frac{\mu}{\Sigma(x)} - \dot\theta^2 & -\ddot\theta & 0 \\ \ddot\theta & \frac{\mu}{\Sigma(x)} - \dot\theta^2 & 0 \\ 0 & 0 & \frac{\mu}{\Sigma(x)} \end{bmatrix}.$$ (7.48)

Since $B(\theta, t, s) = I_3$, this is clearly a fully actuated GSE. The associated polynomial matrix $A(x, \theta, t, s)$ is

$$A(x, \theta, t, s) = M(\dot\theta, \ddot\theta)s^2 + D(\dot\theta, \ddot\theta)s + K(\dot\theta, \ddot\theta)$$

$$= \begin{bmatrix} s^2 + \frac{\mu}{\Sigma(x)} - \dot\theta^2 & -2\dot\theta s - \ddot\theta & 0 \\ 2\dot\theta s + \ddot\theta & s^2 + \frac{\mu}{\Sigma(x)} - \dot\theta^2 & 0 \\ 0 & 0 & s^2 + \frac{\mu}{\Sigma(x)} \end{bmatrix}.$$

In the following sections, we will stress on solution of fully actuated GSEs. Since the results are actually parallel to those in the last four sections in Chapter 6, we will only present the results without giving proofs.

7.4 Fully Actuated Homogeneous GSEs

7.4.1 Forward Solutions

Under Assumption 7.2, a pair of forward solutions of $N(\theta, t, s)$ and $D(\theta, t, s)$ satisfying the generalized RCF (7.24) can be directly given by

$$\begin{cases} N(\theta, t, s) = \mu(\theta, t, s) I_q \\ D(\theta, t, s) = \text{adj}B(\theta, t, s) A(\theta, t, s), \end{cases} \tag{7.49}$$

where $\mu(\theta, t, s)$ is defined in (7.39), which satisfies (7.40).

If, in particular, Assumption 7.3 is met, (7.42) is satisfied, and $\mu(\theta, t, s)$ is not invariant of s, thus $B^{-1}(\theta, t, s)$ is also polynomial matrix in s. In this case, a pair of forward solutions of $N(\theta, t, s)$ and $D(\theta, t, s)$ satisfying the generalized RCF (7.24) can be directly given by

$$\begin{cases} N(\theta, t, s) = I_q \\ D(\theta, t, s) = B^{-1}(\theta, t, s) A(\theta, t, s). \end{cases} \tag{7.50}$$

7.4.1.1 Case of F Being Arbitrary

By applying a slightly generalized version of Theorem 4.7, the following result for solution to the GSE (7.17) under Assumption 7.3 can be obtained, which is a straight forward generalized version of Theorem 6.1.

Theorem 7.4 *Let $A(\theta, t, s) \in \mathbb{R}^{n \times q}[s]$ and $B(\theta, t, s) \in \mathbb{R}^{n \times n}[s]$ be given as in (7.19), and $F \in \mathbb{C}^{p \times p}$. Then,*

1. *When Assumption 7.2 holds, all the solutions to the homogeneous GSE (7.17) are given by*

$$\begin{cases} V(\theta, t) = [\mu(\theta, t, s) Z]\big|_F, \\ W(\theta, t) = [\text{adj}B(\theta, t, s) A(\theta, t, s) Z]\big|_F, \end{cases} \tag{7.51}$$

with $Z \in \mathbb{C}^{q \times p}$ being an arbitrary parameter matrix.
2. *When Assumption 7.3 holds, the aforementioned solution can be replaced by*

$$\begin{cases} V(\theta, t) = Z \\ W(\theta, t) = [B^{-1}(\theta, t, s) A(\theta, t, s) Z]\big|_F. \end{cases} \tag{7.52}$$

7.4.1.2 Case of F Being in Jordan Form

When the matrix F is in the Jordan form of (6.23), by Convention C1 the columns w_{ij} and z_{ij} are well defined. Applying a slightly generalized version of Theorem 4.8

to this special case immediately gives the following result, which is a straightforward generalization of Theorem 6.2.

Theorem 7.5 *Let $A(\theta, t, s) \in \mathbb{R}^{n \times q}[s]$ and $B(\theta, t, s) \in \mathbb{R}^{n \times n}[s]$ be given as in (7.19), and $F \in \mathbb{C}^{p \times p}$ be a Jordan matrix given by (6.23). Then,*

1. *When Assumption 7.2 holds, all the solutions to the GSE (7.17) are given by*

$$
\begin{cases}
v_{ij}(\theta, t) = \sum_{k=0}^{j-1} \frac{1}{k!} \frac{\partial^k}{\partial s^k} \left[\mu(\theta, t, s_i) \right] z_{i,j-k}, \\[4mm]
w_{ij}(\theta, t) = \sum_{k=0}^{j-1} \frac{1}{k!} \frac{\partial^k}{\partial s^k} \left[\mathrm{adj}B(\theta, t, s_i) A(\theta, t, s_i) \right] z_{i,j-k}, \\[4mm]
\qquad j = 1, 2, \ldots, p_i, \quad i = 1, 2, \ldots, w,
\end{cases}
\tag{7.53}
$$

with $Z \in \mathbb{C}^{q \times p}$ being an arbitrary parameter matrix.

2. *When, in particular, Assumption 7.3 holds, the above solution can also be replaced by*

$$
\begin{cases}
V(\theta, t) = Z \\[2mm]
w_{ij}(\theta, t) = \sum_{k=0}^{j-1} \frac{1}{k!} \frac{\partial^k}{\partial s^k} \left[B^{-1}(\theta, t, s_i) A(\theta, t, s_i) \right] z_{i,j-k}, \\[4mm]
\qquad j = 1, 2, \ldots, p_i, \quad i = 1, 2, \ldots, w.
\end{cases}
\tag{7.54}
$$

7.4.1.3 Case of F Being Diagonal

Further, when the matrix F reduces to the diagonal form of (6.27), by Convention C1 the columns w_i and z_i are well defined. Applying a slightly generalized version of Theorem 4.9 to this special case immediately gives the following result, which is a natural generalized version of Theorem 6.3.

Theorem 7.6 *Let $A(\theta, t, s) \in \mathbb{R}^{n \times q}[s]$ and $B(\theta, t, s) \in \mathbb{R}^{n \times n}[s]$ be given as in (7.19), $F \in \mathbb{C}^{p \times p}$ be in the diagonal form of (6.27), and Assumption 7.2 hold. Then all the solutions to the GSE (7.17) are given by*

$$
\begin{cases}
v_i(\theta, t) = z_i \\
w_i(\theta, t) = B^{-1}(\theta, t, s_i) A(\theta, t, s_i) z_i, \quad i = 1, 2, \ldots, p.
\end{cases}
\tag{7.55}
$$

with $z_i \in \mathbb{C}^q$, $i = 1, 2, \ldots, p$, being a group of arbitrary parameter vectors.

Remark 7.1 Simply setting $B(\theta, t, s) = B(\theta, t, s_i) = I_n$ in the three theorems gives general solutions to the special types of fully actuated homogeneous GSE (7.37).

7.4.2 Backward Solutions

In this subsection, we concentrate on the case that $A(\theta, t, s)$ is square, that is, the case of $q = n$.

Again, under Assumption 7.2, a pair of backward solutions of $N(\theta, t, s)$ and $D(\theta, t, s)$ to the generalized RCF (7.24) can be directly given by

$$\begin{cases} N(\theta, t, s) = \mu(\theta, t, s) \operatorname{adj} A(\theta, t, s) \\ D(\theta, t, s) = \pi(\theta, t, s) \operatorname{adj}B(\theta, t, s), \end{cases} \tag{7.56}$$

with $\mu(\theta, t, s)$ given by (7.39), and

$$\pi(\theta, t, s) = \det A(\theta, t, s). \tag{7.57}$$

If, in particular, Assumption 7.3 is met, it is easy to see that $B^{-1}(\theta, t, s)$ is also a polynomial matrix in s, and a pair of backward solutions of $N(\theta, t, s)$ and $D(\theta, t, s)$ to the generalized RCF (7.24) can be directly given by

$$\begin{cases} N(\theta, t, s) = \operatorname{adj} A(\theta, t, s) \\ D(\theta, t, s) = \pi(\theta, t, s) B^{-1}(\theta, t, s). \end{cases} \tag{7.58}$$

If, in addition, $A(\theta, t, s)$ is also unimodular, then $A^{-1}(\theta, t, s)$ is also a polynomial matrix in s, and in this case a pair of polynomial matrices satisfying the generalized RCF (7.24) can be obviously taken as

$$\begin{cases} N(\theta, t, s) = A^{-1}(\theta, t, s) \\ D(\theta, t, s) = B^{-1}(\theta, t, s). \end{cases} \tag{7.59}$$

7.4.2.1 Case of F Being Arbitrary

By applying a slightly generalized version of Theorem 4.7, the following result for solution to the GSE (7.17) under Assumption 7.3 can be easily obtained, which is a natural generalized version of Theorem 6.5.

Theorem 7.7 Let $A(\theta, t, s), B(\theta, t, s) \in \mathbb{R}^{n \times n}[s]$ be given as in (7.19), and $F \in \mathbb{C}^{p \times p}$. Then,

1. *When Assumption 7.2 holds, all the solutions to the fully actuated GSE (7.17) are given by*

$$
\begin{cases}
V\left(\theta, t\right) = \left[\mu\left(\theta, t, s\right) \operatorname{adj} A\left(\theta, t, s\right) Z\right]\big|_F \\
W\left(\theta, t\right) = \left[\pi\left(\theta, t, s\right) \operatorname{adj} B\left(\theta, t, s\right) Z\right]\big|_F,
\end{cases}
\tag{7.60}
$$

with $Z \in \mathbb{C}^{n \times p}$ being an arbitrary parameter matrix.

2. *When, in particular, Assumption 7.3 is met, the above solution can be replaced by*

$$
\begin{cases}
V\left(\theta, t\right) = \left[\operatorname{adj} A\left(\theta, t, s\right) Z\right]\big|_F \\
W\left(\theta, t\right) = \left[\pi\left(\theta, t, s\right) B^{-1}\left(\theta, t, s\right) Z\right]\big|_F.
\end{cases}
\tag{7.61}
$$

3. *In addition, when $A\left(s\right)$ is also unimodular, the above solutions can also be replaced by*

$$
\begin{cases}
V\left(\theta, t\right) = \left[A^{-1}\left(\theta, t, s\right) Z\right]\big|_F \\
W\left(\theta, t\right) = \left[B^{-1}\left(\theta, t, s\right) Z\right]\big|_F.
\end{cases}
\tag{7.62}
$$

7.4.2.2 Case of F Being in Jordan Form

When the matrix F is in the Jordan form of (6.23), by Convention C1 the columns w_{ij} and z_{ij} are well defined. Applying a slightly generalized version of Theorem 4.8 to this special case immediately gives the following result, which is a natural generalized version of Theorem 6.6.

Theorem 7.8 *Let $A\left(\theta, t, s\right)$, $B\left(\theta, t, s\right) \in \mathbb{R}^{n \times n}\left[s\right]$ be given as in (7.19), and $F \in \mathbb{C}^{p \times p}$ be a Jordan matrix given by (6.23). Then,*

1. *When Assumption 7.2 holds, all the solutions to the fully actuated GSE (7.17) are given by*

$$
\begin{cases}
v_{ij}\left(\theta, t\right) = \displaystyle\sum_{k=0}^{j-1} \frac{1}{k!} \frac{\partial^k}{\partial s^k}\left[\mu\left(\theta, t, s_i\right) \operatorname{adj} A\left(\theta, t, s_i\right)\right] z_{i,j-k} \\[2mm]
w_{ij}\left(\theta, t\right) = \displaystyle\sum_{k=0}^{j-1} \frac{1}{k!} \frac{\partial^k}{\partial s^k}\left[\pi\left(\theta, t, s_i\right) \operatorname{adj} B\left(\theta, t, s_i\right)\right] z_{i,j-k}, \\[2mm]
\quad j = 1, 2, \ldots, p_i, \quad i = 1, 2, \ldots, w,
\end{cases}
\tag{7.63}
$$

with $Z \in \mathbb{C}^{n \times p}$ being an arbitrary parameter matrix.

2. When, in particular, Assumption 7.3 holds, the above solution can also be replaced by

$$
\begin{cases}
v_{ij}(\theta, t) = \displaystyle\sum_{k=0}^{j-1} \frac{1}{k!} \frac{\partial^k}{\partial s^k} \left[\operatorname{adj} A(\theta, t, s_i) \right] z_{i,j-k} \\[4mm]
w_{ij}(\theta, t) = \displaystyle\sum_{k=0}^{j-1} \frac{1}{k!} \frac{\partial^k}{\partial s^k} \left[\pi(\theta, t, s_i) B^{-1}(\theta, t, s_i) \right] z_{i,j-k}, \\[4mm]
\qquad j = 1, 2, \ldots, p_i, \quad i = 1, 2, \ldots, w.
\end{cases}
\tag{7.64}
$$

3. In addition, when $A(s)$ is also unimodular, the above solutions can also be replaced by

$$
\begin{cases}
v_{ij}(\theta, t) = \displaystyle\sum_{k=0}^{j-1} \frac{1}{k!} \frac{\partial^k}{\partial s^k} A^{-1}(\theta, t, s_i) z_{i,j-k} \\[4mm]
w_{ij}(\theta, t) = \displaystyle\sum_{k=0}^{j-1} \frac{1}{k!} \frac{\partial^k}{\partial s^k} B^{-1}(\theta, t, s_i) z_{i,j-k}, \\[4mm]
\qquad j = 1, 2, \ldots, p_i, \quad i = 1, 2, \ldots, w.
\end{cases}
\tag{7.65}
$$

7.4.2.3 Case of F Being Diagonal

When the matrix F is in the diagonal form of (6.27), by Convention C1 the columns v_i, w_i and z_i are well defined. Applying Theorem 4.9 to the fully actuated GSE (7.17) immediately gives the following result, which is a natural generalized version of Theorem 6.7.

Theorem 7.9 *Let $A(\theta, t, s)$, $B(\theta, t, s) \in \mathbb{R}^{n \times n}[s]$ be given as in (7.19), $F \in \mathbb{C}^{p \times p}$ be in the diagonal form of (6.27), and Assumption 7.3 hold. Then,*

1. *The general solution to the GSE (7.17) is given by*

$$
\begin{cases}
v_i(\theta, t) = \operatorname{adj} A(\theta, t, s_i) z_i \\
w_i(\theta, t) = \pi(\theta, t, s_i) B^{-1}(\theta, t, s_i) z_i, \quad i = 1, 2, \ldots, p,
\end{cases}
\tag{7.66}
$$

with $Z \in \mathbb{C}^{n \times p}$ being an arbitrary parameter matrix.
2. *In addition, when $A(s)$ is also unimodular, the above solution can also be replaced by*

$$
\begin{cases}
v_i(\theta, t) = A^{-1}(\theta, t, s_i) z_i \\
w_i(\theta, t) = B^{-1}(\theta, t, s_i) z_i, \quad i = 1, 2, \ldots, p.
\end{cases}
\tag{7.67}
$$

Setting $B(s) = I_n$ in the three theorems given in the above subsection immediately produces the following result for solution to the special type of fully actuated higher-order GSEs in the form of (7.17). This result is actually a natural generalized version of Theorem 6.8.

Theorem 7.10 *Let $A(\theta, t, s) \in \mathbb{R}^{n \times n}[s]$ be given by (7.19), and $B(\theta, t, s) = I_n$.*

1. *When $F \in \mathbb{C}^{p \times p}$, the general solution to the fully actuated GSE (7.37) is given by*

$$\begin{cases} V(\theta, t) = [\text{adj}\, A(\theta, t, s)\, Z]\big|_F \\ W(\theta, t) = [\pi(\theta, t, s)\, Z]\big|_F = Z\pi(\theta, t, F), \end{cases} \tag{7.68}$$

or, when $A(s)$ is also unimodular, by

$$\begin{cases} V(\theta, t) = [A^{-1}(\theta, t, s)\, Z]\big|_F \\ W(\theta, t) = Z, \end{cases} \tag{7.69}$$

where $Z \in \mathbb{C}^{n \times p}$ is an arbitrary parameter matrix.

2. *When $F \in \mathbb{C}^{p \times p}$ is in the Jordan form of (6.23), the general solution to the fully actuated GSE (7.37) is given by*

$$\begin{cases} v_{ij}(\theta, t) = \sum_{k=0}^{j-1} \frac{1}{k!} \frac{\partial^k}{\partial s^k} \text{adj}\, A(\theta, t, s_i)\, z_{i,j-k} \\ w_{ij}(\theta, t) = \sum_{k=0}^{j-1} \frac{1}{k!} \frac{\partial^k}{\partial s^k} \pi(\theta, t, s_i)\, z_{i,j-k}, \\ \qquad j = 1, 2, \ldots, p_i, \quad i = 1, 2, \ldots, w, \end{cases} \tag{7.70}$$

or, when $A(s)$ is also unimodular, by

$$\begin{cases} v_{ij}(\theta, t) = \sum_{k=0}^{j-1} \frac{1}{k!} \frac{\partial^k}{\partial s^k} A^{-1}(\theta, t, s_i)\, z_{i,j-k}, \\ w_{ij}(\theta, t) = z_{ij} \\ \qquad j = 1, 2, \ldots, p_i, \quad i = 1, 2, \ldots, w, \end{cases} \tag{7.71}$$

with $z_{ij} \in \mathbb{C}^n$, $j = 1, 2, \ldots, p_i$, $i = 1, 2, \ldots, w$, being a group of arbitrary parameter vectors.

3. *When $F \in \mathbb{C}^{p \times p}$ is in the diagonal form of (6.27), the general solution to the fully actuated GSE (7.37) is given by*

$$\begin{cases} v_i(\theta, t) = \text{adj}\, A(\theta, t, s_i)\, z_i \\ w_i(\theta, t) = \pi(\theta, t, s_i)\, z_i, \quad i = 1, 2, \ldots, p, \end{cases} \tag{7.72}$$

or, when A (s) is also unimodular, by

$$
\begin{cases}
v_i\left(\theta, t\right) = A^{-1}\left(\theta, t, s_i\right) z_i \\
w_i\left(\theta, t\right) = z_i, \quad i = 1, 2, \ldots, p,
\end{cases}
\tag{7.73}
$$

with $z_i \in \mathbb{C}^n$, $i = 1, 2, \ldots, p$, being a group of arbitrary parameter vectors.

7.5 Fully Actuated Nonhomogeneous GSEs

In this section, we investigate fully actuated nonhomogeneous GSEs with varying coefficients. Again, the results in this section limit to the case of $q = n$.

7.5.1 Forward Solutions

When Assumption 7.2 is satisfied, it can be easily verified that a pair of forward solutions of $U\left(\theta, t, s\right)$ and $T\left(\theta, t, s\right)$ to the DPE

$$
A\left(\theta, t, s\right) U\left(\theta, t, s\right) - B\left(\theta, t, s\right) T\left(\theta, t, s\right) = \mu\left(\theta, t, s\right) I_n
\tag{7.74}
$$

can be directly given by

$$
\begin{cases}
U\left(\theta, t, s\right) = \mu\left(\theta, t, s\right) I_n \\
T\left(\theta, t, s\right) = \mathrm{adj}B\left(\theta, t, s\right)\left[A\left(\theta, t, s\right) - I\right],
\end{cases}
\tag{7.75}
$$

where $\mu\left(\theta, t, s\right)$ is given by (7.39).

In particular, when Assumption 7.3 is satisfied, $\mu\left(\theta, t, s\right)$ is nonzero and invariant with s, thus $B^{-1}\left(\theta, t, s\right)$ is also a polynomial matrix. In this case, it can be easily verified that a pair of forward solutions of $U\left(\theta, t, s\right)$ and $T\left(\theta, t, s\right)$ to the DPE

$$
A\left(\theta, t, s\right) U\left(\theta, t, s\right) - B\left(\theta, t, s\right) T\left(\theta, t, s\right) = \mu\left(\theta, t, s\right) I_n
\tag{7.76}
$$

are given by

$$
\begin{cases}
U\left(\theta, t, s\right) = I_n \\
T\left(\theta, t, s\right) = B^{-1}\left(\theta, t, s\right)\left[A\left(\theta, t, s\right) - I\right].
\end{cases}
\tag{7.77}
$$

7.5.1.1 Case of F Being Arbitrary

By using a slightly generalized parameter-varying version of Theorem 5.6, the following result for solution to the fully actuated nonhomogeneous GSE (7.18) under

Assumptions 7.2 and 7.3 can be easily derived, which is clearly a generalized version of Theorems 6.9 and 6.10.

Theorem 7.11 *Let $A(\theta, t, s)$, $B(\theta, t, s) \in \mathbb{R}^{n \times n}[s]$ be given as in (7.19), and $F \in \mathbb{C}^{p \times p}$. Then,*

1. *Under Assumption 7.2, all the solutions to the GSE (7.18) are given by*

$$\begin{cases} V(\theta, t) = Y \\ W(\theta, t) = [\operatorname{adj}B(\theta, t, s)(A(\theta, t, s)Y - R(\theta, t))]\big|_F [\mu(\theta, t, F)]^{-1}, \end{cases}$$
(7.78)

with $Y \in \mathbb{C}^{n \times p}$ being an arbitrary parameter matrix, and by choosing $Y = R(\theta, t)$ produces the following particular solution:

$$\begin{cases} V(\theta, t) = R \\ W(\theta, t) = [\operatorname{adj}B(\theta, t, s)[A(\theta, t, s) - I]R(\theta, t)]\big|_F [\mu(\theta, t, F)]^{-1}; \end{cases}$$
(7.79)

2. *Under Assumption 7.3, all the solutions to the GSE (7.18) are given by*

$$\begin{cases} V(\theta, t) = Y \\ W(\theta, t) = [B^{-1}(\theta, t, s)(A(\theta, t, s)Y - R(\theta, t))]\big|_F, \end{cases}$$
(7.80)

with $Y \in \mathbb{C}^{n \times p}$ being an arbitrary parameter matrix, and by choosing $Y = R(\theta, t)$ gives the following particular solution:

$$\begin{cases} V(\theta, t) = R \\ W(\theta, t) = [B^{-1}(\theta, t, s)[A(\theta, t, s) - I]R(\theta, t)]\big|_F. \end{cases}$$
(7.81)

7.5.1.2 Case of F Being in Jordan Form

When F is a Jordan matrix given by (6.23), we have the following result for solution to the nonhomogeneous GSE (7.18) under Assumptions 7.2 and 7.3, which is clearly a generalized version of Theorems 6.17 and 6.18.

Theorem 7.12 *Let $A(\theta, t, s)$, $B(\theta, t, s) \in \mathbb{R}^{n \times n}[s]$ be given as in (7.19), $F \in \mathbb{C}^{p \times p}$ be in the Jordan form of (6.23). Then,*

1. *When Assumption 7.2 holds, all the solutions to the fully actuated nonhomogeneous GSE (7.18) are given by*

$$
\begin{cases}
v_{ij}(\theta, t) = \sum_{k=0}^{j-1} \frac{1}{k!} \frac{\partial^k}{\partial s^k} \left[\mu(\theta, t, s_i) \right] y_{i,j-k} \\
w_{ij}(\theta, t) = \sum_{k=0}^{j-1} \frac{1}{k!} \frac{\partial^k}{\partial s^k} \left[\mathrm{adj}B(\theta, t, s_i) \left(A(\theta, t, s_i) y_{i,j-k} - r'_{i,j-k} \right) \right], \\
\qquad j = 1, 2, \dots, p_i, \quad i = 1, 2, \dots, w,
\end{cases}
$$

(7.82)

with

$$
R'(\theta, t) = R(\theta, t) \left[\mu(\theta, t, F) \right]^{-1},
$$

and $Y \in \mathbb{C}^{n \times p}$ being an arbitrary parameter matrix, and by setting $Y = R'(\theta, t)$ gives a particular solution as

$$
\begin{cases}
v_{ij}(\theta, t) = \sum_{k=0}^{j-1} \frac{1}{k!} \frac{\partial^k}{\partial s^k} \left[\mu(\theta, t, s_i) \right] r'_{i,j-k}(\theta, t) \\
w_{ij}(\theta, t) = \sum_{k=0}^{j-1} \frac{1}{k!} \frac{\partial^k}{\partial s^k} \left[\mathrm{adj}B(\theta, t, s_i)(A(\theta, t, s_i) - I) \right] r'_{i,j-k}(\theta, t), \\
\qquad j = 1, 2, \dots, p_i, \quad i = 1, 2, \dots, w,
\end{cases}
$$

(7.83)

which reduces to when Assumption 7.3 holds.

2. *When, in particular, Assumption 7.3 holds, all the solutions to the fully actuated nonhomogeneous GSE (7.18) are given by*

$$
\begin{cases}
v_{ij}(\theta, t) = y_{ij} \\
w_{ij}(\theta, t) = \sum_{k=0}^{j-1} \frac{1}{k!} \frac{\partial^k}{\partial s^k} \left[B^{-1}(\theta, t, s_i) \left(A(\theta, t, s_i) y_{i,j-k} - r_{i,j-k}(\theta, t) \right) \right], \\
\qquad j = 1, 2, \dots, p_i, \quad i = 1, 2, \dots, w,
\end{cases}
$$

(7.84)

with $Y \in \mathbb{C}^{n \times p}$ being an arbitrary parameter matrix, and by setting $Y = R(\theta, t)$ gives a particular solution as

$$
\begin{cases}
v_{ij}(\theta, t) = r_{ij}(\theta, t) \\
w_{ij}(\theta, t) = \sum_{k=0}^{j-1} \frac{1}{k!} \frac{\partial^k}{\partial s^k} \left[B^{-1}(\theta, t, s_i)(A(\theta, t, s_i) - I) \right] r_{i,j-k}(\theta, t), \\
\qquad j = 1, 2, \dots, p_i, \quad i = 1, 2, \dots, w.
\end{cases}
$$

(7.85)

7.5.1.3 Case of F *Being Diagonal*

When $F \in \mathbb{C}^{p \times p}$ is a diagonal matrix given by (6.27), we have the following result for solution to the nonhomogeneous GSE (7.18) under Assumptions 7.2 and 7.3, which is clearly a generalized version of Theorems 6.13 and 6.14.

Theorem 7.13 *Let $A\left(\theta, t, s\right), B\left(\theta, t, s\right) \in \mathbb{R}^{n \times n}\left[s\right]$ be given as in (7.19), $F \in \mathbb{C}^{p \times p}$ be in the diagonal form of (6.27), and Assumption 7.2 hold. Then,*

1. *All the solutions to the fully actuated nonhomogeneous GSE (7.18) are given by*

$$
\begin{cases}
v_i\left(\theta, t\right) = y_i \\
w_i\left(\theta, t\right) = B^{-1}\left(\theta, t, s_i\right)\left(A\left(\theta, t, s_i\right)y_i - r_i\left(\theta, t\right)\right), \\
\quad i = 1, 2, \ldots, p,
\end{cases}
\tag{7.86}
$$

with $y_i \in \mathbb{C}^{n \times p}$, $i = 1, 2, \ldots, p$, being a group of arbitrary parameter vectors.

2. *A particular solution to the fully actuated nonhomogeneous GSE (7.18) can be given, by simply choosing $y_i = r_i\left(\theta, t\right)$, $i = 1, 2, \ldots, p$, as*

$$
\begin{cases}
v_i\left(\theta, t\right) = r_i\left(\theta, t\right) \\
w_i\left(\theta, t\right) = B^{-1}\left(\theta, t, s_i\right)\left(A\left(\theta, t, s_i\right) - I\right)r_i\left(\theta, t\right), \\
\quad i = 1, 2, \ldots, p.
\end{cases}
\tag{7.87}
$$

7.5.2 Backward Solutions

Under Assumption 7.2, a pair of polynomial matrices $U\left(\theta, t, s\right)$ and $T\left(\theta, t, s\right)$ satisfying the DPE (7.74) can be directly given by

$$
\begin{cases}
U\left(\theta, t, s\right) = \mu\left(\theta, t, s\right)\operatorname{adj}A\left(\theta, t, s\right) \\
T\left(\theta, t, s\right) = \left(\pi\left(\theta, t, s\right) - 1\right)\operatorname{adj}B\left(\theta, t, s\right),
\end{cases}
\tag{7.88}
$$

where $\mu\left(\theta, t, s\right)$ is given by (7.39).

Particularly, under Assumption 7.3, $\mu\left(\theta, t, s\right)$ becomes a nonzero function, which is invariant of s, thus $B^{-1}\left(\theta, t, s\right)$ is also a polynomial matrix. In this case, a pair of polynomial matrices $U\left(\theta, t, s\right)$ and $T\left(\theta, t, s\right)$ satisfying the DPE (7.76) can be directly given by

$$
\begin{cases}
U\left(\theta, t, s\right) = \operatorname{adj}A\left(\theta, t, s\right) \\
T\left(\theta, t, s\right) = \left(\pi\left(\theta, t, s\right) - 1\right)B^{-1}\left(\theta, t, s\right),
\end{cases}
\tag{7.89}
$$

where $\pi\left(\theta, t, s\right)$ is defined in (7.57).

As in Section 6.5, the solutions (7.88) and (7.89) are backward since they use the "inverse" property of $A(s)$, and thus, the solutions to the nonhomogeneous GSE (7.18) based on (7.88) or (7.89) are also called backward solutions.

7.5.2.1 Case of F Being Arbitrary

When F is an arbitrary matrix, we have, using a generalized parameter-varying version of Theorem 5.6, the following result for solution to the fully actuated nonhomogeneous GSE (7.18) under Assumptions 7.2 and 7.3, which is clearly a generalized version of Theorems 6.15 and 6.16.

Theorem 7.14 *Let $A(\theta, t, s)$, $B(\theta, t, s) \in \mathbb{R}^{n \times n}[s]$ be given as in (7.19), and $F \in \mathbb{C}^{p \times p}$. Then,*

1. *When Assumption 7.2 holds, all the solutions to the fully actuated nonhomogeneous GSE (7.18) are given by*

$$
\begin{cases}
V(\theta, t) = [\mu(\theta, t, s) \operatorname{adj} A(\theta, t, s) Y]\big|_F [\mu(\theta, t, F)]^{-1} \\
W(\theta, t) = [\operatorname{adj} B(\theta, t, s)(\pi(\theta, t, s) Y - R)]\big|_F [\mu(\theta, t, F)]^{-1},
\end{cases}
\tag{7.90}
$$

with $Y \in \mathbb{C}^{n \times p}$ being an arbitrary parameter matrix, and a particular one can be given, by choosing $Y = R(\theta, t)$, as

$$
\begin{cases}
V(\theta, t) = [\mu(\theta, t, s) \operatorname{adj} A(\theta, t, s) R]\big|_F [\mu(\theta, t, F)]^{-1} \\
W(\theta, t) = [(\pi(\theta, t, s) - 1) \operatorname{adj} B(\theta, t, s) R]\big|_F [\mu(\theta, t, F)]^{-1};
\end{cases}
\tag{7.91}
$$

2. *When, in particular, Assumption 7.3 holds, all the solutions to the fully actuated nonhomogeneous GSE (7.18) are given by*

$$
\begin{cases}
V(\theta, t) = [\operatorname{adj} A(\theta, t, s) Y]\big|_F \\
W(\theta, t) = [B^{-1}(\theta, t, s)(\pi(\theta, t, s) Y - R)]\big|_F,
\end{cases}
\tag{7.92}
$$

with $Y \in \mathbb{C}^{n \times p}$ being an arbitrary parameter matrix, and a particular one can be given, by choosing $Y = R(\theta, t)$, as

$$
\begin{cases}
V(\theta, t) = [\operatorname{adj} A(\theta, t, s) R]\big|_F \\
W(\theta, t) = [(\pi(\theta, t, s) - 1) B^{-1}(\theta, t, s) R]\big|_F.
\end{cases}
\tag{7.93}
$$

7.5.2.2 Case of F Being in Jordan Form

When F is a Jordan form matrix given by (6.23), we have, using a generalized parameter varying version of Theorem 5.10, the following result for solution to the nonhomogeneous GSE (7.18) under Assumptions 7.2 and 7.3, which is clearly a generalized version of Theorems 6.17 and 6.18.

Theorem 7.15 *Let $A(\theta, t, s)$, $B(\theta, t, s) \in \mathbb{R}^{n \times n}[s]$ be given as in (7.19), and $F \in \mathbb{C}^{p \times p}$ be a Jordan matrix given by (6.23). Then,*

1. *When Assumption 7.2 holds, all the solutions to the fully actuated nonhomogeneous GSE (7.18) are given by*

$$
\begin{cases}
v_{ij}(\theta, t) = \sum_{k=0}^{j-1} \frac{1}{k!} \frac{\partial^k}{\partial s^k} \left[\mu(\theta, t, s_i) \operatorname{adj} A(\theta, t, s_i) \right] y_{i,j-k} \\
w_{ij}(\theta, t) = \sum_{k=0}^{j-1} \frac{1}{k!} \frac{\partial^k}{\partial s^k} \left[\operatorname{adj} B(\theta, t, s_i) \left(\pi(\theta, t, s_i) y_{i,j-k} - r'_{i,j-k} \right) \right], \\
\qquad\qquad j = 1, 2, \dots, p_i, \quad i = 1, 2, \dots, w,
\end{cases}
\tag{7.94}
$$

with $Y \in \mathbb{C}^{n \times p}$ being an arbitrary parameter matrix, and a particular one can be given, by setting $Y = R'(\theta, t)$, as

$$
\begin{cases}
v_{ij}(\theta, t) = \sum_{k=0}^{j-1} \frac{1}{k!} \frac{\partial^k}{\partial s^k} \left[\mu(\theta, t, s_i) \operatorname{adj} A(\theta, t, s_i) \right] r'_{i,j-k} \\
w_{ij}(\theta, t) = \sum_{k=0}^{j-1} \frac{1}{k!} \frac{\partial^k}{\partial s^k} \left[(\pi(\theta, t, s_i) - 1) \operatorname{adj} B(\theta, t, s_i) \right] r'_{i,j-k}, \\
\qquad\qquad j = 1, 2, \dots, p_i, \quad i = 1, 2, \dots, w;
\end{cases}
\tag{7.95}
$$

2. *When, in particular, Assumption 7.3 holds, all the solutions to the fully actuated nonhomogeneous GSE (7.18) are given by*

$$
\begin{cases}
v_{ij}(\theta, t) = \sum_{k=0}^{j-1} \frac{1}{k!} \frac{\partial^k}{\partial s^k} \operatorname{adj} A(\theta, t, s_i) y_{i,j-k} \\
w_{ij}(\theta, t) = \sum_{k=0}^{j-1} \frac{1}{k!} \frac{\partial^k}{\partial s^k} \left[B^{-1}(\theta, t, s_i) \left(\pi(\theta, t, s_i) y_{i,j-k} - r_{i,j-k} \right) \right], \\
\qquad\qquad j = 1, 2, \dots, p_i, \quad i = 1, 2, \dots, w,
\end{cases}
\tag{7.96}
$$

with $Y \in \mathbb{C}^{n \times p}$ being an arbitrary parameter matrix, and a particular one can be given, by setting $Y = R(\theta, t)$, as

$$
\begin{cases}
v_{ij}(\theta, t) = \displaystyle\sum_{k=0}^{j-1} \frac{1}{k!} \frac{\partial^k}{\partial s^k} \mathrm{adj}\, A(\theta, t, s_i)\, r_{i,j-k} \\
w_{ij}(\theta, t) = \displaystyle\sum_{k=0}^{j-1} \frac{1}{k!} \frac{\partial^k}{\partial s^k} \left[(\pi(\theta, t, s_i) - 1) B^{-1}(\theta, t, s_i) \right] r_{i,j-k}, \\
\qquad j = 1, 2, \ldots, p_i, \quad i = 1, 2, \ldots, w.
\end{cases}
\tag{7.97}
$$

7.5.2.3 Case of F Being Diagonal

When $F \in \mathbb{C}^{p \times p}$ is a diagonal matrix given by (6.27), we have the following result for solution to the fully actuated nonhomogeneous GSE (7.18) under Assumptions 7.2 and 7.3, which is clearly a generalized version of Theorems 6.19 and 6.20.

Theorem 7.16 *Let $A(\theta, t, s) \in \mathbb{R}^{n \times n}[s]$ and $B(\theta, t, s) \in \mathbb{R}^{n \times n}[s]$ be given as in (7.19), $F \in \mathbb{C}^{p \times p}$ be in the diagonal form of (6.27), and Assumption 7.2 hold. Then,*

1. *All the solutions to the fully actuated nonhomogeneous GSE (7.18) are given by*

$$
\begin{cases}
v_i(\theta, t) = \mathrm{adj}\, A(\theta, t, s_i)\, y_i \\
w_i(\theta, t) = B^{-1}(\theta, t, s_i) \left[\pi(\theta, t, s_i)\, y_i - r_i \right], \\
\qquad i = 1, 2, \ldots, p,
\end{cases}
\tag{7.98}
$$

   with $Y \in \mathbb{C}^{n \times p}$ being an arbitrary parameter matrix; and
2. *A particular solution to the fully actuated nonhomogeneous GSE (7.18) can be given, by choosing $Y = R(\theta, t)$, as*

$$
\begin{cases}
v_i(\theta, t) = \mathrm{adj}\, A(\theta, t, s_i)\, r_i \\
w_i(\theta, t) = (\pi(\theta, t, s_i) - 1) B^{-1}(\theta, t, s_i)\, r_i, \\
\qquad i = 1, 2, \ldots, p.
\end{cases}
\tag{7.99}
$$

7.6 Examples

7.6.1 Space Rendezvous Systems

Example 7.8 (Linear Time-Varying Case)

Consider again the time-varying space rendezvous system introduced in Example 7.3, represented by the equations in (7.10) through (7.12). The two polynomial matrices associated with this system are

$$\begin{cases} A(\theta,t,s) = I_3 s^2 + D(\dot{\theta},\ddot{\theta})s + K(\dot{\theta},\ddot{\theta}) \\ \quad = \begin{bmatrix} s^2 - 2k\dot{\theta}^{\frac{3}{2}} - \dot{\theta}^2 & -2\dot{\theta}s - \ddot{\theta} & 0 \\ 2\dot{\theta}s + \ddot{\theta} & s^2 + k\dot{\theta}^{\frac{3}{2}} - \dot{\theta}^2 & 0 \\ 0 & 0 & s^2 + k\dot{\theta}^{\frac{3}{2}} \end{bmatrix} \\ B(\theta,t,s) = I_3. \end{cases}$$

Due to $B(\theta,t,s) = I_3$, the following generalized RCF

$$A(\theta,t,s)N(\theta,t,s) - B(\theta,t,s)D(\theta,t,s) = 0$$

obviously holds for

$$\begin{cases} N(\theta,t,s) = I_3 \\ D(\theta,t,s) = A(\theta,t,s). \end{cases}$$

We can obtain

$$\begin{cases} V(\theta,t) = Z \\ W(\theta,t) = [A(\theta,t,s)Z]\,|_F \\ \qquad\quad = K(\dot{\theta},\ddot{\theta})Z + D(\dot{\theta},\ddot{\theta})ZF + ZF^2. \end{cases}$$

Let

$$\begin{cases} F = \begin{bmatrix} -1 & 1 & 0 \\ -1 & -1 & 0 \\ 0 & 0 & F_0 \end{bmatrix}, \ F_0 = \mathrm{diag}\,(-2,-3,-4,-5) \\ Z = [I_3 \ I_3], \end{cases} \tag{7.100}$$

then,

$$V(\theta,t) = \begin{bmatrix} 1 & 0 & 0 & 1 & 0 & 0 \\ 0 & 1 & 0 & 0 & 1 & 0 \\ 0 & 0 & 1 & 0 & 0 & 1 \end{bmatrix},$$

$$W(\theta,t) = \begin{bmatrix} 2\dot{\theta} - 2k\dot{\theta}^{\frac{3}{2}} - \dot{\theta}^2 & 2\dot{\theta} - \ddot{\theta} - 2 & 0 \\ \ddot{\theta} - 2\dot{\theta} + 2 & 2\dot{\theta}\beta + k\dot{\theta}^{\frac{3}{2}} - \dot{\theta}^2 & 0 \\ 0 & 0 & k\dot{\theta}^{\frac{3}{2}} + 4 \end{bmatrix}$$

$$\begin{bmatrix} 9 - \dot{\theta}^2 - 2k\dot{\theta}^{\frac{3}{2}} & 8\dot{\theta} - \ddot{\theta} & 0 \\ \ddot{\theta} - 6\dot{\theta} & k\dot{\theta}^{\frac{3}{2}} - \dot{\theta}^2 + 16 & 0 \\ 0 & 0 & k\dot{\theta}^{\frac{3}{2}} + 25 \end{bmatrix}.$$

Let

$$\begin{cases} F = \text{diag}\,(-1 \pm i, -2, -3, -4, -5) \\ Z = [I_3 \ I_3], \end{cases} \tag{7.101}$$

then,

$$V\,(\theta, t) = \begin{bmatrix} 1 & 0 & 0 & 1 & 0 & 0 \\ 0 & 1 & 0 & 0 & 1 & 0 \\ 0 & 0 & 1 & 0 & 0 & 1 \end{bmatrix},$$

$$W\,(\theta, t) = \begin{bmatrix} -2i - 2k\dot\theta^{\frac{3}{2}} - \dot\theta^2 & 2\dot\theta\,(1+i) - \ddot\theta & 0 \\ 2\dot\theta\,(-1+i) + \ddot\theta & 2i + k\dot\theta^{\frac{3}{2}} - \dot\theta^2 & 0 \\ 0 & 0 & 4 + k\dot\theta^{\frac{3}{2}} \end{bmatrix}$$

$$\left.\begin{matrix} 9 - 2k\dot\theta^{\frac{3}{2}} - \dot\theta^2 & 8\dot\theta - \ddot\theta & 0 \\ -6\dot\theta + \ddot\theta & 16 + k\dot\theta^{\frac{3}{2}} - \dot\theta^2 & 0 \\ 0 & 0 & 25 + k\dot\theta^{\frac{3}{2}} \end{matrix}\right].$$

Example 7.9 (Quasilinear Case)

Consider the nonlinear space rendezvous system introduced in Example 7.4. The dynamical model in a second-order quasilinear form is represented by the equations (7.13) and (7.14). The two polynomial matrices associated with this system are

$$\begin{cases} A(\theta, t, s) = I_3 s^2 + D(\dot\theta, \ddot\theta)s + K(x, \dot\theta, \ddot\theta) \\ \qquad = \begin{bmatrix} s^2 + \frac{\mu}{\Sigma(x)} - \dot\theta^2 & -2\dot\theta s - \ddot\theta & 0 \\ 2\dot\theta s + \ddot\theta & s^2 + \frac{\mu}{\Sigma(x)} - \dot\theta^2 & 0 \\ 0 & 0 & s^2 + \frac{\mu}{\Sigma(x)} \end{bmatrix} \\ B(\theta, t, s) = I_3. \end{cases}$$

Due to $B(\theta, t, s) = I_3$, the following generalized RCF

$$A(\theta, t, s)N(\theta, t, s) - B(\theta, t, s)D(\theta, t, s) = 0$$

obviously holds for

$$\begin{cases} N(\theta, t, s) = I_3 \\ D(x, \theta, t, s) = A(x, \theta, t, s). \end{cases}$$

We can obtain

$$\begin{cases} V\,(\theta, t) = Z \\ W\,(\theta, t) = [A(x, \theta, t, s)Z]\,|_F \\ \qquad = K(x, \dot\theta, \ddot\theta)Z + D(\dot\theta, \ddot\theta)ZF + ZF^2. \end{cases}$$

When F and Z are chosen the same as in (7.100), we have

$$V_e\,(\theta, t) = \begin{bmatrix} 1 & 0 & 0 & 1 & 0 & 0 \\ 0 & 1 & 0 & 0 & 1 & 0 \\ 0 & 0 & 1 & 0 & 0 & 1 \end{bmatrix},$$

$$W\,(\theta, t) = \begin{bmatrix} -\dot{\theta}^2 + 2\dot{\theta} + \frac{\mu}{\Sigma(x)} & 2\dot{\theta} - \ddot{\theta} - 2 & 0 \\ \ddot{\theta} - 2\dot{\theta} + 2 & -\dot{\theta}^2 + 2\dot{\theta} + \frac{\mu}{\Sigma(x)} & 0 \\ 0 & 0 & \frac{\mu}{\Sigma(x)} + 4 \end{bmatrix}$$

$$\left.\begin{matrix} -\dot{\theta}^2 + \frac{\mu}{\Sigma(x)} + 9 & 8\dot{\theta} - \ddot{\theta} & 0 \\ \ddot{\theta} - 6\dot{\theta} & -\dot{\theta}^2 + \frac{\mu}{\Sigma(x)} + 16 & 0 \\ 0 & 0 & \frac{\mu}{\Sigma(x)} + 25 \end{matrix}\right].$$

When F and Z are chosen the same as in (7.101), we have,

$$V_e\,(\theta, t) = \begin{bmatrix} 1 & 0 & 0 & 1 & 0 & 0 \\ 0 & 1 & 0 & 0 & 1 & 0 \\ 0 & 0 & 1 & 0 & 0 & 1 \end{bmatrix},$$

$$W\,(\theta, t) = \begin{bmatrix} -2\mathrm{i} + \frac{\mu}{\Sigma(x)} - \dot{\theta}^2 & 2\dot{\theta}\,(1 + \mathrm{i}) - \ddot{\theta} & 0 \\ 2\dot{\theta}\,(-1 + \mathrm{i}) + \ddot{\theta} & 2\mathrm{i} + \frac{\mu}{\Sigma(x)} - \dot{\theta}^2 & 0 \\ 0 & 0 & 4 + \frac{\mu}{\Sigma(x)} \end{bmatrix}$$

$$\left.\begin{matrix} 9 + \frac{\mu}{\Sigma(x)} - \dot{\theta}^2 & 8\dot{\theta} - \ddot{\theta} & 0 \\ -6\dot{\theta} + \ddot{\theta} & 16 + \frac{\mu}{\Sigma(x)} - \dot{\theta}^2 & 0 \\ 0 & 0 & 25 + \frac{\mu}{\Sigma(x)} \end{matrix}\right].$$

7.6.2 Robotic Systems

Consider a type of robotic systems described by the following model:

$$H\,(q)\,\ddot{q} + C\,(q, \dot{q})\,\dot{q} = u, \tag{7.102}$$

where $H\,(q) > 0$ is the inertia matrix, $C\,(q, \dot{q})\,\dot{q}$ is the damping term, and u is the control torque.

Example 7.10

The homogeneous GSE corresponding to the robotic system (7.102) is

$$H\,(q)\,VF^2 + C\,(q, \dot{q})\,VF = W.$$

Note that $B(s) = I$, Assumption 7.3 holds. Thus, according to the theorems in this section the general solution to this GSE is given by

$$\begin{cases} V(q, \dot{q}) = Z \\ W(q, \dot{q}) = C(q, \dot{q}) ZF + H(q) ZF^2, \end{cases} \tag{7.103}$$

with Z being an arbitrary parameter matrix. Further, when the matrix F is in the Jordan form of (6.23), the general solution to this GSE is given by

$$\begin{cases} V(q, \dot{q}) = Z \\ w_{i1}(q, \dot{q}) = \Phi_2(s_i) z_{i,1} \\ w_{i2}(q, \dot{q}) = \Phi_2(s_i) z_{i,2} + \Phi_1(s_i) z_{i,1} \\ w_{ij}(q, \dot{q}) = \Phi_2(s_i) z_{i,j} + \Phi_1(s_i) z_{i,j-1} + H(q) z_{i,j-2}, \\ \qquad j = 3, 4, \dots, p_i, \quad i = 1, 2, \dots, w, \end{cases} \tag{7.104}$$

where

$$\Phi_2(s) = H(q) s^2 + C(q, \dot{q}) s, \quad \Phi_1(s) = 2H(q) s + C(q, \dot{q}).$$

This formula obviously reduces, when F is in the diagonal form of (6.27), to

$$\begin{cases} V(q, \dot{q}) = Z \\ w_i(q, \dot{q}) = \left[H(q) s_i^2 + C(q, \dot{q}) s_i \right] z_i, \quad i = 1, 2, \dots, p, \end{cases}$$

with Z being an arbitrary parameter matrix.

Example 7.11

The nonhomogeneous GSE corresponding to the robotic system (7.102) is

$$H(q) VF^2 + C(q, \dot{q}) VF = W + R.$$

Note that $B(s) = I$, Assumption 7.3 holds. Thus, by Theorem 7.11, the general solution to this GSE is given by

$$\begin{cases} V(q, \dot{q}) = Y \\ W(q, \dot{q}) = H(q) YF^2 + C(q, \dot{q}) YF - R. \end{cases} \tag{7.105}$$

When F is in the Jordan form of (6.23), by Theorem 7.12, the general solution is given by

$$\begin{cases} V(q, \dot{q}) = Y \\ w_{i1}(q, \dot{q}) = \Phi_2(s_i) y_{i,1} - r_{i,1} \\ w_{i2}(q, \dot{q}) = \Phi_2(s_i) y_{i,2} + \Phi_1(s_i) y_{i,1} - r_{i,2} \\ w_{ij}(q, \dot{q}) = \Phi_2(s_i) y_{i,j} + \Phi_1(s_i) y_{i,j-1} + H(q) y_{i,j-2} - r_{i,j}, \\ \qquad j = 3, 4, \dots, p_i, \quad i = 1, 2, \dots, w, \end{cases} \tag{7.106}$$

which reduces, when F is in the diagonal form of (6.27), to

$$
\begin{cases}
V\left(q,\dot{q}\right) = Y \\
w_i\left(q,\dot{q}\right) = \left[\left(H\left(q\right)s_i^2 + C\left(q,\dot{q}\right)s_i\right)y_i - r_i\right], \\
\qquad i = 1, 2, \ldots, p,
\end{cases}
$$

with Y being an arbitrary parameter matrix.

7.7 Notes and References

7.7.1 Further Comments

This world has a varying and nonlinear nature! Nothing is really constant, nothing is really linear. Speaking of dynamical systems, most of them are nonlinear and time-varying, while constant linear ones are just approximations under some circumstances. Eventually, GSEs with varying coefficients are met when dealing with certain control problems of nonlinear and time-varying systems.

In this chapter, it is shown that many results about GSEs with constant coefficients still hold for GSEs with varying coefficients, and general solutions to the several types of homogeneous and nonhomogeneous GSEs are investigated, with an emphasis on the fully actuated GSEs with varying coefficients. Therefore, the results have a close relation to those in Chapter 6 (Figure 7.1). Again, due to similarities of results, we have not gone to cover all types of GSEs. Those cases that are really treated in this chapter are shown in Table 7.1. Readers are suggested to give the presentations of the results for the rest of the cases by themselves.

The space rendezvous problem has appeared at several different places in the book. Yet it is in this chapter the problem is really stated original and appears as a nonlinear one (see Examples 7.4 and 7.9).

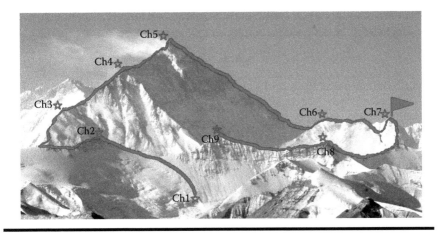

Figure 7.1   We are here. (Modified from http://go.jutuw.com/zhumulangmafeng/ photo/.)

Table 7.1 GSEs with Varying Coefficients Treated

Cases	F Arbitrary	F Jordan	F Diagonal
Higher-order	Yes	Yes	Yes
Second-order	Yes	–	–
First-order (descriptor)	–	–	–
First-order (normal)	–	–	–

Control of nonlinear and/or time-varying systems has always been challenging since it is usually hard to guarantee closed-loop stability. In the following, we show with the nonlinear space rendezvous problem that control of fully actuated higher-order quasilinear systems can be well solved using the direct parametric design approach.

The treatment here is a direct generalization of that given in Section 6.7.3 for the constant linear rendezvous problem described by C-W equation.

7.7.2 Space Rendezvous Control: The General Case

Consider the nonlinear fully actuated second-order spacecraft rendezvous system in the nonlinear matrix second form (7.13) through (7.16). It is easy to note that the parameter $\theta(t)$ in the spacecraft rendezvous system model (7.13) through (7.16), as well as its first- and second-order derivatives, are all continuous periodic variables and hence are uniformly bounded.

7.7.2.1 Problem

For control of the nonlinear system in the matrix second form (7.13) through (7.16), the controller to be designed is composed of two parts:

$$u = u_c + u_f, \tag{7.107}$$

where u_c compensates the term $\xi(x)$ in the system model, and is simply given by

$$u_c = \xi(x) = \begin{bmatrix} \dfrac{\mu R}{\Sigma(x)} - \dfrac{\mu}{R^2} \\ 0 \\ 0 \end{bmatrix}; \tag{7.108}$$

while u_f is a proportional plus derivative state feedback in the following form:

$$u_f = K_0(\theta, x, \dot{x})x + K_1(\theta, x, \dot{x})\dot{x} + v$$

$$= \begin{bmatrix} K_0(\theta, x, \dot{x}) & K_1(\theta, x, \dot{x}) \end{bmatrix} \begin{bmatrix} x \\ \dot{x} \end{bmatrix} + v, \tag{7.109}$$

where $K_0\left(\theta, x, \dot{x}\right), K_1\left(\theta, x, \dot{x}\right) \in \mathbb{R}^{3\times 3}$ are the feedback gains to be designed, they are piecewise continuous functions with respect to x and $\dot{x}$, and v is an external signal.

With this controller applied to the fully actuated system (7.13) through (7.16), the closed-loop system is obviously obtained as

$$\ddot{x} + A_1^c\left(\theta, x, \dot{x}\right)\dot{x} + A_0^c\left(\theta, x, \dot{x}\right)x = v, \tag{7.110}$$

or

$$\dot{X} = A_c\left(\theta, x, \dot{x}\right)X + B_c v, \tag{7.111}$$

with

$$X = \begin{bmatrix} x \\ \dot{x} \end{bmatrix},$$

$$A_c\left(\theta, x, \dot{x}\right) = \begin{bmatrix} 0 & I_n \\ -A_0^c\left(\theta, x, \dot{x}\right) & -A_1^c\left(\theta, x, \dot{x}\right) \end{bmatrix}, \tag{7.112}$$

$$B_c\left(x\right) = \begin{bmatrix} 0 \\ I_3 \end{bmatrix}, \tag{7.113}$$

and

$$\begin{cases} A_0^c\left(\theta, x, \dot{x}\right) = K\left(x, \dot{\theta}, \ddot{\theta}\right) - K_0\left(\theta, x, \dot{x}\right) \\ A_1^c\left(\theta, x, \dot{x}\right) = D\left(\dot{\theta}\right) - K_1\left(\theta, x, \dot{x}\right). \end{cases} \tag{7.114}$$

Our design purpose is to let $A_c\left(\theta, x, \dot{x}\right)$ be similar to an arbitrary given constant matrix of the same dimensions.

Problem 7.1   *Given the rendezvous system model (7.13) through (7.16), and an arbitrarily chosen matrix $F \in \mathbb{R}^{6\times 6}$, find a constant nonsingular matrix $V_e \in \mathbb{R}^{6\times 6}$, and a pair of gain matrices $K_0\left(\theta, x, \dot{x}\right)$ and $K_1\left(\theta, x, \dot{x}\right) \in \mathbb{R}^{3\times 3}$, such that,*

$$V_e^{-1}A_c\left(\theta, x, \dot{x}\right)V_e = F. \tag{7.115}$$

As a consequence of the requirement in the above problem, the closed-loop system matrix

$$A_c\left(\theta, x, \dot{x}\right) = V_e F V_e^{-1} \tag{7.116}$$

is a constant one and possesses the same set of eigenvalues as F.

7.7.2.2 Direct Parametric Approach

Rewrite (7.115) as

$$A_c\left(\theta, x, \dot{x}\right) V_e = V_e F. \tag{7.117}$$

Denote

$$V_e = \begin{bmatrix} V \\ V' \end{bmatrix}, \tag{7.118}$$

and use the expression of $A_c\left(\theta, x, \dot{x}\right)$ in (7.112), we can further convert (7.117) into

$$V' = VF, \tag{7.119}$$

and

$$A_0^c\left(\theta, x, \dot{x}\right) V + A_1^c\left(\theta, x, \dot{x}\right) V' + V'F = 0. \tag{7.120}$$

Substituting (7.119) into (7.120), and using (7.114), gives

$$K\left(x, \dot{\theta}, \ddot{\theta}\right) V + D\left(\dot{\theta}\right) VF + VF^2 = W, \tag{7.121}$$

where

$$W = K_0\left(\theta, x, \dot{x}\right) V + K_1\left(\theta, x, \dot{x}\right) VF. \tag{7.122}$$

Clearly, (7.121) is a second-order fully actuated GSE with varying coefficients. Define the set

$$\mathbb{F} = \left\{ F \mid F \in \mathbb{R}^{6 \times 6},\ \exists Z \in \mathbb{R}^{3 \times 6},\ \text{s.t. } \det\begin{bmatrix} Z \\ ZF \end{bmatrix} \neq 0 \right\}.$$

Then, based on the above deduction and solutions to fully actuated GSEs with varying coefficients proposed in this chapter, we can derive the following result regarding solution to Problem 7.1.

Theorem 7.17 *Problem 7.1 has a solution if and only if $F \in \mathbb{F}$, and in this case all the solutions to Problem 7.1 are parameterized as*

$$V = V\left(Z, F\right) = \begin{bmatrix} Z \\ ZF \end{bmatrix}, \tag{7.123}$$

and

$$\begin{bmatrix} K_0\left(x, \dot{x}\right) & K_1\left(x, \dot{x}\right) \end{bmatrix} = \begin{bmatrix} K\left(x, \dot{\theta}, \ddot{\theta}\right) V + D\left(\dot{\theta}\right) VF + VF^2 \end{bmatrix} V\left(Z, F\right)^{-1}, \tag{7.124}$$

where $Z \in \mathbb{R}^{3 \times 6}$ is an arbitrary parameter matrix satisfying

$$\det \begin{bmatrix} Z \\ ZF \end{bmatrix} \neq 0. \tag{7.125}$$

Based on Theorem 7.17, we can give a procedure for carrying out the direct parametric control design of the spacecraft rendezvous system model (7.13) through (7.16).

Step 1. *Defining the structure of matrix F*
The structure of the matrix F is usually in a Jordan form or a diagonal form. To make sure that it is Hurwitz, it is required that the eigenvalues of the matrix lie in the left-hand complex plane, that is,

$$\lambda_i(F) \in \mathbb{C}^-, \quad i = 1, 2, \ldots, 6. \tag{7.126}$$

In certain cases, this matrix may be simply chosen to be a specific Hurwitz matrix.

Step 2. *Forming an optimization problem*
According to the system requirements, establish an index

$$J = J(F, Z),$$

which is a scalar function with respect to the design parameters F and Z, and then form an optimization problem of the following form:

$$\begin{aligned} \min & J(F, Z) \\ \text{s.t.} & \quad (7.125), (7.126). \end{aligned} \tag{7.127}$$

Depending on the specific problem, there may be other constraints added to the above optimization. Also, in many practical applications, the constraint (7.125) can be often neglected since it is satisfied for almost any matrix Z.

Step 3. *Seeking parameters*
Find the optimal (or suboptimal) parameters F and Z by solving the above optimization problem (7.127) using some proper optimization algorithm.

Step 4. *Computing the controller gains*
Compute the controller gains according to the parametric expression of the feedback gains given in formulas (7.123) and (7.124). In certain cases, the closed-loop eigenvector matrix V may also need to be obtained by the expression (7.123) and the closed-loop system matrix may be obtained as $A_c = VFV^{-1}$.

7.7.2.3 Example

Let us design specifically a controller for the spacecraft rendezvous system following the procedure given above.

Step 1. Without loss of generality, let us take

$$F = \text{blockdiag}\left(\begin{bmatrix} -1 & 1 \\ -1 & -1 \end{bmatrix}, -3, -4, -5, -6\right),$$

whose set of eigenvalues is

$$\text{eig}\,(F) = \{-1 \pm i, -3, -4, -5, -6\}.$$

Correspondingly, we have

$$J_1 = \begin{bmatrix} -1 & 1 & 0 \\ -1 & -1 & 0 \\ 0 & 0 & -3 \end{bmatrix}, \quad J_2 = \begin{bmatrix} -4 & 0 & 0 \\ 0 & -5 & 0 \\ 0 & 0 & -6 \end{bmatrix}.$$

Step 2. Due to space limitation, optimization of parameter Z is not considered.
Step 3. For simplicity, we just choose

$$Z = \begin{bmatrix} I_3 & I_3 \end{bmatrix}.$$

It can be easily checked that

$$V = \begin{bmatrix} I_3 & I_3 \\ J_1 & J_2 \end{bmatrix} = \begin{bmatrix} 1 & 0 & 0 & 1 & 0 & 0 \\ 0 & 1 & 0 & 0 & 1 & 0 \\ 0 & 0 & 1 & 0 & 0 & 1 \\ -1 & 1 & 0 & -4 & 0 & 0 \\ -1 & -1 & 0 & 0 & -5 & 0 \\ 0 & 0 & -3 & 0 & 0 & -6 \end{bmatrix}$$

is nonsingular, that is, the constraint (7.125) is met, and

$$V^{-1} = \frac{1}{39} \begin{bmatrix} 48 & -15 & 0 & 12 & -3 & 0 \\ 12 & 45 & 0 & 3 & 9 & 0 \\ 0 & 0 & 78 & 0 & 0 & 13 \\ -9 & 15 & 0 & -12 & 3 & 0 \\ -12 & -6 & 0 & -3 & -9 & 0 \\ 0 & 0 & -39 & 0 & 0 & -13 \end{bmatrix}.$$

Step 4. Note that

$$ZFV^{-1} = \begin{bmatrix} 0_{3\times3} & I_3 \end{bmatrix},$$

$$ZF^2 V^{-1} = \frac{1}{39} \begin{bmatrix} -168 & 150 & 0 & -198 & 30 & 0 \\ -204 & -180 & 0 & -51 & -231 & 0 \\ 0 & 0 & -702 & 0 & 0 & -351 \end{bmatrix},$$

and

$$D(\dot{\theta}) ZFV^{-1} = \begin{bmatrix} 0_{3\times3} & D(\dot{\theta}) \end{bmatrix},$$

$$K(\dot{\theta},\ddot{\theta},x) ZV^{-1} = \begin{bmatrix} K(\dot{\theta},\ddot{\theta},x) & 0_{3\times3} \end{bmatrix}.$$

Thus, it follows from

$$\begin{bmatrix} K_0(x,\dot{x}) & K_1(x,\dot{x}) \end{bmatrix} = ZF^2 V^{-1} + D(\dot{\theta}) ZFV^{-1} + K(\dot{\theta},\ddot{\theta},x) ZV^{-1},$$

that the gain matrices are

$$K_0(x,\dot{x}) = \frac{1}{39} \begin{bmatrix} -168 & 150 & 0 \\ -204 & -180 & 0 \\ 0 & 0 & -702 \end{bmatrix} + K(\dot{\theta},\ddot{\theta},x), \qquad (7.128)$$

and

$$K_1(x,\dot{x}) = \frac{1}{39} \begin{bmatrix} -198 & 30 & 0 \\ -51 & -231 & 0 \\ 0 & 0 & -351 \end{bmatrix} + D(\dot{\theta}). \qquad (7.129)$$

Therefore, the controller designed for this system is

$$u = \frac{1}{39} \times \begin{bmatrix} \left[39\left(\frac{\mu}{\Sigma(x)} - \dot{\theta}^2\right) - 168 \right] x_r + (150 - 39\ddot{\theta}) y_r \\ (39\ddot{\theta} - 204) x_r + \left[39\left(\frac{\mu}{\Sigma(x)} - \dot{\theta}^2\right) - 180 \right] y_r \\ \left(39\frac{\mu}{\Sigma(x)} - 702\right) z_r \end{bmatrix}$$

$$+ \frac{1}{39} \begin{bmatrix} -198\dot{x}_r + (30 - 78\dot{\theta}) \dot{y}_r \\ (78\dot{\theta} - 51) \dot{x}_r - 231\dot{y}_r \\ 0 - 351\dot{z}_r \end{bmatrix} + \begin{bmatrix} \frac{\mu R}{\Sigma(x)} - \frac{\mu}{R^2} \\ 0 \\ 0 \end{bmatrix} + v. \qquad (7.130)$$

With the above design controller, it can be checked that the closed-loop system is

$$\dot{x} = A_c x + B_c v,$$

with

$$
A_c = \frac{1}{39}
\begin{bmatrix}
0 & 0 & 0 & 39 & 0 & 0 \\
0 & 0 & 0 & 0 & 39 & 0 \\
0 & 0 & 0 & 0 & 0 & 39 \\
-168 & 150 & 0 & -198 & 30 & 0 \\
-204 & -180 & 0 & -51 & -231 & 0 \\
0 & 0 & -702 & 0 & 0 & -351
\end{bmatrix},
$$

and

$$
B_c = \begin{bmatrix} 0_{3\times3} \\ I_3 \end{bmatrix}.
$$

Remark 7.2 Due to limitations of control strategies, the model for spacecraft rendezvous is often simplified to those represented by the C-W equation or the T-H equation; this definitely affects the application of the proposed designs. The above established direct parametric approach for spacecraft rendezvous control is general in the sense that it allows application to the originally established nonsimplified nonlinear model.

Remark 7.3 Again, different from many previously reported results, the above approach treats the spacecraft rendezvous control problem in a quasilinear matrix second-order frame. It is shown that for this model a simple controller parametrization exists in the form of state proportional plus derivative feedback. An important consequence of this set of controllers is that the resulted closed-loop system is a linear constant one with a desired eigenstructure.

Remark 7.4 For a more detailed treatment of the above nonlinear space rendezvous problem, please refer to Duan (2014a). We mention that the direct parametric approach for the nonlinear space rendezvous control has been generalized by the author to fully actuated second-order quasilinear systems (Duan 2014e,f), and also to fully actuated higher-order quasilinear systems (Duan 2014c,d), and the proposed direct parametric approach has also been applied to noncooperative rendezvous control (Duan 2014h), satellite attitude control (Duan 2014m), and missile guidance and control (Duan 2014b,g).

Chapter 8

Rectangular NSEs

Chapters 4 through 7 are all focused on parametric solutions to GSEs. From this chapter on, we turn to investigate the solution to the NSEs (1.74) through (1.78).

In this chapter, we investigate rectangular NSEs, which are, as we will find out, in fact a different type of representation of GSEs. In the next chapter, we will concentrate our attention to square NSEs.

8.1 Rectangular NSEs versus GSEs

8.1.1 Rectangular NSEs

This chapter studies solution to general higher-order NSEs, namely, the following homogeneous NSE

$$A_m V F^m + \cdots + A_1 V F + A_0 V = 0, \tag{8.1}$$

and the following nonhomogeneous one

$$A_m V F^m + \cdots + A_1 V F + A_0 V = R, \tag{8.2}$$

where

- $A_i \in \mathbb{R}^{n \times q}$, $i = 0, 1, \ldots, m$, $F \in \mathbb{C}^{p \times p}$, and $R \in \mathbb{C}^{n \times p}$ are the parameter matrices
- $V \in \mathbb{C}^{q \times p}$ is the matrix to be determined

Again, the polynomial matrix associated with this equation takes the following form:

$$A(s) = A_m s^m + \cdots + A_1 s + A_0, \quad A_i \in \mathbb{R}^{n \times q}. \tag{8.3}$$

These equations are generally called rectangular NSEs since the polynomial matrix $A(s)$ is allowed to be rectangular. They are said to be square if $q = n$. Square ones are to be considered in the next chapter. Furthermore, (8.1) is called a homogeneous NSE, while the NSE (8.2) with $R \neq 0$ is called a nonhomogeneous NSE.

When the matrix R is restricted to possess the following special form

$$R = C_\psi R^* F^\psi + \cdots + C_1 R^* F + C_0 R^*, \tag{8.4}$$

where $C_i \in \mathbb{R}^{n \times d}$, $i = 0, 1, \ldots, \psi$, and $R^* \in \mathbb{C}^{d \times p}$ are given matrices, the above nonhomogeneous NSE (8.2) can be written as

$$A_m VF^m + \cdots + A_1 VF + A_0 V = C_\psi R^* F^\psi + \cdots + C_1 R^* F + C_0 R^*. \tag{8.5}$$

Other important special forms of this nonhomogeneous NSE (8.2) include the second-order nonhomogeneous NSE

$$MVF^2 + DVF + KV = R, \tag{8.6}$$

as well as the following first-order ones

$$EVF - AV = R, \tag{8.7}$$

and

$$VF - AV = R. \tag{8.8}$$

Like the case of GSEs, the homogeneous NSE (8.1) always has a solution since $V = 0$ satisfies the equation, while generally the nonhomogeneous NSE (8.2) needs a condition for a solution to exist.

As the cases in Chapter 5, the NSE (8.5) is a special case of the NSE (8.2) (see Remark 5.8). Thus in this chapter, we only stress on solution to the NSE (8.2). To obtain a solution to the NSE (8.5), one suffices only to restrict the R matrix in the solution to NSE (8.2) to be the one given in (8.4).

Example 8.1

Again, consider the well-known space rendezvous system described by the C-W equation, with a failed thruster, treated in Examples 3.1, 4.6, and 5.5. The system has a standard matrix second-order form of

$$\ddot{x} + D\dot{x} + Kx = Bu,$$

with

$$D = \begin{bmatrix} 0 & -2\omega & 0 \\ 2\omega & 0 & 0 \\ 0 & 0 & 0 \end{bmatrix}, \quad K = \begin{bmatrix} -3\omega^2 & 0 & 0 \\ 0 & 0 & 0 \\ 0 & 0 & \omega^2 \end{bmatrix}, \quad B = \begin{bmatrix} 1 & 0 \\ 0 & 0 \\ 0 & 1 \end{bmatrix}.$$

As shown in Example 3.1, this system is not controllable, it has an uncontrollable mode at the origin.

Let

$$A_2 = [I_3 \ 0_{3\times2}],$$

$$A_1 = \begin{bmatrix} 0 & -2\omega & 0 & 0 & 0 \\ 2\omega & 0 & 0 & 0 & 0 \\ 0 & 0 & 0 & 0 & 0 \end{bmatrix},$$

$$A_0 = \begin{bmatrix} -3\omega^2 & 0 & 0 & -1 & 0 \\ 0 & 0 & 0 & 0 & 0 \\ 0 & 0 & \omega^2 & 0 & -1 \end{bmatrix},$$

then the NSE corresponding to this system is

$$A_2 VF^2 + A_1 VF + A_0 V = R. \tag{8.9}$$

8.1.2 Deriving NSEs by Specifying GSEs

There are several ways to derive the general NSEs in the form of (8.2). Concretely, from nonhomogeneous GSEs, we have the following three ways:

1. From the nonhomogeneous GSE (5.1) through letting $B(s) = 0_{n\times r}$.
2. From the nonhomogeneous fully actuated GSE (6.9) through letting $B(s) = I$, $R = 0$ and fixing the matrix W.
3. From the nonhomogeneous standard fully actuated GSE (6.11) through letting $R = 0$ and fixing the matrix W.

To derive the general NSEs from homogeneous GSEs, we also have three ways:

1. From the homogeneous GSE (4.50) through letting $r = n$, $B(s) = I_n$, and fixing the matrix W.
2. From the homogeneous fully actuated GSE (6.8) through letting $B(s) = I_n$ and fixing the matrix W.
3. From the homogeneous standard fully actuated GSE (6.10) through fixing the matrix W.

These relations are shown in Figure 8.1.

General solutions to the NSE (8.2) can be derived through any of these six ways. Yet maybe the most direct way is through the last option, that is, using results for the homogeneous and nonhomogeneous standard fully actuated GSE (6.10). As a matter of fact, Theorems 6.4 and 6.8, which are for general solutions to the homogeneous standard fully actuated GSE (6.10), have really provided us with ready tools for getting the general solutions to the types of NSEs.

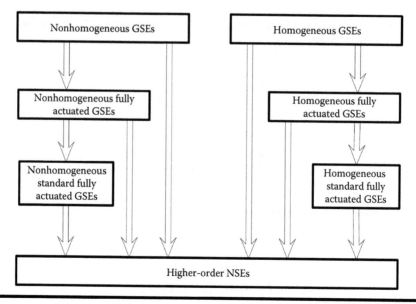

Figure 8.1   Derivation of NSEs.

8.1.3 *Converting GSEs into NSEs*

While in the last subsection we have shown that NSEs can be obtained from GSEs, in this subsection we further show that a general GSE can also be presented in the form of an NSE.

Rewrite the general nonhomogeneous GSE (5.1) as

$$\sum_{i=0}^{m} \left[(A_i V - B_i W) F^i \right] = R.$$

Letting

$$A_i' = \begin{bmatrix} A_i & -B_i \end{bmatrix}, \quad V' = \begin{bmatrix} V \\ W \end{bmatrix},$$

we can write the GSE as the following NSE:

$$\sum_{i=0}^{m} A_i' V' F^i = R.$$

This process states that any GSE in the form of (5.1) can be equivalently converted into a rectangular NSE.

We can also consider the more general type of GSEs in the following form:

$$\sum_{i=0}^{m}\sum_{j=1}^{p} A_{ij} V_j F^i = \sum_{i=0}^{m}\sum_{j=1}^{q} B_{ij} W_j F^i + R. \tag{8.10}$$

Let

$$A_i = \begin{bmatrix} A_{i1} & A_{i2} & \cdots & A_{ip} \end{bmatrix},$$

$$B_i = \begin{bmatrix} B_{i1} & B_{i2} & \cdots & B_{iq} \end{bmatrix},$$

and

$$V = \begin{bmatrix} V_1 \\ V_2 \\ \vdots \\ V_p \end{bmatrix}, \quad W = \begin{bmatrix} W_1 \\ W_2 \\ \vdots \\ W_q \end{bmatrix},$$

the GSE (8.10) can be converted into an GSE in the form of (5.1), and hence can be further converted into an NSE in the form of (8.2).

Nevertheless, please bear in mind that this conversion is only feasible due to the generalization of square GSEs and NSEs to rectangular ones.

8.1.4 Assumption

In this chapter, we seek the solution to the NSEs (8.1) and (8.2). In order to cope with more general cases, we impose the following general assumption.

Assumption 8.1   *A(s) is of maximum rank α over* eig (F).

The above assumption means

$$\begin{cases} \operatorname{rank} A(s) \le \alpha \le q, \ \forall s \in \mathbb{C} \\ \operatorname{rank} A(s) = \alpha, \ \forall s \in \operatorname{eig}(F), \end{cases} \tag{8.11}$$

or, equivalently,

$$\max_{\lambda \in \mathbb{C}}\{\operatorname{rank} A(\lambda)\} = \operatorname{rank} A(s) = \alpha \le q, \ \forall s \in \operatorname{eig}(F). \tag{8.12}$$

Recall from Definition 3.8 that a $\lambda \in \mathbb{C}$ is called an essential zero of $A(s)$ if

$$\operatorname{rank} A (\lambda) < \max_{s \in \mathbb{C}}\{\operatorname{rank}A(s)\} \leq \min\{n, q\}. \tag{8.13}$$

Using the concept essential zeros, we can give the following interpretation of Assumption 8.1.

Proposition 8.1   *Let $A(s) \in \mathbb{R}^{n \times q} [s]$ be given by (8.3), and $F \in \mathbb{C}^{p \times p}$. Then $A(s)$ is of maximum rank α over eig (F) if and only if the eigenvalues of F are different from the essential zeros of $A(s)$.*

Proof. Necessity. Suppose $A(s)$ is of maximum rank α over eig (F), then the relations in (8.11) hold. Let $\lambda \in \operatorname{eig}(F)$, we thus have

$$\operatorname{rank} A (\lambda) = \alpha.$$

Therefore, it follows from the above definition that λ is not an essential zero of $A(s)$.

Sufficiency. Suppose that $\lambda \in \operatorname{eig}(F)$, and λ is not an essential zero of $A(s)$. Thus by definition, we have

$$\operatorname{rank} A (\lambda) \geq \alpha. \tag{8.14}$$

Note the assumption of

$$\alpha = \max_{\lambda \in \mathbb{C}}\{\operatorname{rank} A (\lambda)\},$$

(8.14) becomes

$$\operatorname{rank} A (\lambda) = \alpha. \tag{8.15}$$

This implies that $A(s)$ is of maximum rank α over eig (F). ■

Due to the linear nature of the NSEs (8.2) and (8.6) through (8.8), we can obtain the solutions to these equations using Kronecker product. In fact, taking the vec($\cdot$) operation over both sides of (8.2), and using (A.23), gives

$$\left(\sum_{i=0}^{m} \left(F^{\mathrm{T}}\right)^{i} \otimes A_{i} \right) \operatorname{vec} (V) = \operatorname{vec} (W).$$

Clearly, this is a linear equation in vec(V). Therefore, the solution to the NSEs (8.2) can be easily obtained from the above linear equation.

However, the above method has a main drawback in applications: *it does not work when the matrix F and/or W are undetermined.* While in many applications, these two matrices are not prescribed, but are set undetermined and are used as parts of the design degrees of freedom to be optimized.

The purpose of this chapter is to present, under Assumption 8.1 and based on the results obtained in Chapters 4 through 6, explicit analytical solutions to rectangular NSEs, which allow the matrices F and W to be set undetermined.

8.2 Case of *F* Being Arbitrary

Starting from this section, we consider, based on the SFR of $A(s)$, solution to the rectangular NSEs (8.1) and (8.2) satisfying Assumption 8.1.

8.2.1 SFR of A(s)

Let $A(s) \in \mathbb{R}^{n \times q}[s]$. Then, under Assumption 8.1, there exist two unimodular matrices $P(s) \in \mathbb{R}^{n \times n}[s]$ and $Q(s) \in \mathbb{R}^{q \times q}[s]$ and a diagonal polynomial matrix $\Sigma(s) \in \mathbb{R}^{\alpha \times \alpha}[s]$ satisfying

$$P(s)A(s)Q(s) = \begin{bmatrix} \Sigma(s) & 0 \\ 0 & 0 \end{bmatrix}, \tag{8.16}$$

and

$$\Delta(s) = \det \Sigma(s) \neq 0, \ \forall s \in \text{eig}(F). \tag{8.17}$$

Partition the unimodular matrix $P(s)$ as

$$P(s) = \begin{bmatrix} P_1(s) \\ P_2(s) \end{bmatrix}, \ P_1(s) \in \mathbb{R}^{\alpha \times n}[s], \tag{8.18}$$

and partition the unimodular matrix $Q(s)$ as

$$Q(s) = \begin{bmatrix} U(s) & N(s) \end{bmatrix}, \tag{8.19}$$

where $U(s) \in \mathbb{R}^{q \times \alpha}[s]$, $N(s) \in \mathbb{R}^{q \times \beta}[s]$, with

$$\beta = q - \alpha.$$

Then, it follows from the SFR (8.16) that the polynomial matrix $N(s)$ satisfies

$$A(s)N(s) = 0, \tag{8.20}$$

and the polynomial matrix $U(s)$ satisfies

$$A(s)U(s) = C(s), \tag{8.21}$$

where $C(s) \in \mathbb{R}^{n \times \alpha}[s]$ is given by

$$C(s) = P^{-1}(s) \begin{bmatrix} \Sigma(s) \\ 0 \end{bmatrix}. \tag{8.22}$$

If we denote

$$U(s) = \left[U_{ij}(s) \right]_{q \times \alpha}, \quad N(s) = \left[N_{ij}(s) \right]_{q \times \beta},$$

and let

$$\varphi = \max \left\{ \deg \left(U_{ij}(s) \right), \quad i = 1, 2, \ldots, q, \quad j = 1, 2, \ldots, \alpha \right\},$$

$$\omega = \max \left\{ \deg \left(N_{ij}(s) \right), \quad i = 1, 2, \ldots, q, \quad j = 1, 2, \ldots, \beta \right\},$$

then $U(s)$ and $N(s)$ can be written in the form of

$$U(s) = \sum_{i=0}^{\varphi} U_i s^i, \quad U_i \in \mathbb{R}^{q \times \alpha}, \tag{8.23}$$

and

$$N(s) = \sum_{i=0}^{\omega} N_i s^i, \quad N_i \in \mathbb{R}^{q \times \beta}, \tag{8.24}$$

respectively.

8.2.2 Homogeneous NSEs

Regarding the general solution to the mth order NSE (8.1), we have the following result represented in terms of the above polynomial matrix $N(s)$.

Theorem 8.1 *Let $A(s) \in \mathbb{R}^{n \times q}[s]$, $F \in \mathbb{C}^{p \times p}$ satisfy Assumption 8.1, and $N(s) \in \mathbb{R}^{q \times \beta}[s]$ be given by (8.19), with $Q(s) \in \mathbb{R}^{q \times q}[s]$ satisfying the SFR (8.16) and (8.17). Then,*

1. *When β > 0, the general complete solution V ∈ $\mathbb{C}^{q \times p}$ to the mth order NSE (8.1) is given by*

$$V = [N(s)Z]\big|_F = N_0 Z + N_1 ZF + \cdots + N_\omega ZF^\omega, \qquad (8.25)$$

where Z ∈ $\mathbb{C}^{\beta \times p}$ is an arbitrary matrix representing the degrees of freedom.
2. *When β = 0, the mth order NSE (8.1) has a unique solution V = 0.*

Proof. Let us note the following observations:

1. The *m*th order homogeneous NSE (8.1) can be viewed as a special homogeneous GSE in the form of (4.50) with $B(s) = 0$.
2. When $B(s) = 0$ the generalized RCF (4.56) becomes equation (8.20).
3. The polynomial matrix $N(s) \in \mathbb{R}^{q \times \beta}[s]$ given by (8.19) satisfies equation (8.20).

Thus, by applying Theorem 4.7 to equation (8.1), and looking up on equation (8.1) as a special GSE, we obtain the general complete solution (8.25) to the *m*th order NSE (8.1). The first conclusion is thus proven.

When $β = 0$, we have $α = q$. This implies that $A(s)$ is unimodular, hence in this case the *m*th order NSE (8.1) has a unique zero solution. ∎

Remark 8.1 The proposed solution (8.25) is very simple and neat. Furthermore, it allows the matrix F to be set undetermined. Such a property may give great convenience and advantages to some analysis and design problems in control system theory. This matrix F, together with the parameter matrix Z, can be optimized to achieve some better performance in applications.

8.2.3 Nonhomogeneous NSEs

8.2.3.1 Particular Solution

Regarding solution to the nonhomogeneous NSE (8.2), we have the following result, which is based on SFR of $A(s)$.

Theorem 8.2 *Let $A(s) \in \mathbb{R}^{n \times q}[s]$, $F \in \mathbb{C}^{p \times p}$ satisfy Assumption 8.1. Further, let*

- *$P(s) \in \mathbb{R}^{n \times n}[s]$, $Q(s) \in \mathbb{R}^{q \times q}[s]$ and $\Sigma(s) \in \mathbb{R}^{\alpha \times \alpha}[s]$ be given by SFR (8.16) and (8.17)*
- *$P_1(s) \in \mathbb{R}^{\alpha \times n}[s]$ and $P_2(s) \in \mathbb{R}^{(n-\alpha) \times n}[s]$ be given by (8.18)*
- *$U(s) \in \mathbb{R}^{q \times \alpha}[s]$ and $N(s) \in \mathbb{R}^{q \times \beta}[s]$ be given by (8.19)*

Then the NSE (8.2) has a solution if and only if

$$P_2(s)R = 0, \ \forall s \in \mathbb{C}, \tag{8.26}$$

and in this case, a particular solution is given by

$$V = [U(s)\text{adj}\Sigma(s)P_1(s)R]\big|_F [\Delta(F)]^{-1}. \tag{8.27}$$

Proof. Let us note the following observations:

1. The mth order nonhomogeneous NSE (8.2) can be viewed as a special nonhomogeneous GSE in the form of (5.1) with $B(s) = 0$.
2. When $B(s) = 0$ the DPE (5.7) becomes equation (8.21).
3. The polynomial matrix $U(s) \in \mathbb{R}^{q \times \beta}[s]$ given by (8.19) satisfies equation (8.21) with $C(s)$ given by (8.22).

Thus, by applying Theorem 5.1 to equation (8.2), and looking upon equation (8.2) as a special GSE, we obtain the condition (8.26) for existence of solutions as well as the particular complete solution (8.27) to the mth order NSE (8.1). ■

Noting that $\Sigma(s)$ is diagonal, both $\text{adj}\Sigma(s)$ and $\det \Sigma(s)$ are very easy to be derived.

The following corollary further specifies the solutions to the NSE (8.2) in several special cases.

Corollary 8.1 *Given conditions of Theorem 8.2, then*

1. *When $A(s) \in \mathbb{R}^{n \times q}[s]$ is of rank α over $\mathbb{C}$, the NSE (8.2) has a solution if and only if (8.26) holds, and in this case, a particular solution is given by*

$$V = [U(s)P_1(s)R]\big|_F. \tag{8.28}$$

2. *When $A(s) \in \mathbb{R}^{n \times q}[s]$ is of rank n over $\text{eig}(F)$, the NSE (8.2) always has a solution, and a particular solution is given by*

$$V = [U(s)\text{adj}\Sigma(s)P(s)R]\big|_F. \tag{8.29}$$

3. *When $A(s) \in \mathbb{R}^{n \times q}[s]$ is of rank n over $\mathbb{C}$, the NSE (8.2) always has a solution, and a particular solution is given by*

$$V = [U(s)P(s)R]\big|_F. \tag{8.30}$$

8.2.3.2 *General Solution*

Using Lemma 5.1 and Theorems 8.1 and 8.2, we can immediately derive the following result about a general solution to the NSE (8.2).

Theorem 8.3 *Under the condition of Theorem 8.2, the general solution to the NSE (8.2) is given by*

$$V = [U(s)\mathrm{adj}\Sigma(s)P_1(s)R + N(s)Z]\big|_F [\Delta(F)]^{-1}, \tag{8.31}$$

where $Z \in \mathbb{C}^{\beta \times p}$ *is an arbitrary parameter matrix that represents the degrees of freedom in the solution.*

It may be noted that the solution (8.31) can also be expressed by the unimodular matrix $Q(s)$ as follows:

$$V = Q(s) \begin{bmatrix} \mathrm{adj}\Sigma(s)P_1(s) & 0 \\ 0 & I \end{bmatrix} \begin{bmatrix} R \\ Z \end{bmatrix}\Bigg|_F [\Delta(F)]^{-1}.$$

Remark 8.2 The above theorem gives a very neat solution to the matrix equation (8.2). This solution is obviously in a linear explicit form with respect to R, and therefore allows the matrix R to be set undetermined. Furthermore, note that the only requirement on the matrix F is to make $A(s)$ be of rank α over F, thus the matrix F can be arbitrarily chosen with eigenvalues different from the essential zeros of $A(s)$. Such a property may give great convenience and advantages to some analysis and design problems in control system theory. These matrices F and R, together with the parameter matrix Z, can be optimized to achieve some better performance in applications.

8.3 Case of *F* Being in Jordan Form

In this section, we will give complete parametric solutions to the NSEs (8.1) and (8.2) for the case that the matrix F is a Jordan matrix of the following form:

$$\begin{cases} F = \mathrm{blockdiag}\,(F_1, F_2, \ldots, F_w) \\ F_i = \begin{bmatrix} s_i & 1 & & \\ & s_i & \ddots & \\ & & \ddots & 1 \\ & & & s_i \end{bmatrix}_{p_i \times p_i} \end{cases}, \tag{8.32}$$

where s_i, $i = 1, 2, \ldots, w$, are obviously the eigenvalues of the matrix F, and p_i, $i = 1, 2, \ldots, w$, are the geometric multiplicities corresponding to the eigenvalues s_i, $i = 1, 2, \ldots, w$, and satisfy

$$\sum_{i=1}^{w} p_i = p.$$

By the structure of the F matrix, the columns of the matrices V, Z and R, namely, v_{ij}, z_{ij} and r_{ij}, are well defined according to Convention C1 introduced in Chapter 4. Further, Assumption 8.1 becomes

Assumption 8.2 $\begin{cases} \text{rank} A(s) \leq \alpha, \ \forall s \in \mathbb{C} \\ \text{rank} A(s_i) = \alpha, \quad i = 1, 2, \ldots, w, \end{cases}$

which is clearly equivalent to

$$\max_{s \in \mathbb{C}} \{\text{rank} A(s)\} = \text{rank} A(s_i) = \alpha, \quad i = 1, 2, \ldots, w.$$

8.3.1 Homogeneous NSEs

The following theorem gives the general solution to the homogeneous NSE (8.1) with F being the Jordan form given by (8.32).

Theorem 8.4 *Let $A(s) \in \mathbb{R}^{n \times q} [s]$, $F \in \mathbb{C}^{p \times p}$ be a Jordan matrix given by (8.32), and Assumption 8.2 be satisfied. Further, let $N(s) \in \mathbb{R}^{q \times \beta} [s]$ be given by (8.19), with $Q(s) \in \mathbb{R}^{q \times q}[s]$ satisfying the SFR (8.16) and (8.17). Then*

1. *When $\beta > 0$, a complete general solution to the homogeneous NSE (8.1) is given by*

$$v_{ij} = \sum_{k=0}^{j-1} \frac{1}{k!} \frac{d^k}{ds^k} N(s_i) z_{i,j-k}, \tag{8.33}$$

$$j = 1, 2, \ldots, p_i, \quad i = 1, 2, \ldots, w,$$

where $z_{ij} \in \mathbb{C}^\beta$, $j = 1, 2, \ldots, p_i$, $i = 1, 2, \ldots, w$, are a group of arbitrary parameter vectors.

2. *When $\beta = 0$, the homogeneous NSE (8.1) has a unique zero solution.*

Proof. Let us note the following observations:

1. The mth order homogeneous NSE (8.1) can be viewed as a special homogeneous GSE in the form of (4.50) with $B(s) = 0$.
2. When $B(s) = 0$ the generalized RCF (4.56) becomes equation (8.20).
3. The polynomial matrix $N(s) \in \mathbb{R}^{q \times \beta}[s]$ given by (8.19) satisfies equation (8.20).

Thus, when the matrix $F \in \mathbb{C}^{p \times p}$ is in the Jordan form of (8.32), by applying Theorem 4.8 to equation (8.1), which is looked upon as a special GSE, we obtain the general complete solution (8.33) to the mth order NSE (8.1). The first conclusion is thus proven.

The second conclusion is obvious. ■

8.3.2 Nonhomogeneous NSEs

For a particular solution to the nonhomogeneous NSE (8.2) with F being given in the Jordan form (8.32), we have the following result.

Theorem 8.5 *Let $A(s) \in \mathbb{R}^{n \times q}[s]$, $F \in \mathbb{C}^{p \times p}$ be in the Jordan form (8.32), and Assumption 8.2 be met. Further, let*

- *$P(s) \in \mathbb{R}^{n \times n}[s]$, $Q(s) \in \mathbb{R}^{q \times q}[s]$ and $\Sigma(s) \in \mathbb{R}^{\alpha \times \alpha}[s]$ be given by SFR (8.16) and (8.17)*
- *$P_1(s) \in \mathbb{R}^{\alpha \times n}[s]$ and $P_2(s) \in \mathbb{R}^{(n-\alpha) \times n}[s]$ be given by (8.18)*
- *$U(s) \in \mathbb{R}^{q \times \alpha}[s]$ be given by (8.19)*

Then the NSE (8.2) has a solution if and only if (8.26) holds, and in this case, a particular solution is given by

$$
\begin{cases}
V = \hat{V}\left[\Delta\left(F\right)\right]^{-1} \\
\hat{v}_{ij} = \sum_{k=0}^{j-1} \frac{1}{k!} \frac{d^k}{ds^k} \hat{U}\left(s_i\right) r_{i,j-k}, \\
\qquad j = 1, 2, \ldots, p_i, \quad i = 1, 2, \ldots, w,
\end{cases}
\tag{8.34}
$$

with

$$
\hat{U}(s) = U\left(s_i\right) \operatorname{adj}\Sigma\left(s_i\right) P_1\left(s_i\right).
\tag{8.35}
$$

Proof. Let us note the following observations:

1. The mth order nonhomogeneous NSE (8.2) can be viewed as a special GSE in the form of (5.1) with $B(s) = 0$.
2. When $B(s) = 0$ the DPE (5.7) becomes equation (8.21).
3. The polynomial matrix $U(s) \in \mathbb{R}^{q \times \beta} [s]$ given by (8.19) satisfies equation (8.21) with $C(s)$ given by (8.22).

Thus, when the matrix $F \in \mathbb{C}^{p \times p}$ is in the Jordan form of (8.32), by applying Theorem 5.12 to equation (8.2), which is viewed as a special nonhomogeneous GSE, we obtain the condition (8.26) for existence of solutions as well as the particular complete solution (8.34) to the mth order NSE (8.2). ■

Corresponding to Corollary 5.2, we also have the following results.

Corollary 8.2 *Let conditions of Theorem 8.5 be met, then,*

1. *When $A(s) \in \mathbb{R}^{n \times q} [s]$ is of rank α over $\mathbb{C}$, the NSE (8.2) has a solution if and only if (8.26) holds, and in this case, a particular solution is given by*

$$v_{ij} = \sum_{k=0}^{j-1} \frac{1}{k!} \frac{d^k}{ds^k} \hat{U} (s_i) \, r_{i,j-k}, \tag{8.36}$$

$$j = 1, 2, \dots, p_i, \quad i = 1, 2, \dots, w, \tag{8.37}$$

where $\hat{U}(s)$ is defined by (8.35).

2. *When $A(s) \in \mathbb{R}^{n \times q} [s]$ is of rank n over $\mathrm{eig}(F)$, the NSE (8.2) always has a solution, and a particular solution is given by (8.34) with*

$$\hat{U}(s) = U(s) \mathrm{adj}\Sigma (s) P(s). \tag{8.38}$$

3. *When $A(s) \in \mathbb{R}^{n \times q} [s]$ is of rank n over $\mathbb{C}$, the NSE (8.2) always has a solution, and a particular solution is given by (8.36) with*

$$\hat{U}(s) = U(s) P(s). \tag{8.39}$$

Remark 8.3 The aforementiond theorem gives a solution to the matrix equation (8.2) for the case of F being a Jordan matrix, with all the degrees of freedom represented by the set of vectors z_{ij}, $j = 1, 2, \dots, p_i$, $i = 1, 2, \dots, w$. This solution allows the matrix R to be set undetermined, and also allows the eigenvalues of the matrix F to be set undetermined, but restricted to be different from the essential zeros of $A(s)$. Particularly, in the case that $A(s)$ is of full row rank, the matrix F can be arbitrarily chosen. These degrees of freedom may give great convenience and advantages to some analysis and design problems in control system theory.

8.4 Case of *F* Being Diagonal

In many applications, the matrix F in the higher-order NSE (8.2) is a diagonal matrix, that is,

$$F = \text{diag}\left(s_1, s_2, \ldots, s_p\right), \qquad (8.40)$$

where s_i, $i = 1, 2, \ldots, p$, may not be distinct. Such a special case is often encountered in practical applications and hence is very important. In this subsection, we provide a complete parametric general solution to the NSE (8.2) for this important special case of F being diagonal.

When the F matrix is in the diagonal form of (8.40), by convention C1 the columns v_{i1}, z_{i1}, r_{i1}, and r'_{i1} of matrices V, Z, R, and R', respectively, are well-defined. Without loss of generality, we can further denote v_{i1}, z_{i1}, r_{i1}, and r'_{i1} simply by v_i, z_i, r_i, and r'_i. Also, Assumption 8.1 simply becomes

Assumption 8.3 $\begin{cases} \text{rank } A(s) \le \alpha, & \forall s \in \mathbb{C} \\ \text{rank } A(s_i) = \alpha, & i = 1, 2, \ldots, p, \end{cases}$

which is clearly equivalent to

$$\max_{s \in \mathbb{C}}\{\text{rank } A(s)\} = \text{rank} A(s_i) = \alpha, \quad i = 1, 2, \ldots, p.$$

8.4.1 Homogeneous NSEs

For a general solution to the homogeneous NSE (8.1) with F being given by (8.40), we have the following result.

Theorem 8.6 *Let $A(s) \in \mathbb{R}^{n \times q}[s]$, $F \in \mathbb{C}^{p \times p}$ be given in the diagonal form (8.40), and Assumption 8.3 hold. Further, let $N(s) \in \mathbb{R}^{q \times \beta}[s]$ be given by (8.24) and satisfy (8.20). Then*

1. *When $\beta > 0$, a general complete parametric solution V to the NSE (8.1) is given by*

$$v_i = N(s_i) z_i, \quad i = 1, 2, \ldots, p, \qquad (8.41)$$

where $z_i \in \mathbb{C}^\beta$, $i = 1, 2, \ldots, p$, are a group of arbitrary parameter vectors that represents the degrees of freedom in the solution.

2. *When $\beta = 0$, the NSE (8.1) has a unique zero solution.*

Proof. Let us note the following observations:

1. The mth order homogeneous NSE (8.1) can be viewed as a special homogeneous GSE in the form of (4.50) with $B(s) = 0$.
2. When $B(s) = 0$ the generalized RCF (4.56) becomes equation (8.20).
3. The polynomial matrix $N(s) \in \mathbb{R}^{q \times \beta}[s]$ given by (8.19) satisfies equation (8.20).

Thus, when the matrix $F \in \mathbb{C}^{p \times p}$ is in the diagonal form (8.40), by applying Theorem 4.9 to equation (8.1), which is viewed as a special GSE, we obtain the general complete solution (8.41) to the mth order NSE (8.1). The first conclusion is thus proven.

The second conclusion is obvious. ■

Note that a diagonal matrix is also a Jordan matrix. Simply by replacing the Jordan matrix F in Theorem 8.4 with the diagonal matrix F in the form of (8.40), we can also obtain the general solution (8.41) to the NSE (8.1) with F being given by (8.40).

Remark 8.4 It is easily observed from the above theorem that, in case of F being a diagonal matrix the solution to the matrix equation (8.1) turns out to be extremely neat and simple. The degrees of freedom are represented by the set of vectors z_i, $i = 1, 2, \ldots, p$. This solution allows the eigenvalues of the matrix F to be set undetermined, but restricted to be different from the essential zeros of $A(s)$. These degrees of freedom may give great convenience and advantages to some analysis and design problems in control system theory.

8.4.2 Nonhomogeneous NSEs

When F is given in the diagonal form of (8.40), by simplifying Theorem 5.12, we can obtain a special solution to the NSE (8.2).

Theorem 8.7 *Let $A(s) \in \mathbb{R}^{n \times q}[s]$, $F \in \mathbb{C}^{p \times p}$ be in the diagonal form of (8.40), and Assumption 8.3 is satisfied. Further, let*

- *$P(s) \in \mathbb{R}^{n \times n}[s]$, $Q(s) \in \mathbb{R}^{q \times q}[s]$ and $\Sigma(s) \in \mathbb{R}^{\alpha \times \alpha}[s]$ be given by SFR (8.16) and (8.17)*
- *$P_1(s) \in \mathbb{R}^{\alpha \times n}[s]$ and $P_2(s) \in \mathbb{R}^{(n-\alpha) \times n}[s]$ be given by (8.18)*
- *$U(s) \in \mathbb{R}^{q \times \alpha}[s]$ be given by (8.19)*

Then the NSE (8.2) has a solution if and only if (8.26) holds, and in this case, a particular solution is given by

$$v_i = U(s_i) \Sigma^{-1}(s_i) P_1(s_i) r_i, \quad i = 1, 2, \ldots, p. \tag{8.42}$$

Proof. Let us note the following observations:

1. The mth order nonhomogeneous NSE (8.2) can be viewed as a special GSE in the form of (5.1) with $B(s) = 0$.
2. When $B(s) = 0$ the DPE (5.7) becomes equation (8.21).
3. The polynomial matrix $U(s) \in \mathbb{R}^{q \times \beta}[s]$ given by (8.19) satisfies equation (8.21) with $C(s)$ given by (8.22).

Thus, when the matrix $F \in \mathbb{C}^{p \times p}$ is in the diagonal form (8.40), by applying Theorem 5.16 to the equation (8.2), which is viewed as a special nonhomogeneous GSE, we obtain the condition (8.26) for existence of solutions as well as the general complete solution (8.42) to the mth order NSE (8.2). ■

The result can also be obtained by specifying in Theorem 8.5 the matrix F to be a diagonal one in the form of (8.40).

Corresponding to Corollary 5.3, we also have the following results.

Corollary 8.3 *Given conditions of Theorem 8.7, then,*

1. *When $A(s) \in \mathbb{R}^{n \times q}[s]$ is of rank α over $\mathbb{C}$, the NSE (8.2) has a solution if and only if (8.26) holds, and in this case, a particular solution is given by*

$$v_i = U(s_i) P_1(s_i) r_i, \quad i = 1, 2, \ldots, p. \tag{8.43}$$

2. *When $A(s) \in \mathbb{R}^{n \times q}[s]$ is of rank n over eig(F), the NSE (8.2) always has a solution, and a particular solution is given by*

$$v_i = U(s_i) \Sigma^{-1}(s_i) P(s_i) r_i, \quad i = 1, 2, \ldots, p. \tag{8.44}$$

3. *When $A(s) \in \mathbb{R}^{n \times q}[s]$ is of rank n over $\mathbb{C}$, the NSE (8.2) always has a solution, and a particular solution is given by*

$$v_i = U(s_i) P(s_i) r_i, \quad i = 1, 2, \ldots, p. \tag{8.45}$$

Remark 8.5 Again, the general complete parametric solution to the nonhomogeneous GSE (8.2) for the case of F being a diagonal matrix turns out to be extremely neat and simple. Again, all the degrees of freedom are represented by the set of vectors z_j, $j = 1, 2, \ldots, p$. This solution allows the matrix R to be set undetermined, and also allows the eigenvalues of the matrix F to be set undetermined, but restricted to be different from the essential zeros of $A(s)$.

8.4.3 Example

Example 8.2

Consider the following NSE given in Example 8.1:

$$A_2 VF^2 + A_1 VF + A_0 V = R,$$

with

$$A_2 = [I_3 \ 0_{3\times2}],$$

$$A_1 = \begin{bmatrix} 0 & -2w & 0 & 0 & 0 \\ 2w & 0 & 0 & 0 & 0 \\ 0 & 0 & 0 & 0 & 0 \end{bmatrix},$$

$$A_0 = \begin{bmatrix} -3w^2 & 0 & 0 & -1 & 0 \\ 0 & 0 & 0 & 0 & 0 \\ 0 & 0 & w^2 & 0 & -1 \end{bmatrix}.$$

Thus, the polynomial matrix associated with this NSE is

$$A(s) = \begin{bmatrix} s^2 - 3w^2 & -2ws & 0 & -1 & 0 \\ 2ws & s^2 & 0 & 0 & 0 \\ 0 & 0 & s^2 + w^2 & 0 & -1 \end{bmatrix},$$

and its SFR is given by (8.16), with $P(s) = I_3$,

$$Q(s) = \begin{bmatrix} 0 & \frac{1}{2w} & 0 & -s & 0 \\ 0 & 0 & 0 & 2w & 0 \\ 0 & 0 & 0 & 0 & 1 \\ -1 & \frac{1}{2w}(s^2 - 3w^2) & 0 & -s(s^2 + w^2) & 0 \\ 0 & 0 & -1 & 0 & s^2 + w^2 \end{bmatrix},$$

and

$$\Sigma(s) = \begin{bmatrix} 1 & 0 & 0 \\ 0 & s & 0 \\ 0 & 0 & 1 \end{bmatrix}.$$

Due to the expression of $\Sigma(s)$, we should impose the assumption

$$\mathrm{rank} A(s) = 3, \ \forall s \neq 0,$$

that is, the matrix F should be chosen not to possess zero eigenvalues. Meanwhile, from the polynomial matrix $Q(s)$ we obtain

$$N(s) = \begin{bmatrix} -s & 0 \\ 2\omega & 0 \\ 0 & 1 \\ -s\left(s^2 + \omega^2\right) & 0 \\ 0 & s^2 + \omega^2 \end{bmatrix},$$

and

$$U(s) = \frac{1}{2\omega} \begin{bmatrix} 0 & 1 & 0 \\ 0 & 0 & 0 \\ 0 & 0 & 0 \\ -2\omega & s^2 - 3\omega^2 & 0 \\ 0 & 0 & -2\omega \end{bmatrix}.$$

Denote

$$z_i = \begin{bmatrix} \alpha_i \\ \beta_i \end{bmatrix}, \quad i = 1, 2, \ldots, p,$$

then it follows from Theorem 8.6 the general solution to the corresponding homogeneous NSE is given by

$$v_i = N(s_i) z_i = \begin{bmatrix} -\alpha_i s_i \\ 2\alpha_i \omega \\ \beta_i \\ -s_i \alpha_i \left(s_i^2 + \omega^2\right) \\ \beta_i \left(s_i^2 + \omega^2\right) \end{bmatrix}, \quad i = 1, 2, \ldots, p.$$

Meanwhile, let

$$r_i = \begin{bmatrix} 0 \\ \gamma_i \\ -1 \end{bmatrix}, \quad i = 1, 2, \ldots, p,$$

it follows from Theorem 8.7 a particular solution to the nonhomogeneous NSE is given by

$$v_i = U(s_i) \Sigma^{-1}(s_i) r_i$$

$$= \frac{1}{2\omega s_i} \begin{bmatrix} 0 & 1 & 0 \\ 0 & 0 & 0 \\ 0 & 0 & 0 \\ -2\omega s_i & s_i^2 - 3\omega^2 & 0 \\ 0 & 0 & -2\omega s_i \end{bmatrix} \begin{bmatrix} 0 \\ \gamma_i \\ 1 \end{bmatrix}$$

$$= \frac{1}{2\omega s_i} \begin{bmatrix} \gamma_i \\ 0 \\ 0 \\ \gamma_i \left(s_i^2 - 3\omega^2\right) \\ -2\omega s_i \end{bmatrix}, \quad i = 1, 2, \ldots, p.$$

8.5 Case of rank $A(s) = n$, $\forall s \in \mathbb{C}$

In this section, let us give a special care of rectangular NSEs satisfying the following assumption.

Assumption 8.4 *The polynomial matrix $A(s)$ is of rank n over $\mathbb{C}$.*

This important special case corresponds to the controllable case of GSEs treated in Section 5.4.

Under the above assumption, the SFR (8.16) reduces to

$$P(s)A(s)Q'(s) = \begin{bmatrix} I_n & 0 \end{bmatrix}. \tag{8.46}$$

In this case, we have $\Sigma(s) = I_n$ and $\Delta(s) = 1$. Furthermore, we point out that in this case the unimodular matrix $P(s)$ can always be taken to be identity, since otherwise we may choose

$$Q(s) = Q'(s) \begin{bmatrix} P(s) & 0 \\ 0 & I_{q-n} \end{bmatrix},$$

and with this $Q(s)$, we clearly have

$$A(s)Q(s) = \begin{bmatrix} I_n & 0 \end{bmatrix}. \tag{8.47}$$

Therefore, the polynomial matrices $U(s) \in \mathbb{R}^{q \times n}[s]$ and $N(s) \in \mathbb{R}^{q \times (q-n)}[s]$ which satisfy the equations (8.20) and (8.21), respectively, are given by the following partition:

$$Q(s) = \begin{bmatrix} U(s) & N(s) \end{bmatrix}. \tag{8.48}$$

Furthermore, since in the case of (8.47) we have $P_1(s) = P(s) = I$, and $P_2(s)$ vanishes, the condition (8.26) holds automatically. In other words, in this case the nonhomogeneous NSE (8.2) always has a solution.

With the knowledge gained in the previous three sections, here we only give the results without proofs.

8.5.1 Homogeneous NSEs

For general solution to the mth order homogeneous NSE (8.1) under Assumption 8.4, we have the following results.

Theorem 8.8 *Let $A(s) \in \mathbb{R}^{n \times q}[s]$, with $q > n$, $F \in \mathbb{C}^{p \times p}$, and Assumption 8.4 be met. Further, let $N(s) \in \mathbb{R}^{q \times (q-n)}[s]$ be given by (8.48), with $Q(s) \in \mathbb{R}^{q \times q}[s]$ a unimodular polynomial matrix satisfying (8.47). Then,*

1. When $F \in \mathbb{C}^{p \times p}$ is an arbitrary matrix, a general complete parametric solution $V \in \mathbb{C}^{q \times p}$ to the mth order homogeneous NSE (8.1) is given by

$$V = [N(s)Z]\big|_F = N_0 Z + N_1 ZF + \cdots + N_\omega ZF^\omega, \tag{8.49}$$

where $Z \in \mathbb{C}^{(q-n) \times p}$ is an arbitrary matrix representing the degrees of freedom.

2. When $F \in \mathbb{C}^{p \times p}$ is a Jordan matrix in the form of (8.32), the general complete parametric solution $V \in \mathbb{C}^{q \times p}$ to the mth order homogeneous NSE (8.1) is given by

$$v_{ij} = \sum_{k=0}^{j-1} \frac{1}{k!} \frac{d^k}{ds^k} N(s_i)\, z_{i,j-k}, \tag{8.50}$$

$$j = 1, 2, \ldots, p_i, \quad i = 1, 2, \ldots, w,$$

where $z_{ij} \in \mathbb{C}^{q-n}$, $j = 1, 2, \ldots, p_i$, $i = 1, 2, \ldots, w$, are a group of arbitrary parameter vectors.

3. When $F \in \mathbb{C}^{p \times p}$ is a diagonal matrix in the form of (8.40), the general complete parametric solution $V \in \mathbb{C}^{q \times p}$ to the mth order homogeneous NSE (8.1) is given by

$$v_i = N(s_i)\, z_i, \quad i = 1, 2, \ldots, p, \tag{8.51}$$

where $z_i \in \mathbb{C}^{q-n}$, $i = 1, 2, \ldots, p$, are a group of arbitrary parameter vectors.

8.5.2 Nonhomogeneous NSEs

For solution to the mth order nonhomogeneous NSE (8.2) under Assumption 8.4, we have the following results.

Theorem 8.9 Let $A(s) \in \mathbb{R}^{n \times q}[s]$, with $q > n$, $F \in \mathbb{C}^{p \times p}$, and Assumption 8.4 be met, then the nonhomogeneous NSE (8.2) always has a solution. Further, let $Q(s) \in \mathbb{R}^{q \times q}[s]$ be a unimodular matrix given by (8.47), and $U(s) \in \mathbb{R}^{q \times n}[s]$ and $N(s) \in \mathbb{R}^{q \times (q-n)}[s]$ be given by (8.48). Then

1. When $F \in \mathbb{C}^{p \times p}$ is an arbitrary matrix, a particular solution $V \in \mathbb{C}^{q \times p}$ to the mth order nonhomogeneous NSE (8.2) is given by

$$V = [U(s)R]\big|_F. \tag{8.52}$$

2. When $F \in \mathbb{C}^{p \times p}$ is a Jordan matrix in the form of (8.32), a particular solution $V \in \mathbb{C}^{q \times p}$ to the mth order nonhomogeneous NSE (8.2) is given by

$$
\begin{cases}
v_{ij} = \sum_{k=0}^{j-1} \frac{1}{k!} \frac{d^k}{ds^k} U(s_i) \, r_{i,j-k}, \\
j = 1, 2, \dots, p_i, \quad i = 1, 2, \dots, w.
\end{cases}
\tag{8.53}
$$

3. When $F \in \mathbb{C}^{p \times p}$ is a diagonal matrix in the form of (8.40), a particular solution $V \in \mathbb{C}^{q \times p}$ to the mth order nonhomogeneous NSE (8.2) is given by

$$
v_i = U(s_i) \, r_i, \quad i = 1, 2, \dots, p.
\tag{8.54}
$$

With the two theorems, a general solution to the mth order nonhomogeneous NSE (8.2) can be easily presented.

8.5.3 Example

Example 8.3

Consider the NSE corresponding to the satellite attitude system treated in Duan and Yu (2013), and in Example 6.2 and Section 6.6:

$$
A_2 VF^2 + A_1 VF + A_0 V = R,
\tag{8.55}
$$

where

$$
A_2 = [M \; 0_{3 \times 3}],
$$

$$
A_1 = [H \; 0_{3 \times 3}],
$$

$$
A_0 = [G \; -I_3],
$$

with

$$
M = \mathrm{diag}\,(I_x, \, I_y, \, I_z),
$$

$$
H = w_0 (I_y - I_x - I_z) \begin{bmatrix} 0 & 0 & 1 \\ 0 & 0 & 0 \\ -1 & 0 & 0 \end{bmatrix},
$$

$$
G = \mathrm{diag}\left(4w_0^2(I_y - I_z), \, 3w_0^2(I_x - I_z), \, w_0^2(I_y - I_x)\right),
$$

here I_x, I_y, and I_z are the inertia matrices of the three channels, and $w_0 = 7.292115 \times 10^{-5}$ rad/s is the rotational-angular velocity of the earth.

For this NSE, the associated polynomial matrix is

$$A(s) = [\Phi(s) \quad -I_3],$$

where

$$\Phi(s) = \begin{bmatrix} s^2 I_x + 4\omega_0^2 I_{y,z} & 0 & -s\omega_0 I_0 \\ 0 & s^2 I_y + 3\omega_0^2 I_{x,z} & 0 \\ s\omega_0 I_0 & 0 & s^2 I_z - \omega_0^2 I_{x,y} \end{bmatrix},$$

with

$$\begin{cases} I_0 = I_x - I_y + I_z \\ I_{a,b} = I_a - I_b, \quad a, b = x, y, z. \end{cases} \tag{8.56}$$

Performing the SFR of $A(s)$, we can easily obtain (8.47) with

$$Q(s) = \begin{bmatrix} 0 & I_3 \\ -I_3 & \Phi(s) \end{bmatrix}.$$

This gives

$$U(s) = \begin{bmatrix} 0 \\ -I_3 \end{bmatrix}, \quad N(s) = \begin{bmatrix} I_3 \\ \Phi(s) \end{bmatrix}.$$

1. *Solution to Homogeneous NSE*

   Using Theorem 8.8, we have the following conclusions about the solution to the considered homogeneous NSE:

   ■ For an arbitrary matrix F, the general solution to this NSE is given by

   $$V = \left[\begin{bmatrix} I_3 \\ \Phi(s) \end{bmatrix} Z \right]\Bigg|_F = \begin{bmatrix} Z \\ [\Phi(s)Z]\big|_F \end{bmatrix}. \tag{8.57}$$

   ■ When F is taken to be the following Jordan matrix

   $$F = \begin{bmatrix} \lambda & 1 \\ 0 & \lambda \end{bmatrix}, \tag{8.58}$$

   the general solution can be also given by

   $$v_{11} = N(\lambda) z_{11} = \begin{bmatrix} z_{11} \\ \Phi(\lambda) z_{11} \end{bmatrix}$$

   $$v_{12} = N(\lambda) z_{12} + \begin{bmatrix} 0 \\ 2\lambda M + D \end{bmatrix} z_{11}$$

   $$= \begin{bmatrix} z_{12} \\ \Phi(\lambda) z_{12} + (2\lambda M + D) z_{11} \end{bmatrix}. \tag{8.59}$$

■ When F is taken to be the following diagonal matrix

$$F = \text{diag}\,(s_1, s_2), \qquad (8.60)$$

the general solution to this equation is given by

$$v_i = N\,(s_i)\,z_i = \begin{bmatrix} z_i \\ \Phi\,(s_i)\,z_i \end{bmatrix}, \quad i = 1, 2, \qquad (8.61)$$

where in the equations in (8.57), (8.59), and (8.61), the matrix $Z \in \mathbb{C}^{3\times 2}$ represents an arbitrary parameter matrix.
Particularly, when

$$F = \text{diag}\,(-1 \pm \text{i}),$$

and

$$Z = \begin{bmatrix} 1 & 0 \\ 0 & 1 \\ 0 & 0 \end{bmatrix},$$

where i represents the imaginary unit, it can be verified that both the above formulas (8.57) and (8.61) give the following same result:

$$V = \begin{bmatrix} 1 & 0 \\ 0 & 1 \\ 0 & 0 \\ 4w_0^2 I_{y,z} - 1 - 2I_x \text{i} & 0 \\ 0 & 3w_0^2 I_{x,z} - 1 + 2I_y \text{i} \\ w_0\,(\text{i} - 1)\,I_0 & 0 \end{bmatrix},$$

where the notions $I_{x,y}$, $I_{x,z}$, $I_{y,z}$, and I_0 are defined in (8.56).

2. *Solution to Nonhomogeneous NSE*

According to Theorem 8.9, we also have the following conclusions about solution to the nonhomogeneous NSE (8.55):

■ When $F \in \mathbb{C}^{p\times p}$, the general solution to this GSE is given by

$$V = \left[\begin{bmatrix} 0 \\ -I_3 \end{bmatrix} R \right]\bigg|_F = \begin{bmatrix} 0 \\ -R \end{bmatrix}. \qquad (8.62)$$

■ When F is taken as in (8.58), the general solution can be also given by

$$\begin{cases} v_{11} = \begin{bmatrix} 0 \\ -I_3 \end{bmatrix} r_{11} = \begin{bmatrix} 0 \\ -r_{11} \end{bmatrix} \\[3mm] v_{12} = \begin{bmatrix} 0 \\ -I_3 \end{bmatrix} r_{1,2} = \begin{bmatrix} 0 \\ -r_{1,2} \end{bmatrix}. \end{cases} \qquad (8.63)$$

▪ When F is taken as in (8.60), the general solution is given by

$$v_i = U\left(s_i\right) r_i = \begin{bmatrix} 0 \\ -r_i \end{bmatrix}, \quad i = 1, 2. \tag{8.64}$$

Summing up the aforementioned three cases, it is easy to see that for this particular NSE, there exists a particular solution

$$V = \begin{bmatrix} 0 \\ -R \end{bmatrix},$$

which is not dependent on matrix F.

8.6 Case of *F* Being Diagonally Known

In Section 8.4, solution to the NSE (8.2) with the matrix F being diagonal is considered, where the eigenvalues of the matrix F is not needed until the very last step to express the solutions. In this section, we still treat the case that the matrix F is in the diagonal form of (8.40), but with the eigenvalues s_i, $i = 1, 2, \ldots, p$, being known.

It is clearly observed from Section 8.4 that, when the matrix F is diagonal, solutions to the NSEs (8.1) and (8.2) can be immediately written out when the following polynomial matrices are obtained under Assumption 8.3:

▪ $A(s) \in \mathbb{R}^{n \times q}[s]$ satisfying Assumption 8.3.
▪ $P(s) \in \mathbb{R}^{n \times n}[s]$, $Q(s) \in \mathbb{R}^{q \times q}[s]$ and $\Sigma(s) \in \mathbb{R}^{n \times n}[s]$ given by SFR (8.16) and (8.17).
▪ $P_1(s) \in \mathbb{R}^{\alpha \times n}[s]$ and $P_2(s) \in \mathbb{R}^{(n-\alpha) \times n}[s]$ given by (8.18).
▪ $N(s) \in \mathbb{R}^{q \times \beta}[s]$ and $U(s) \in \mathbb{R}^{q \times \alpha}[s]$ given by (8.19).

More importantly, it can be observed that it is the values of these polynomials at s_i, $i = 1, 2, \ldots, p$, namely, $N(s_i)$, $U(s_i)$, $C(s_i)$, $\Delta(s_i)$, $P(s_i)$, $Q(s_i)$ and $\Sigma(s_i)$, $i = 1, 2, \ldots, p$, that are really used in the solutions. Therefore, in the case that the eigenvalues s_i, $i = 1, 2, \ldots, p$, are prescribed, we would naturally ask the following question:

Can we find a way to compute these values directly instead of solving these polynomials?

In this section, we show that the answer to the above question is positive and the well-known SVD provides a perfect technique to fulfil this task. This technique is first presented in Section 3.6, with strict proof for the controllable case, and then used in Sections 4.6.2 and 5.7 for solving homogeneous and nonhomogeneous GSEs, respectively, with a prescribed diagonal matrix F. In this section, results are presented without strict proofs.

8.6.1 SFR and SVD

When F is diagonal and Assumption 8.3 is met, we have the following comparison of SFR and SVD:

SFR

$$\begin{cases} P(s)A(s)Q(s) = \begin{bmatrix} \Sigma(s) & 0 \\ 0 & 0 \end{bmatrix} \\ \Sigma(s) \in \mathbb{R}^{\alpha \times \alpha}[s] \\ \det \Sigma(s_i) \neq 0, \end{cases}$$

SVD

$$\rightleftharpoons \quad \begin{cases} P_i A(s_i) Q_i = \begin{bmatrix} \Sigma_i & 0 \\ 0 & 0 \end{bmatrix} \\ \Sigma_i \in \mathbb{R}^{\alpha \times \alpha} \\ \det \Sigma_i \neq 0, \end{cases}$$

$$\begin{cases} Q(s) = \begin{bmatrix} U(s) & N(s) \end{bmatrix} \\ U(s) \in \mathbb{R}^{q \times \alpha}[s], \ N(s) \in \mathbb{R}^{q \times \beta}[s], \end{cases} \quad \rightleftharpoons \quad \begin{cases} Q_i = \begin{bmatrix} U_i & N_i \end{bmatrix} \\ U_i \in \mathbb{R}^{q \times \alpha}, \ N_i \in \mathbb{R}^{q \times \beta}, \end{cases}$$

$$A(s)N(s) = 0, \quad \rightleftharpoons \quad A(s_i)N_i = 0,$$

$$\begin{cases} A(s)U(s) = C(s) \\ C(s) = P^{-1}(s) \begin{bmatrix} \Sigma(s) \\ 0 \end{bmatrix}, \\ i = 1, 2, \ldots, p. \end{cases} \quad \rightleftharpoons \quad \begin{cases} A(s_i)U_i = C_i \\ C_i = P_i^{-1} \begin{bmatrix} \Sigma_i \\ 0 \end{bmatrix}, \\ i = 1, 2, \ldots, p. \end{cases}$$

$$(8.65)$$

Comparison of the above two aspects clearly suggests that

$$\begin{cases} P_i = P(s_i) \\ Q_i = Q(s_i) \\ \Sigma_i = \Sigma(s_i) \\ U_i = U(s_i) \\ N_i = N(s_i), \quad i = 1, 2, \ldots, p. \end{cases} \quad (8.66)$$

8.6.2 Solutions

With the above preparation, and using Theorem 8.6, we immediately have the following result about a general complete solution to the homogeneous NSE (8.1).

Theorem 8.10 *Let $A(s) \in \mathbb{R}^{n \times q}[s]$, $F \in \mathbb{C}^{p \times p}$ be a diagonal matrix given by (8.40), and Assumption 8.3 hold. Further, let $N_i \in \mathbb{R}^{q \times \beta}$, $i = 1, 2, \ldots, p$, be given by the right side in (8.65). Then,*

1. *When $\beta > 0$, a general solution V to the NSE (8.1) is given by*

$$\begin{cases} V = \begin{bmatrix} v_1 & v_2 & \cdots & v_p \end{bmatrix} \\ v_i = N_i z_i, \quad i = 1, 2, \ldots, p, \end{cases} \quad (8.67)$$

where $z_i \in \mathbb{C}^\beta$, $i = 1, 2, \ldots, p$, are a group of arbitrary parameter vectors that represent the degrees of freedom in the solution.

2. *When $\beta = 0$, the homogeneous NSE (8.1) has a unique zero solution.*

Again, with the above preparation, and using Theorem 8.7, we immediately have the following result about a particular solution to the nonhomogeneous NSE (8.2).

Theorem 8.11   *Let $A(s) \in \mathbb{R}^{n \times q}[s]$, $F \in \mathbb{C}^{p \times p}$ be in the diagonal form of (8.40), and Assumption 8.3 hold. Further, let $P_i \in \mathbb{R}^{n \times n}$, $U_i \in \mathbb{R}^{q \times \alpha}$, and $\Sigma_i \in \mathbb{R}^{n \times \alpha}$ be given by the SVD column in (8.65). Then*

1. *The NSE (8.2) has a solution if and only if*

$$\begin{bmatrix} 0 & I_{n-\alpha} \end{bmatrix} P_i R = 0, \quad i = 1, 2, \ldots, p. \tag{8.68}$$

2. *When the above condition is met, the matrix V given by*

$$\begin{cases} V = \begin{bmatrix} v_1 & v_2 & \cdots & v_p \end{bmatrix} \\ v_i = U_i \Sigma_i^{-1} \begin{bmatrix} I_\alpha & 0 \end{bmatrix} P_i r_i, \quad i = 1, 2, \ldots, p, \end{cases} \tag{8.69}$$

satisfies the NSE (8.2).

In the above solutions, polynomial matrix operations are no longer needed. This obviously gives great convenience to the computation of the solution. Moreover, note that SVD is well-known for its numerical stability, and the solution can be immediately obtained as soon as the set of SVDs in (8.65) are carried out, the solution procedure of this solution is extremely numerically simple and reliable.

Corresponding to Corollary 5.6, we also have the following results.

Corollary 8.4   *Let conditions of Theorem 8.11 be met, then,*

1. *When $A(s) \in \mathbb{R}^{n \times q}[s]$ is of rank α over $\mathbb{C}$, the NSE (8.2) has a solution if and only if (8.68) holds, and in this case, a particular solution is given by*

$$v_i = U_i \begin{bmatrix} I_\alpha & 0 \end{bmatrix} P_i r_i, \quad i = 1, 2, \ldots, p. \tag{8.70}$$

2. *When $A(s) \in \mathbb{R}^{n \times q}[s]$ is of rank n over $\text{eig}(F)$, the NSE (8.2) always has a solution, and a particular solution is given by*

$$v_i = U_i \Sigma_i^{-1} P_i r_i, \quad i = 1, 2, \ldots, p. \tag{8.71}$$

3. When $A(s) \in \mathbb{R}^{n \times q}[s]$ is of rank n over $\mathbb{C}$, the NSE (8.2) always has a solution, and a particular solution is given by

$$v_i = U_i P_i r_i, \quad i = 1, 2, \ldots, p. \tag{8.72}$$

8.6.3 Example

Example 8.4

Again, let us consider the space rendezvous system described by the C-W equation, with a failed thruster, treated in Examples 3.1, 4.6, 5.5, and 5.6. The system has a standard matrix second-order form of

$$\ddot{x} + D\dot{x} + Kx = Bu,$$

with

$$D = \begin{bmatrix} 0 & -2\omega & 0 \\ 2\omega & 0 & 0 \\ 0 & 0 & 0 \end{bmatrix}, \ K = \begin{bmatrix} -3\omega^2 & 0 & 0 \\ 0 & 0 & 0 \\ 0 & 0 & \omega^2 \end{bmatrix}, \ B = \begin{bmatrix} 1 & 0 \\ 0 & 0 \\ 0 & 1 \end{bmatrix}.$$

The NSE corresponding to this system is

$$A_2 V F^2 + A_1 V F + A_0 V = R,$$

with

$$A_2 = [I \ \ 0_{3 \times 2}],$$
$$A_1 = [D \ \ 0_{3 \times 2}],$$
$$A_0 = [K \ \ B].$$

Thus,

$$A(s) = \begin{bmatrix} s^2 - 3\omega^2 & -2\omega s & 0 & -1 & 0 \\ 2\omega s & s^2 & 0 & 0 & 0 \\ 0 & 0 & s^2 + \omega^2 & 0 & -1 \end{bmatrix}.$$

In the following, let us assume that the target is moving on a geosynchronous orbit, with $\omega = 7.292115 \times 10^{-5}$ rad/s. Also, let us choose

$$F = \text{diag}(-1, -2, -3, -4, -5).$$

Then, by performing the SVDs of $A\,(s_i)$, $i = 1, 2, \ldots, 5$, we obtain P_i, Q_i, and Σ_i, $i = 1, 2, \ldots, 5$, and based on these we further derive

$$N_1 = \begin{bmatrix} 0.707106775546493 & 0 \\ 0.000103126078491 & 0 \\ 0 & 0.707106779306529 \\ 0.707106779306530 & 0 \\ 0 & 0.707106783066566 \end{bmatrix},$$

$$N_2 = \begin{bmatrix} 0.242535624694947 & 0 \\ 0.000017685976669 & 0 \\ 0 & 0.242535624732878 \\ 0.970142500069468 & 0 \\ 0 & 0.970142500221196 \end{bmatrix},$$

$$N_3 = \begin{bmatrix} 0.110431526008804 & 0 \\ 0.000005368529249 & 0 \\ 0 & 0.110431526010396 \\ 0.993883734666458 & 0 \\ 0 & 0.993883734680780 \end{bmatrix},$$

$$N_4 = \begin{bmatrix} 0.062378286134369 & 0 \\ 0.000002274348180 & 0 \\ 0 & 0.062378286134530 \\ 0.998052578481598 & 0 \\ 0 & 0.998052578484179 \end{bmatrix},$$

$$N_5 = \begin{bmatrix} 0.039968038340357 & 0 \\ 0.000001165806128 & 0 \\ 0 & 0.039968038340384 \\ 0.999200958721450 & 0 \\ 0 & 0.999200958722129 \end{bmatrix},$$

and also the matrices $U_i' = U_i \Sigma_i^{-1} P_i$, $i = 1, 2, \ldots, 5$, as

$$U_1' = \begin{bmatrix} 0.49999999 & -0.00014584 & 0 \\ 0.00007292 & 0.99999998 & 0 \\ 0 & 0 & 0.50000000 \\ -0.50000000 & 0.00000000 & 0 \\ 0 & 0 & -0.50000000 \end{bmatrix},$$

$$U_2' = \begin{bmatrix} 0.23529412 & -0.00001823 & 0 \\ 0.00001716 & 0.25000000 & 0 \\ 0 & 0 & 0.23529412 \\ -0.05882353 & 0.00000000 & 0 \\ 0 & 0 & -0.05882353 \end{bmatrix},$$

$$U_3' = \begin{bmatrix} 0.10975610 & -0.00000540 & 0 \\ 0.00000534 & 0.11111111 & 0 \\ 0 & 0 & 0.10975610 \\ -0.01219512 & 0.00000000 & 0 \\ 0 & 0 & -0.01219512 \end{bmatrix},$$

$$U_4' = \begin{bmatrix} 0.06225681 & -0.00000228 & 0 \\ 0.00000227 & 0.06250000 & 0 \\ 0 & 0 & 0.06225681 \\ -0.00389105 & 0.00000000 & 0 \\ 0 & 0 & -0.00389105 \end{bmatrix},$$

$$U_5' = \begin{bmatrix} 0.03993610 & -0.00000117 & 0 \\ 0.00000116 & 0.04000000 & 0 \\ 0 & 0 & 0.03993610 \\ -0.00159744 & 0.00000000 & 0 \\ 0 & 0 & -0.00159744 \end{bmatrix}.$$

With the above matrices N_i, $i = 1, 2, \ldots, 5$, obtained, the general solution to the homogeneous NSE is given by

$$v_i = N_i z_i, \quad i = 1, 2, \ldots, 5.$$

Particularly, choosing

$$z_i = \begin{bmatrix} 1 \\ 1 \end{bmatrix}, \quad i = 1, 2, \ldots, 5,$$

gives the following solution

$$V = \begin{bmatrix} 0.70710678 & 0.24253562 & 0.11043153 & 0.06237827 & 0.03996804 \\ 0.00010313 & 0.00001769 & 0.00000537 & 0.00000227 & 0.00000117 \\ 0.70710678 & 0.24253562 & 0.11043153 & 0.06237829 & 0.03996804 \\ 0.70710678 & 0.97014250 & 0.99388373 & 0.99805258 & 0.99920096 \\ 0.70710678 & 0.97014250 & 0.99388373 & 0.99805258 & 0.99920096 \end{bmatrix}.$$

It can be verified that, with the obtained matrix V, we have

$$\left\| A_2 V F^2 + A_1 V F + A_0 V \right\|_{fro} = 3.0758 \times 10^{-7}.$$

With the above matrices U_i', $i = 1, 2, \ldots, 5$, determined, a particular solution to the nonhomogeneous NSE is given by

$$v_i = U_i' r_i, \quad i = 1, 2, \ldots, 5.$$

Particularly, choosing

$$r_i = \begin{bmatrix} i - 2 \\ -i + 3 \\ 1 \end{bmatrix}, \quad i = 1, 2, \ldots, 5,$$

gives the following solutions

$$
V =
\begin{bmatrix}
-0.50029168 & -0.00001823 & 0.10975610 & 0.12451590 & 0.11981064 \\
1.99992704 & 0.25000000 & 0.00000534 & -0.06249546 & -0.07999651 \\
0.50000000 & 0.23529412 & 0.10975610 & 0.06225681 & 0.03993610 \\
0.50000000 & 0.00000000 & -0.01219512 & -0.00778210 & -0.00479233 \\
-0.50000000 & -0.05882353 & -0.01219512 & -0.00389105 & -0.00159744
\end{bmatrix}.
$$

It can be verified that, with the matrix V, we have

$$
\left\| A_2 VF^2 + A_1 VF + A_0 V - R \right\|_{fro} = 1.40125764 \times 10^{-7}.
$$

8.7 Notes and References

8.7.1 Comments

In this chapter, several types of rectangular NSEs are proposed, and general solutions to these rectangular NSEs are investigated. In Chapter 9, square NSEs will be investigated (Figure 8.2).

As in the previous several chapters, we have not gone to cover all the cases. Those cases that are really tackled in this chapter are shown in Table 8.1. Readers are suggested to give the presentations of the results for the rest of the cases by themselves, particularly for the case of rectangular NSEs with varying coefficients.

Regarding the results presented in this chapter, one can also refer to Duan (2014k) and Duan (2014l).

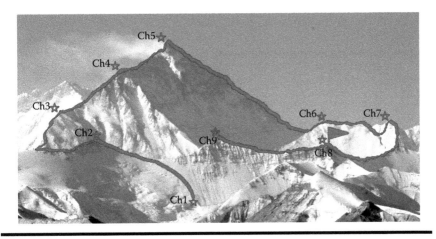

Figure 8.2 We are here. (Modified from http://go.jutuw.com/zhumulangmafeng/photo/.)

Table 8.1   Rectangular NSEs Treated in the Chapter

Cases	F Arbitrary	F Jordan	F Diagonal
Higher-order	Yes	Yes	Yes
Second-order	—	—	—
First-order (descriptor)	—	—	—
First-order (normal)	—	—	—
Varying coefficients	—	—	—

To most readers, it may be taken granted that NSEs are special cases of GSEs, but not vice versa. Yet for the type of rectangular NSEs, as we have seen from the first section in this chapter, they are just a different representation of GSEs. What is more, in the following we further show that combined GSEs can also be represented as an NSE.

8.7.2 Combined GSEs

Combined NSEs are often encountered in applications. The following two facts can be observed from Chapter 2:

1. The problem of model reference control can be solved via finding a pair of matrices G and H satisfying the following combined GSEs (see also Duan et al. 1994, 2001b):

$$\begin{cases} AG + BH = GA_m \\ CG + DH = C_m. \end{cases} \tag{8.73}$$

2. The problem of disturbance rejection can be solved via finding a pair of matrices V and W satisfying the following combined GSEs:

$$\begin{cases} AV + BW = VF - E_w \\ C_r V + D_{ru} W = -D_{ru}. \end{cases} \tag{8.74}$$

In general, we can propose the following combined first-order GSEs

$$\begin{cases} A_{11}X + A_{12}Y = E_{11}XF + E_{12}YF + R \\ A_{21}X + A_{22}Y = E_{21}XF + E_{22}YF + L. \end{cases} \tag{8.75}$$

where $A_{11}, E_{11} \in \mathbb{R}^{n_1 \times n_1}$, $A_{22}, E_{22} \in \mathbb{R}^{n_2 \times n_2}$, $A_{12}, E_{12} \in \mathbb{R}^{n_1 \times n_2}$, $A_{21}, E_{21} \in \mathbb{R}^{n_2 \times n_1}$, $R \in \mathbb{R}^{n_1 \times p}$, $L \in \mathbb{R}^{n_2 \times p}$, $F \in \mathbb{C}^{p \times p}$, and X and Y are the unknowns to be determined. The following lemma states an interesting phenomenon (Duan 2004b).

Proposition 8.2   *Let*

$$V = \begin{bmatrix} X \\ Y \end{bmatrix}, \tag{8.76}$$

then the combined two GSEs in (8.75) can be equivalently converted into the following NSE

$$EVF - AV = W, \tag{8.77}$$

with

$$A = \begin{bmatrix} A_{11} & A_{12} \\ A_{21} & A_{22} \end{bmatrix}, \; E = \begin{bmatrix} E_{11} & E_{12} \\ E_{21} & E_{22} \end{bmatrix}, \; W = -\begin{bmatrix} R \\ L \end{bmatrix}. \tag{8.78}$$

Due to this interesting fact, in applications involving combined GSEs we may consider solving the extended NSE instead of solving the two separated GSEs. Furthermore, we remark that the above fact can also be generalized to the higher-order case.

Chapter 9

Square NSEs

This chapter treats square NSEs. Based on the results for GSEs presented in the previous chapters, we will give analytical solutions to the square NSEs (1.74) through (1.78) as well as the Lyapunov matrix equations (1.79) and (1.81).

Consider, again, the following higher-order NSE

$$A_m V F^m + \cdots + A_1 V F + A_0 V = W, \tag{9.1}$$

whose associated polynomial matrix is

$$A(s) = A_m s^m + \cdots + A_1 s + A_0. \tag{9.2}$$

Different from Chapter 8, here $A_i \in \mathbb{R}^{n \times n}$, $i = 0, 1, \ldots, m$, and $F \in \mathbb{C}^{p \times p}$ are square coefficient matrices. Again, different from Chapters 4 through 7, in this chapter the matrix $W \in \mathbb{C}^{n \times p}$ is no longer an unknown. The only matrix to be determined is the matrix $V \in \mathbb{C}^{n \times p}$.

The matrix W is certainly independent on the matrix V, but it may be dependent on the matrix F. Generally, we can assume

$$W = f(F), \tag{9.3}$$

where $f : \mathbb{R}^{p \times p} \longrightarrow \mathbb{R}^{n \times p}$ is some given mapping. Particularly, when

$$W = \sum_{i=0}^{\psi} H_i W^* F^i, \tag{9.4}$$

the equation NSE (9.1) becomes the following one:

$$A_m VF^m + \cdots + A_1 VF + A_0 V = H_\psi W^* F^\psi + \cdots + H_1 W^* F + H_0 W^*, \quad (9.5)$$

where $H_i \in \mathbb{R}^{n \times d}$, $i = 0, 1, \ldots, \psi$, and $W^* \in \mathbb{C}^{d \times p}$ are given matrices.

General solutions to the NSE (9.1) can be derived through many ways. Of course, the results obtained in Chapter 8 for rectangular NSE can be readily applied to solve square NSEs. Yet maybe the most direct way is through using results for the standard fully actuated GSE (6.10). In this way, conditions of existence and uniqueness of solutions to the NSEs are naturally found. Thus in this chapter *it is the results in Chapter 6 but not those in Chapter 8 are used to derive the solutions to square NSEs.* As a matter of fact, Theorems 6.4 and 6.8, which are for general solutions to the homogeneous standard fully actuated GSE (6.10), have really provided us with ready tools for getting the general solutions to the various types of NSEs.

9.1 Case of *F* Being Arbitrary

In this section, we concentrate on the case that $F \in \mathbb{C}^{p \times p}$ is an arbitrary matrix and provide solution to the *m*th order square NSE (9.1).

9.1.1 Solution

Based on Theorem 6.8, we can derive the following result about solution to the *m*th order NSE (9.1).

Theorem 9.1 *Let $A(s) \in \mathbb{R}^{n \times n}[s]$ be given in (9.2), $W \in \mathbb{C}^{n \times p}$, $F \in \mathbb{C}^{p \times p}$, and denote*

$$\pi(s) = \det A(s).$$

Then,

1. *The mth order NSE (9.1) has a solution with respect to the matrix V if and only if*

$$\mathrm{rank} \begin{bmatrix} \pi(F) \\ W \end{bmatrix} = \mathrm{rank}\pi(F), \quad (9.6)$$

and in this case there exists a matrix Z satisfying

$$W = Z\pi(F), \quad (9.7)$$

and a solution to the NSE (9.1) is given by

$$V = [\text{adj}A(s)Z]\big|_F. \tag{9.8}$$

2. *The mth order NSE (9.1) has a unique solution with respect to the matrix V if and only if the zeros of det A(s) are different from the eigenvalues of the matrix F, that is,*

$$\{s \mid \det A(s) = 0\} \cap \text{eig}(F) = \varnothing, \tag{9.9}$$

or, equivalently,

$$\det \pi(F) \neq 0. \tag{9.10}$$

When condition (9.10) is satisfied, the unique solution to the mth order NSE (9.1) is given by

$$V = \left[\text{adj}A(s)\,W\,[\pi(F)]^{-1}\right]\Big|_F. \tag{9.11}$$

Proof. Proof of conclusion 1. When W is viewed as an unknown and the mth order NSE (9.1) is viewed as a standard fully actuated homogeneous GSE with $B(s) = I$, it follows from the first conclusion of Theorem 6.8 that the general solution to the standard fully actuated GSE (9.1) is given by

$$\begin{cases} V = [\text{adj}A(s)Z]\big|_F \\ W = Z\pi(F). \end{cases}$$

Therefore, for a fixed W, the NSE (9.1) has a solution if and only if (9.7) has a solution with respect to Z. Thus, the conclusion holds according to theory for linear equation groups.

Proof of conclusion 2. It further follows from the above that the NSE (9.1) has a unique solution if and only if (9.7) has a unique solution with respect to Z. While it is easy to see that (9.7) has a unique solution with respect to Z if and only if (9.10) holds. Further, utilizing Lemma 5.2, we know that (9.10) holds if and only if

$$\pi(s) \neq 0, \ \forall s \in \text{eig}(F).$$

Recall the definition of $\pi(s)$, we can write above condition as

$$\det A(s) \neq 0, \ \forall s \in \text{eig}(F).$$

This implies that all the eigenvalues of the matrix F are not zeros of $\det A(s)$. Therefore, (9.10) holds if and only if the zeros of $\det A(s)$ are different from the eigenvalues of the matrix F.

When condition (9.10) is met, by (9.7) the parameter Z is uniquely given by

$$Z = W \left[\pi(F) \right]^{-1} . \tag{9.12}$$

Substituting the above relation into (9.8) gives the solution (9.11) to the mth order NSE (9.1). ■

Remark 9.1 To obtain a solution to the GSE (9.5), we need only to substitute the matrix W in Theorem 9.1 by the one given in (9.4). Such a similar fact will not be mentioned again in the rest of the chapter.

The following is a further corollary of Theorem 9.1, which further clarifies certain special cases.

Corollary 9.1 *Let $A(s) \in \mathbb{R}^{n \times n}[s]$ be given in (9.2), $W \in \mathbb{C}^{n \times p}$, $F \in \mathbb{C}^{p \times p}$. Then,*

1. *When $A(s)$ is irregular, the mth order NSE (9.1) has a solution if and only if $W = 0$, and in this case all the solutions are given by (9.8) with $Z \in \mathbb{C}^{n \times p}$ being an arbitrary parameter matrix.*
2. *When $A(s)$ is regular and has rank n over F, the mth order NSE (9.1) has a unique solution $V = 0$ when $W = 0$.*
3. *When $A(s)$ is unimodular, the mth order NSE (9.1) has a unique solution, which is given by*

$$V = \left[A^{-1}(s) W \right] \Big|_F . \tag{9.13}$$

Proof. Proof of the first conclusion. When $A(s)$ is irregular, we have

$$\pi(s) = \det A(s) = 0, \ \forall s \in \mathbb{C}.$$

Thus, the necessary and sufficient condition (9.6) becomes $W = 0$, and meanwhile, (9.7) holds for arbitrary matrix Z. Therefore, all the solutions to the mth order NSE (9.1) are given by (9.8) with Z being an arbitrary parameter matrix.

Proof of the second conclusion. When $A(s)$ is regular and has rank n over F, we have $\pi(s) = \det A(s) \neq 0$, then $\pi(s)$ is nonzero constant, and thus

$$\pi(s) = \det A(s) \neq 0, \ \forall s \in \text{eig}(F).$$

Thus, we have

$$\det \pi(F) \neq 0,$$

the conclusion clearly follows.

Proof of the third conclusion. When $A(s)$ is unimodular, we have $\pi(s) = \det A(s) \neq 0$, then $\pi(s)$ is nonzero constant, and thus

$$\pi \triangleq \pi(s) \neq 0, \ \forall s \in \mathbb{C}.$$

Therefore,

$$\pi(F) = \pi I,$$

and

$$\det \pi(F) = \pi^n \neq 0.$$

Thus, condition (9.10) holds, and by the above theorem the equation has a unique solution.

By (9.11), in this case the unique solution is given by

$$V = \left[\text{adj}A(s) W \left[\pi I \right]^{-1} \right] \Big|_F \tag{9.14}$$

$$= \left[\frac{1}{\pi} \text{adj}A(s) W \right] \Big|_F \tag{9.15}$$

$$= \left[A^{-1}(s) W \right] \Big|_F, \tag{9.16}$$

which coincides with solution (9.13). ■

9.1.2 Special Cases

To derive the solution to the first-order NSE (1.77), that is,

$$EVF - AV = W, \tag{9.17}$$

and the second-order NSE (1.76), that is,

$$MVF^2 + DVF + KV = W, \tag{9.18}$$

we suffice only to substitute the general polynomial matrix $A(s)$ in Theorem 9.1 by

$$A_1(s) = sE - A,$$

and

$$A_2(s) = Ms^2 + Ds + K,$$

respectively. In the following, let us look into the case of first-order GSEs.

9.1.2.1 First-Order NSEs

For special importance of the first-order case, we here give the solution to the first-order NSE (9.17). Applying the above theorem to the equation, we obtain the following result.

Theorem 9.2 *Let E, $A \in \mathbb{R}^{n \times n}$, $W \in \mathbb{C}^{n \times p}$, $F \in \mathbb{C}^{p \times p}$, and denote*

$$\pi_{e,a}(s) = \det(sE - A).$$

Then,

1. *The first-order NSE (9.17) has a solution with respect to the matrix V if and only if*

$$\mathrm{rank} \begin{bmatrix} \pi_{e,a}(F) \\ W \end{bmatrix} = \mathrm{rank}\pi_{e,a}(F),$$

and in this case there exists a matrix Z satisfying

$$W = Z\pi_{e,a}(F), \tag{9.19}$$

and a solution to the first-order NSE (9.17) is given by

$$V = [\mathrm{adj}(sE - A)Z]\big|_F. \tag{9.20}$$

2. *The first-order NSE (9.17) has a unique solution with respect to the matrix V if and only if the relative finite eigenvalues of the matrix pair (E, A) are different from the eigenvalues of the matrix F, that is,*

$$\{s \mid \det(sE - A) = 0\} \cap \mathrm{eig}(F) = \varnothing, \tag{9.21}$$

or, equivalently,

$$\det \pi_{e,a}(F) \neq 0, \tag{9.22}$$

and when condition (9.22) is met, the unique solution to the first-order NSE (1.77) is given by

$$V = \left[\text{adj} \, (sE - A) \, W \, [\pi_{e,a}(F)]^{-1} \right] \Big|_F, \tag{9.23}$$

which reduces to

$$V = \left[(sE - A)^{-1} \, W \right] \Big|_F, \tag{9.24}$$

when $sE - A$ is further unimodular, in which case $\pi_{e,a}(s)$ is a nonzero constant.

Remark 9.2 Setting the matrix E to identity in the above theorem gives solution to the NSE (1.78), that is,

$$VF + AV = W. \tag{9.25}$$

Obviously, this is the well-known Sylvester equation, or sometimes is called the generalized continuous-time Lyapunov equation. Please note that in this case the existence and uniqueness condition in the second conclusion of the theorem becomes that the matrices A and F do not have common eigenvalues.

9.1.2.2 Lyapunov Equations

Based on Theorem 9.2, by setting $E = I$ and $A = -F^T$ we can easily derive the following result about solution to the continuous-time Lyapunov equation (1.79), that is,

$$VF + F^T V = W. \tag{9.26}$$

Corollary 9.2 *Let $F \in \mathbb{C}^{n \times n}$, $W \in \mathbb{C}^{n \times n}$, and*

$$\pi_f(s) = \det \left(sI + F^T \right).$$

Then,

1. *The continuous-time Lyapunov equation (9.26) has a solution with respect to the matrix V if and only if*

$$\text{rank} \begin{bmatrix} \pi_f(F) \\ W \end{bmatrix} = \text{rank} \pi_f(F),$$

and in this case there exists a matrix Z satisfying

$$W = Z\pi_f(F), \tag{9.27}$$

and a solution to the continuous-time Lyapunov equation (9.26) is given by

$$V = \left[\text{adj}\left(sI + F^{\mathrm{T}} \right) Z \right] \Big|_F. \tag{9.28}$$

2. *The continuous-time Lyapunov equation (9.26) has a unique solution with respect to the matrix V if and only if the matrix F does not possess eigenvalues on the imaginary axis, or equivalently, there holds*

$$\det \pi_f(F) \neq 0,$$

and when this condition is met, the unique solution is given by

$$V = \left[\text{adj}\left(sI + F^{\mathrm{T}} \right) W \left[\pi_f(F) \right]^{-1} \right] \Big|_F. \tag{9.29}$$

Again, using Theorem 9.2, and setting $A = I$, we can easily derive the following result about solution to the generalized discrete-time Lyapunov equation or Kalman–Yakubovich equation (1.80), that is,

$$EVF - V = W. \tag{9.30}$$

Corollary 9.3 *Let $E \in \mathbb{R}^{n \times n}$, $W \in \mathbb{C}^{n \times p}$, $F \in \mathbb{C}^{p \times p}$, and denote*

$$\pi_e(s) = \det(sE - I).$$

Then,

1. *The generalized discrete-time Lyapunov equation (9.30) has a solution with respect to the matrix V if and only if*

$$\text{rank} \begin{bmatrix} \pi_e(F) \\ W \end{bmatrix} = \text{rank}\pi_e(F),$$

and in this case there exists a matrix Z satisfying

$$W = Z\pi_e(F), \tag{9.31}$$

and a solution to the generalized discrete-time Lyapunov equation (9.30) is given by

$$V = \left[\text{adj} \, (sE - I) \, Z \right] \big|_F . \tag{9.32}$$

2. *The generalized discrete-time Lyapunov equation (9.30) has a unique solution with respect to the matrix V if and only if*

$$\lambda \, (E) \, \lambda \, (F) \neq 1, \tag{9.33}$$

and when this condition is met, the unique solution to the generalized discrete-time Lyapunov equation (9.30) is given by

$$V = \left[\text{adj} \, (sE - I) \, W \left[\pi_e(F) \right]^{-1} \right] \Big|_F , \tag{9.34}$$

which reduces, when sE − I is unimodular, to

$$V = \left[(sE - I)^{-1} \, W \right] \big|_F . \tag{9.35}$$

Proof. Here we only prove condition (9.33). All the other aspects are natural implication of corresponding conclusions of Theorem 9.2.

According to Theorem 9.2, the condition for existence and uniqueness of solutions is

$$\mathbb{E} \triangleq \{ s \mid \det (sE - I) = 0 \} \cap \text{eig} \, (F) = \varnothing. \tag{9.36}$$

Note that

$$\begin{aligned} \mathbb{E} &\triangleq \{ s \mid \det (sE - I) = 0 \} \cap \text{eig} \, (F) \\ &= \{ s \mid \det (sE - I) = 0, \, s \in \text{eig} \, (F) \} \\ &= \{ \beta \mid \det (E - \beta I) = 0, \, \frac{1}{\beta} \in \text{eig} \, (F) \} \\ &= \{ \beta \mid \det (\beta I - E) = 0, \, \frac{1}{\beta} \in \text{eig} \, (F) \} \\ &= \{ \beta \mid \det (\beta I - E) = 0, \, \beta \lambda \, (F) = 1 \}. \end{aligned}$$

Therefore,

$$\mathbb{E} = \varnothing \iff \lambda \, (E) \, \lambda \, (F) \neq 1,$$

thus, the condition for existence and uniqueness of solutions is given by (9.33). ■

Simply setting $E = F^T$ in the above corollary gives result about solution to the discrete-time Lyapunov equation, or Stein equation (1.81), that is,

$$F^T VF - V = W. \tag{9.37}$$

The condition for existence and uniqueness of a solution for this equation with respect to the matrix V is

$$\lambda\left(F^T\right)\lambda(F) \neq 1, \tag{9.38}$$

which can obviously be represented as

$$\lambda^{-1} \notin \text{eig}(F), \quad \forall \lambda \in \text{eig}(F). \tag{9.39}$$

9.2 Case of *F* Being in Jordan Form

In this section, we further investigate the case that the matrix F is in the following Jordan form:

$$\begin{cases} F = \text{blockdiag}\,(F_1, F_2, \ldots, F_w) \\ F_i = \begin{bmatrix} s_i & 1 & & \\ & s_i & \ddots & \\ & & \ddots & 1 \\ & & & s_i \end{bmatrix}_{p_i \times p_i} \end{cases}, \tag{9.40}$$

where s_i, $i = 1, 2, \ldots, w$, are obviously the eigenvalues of the matrix F, and p_i, $i = 1, 2, \ldots, w$, are the geometric multiplicities corresponding to the eigenvalues s_i, $i = 1, 2, \ldots, w$, and satisfy $\sum_{i=1}^{w} p_i = p$.

9.2.1 General Solution

Based on the second conclusion in Theorem 6.8, we can derive the solution to the mth order NSE (9.1). Please recall the notation

$$\pi(s) = \det A(s),$$

which is to be used again.

Theorem 9.3 *Let $A(s) \in \mathbb{R}^{n \times n}[s]$ be given in (9.2), $W \in \mathbb{C}^{n \times p}$, and $F \in \mathbb{C}^{p \times p}$ be in the Jordan form of (9.40). Then,*

1. *The mth order NSE (9.1) has a unique solution with respect to the matrix V if and only if s_i, $i = 1, 2, \ldots, p$, are different from the zeros of $A(s)$, that is,*

$$\pi(s_i) = \det A(s_i) \neq 0, \quad i = 1, 2, \ldots, p. \tag{9.41}$$

2. *Under the condition (9.41), the unique solution to the mth order NSE (9.1) is given iteratively by*

$$v_{ij} = A^{-1}(s_i) \left[w_{ij} - \sum_{k=1}^{j-1} \frac{1}{k!} \frac{d^k}{ds^k} A(s_i) v_{i,j-k} \right], \tag{9.42}$$

$$j = 1, 2, \ldots, p_i, \quad i = 1, 2, \ldots, w,$$

or, analytically by

$$v_{ij} = \sum_{k=0}^{j-1} \frac{1}{k!} \frac{d^k}{ds^k} \mathrm{adj} A(s_i) z_{i,j-k}, \tag{9.43}$$

$$j = 1, 2, \ldots, p_i, \quad i = 1, 2, \ldots, w,$$

with Z being given iteratively by

$$z_{ij} = \frac{1}{\pi(s_i)} \left[w_{ij} - \sum_{k=1}^{j-1} \frac{1}{k!} \frac{d^k}{ds^k} \pi(s_i) z_{i,j-k} \right], \tag{9.44}$$

$$j = 1, 2, \ldots, p_i, \quad i = 1, 2, \ldots, w.$$

Proof. Proof of conclusion 1. When W is viewed as an unknown and the mth order NSE (9.1) is viewed as a standard fully actuated homogeneous GSE with $B(s) = I$, it follows from the second conclusion of Theorem 6.8 that the general solution to the standard fully actuated GSE (9.1) is given by

$$
\begin{cases}
v_{ij} = \sum_{k=0}^{j-1} \frac{1}{k!} \frac{d^k}{ds^k} \mathrm{adj} A(s_i) z_{i,j-k} \\[2mm]
w_{ij} = \sum_{k=0}^{j-1} \frac{1}{k!} \frac{d^k}{ds^k} \pi(s_i) z_{i,j-k}, \\[2mm]
j = 1, 2, \ldots, p_i, \quad i = 1, 2, \ldots, w.
\end{cases}
$$

Therefore, for a fixed W, the NSE (9.1) has a solution if and only if

$$w_{ij} = \sum_{k=0}^{j-1} \frac{1}{k!} \frac{d^k}{ds^k} \pi(s_i) z_{i,j-k}, \tag{9.45}$$

$$j = 1, 2, \ldots, p_i, \quad i = 1, 2, \ldots, w,$$

has a solution with respect to Z. Rewrite the above equations in (9.45) as

$$w_{ij} = \pi(s_i) z_{ij} + \sum_{k=1}^{j-1} \frac{1}{k!} \frac{d^k}{ds^k} \pi(s_i) z_{i,j-k}, \tag{9.46}$$

$$j = 1, 2, \ldots, p_i, \quad i = 1, 2, \ldots, w,$$

and further shift the second right-hand term to the left, we obtain

$$\pi(s_i) z_{ij} = w_{ij} - \sum_{k=1}^{j-1} \frac{1}{k!} \frac{d^k}{ds^k} \pi(s_i) z_{i,j-k}, \tag{9.47}$$

$$j = 1, 2, \ldots, p_i, \quad i = 1, 2, \ldots, w.$$

From this relation, it is easy to see that (9.45) has a solution with respect to Z if and only if the relations in (9.41) hold.

Proof of conclusion 2. It follows from the above proof of conclusion 1 that the solution to the NSE is given by (9.43) with matrix Z determined by (9.47). Under the condition of (9.41), the iterative formula (9.44) can be immediately obtained from the above relations in (9.47).

Now let us prove the solution (9.42). Again, when W is viewed as an unknown and the mth order NSE (9.1) is viewed as a standard fully actuated homogeneous GSE, it follows from Theorem 6.4 that the general solution to the standard fully actuated GSE (9.1) is given by

$$\begin{cases} V = Z \\ w_{ij} = \sum_{k=0}^{j-1} \frac{1}{k!} \frac{d^k}{ds^k} A(s_i) z_{i,j-k}, \\ j = 1, 2, \ldots, p_i, \quad i = 1, 2, \ldots, w. \end{cases} \tag{9.48}$$

Therefore, when W is fixed, the matrix V is determined by

$$w_{ij} = \sum_{k=0}^{j-1} \frac{1}{k!} \frac{d^k}{ds^k} A(s_i) v_{i,j-k}, \tag{9.49}$$

$$j = 1, 2, \ldots, p_i, \quad i = 1, 2, \ldots, w.$$

Rewrite the above equations as

$$w_{ij} = A(s_i)v_{ij} + \sum_{k=1}^{j-1} \frac{1}{k!} \frac{d^k}{ds^k} A(s_i)v_{i,j-k}, \tag{9.50}$$

$$j = 1, 2, \ldots, p_i, \quad i = 1, 2, \ldots, w,$$

we can easily obtain the solution (9.42). ■

Suppose that the *i*th Jordan block is a third-order one, that is,

$$J_i = \begin{bmatrix} s_i & 1 & 0 \\ 0 & s_i & 1 \\ 0 & 0 & s_i \end{bmatrix},$$

then in the following formula (9.42) we can compute the vectors v_{ij}, $j = 1, 2, 3$, iteratively as follows:

$$\begin{cases} v_{i1} = A^{-1}(s_i)w_{i1} \\ v_{i2} = A^{-1}(s_i)\left[w_{i2} - \frac{d}{ds}A(s_i)v_{i1}\right] \\ v_{i3} = A^{-1}(s_i)\left[w_{i3} - \frac{d}{ds}A(s_i)v_{i2} - \frac{1}{2}\frac{d^2}{ds^2}A(s_i)v_{i1}\right]. \end{cases} \tag{9.51}$$

Note that when $A(s) \in \mathbb{R}^{n \times n}[s]$ is given in (9.2) and unimodular, condition (9.41) holds. This fact together with the above result leads to the following result, which corresponds to Corollary 9.1.

Corollary 9.4 *Let $A(s) \in \mathbb{R}^{n \times n}[s]$ be given in (9.2) and be unimodular, $W \in \mathbb{C}^{n \times p}$, and $F \in \mathbb{C}^{p \times p}$ be in the Jordan form of (9.40). Then, the mth order NSE (9.1) has a unique solution, which can be given by*

$$v_{ij} = \sum_{k=0}^{j-1} \frac{1}{k!} \frac{d^k}{ds^k} A^{-1}(s_i)\, w_{i,j-k}, \tag{9.52}$$

$$j = 1, 2, \ldots, p_i, \quad i = 1, 2, \ldots, w.$$

Proof. When $A(s)$ is unimodular,

$$\pi(s) = \det A(s) = \pi$$

is a nonzero constant, thus condition (9.41) obviously follows.

When this condition is met, according to (9.44), we have

$$z_{ij} = \frac{1}{\pi} \left[w_{ij} - \sum_{k=1}^{j-1} \frac{1}{k!} \left(\frac{d^k}{ds^k} \pi \right) z_{i,j-k} \right]$$

$$= \frac{1}{\pi} w_{ij}, \quad j = 1, 2, \ldots, p_i, \quad i = 1, 2, \ldots, w. \tag{9.53}$$

Substituting this into (9.43) gives

$$v_{ij} = \sum_{k=0}^{j-1} \frac{1}{k!} \frac{d^k}{ds^k} \text{adj} A(s_i) \frac{1}{\pi} w_{i,j-k}$$

$$= \sum_{k=0}^{j-1} \frac{1}{k!} \frac{d^k}{ds^k} \text{adj} A^{-1}(s_i) w_{i,j-k}, \tag{9.54}$$

$$j = 1, 2, \ldots, p_i, \quad i = 1, 2, \ldots, w,$$

which coincides with (9.52). ■

9.2.2 Special Cases

To derive solution to the first-order NSE (1.77), that is, (9.17), and the second-order NSE (1.76), that is, (9.18), we suffice only to substitute the general polynomial matrix $A(s)$ in Theorem 9.3 by

$$A_1(s) = sE - A,$$

and

$$A_2(s) = Ms^2 + Ds + K,$$

respectively.

9.2.2.1 First-Order NSEs

Due to special importance of the first-order case, we here give the solution to the first-order NSE (9.17) with F being in Jordan form. It is reminded that the following notation is used again:

$$\pi_{e,a}(s) = \det(sE - A).$$

Theorem 9.4 *Let E, $A \in \mathbb{R}^{n \times n}$, $W \in \mathbb{C}^{n \times p}$, and $F \in \mathbb{C}^{p \times p}$ be in the Jordan form of (9.40). Then,*

1. *The first-order NSE (9.17) has a unique solution with respect to the matrix V if and only if s_i, $i = 1, 2, \ldots, p$, are not the relative finite eigenvalues of the matrix pair (E, A), that is,*

$$\pi_{e,a}(s_i) = \det (s_i E - A) \neq 0, \quad i = 1, 2, \ldots, p. \tag{9.55}$$

2. *Under the condition (9.55), the unique solution to the first-order NSE (9.17) is given iteratively by*

$$\begin{cases} v_{i1} = (s_i E - A)^{-1} w_{i1} \\ v_{ij} = (s_i E - A)^{-1} \left[w_{ij} - E v_{i,j-1} \right], \\ \qquad j = 2, 3, \ldots, p_i, \quad i = 1, 2, \ldots, w, \end{cases} \tag{9.56}$$

or given by

$$v_{ij} = \sum_{k=0}^{j-1} \frac{1}{k!} \frac{d^k}{ds^k} \mathrm{adj}\,(s_i E - A)\, z_{i,j-k},$$

$$j = 1, 2, \ldots, p_i, \quad i = 1, 2, \ldots, w,$$

with Z being given iteratively by

$$z_{ij} = \frac{1}{\pi_{e,a}(s_i)} \left[w_{ij} - \sum_{k=1}^{j-1} \frac{1}{k!} \frac{d^k}{ds^k} \pi_{e,a}(s_i)\, z_{i,j-k} \right], \tag{9.57}$$

$$j = 1, 2, \ldots, p_i, \quad i = 1, 2, \ldots, w.$$

For the first-order NSE (9.17), the following result immediately follows from Corollary 9.4.

Corollary 9.5 *If $sE - A$ is unimodular, then the first-order NSE (9.17) has a unique solution, which is given by*

$$v_{ij} = \sum_{k=0}^{j-1} \frac{1}{k!} \frac{d^k}{ds^k} (s_i E - A)^{-1} w_{i,j-k}, \tag{9.58}$$

$$j = 1, 2, \ldots, p_i, \quad i = 1, 2, \ldots, w.$$

9.2.2.2 Lyapunov Equations

Based on Theorem 9.4, by setting $E = I$ and $A = -F^T$, we can easily derive the following result about solution to the continuous-time Lyapunov equation (9.26), where the notation

$$\pi_f(s) = \det\left(sI + F^T\right),$$

is again used.

Corollary 9.6 *Let $W \in \mathbb{C}^{n \times p}$, and $F \in \mathbb{C}^{p \times p}$ be in the Jordan form of (9.40). Then,*

1. *The continuous-time Lyapunov equation (9.26) has a unique solution with respect to the matrix V if and only if the eigenvalues of matrix F are different from zeros of $\pi_f(s)$, or equivalently,*

$$\pi_f(s_i) = \det(s_iI + F) \neq 0, \quad i = 1, 2, \dots, p. \tag{9.59}$$

2. *Under the condition (9.59), the unique solution to the continuous-time Lyapunov equation (9.26) is given iteratively by*

$$\begin{cases} v_{i1} = \left(s_iI + F^T\right)^{-1} w_{i1} \\ v_{ij} = \left(s_iI + F^T\right)^{-1} \left[w_{ij} - v_{i,j-1}\right], \\ \quad j = 2, 3, \dots, p_i, \quad i = 1, 2, \dots, w, \end{cases} \tag{9.60}$$

or given by

$$v_{ij} = \sum_{k=0}^{j-1} \frac{1}{k!} \frac{d^k}{ds^k} \mathrm{adj}\left(s_iI + F^T\right) z_{i,j-k},$$

$$j = 1, 2, \dots, p_i, \quad i = 1, 2, \dots, w,$$

with Z being given iteratively by

$$z_{ij} = \frac{1}{\pi_f(s_i)} \left[w_{ij} - \sum_{k=1}^{j-1} \frac{1}{k!} \frac{d^k}{ds^k} \pi_f(s_i) z_{i,j-k}\right], \tag{9.61}$$

$$j = 1, 2, \dots, p_i, \quad i = 1, 2, \dots, w.$$

Setting $A = I$, using Theorem 9.4 and the notation

$$\pi_e(s) = \det(sE - I),$$

again, we can give the following result about solution to the generalized discrete-time Lyapunov equation (9.30) for the case that the matrix F is a Jordan form.

Corollary 9.7 *Let $E \in \mathbb{R}^{n \times n}$, $W \in \mathbb{C}^{n \times p}$, and $F \in \mathbb{C}^{p \times p}$ be in the Jordan form of (9.40). Then,*

1. *The generalized discrete-time Lyapunov equation (9.30) has a unique solution with respect to the matrix V if and only if*

$$\pi_e(s_i) = \det(s_i E - I) \neq 0, \quad i = 1, 2, \dots, p, \tag{9.62}$$

or, equivalently,

$$\lambda_j(E)\, s_i \neq 1, \quad i = 1, 2, \dots, p, \quad j = 1, 2, \dots, n.$$

2. *Under the condition (9.62), the unique solution to the generalized discrete-time Lyapunov equation (9.30) is given iteratively by*

$$\begin{cases} v_{i1} = (s_i E - I)^{-1} w_{i1} \\ v_{ij} = (s_i E - I)^{-1} \left[w_{ij} - E v_{i,j-1} \right], \\ \quad j = 2, 3, \dots, p_i, \quad i = 1, 2, \dots, w, \end{cases} \tag{9.63}$$

or given by

$$v_{ij} = \sum_{k=0}^{j-1} \frac{1}{k!} \frac{d^k}{ds^k} \mathrm{adj}\,(s_i E - I)\, z_{i,j-k},$$

$$j = 1, 2, \dots, p_i, \quad i = 1, 2, \dots, w,$$

with Z being given iteratively by

$$z_{ij} = \frac{1}{\pi_e(s_i)} \left[w_{ij} - \sum_{k=1}^{j-1} \frac{1}{k!} \frac{d^k}{ds^k} \pi_e(s_i)\, z_{i,j-k} \right], \tag{9.64}$$

$$j = 1, 2, \dots, p_i, \quad i = 1, 2, \dots, w.$$

It can be easily shown that, when $(sE - I)$ is unimodular, the condition (9.62) holds, and in this case the unique solution to the generalized discrete-time Lyapunov equation (9.30) is given by

$$v_{ij} = \sum_{k=0}^{j-1} \frac{1}{k!} \frac{d^k}{ds^k} (s_i E - I)^{-1} w_{i,j-k}, \tag{9.65}$$

$$j = 1, 2, \dots, p_i, \quad i = 1, 2, \dots, w.$$

9.3 Case of *F* Being Diagonal

In this section, we further investigate the case that the matrix F is in the diagonal form of

$$F = \text{diag} \left(s_1, s_2, \ldots, s_p \right), \tag{9.66}$$

where s_i, $i = 1, 2, \ldots, p$, are a group of self-conjugate complex numbers, which are not necessarily distinct.

9.3.1 General Solution

Based on the third conclusion in Theorem 6.8, or through directly simplifying the results in Theorem 9.3, we can derive the following result about solution to the mth order NSE (9.1).

Theorem 9.5 *Let $A(s) \in \mathbb{R}^{n \times n}[s]$ be given in (9.2), $W \in \mathbb{C}^{n \times p}$, and F be in the diagonal form of (9.66). Then,*

1. *The mth order NSE (9.1) has a unique solution with respect to the matrix V if and only if s_i, $i = 1, 2, \ldots, p$, are different from the zeros of $A(s)$, that is,*

$$\det A(s_i) \neq 0, \quad i = 1, 2, \ldots, p. \tag{9.67}$$

2. *Under the condition (9.67), the unique solution to the mth order NSE (9.1) is given by*

$$v_i = A^{-1} \left(s_i \right) w_i, \quad i = 1, 2, \ldots, p. \tag{9.68}$$

Proof. This is a special case of Theorem 9.3. It is easy to see that the condition of existence and uniqueness remains the same. When the matrix F is in the diagonal form of (9.66), we have $p_i = 1$, $i = 1, 2, \ldots, p$. Thus, the j subscript in v_{ij} can be omitted, and it is easy to see that solution (9.42) reduces to (9.68), while solution (9.43) reduces to

$$v_i = \frac{1}{\pi (s_i)} \text{adj} A \left(s_i \right) w_i, \quad i = 1, 2, \ldots, p,$$

which is in fact the same as solution (9.68). ■

9.3.2 First-Order NSEs and Lyapunov Equations

To derive the solution to the first-order NSE (9.17) and the second-order NSE (9.18), we suffice only to substitute the general polynomial matrix $A(s)$ in Theorem 9.5 by

$$A_1(s) = sE - A,$$

and

$$A_2(s) = Ms^2 + Ds + K,$$

respectively.

9.3.2.1 First-Order NSEs

Due to special importance of the first-order case, we here give the solution to the first-order NSE (9.17).

Theorem 9.6 *Let E, $A \in \mathbb{R}^{n \times n}$, $W \in \mathbb{C}^{n \times p}$, and F be in the diagonal form of (9.66). Then,*

1. *The first-order NSE (9.17) has a unique solution with respect to the matrix V if and only if s_i, $i = 1, 2, \ldots, p$, are different from the finite relative eigenvalues of the matrix pair (E, A), that is,*

$$\det(s_i E - A) \neq 0, \quad i = 1, 2, \ldots, p. \tag{9.69}$$

2. *Under the condition (9.69), the unique solution to the first-order NSE (9.17) is given by*

$$v_i = -(s_i E - A)^{-1} w_i, \quad i = 1, 2, \ldots, p. \tag{9.70}$$

9.3.2.2 Lyapunov Equations

In this subsection, we simply use v_{ij} and w_{ij} to denote the ith column and jth row element in the matrices V and W. Please keep in mind that these are not the notations by Convention C1.

Based on Theorem 9.6, by setting $E = -I$ and $A = F^{\mathrm{T}}$ we can easily derive the following result about solution to the continuous-time Lyapunov equation (9.26).

Corollary 9.8 *Let $W \in \mathbb{C}^{n \times p}$, and F be in the diagonal form of (9.66). Then,*

1. *The continuous-time Lyapunov equation (9.26) has a unique solution with respect to the matrix V if and only if*

$$s_i + s_j \neq 0, \quad i, j = 1, 2, \ldots, p. \tag{9.71}$$

2. *Under the condition (9.71), the unique solution to the continuous-time Lyapunov equation (9.26) is given by*

$$v_{ij} = \frac{w_{ij}}{s_i + s_j}, \quad i,j = 1,2,\ldots,p. \tag{9.72}$$

Proof. Proof of conclusion 1. Based on the first conclusion of Theorem 9.6, setting $E = -I$ and $A = F^{\mathrm{T}}$ in the condition (9.69), gives

$$\pi_c(s_i) = -\det\left(s_i I + F^{\mathrm{T}}\right) \neq 0, \quad i = 1,2,\ldots,p. \tag{9.73}$$

Further, in view of the diagonal form of F, it is easily observed that the above relation is

$$\pi_c(s_i) = -\det\left(\mathrm{diag}\left(s_i + s_1, s_i + s_2, \ldots, s_i + s_p\right)\right)$$
$$= \prod_{j=1}^{p}\left(s_i + s_j\right) \neq 0, \quad i = 1,2,\ldots,p, \tag{9.74}$$

which is clearly equivalent to (9.71).

Proof of conclusion 2. Based on the second conclusion of Theorem 9.6, by setting $E = -I$ and $A = F^{\mathrm{T}}$ the unique solution to the continuous-time Lyapunov equation (9.26) is obtained as

$$v_i = (s_i I + F)^{-1} w_i, \quad i = 1,2,\ldots,p, \tag{9.75}$$

which can be written as

$$\begin{bmatrix} v_{i1} \\ v_{i2} \\ \vdots \\ v_{ip} \end{bmatrix} = \begin{bmatrix} (s_i + s_1)^{-1} w_{i1} \\ (s_i + s_2)^{-1} w_{i2} \\ \vdots \\ (s_i + s_p)^{-1} w_{ip} \end{bmatrix}, \quad i = 1,2,\ldots,p.$$

This clearly gives the formula (9.72). ■

Again, using Theorem 9.6, and setting $E = F^{\mathrm{T}}$ and $A = I$, we can easily derive the following result about solution to the discrete-time Lyapunov equation (1.81), that is,

$$V - F^{\mathrm{T}} V F = W. \tag{9.76}$$

Corollary 9.9 *Let* $W \in \mathbb{C}^{n \times p}$, *and* F *be in the diagonal form of* (9.66). *Then,*

1. *The discrete-time Lyapunov equation* (9.76) *has a unique solution with respect to the matrix* V *if and only if*

$$s_i s_j \neq 1, \quad i, j = 1, 2, \ldots, p. \tag{9.77}$$

2. *Under the condition* (9.77), *the unique solution to the discrete-time Lyapunov equation* (9.76) *is given by*

$$v_{ij} = \frac{w_{ij}}{1 - s_i s_j}, \quad i, j = 1, 2, \ldots, p. \tag{9.78}$$

Proof. *Proof of conclusion 1.* Using Theorem 9.6 and setting $E = F^{\mathrm{T}}$ and $A = I$ in the condition (9.69) give obviously the condition

$$\pi_d(s_i) = \det(s_i F - I) \neq 0, \quad i = 1, 2, \ldots, p. \tag{9.79}$$

Further, note the diagonal form of the matrix F, it is easy to see that condition (9.79) is equivalent to

$$\pi_d(s_i) = \det\left(\mathrm{diag}\left(s_i s_1 - 1, s_i s_2 - 1, \ldots, s_i s_p - 1\right)\right)$$

$$= \prod_{j=1}^{p} \left(s_i s_j - 1\right) \neq 0, \quad i = 1, 2, \ldots, p.$$

This is obviously equivalent to condition (9.77).

Proof of conclusion 2. Again, using Theorem 9.6, and setting $E = F^{\mathrm{T}}$ and $A = I$, we obtain the unique solution to the first-order NSE (1.81) as

$$v_i = -(s_i F - I)^{-1} w_i, \quad i = 1, 2, \ldots, p. \tag{9.80}$$

Due to the diagonal form of F, the above relations can be written as

$$\begin{bmatrix} v_{i1} \\ v_{i2} \\ \vdots \\ v_{ip} \end{bmatrix} = \begin{bmatrix} (1 - s_i s_1)^{-1} w_{i1} \\ (1 - s_i s_2)^{-1} w_{i2} \\ \vdots \\ (1 - s_i s_p)^{-1} w_{ip} \end{bmatrix}, \quad i = 1, 2, \ldots, p.$$

Comparing the corresponding elements on both sides of the above equations immediately gives the formulas in (9.78). ■

Remark 9.3 It is observed from the above that in the case of F being diagonal, solutions to both the continuous-time and discrete-time Lyapunov equations

(9.26) and (9.76) can be immediately written out based on the given matrix W and the diagonal elements of F. When the matrix F is not diagonal but nondefective, a similarity transformation can first be applied to convert the matrix F into a diagonal one.

9.4 Example: Constrained Mechanical System

In this section, we demonstrate our results proposed in this chapter with an example that are originated from the constrained mechanical system introduced in Section 1.2.

Example 9.1 (Constrained Mechanical System in Second-Order Form)

Consider again the constrained mechanical system treated in Examples 1.3 and 4.9. As we have seen in Example 1.3 that the model of this system is established in a matrix second-order form with the following coefficient matrices:

$$A_2 = \begin{bmatrix} 1 & 0 & 0 \\ 0 & 1 & 0 \\ 0 & 0 & 0 \end{bmatrix}, A_1 = \begin{bmatrix} 1 & 1 & 0 \\ 1 & 1 & 0 \\ 0 & 0 & 0 \end{bmatrix},$$

$$A_0 = \begin{bmatrix} 2 & 0 & -1 \\ 0 & 1 & -1 \\ 1 & 1 & 0 \end{bmatrix}, B = \begin{bmatrix} 1 \\ -1 \\ 0 \end{bmatrix}.$$

Correspondingly, let us consider the following NSE:

$$A_2 VF^2 + A_1 VF + A_0 V = I_3. \tag{9.81}$$

Note that for this equation we have

$$A(s) = A_2 s^2 + A_1 s + A_0 = \begin{bmatrix} s^2 + s + 2 & s & -1 \\ s & s^2 + s + 1 & -1 \\ 1 & 1 & 0 \end{bmatrix}.$$

Thus,

$$\pi(s) = \det \begin{bmatrix} s^2 + s + 2 & s & -1 \\ s & s^2 + s + 1 & -1 \\ 1 & 1 & 0 \end{bmatrix} = 2s^2 + 3.$$

Therefore, for any matrix F, which do not possess eigenvalues $\pm\sqrt{\frac{3}{2}}i$, this equation has a unique solution for an arbitrary W.

In the following, we consider three different choices of the F matrix.

Case I: F *Being Arbitrarily Chosen*
In this case, the matrix F is chosen to be

$$F = \begin{bmatrix} -1 & 1 & 0 \\ -1 & -1 & 0 \\ 0 & 0 & -1 \end{bmatrix},$$

which possesses the eigenvalues $-1, -1 \pm i$.

In this case, we can find the solution according to formula (9.11). Since

$$\text{adj}A(s) = \begin{bmatrix} 1 & -1 & s^2 + 1 \\ -1 & 1 & s^2 + 2 \\ -s^2 - 1 & -s^2 - 2 & s^4 + 2s^3 + 3s^2 + 3s + 2 \end{bmatrix}$$

$$= G_4 s^4 + G_3 s^3 + G_2 s^2 + G_1 s + G_0,$$

with

$$G_4 = \begin{bmatrix} 0 & 0 & 0 \\ 0 & 0 & 0 \\ 0 & 0 & 1 \end{bmatrix}, \qquad G_3 = \begin{bmatrix} 0 & 0 & 0 \\ 0 & 0 & 0 \\ 0 & 0 & 2 \end{bmatrix},$$

$$G_2 = \begin{bmatrix} 0 & 0 & 1 \\ 0 & 0 & 1 \\ -1 & -1 & 3 \end{bmatrix}, \qquad G_1 = \begin{bmatrix} 0 & 0 & 0 \\ 0 & 0 & 0 \\ 0 & 0 & 3 \end{bmatrix},$$

and

$$G_0 = \begin{bmatrix} 1 & -1 & 1 \\ -1 & 1 & 2 \\ -1 & -2 & 2 \end{bmatrix},$$

and

$$\pi(F) = 2F^2 + 3I = \begin{bmatrix} 3 & -4 & 0 \\ 4 & 3 & 0 \\ 0 & 0 & 5 \end{bmatrix},$$

$$[\pi(F)]^{-1} = \frac{1}{25} \begin{bmatrix} 3 & 4 & 0 \\ -4 & 3 & 0 \\ 0 & 0 & 5 \end{bmatrix},$$

we thus have the solution to this NSE as

$$V = \left[\text{adj}A(s) W \left[\pi(F)\right]^{-1} \right] \Big|_F$$

$$= G_0 \left[\pi(F)\right]^{-1} + G_1 \left[\pi(F)\right]^{-1} F + \cdots + G_4 \left[\pi(F)\right]^{-1} F^4$$

$$= \frac{1}{25} \begin{bmatrix} 7 & 1 & 10 \\ -7 & -1 & 15 \\ -9 & -12 & 5 \end{bmatrix}.$$

Case II: F *Being a Jordan Matrix*

In this case, the matrix F is chosen to be the following Jordan block

$$F = \begin{bmatrix} -1 & 1 & 0 \\ 0 & -1 & 1 \\ 0 & 0 & -1 \end{bmatrix}.$$

In this case, the solution can be solved using formula (9.42). Noting that

$$\frac{d}{ds}A(-1) = \begin{bmatrix} 2s+1 & 1 & 0 \\ 1 & 2s+1 & 0 \\ 0 & 0 & 0 \end{bmatrix}_{s=-1} = \begin{bmatrix} -1 & 1 & 0 \\ 1 & -1 & 0 \\ 0 & 0 & 0 \end{bmatrix},$$

$$\frac{d^2}{ds^2}A(-1) = \begin{bmatrix} 2 & 0 & 0 \\ 0 & 2 & 0 \\ 0 & 0 & 0 \end{bmatrix},$$

and

$$A^{-1}(-1) = \frac{1}{5}\begin{bmatrix} 1 & -1 & 2 \\ -1 & 1 & 3 \\ -2 & -3 & 1 \end{bmatrix},$$

we have

$$v_{11} = A^{-1}(-1)\,w_{11} = \frac{1}{5}\begin{bmatrix} 1 \\ -1 \\ -2 \end{bmatrix}, \tag{9.82}$$

$$v_{12} = A^{-1}(-1)\left[w_{12} - \frac{d}{ds}A(s_1)v_{11}\right] = \frac{1}{25}\begin{bmatrix} -1 \\ 1 \\ -13 \end{bmatrix}, \tag{9.83}$$

and

$$v_{13} = A^{-1}(-1)\left[w_{13} - \frac{d}{ds}A(s_1)v_{12} - \frac{1}{2}\frac{d^2}{ds^2}A(s_1)v_{11}\right]$$

$$= \frac{1}{125}\begin{bmatrix} 36 \\ 89 \\ 18 \end{bmatrix}, \tag{9.84}$$

Therefore, the solution to the NSE is

$$V = \frac{1}{125} \begin{bmatrix} 25 & -5 & 36 \\ -25 & 5 & 89 \\ -50 & -65 & 18 \end{bmatrix}.$$

Case III: F Being Diagonal
In this case, the matrix F is chosen to be the following diagonal one:

$$F = \text{diag}(-1, -2, -3).$$

For this diagonal case, the solution can be obtained by formula (9.68). Recalling that

$$A^{-1}(-1) = \frac{1}{5} \begin{bmatrix} 1 & -1 & 2 \\ -1 & 1 & 3 \\ -2 & -3 & 1 \end{bmatrix},$$

and

$$A^{-1}(-2) = \frac{1}{11} \begin{bmatrix} 1 & -1 & 5 \\ -1 & 1 & 6 \\ -5 & -6 & 8 \end{bmatrix},$$

$$A^{-1}(-3) = \frac{1}{21} \begin{bmatrix} 1 & -1 & 10 \\ -1 & 1 & 11 \\ -10 & -11 & 47 \end{bmatrix},$$

we have

$$v_1 = A^{-1}(-1)\, w_1 = \frac{1}{5} \begin{bmatrix} 1 \\ -1 \\ -2 \end{bmatrix},$$

$$v_2 = A^{-1}(-2)\, w_2 = \frac{1}{11} \begin{bmatrix} -1 \\ 1 \\ -6 \end{bmatrix},$$

$$v_3 = A^{-1}(-3)\, w_3 = \frac{1}{21} \begin{bmatrix} 10 \\ 11 \\ 47 \end{bmatrix}.$$

These give the following solution to this NSE:

$$V = \frac{1}{1155} \begin{bmatrix} 231 & -105 & 550 \\ -231 & 105 & 605 \\ -462 & -630 & 2585 \end{bmatrix}.$$

9.5 NSEs with Varying Coefficients

In this section, we briefly consider the following NSE with varying coefficients:

$$\sum_{i=0}^{m} A_i(\theta, t) V(\theta, t) F^i = W(\theta, t), \tag{9.85}$$

where $\theta(t) : [0, +\infty) \rightarrow \Omega \subset \mathbb{R}^q$, is a time-varying parameter vector, $\Omega \subset \mathbb{R}^q$ is some compact set. Without loss of generality, $\theta(t)$ is assumed to be piecewise continuous. The associated polynomial matrix is

$$A(\theta, t, s) = A_m(\theta, t)s^m + \cdots + A_1(\theta, t)s + A_0(\theta, t), \tag{9.86}$$

where $A_i(\theta, t) \in \mathbb{R}^{n \times n}$, $i = 0, 1, \ldots, m$, $W(\theta, t) \in \mathbb{C}^{n \times p}$ and $F \in \mathbb{C}^{p \times p}$ are the coefficient matrices.

We remark that the results for NSEs with constant coefficients presented in the previous sections can be naturally generalized to the case of NSEs with varying coefficients. Here in this section, we only give the results associated with the general NSE (9.85), while omitting the results for all the special ones. Furthermore, proofs of results are neither presented. Readers may refer to the corresponding proofs for the constant coefficient cases presented in Sections 9.1 through 9.3.

9.5.1 Case of F Being Arbitrary

For the case that $F \in \mathbb{C}^{p \times p}$ is an arbitrary matrix, based on Theorem 7.10, we can derive the following result about solution to the mth order NSE (9.85).

Theorem 9.7 *Let $A(\theta, t) \in \mathbb{R}^{n \times n}[s]$ be given in (9.86), $W(\theta, t) \in \mathbb{C}^{n \times p}$, $F \in \mathbb{C}^{p \times p}$, and denote*

$$\pi(\theta, t, s) = \det A(\theta, t, s).$$

Then,

1. *The mth order NSE (9.85) has a solution with respect to the matrix V if and only if*

$$\text{rank} \begin{bmatrix} \pi(\theta, t, F) \\ W(\theta, t) \end{bmatrix} = \text{rank}\pi(\theta, t, F), \ \forall \theta \in \Omega, \ t \in [0, +\infty),$$

and in this case there exists a matrix $Z(\theta, t)$ satisfying

$$W(\theta, t) = Z(\theta, t)\pi(\theta, t, F),$$

and a solution to the NSE (9.85) is given by

$$V(\theta, t) = \left[\text{adj}A(\theta, t, s)Z(\theta, t) \right] \big|_F.$$

2. *The mth order NSE (9.85) has a unique solution with respect to the matrix V if and only if the zeros of $\det A(\theta, t, s)$ are different from the eigenvalues of the matrix F, that is,*

$$\{s \mid \det A(\theta, t, s) = 0\} \cap \text{eig}(F) = \varnothing, \ \forall \theta \in \Omega, \ t \in [0, +\infty),$$

or, equivalently,

$$\det \pi(\theta, t, F) \neq 0, \ \forall \theta \in \Omega, \ t \in [0, +\infty), \tag{9.87}$$

and when condition (9.87) is met, the unique solution to the mth order NSE (9.85) is given by

$$V(\theta, t) = \left[\text{adj}A(\theta, t, s) W(\theta, t) \left[\pi(\theta, t, F) \right]^{-1} \right] \big|_F.$$

It can also be easily shown that, if $A(\theta, t, s)$ is unimodular, that is,

$$\det A(\theta, t, s) \neq 0, \ \forall \theta \in \Omega, \ t \in [0, +\infty), \ s \in \mathbb{C},$$

then condition (9.87) holds, and in this case the unique solution to the *m*th order NSE (9.85) is given by

$$V(\theta, t) = \left[A^{-1}(\theta, t, s) W(\theta, t) \right] \big|_F.$$

9.5.2 Case of F Being in Jordan Form

In the case that the matrix $F \in \mathbb{C}^{p \times p}$ is in the Jordan form of (9.40), based on the second conclusion in Theorem 7.10, we can derive the following result about solution to the mth order NSE (9.85).

Theorem 9.8 *Let $A(\theta, t, s) \in \mathbb{R}^{n \times n}[s]$ be given in (9.86), $W(\theta, t) \in \mathbb{C}^{n \times p}$, and $F \in \mathbb{C}^{p \times p}$ be in the Jordan form of (9.40). Further, denote*

$$\pi(\theta, t, s) = \det A(\theta, t, s).$$

Then,

1. *The mth order NSE (9.85) has a unique solution with respect to the matrix V if and only if s_i, $i = 1, 2, \ldots, p$, are different from the zeros of $A(\theta, t, s)$, that is,*

$$\pi(\theta, t, s_i) = \det A(\theta, t, s_i) \neq 0, \quad i = 1, 2, \ldots, p. \quad (9.88)$$

2. *Under the condition (9.88), the unique solution to the mth order NSE (9.85) is given iteratively by*

$$v_{ij}(\theta, t) = A^{-1}(\theta, t, s_i) \left[w_{ij}(\theta, t) - \sum_{k=1}^{j-1} \frac{1}{k!} \frac{\partial^k}{\partial s^k} A(\theta, t, s_i) v_{i,j-k} \right], \quad (9.89)$$

$$j = 1, 2, \ldots, p_i, \quad i = 1, 2, \ldots, w,$$

or given by

$$v_{ij}(\theta, t) = \sum_{k=0}^{j-1} \frac{1}{k!} \frac{\partial^k}{\partial s^k} \mathrm{adj} A(\theta, t, s_i) z_{i,j-k}, \quad (9.90)$$

$$j = 1, 2, \ldots, p_i, \quad i = 1, 2, \ldots, w,$$

with Z being given iteratively by

$$z_{ij} = \frac{1}{\pi(\theta, t, s_i)} \left[w_{ij}(\theta, t) - \sum_{k=1}^{j-1} \frac{1}{k!} \frac{\partial^k}{\partial s^k} \pi(\theta, t, s_i) z_{i,j-k} \right],$$

$$j = 1, 2, \ldots, p_i, \quad i = 1, 2, \ldots, w.$$

It can be easily proven that, if $A(\theta, t, s)$ is unimodular, that is,

$$\det A(\theta, t, s) \neq 0, \ \forall \theta \in \Omega, \ t \in [0, +\infty), \ s \in \mathbb{C},$$

then condition (9.41) holds, and in this case the unique solution to the mth order NSE (9.85) is given by

$$v_{ij}(\theta, t) = \sum_{k=0}^{j-1} \frac{1}{k!} \frac{\partial^k}{\partial s^k} A^{-1}(\theta, t, s_i) \, w_{i,j-k}, \tag{9.91}$$

$$j = 1, 2, \ldots, p_i, \quad i = 1, 2, \ldots, w.$$

9.5.3 Case of F Being Diagonal

In the case that the matrix F is in the diagonal form of (9.66), based on the third conclusion in Theorem 7.10, or through directly simplifying the results in Theorem 9.8, we can derive the following result about solution to the mth order NSE (9.85).

Theorem 9.9 *Let $A(\theta, t, s) \in \mathbb{R}^{n \times n}[s]$ be given in (9.86), $W(\theta, t) \in \mathbb{C}^{n \times p}$, and $F \in \mathbb{C}^{p \times p}$ be in the diagonal form of (9.66). Then,*

1. *The mth order NSE (9.85) has a unique solution with respect to the matrix V if and only if s_i, $i = 1, 2, \ldots, p$, are not the zeros of $A(\theta, t, s)$, that is,*

$$\det A(\theta, t, s_i) \neq 0, \quad i = 1, 2, \ldots, p. \tag{9.92}$$

2. *Under the condition (9.92), the unique solution to the mth order NSE (9.85) is given by*

$$v_i = A^{-1}(\theta, t, s_i) \, w_i, \quad i = 1, 2, \ldots, p.$$

Example 9.2 (Space Rendezvous System—The T-H Equation)

Consider the time-varying space rendezvous problem mentioned in Example 7.3 again, the relative equation of motion is governed by the well-known T-H equation and appears, when arranged into the second-order system form, as

$$\ddot{x} + D(\dot{\theta})\dot{x} + K(\dot{\theta}, \ddot{\theta})x = u, \tag{9.93}$$

with

$$x = \begin{bmatrix} x_r & y_r & z_r \end{bmatrix}^{\mathrm{T}},$$

$$D(\dot{\theta}) = \begin{bmatrix} 0 & -2\dot{\theta} & 0 \\ 2\dot{\theta} & 0 & 0 \\ 0 & 0 & 0 \end{bmatrix}, \tag{9.94}$$

$$K(\dot{\theta}, \ddot{\theta}) = \begin{bmatrix} -2k\dot{\theta}^{\frac{3}{2}} - \dot{\theta}^2 & -\ddot{\theta} & 0 \\ \ddot{\theta} & k\dot{\theta}^{\frac{3}{2}} - \dot{\theta}^2 & 0 \\ 0 & 0 & k\dot{\theta}^{\frac{3}{2}} \end{bmatrix}, \tag{9.95}$$

where θ is the true anomaly. The corresponding NSE to be solved is

$$VF^2 + D(\dot{\theta}, \ddot{\theta})VF + K(\dot{\theta}, \ddot{\theta})KV = W,$$

where the matrices F and W are taken to be

$$F = \begin{bmatrix} -1 & 0 & 0 \\ 0 & -2 & 0 \\ 0 & 0 & -3 \end{bmatrix}, \quad W = \begin{bmatrix} 0 & 0 & 1 \\ 0 & 1 & 0 \\ 1 & 0 & 0 \end{bmatrix}.$$

Denoting

$$\theta_1 = \dot{\theta}, \ \theta_2 = \ddot{\theta},$$

we have

$$A(\theta_1, \theta_2, s) = M(\dot{\theta}, \ddot{\theta})s^2 + D(\dot{\theta}, \ddot{\theta})s + K(\dot{\theta}, \ddot{\theta})$$

$$= \begin{bmatrix} s^2 - 2k\theta_1^{\frac{3}{2}} - \theta_1^2 & -2\theta_1 s - \theta_2 & 0 \\ 2\theta_1 s + \theta_2 & s^2 + k\theta_1^{\frac{3}{2}} - \theta_1^2 & 0 \\ 0 & 0 & s^2 + k\theta_1^{\frac{3}{2}} \end{bmatrix}.$$

It can then be obtained that

$$A^{-1}(\theta_1, \theta_2, s)$$

$$= \frac{1}{\Delta(\theta_1, \theta_2, s)} \begin{bmatrix} k\theta_1^{\frac{3}{2}} - \theta_1^2 + s^2 & \theta_2 + 2s\theta_1 & 0 \\ -\theta_2 - 2s\theta_1 & s^2 - 2k\theta_1^{\frac{3}{2}} - \theta_1^2 & 0 \\ 0 & 0 & \frac{\Delta(s)}{k\theta_1^{\frac{3}{2}} + s^2} \end{bmatrix}, \tag{9.96}$$

with

$$\Delta(\theta_1, \theta_2, s) = \det \begin{bmatrix} s^2 - 2k\theta_1^{\frac{3}{2}} - \theta_1^2 & -2\theta_1 s - \theta_2 \\ 2\theta_1 s + \theta_2 & s^2 + k\theta_1^{\frac{3}{2}} - \theta_1^2 \end{bmatrix}$$

$$= 2s^2\theta_1^2 - 2k^2\theta_1^3 + \theta_2^2 + \theta_1^4 + k\theta_1^{\frac{7}{2}} + s^4 - ks^2\theta_1^{\frac{3}{2}} + 4s\theta_1\theta_2.$$

Since

$$\Delta(\theta_1, \theta_2, -1) = 2\theta_1^2 - 2k^2\theta_1^3 + \theta_2^2 + \theta_1^4 - 4\theta_1\theta_2 - k\theta_1^{\frac{3}{2}} + k\theta_1^{\frac{7}{2}} + 1,$$

$$\Delta(\theta_1, \theta_2, -2) = 8\theta_1^2 - 2k^2\theta_1^3 + \theta_2^2 + \theta_1^4 - 8\theta_1\theta_2 - 4k\theta_1^{\frac{3}{2}} + k\theta_1^{\frac{7}{2}} + 16,$$

$$\Delta(\theta_1, \theta_2, -3) = 18\theta_1^2 - 2k^2\theta_1^3 + \theta_2^2 + \theta_1^4 - 12\theta_1\theta_2 - 9k\theta_1^{\frac{3}{2}} + k\theta_1^{\frac{7}{2}} + 81,$$

are generally nonzero, the NSE has a unique solution, which is given by

$$v_i = A^{-1}(\theta_1, \theta_2, s_i)w_i, \quad i = 1, 2, 3.$$

Using the expression of in (9.96), and substituting the values of s_i and w_i, $i = 1, 2, 3$, into the above formula, gives the following solution to the NSE:

$$V = \begin{bmatrix} 0 & \frac{\theta_2 - 4\theta_1}{\Delta(\theta_1, \theta_2, -2)} & \frac{k\theta_1^{\frac{3}{2}} - \theta_1^2 + 9}{\Delta(\theta_1, \theta_2, -3)} \\ 0 & \frac{4 - 2k\theta_1^{\frac{3}{2}} - \theta_1^2}{\Delta(\theta_1, \theta_2, -2)} & \frac{6\theta_1 - \theta_2}{\Delta(\theta_1, \theta_2, -3)} \\ \left(k\theta_1^{\frac{3}{2}} + 1\right)^{-1} & 0 & 0 \end{bmatrix}.$$

9.6 Notes and References

In this last chapter of the book, analytical solutions in closedforms to square NSEs are presented (Figure 9.1). Of the several types of NSEs, the ones that are really tackled in this chapter are shown in Table 9.1. Readers may give the presentations of the results for the rest cases by themselves.

9.6.1 Comments on Results

As in the case of GSEs, the obtained solutions to the various NSEs and their special cases are also highly unified. It is obviously observed that the condition of existence of a solution and the solution itself are both dependent on the function

$$\pi(s) = \det A(s).$$

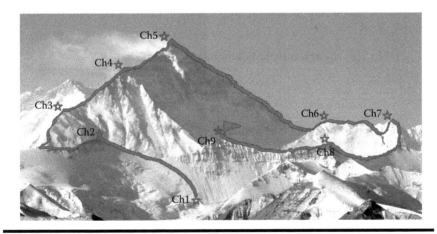

Figure 9.1   We are here. Journey finished. (Modified from http://go.jutuw.com/ zhumulangmafeng/photo/.)

Table 9.1   Square NSEs Treated in the Chapter

Cases	F Arbitrary	F Jordan	F Diagonal
Higher-order	Yes	Yes	Yes
Second-order	—	—	—
First-order (descriptor)	Yes	Yes	Yes
First-order (normal)	—	—	—
Lyapunov (continuous-time)	Yes	Yes	Yes
Lyapunov (discrete-time)	Yes	Yes	Yes

When the characteristic polynomial matrix $A(s)$ is chosen to be the special forms listed in Table 9.2 (where the K-Y equation stands for Kalman–Yakubovich equation), solutions to the corresponding NSEs are obtained.

Different from the cases of GSEs and rectangular NSEs, for a square NSE, it is important to know when it possesses a unique solution. The general condition can be unified as follows for all different square NSEs:

$$\det \pi (F) \neq 0.$$

More explicitly, the condition can be equivalently replaced by (9.9), which clearly reduces to those listed in Table 9.3 for the other special types of NSEs.

Regarding the proposed solutions, they are all in simple analytical closedforms. Particularly, the solutions of the various NSEs with a diagonal matrix F turn out to be extremely simple and neat. More importantly, it can be easily observed that the

Table 9.2   Characteristic Polynomial Matrix

Name	Equation	Characteristic Polynomial Matrix
Higher-order NSE	(1.74)/(9.1)	$A(s)$
Second-order NSE	(1.76)/(9.18)	$Ms^2 + Ds + K$
First-order NSE	(1.77)/(9.17)	$sE - A$
First-order NSE	(1.78)/(9.25)	$sI + A$
Lyapunov equation	(1.79)/(9.26)	$sI + F^{\mathrm{T}}$
K-Y equation	(1.80)/(9.30)	$sE - I$
Stein equation	(1.81)/(9.37)	$sF^{\mathrm{T}} - I$

Table 9.3 Condition for Existence and Uniqueness of Solutions

Name	Equation	Existence and Uniqueness of Solution
Higher-order NSE	(1.74)/(9.1)	$\{s\mid \det A(s) = 0\} \cap \mathrm{eig}(F) = \varnothing$
Second-order NSE	(1.76)/(9.18)	$\{s\mid \det\left(Ms^2 + Ds + K\right) = 0\} \cap \mathrm{eig}(F) = \varnothing$
First-order NSE	(1.77)/(9.17)	$\{s\mid \det(sE - A) = 0\} \cap \mathrm{eig}(F) = \varnothing$
First-order NSE	(1.78)/(9.25)	$\{s\mid \det(sI + A) = 0\} \cap \mathrm{eig}(F) = \varnothing$
Lyapunov equation	(1.79)/(9.26)	$\mathrm{eig}(-F) \cap \mathrm{eig}(F) = \varnothing$
K-Y equation	(1.80)/(9.30)	$\lambda(E)\lambda(F) \neq 1$
Stein equation	(1.81)/(9.37)	$\lambda^{-1} \notin \mathrm{eig}(F),\ \forall \lambda \in \mathrm{eig}(F)$

solutions are explicit and linear with respect to the matrix W. This property allows us to set the matrix W undetermined and used as a design parameter in many analysis and design problems. Moreover, the linearity relation provides great convenience in many applications, especially for those involving optimizations.

Clearly, the proposed solutions involve the determinants and the adjoint matrices of the characteristic polynomial matrices associated with these equations. We remark that for all the first-order cases the well-known Leverrier algorithm can be readily applied to obtain the determinants and adjoint matrices.

To conclude this subsection, let us point out that the results in this chapter can also be easily obtained by specifying the results about nonhomogeneous GSEs proposed in Chapter 5.

9.6.2 Existing Solutions

Regarding existing solutions to square NSEs, we would like first to mention the preliminary paper, Duan (2005a), which has given a systematic discussion on solutions to both GSEs and square NSEs.

9.6.2.1 NSEs

For solutions to the NSEs (1.74) through (1.78), except a few studies, for example, Duan (2005a), almost all of the results are focused on the first-order ones (1.77) and (1.78), while little attention has been given to the second-order equation (1.76) or (9.18), and higher-order equation (1.74) or (9.1).

As is well known, the NSEs (1.77) and (1.78) have important applications in stability analysis and eigenvalue assignment in linear descriptor and normal systems (Brierley and Lee 1984, Lewis and Mertzios 1987). For solutions to equations (1.77) and (1.78), there have been some numerical computational algorithms, for example, Golub et al. (1979) and Lewis and Mertzios (1987).

Equation (1.77) is a more generalized form of the usual NSE (1.78), but it is not studied as widely as (1.78) in the literature. Lewis and Mertzios (1987) have used this equation in the analysis of singular systems and proposed a generalized Bartels–Stewart algorithm for its solution using the QZ algorithm. Beitia and Gracia (1994) give topological properties of a matrix equation of the type of (1.77). This equation is related to the block similarity between rectangular matrices, and the passage matrices in this equivalence relation are solutions. A local criterion for that similarity is exposed. The points of continuity of the map that associates with the coefficient matrices and the solution space of that equation are determined. Furthermore, Ramadan et al. (2010) propose a Hessenberg method for the numerical solutions to types of block Sylvester matrix equation, which utilizes the technique consisting of orthogonal reduction of the matrix A to a block upper Hessenberg form.

Feng Ding and his coauthors have proposed several iterative algorithms for solving Sylvester-like equations (see Ding and Chen 2005a, Ding et al. 2008, Xie et al. 2009). Particularly, Ding and Chen (2005a) propose gradient based iterative algorithms for solving the Sylvester and Lyapunov matrix equations by minimizing certain criterion functions. Ding et al. (2008) propose a gradient based and a least-squares based iterative algorithms for the solutions of the generalized Sylvester matrix equation

$$AXB + CXD = F \tag{9.97}$$

by using the hierarchical identification principle. While Xie et al. (2009) propose by extending the Jacobi iteration and by applying the hierarchical identification principle a gradient-based iterative algorithm for solving a group of linear matrix equations that include some Sylvester- and Lyapunov-types equations. Furthermore, they have also studied solutions to coupled Sylvester matrix equations. Specifically, Zhang and Ding (2014) present a family of iterative algorithms coupled Sylvester matrix equations using some property of the eigenvalues of symmetric positive definite matrices. Ding and Chen (2005b) propose by applying a hierarchical identification principle and by introducing the block-matrix inner product a general family of iterative methods to solve coupled Sylvester matrix equations, which includes the well-known Jacobi and Gauss–Seidel iterations as its special cases. While Ding and Chen (2006) extend the well-known Jacobi and Gauss–Seidel iterations and present a large family of iterative methods, which are applied to develop iterative solutions to coupled Sylvester matrix equations.

For explicit solutions, perhaps the most well-known ones are the integral forms in Lewis and Mertzios (1987) of the unique solution to equation (1.78). For the NSE (1.78), Ma (1966) has provided an explicit solution in the form of finite double matrix series for the case of A and F being both Jordan forms, while Kucera (1974) has presented for this equation another general solution in the form of $V = YX^{-1}$ with the columns of the matrices Y and X being the eigenvectors of a certain composite matrix associated with the eigenvalues of the matrix F. Some most up-to-date results on this equation can be found in Bouhamidi et al. (2013), Chen and Lu (2013), Flagg and Gugercin (2013), and Kuzmanovic and Truhar (2013). Besides these Duan and Patton (1998c) propose new analytical solutions to both the two equations (1.77) and (1.78) for the case that the matrix F is in a Jordan form.

For the higher-order NSE (1.74), Lin (2005) proposes the implicitly restarted global full orthogonalization method (FOM) and generalized minimum residual method (GMRES) algorithms, and proves that global GMRES and global FOM methods for matrix equations are equivalent with the corresponding methods for linear equations and proposed implicitly restarted global FOM and GMRES.

Two Iranian scholars, Dehghan Mehdi and Masoud Hajarian, have done tremendous amount of work on this aspect. They have given iterative algorithms for symmetric and/or reflexive solutions of many types of generalized Kalman–Yakubovich type equations, including single univariable ones (Dehghan and Hajarian 2011b,c,f, 2012a), coupled univariable ones (Dehghan and Hajarian 2011d, 2012c, 2013, 2014), single multivariable ones (Dehghan and Hajarian 2011e) and coupled multivariable ones (Dehghan and Hajarian 2008b, 2010a,b,c,d, 2011a, 2012b,d).

9.6.2.2 Lyapunov Matrix Equations

We have to mention that the Lyapunov matrix equations (1.79) and (1.81) have attracted so much attention ever since the 1960s that there have been numerous reported results. For a detailed discussion on these equations, reader can further refer to the book Gajic and Qureshi (2008).

It is seen from Chapter 1 that the Lyapunov matrix equations (1.79) and (1.81) are actually special forms of the NSE (1.77) and are the most simple ones in the Sylvester family.

For solutions to the continuous-time Lyapunov matrix equation in the form of (1.79), and the discrete-time Lyapunov matrix equation in the form of (1.81), there have been quite some numerical computational algorithms, for example, Hoskins et al. (1977), Barraud (1977), Berger (1971), and Jbilou et al. (1999). Particularly, we have presented a finite iterative algorithm for solving coupled Lyapunov equations appearing in discrete-time Markov jump linear systems (Tong et al. 2010), and also have given Smith-type iterative algorithms for Stein matrix equation (Zhou et al. 2009c).

For explicit solutions, perhaps the most well-known ones are the integral forms in Brockett (1970) of the unique solution to equation (1.79), and the matrix power form in Young (1980) of the unique solution to equation (1.81). For the continuous-time Lyapunov matrix equation (1.79), Ziedan (1972) has also proposed an explicit solution in the form of a summation of n matrices with each term a function of the matrices F and W as well as elements of the related Schwarz form, and Mori et al. (1986) also propose an explicit solution to equation (1.79), but in terms of the controllability matrix of (F, G), with G being the square root of the matrix W, which is assumed to be positive semi-definite. For the discrete-time Lyapunov matrix equation (1.81), Bitmead and Weiss (1979) and Ptak (1981) both have considered the case that the matrix F is in companion form and

$$W = \text{diag}\,(0, \ldots 0, 1),\qquad(9.98)$$

and proved that solution to this equation is the inverse of the Schur–Cohn matrix corresponding to the characteristic polynomial of the matrix F. While Young (1980) has obtained an explicit solution for the case that the matrix F is also in the companion form but with W in the form of (9.98), and also presented an algorithm for the general case based on this explicit solution. Besides these, Duan and Patton (1998b) propose new analytical solutions to both the two equations (1.79) and (1.81) for the case that the matrix F is in Jordan form.

Finally, we mention that the author and his coauthors, for example, Wu et al. (2009b), Wu et al. (2006a), and Wu et al. (2009d), have given solutions to the Lyapunov-like conjugate matrix equations. Specifically, Wu et al. (2009b) give loosed-form solutions to the nonhomogeneous Yakubovich-conjugate matrix equation, Wu et al. (2006a) propose solutions to the matrix equations

$$XF - AX = C$$

and

$$XF - A\bar{X} = C,$$

while Wu et al. (2009d) further generalize the results to the case of

$$X - AXF = C$$

and

$$X - A\bar{X}F = C.$$

Similar to these results, Song and Feng (2014) have presented explicit solution to the Kalman–Yakubovich-transpose equation

$$X - AX^T B = C,$$

and the Sylvester-conjugate matrix equation (Song et al. 2014d)

$$AX - \bar{X}B = C.$$

Also, Song et al. (2014a) have provided finite iterative method for solving coupled Sylvester-transpose matrix equations by extending the idea of conjugate gradient method.

Appendix A: Proofs of Theorems

A.1 Proof of Theorem 3.6

A.1.1 Preliminary Lemma

To prove this theorem, the following lemma is needed.

Lemma A.1 *Let λ be a scalar,*

$$E = \begin{bmatrix} 0 & 1 & & \\ & 0 & \ddots & \\ & & \ddots & 1 \\ & & & 0 \end{bmatrix}_{q \times q} = \begin{bmatrix} 0 & I_{q-1} \\ 0 & 0 \end{bmatrix}_{q \times q},$$

and

$$J = \lambda I_q + E.$$

Then,

1. *The matrix E is a nilpotent matrix of order q, and*

$$E^k = \begin{bmatrix} 0 & I_{q-k} \\ 0 & 0 \end{bmatrix}, \qquad (A.1)$$

2. *The matrix J is a Jordan block of order q, and*

$$J^k = \sum_{j=0}^{k} \lambda^{k-j} C_k^j E_i^j, \qquad (A.2)$$

$$= \lambda^k I_q + \lambda^{k-1} C_k^1 E^1 + \cdots + \lambda C_k^k E^k. \qquad (A.3)$$

Proof. Denote by e_i the vector with the ith element being 1 while all the other ones being zeros. Then it is easy to show

$$e_i^T E = e_{i+1}^T.$$

Using this relation, we have

$$\begin{cases} e_i^T E^2 = e_{i+1}^T E = e_{i+2}^T \\ e_i^T E^3 = e_{i+2}^T E = e_{i+3}^T \\ \vdots \\ e_i^T E^k = e_{i+k-1}^T E = e_{i+k}^T \end{cases} \tag{A.4}$$

Further, note that

$$E = \begin{bmatrix} e_2^T \\ e_3^T \\ \vdots \\ e_q^T \\ 0_{1 \times q} \end{bmatrix}, \quad \begin{bmatrix} 0 & I_{q-k} \\ 0 & 0 \end{bmatrix}_{q \times q} = \begin{bmatrix} e_{k+1}^T \\ e_{k+2}^T \\ \vdots \\ e_q^T \\ 0_{k \times q} \end{bmatrix},$$

we thus have, using the equations in (A.4),

$$E^k = E E^{k-1} = \begin{bmatrix} e_2^T E^{k-1} \\ e_3^T E^{k-1} \\ \vdots \\ e_q^T E^{k-1} \\ 0_{1 \times q} \end{bmatrix} = \begin{bmatrix} e_{k+1}^T \\ e_{k+2}^T \\ \vdots \\ e_q^T \\ 0_{k \times q} \end{bmatrix} = \begin{bmatrix} 0 & I_{q-k} \\ 0 & 0 \end{bmatrix}_{q \times q}.$$

Hence, the first conclusion holds.

Using the Binomial Theorem, we have

$$J^k = \left(\lambda I_q + E \right)^k$$

$$= \sum_{j=0}^{k} C_k^{k-j} \left(\lambda I_q \right)^j E^{k-j}.$$

This clearly gives (A.2). ▪

A.1.2 Proof of Theorem 3.6

With the help of Lemma A.1, we can now prove Theorem 3.6.

Let the Jordan form of the matrix F be as follows:

$$\begin{cases} J = \text{blockdiag}\,(J_1, J_2, \ldots, J_w) \\ J_i = \begin{bmatrix} s_i & 1 & & \\ & s_i & \ddots & \\ & & \ddots & 1 \\ & & & s_i \end{bmatrix}_{p_i \times p_i} \end{cases},$$

where $s_i, i = 1, 2, \ldots, w$, are obviously the eigenvalues of the matrix F (which are not necessarily distinct). Further, let the corresponding eigenvector matrix of F be P, then we have

$$F = PJP^{-1}. \tag{A.5}$$

Substituting equation (A.5) into the left-hand side of (3.40) yields

$$\sum_{i=0}^{\omega} \left(F^i \otimes \begin{bmatrix} N_i \\ D_i \end{bmatrix} \right)$$

$$= \sum_{i=0}^{\omega} \left((PJP^{-1})^i \otimes \begin{bmatrix} N_i \\ D_i \end{bmatrix} \right)$$

$$= (P \otimes I_{n+r}) \sum_{i=0}^{\omega} \left(J^i \otimes \begin{bmatrix} N_i \\ D_i \end{bmatrix} \right) (P^{-1} \otimes I_r).$$

Since $P \otimes I_{n+r}$ and $P^{-1} \otimes I_r$ are nonsingular, we have

$$\text{rank} \left[\sum_{i=0}^{\omega} F^i \otimes \begin{bmatrix} N_i \\ D_i \end{bmatrix} \right]$$

$$= \text{rank} \sum_{i=0}^{\omega} \left(J^i \otimes \begin{bmatrix} N_i \\ D_i \end{bmatrix} \right)$$

$$= \sum_{j=1}^{w} \text{rank} \left[\sum_{i=0}^{\omega} J_j^i \otimes \begin{bmatrix} N_i \\ D_i \end{bmatrix} \right]. \tag{A.6}$$

Define a nilpotent matrix

$$E_j = \begin{bmatrix} 0 & I_{p_j-1} \\ 0 & 0 \end{bmatrix}_{p_j \times p_j}, \quad j = 1, 2, \ldots, w,$$

then we have

$$J_j = s_j I_{p_j} + E_j, \quad j = 1, 2, \ldots, w,$$

and following Lemma A.1, we further have

$$E_j^l = \begin{bmatrix} 0 & I_{p_j - l} \\ 0 & 0 \end{bmatrix} \tag{A.7}$$

and

$$J_j^i = s_j^i I_{p_j} + s_j^{i-1} C_i^1 E_j^1 + \cdots + s_j^0 C_i^i E_j^i. \tag{A.8}$$

Using the above relation, we have

$$\sum_{i=0}^{\omega} \left(J_j^i \otimes \begin{bmatrix} N_i \\ D_i \end{bmatrix} \right)$$

$$= \sum_{i=0}^{\omega} \left(s_j^i I_{p_j} + s_j^{i-1} C_i^1 E_j^1 + \cdots + s_j^0 C_i^i E_j^i \right) \otimes \begin{bmatrix} N_i \\ D_i \end{bmatrix}$$

$$= \sum_{i=0}^{\omega} \left(s_j^i I_{p_j} C_i^0 \otimes \begin{bmatrix} N_i \\ D_i \end{bmatrix} \right)$$

$$+ \sum_{i=0}^{\omega-1} \left(s_j^i E_j^1 C_{i+1}^1 \otimes \begin{bmatrix} N_{i+1} \\ D_{i+1} \end{bmatrix} \right)$$

$$+ \cdots + \sum_{i=0}^{1} \left(s_j^i E_j^{\omega-1} C_{i+\omega-1}^{\omega-1} \otimes \begin{bmatrix} N_{i+\omega-1} \\ D_{i+\omega-1} \end{bmatrix} \right)$$

$$+ \sum_{i=0}^{0} \left(s_j^i E_j^\omega C_{i+\omega}^\omega \otimes \begin{bmatrix} N_{i+\omega} \\ D_{i+\omega} \end{bmatrix} \right).$$

If we denote

$$\theta_j^{\omega-k} = \sum_{i=0}^{k} \left(s_j^i C_{i+\omega-k}^{\omega-k} \begin{bmatrix} N_{i+\omega-k} \\ D_{i+\omega-k} \end{bmatrix} \right), \tag{A.9}$$

$$k = 0, \ldots, \omega,$$

then the above equation can be simplified to

$$\sum_{i=0}^{\omega}\left(J_j^i \otimes \begin{bmatrix} N_i \\ D_i \end{bmatrix}\right)$$

$$= I_{P_j} \otimes \theta_j^0 + \cdots + E_j^{\omega} \otimes \theta_j^{\omega}$$

$$= \begin{bmatrix} \theta_j^0 & \theta_j^1 & \cdots & \theta_j^{\omega} & 0 & \cdots & 0 \\ & \theta_j^0 & \theta_j^1 & \ddots & \ddots & \ddots & \vdots \\ & & \theta_j^0 & \ddots & \ddots & \ddots & 0 \\ & & & \ddots & \ddots & \ddots & \theta_j^{\omega} \\ & & & & \theta_j^0 & \theta_j^1 & \vdots \\ & & & & & \theta_j^0 & \theta_j^1 \\ & & & & & & \theta_j^0 \end{bmatrix}, \tag{A.10}$$

which gives

$$\text{rank} \sum_{i=0}^{\omega}\left(J_j^i \otimes \begin{bmatrix} N_i \\ D_i \end{bmatrix}\right) = p_j \text{rank} \theta_j^0. \tag{A.11}$$

From (A.9) and (3.39) we can get

$$\theta_j^0 = \sum_{i=0}^{k} s_j^i \begin{bmatrix} N_i \\ D_i \end{bmatrix} = \begin{bmatrix} N(s_j) \\ D(s_j) \end{bmatrix}.$$

Therefore, it follows from the above relation and (A.11) that

$$\text{rank} \begin{bmatrix} N(s_j) \\ D(s_j) \end{bmatrix} = \alpha, \tag{A.12}$$

if and only if

$$\text{rank} \sum_{i=0}^{\omega}\left(J_j^i \otimes \begin{bmatrix} N_i \\ D_i \end{bmatrix}\right) = \alpha p_j.$$

Further, in view of (A.6), the above is easily seen to be equivalent to

$$\text{rank} \left[\sum_{i=0}^{\omega} F^i \otimes \begin{bmatrix} N_i \\ D_i \end{bmatrix}\right] = \sum_{j=1}^{w} \alpha p_j = \alpha p.$$

Therefore, (A.12) holds for $j = 1, 2, \ldots, w$, if and only if (3.40) holds. Further recall that s_j, $j = 1, 2, \ldots, w$, are the eigenvalues of matrix F, the conclusion clearly follows.

A.2 Proof of Theorem 3.13

In order to prove this theorem, we need several preliminary lemmas.

A.2.1 Preliminary Lemmas

Firstly, due to this controllability condition (3.85), we have the following result.

Lemma A.2 *Let $A(s) \in \mathbb{R}^{n \times q}[s]$, $B(s) \in \mathbb{R}^{n \times r}[s]$, be two polynomial matrices satisfying the controllability condition (3.85). Given the SVDs of $\begin{bmatrix} A(s_i) & -B(s_i) \end{bmatrix}$ in (3.92) for an arbitrary group of $s_i \in \mathbb{C}$, $i = 0, 1, 2, \ldots, N$, then,*

$$\det \Sigma_i = \sigma_{i1} \sigma_{i2} \cdots \sigma_{in} = constant, \tag{A.13}$$

$$i = 0, 1, 2, \ldots, N.$$

Proof. Define

$$Z(s) = [A(s) \quad B(s)] \begin{bmatrix} A^{\mathrm{T}}(s) \\ B^{\mathrm{T}}(s) \end{bmatrix},$$

then, in view of the controllability condition (3.85), we have

$$\det Z(s) \neq 0, \quad \forall s \in \mathbb{C}.$$

Therefore, $Z(s)$ is a unimodular matrix, and there exists a nonzero constant C such that

$$\det Z(s) = C \neq 0, \quad \forall s \in \mathbb{C}. \tag{A.14}$$

On the other hand, according to the definition of singular values, we know that $\sigma_{i1}, \sigma_{i2}, \ldots, \sigma_{in}$ are the eigenvalues of $Z(s_i)$, thus we have

$$\det Z(s) = \sigma_{i1} \sigma_{i2} \cdots \sigma_{in}.$$

Combining this with (A.14) gives (A.13). ■

Secondly, let us state without proofs the following two results which perform an important role in the proof of the theorem.

Lemma A.3 *Let $X(s) \in \mathbb{R}^{q \times r}[s]$ be a real-coefficient polynomial matrix of order n. If for a sufficiently large N there hold*

$$X(s_i) = 0, \quad i = 0, 1, 2, \ldots, N, \tag{A.15}$$

for a group of distinct complex numbers s_i, $i = 0, 1, 2, \ldots, N$, then

$$X(s) = 0, \; \forall s \in \mathbb{C}.$$

Lemma A.4 *Let $X(s) \in \mathbb{R}^{r \times r}[s]$ be a real-coefficient polynomial matrix of order n. If for an integer $N \geq nr$, there hold*

$$\det X(s_i) = C, \quad i = 0, 1, 2, \ldots, N, \quad\quad\quad (A.16)$$

for a group of distinct complex numbers s_i, $i = 0, 1, 2, \ldots, N$, then

$$\det X(s) = C, \; \forall s \in \mathbb{C}.$$

A.2.2 Proof of Theorem 3.13

Firstly, let us show that $P(s)$ and $Q(s)$ satisfy the relation (3.86).
  With the obtained polynomial matrices $P(s)$ and $Q(s)$, the relations in (3.95) hold. Thus we have

$$P(s_i) \begin{bmatrix} A(s_i) & -B(s_i) \end{bmatrix} Q(s_i) = \Sigma_i^{-1} U_i \begin{bmatrix} A(s_i) & -B(s_i) \end{bmatrix} V_i, \quad\quad (A.17)$$
$$i = 0, 1, 2, \ldots, N.$$

Let

$$R(s) = P(s) \begin{bmatrix} A(s) & -B(s) \end{bmatrix} Q(s) - \begin{bmatrix} I_n & 0 \end{bmatrix},$$

then we have

$$\begin{aligned} R(s_i) &= P(s_i) \begin{bmatrix} A(s_i) & -B(s_i) \end{bmatrix} Q(s_i) - \begin{bmatrix} I_n & 0 \end{bmatrix} \\ &= \Sigma_i^{-1} U_i \begin{bmatrix} A(s_i) & -B(s_i) \end{bmatrix} V_i - \begin{bmatrix} I_n & 0 \end{bmatrix} \\ &= 0, \quad i = 0, 1, 2, \ldots, N. \end{aligned}$$

Therefore, it follows from Lemma A.3 that, when N is sufficiently large, the above relations imply $R(s) = 0$, which gives equation (3.86). Furthermore, it can be easily understood that the uniqueness of $P(s)$ and $Q(s)$ are guaranteed by the second conclusion of Theorem 3.12.
  Secondly, let us show the unimodularity of $Q(s)$.
  Recall again that

$$Q(s_i) = V_i, \quad i = 0, 1, 2, \ldots, N.$$

Thus we have, in view of (3.104),

$$\det Q\,(s_i) = \det V_i = 1,$$
$$i = 0, 1, 2, \ldots, N.$$

Therefore, it follows from Lemma A.4 that, when N is sufficiently large, we have

$$\det Q\,(s) = 1, \quad \forall s \in \mathbb{C}.$$

Finally, let us prove the unimodularity of $P\,(s)$.
  Since

$$P\,(s_i) = \Sigma_i U_i, \quad i = 0, 1, 2, \ldots, N,$$

we have, in view of (3.104),

$$\det P\,(s_i) = \det \Sigma_i, \quad i = 0, 1, 2, \ldots, N.$$

Further, using Lemma A.2, we get

$$\det P\,(s_i) = \det \Sigma_i = C,$$
$$i = 0, 1, 2, \ldots, N.$$

Therefore, it follows from Lemma A.4 that, when N is sufficiently large, we have

$$\det P\,(s) = C, \quad \forall s \in \mathbb{C}.$$

This indicates that the polynomial matrix $P\,(s)$ is unimodular.

A.3 Proof of Theorem 4.1

A.3.1 Proof of Conclusion 1

By definition, and using the commutativity of F and G, we have

$$
\begin{aligned}
\left[P\,(s)\,ZG\right]\big|_F &= \sum_{i=0}^{k} P_i ZGF^i \\
&= \sum_{i=0}^{k} P_i ZF^i G \\
&= \left[P\,(s)\,Z\right]\big|_F\, G.
\end{aligned}
$$

This is the conclusion.

A.3.2 Proof of Conclusion 2

Sufficiency. Let (4.7) hold, then for arbitrary $F \in \mathbb{C}^{p \times p}$ we have

$$P_i Z F^i = 0, \quad i = 0, 1, \ldots, k, \tag{A.18}$$

which gives

$$[P(s) Z]\big|_F = \sum_{i=0}^{k} P_i Z F^i = 0.$$

Necessity. Let (4.5) hold for arbitrary $F \in \mathbb{C}^{p \times p}$, that is,

$$\sum_{i=0}^{l} P_i Z F^i = 0, \quad \forall F \in \mathbb{C}^{p \times p}.$$

Choosing a series of matrices $F_j \in \mathbb{R}^{p \times p}$, $j = 0, 1, \ldots, k$, which are mutually commutative and do not have common eigenvalues, then we have

$$\sum_{i=0}^{k} P_i Z F_j^i = 0, \quad j = 0, 1, \ldots, k.$$

This set of equations can be written compactly as

$$[P_0 Z \ \ P_1 Z \ \cdots \ P_k Z] \, V(F_0, F_1, \ldots, F_k) = 0, \tag{A.19}$$

where $V(F_0, F_1, \ldots, F_k)$ is the generalized Vandermonde matrix formed by $F_j \in \mathbb{R}^{p \times p}, j = 0, 1, \ldots, k$, that is,

$$V(F_0, F_1, \ldots, F_k) = \begin{bmatrix} I_p & I_p & I_p & \cdots & I_p \\ F_0 & F_1 & F_2 & \cdots & F_k \\ F_0^2 & F_1^2 & F_2^2 & \cdots & F_k^2 \\ \vdots & \vdots & \vdots & \vdots & \vdots \\ F_0^k & F_1^k & F_2^k & \cdots & F_k^k \end{bmatrix}.$$

Note that $\det V(F_0, F_1, \ldots, F_k) \neq 0$ due to the choices of $F_j \in \mathbb{R}^{p \times p}, j = 0, 1, \ldots, k$ (Duan and Yuan (1991)), equation (A.19) clearly implies (4.7).

A.3.3 Proof of Conclusion 3

Denote

$$Q(s) = \sum_{i=0}^{\beta} Q_i s^i,$$

thus, by definition, we have

$$[Q(s)X]|_F = \sum_{i=0}^{\beta} Q_i XF^i.$$

Thus,

$$[P(s)[Q(s)X]|_F]|_F = \sum_{i=0}^{k} P_i[Q(s)X]|_F F^i$$

$$= \sum_{i=0}^{k} P_i \left(\sum_{j=0}^{\beta} Q_j XF^j \right) F^i$$

$$= \sum_{i=0}^{k} \sum_{j=0}^{\beta} P_i Q_j XF^{i+j}.$$

On the other hand,

$$[P(s)Q(s)X]|_F = \left[\left(\sum_{i=0}^{k} P_i s^i \sum_{j=0}^{\beta} Q_j s^j \right) X \right]\Bigg|_F$$

$$= \left[\left(\sum_{i=0}^{k} \sum_{j=0}^{\beta} P_i Q_j s^{i+j} \right) X \right]\Bigg|_F$$

$$= \sum_{i=0}^{m} \sum_{j=0}^{\beta} P_i Q_j XF^{i+j}.$$

Comparing the above two relations immediately gives the equation (4.8).

A.3.4 Proof of Conclusion 4

Let $P(s)$ be given as in (4.1), and denote

$$\tilde{P}(s) = \sum_{i=0}^{\beta} \tilde{P}_i s^i.$$

Then there holds

$$\left[P(s)Z + \tilde{P}(s)\tilde{Z} \right]\Big|_F = \left[\sum_{i=0}^{k} P_i Z^i + \sum_{i=0}^{\beta} \tilde{P}_i \tilde{Z} s^i \right]\Bigg|_F. \tag{A.20}$$

Denote

$$\gamma = \max\{k, \beta\},$$

and define

$$P_i = 0, \quad k < i \leq \gamma, \tag{A.21}$$
$$\tilde{P}_i = 0, \quad \beta < i \leq \gamma. \tag{A.22}$$

Then from (A.20) we have

$$
\begin{aligned}
\left[P(s)Z + \tilde{P}(s)\tilde{Z} \right]\Big|_F &= \left[\sum_{i=0}^{\gamma} \left(P_i Z + \tilde{P}_i \tilde{Z} \right) s^i \right]\Big|_F \\
&= \sum_{i=0}^{\gamma} \left(P_i Z + \tilde{P}_i \tilde{Z} \right) F^i \\
&= \sum_{i=0}^{\gamma} \left(P_i Z F^i + \tilde{P}_i \tilde{Z} F^i \right) \\
&= \sum_{i=0}^{k} P_i Z F^i + \sum_{i=0}^{\beta} \tilde{P}_i \tilde{Z} F^i \\
&= [P(s)Z]\Big|_F + \left[\tilde{P}(s)\tilde{Z} \right]\Big|_F.
\end{aligned}
$$

This gives equation (4.9).

Again, using (A.20) through (A.22) gives

$$
\begin{aligned}
\left[P(s)Z + \tilde{P}(s)\tilde{Z} \right]\Big|_F &= \left[\sum_{i=0}^{\gamma} \left(P_i Z + \tilde{P}_i \tilde{Z} \right) s^i \right]\Big|_F \\
&= \sum_{i=0}^{\gamma} \left(P_i Z + \tilde{P}_i \tilde{Z} \right) F^i \\
&= \sum_{i=0}^{\gamma} \left[\, P_i \quad \tilde{P}_i \,\right] \left[\begin{array}{c} Z \\ \tilde{Z} \end{array} \right] F^i \\
&= [R(s) Z_e]\Big|_F.
\end{aligned}
$$

Thus equation (4.10) is also proven.

A.4 Proofs of Theorems 4.2, 4.4, and 4.6

For an $m \times n$ dimensional matrix $R = [r_{ij}]$, the so-called stretching function $\text{vec}(R)$ is defined as

$$\text{vec}(R) = \begin{bmatrix} r_{11} & r_{21} & \cdots & r_{m1} & \cdots & r_{1n} & r_{2n} & \cdots & r_{mn} \end{bmatrix}^{\mathrm{T}}.$$

Regarding the stretching operation, we have the following well-known result.

Lemma A.5 *Let $M, X,$ and N be matrices with appropriate dimensions, then*

$$\text{vec}(MXN) = \left(N^{\mathrm{T}} \otimes M\right) \text{vec}(X). \tag{A.23}$$

Putting $\text{vec}(\cdot)$ on both sides of the homogeneous GSE (4.50) and using (A.23), we obtain

$$\begin{bmatrix} \Phi & \Psi \end{bmatrix} \begin{bmatrix} \text{vec}(V) \\ \text{vec}(W) \end{bmatrix} = 0, \tag{A.24}$$

where

$$\begin{cases} \Phi = \sum_{i=0}^{m} \left(F^{\mathrm{T}}\right)^{i} \otimes A_{i} \\ \Psi = -\sum_{i=0}^{m-1} \left(F^{\mathrm{T}}\right)^{i} \otimes B_{i}. \end{cases} \tag{A.25}$$

Clearly, this is an equivalent form of equation (4.50). Let P and J be the eigenvector matrix and the Jordan form of matrix F^{T}, respectively. Then we have

$$F^{\mathrm{T}} = PJP^{-1}. \tag{A.26}$$

Substituting (A.26) into (A.25) yields

$$\Phi = P \otimes I_{n} \left(\sum_{i=0}^{m} J^{i} \otimes A_{i}\right) Q,$$

$$\Psi = -P \otimes I_{n} \left(\sum_{i=0}^{m} J^{i} \otimes B_{i}\right) Q,$$

with

$$Q = \begin{bmatrix} P^{-1} \otimes I_n & 0 \\ 0 & -P^{-1} \otimes I_r \end{bmatrix}.$$

Noting that $P \otimes I_n$ and Q are both nonsingular, we have

$$\mathrm{rank}\Phi = \mathrm{rank}\left(\sum_{i=0}^{m} J^i \otimes A_i\right)$$

$$= \mathrm{rank}\begin{bmatrix} A(s_1) & * & 0 & 0 \\ 0 & A(s_2) & \ddots & 0 \\ \vdots & & \ddots & \ddots & * \\ 0 & & \cdots & 0 & A(s_p) \end{bmatrix},$$

and

$$\mathrm{rank}\Psi = \mathrm{rank}\left(\sum_{i=0}^{m} J^i \otimes B_i\right)$$

$$= \mathrm{rank}\begin{bmatrix} B(s_1) & * & 0 & 0 \\ 0 & B(s_2) & \ddots & 0 \\ \vdots & & \ddots & \ddots & * \\ 0 & & \cdots & 0 & B(s_p) \end{bmatrix},$$

where the terms denoted by $*$ may be zero and s_i, $i = 1, 2, \ldots, p$, are the eigenvalues of matrix F (not necessarily distinct). Using the above two relations, we clearly have

$$\mathrm{rank}\begin{bmatrix} \Phi & \Psi \end{bmatrix} = \mathrm{rank}\begin{bmatrix} \Omega(s_1) & * & 0 & 0 \\ 0 & \Omega(s_2) & \ddots & 0 \\ \vdots & & \ddots & \ddots & * \\ 0 & & \cdots & 0 & \Omega(s_p) \end{bmatrix}, \qquad (A.27)$$

where

$$\Omega(s) = \begin{bmatrix} A(s) & B(s) \end{bmatrix}.$$

It thus follows from the above relation that

$$\mathrm{rank}\Phi = \alpha p \qquad (A.28)$$

if and only if (4.53) holds.

When (A.28) holds, according to linear equation theory the maximum number of free parameters in the solution (V, W) to equation (A.24), hence (4.50), is

$$\pi = np + rp - \text{rank}\begin{bmatrix} \Phi & \Psi \end{bmatrix} = \beta p.$$

With this we also complete the proof of the second part of the conclusion.

A.5 Proofs of Theorems 4.3, 4.5, and 4.7

The proofs of the sufficient parts of these theorems have been given in Chapter 4. The necessity parts of these theorems are the same and given below.

In order to prove the second conclusions in Theorems 4.3, 4.5, and 4.7, putting $\text{vec}(\cdot)$ on both sides of (4.59) and using the equation (A.23), we obtain

$$\begin{cases} \text{vec}(V) = \left[\sum_{i=0}^{\omega} \left((F^T)^i \otimes N_i \right) \right] \text{vec}(Z) \\ \text{vec}(W) = \left[\sum_{i=0}^{\omega} \left((F^T)^i \otimes D_i \right) \right] \text{vec}(Z), \end{cases}$$

or equivalently,

$$\begin{bmatrix} \text{vec}(V) \\ \text{vec}(W) \end{bmatrix} = \begin{bmatrix} \sum_{i=0}^{\omega} \left((F^T)^i \otimes N_i \right) \\ \sum_{i=0}^{\omega} \left((F^T)^i \otimes D_i \right) \end{bmatrix} \text{vec}(Z). \tag{A.29}$$

According to Theorem 4.6, the number of free parameters of the solution (V, W) is βp. Recalling the fact that $Z \in \mathbb{C}^{\beta \times p}$ is an arbitrary parameter matrix, we need only to validate that each element in Z contributes independently to (V, W) if and only if the condition (3.33) holds. It follows from (A.29) that each element in Z contributes independently to (V, W) if and only if

$$\text{rank} \begin{bmatrix} \sum_{i=0}^{\omega} \left((F^T)^i \otimes N_i \right) \\ \sum_{i=0}^{\omega} \left((F^T)^i \otimes D_i \right) \end{bmatrix} = \beta p. \tag{A.30}$$

Therefore, in the following we suffice only to show that (A.30) holds if and only if $N(s)$ and $D(s)$ are F-right coprime with rank α.

By the definition of Kronecker product, we have

$$
\text{rank}
\begin{bmatrix}
\sum\limits_{i=0}^{\omega} \left((F^{\mathrm{T}})^i \otimes N_i \right) \\[2mm]
\sum\limits_{i=0}^{\omega} \left((F^{\mathrm{T}})^i \otimes D_i \right)
\end{bmatrix}
$$

$$
= \text{rank}
\begin{bmatrix}
\sum\limits_{i=0}^{\omega}
\begin{bmatrix}
(F^{\mathrm{T}})^i_{11} N_i & \cdots & (F^{\mathrm{T}})^i_{1p} N_i \\
\vdots & \ddots & \vdots \\
(F^{\mathrm{T}})^i_{p1} N_i & \cdots & (F^{\mathrm{T}})^i_{pp} N_i
\end{bmatrix} \\[4mm]
\sum\limits_{i=0}^{\omega}
\begin{bmatrix}
(F^{\mathrm{T}})^i_{11} D_i & \cdots & (F^{\mathrm{T}})^i_{1p} D_i \\
\vdots & \ddots & \vdots \\
(F^{\mathrm{T}})^i_{p1} D_i & \cdots & (F^{\mathrm{T}})^i_{pp} D_i
\end{bmatrix}
\end{bmatrix}.
$$

where $(F^{\mathrm{T}})^i_{kj}$ denotes the element in the kth row and jth column of the matrix $(F^{\mathrm{T}})^i$.
By exchanging certain rows of the matrix in the above equation, we further get

$$
\text{rank}
\begin{bmatrix}
\sum\limits_{i=0}^{\omega} \left((F^{\mathrm{T}})^i \otimes N_i \right) \\[2mm]
\sum\limits_{i=0}^{\omega} \left((F^{\mathrm{T}})^i \otimes D_i \right)
\end{bmatrix}
$$

$$
= \text{rank}
\left[
\sum\limits_{i=0}^{\omega}
\begin{bmatrix}
(F^{\mathrm{T}})^i_{11} \begin{bmatrix} N_i \\ D_i \end{bmatrix} & \cdots & (F^{\mathrm{T}})^i_{1p} \begin{bmatrix} N_i \\ D_i \end{bmatrix} \\
\vdots & \ddots & \vdots \\
(F^{\mathrm{T}})^i_{p1} \begin{bmatrix} N_i \\ D_i \end{bmatrix} & \cdots & (F^{\mathrm{T}})^i_{pp} \begin{bmatrix} N_i \\ D_i \end{bmatrix}
\end{bmatrix}
\right]
$$

$$
= \text{rank}
\left[
\sum\limits_{i=0}^{\omega} \left((F^{\mathrm{T}})^i \otimes \begin{bmatrix} N_i \\ D_i \end{bmatrix} \right)
\right],
$$

By Theorem 3.6, (A.30) holds if and only if

$$
\text{rank} \begin{bmatrix} N(\lambda) \\ D(\lambda) \end{bmatrix} = \alpha, \ \forall \lambda \in \text{eig}\left(F^{\mathrm{T}} \right).
$$

Since F and F^{T} have the same eigenvalues, the above condition is equivalent to the F-right coprimeness of $N(s)$ and $D(s)$. With this we complete the proof.

References

Almuthairi, N. F. and Bingulac, S. (1994). On coprime factorization and minimal-realization of transfer-function matrices using the pseudo-observability concept. *International Journal of Computer and Systems Sciences*, 25(11):1819–1844.

Altman, R. B., Dunker, A. K., Hunter, L., and Murray, T. (2006). *Pacific Symposium on Biocomputing 2007*. World Scientific Publishing Company, Inc., Hackensack, NJ.

Anderson, E., Bai, Z., Bischof, C., and Blackford, S. (1999). *LAPACK Users' Guide*, 3rd edn. Software, Environments and Tools. Society for Industrial and Applied Mathematics, Philadelphia, PA.

Armstrong, E. S. (1994). Coprime factorization approach to robust stabilization of control-structures interaction evolutionary model. *Journal of Guidance Control and Dynamics*, 17(5):935–941.

Asada, H. and Slotine, J. J. E. (1986). *Robot Analysis and Control*. John Wiley & Sons, New York.

Ashour, O. N. and Nayfeh, A. H. (2002). Adaptive control of flexible structures using a nonlinear vibration absorber. *Nonlinear Dynamics*, 28(3–4):309–322.

Balas, M. J. (1982). Trends in large space structure control theory: Fondest hopes, wildest dreams. *IEEE Transactions on Automatic Control*, 27:522–535.

Barlow, J. B., Monahemt, M. M., and Oleary, D. P. (1992). Constrained matrix Sylvester equations. *SIAM Journal on Matrix Analysis and Applications*, 13(1):1–9.

Barraud, A. Y. (1977). A numerical algorithm in solve $A^{\mathrm{T}}XA - X = Q$. *IEEE Transactions on Automatic Control*, AC-22:883–885.

Beelen, T. G. J. and Veltkamp, G. W. (1987). Numerical computation of a coprime factorization of a transfer-function matrix. *Systems & Control Letters*, 9(4):281–288.

Beitia, M. A. and Gracia, J. M. (1994). Local behavior of Sylvester matrix equations related to block similarity. *Linear Algebra and Its Applications*, 199:253–279.

Beitia, M. A. and Gracia, J. M. (1996). Sylvester matrix equation for matrix pencils. *Linear Algebra and Its Applications*, 232:155–197.

Benner, P., Mehrmann, V., and Sorensen, D. C. (2005). *Proceedings of a Workshop on Dimension Reduction of Large-Scale Systems*. Lecture Notes in Computational Science and Engineering. Springer, Berlin, Germany.

Benzaouia, A. (2012). *Saturated Switching Systems*. Lecture Notes in Control and Information Sciences. Springer, Berlin, Germany.

Berger, C. S. (1971). A numerical solution of the matrix equation. *IEEE Transactions on Automatic Control*, AC-16:381–382.

Bhaya, A. and Desoer, C. (1985). On the design of large flexible space structures. *IEEE Transactions on Automatic Control*, 30:1118–1120.

Bingulac, S. and Almuthairi, N. F. (1995). Novel-approach to coprime factorization and minimal-realization of transfer-function matrices. *Journal of the University of Kuwait-Science*, 22(1):24–43.

Bitmead, R. B. and Weiss, H. (1979). On the solution of the discrete-time Lyapunov matrix equation in controllable canonical form. *IEEE Transactions on Automatic Control*, AC-24:481–482.

Bittanti, S. and Colaneri, P. (2002). *Periodic Control Systems 2001*. IFAC Proceedings Volumes. Pergamon, Oxford, U.K.

Bongers, P. M. M. and Heuberger, P. S. C. (1990). Discrete normalized coprime factorization. *Lecture Notes in Control and Information Sciences*, 144:307–313.

Bouhamidi, A., Hached, M., Heyouni, M., and Jbilou, K. (2013). A preconditioned block Arnoldi method for large Sylvester matrix equations. *Numerical Linear Algebra with Applications*, 20(2):208–219.

Brierley, S. D. and Lee, E. B. (1984). Solution of the equation $A(z)X(z)+X(z)B(z) = C(z)$ and its application to the stability of generalized linear systems. *International Journal of Control*, 40:1065–1075.

Brockett, R. W. (1970). *Introduction to Matrix Analysis*. John Wiley & Sons, New York.

Cai, G. B., Hu, C. H., and Duan, G. R. (2011). Eigenstructure assignment for linear parameter-varying systems with applications. *Mathematical and Computer Modelling*, 53(5–6):861–870.

Calvetti, D., Lewis, B., and Reichel, L. (2001). On the solution of large Sylvester-observer equations. *Numerical Linear Algebra with Applications*, 8(6–7):435–451.

Carvalho, J., Datta, K., and Hong, Y. P. (2003). New block algorithm for full-rank solution of the Sylvester-observer equation. *IEEE Transactions on Automatic Control*, 48(12): 2223–2228.

Carvalho, J. B. and Datta, B. N. (2011). A new algorithm for generalized Sylvester-observer equation and its application to state and velocity estimations in vibrating systems. *Numerical Linear Algebra with Applications*, 18:719–732.

Castelan, E. B. and Silva, V. G. D. (2005). On the solution of a Sylvester equation appearing in descriptor systems control theory. *Systems & Control Letters*, 54(2):109–117.

Chen, C. T. (1984). *Linear System Theory and Design*. Holt, Rinchart and Winston, New York.

Chen, Z. and Lu, L. Z. (2013). A gradient based iterative solutions for Sylvester tensor equations. *Mathematical Problems in Engineering*, doi:10.1155/2013/819479.

Choi, J. W. (1998). Left eigenstructure assignment via Sylvester equation. *KSME International Journal*, 12(6):1034–1040.

Choi, J. W., Lee, H. C., and Yoo, W. S. (1999). Eigenstructure assignment by the differential Sylvester equation for linear time-varying systems. *KSME International Journal*, 13(9):609–619.

Chu, E. K. and Datta, B. N. (1996). Numerically robust pole assignment for second-order systems. *International Journal of Control*, 64(4):1113–1127.

Ciegis, R., Henty, D., Kågström, B., and Zilinskas, J. (2008). *Parallel Scientific Computing and Optimization: Advances and Applications*. Springer Optimization and Its Applications. Springer, New York.

Clohessy, W. H. and Wiltshire, R. S. (1960). A terminal guidance system for spacecraft rendezvous. *Journal of Aerospace Sciences*, 27(9):653–658.

Dai, L. (1989). *Singular Control Systems. Lecture Notes in Control and Information Sciences*. Springer, Berlin, Germany.

Danelutto, M., Vanneschi, M., and Laforenza, D. (2004). *Proceedings of the 10th International Euro-Par Conference on Parallel Processing*. Lecture Notes in Computer Science. Springer, Berlin, Germany.

Darouach, M. (2006). Solution to Sylvester equation associated to linear descriptor systems. *Systems & Control Letters*, 55(10):835–838.

Datta, B. N. (1999). *Applied and Computational Control, Signals, and Circuits: Volume 1*. Birkhäuser, Boston, MA.

Datta, B. N., Heyouni, M., and Jbilou, K. (2010). The global Arnoldi process for solving the Sylvester-observer equation. *Computational and Applied Mathematics*, 29:527–544.

Datta, B. N. and Saad, Y. (1991). Arnoldi method for large Sylvester-like observer matrix equations, and an associated algorithm for partial spectrum assignment. *Linear Algebra and Its Applications*, 154:225–244.

Daydé, M., Dongarra, J., Hernández, V., and Palma, J. M. L. M. (2005). *Proceedings of the 6th International Conference on High Performance Computing for Computational Science (VECPAR 2004)*. Lecture Notes in Computer Science/Theoretical Computer Science and General Issues. Springer, Berlin, Germany.

Dehghan, M. and Hajarian, M. (2008a). An iterative algorithm for the reflexive solutions of the generalized coupled Sylvester matrix equations and its optimal approximation. *Applied Mathematics and Computation*, 202(2):571–588.

Dehghan, M. and Hajarian, M. (2008b). An iterative algorithm for the reflexive solutions of the generalized coupled Sylvester matrix equations and its optimal approximation. *Applied Mathematics and Computation*, 202(2):571–588.

Dehghan, M. and Hajarian, M. (2009). Efficient iterative method for solving the second-order Sylvester matrix equation $EVF^2 - AVF - CV = BW$. *IET Control Theory and Applications*, 3(10):1401–1408.

Dehghan, M. and Hajarian, M. (2010a). An efficient algorithm for solving general coupled matrix equations and its application. *Mathematical and Computer Modelling*, 51(9–10):1118–1134.

Dehghan, M. and Hajarian, M. (2010b). The general coupled matrix equations over generalized bisymmetric matrices. *Linear Algebra and Its Applications*, 432(6):1531–1552.

Dehghan, M. and Hajarian, M. (2010c). An iterative method for solving the generalized coupled Sylvester matrix equations over generalized bisymmetric matrices. *Applied Mathematical Modelling*, 34(3):639–654.

Dehghan, M. and Hajarian, M. (2010d). On the reflexive and anti-reflexive solutions of the generalised coupled Sylvester matrix equations. *International Journal of Systems Science*, 41(6):607–625.

Dehghan, M. and Hajarian, M. (2011a). Analysis of an iterative algorithm to solve the generalized coupled Sylvester matrix equations. *Applied Mathematical Modelling*, 35(7): 3285–3300.

Dehghan, M. and Hajarian, M. (2011b). Convergence of an iterative method for solving Sylvester matrix equations over reflexive matrices. *Journal of Vibration and Control*, 17(9):1295–1298.

Dehghan, M. and Hajarian, M. (2011c). SSHI methods for solving general linear matrix equations. *Engineering Computations*, 28(7–8):1028–1043.

Dehghan, M. and Hajarian, M. (2011d). On the generalized bisymmetric and skew-symmetric solutions of the system of generalized Sylvester matrix equations. *Linear and Multilinear Algebra*, 59(11):1281–1309.

Dehghan, M. and Hajarian, M. (2011e). Solving the generalized Sylvester matrix equation $\Sigma_{i=1}^{p} A_i X B_i + \Sigma_{j=1}^{q} C_j Y D_j = E$ over reflexive and anti-reflexive matrices. *International Journal of Control Automation and Systems*, 9(1):118–124.

Dehghan, M. and Hajarian, M. (2011f). Two algorithms for finding the Hermitian reflexive and skew-Hermitian solutions of Sylvester matrix equations. *Applied Mathematics Letters*, 24(4):444–449.

Dehghan, M. and Hajarian, M. (2012a). The generalised Sylvester matrix equations over the generalised bisymmetric and skew-symmetric matrices. *International Journal of Systems Science*, 43(8):1580–1590.

Dehghan, M. and Hajarian, M. (2012b). Iterative algorithms for the generalized centro-symmetric and central anti-symmetric solutions of general coupled matrix equations. *Engineering Computations*, 29(5–6):528–560.

Dehghan, M. and Hajarian, M. (2012c). On the generalized reflexive and anti-reflexive solutions to a system of matrix equations. *Linear Algebra and Its Applications*, 437(11): 2793–2812.

Dehghan, M. and Hajarian, M. (2012d). Solving coupled matrix equations over generalized bisymmetric matrices. *International Journal of Control Automation and Systems*, 10(5): 905–912.

Dehghan, M. and Hajarian, M. (2013). Construction of an iterative method for solving generalized coupled Sylvester matrix equations. *Transactions of the Institute of Measurement and Control*, 35(8):961–970.

Dehghan, M. and Hajarian, M. (2014). Solving the system of generalized Sylvester matrix equations over the generalized centro-symmetric matrices. *Journal of Vibration and Control*, 20(6):838–846.

Ding, F. and Chen, T. W. (2005a). Gradient based iterative algorithms for solving a class of matrix equations. *IEEE Transactions on Automatic Control*, 50(8):1216–1221.

Ding, F. and Chen, T. W. (2005b). Iterative least-squares solutions of coupled Sylvester matrix equations. *Systems & Control Letters*, 54(2):95–107.

Ding, F. and Chen, T. W. (2006). On iterative solutions of general coupled matrix equations. *SIAM Journal on Control and Optimization*, 44(6):2269–2284.

Ding, F., Liu, P. X., and Ding, J. (2008). Iterative solutions of the generalized Sylvester matrix equations by using the hierarchical identification principle. *Applied Mathematics and Computation*, 197(1):41–50.

Dorf, R. C. and Bishop, R. H. (2010). *Modern Control Systems*. Prentice Hall, Englewood Cliffs, NJ.

Duan, G. R. (1991a). Eigenstructure assignment in multivariable linear systems via decentralized state feedback. In *Proceedings of European Control Conference*, pp. 2530–2533, July 2–5, Juillet, France.

Duan, G. R. (1991b). A parametric approach for eigenstructure assignment via compensators. In *Proceedings of the Fifth IFAC/IMACS Symposium on Computer Aided Design in Control Systems*, July 15–17, Swansea, U.K.

Duan, G. R. (1992a). Simple algorithm for robust pole assignment in linear output feedback. *IEE Proceedings, Part D: Control Theory and Applications*, 139(5):465–469. Also, in *IEE Conference Publication*, 1991, 1(332):682–688.

Duan, G. R. (1992b). Solution to matrix equation $AV + BW = EVF$ and eigenstructure assignment for descriptor systems. *Automatica*, 28(3):639–643.

Duan, G. R. (1993a). Robust eigenstructure assignment via dynamical compensators. *Automatica*, 29(2):469–474.

Duan, G. R. (1993b). Solutions of the equation $AV + BW = VF$ and their application to eigenstructure assignment in linear systems. *IEEE Transactions on Automatic Control*, 38(2):276–280.

Duan, G. R. (1994). Eigenstructure assignment by decentralized output feedback— A complete parametric approach. *IEEE Transactions on Automatic Control*, 39(5): 1009–1014.

Duan, G. R. (1995). Parametric approach for eigenstructure assignment in descriptor systems via output feedback. *IEE Proceedings: Control Theory and Applications*, 142(6):611–616.

Duan, G. R. (1996). On the solution to the Sylvester matrix equation $AV + BW = EVF$. *IEEE Transactions on Automatic Control*, 41(4):612–614.

Duan, G. R. (1998a). Eigenstructure assignment and response analysis in descriptor linear systems with state feedback control. *International Journal of Control*, 69(5):663–694.

Duan, G. R. (1998b). Right coprime factorization for single input systems using Hessenberg forms. In *Proceedings of the Sixth IEEE Mediterranean Conference on Control and Systems*, pp. 573–577, June 9–11, Sardinia, Italy.

Duan, G. R. (1999). Eigenstructure assignment in descriptor systems via output feedback: A new complete parametric approach. *International Journal of Control*, 72(4):345–364.

Duan, G. R. (2001). Right coprime factorisations using system upper Hessenberg forms - the multi-input system case. *IEE Proceedings: Control Theory and Applications*, 148(6): 433–441. Also, in *Proceedings of 39th IEEE Conference on Decision and Control*, 2000, pp. 1960–1965, Sydney, New South Wales, Australia.

Duan, G. R. (2002a). Parametric eigenstructure assignment via state feedback: A simple numerically stable approach. In *Proceedings of the Fourth World Congress on Intelligent Control and Automation*, pp. 165–173, June 10–14, Shanghai, China.

Duan, G. R. (2002b). Right coprime factorizations for single-input descriptor linear systems: A simple numerically stable algorithm. *Asian Journal of Control*, 4(2):146–158.

Duan, G. R. (2003). Parametric eigenstructure assignment via output feedback based on singular value decompositions. *IEE Proceedings: Control Theory and Applications*, 150(1): 93–100. Also, in *Proceedings of the 40th IEEE Conference on Decision and Control*, 2001, pp. 2665–2670, Orlando, FL.

Duan, G. R. (2004a). *Linear Systems Theory*, 2nd edn. (in Chinese). Harbin Institute of Technology Press, Harbin, China.

Duan, G. R. (2004b). A note on combined generalized sylvester matrix equations. *Journal of Control Theory and Applications*, 2(4):397–400.

Duan, G. R. (2004c). Parametric eigenstructure assignment in second-order descriptor linear systems. *IEEE Transactions on Automatic Control*, 49(10):1789–1795.

Duan, G. R. (2004d). The solution to the matrix equation $AV + BW = EVJ + R$. *Applied Mathematics Letters*, 17(10):1197–1202.

Duan, G. R. (2005a). Generalized Sylvester matrix equations in control systems theory. In *Proceedings of the 17th Chinese Control and Decision Conference*, pp. 32–57, June, Harbin, China.

Duan, G. R. (2005b). Parametric approaches for eigenstructure assignment in high-order linear systems. *International Journal of Control Automation and Systems*, 3(3):419–429.

Duan, G. R. (2008). On numerical reliability of pole assignment algorithms—A case study. In *Proceedings of the 27th Chinese Control Conference*, pp. 189–194, July 16–18, Kunming, China.

Duan, G. R. (2010). *Analysis and Design of Descriptor Linear Systems*. Advances in Mechanics and Mathematics. Springer, New York.

Duan, G. R. (2012). An LMI approach to robust attitude control of BTT missiles. Technical report, *The Fifth International Conference on Optimizaiton and Control with Applications*, Beijing, China.

Duan, G. R. (2013a). On a type of generalized Sylvester equations. In *Proceedings of the 25th Chinese Control and Decision Conference*, pp. 1264–1269, May 25–27, Guiyang, China.

Duan, G. R. (2013b). On a type of high-order generalized Sylvester equations. In *Proceedings of the 32nd Chinese Control Conference*, pp. 328–333, July 26–28, Xi'an, China.

Duan, G. R. (2013c). On a type of second-order generalized Sylvester equations. In *Proceedings of the Ninth Asian Control Conference (ASCC 2013)*, June 23–26, Istanbul, Turkey.

Duan, G. R. (2013d). Solution to a type of high-order nonhomogeneous generalized Sylvester equations. In *Proceedings of the 32nd Chinese Control Conference*, pp. 322–327, July 26–28, Xi'an, China.

Duan, G. R. (2013e). Solution to a type of nonhomogeneous generalized Sylvester equations. In *Proceedings of the 25th Chinese Control and Decision Conference*, pp. 163–168, May 25–27, Guiyang, China.

Duan, G. R. (2013f). Solution to second-order nonhomogeneous generalized Sylvester equations. In *Proceedings of the Ninth Asian Control Conference*, June 23–26, Istanbul, Turkey.

Duan, G. R. (2014a). Cooperative spacecraft rendezvous—A direct parametric control approach. In *Proceedings of the 11th World Congress on Intelligent Control and Automation*, June 29–July 4, Shenyang, China.

Duan, G. R. (2014b). A direct parametric approach for missile guidance—Case of sea targets. In *Proceedings of the 33rd Chinese Control Conference*, July 28–30, Nanjing, China.

Duan, G. R. (2014c). Direct parametric control of fully-actuated high-order nonlinear systems—The descriptor case. In *SICE Annual Conference 2014*, September 9–12, Hokkaido University, Sapporo, Japan.

Duan, G. R. (2014d). Direct parametric control of fully-actuated high-order nonlinear systems—The normal case. In *Proceedings of the 11th World Congress on Intelligent Control and Automation*, June 29–July 4, Shenyang, China.

Duan, G. R. (2014e). Direct parametric control of fully-actuated second-order nonlinear systems—The descriptor case. In *Proceedings of the 11th World Congress on Intelligent Control and Automation*, June 29–July 4, Shenyang, China.

Duan, G. R. (2014f). Direct parametric control of fully-actuated second-order nonlinear systems—The normal case. In *Proceedings of the 33rd Chinese Control Conference*, July 28–30, Nanjing, China.

Duan, G. R. (2014g). Missile attitude control—A direct parametric approach. In *Proceedings of the 33rd Chinese Control Conference*, July 28–30, Nanjing, China.

Duan, G. R. (2014h). Non-cooperative rendezvous and interception—A direct parametric control. In *Proceedings of the 11th World Congress on Intelligent Control and Automation*, June 29–July 4, Shenyang, China.

Duan, G. R. (2014i). Parametric solutions to fully-actuated generalized Sylvester equations—The homogeneous case. In *Proceedings of the 33rd Chinese Control Conference*, July 28–30, Nanjing, China.

Duan, G. R. (2014j). Parametric solutions to fully-actuated generalized Sylvester equations—The nonhomogeneous case. In *Proceedings of the 33rd Chinese Control Conference*, July 28–30, Nanjing, China.

Duan, G. R. (2014k). Parametric solutions to rectangular high-order Sylvester equations—Case of *F* arbitrary. In *SICE Annual Conference 2014*, September 9–12, Hokkaido University, Sapporo, Japan.

Duan, G. R. (2014l). Parametric solutions to rectangular high-order Sylvester equations—Case of *F* Jordan. In *SICE Annual Conference 2014*, September 9–12, Hokkaido University, Sapporo, Japan.

Duan, G. R. (2014m). Satellite attitude control—A direct parametric approach. In *Proceedings of the 11th World Congress on Intelligent Control and Automation*, June 29–July 4, Shenyang, China.

Duan, G. R., Gu, D. K., and Li, B. (2010). Optimal control for final approach of rendezvous with non-cooperative target. *Pacific Journal of Optimization*, 6(3):521–532.

Duan, G. R. and Howe, D. (2003). Robust magnetic bearing control via eigenstructure assignment dynamical compensation. *IEEE Transactions on Control Systems Technology*, 11(2):204–215.

Duan, G. R., Howe, D., and Liu, G. P. (1999a). Complete parametric approach for eigenstructure assignment in a class of second-order linear systems. In *Proceedings of IFAC World Congress'99*, pp. 213–218, July 5–8, Beijing, China.

Duan, G. R., Howe, D., and Patton, R. J. (2002a). Robust fault detection in descriptor linear systems via generalized unknown input observers. *International Journal of Systems Science*,

33(5):369–377. Also, in *Proceedings of the IFAC World Congress*, 1999, pp. 43–48, July 5–8, Beijing, China.

Duan, G. R. and Huang, L. (2006). Disturbance attenuation in model following designs of a class of second-order systems: A parametric approach. In *Proceedings of 2006 SICE-ICASE International Joint Conference*, pp. 5662–5667, October 18–21, Busan, South Korea.

Duan, G. R. and Huang, L. (2007). Robust pole assignment in descriptor second-order dynamical systems. *Zidonghua Xuebao*, 33(8):888–892.

Duan, G. R. and Huang, L. (2008). Robust model following control for a class of second-order dynamical systems subject to parameter uncertainties. *Transactions of the Institute of Measurement and Control*, 30(2):115–142.

Duan, G. R., Irwin, G. W., and Liu, G. P. (1999b). A complete parametric approach to partial eigenstructure assignment. In *Proceedings of European Control Conference 1999 (ECC'99)*, August 31–September 3, Karlsruhe, Germany.

Duan, G. R., Irwin, G. W., and Liu, G. P. (1999c). Disturbance decoupling with eigenstructure assignment in linear systems via output dynamical feedback control. In *Proceedings of European Control Conference 1999 (ECC'99)*, August 31–September 3, Karlsruhe, Germany.

Duan, G. R., Irwin, G. W., and Liu, G. P. (1999d). Robust stabilization of descriptor linear systems via proportional-plus-derivative state feedback. In *Proceedings of 1999 American Control Conference*, pp. 1304–1308, June 2–4, San Diego, CA.

Duan, G. R., Irwin, G. W., and Liu, G. P. (2000a). Disturbance attenuation in linear systems via dynamical compensators: A parametric eigenstructure assignment approach. *IEE Proceedings: Control Theory and Applications*, 147(2):129–136.

Duan, G. R. and Liu, G. P. (2002). Complete parametric approach for eigenstructure assignment in a class of second-order linear systems. *Automatica*, 38(4):725–729.

Duan, G. R., Liu, G. P., and Thompson, S. (2000b). Disturbance attenuation in Luenberger function observer designs—A parametric approach. In *Proceedings of IFAC Symposium on Robust Control*, pp. 41–46, June 21–23, Prague, Czech Republic.

Duan, G. R., Liu, G. P., and Thompson, S. (2000c). Disturbance decoupling in descriptor systems via output feedback—A parametric eigenstructure assignment approach. In *Proceedings of the 39th IEEE Conference on Decision and Control*, pp. 3660–3665, December 12–15, Sydney, New South Wales, Australia.

Duan, G. R., Liu., G. P., and Thompson, S. (2001a). Eigenstructure assignment design for proportional-integral observers: Continuous-time case. *Proceedings of the Institution of Mechanical Engineers. Part I: Journal of Systems and Control Engineering*, 148(3): 263–267.

Duan, G. R., Liu., G. P., and Thompson, S. (2003). Eigenstructure assignment design for proportional-integral observers: The discrete-time case. *International Journal of Systems Science*, 34(5):357–363. Also, in *Proceedings of the Eighth IFAC Symposium on Computer Aided Control System Design (CACSD 2000)*, Salford, U.K.

Duan, G. R., Liu, W. Q., and Liu, G. P. (2001b). Robust model reference control for multivariable linear systems subject to parameter uncertainties. *Proceedings of the Institution of Mechanical Engineers. Part I: Journal of Systems and Control Engineering*, 215(6): 599–610.

Duan, G. R., Lv, L. L., and Zhou, B. (2009a). Robust pole assignment for discrete-time linear periodic systems via output feedback. In *Proceedings of 2009 Joint 48th IEEE Conference on Decision and Control (CDC) and 28th Chinese Control Conference*, pp. 1729–1733, December 15–18, Shanghai, China.

Duan, G. R. and Ma, K. M. (1995). Robust Luenberger function observers for linear systems. In *Pre-prints of IFAC Youth Automatic Conference (IFAC YAC'95)*, pp. 382–387, August 22–25, Beijing, China.

Duan, G. R., Nichols, N. K., and Liu, G. P. (2002b). Robust pole assignment in descriptor linear systems via state feedback. *European Journal of Control*, 8(2):136–149. Also, in *Proceedings of the European Control Conference*, 2001, pp. 2386–2391.

Duan, G. R. and Patton, R. J. (1997). Eigenstructure assignment in descriptor systems via proportional plus derivative state feedback. *International Journal of Control*, 68(5): 1147–1162.

Duan, G. R. and Patton, R. J. (1998a). Eigenstructure assignment in descriptor systems via state feedback—A new complete parametric approach. *International Journal of Systems Science*, 29(2):167–178.

Duan, G. R. and Patton, R. J. (1998b). Explicit and analytical solutions to Lyapunov algebraic matrix equations. *Journal of Engineering and Applied Science*, 455(2):1397–1402.

Duan, G. R. and Patton, R. J. (1998c). Explicit and analytical solutions to Sylvester algebraic matrix equations. *Journal of Engineering and Applied Science*, 455(2):1563–1568.

Duan, G. R. and Patton, R. J. (1998d). Robust fault detection in linear systems using Luenberger observers. *Journal of Engineering and Applied Science*, 455(2):1468–1473.

Duan, G. R. and Patton, R. J. (1999). Robust pole assignment in descriptor systems via proportional plus partial derivative state feedback. *International Journal of Control*, 72(13):1193–1203.

Duan, G. R. and Patton, R. J. (2001). Robust fault detection using Luenberger-type unknown input observers—A parametric approach. *International Journal of Systems Science*, 32(4):533–540.

Duan, G. R., Patton, R. J., Chen, J., and Chen, Z. (1997). A parametric approach for fault detection in linear systems with unknown disturbances. In *Proceedings of IFAC Symposium on Fault Detection, Supervision and Safety for Technical Processes, SAFEPROCESS'97*, pp. 318–322, August 26–28, Kingston Upon Hull, U.K.

Duan, G. R., Qiang, W. Y., Feng, W. J., and Sun, L. J. (1994). A complete parametric approach for model reference control system design (in Chinese). *Journal of Astronautics*, 15(2):7–13.

Duan, G. R., Thompson, S., and Liu, G. P. (1999e). On solution to the matrix equation $AV + EVJ = BW + G$. In *Proceedings of the 38th IEEE Conference on Decision and Control*, pp. 2742–2743, Phoenix, AZ.

Duan, G. R., Thompson, S., and Liu, G. P. (1999f). Separation principle for robust pole assignment—An advantage of full-order state observers. In *Proceedings of 1999 IEEE Conference on Decision and Control*, pp. 76–78, December 7–10, Phoenix, AZ.

Duan, G. R. and Wang, G. S. (2003). Partial eigenstructure assignment for descriptor linear systems: A complete parametric approach. In *Proceedings of IEEE 2003 Conference on Decision and Control*, pp. 3402–3407, December 9–12, Maui, HI.

Duan, G. R. and Wang, G. S. (2004). P-D feedback eigenstructure assignment with minimum control effort in second-order dynamic systems. In *Proceedings of IEEE Conference of Computer Aid Control System Design*, pp. 344–349, Taibei, China.

Duan, G. R. and Wang, G. S. (2005). Eigenstructure assignment in a class of second-order descriptor linear systems: A complete parametric approach. *International Journal of Control, Automation, and Systems*, 2(1):1–5.

Duan, G. R., Wang, G. S., and Choi, J. W. (2002c). Eigenstructure assignment in a class of second-order linear systems: A complete parametric approach. In *Proceedings of the Eighth Annual Chinese Automation and Computer Society Conference*, pp. 89–96, Manchester, U.K.

Duan, G. R. and Wang, Q. C. (1992). Modes decoupling control for linear systems (in Chinese). *Journal of Astronautics*, 13(2):7–13.

Duan, G. R., Wu, A. G., and Hou, W. N. (2007). Parametric approach for Luenberger observers for descriptor linear systems. *Bulletin of the Polish Academy of Sciences: Technical Sciences*, 55(1):15–18.

Duan, G. R., Wu, G. Y., and Huang, W. H. (1991a). Eigenstructure assignment for time-varying linear-systems. *Science China Series A—Mathematics Physics Astronomy and Technological Sciences*, 34(2):246–256.

Duan, G. R. and Wu, Y. L. (2004a). Dual observer design for matrix second-order linear systems. In *IEE Control'04*, Bath, U.K.

Duan, G. R. and Wu, Y. L. (2004b). Generalized Luenberger observer design for matrix second-order linear systems. In *IEEE Conference on Control Applications*, pp. 1739–1743, September 2–4, Taibei, China.

Duan, G. R. and Wu, Y. L. (2004c). Robust fault detection in matrix second-order linear systems via unknown input observers—A parametric approach. In *Proceedings of the Eighth International Conference on Control, Automation, Robotics and Vision*, pp. 1847–1852, December 6–9, Kunming, China.

Duan, G. R. and Wu, Y. L. (2005). Robust pole assignment in matrix descriptor second-order linear systems. *Transactions of the Institute of Measurement and Control*, 27(4):279–295.

Duan, G. R., Wu, Y. L., and Zhang, M. R. (2004). Robust fault detection in matrix second-order linear systems via Luenberger-type unknown input observers: A parametric approach. In *Proceedings of the Eighth International Conference on Control, Automation, Robotics and Vision*, pp. 1847–1852, Kunming, China.

Duan, G. R., Wu, Z. Y., Bingham, C., and Howe, D. (2000d). Robust magnetic bearing control using stabilizing dynamical compensators. *IEEE Transactions on Industry Applications*, 36(6):1654–1660.

Duan, G. R., Wu, Z. Y., and Howe, D. (1999g). Explicit parametric solution to observer-based control of self-sensing magnetic bearings. In *Proceedings of IFAC World Congress'99*, pp. 379–384, July 5–8, Beijing, China.

Duan, G. R., Wu, Z. Y., and Howe, D. (2001c). Robust control of a magnetic-bearing flywheel using dynamical compensators. *Transactions of the Institute of Measurement and Control*, 23(4):249–278.

Duan, G. R. and Xue, Y. (2005). Parametric eigenstructure assignment for linear systems subject to input saturation via state feedback. In *Proceedings of the Fifth International Conference on Control and Automation*, pp. 757–760, June 26–29, Hungarian Academy of Sciences, Budapest, Hungary.

Duan, G. R. and Yu, H. H. (2006a). Complete eigenstructure assignment in high-order descriptor linear systems via proportional plus derivative state feedback. In *Proceedings of World Congress on Intelligent Control and Automation*, pp. 500–505, June 21–23, Dalian, China.

Duan, G. R. and Yu, H. H. (2006b). Parametric approaches for eigenstructure assignment in high-order descriptor linear systems. In *Proceedings of the 45th IEEE Conference on Decision and Control*, pp. 1399–1404, December 13–15, San Diego, CA.

Duan, G. R. and Yu, H. H. (2008). Robust pole assignment in high-order descriptor linear systems via proportional plus derivative state feedback. *IET Control Theory and Applications*, 2(4):277–287.

Duan, G. R. and Yu, H. H. (2013). *LMIs in Control Systems: Analysis, Design and Applications*. CRC Press, Boca Raton, FL.

Duan, G. R., Yu, H. H., and Tan, F. (2009b). Parametric control systems design with applications in missile control. *Science China Series F—Information Sciences*, 52(11): 2190–2200.

Duan, G. R., Yu, H. H., Wu, A. G., and Zhang, X. (2012). *Analysis and Design of Descriptor Linear Systems (in Chinese)*. Science Press, Beijing, China.

Duan, G. R. and Yuan, J. P. (1991). Determinant and inverse of the generalized vendermonde matrix (in Chinese). *Electric Machines and Control*, 14(4):399–403.

Duan, G. R. and Zhang, B. (2006). A parametric method for model reference control in descriptor linear systems. In *Proceedings of the Sixth World Congress on Intelligent Control and Automation*, pp. 495–499, June 21–23, Dalian, China.

Duan, G. R. and Zhang, B. (2007a). Robust control system design using proportional plus partial derivative state feedback. *Zidonghua Xuebao*, 33(5):506–510.

Duan, G. R. and Zhang, B. (2007b). Robust model-reference control for descriptor linear systems subject to parameter uncertainties. *Journal of Control Theory and Applications*, 5(3):213–220.

Duan, G. R. and Zhang, B. (2007c). Robust pole assignment via output feedback in descriptor linear systems with structural parameter perturbations. *Asian Journal of Control*, 9(2):201–207.

Duan, G. R. and Zhou, B. (2005). Solution to the equation $MVF^2 + DVF + KV = BW$— The nonsingular case. In *Proceedings of the Second IASTED International Multi-Conference on Automation, Control, and Information Technology-Automation, Control, and Applications*, pp. 259–264, Novosibirsk, Russia.

Duan, G. R. and Zhou, B. (2006). Solution to the second-order Sylvester matrix equation $MVF^2 + DVF + KV = BW$. *IEEE Transactions on Automatic Control*, 51(5):805–809.

Duan, G. R., Zhou, L. S., and Xu, Y. M. (1991b). A parametric approach for observer-based control system design. In *Proceedings of Asia-Pacific Conference on Measurement and Control*, pp. 295–300, August 21–23, Guangzhou, China.

Emirsajlow, Z. (2012). Infinite-dimensional Sylvester equations: Basic theory and application to observer design. *International Journal of Applied Mathematics and Computer Science*, 22(2):245–257.

Fagerholm, J., Haataja, J., Järvinen, J., and Lyly, M. (2002). *Applied Parallel Computing, Proceedings of the Sixth International Conference on Advanced Scientific Computing*. Lecture Notes in Computer Science. Springer, Berlin, Germany.

Fei, M., Li, J., and Irwin, G. W. (2010). *Proceedings of the International Conference on Life System Modeling and Intelligent Computing.* Lecture Notes in Computer Science/Theoretical Computer Science and General Issues. Springer, Berlin, Germany.

Flagg, G. M. and Gugercin, S. (2013). On the ADI method for the Sylvester equation and the optimal-H_2 points. *Applied Numerical Mathematics*, 64:50–58.

Fletcher, L. R. (1997). Pole assignment and controllability subspaces in descriptor systems. *International Journal of Control*, 66(5):677–709.

Fu, Y. M., Chai, Q. X., and Duan, G. R. (2005). Robust guaranteed cost observer for Markovian jumping systems with state delays. In *Proceedings of International Conference on Control and Automation*, pp. 245–248, June 26–29, Hungarian Academy of Sciences, Budapest, Hungary.

Fu, Y. M., Duan, G. R., and Song, S. M. (2004). Design of unknown input observer for linear time-delay systems. *International Journal of Control, Automation and Systems*, 2(4): 530–535.

Fu, Y. M., Wu, D., Zhang, P., and Duan, G. R. (2006). Design of unknown input observer with H_∞ performance for linear time-delay systems. *Journal of Systems Engineering and Electronics*, 17(3):606–610.

Fu, Y. M., Zhang, B., and Duan, G. R. (2008). Robust guaranteed cost observer design for linear uncertain jump systems with state delays. *Journal of Harbin Institute of Technology (New Series)*, 15(6):826–830.

Gajic, Z. and Qureshi, M. T. J. (2008). *Lyapunov Matrix Equation in System Stability and Control.* Dover Publications, Mineola, NY.

Gao, X. Y., Teo, K. L., and Duan, G. R. (2012a). Non-fragile robust H_∞ control for uncertain spacecraft rendezvous system with pole and input constraints. *International Journal of Control*, 85(7):933–941.

Gao, X. Y., Teo, K. L., and Duan, G. R. (2012b). Robust H_∞ control of spacecraft rendezvous on elliptical orbit. *Journal of the Franklin Institute—Engineering and Applied Mathematics*, 349(8):2515–2529.

Gao, X. Y., Teo, K. L., and Duan, G. R. (2013). An optimal control approach to robust control of nonlinear spacecraft rendezvous system with $\theta - D$ technique. *International Journal of Innovative Computing, Information and Control*, 9(5):2099–2110.

Golnaraghi, F. and Kuo, B. C. (2009). *Automatic Control Systems*, 9th edn. John Wiley & Sons, Hoboken, NJ.

Golub, G. H. and Loan, C. F. V. (1996). *Matrix Computations.* John Hopkins University Press, Baltimore, MD.

Golub, G. H., Nash, S., and Loan, C. V. (1979). A Hessenberg-Schur method for the problem $AC + XB = C$. *IEEE Transactions on Automatic Control*, AC-24:909–913.

Gray, J. O. (2001). *Computer Aided Control Systems Design 2000.* IFAC Proceedings Volumes. Pergamon, Oxford, U.K.

Green, M. (1992). H_∞ controller synthesis by J-lossless coprime factorization. *SIAM Journal on Control and Optimization*, 30(3):522–547.

Guan, X. P. and Duan, G. R. (1999). Function observer-based robust stabilization for delay systems with parameter perturbations. In *Proceedings of IFAC World Congress'99*, pp. 213–218, July 5–8, Beijing, China.

Guan, X. P., Lin, Z. Y., Liu, Y. C., and Duan, G. R. (2000a). H$_\infty$ observer design for discrete delay systems. In *Proceedings of International Conference on Differential Equations and Computational Simulations*, pp. 98–103, June 13–18, Chengdu, China.

Guan, X. P., Liu, Y. C., and Duan, G. R. (2000b). Observer-based H$_\infty$ robust control for multi-delays uncertain systems. In *Proceedings of the Third Asian Control Conference (ASCC'2000)*, pp. 700–704, July 4–7, Shanghai, China.

Guan, X. P., Liu, Y. C., and Duan, G. R. (2000c). Observer-based robust control for uncertain time delay systems. In *Proceedings of the Third World Congress on Intelligent Control and Automation*, pp. 3333–3337, Hefei, China.

Habets, L. C. G. J. M., Kloetzer, M., and Belta, C. (2006). Control of rectangular multi-affine hybrid systems. In *Proceedings of the 45th IEEE Conference on Decision & Control*, December 13–15, Manchester Grand Hyatt Hotel, San Diego, CA.

Havelock, D., Kuwano, S., and Vorländer, M. (2008). *Handbook of Signal Processing in Acoustics: Volume 1*. Springer, New York.

Hazewinkel, M. (1996). *Handbook of Algebra: Volume 1*. North Holland, Amsterdam, the Netherlands.

He, L. and Duan, G. R. (2006). Robust H-infinity control with pole placement constraints for T-S fuzzy systems. *Advances in Machine Learning and Cybernetics*, 3930: 338–346.

He, L., Duan, G. R., and Wu, A. G. (2006). Robust L$_1$ filtering with pole constraint in a disk via parameter-dependent Lyapunov functions. In *Proceedings of SICE-ICASE International Joint Conference*, pp. 833–836, Busan, South Korea.

He, L., Fu, Y. M., and Duan, G. R. (2004). Multiobjective control synthesis based on parametric eigenstructure assignment. In *Proceedings of International Conference on Control, Automation, Robotics and Vision*, pp. 1838–1841, Kunming, China.

Heyouni, M. (2011). Extended Arnoldi methods for large low-rank Sylvester matrix equations. *Applied Numerical Mathematics*, 60:1171–1182.

Higham, N. J. (1996). *Accuracy and Stability of Numerical Algorithms*. Society for Industrial and Applied Mathematics, Philadelphia, PA.

Higham, N. J. (2008). *Functions of Matrices: Theory and Computation*. Other Titles in Applied Mathematics. Society for Industrial and Applied Mathematics, Philadelphia, PA.

Hodel, A. S. and Misra, P. (1996). Solution of underdetermined Sylvester equations in sensor array signal processing. *Linear Algebra and Its Applications*, 249:1–14.

Hoskins, W. D., Meek, D. S., and Walton, D. J. (1977). The numerical solution of $AQ^T + QA = -C$. *IEEE Transactions on Automatic Control*, AC-22:882–883.

Hou, M. (2004). Controllability and elimination of impulsive modes in descriptor systems. *IEEE Transactions on Automatic Control*, 49(10):1723–1727.

Huang, G. X., Wu, N., Yin, F., Zhou, Z. L., and Guo, K. (2012). Finite iterative algorithms for solving generalized coupled Sylvester systems—Part I: One-sided and generalized coupled Sylvester matrix equations over generalized reflexive solutions. *Applied Mathematical Modelling*, 36(4):1589–1603.

Huang, L., Wei, Y. Y., and Duan, G. R. (2006). Disturbance attenuation in model following designs: A parametric approach. In *Proceedings of the 25th Chinese Control Conference*, pp. 2056–2059, August 7–11, Harbin, China.

Ilchmann, A. and Reis, T. (2013). *Surveys in Differential-Algebraic Equations I*. Differential-Algebraic Equations Forum. Springer, Berlin, Germany.

Ishihara, J. Y. and Terra, M. H. (2001). Impulse controllability and observability of rectangular descriptor systems. *IEEE Transactions on Automatic Control*, 46(6):991–994.

Jbilou, K. (2006). Low rank approximate solutions to large Sylvester matrix equations. *Applied Mathematics and Computation*, 177(1):365–376.

Jbilou, K., A. Messaoudi, H. Sadok. (1999). Global FOM and GMRES algorithms for matrix equations. *Applied Numerical Mathematics*, 31(1):49–63.

Jonsson, I. and Kagstrom, B. (2002). Recursive blocked algorithms for solving triangular systems—Part I: One-sided and coupled Sylvester-type matrix equations. *ACM Transactions on Mathematical Software*, 28(4):392–415.

Juang, J. N., Lim, K. B., and Junkins, J. L. (1989). Robust eigensystem assignment for flexible structures. *Journal of Guidance, Control and Dynamics*, 12(3):381–387.

Kagstrom, B. (1994). A perturbation analysis of the generalized Sylvester equation $(AR - LB, DR - LE) = (C, F)$. *SIAM Journal on Analysis and Applications*, 15(4): 1045–1060.

Kagstrom, B. and Poromaa, P. (1996). Lapack-style algorithms and software for solving the generalized Sylvester equation and estimating the separation between regular matrix pairs. *ACM Transactions on Mathematical Software*, 22(2):78–103.

Kagstrom, B. and Westin, L. (1989). Generalized Schur methods with condition estimators for solving the generalized Sylvester equations. *IEEE Transactions on Automatic Control*, 34(7):745–751.

Keshmiri, S., Colgren, R., and Mirmirani, M. (2005). Development of an aerodynamic database for a generic hypersonic air vehicle. In *AIAA Guidance, Navigation, and Control Conference and Exhibit*, August 15–18, San Francisco, CA.

Kimura, H. (1977). A further result on the problem of pole assignment by output feedback. *IEEE Transactions on Automatic Control*, AC-22:458–463.

Kong, H., Duan, G. R., and Zhou, B. (2009). A stein equation approach for solutions to the Bezout identity and the generalized Bezout identity. In *Proceedings of the Seventh Asian Control Conference*, pp. 1515–1519, August 27–29, Hong Kong China.

Kosch, H., Böszörményi, L., and Hellwagner, H. (2003). *Proceedings of the Ninth International Euro-Par Conference on Parallel Processing*. Lecture Notes in Computer Science. Springer, Berlin, Germany.

Kressner, D. (2005). *Numerical Methods for General and Structured Eigenvalue Problems*. Lecture Notes in Computational Science and Engineering. Springer, Berlin, Germany.

Kucera, V. (1974). The matrix equation $AX + XB = C$. *SIAM Journal on Applied Mathematics*, 26:15–25.

Kucera, V. and Sebek, M. (2005). *Robust Control Design 2000*. IFAC Proceedings Volumes. Pergamon, Oxford, U.K.

Kuzmanovic, I. and Truhar, N. (2013). Optimization of the solution of the parameter-dependent Sylvester equation and applications. *Journal of Computational and Applied Mathematics*, 237(1):136–144.

Leondes, C. T. (1995). *Multidimensional Systems: Signal Processing and Modeling Techniques*. Academic Press, San Diego, CA.

Lewis, F. L. (1986). A survey of linear singular systems. *Circuit System Signal Processing*, 5:3–36.

Lewis, F. L. and Mertzios, B. G. (1987). Analysis of singular systems using orthogonal functions. *IEEE Transactions on Automatic Control*, AC-32:527–530.

Li, F. M., Zhao, L. J., and Duan, G. R. (2006). H_∞ fault-tolerant controller design for time-delay systems based on a state observer. In *Proceedings of the 25th Chinese Control Conference*, pp. 334–337, August 7–11, Harbin, China.

Li, Z. Y., Zhou, B., Wang, Y., and Duan, G. R. (2010). Numerical solution to linear matrix equation by finite steps iteration. *IET Control Theory and Applications*, 4(7): 1245–1253.

Liang, B., Chang, T. Q., and Wang, G. S. (2011). Robust H_∞ fault-tolerant control against sensor and actuator failures for uncertain descriptor systems. *Procedia Engineering*, 15:979–983.

Liang, B. and Duan, G. R. (2004a). Observer-based fault-tolerant control for descriptor linear systems. In *Proceedings of the Eighth International Conference on Control, Automation, Robotics and Vision*, pp. 2233–2237, December 6–9, Kunming, China.

Liang, B. and Duan, G. R. (2004b). Observer-based H_∞ fault-tolerant control against actuator failures for descriptor systems. In *Proceedings of the Fifth World Congress on Intelligent Control and Automation*, pp. 1007–1011, June 15–19, Hangzhou, China.

Liang, B. and Duan, G. R. (2004c). Observer-based H_∞ fault-tolerant control for descriptor linear systems with sensor failures. In *Proceedings of the Fifth World Congress on Intelligent Control and Automation*, pp. 1012–1016, June 15–19, Hangzhou, China.

Lin, Y. Q. (2005). Implicitly restarted global FOM and GMRES for nonsymmetric matrix equations and Sylvester equations. *Applied Mathematics and Computation*, 167(2): 1004–1025.

Lin, Y. Q. and Wei, Y. M. (2007). Condition numbers of the generalized Sylvester equation. *IEEE Transactions on Automatic Control*, 52(12):2380–2385.

Liu, D., Zhang, H., Polycarpou, M., and Alippi, C. (2011). *Proceedings of the Eighth International Symposium on Neural Networks (Advances in Neural Networks)*. Lecture Notes in Computer Science/Theoretical Computer Science and General Issues. Springer, Berlin, Germany.

Liu, G. P., Daley, S., and Duan, G. R. (2001). On stability of dynamical controllers using pole assignment. *European Journal of Control*, 7(1):58–66. Also, in *Proceedings of European Control Conference*, 1999, August 31–September 3, Karlsruhe, Germany.

Liu, G. P. and Duan, G. R. (1998). Eigenstructure assignment with mixed performance specifications. In *Proceedings of the Sixth IEEE Mediterranean Conference on Control and Systems*, pp. 690–695, June 9–11, Sardinia, Italy.

Liu, G. P. and Duan, G. R. (2000). Robust eigenstructure assignment using multi-objective optimization techniques. In *Proceedings of the Third Asian Control Conference (ASCC'2000)*, July 4–7, Shanghai, China.

Liu, G. P., Duan, G. R., and Daley, S. (2000a). Design of stable observer based controllers for robust pole assignment. In *Proceedings of IFAC Symposium on Robust Control (ROCOND 2000)*, pp. 71–76, June 21–23, Prague, Czech Republic.

Liu, G. P., Duan, G. R., and Daley, S. (2000b). Stable dynamical controller design using output-feedback eigenstructure assignment. In *Proceedings of the Third Asian Control Conference (ASCC'2000)*, July 4–7, Shanghai, China.

Liu, G. P., Duan, G. R., and Daley, S. (2000c). Stable observer-based controller design for robust state-feedback pole assignment. *Proceedings of the Institution of Mechanical Engineers. Part I: Journal of Systems and Control Engineering*, 214(4):313–318.

Luo, Y. Z., Zhang, J., and Tang, G. J. (2013). Survey of orbital dynamics and control of space rendezvous. *Chinese Journal of Aeronautics*, 27(1):1–11.

Luque, E., Margalef, T., and Benítez, D. (2008). *Proceedings of the 14th International Euro-Par Conference on Parallel Processing.* Lecture Notes in Computer Science/Theoretical Computer Science and General Issues. Springer, Berlin, Germany.

Lv, L. L. and Duan, G. R. (2010). Parametric observer-based control for linear discrete periodic systems. In *Proceedings of the Eighth World Congress on Intelligent Control and Automation*, pp. 313–316, July 7–9, Jinan, China.

Lv, L. L., Duan, G. R., and Zhou, B. (2010). Parametric pole assignment and robust pole assignment for discrete-time linear periodic systems. *SIAM Journal on Control and Optimization*, 48(6):3975–3996.

Ma, E. C. (1966). A finite series solution of the matrix equation $AX - XB = C$. *SIAM Journal on Applied Mathematics*, 14:490–495.

Marino, R. and Spong, M. W. (1986). Nonlinear control techniques for flexible joint manipulators: A single link case study. In *Proceedings of 1986 IEEE International Conference on Robotics and Automation*, vol. 3, pp. 1030–1036, San Francisco, CA.

Meirovitch, L., Baruh, H. J., and Oz, H. (1983). A comparison of control techniques for large flexible systems. *Journal of Guidance, Control and Dynamics*, 6:302–310.

Moonen, M. S., Golub, G. H., and de Moor, B. L. (2010). *Linear Algebra for Large Scale and Real-Time Applications.* Nato Science Series E: (closed). Springer, Berlin, Germany.

Mori, T., Fukuma, N., and Kuwahara, M. (1986). Explicit solution and eigenvalue bounds in the Lyapunov matrix equation. *IEEE Transactions on Automatic Control*, AC-31: 656–658.

Ogata, K. (2009). *Modern Control Engineering*, 5th edn. Prentice Hall, Englewood Cliffs, NJ.

Ohishi, K., Miyazaki, T., and Nakamura, Y. (1996). High performance ultra-low speed servo system based on doubly coprime factorization and instantaneous speed observer. *IEEE-ASME Transactions on Mechatronics*, 1(1):89–98.

Palma, J. M. L. M., Dongarra, J., and Hernandez, V. (2001). *Proceedings of the Fourth International Conference on Applied Parallel Computing (Advanced Scientific Computing).* Lecture Notes in Computer Science. Springer, Berlin, Germany.

Papadopoulos, E. and Dubowsky, S. (1991). On the nature of control algorithms for free-floating space manipulators. *IEEE Transactions on Robotics & Automation*, 7(6): 750–758.

Parker, J. T., Serrani, A., Yurkovich, S., Bolender, M. A., and Doman, D. B. (2007). Control-oriented modeling of an air-breathing hypersonic vehicle. *Journal of Guidance, Control, and Dynamics*, 30(3):856–869.

Poromaa, P. (1998). Parallel algorithms for triangular Sylvester equations: Design, scheduling and scalability issues. *Applied Parallel: Large Scale Scientific And Industrial Problems*, 1541:438–446.

Ptak, V. (1981). The discrete Lyapunov equation in controllable canonical form. *IEEE Transactions on Automatic Control*, AC-26:580–581.

Putinar, M. and Sullivant, S. (2010). *Emerging Applications of Algebraic Geometry*. The IMA Volumes in Mathematics and its Applications. Springer, New York.

Ramadan, M. A., El-Danaf, T. S., and Bayoumi, A. M. E. (2013). A finite iterative algorithm for the solution of Sylvester-conjugate matrix equations $AV + BW = E\bar{V}F + C$ and $AV + B\bar{W} = E\bar{V}F + C$. *Mathematical and Computer Modelling*, 58(11-12):1738–1754.

Ramadan, M. A., El-Shazly, N. M., and Selim, B. I. (2010). A Hessenberg method for the numerical solutions to types of block Sylvester matrix equation. *Mathematical and Computer Modelling*, 52(9–10):1716–1727.

Ramadan, M. A., Naby, M. A. A., and Bayoumi, A. M. E. (2009). On the explicit solutions of forms of the Sylvester and the Yakubovich matrix equations. *Mathematical and Computer*, 50(9–10):1400–1408.

Rincon, F. (1992). Feedback stabilization of second-order models. PhD dissertation, Northern Illinois University, De Kalb, IL.

Robbe, M. and Sadkane, M. (2008). Use of near-breakdowns in the block Arnoldi method for solving large Sylvester equations. *Applied Number Mathematics*, 58(4):486–498.

Saberi, A., Stoorvogel, A. A., and Sannuti, P. (1999). *Control of Linear Systems with Regulation and Input Constraints*. Springer, London, U.K.

Schaub, H. and Junkins, J. L. (2003). *Analytical Mechanics of Space Systems*. AIAA Education Series. AIAA, Reston, VA, pp. 593–601.

Schmidt, T. (1994). *Parametrschaetzung bei mehrkoerpersystemen mit zwangsbedingungen*. VDI-Verlag.

Shahzad, A., Jones, B. L., Kerrigan, E. C., and Constantinides, G. A. (2011). An efficient algorithm for the solution of a coupled Sylvester equation appearing in descriptor systems. *Automatica*, 47:244–248.

Skelton, R. E., Iwasaki, T., and Grigoriadis, K. M. (1997). *A Unified Algebraic Approach to Control Design*. Taylor & Francis, London, U.K.

Slotine, J. E. and Li, W. P. (1991). *Applied Nonlinear Control*. Prentice Hall, Englewood Cliffs, NJ.

Song, C. Q. and Feng, J. E. (2014). Polynomial solutions to the matrix equation. *Journal of Applied Mathematics*, 2014, Article ID 710458, 8pp.

Song, C. Q., Feng, J. E., Wang, X. D., and Zhao, J. L. (2014a). Finite iterative method for solving coupled Sylvester-transpose matrix equations. *Journal of Applied Mathematics and Computing*, 46:351–372.

Song, C. Q., Feng, J. E., Wang, X. D., and Zhao, J. L. (2014b). Parametric solutions to the generalized discrete Yakubovich-transpose matrix equation. *Asian Journal of Control*, 16(4):1–8.

Song, C. Q., Feng, J. E., Wang, X. D., and Zhao, J. L. (2014c). A real representation method for solving Yakubovich-j-conjugate quaternion matrix equation. *Abstract and Applied Analysis*, 2014, Article ID 285086, 9pp.

Song, C. Q., Feng, J. E., and Zhao, J. L. (2014d). A new technique for solving continuous Sylvester-conjugate matrix equation. *Transactions of the Institute of Measurement and Control,* 36:946–953.

Song, C. Q., Rui, H. X., Wang, X. D., and Zhao, J. L. (2014e). Closed-form solutions to the non-homogeneous Yakubovich-transpose matrix equation. *Journal of Computational and Applied Mathematics,* 267:72–81.

Sorevik, T., Manne, F., Gebremedhin A. H., M. R. (2006). *Proceedings of the Fifth International Workshop on Applied Parallel Computing (New Paradigms for HPC in Industry and Academia 2000).* Lecture Notes in Computer Science. Springer, Berlin, Germany.

Sorevik, T., Manne, F., Moe, R., and Gebremedhin, A. H. (2001). *Proceedings of the Fifth International Workshop on Applied Parallel Computing (New Paradigms for HPC in Industry and Academia).* Lecture Notes in Computer Science. Springer, Berlin, Germany.

Spong, M. W., Hutchinson, S., and Vidyasagar, M. (2008). *Robot Dynamics and Control,* 2nd edn. John Wiley & Sons, New York.

Srivastava, A., Sylvester, D., and Blaauw, D. (2006). *Statistical Analysis and Optimization for VLSI: Timing and Power.* Integrated Circuits and Systems. Springer, New York.

Sun, C. Y., Yu, Y. H., and Wang, G. S. (2010). Solutions on a class of uncertain second-order matrix equations. In *Proceedings of the 22th Chinese Control and Decision Conference,* pp. 820–823, May 26–28, Xuzhou, China.

Syrmos, V. L. (1994). Disturbance decoupling using constrained Sylvester equations. *IEEE Transactions on Automatic Control,* 39(4):797–803.

Syrmos, V. L. and Lewis, F. L. (1993). Output-feedback eigenstructure assignment using 2 Sylvester equations. *IEEE Transactions on Automatic Control,* 38(3):495–499.

Syrmos, V. L. and Lewis, F. L. (1994). Coupled and constrained Sylvester equations in system-design. *Circuits Systems and Signal Processing,* 13(6):663–694.

Tamaki, S. A., Oshiro, N. B., Yamamoto, T. A., and Kinjo, H. A. (1996). Design of optimal digital feedback regulator based on first and second order information and its application to vibration control. *JSME International Journal, Series C: Dynamics, Control, Robotics, Design and Manufacturing,* 39(1):41–48.

Tong, L., Wu, A. G., and Duan, G. R. (2010). Finite iterative algorithm for solving coupled Lyapunov equations appearing in discrete-time Markov jump linear systems. *IET Control Theory and Applications,* 4(10):2223–2231.

Trinh, H. and Fernando, T. (2011). *Functional Observers for Dynamical Systems.* Lecture Notes in Control and Information Sciences. Springer, Berlin, Germany.

Truhar, N., Tomljanovic, Z., and Li, R. C. (2010). Analysis of the solution of the Sylvester equation using low-rank ADI with exact shifts. *Systems & Control Letters,* 59: 248–257.

Tsui, C. C. (1987). A complete analytical solution to the equation $TA - FT = LC$ and its applications. *IEEE Transactions on Automatic Control,* 32:742–744.

Ulrich, S. and Sasiadek, J. Z. (2010). Modified simple adaptive control for a two-link space robot. In *Proceedings of the 2010 American Control Conference,* pp. 3654–3659, Baltimore, MD.

van Dooren, P. (1984). Reduced order observers: A new algorithm and proof. *Systems & Control Letters,* 4:243–251.

van Dooren, P. M., Hadjidimos, A., and van der Vorst, H. A. (2001). *Linear Algebra-Linear Systems and Eigenvalues: Volume 3*. Numerical Analysis 2000. North Holland, Amsterdam, the Netherlands.

Voicu, M. (2003). *Advances in Automatic Control*. The Springer International Series in Engineering and Computer Science. Springer, Berlin, Germany.

Wachspress, E. (2013). *The ADI Model Problem*. Springer, New York.

Wang, A. P., Liu, S. F., Zhang, X., and Duan, G. R. (2009a). A note on 'the parametric solutions of eigenstructure assignment for controllable and uncontrollable singular systems'. *Journal of Applied Mathematics and Computing*, 31(1–2):145–150.

Wang, G., Liang, B., Lv, Q., and Duan, G. R. (2007a). Eigenstructure assignment in second-order linear systems: A parametric design method. In *Proceedings of the 26th Chinese Control Conference*, pp. 9–13, July 26–31, Zhangjiajie, China.

Wang, G. S., Chang, T. Q., Liang, B., and Liu, F. (2010). A parametric solution of second-order vibration matrix equations and its control applications. In *Proceedings of the Eighth World Congress on Intelligent Control and Automation*, pp. 3342–3346, July 6–9, Jinan, China.

Wang, G. S. and Duan, G. R. (2003). Eigenstructure assignment with disturbance decoupling and minimum eigenvalue sensitivities. In *Proceedings of International Conference on Control Science and Engineering*, December 18–20, Harbin, China.

Wang, G. S. and Duan, G. R. (2004a). Robust pole assignment via P-D feedback in a class of second-order dynamic systems. In *Proceedings of the Eighth International Conference on Control, Automation, Robotics and Vision*, pp. 1152–1156, December 6–9, Kunming 2004.

Wang, G. S. and Duan, G. R. (2004b). State feedback eigenstructure assignment with minimum control effort. In *Proceedings of the Fifth World Congress on Intelligent Control and Automation*, pp. 35–38, June 15–19, Hangzhou, China.

Wang, G. S. and Duan, G. R. (2007). Parameterisation of PID eigenstructure assignment in second-order linear systems. *International Journal of Modelling, Identification and Control*, 2(2):100–105.

Wang, G. S. and Duan, G. R. (2008). Parameterisation of reconfiguring second-order linear systems via eigenstructure assignment. *International Journal of Modelling, Identification and Control*, 3(2):124–130.

Wang, G. S., Liang, B., and Duan, G. R. (2005a). Reconfiguring second-order dynamic systems via state feedback eigenstructure assignment. *International Journal of Control, Automation, and Systems*, 3(1):109–116.

Wang, G. S., Liang, B., and Duan, G. R. (2006a). Parameterization of high order PI observers for second-order linear systems. In *Proceedings of the 25th Chinese Control Conference*, pp. 1–4, August 7–11, Harbin, China.

Wang, G. S., Liang, B., and Tang, Z. X. (2011). A parameterized design of reduced-order state observer in linear control systems. *Procedia Engineering*, 15:974–978.

Wang, G. S., Liu, F., Liang, B., and Duan, G. R. (2007b). Design of full-order PD observers for second-order dynamic systems. In *Proceedings of the 26th Chinese Control Conference*, pp. 5–8, July 26–31, Zhangjiajie, China.

Wang, G. S., Liu, F., Lv, Q., and Duan, G. R. (2008a). Parameterization of full-order PI observers in second-order linear systems. In *Proceedings of the 27th Chinese Control Conference*, pp. 152–155, July 16–18, Kunming, China.

Wang, G. S., Lv, Q., and Duan, G. R. (2006b). Eigenstructure assignment in a class of second-order dynamic systems. *Journal of Control Theory and Applications*, 4(3):302–308.

Wang, G. S., Lv, Q., and Duan, G. R. (2006c). H_2-optimal control with regional pole assignment via state feedback. *International Journal of Control, Automation, and Systems*, 4(5):653–659.

Wang, G. S., Lv, Q., and Duan, G. R. (2006d). Partial eigenstructure assignment via $P - D$ feedback in second-order descriptor linear systems. *Dynamics of Continuous, Discrete and Impulsive Systems: Part 2 Suppl. S*, 3:1022–1029.

Wang, G. S., Lv, Q., and Duan, G. R. (2007c). On the parametric solution to the second-order sylvester matrix equation $EVF^2 - AVF - CV = BW$. *Mathematical Problems in Engineering*, 2007.

Wang, G. S., Lv, Q., Liang, B., and Duan, G. R. (2005b). Eigenstructure assignment for a class of composite systems: A complete parametric method. In *Proceedings of the 24th Chinese Control Conference*, pp. 7–11, July 15–18, Guangzhou, China.

Wang, G. S., Lv, Q., Liang, B., and Duan, G. R. (2006e). Design of robust tracking observer for perturbed control systems. In *Proceedings of the Sixth World Congress on Intelligent Control and Automation*, pp. 506–510, June 21–23, Dalian, China.

Wang, G. S., Lv, Q., Mu, Q., and Duan, G. R. (2006f). Design of robust tracking observer for perturbed descriptor linear systems. In *Proceedings of the First International Sympo-sium on Systems and Control in Aerospace and Astronautics*, pp. 1180–1183, January 19–21, Harbin, China.

Wang, G. S., Wang, H. Q., and Duan, G. R. (2009b). On the robust solution to a class of perturbed second-order Sylvester equation. *Dynamics of Continuous, Discrete and Impulsive Systems Series A: Mathematical Analysis*, 16:439–449.

Wang, G. S., Xia, F., Liang, B., Guo, F., and Feng, L. (2014). A parametric design method of finite time state observers in linear time-invariant systems. In *Proceedings of the 26th Chinese Control and Decision Conference*, pp. 795–799, May 31–June 2, Changsha, China.

Wang, G. S., Xia, F., and Yang, W. L. (2013). Design of robust finite time func-tional observers in uncertain linear systems. *International Journal of Advanced Mechatronic Systems*, 5(4):223–231.

Wang, H. L., Lv, Q., and Duan, G. R. (2008b). PID eigenstructure assignment in second-order dynamic systems: A parametric method. In *Proceedings of the Seventh World Congress on Intelligent Control and Automation*, pp. 856–859, June 25–27, Chongqing, China.

Wang, Q. W., Sun, J. H., and Li, S. Z. (2002). Consistency for bi (skew) symmetric solutions to systems of generalized Sylvester equations over a finite central algebra. *Linear Algebra and Its Applications*, 353:169–182.

Wang, Y. Y. and Yu, H. H. (2014). Robust pole assignment of uncertain discrete systems with input time-delay. In *Proceedings of the 11th World Congress on Intelligent Control and Automation*, June 29–July 4, Shenyang, China.

Watkins, D. S. (2007). *The Matrix Eigenvalue Problem: GR and Krylov Subspace Methods*. Society for Industrial and Applied Mathematics, Philadelphia, PA.

Wimmer, H. K. (1994). Consistency of a paid of generalized Sylvester equations. *IEEE Transactions on Automatic Control*, 39(5):1014–1016.

Wu, A. G. and Duan, G. R. (2006a). Design of generalized PI observers for descriptor linear systems. *IEEE Transactions on Circuits and Systems*, 53(12):2828–2837.

Wu, A. G. and Duan, G. R. (2006b). Design of PI observers for continuous-time descriptor linear systems. *IEEE Transactions on Systems, Man, and Cybernetics, Part B: Cybernetics*, 36(6):1423–1431.

Wu, A. G. and Duan, G. R. (2007a). Design of PD observers in descriptor linear systems. *International Journal of Control, Automation and Systems*, 5(1):93–98.

Wu, A. G. and Duan, G. R. (2007b). IP observer design for descriptor linear systems. *IEEE Transactions on Circuits and Systems II: Express Briefs*, 54(9):815–819.

Wu, A. G. and Duan, G. R. (2007c). Solution to the generalised Sylvester matrix equation $AV + BW = EVF$. *IET Control Theory and Applications*, 1(1):402–408.

Wu, A. G. and Duan, G. R. (2008a). Explicit general solution to the matrix equation $AV + BW = EVF + R$. *IET Control Theory and Applications*, 2(1):56–60.

Wu, A. G. and Duan, G. R. (2008b). Generalized PI observer design for linear systems. *IMA Journal of Mathematical Control and Information*, 25(2):239–250.

Wu, A. G., Duan, G. R., Dong, J., and Fu, Y. M. (2009a). Design of proportional-integral observers for discrete-time descriptor linear systems. *IET Control Theory and Applications*, 3(1):79–87.

Wu, A. G., Duan, G. R., and Fu, Y. M. (2007a). Generalized PID observer design for descriptor linear systems. *IEEE Transactions on Systems, Man, and Cybernetics, Part B: Cybernetics*, 37(5):1390–1395.

Wu, A. G., Duan, G. R., Fu, Y. M., and Wu, W. J. (2010a). Finite iterative algorithms for the generalized sylvester-conjugate matrix equation $AX + BY = E\bar{X}F + S$. *Computing*, 89(3–4):147–170.

Wu, A. G., Duan, G. R., and Hou, M. Z. (2012a). Parametric design approach for proportional multiple-integral derivative observer in descriptor linear systems. *Asian Journal of Control*, 14(6):1683–1689.

Wu, A. G., Duan, G. R., and Liu, W. Q. (2012b). Proportional multiple-integral observer design for continuous-time descriptor linear systems. *Automatica*, 14(2): 476–488.

Wu, A. G., Duan, G. R., and Xue, Y. (2007b). Kronecker maps and Sylvester-polynomial matrix equations. *IEEE Transactions on Automatic Control*, 52(5):905–910.

Wu, A. G., Duan, G. R., and Yu, H. H. (2006a). On solutions of the matrix equations $XF - AX = C$ and $XF - A\bar{X} = C$. *Applied Mathematics and Computation*, 183(2): 932–941.

Wu, A. G., Duan, G. R., and Zhou, B. (2008a). Solution to generalized Sylvester matrix equations. *IEEE Transactions on Automatic Control*, 53(5):811–815.

Wu, A. G., Feng, G., and Duan, G. R. (2012c). Proportional multiple-integral observer design for discrete-time descriptor linear systems. *International Journal of Systems Science*, 43(8):1492–1503.

Wu, A. G., Feng, G., Duan, G. R., and Wu, W. J. (2010b). Closed-form solutions to Sylvester-conjugate matrix equations. *Computers and Mathematics with Applications*, 60(1):95–111.

Wu, A. G., Feng, G., Duan, G. R., and Wu, W. J. (2010c). Finite iterative solutions to a class of complex matrix equations with conjugate and transpose of the unknowns. *Mathematical and Computer Modelling*, 52(9–10):1463–1478.

Wu, A. G., Feng, G., Duan, G. R., and Wu, W. J. (2010d). Iterative solutions to coupled Sylvester-conjugate matrix equations. *Computers and Mathematics with Applications*, 60(1):54–66.

Wu, A. G., Feng, G., Hu, J. Q., and Duan, G. R. (2009b). Closed-form solutions to the nonhomogeneous Yakubovich-conjugate matrix equation. *Applied Mathematics and Computation*, 214(2):442–450.

Wu, A. G., Fu, Y. M., and Duan, G. R. (2008b). On solutions of matrix equations $V - AVF = BW$ and $V - A\bar{V}F = BW$. *Mathematical and Computer Modelling*, 47(11–12):1181–1197.

Wu, A. G., Hu, J. Q., and Duan, G. R. (2009c). Solutions to the matrix equation $AX - EXF = BY$. *Journal of Applied Mathematics and Computing*, 58(10):1891–1900.

Wu, A. G., Li, B., Zhang, Y., and Duan, G. R. (2011a). Finite iterative solutions to coupled Sylvester-conjugate matrix equations. *Applied Mathematical Modelling*, 35(3): 1065–1080.

Wu, A. G., Liang, B., and Duan, G. R. (2005). Reconfiguring second-order dynamic systems via P-D feedback eigenstructure assignment: A parametric method. *International Journal of Control, Automation and Systems*, 3(1):109–116.

Wu, A. G., Lv, L. L., Duan, G. R., and Liu, W. Q. (2011b). Corrigendum to 'parametric solutions to Sylvester-conjugate matrix equations'. *Computers and Mathematics with Applications*, 62(12):4806–4806.

Wu, A. G., Lv, L. L., Duan, G. R., and Liu, W. Q. (2011c). Parametric solutions to Sylvester-conjugate matrix equations. *Computers and Mathematics with Applications*, 62(9):3317–3325.

Wu, A. G., Sun, Y., and Feng, G. (2010e). Closed-form solution to the non-homogeneous generalised Sylvester matrix equation. *IET Control Theory and Applications*, 4(10): 1914–1921.

Wu, A. G., Wang, H. Q., and Duan, G. R. (2009d). On matrix equations $X - AXF = C$ and $X - A\bar{X}F = C$. *Journal of Computational and Applied Mathematics*, 230(2):690–698.

Wu, A. G., Yang, G. Z., and Duan, G. R. (2007c). Partial pole assignment via constant gain feedback in two classes of frequency-domain models. *International Journal of Control, Automation and Systems*, 5(2):111–116.

Wu, A. G., Zeng, X. L., Duan, G. R., and Wu, W. J. (2010f). Iterative solutions to the extended Sylvester-conjugate matrix equations. *Applied Mathematics and Computation*, 217(1):130–142.

Wu, A. G., Zhang, E. Z., and Liu, F. C. (2012d). On closed-form solutions to the generalized Sylvester-conjugate matrix equation. *Applied Mathematics and Computation*, 218(19):9730–9741.

Wu, A. G. and Zhang, Y. (2015). *Complex Conjugate Matrix Equations*. Springer, New York.

Wu, A. G., Zhao, S. M., and Duan, G. R. (2008c). Solving the generalized Sylvester matrix equation $AV + BW = VF$ via Kronecker map. *Journal of Control Theory and Applications*, 6(3):330–332.

Wu, A. G., Zhu, F., Duan, G. R., and Zhang, Y. (2008d). Solving the generalized Sylvester matrix equation $AV + BW = EVF$ via Kronecker map. *Applied Mathematics Letters*, 21(10):1069–1073.

Wu, Y. L. and Duan, G. R. (2004). Reduced-order observer design for matrix second-order linear systems. In *Proceedings of the Fifth World Congress on Intelligent Control and Automation*, pp. 28–31, June 15–19, Hangzhou, China.

Wu, Y. L. and Duan, G. R. (2005). Unified parametric approaches for observer design in matrix second-order linear systems. *International Journal of Control, Automation and Systems*, 3(2):159–165.

Wu, Y. L. and Duan, G. R. (2006c). Design of Luenberger function observer with disturbance decoupling for matrix second-order linear systems—A parametric approach. *Journal of Systems Engineering and Electronics*, 17(1):156–162.

Wu, Y. L., Li, Z. B., and Duan, G. R. (2006b). Observer design for matrix second order linear systems with uncertain disturbance input—A parametric approach. *Journal of Systems Engineering and Electronics*, 17(4):811–816.

Xie, L., Ding, J., and Ding, F. (2009). Gradient based iterative solutions for general linear matrix equations. *Computers & Mathematics with Applications*, 58(7):1441–1448.

Xu, H. J., Mirmirani, M. D., and Ioannou, P. A. (2004). Adaptive sliding mode control design for a hypersonic flight vehicle. *Journal of Guidance, Control, and Dynamics*, 27(5):829–838.

Xue, Y. and Duan, G. R. (2005a). Eigenstructure assignment for linear discrete-time systems subject to input saturation via decentralized state feedback—A parametric approach. In *Proceedings of 2005 International Conference on Machine Learning and Cybernetics*, pp. 1460–1465, August 18–21, Guangzhou, China.

Xue, Y. and Duan, G. R. (2005b). Eigenstructure assignment for linear systems with constrained output via state feedback—A parametric approach. In *Proceedings of 2005 International Conference on Machine Learning and Cybernetics*, pp. 1454–1459, August 18–21, Guangzhou, China.

Xue, Y. and Duan, G. R. (2006a). Eigenstructure assignment for descriptor linear systems subject to input saturation via state feedback—A parametric approach. *Dynamics of Continuous Discrete and Impulsive Systems-Series A: Mathematical Analysis*, 13:1181–1188.

Xue, Y. and Duan, G. R. (2006b). Eigenstructure assignment for linear systems with constraints on input and its rate via state feedback—A parametric approach. In *Proceedings of SICE-ICASE International Joint Conference*, pp. 4572–4577, August 7–11, Harbin, China.

Xue, Y. and Duan, G. R. (2006c). Parametric, eigenstructure assignment for linear systems with constraints on input and its rate via decentralized state feedback. In *Proceedings of International Conference on Sensing, Computing and Automation*, pp. 2786–2790, May 8–11, Chongqing, China.

Xue, Y., Wei, Y. Y., and Duan, G. R. (2006). Eigenstructure assignment for linear systems with constrained input via state feedback—A parametric approach. In *Proceedings of the 25th Chinese Control Conference*, pp. 90–95, August 7–11, Harbin, China.

Yamanaka, K. and Ankersen, F. (2002). New state transition matrix for relative motion on an arbitrary elliptical orbit. *Journal of Guidance, Control, and Dynamics*, 25(1):60–66.

Yan, Y. X., Chai, Q. X., and Duan, G. R. (2005). Observer-based controller design for disturbance attenuation in linear system. In *Proceedings of the 17th Chinese Control and Decision Conference*, pp. 807–811, Harbin, China.

Yang, C. L., Liu, J. Z., and Liu, Y. (2012). Solutions of the generalized Sylvester matrix equation and the application in eigenstructure assignment. *Asian Journal of Control*, 14(6):1669–1675.

Yang, J., Li, S. H., Sun, C. Y., and Guo, L. (2013). Nonlinear-disturbance-observer-based robust flight control for airbreathing hypersonic vehicles. *IEEE Transactions on Aerospace and Electronic Systems*, 49(2):1263–1275.

Yin, F., Huang, G. X., and Chen, D. Q. (2012). Finite iterative algorithms for solving generalized coupled Sylvester systems—Part II: Two-sided and generalized coupled Sylvester matrix equations over reflexive solutions. *Applied Mathematical Modelling*, 36(4):1604–1614.

Young, N. J. (1980). Formulae for the solution of Lyapunov matrix equation. *International Journal of Control*, 31:159–179.

Yu, H. H. and Bi, D. G. (2012a). Parametric approaches for eigenstructure assignment in high-order linear systems via output feedback. In *Proceedings of 24th Chinese Control and Decision Conference*, pp. 459–464, May 23–25, Taiyuan, China.

Yu, H. H. and Bi, D. G. (2012b). Parametric approaches for observer design in high-order descriptor linear systems. In *Proceedings of 24th Chinese Control and Decision Conference*, pp. 465–469, May 23–25, Taiyuan, China.

Yu, H. H. and Bi, D. G. (2014). Solution to generalized matrix equation $AV - EVJ = B_D W_D J + B_P W_P$. In *Proceedings of 33th Chinese Control Conference*, July 28–30, Nanjing, China.

Yu, H. H. and Duan, G. R. (2009a). ESA in high-order linear system via output feedback. *Asian Journal of Control*, 11(3):336–343.

Yu, H. H. and Duan, G. R. (2009b). Pole assignment of large-scale systems via decentralized state feedback control. In *2009 Chinese Control and Decision Conference*, pp. 1086–1089, June 17–19, Guilin China.

Yu, H. H. and Duan, G. R. (2010). ESA in high-order descriptor linear systems via output feedback. *International Journal of Control Automation and Systems*, 8(2):408–417.

Yu, H. H. and Duan, G. R. (2011). The analytical general solutions to the higher-order Sylvester matrices equation. *Control Theory and Applications*, 28(5):698–702.

Yu, H. H. and Wang, Y. Y. (2013). ESA in a type of discrete time-delay linear system via state feedback. In *Proceedings of Second International Conference on Measurement, Information and Control*, pp. 797–800, August 16–18, Harbin, China.

Yu, H. H., Wang, Z. H., and Duan, G. R. (2005). Pole assignment in descriptor linear systems via proportional plus derivative state feedback. In *Proceedings of Chinese Control and Decision Conference*, pp. 899–902, Harbin, China.

Zhang, B. (2008). Parametric eigenstructure assignment by state feedback in descriptor systems. *IET Control Theory and Applications*, 2(4):303–309.

Zhang, B. (2013). Eigenvalue assignment in linear descriptor systems via output feedback. *IET Control Theory and Applications*, 7(15):1906–1913.

Zhang, B. and Duan, G. R. (2002). Eigenstructure assignment for stabilizable linear systems via state feedback. In *Proceedings of the Fourth World Congress on Intelligent Control and Automation (WCICA'02)*, pp. 184–188, June 10–14, Shanghai, China.

Zhang, G. S. (2006). Regularizability, controllability and observability of rectangular descriptor systems by dynamic compensation. In *Proceedings of the 2006 American Control Conference*, June 14–16, Minneapolis, MN.

Zhang, H. M. and Ding, F. (2014). A property of the eigenvalues of the symmetric positive definite matrix and the iterative algorithm for coupled Sylvester matrix equations. *Journal of the Franklin Institute—Engineering and Applied Mathematics*, 351(1):340–357.

Zhang, J. F. (2002). Optimal control for mechanical vibration systems based on second-order matrix equations. *Mechanical Systems and Signal Processing*, 16(1):61–67.

Zhang, L. and Duan, G. R. (2012). Robust poles assignment for a kind of second-order linear time-varying systems. In *Proceedings of the 31st Chinese Control Conference*, pp. 2602–2606, July 25–27, Heifei, China.

Zhang, Q. L. and Yang, D. M. (2003). *Analysis and Synthesis of Uncertain Descriptor Linear Systems (in Chinese)*. The Northeastern University Press, Shenyang, China.

Zhang, X., Thompson, S., and Duan, G. R. (2004). Full-column rank solutions of the matrix equation $AV = EVJ$. *Applied Mathematics and Computation*, 151(3):815–826.

Zhang, Y. and Duan, G. R. (2005). Guaranteed cost observer for uncertain discrete-time switched systems with time-delay. In *Proceedings of Chinese Control and Decision Conference*, pp. 912–916, August 18–21, Guangzhou, China.

Zhao, L. B. and Wang, G. S. (2012). Design of finite time functional observers in linear control systems. In *Proceedings of the Third International Conference on Intelligent Control and Information Processing*, pp. 303–307, July 15–17, Dalian, China.

Zhou, B., Cui, N. G., and Duan, G. R. (2012). Circular orbital rendezvous with actuator saturation and delay: A parametric Lyapunov equation approach. *IET Control Theory and Applications*, 6(9):1281–1287.

Zhou, B., Ding, B. C., and Duan, G. R. (2006). Observer-based output stabilization of integrators system with Lipschitz nonlinear term by bounded control. In *Proceedings of the 25th Chinese Control Conference*, pp. 1457–1462, August 7–11, Harbin, China.

Zhou, B. and Duan, G. R. (2005). An explicit solution to the matrix equation $AX - XF = BY$. *Linear Algebra and Its Applications*, 402(1–3):345–366.

Zhou, B. and Duan, G. R. (2006a). A new solution to the generalized Sylvester matrix equation $AV - EVF = BW$. *Systems & Control Letters*, 55(3):193–198.

Zhou, B. and Duan, G. R. (2006b). Parametric approach for the normal Luenberger function observer design in second-order linear systems. In *Proceedings of the 45th IEEE Conference on Decision and Control*, pp. 2788–2793, San Diego, CA.

Zhou, B. and Duan, G. R. (2007a). Parametric solutions to the generalized Sylvester matrix equation $AX - XF = BY$ and the regulator equation $AX - XF = BY + R$. *Asian Journal of Control*, 9(4):475–483.

Zhou, B. and Duan, G. R. (2007b). Solutions to generalized Sylvester matrix equation by Schur decomposition. *International Journal of Systems Science*, 38(5):369–375.

Zhou, B. and Duan, G. R. (2008). On the generalized Sylvester mapping and matrix equations. *Systems & Control Letters*, 57(3):200–208.

Zhou, B. and Duan, G. R. (2009). Closed-form solutions to the matrix equation $AX - EXF = BY$ by with F in companion form. *International Journal of Automation and Computing*, 6(2):204–209.

Zhou, B. and Duan, G. R. (2012). Periodic Lyapunov equation based approaches to the stabilization of continuous-time periodic linear systems. *IEEE Transactions on Automatic Control*, 57(8):2139–2146.

Zhou, B., Duan, G. R., and Li, Z. Y. (2009a). Gradient based iterative algorithm for solving coupled matrix equations. *Systems & Control Letters*, 58(5):327–333.

Zhou, B., Duan, G. R., and Li, Z. Y. (2009b). A Stein matrix equation approach for computing coprime matrix fraction description. *IET Control Theory and Applications*, 3(6):691–700.

Zhou, B., Lam, J., and Duan, G. R. (2009c). On Smith-type iterative algorithms for the Stein matrix equation. *Applied Mathematics Letters*, 22(7):1038–1044.

Zhou, B., Lam, J., and Duan, G. R. (2010a). Gradient-based maximal convergence rate iterative method for solving linear matrix equations. *International Journal of Computer Mathematics*, 87(3):515–527.

Zhou, B., Li, Z. Y., Duan, G. R., and Wang, Y. (2009d). Optimal pole assignment for discrete-time systems via Stein equations. *IET Control Theory and Applications*, 3(8):983–994.

Zhou, B., Li, Z. Y., Duan, G. R., and Wang, Y. (2009e). Solutions to a family of matrix equations by using the Kronecker matrix polynomials. *Applied Mathematics and Computation*, 212(2):327–336.

Zhou, B., Li, Z. Y., Duan, G. R., and Wang, Y. (2009f). Weighted least squares solutions to general coupled Sylvester matrix equations. *Journal of Computational and Applied Mathematics*, 224(2):759–776.

Zhou, B., Lin, Z. L., and Duan, G. R. (2011). Lyapunov differential equation approach to elliptical orbital rendezvous with constrained controls. *Journal of Guidance Control and Dynamics*, 34(2):345–358.

Zhou, B. and Yan, Z. B. (2008). Solutions to right coprime factorizations and generalized Sylvester matrix equations. *Transactions of the Institute of Measurement and Control*, 30(5):397–426.

Zhou, B., Yan, Z. B., and Duan, G. R. (2010b). Unified parametrization for the solutions to the polynomial Diophantine matrix equation and the generalized Sylvester matrix equation. *International Journal of Control Automation and Systems*, 8(1):29–35. Also, in *Proceedings of 20th Chinese Control and Decision Conference*, 2008, pp. 4075–4080, Yantai, China.

Ziedan, I. E. (1972). Explicit solution of the Lyapunov-matrix equation. *IEEE Transactions on Automatic Control*, AC-17:379–381.

Zou, A. M., Kumar, K., and Hou, Z. G. (2012). Attitude coordination control for a group of spacecraft without velocity measurements. *IEEE Transactions on Control Systems Technology*, 20(5):1160–1174.

Index